Writing from Sources

FOURTH EDITION

Brenda Spatt

The City University of New York

St. Martin's Press

New York

Editor: Jimmy Fleming
Development editor: John Elliott
Manager, publishing services: Emily Berleth
Project management: Books By Design, Inc.
Production supervisor: Scott Lavelle
Cover design: Rod Hernandez
Cover photo: Tony Stone Images

Library of Congress Catalog Card Number: 95-67059

For information, write:
St. Martin's Press, Inc.
175 Fifth Avenue
New York, NY 10010

ISBN: 0-312-10132-5

Acknowledgments

Leach, William, specified excerpt from pages 131–132 in *Land of Desire: Merchants, Power, and the Rise of a New American Culture.* Copyright © 1993 by William Leach. Reprinted by permission of Pantheon Books, a division of Random House, Inc.

Guterson, David, "Enclosed. Encyclopedic. Endured. One Week at the Mall of America." Copyright © 1993 by David Guterson. Reprinted by permission of Georges Borchardt, Inc. for the author. This essay originally appeared in *Harper's* magazine.

Blank, Blanche D., "A Question of Degree." Excerpt from "Degrees: Who Needs Them?" by Blanche Blank. Autumn 1972, *AAUP Bulletin,* a publication of the American Association of University Professors. Reprinted by permission.

Edwards, Owen, "Thrice-Told Tales." *The New York Times,* March 20, 1988. Copyright © 1988 by the New York Times Company. Reprinted by permission.

Halpern, Sue, specified excerpt from *Migrations to Solitude,* pp. 3–8, by Sue Halpern. Copyright © 1992 by Sue Halpern. Reprinted by permission of Pantheon Books, a division of Random House, Inc.

Acknowledgments and copyrights are continued at the back of the book on pages 542–544, which constitute an extension of the copyright page.

Contents

PART II
WRITING FROM SOURCES 143

List of Exercises, Assignments, and Readings

To the Instructor

When I wrote the first edition of *Writing from Sources,* the book distilled my experience teaching freshman composition courses for over a decade at Lehman College of The City University of New York. Most of the students who tested *Writing from Sources* were typical of freshmen enrolled in a public urban university committed to a policy of open access. Many were older students, holding down full- or part-time jobs, burdened with work and family responsibilities. Whatever their ambitions and talents, they often lacked the time and energy to redeem the flawed education received in a decaying public school system. All of my students had completed at least one semester of freshman composition at Lehman or at a community college; many had previously taken one or more remedial writing courses or intensive classes in ESL. Nevertheless, most were still poorly prepared for college work.

For these students, weaknesses of syntax and style, while still a problem, were not the major issue. Nor were they hesitant about speaking their minds on paper and expressing their views. What gave them the most trouble was dealing with the disparate sources and the abstract ideas typically found in general education and major courses. They didn't know how to take good lecture notes, to pinpoint and paraphrase the key ideas of a chapter in a textbook, to evaluate a group of readings, or to undertake the extended synthesis necessary for presenting research. Unaccustomed to careful reading, analysis, and synthesis, these students felt impotent and frustrated when confronted by term paper assignments and essay examinations requiring the presentation of sources.

Students like those that I taught at Lehman in the 1970s and the 1980s can be found in every classroom at every college in this country—from research university to community college—during the 1990s. For a variety of educational, sociological, and economic reasons, more and more of our incoming students lack the academic preparation in reading, analysis, and writing that is essential if they are to progress through college and earn meaningful degrees. Even after graduation, without the generic analytical and communication skills specified in most job descriptions, our students may be hindered from achieving professional success as they follow the anticipated twenty-first-century pattern of seven or more successive positions over a lifetime's career. Preparing cogent memos and reports calls upon skills of analysis and synthesis to explain, evaluate, and integrate opinions and facts taken from a wide range of data. The object of *Writing from Sources* is to provide students with the tools for successful academic and professional writing and thus to raise the standard of writing across the college curriculum and, ultimately, in the workplace.

Poor preparation for academic writing is not a new problem. Almost forty years ago, during my own freshman year at a highly prestigious research university, I had no idea how to write about sources. Nor did I acquire those skills in freshman composition or in any other college course. Indeed, I produced my first successful term paper twenty-five years later, after I had figured out how to teach my students academic and professional writing and began to apply the principles to my own work. For ten years, my effectiveness as an administrator at The City University of New York has depended on following my own step-by-step techniques in the preparation of an endless succession of documents. I would urge instructors, as well as students, to become active participants in the process of writing from sources and to observe the increased facility and success with which they pursue their academic and professional writing.

Writing from Sources is based on the premise that an entire semester's work in composition should be structured around sources, with major emphasis on the analysis and synthesis of ideas and evidence so that the research essay becomes the course's natural conclusion. When (as has traditionally been the case in composition courses) the treatment of sources is introduced at the end of the semester, the assignment of the research essay becomes an unfair test of abilities that students have not been given the opportunity or the means to develop. In teaching the research essay, many instructors emphasize library work to the exclusion of virtually every other part of the process. But locating sources, especially in a modern, computerized library, is largely a mechanical task, unlikely in itself to teach students to think or write about what they have read. Knowing how to compile an impressive bibliography through CD-ROM will not enable students to select appropriate materials and integrate them into a coherent essay.

I believe that students learn best if skills are presented gradually, in lessons and assignments of progressive difficulty. In *Writing from Sources*, composition and organizational skills are broken into separate units and presented in discrete stages. In this sequential approach, each technique is first considered as an end in itself, to be explained, demonstrated, and practiced in isolation, like the skills necessary for mastering a sport. The use of quotation, for example, is thoroughly taught and applied before the student learns about paraphrase. Simple operations are practiced again and again so that they are thoroughly learned before the student goes on to attempt more complex variations. *Writing from Sources* is packed with materials and exercises—too many to be assigned to every class in a single semester—to ensure that students get precisely the practice they need at an appropriate level and with compatible texts. By the time the instructor assigns the research essay, the writing process and the handling of texts have become so familiar that students can focus on evaluating and selecting material gathered through research and on documenting their sources.

The fourth edition of *Writing from Sources* contains many new features to enhance its usefulness as a text, a reader, an exercise book, and a research-essay handbook.

- The chapter on library research has been greatly revised and expanded to reflect the shift toward *computerization*. Students are taken, step by step, through the process of acquiring information about a topic using on-line and CD-ROM sources. In addition, brief explanations about using the computer to take notes and to organize the research essay are incorporated into the text.

- The chapter on *documentation* contains a greatly expanded presentation of *MLA style*, with a wide variety of examples to illustrate the use of parenthetical notes as well as a sample page of a research essay with different kinds of parenthetical notes clearly indicated.

- An expanded Appendix B provides a comprehensive listing of *forms for bibliographical entries* based on the fourth edition of the *MLA Handbook*, as well as brief presentations and useful selections of *APA* and *endnote/footnote* forms.

- One of the three *sample research essays*, illustrating the use of endnotes, has been replaced with an essay about the 1972 plane crash of a Uruguayan rugby team in the Andes. The research essay on euthanasia, illustrating MLA documentation, has been brought up to date.

- The section on *logic* in Chapter 1 has doubled in length, with a presentation of argumentation that includes *deductive and inductive reasoning*.

- A new appendix (Appendix C) discusses the techniques of *interviewing* and *field research* to enable students to maintain academic rigor in and get the maximum amount of value from interviews and direct observation as sources for research and other essays.

- The Instructor's Manual emphasizes the possible use of *collaborative activities* in preparing many of the exercises and assignments—even the research essay. Potentially collaborative assignments are flagged in the Instructor's Manual.

- For instructors who want their classes to engage in pre-writing, the Instructor's Manual includes suggestions for *brainstorming* activities to encourage the rigorous exploration of topics.

Like its predecessors, this edition of *Writing from Sources* includes enough reprinted articles and essays to make supplements and handouts unnecessary. The readings, drawn from a variety of disciplines ranging from anthropology to statistics, provide an assortment of topics that should interest both students and instructors; these include white-collar crime, beer commercials, grade inflation, the spread of viruses, the culture of pain, the unavailability of jobs for college graduates, the desirability of school uniforms, the lack of leisure time in America, violence in English football, the wonders of the mall, and the pleasures of solitude. There are also several narrative essays placed early in the book to encourage an easier transition to academic writing. As it did in previous editions, the text can serve as a casebook, for it includes a group of articles on two overlapping topics—changing concepts of masculinity and violence in sports—that will enable students to complete a research essay assignment without using the library.

In preparing the fourth edition of *Writing from Sources,* I remain grateful to the hundreds of my students who first taught me how to teach the research essay and to the thousands of students using the first three editions who, through their instructors, have expressed their approval of the book and have suggested changes to make it more useful and effective. I would like to thank the following instructors who reviewed the text: Dennis Barron, University of Illinois at Urbana-Champaign; Margaret Borden, Willmar Community College; Sandra Clark, Anderson University; Joyce Durham, University of Dayton; John R. Ford, Delta State University; Elizabeth Fischel, Hawaii Pacific University; Mareen Goldman, Bentley College; Gary Lane Hatch, Brigham Young University; Maurice Hunt, Baylor University; Kenneth Larson, Rochester Community College; Jo McDougall, Pittsburgh State University; Doris Myers, University of Northern Colorado; Margaret Smith, University of Texas at El Paso; and Heidi Weidner, Texas Tech University. John Elliott of St. Martin's Press has been patient and kindly throughout the preparation of this edition.

Full-time administration does not lend itself to the timely completion of new editions of textbooks. The fourth edition of *Writing from Sources* would not exist were it not for the efforts of Marybeth McMahon, Eric Wilson, and—most particularly—Marianne Ahokas; the latter made invaluable contributions to the revision of exercises and to the preparation of the Instructor's Manual. I am particularly grateful to Eve Zarin for her contributions to the Instructor's Manual and for her preparation of the first draft of Appendix C. Moral support for the enterprise came from Richard Barsam, Diane Dettmore, and Dolly Martinez, to all of whom I owe special gratitude and affection.

Brenda Spatt

To the Student

Every day, as you talk, write, and work, you use sources. Most of the knowledge and many of the ideas that you express to others originate outside yourself. You have learned from your formal schooling and from observing the world around you, from reading, from watching television and movies, and from a multitude of other experiences. Most of the time, you do not consciously think about where you got the information; you simply go about your activities, communicating with others and making decisions based on your acquired knowledge.

In college, however, using sources becomes more concentrated and deliberate. Each course bombards you with new facts and ideas. Your academic success depends on how well you can understand what you read and hear in your courses, distinguish the more important from the less important, relate new facts or ideas to what you already have learned, and, especially, communicate your findings to others.

Most college writing is both informative and interpretive; that is, it contains material that you take from sources and ideas that are your own. Depending on the individual course and assignment, a college paper may emphasize your own conclusions supported by knowledge you have gathered, or it may emphasize that knowledge, showing that you have mastered a certain body of information. In any case it will contain something of others and something of you. If twenty students in your class are all assigned the same topic, the other nineteen papers will all be somewhat different from yours.

The main purpose of college writing assignments is to help you consolidate what you have learned and to expand your capacity for constructive thinking and clear communication. These are not merely academic skills; there are few careers in which success does not depend on these abilities. You will listen to the opinions of your boss, your colleagues, and your customers; or read the case histories of your clients or patients; or study the marketing reports of your salespeople or the product specifications of your suppliers; or perhaps even analyze the papers of your students! Whatever your job, the decisions that you make and the actions that you take will depend on your ability to understand and evaluate what your sources are saying (whether orally or in writing), to recognize any important pattern or theme, and to form conclusions. As you build on other people's ideas, you certainly will be expected to remember which facts and opinions came from which source and to give appropriate credit. Chances are that you will also be expected to draft a memo, a letter, a report, or a case history that will summarize your information and present and support your conclusions.

To help you see the connection between college and professional writing, here are some typical essay topics for various college courses, each followed by a parallel writing assignment that you might have to do on the job. Notice that all of the pairs of assignments call for much the same skills: the writer must consult a variety of sources, present what he or she has learned from those sources, and interpret that knowledge in the light of experience.

ACADEMIC ASSIGNMENT	PROFESSIONAL ASSIGNMENT	SOURCES
For a *political science* course, you choose a law presently being debated in Congress or the state legislature, and argue for its passage.	As a *lobbyist, consumer advocate*, or *public relations expert*, you prepare a pamphlet to arouse public interest in your agency's program.	debates Congressional Record editorials periodical articles your opinions
For a *health sciences* course, you summarize present knowledge about the appropriate circumstances for prescribing tranquilizers and suggest some safeguards for their use.	As a *member of a medical research team*, you draft a report summarizing present knowledge about a specific medication and suggesting likely directions for your team's research.	books journals government and pharmaceutical industry reports on-line abstracts
For a *psychology* course, you analyze the positive and negative effects of peer group pressure.	As a *social worker* attached to a halfway house for adolescents, you write a case history of three boys, determining whether they are to be sent to separate homes or kept in the same facility.	textbooks journals case studies interviews personal experience
For a *business management* course, you decide which department or service of your college should be eliminated if the budget were cut by 3 percent next year; you defend your choice.	As an *assistant to a management consultant*, you draft a memo recommending measures to save a manufacturing company that is in severe financial trouble.	ledgers interviews newspapers journals
For a *sociology* or *history* course, you compare reactions to unemployment in the 1990s with reactions in the 1930s.	As a *staff member in the social services agency* of a small city, you prepare a report on the social consequences that would result from closing of major factory.	newspapers magazines books interviews

ACADEMIC ASSIGNMENT	PROFESSIONAL ASSIGNMENT	SOURCES
For a *physical education* course, you classify the ways in which a team can react to a losing streak and recommend some ways in which coaches can maintain team morale.	As a *member of a special committee of physical-education teachers,* you help plan an action paper that will improve your district's performance in interscholastic sports.	textbooks articles observation and personal experience
For an *anthropology* course, you contrast the system of punishment used by a tribe that you have studied with the penal code used in your home or college town.	As *assistant to the head of the local correction agency,* you prepare a report comparing the success of eight minimum-security prisons around the country.	textbooks lectures articles observation and personal experience
For a *physics* course, you write a definition of "black holes" and explain why theories about them were fully developed in the second half of the twentieth century—not earlier, not later.	As a *physicist* working for a university research team, you write a grant application based on an imminent breakthrough in your field.	books journals on-line abstracts E-mail
For a *nutrition* course, you explain why adolescents prefer junk food.	As a *dietician* at the cafeteria of a local high school, you write a memo that accounts for the increasing waste of food and recommends changes in the lunch menu.	textbooks articles interviews observation
For an *engineering* course, you describe changes and improvements in techniques of American coal mining over the last hundred years.	As a *mining engineer,* you write a report determining whether it is cost-effective for your company to take over the derelict mine that you were sent to survey.	books articles observation and experience E-mail

Writing from Sources will help you learn the basic procedures that are common to all kinds of academic and professional writing and will provide enough practice in these skills to enable you to write from sources confidently and successfully. Here are the basic skills.

1. *Choosing a topic:* deciding what you are actually writing about; interpreting the requests of your instructor, boss, or client, and determining the scope and limits of the assignment; making the project manageable.
2. *Finding sources and acquiring information:* deciding how much supporting information you are going to need (if any) and locating it; evaluating

sources and determining which are most suitable and trustworthy for your purpose; taking notes on your sources and on your own reactions; judging when you have sufficient information.

3. *Determining your main idea:* determining the purpose of what you are writing and your probable conclusions; redefining the scope and objective in the light of what you have learned from your sources.

4. *Taking notes:* presenting your sources through summary, outline, paraphrase, and quotation; learning when each skill is most appropriate.

5. *Organizing your material:* determining what must be included and what may be eliminated; arranging your evidence in the most efficient and convincing way, so that your reader will reach the same conclusions as you; calling attention to common patterns and ideas that will reinforce your thesis; making sure that your presentation has a beginning, middle, and end, and that the stages are in logical order.

6. *Writing your assignment:* breaking down the mass of information into easily understood units or paragraphs; constructing each paragraph so that the reader will receive a general idea that will advance your main idea, as well as providing supporting examples and details that will make it convincing.

7. *Giving credit to your sources:* ensuring that your reader knows who is responsible for which idea; distinguishing between the evidence of your sources and your own interpretation and evaluation; assessing the relative reliability and usefulness of each source so that the reader can appreciate your basis for judgment.

This list of skills may seem overwhelming right now. But remember: you will be learning these procedures *gradually.* In Part I, you will learn how to get the most out of what you read and how to use the skills of summary, quotation, and paraphrase to provide accurate accounts of your sources. In Part II, you will begin to apply these skills as you prepare an essay based on a single reading and then a synthesis essay drawing on a group of sources. Finally, in Part III, you will go to the library to locate your own sources and begin the complex process of research. The gradual increase in the number of sources will make each stage of the process more complex and demanding, but not essentially different.

The best way to gain confidence and facility in writing from sources is to master each skill so thoroughly that it becomes automatic, like riding a bicycle or driving a car. To help you break the task down into workable units, each procedure will first be illustrated with a variety of models and then followed by exercises to give you as much practice as you need before going on to the next step. As you go on to write essays for other courses, you can concentrate more and more on *what* you are writing and forget about *how* to write from sources, for these methods will have become natural and automatic.

Part I

MAKING YOUR SOURCES YOUR OWN

Academic writers continually study and use the ideas of others. However good and original their own ideas may be, academic writers must explore the work of authorities in their field, to estimate its value and its relevance to their own work, and then to place the ideas and the words of others side by side with their own. We call this process *research*.

To make use of another person's ideas in developing your own work, you need to appreciate (and even temporarily share) that person's point of view. Naturally, you need to read extensively and learn to understand what you read. In Chapter 1, you will learn to distinguish the main ideas of an essay and to grasp its strategy and development. You can measure your comprehension by your ability to sum up a group of related ideas briefly, yet completely. Chapter 1 ends with some practice in presenting a source through *summary*.

In order to use what you have learned from your reading and to write about your sources in essays, you must learn two other basic methods of presenting sources. Chapter 2 will show you how to use *quotation* and *paraphrase* to represent your sources fairly. You must make it clear to your reader whether a specific idea, sentence, or group of sentences is the product of your work or that of another.

- *Quotation* shows that someone else is responsible for the precise phrasing, as well as the ideas, in the quoted sentences.
- Through *paraphrase,* you express the ideas of others in your own words and so demonstrate your understanding of the source and your ability to integrate these ideas into your own work.

Using quotation or paraphrase and including the source's name helps you to avoid the dishonest "borrowings," called *plagiarism*, that occur when the reader cannot tell who wrote what and so gives you credit for work that you did not do. Finally, whether you paraphrase or quote, you must always acknowledge your source with a clear citation of the writer's name.

Although these methods of presentation are somewhat technical, requiring a high standard of accuracy, they are used throughout the academic and professional world. You will use them again and again, until they become automatic.

·1·

Reading for Understanding

Before class began, I happened to walk around the room and I glanced at some of the books lying open on the desks. Not one book had a mark in it! Not one underlining! Every page was absolutely clean! These twenty-five students all owned the book, and they'd all read it. They all knew that there'd be an exam at the end of the week; and yet not one of them had had the sense to make a marginal note!

Teacher of an English honors class

Why was this teacher so horrified? The students had fulfilled their part of the college contract by reading the book and coming to class. Why write anything down, they might argue, when the ideas are already printed on the page. All you have to do is read the assignment and, later on, review by skimming it again. Sometimes it pays to underline an important point, but only in very long chapters, so that you don't have to read every word all over again. Taking notes wastes a lot of time, and anyway, there's never enough space in the margins.

The last point is true: narrow margins do discourage students from making notes. But the other comments are all typical of passive readers, who think that they are working when their eyes rove over every page, line after line, chapter after chapter, until the entire assignment has been "read." In fact, they are looking, not reading.

Effective reading—reading that is active, not passive—requires concentration. Reading is hard work.

Responding to what you are reading and participating in a mental dialogue between yourself and an author can be challenging but difficult. But only this kind of involvement can prevent your eyes from glazing over and your thoughts from wandering off to next weekend or next summer.

3

> ## Guidelines for Effective Reading
>
> - As you read and reread, notice which ideas make you react.
> - Pause frequently—not to take a break but to think about and respond to what you have read. If the reading has been difficult, these pauses will provide time for you to figure out what questions you need to ask yourself to gain full understanding.
> - As you read, have a pencil in your hand so that you can make lines, checks, and comments in and around what you are reading. You may even want to use several colored pens to help you distinguish between different ideas or themes as they recur. Of course, if you don't own the book, always take notes on separate paper. If you underline or write in a library book, you are committing an act of vandalism, like writing graffiti on a wall. Others will be using the book after you and will not benefit from your notes.

Pause Frequently

As with any job, active reading seems more rewarding if you have a product to show for your labors. *In active reading, this product is notes:* the result of contact (even friction) between your mind and the author's.

UNDERLINING

Underlining is used for selection and emphasis. *When you underline, you are distinguishing between what is important (and worth rereading) and what you can skip on later readings.* Such discrimination is never easy. In fact, it's usually hard to underline a text on a first reading, since you don't yet know what is crucial to the work's main ideas. Underlining, then, can be a sophisticated analytical skill.

On the other hand, underlining can also be the active sign of passive reading. You can underline while you are half-asleep: the brain doesn't need to work in order to make the pencil move across the page. Too often, underlining merely represents so many minutes spent on an assignment: the pencil running over the page indicates that the eyes have run over the same lines. Many pages are underlined or colored with "hi-liter" so completely that there is hardly anything left over. *Everything* has been chosen for emphasis.

Underlining means selection. Some points are worth reviewing, and some are not. Try *underlining* and also *circling* and *bracketing* words and phrases that seem worth rereading and remembering. You probably would want to underline:

- *important generalizations* and *topic sentences*
- *examples* that have helped you understand a difficult idea
- *transitional points,* where the argument changes

Or try "underlining" by using *checks in the margin.* Either way, deciding *what* to mark is the important step.

ANNOTATING

Annotation refers to the comments you write in the margins when you interpret, evaluate, or question the author's meaning, define a word or phrase, or clarify a point. You are annotating when you jot down short explanations, summaries, or definitions in the margin. You are also annotating when you note down an idea of your own: a question or counterargument, perhaps, or a point for comparison. Annotation is different from taking notes on a separate page (a procedure that will be discussed in Chapter 8). *Not every reading deserves to be annotated.* Since the process takes time and concentration, save your marginal notes for material that is especially difficult or stimulating.

Here is an example of a passage that has been annotated on the second reading. Difficult words have been defined; a few ideas have been summarized; and some problems and questions have been raised.

from LAND OF DESIRE

William Leach

why quotes? — To make customers feel welcome, merchants trained workers to treat them as "special people" and as "guests." The numbers of service workers, including those

entrust: customers are precious possessions — entrusted with the care of customers, rose fivefold between 1870 and 1910, at two and a half times the rate of increase of industrial workers. Among them were the restaurant and hotel employees hired to wait on tables in exchange for wages and

all European — "tips," nearly all recent immigrants, mostly poor Germans and Austrians, but also Italians, Greeks, and Swiss, who suffered nerve-wracking seven-day weeks, eleven-hour days, low wages, and the sometimes terrible heat of the kitchens. Neglected

True of all service workers? — by major unions until just before World War I, they endured sweated conditions equal in their misery only to those of the garment and textile workers of the day.

depends on luck, not good service — Tipping was supposed to encourage waiters and waitresses to tolerate these conditions in exchange for possible windfalls from customers. Tipping was an un-

tastes and manners of the upper classes — usual practice in the United States before 1890 (although common in the luxurious and aristocratic European hotels), when the prevailing "American Plan" entailed serving meals at fixed times, no frills, no tipping, and little or no follow-up service.

meals at any time; more choice in return for higher prices — After 1900 the European system of culinary service expanded very quickly in the United States, introduced first to the fancy establishments and then, year by year, to the more popularly priced places. By 1913 some European tourists were even expressing "outrage" at the extent of tipping in the United States. Its effect on

Why extremely? — workers was extremely mixed. On the one hand, it helped keep wages low, increased the frenzy and tension of waiting, and lengthened the hours. "The tipping business is a great evil," wrote an old, retired waiter in the 1940s. "It gives the

Waiter portrayed as victim — waiter an inferiority complex—makes him feel he is at the mercy of the customers all the time." On the other hand, some waiters were stirred by the "speculative excitement" of tipping, the risk and chance. *chance = luck, not opportunity*

cliché — For customers, however, tipping was intended to have only one effect—to make them feel at home and in the lap of luxury. On the backs of an ever-growing sweated

[right margin annotations:]

1
service grew faster than industry (same in 1980s & 90s)

Did they speak English? Who trained them?

sweatshop = long hours / low wages

2
barely endure

"American Plan" based on middle-class culture

luxurious? expensive?

middle class attracted by upper class style

Hours were longer because of tipping or because of greater service?

3

statement of theme expressed in parag. 2

all these quotation marks are distracting

all an illusion

workforce, it aristocratized consumption, <u>integrating upper-class patterns of comfort into the middle-class lifestyle.</u> Tips rewarded waiters and waitresses for making the customer "feel like 'somebody,'" as one restaurant owner put it. Such a "feeling," he wrote, "depends" on the "service of the waiter," who ushers us to "our table" and "anticipates our every want or whim." "Courteous service is a valuable asset to the restaurateur. There is a curious little twist to most of us: We enjoy the luxurious feeling of affluence, of being 'somebody,' of having our wishes catered to."

tipping as a marketing device

it's the customer who has the inferiority complex

As this annotated passage demonstrates, *annotation works best as an aid to memory,* reminding you of ideas that you have thought about and understood. Some of these notes provide no more than a shorter version of the major ideas of the passage. However, marginal notes can also remind you of places where you disagreed with the author, looked at the ideas in a new way, or thought of fresh evidence. Your marginal notes can even suggest the topic for an essay of your own.

Finally, when you write marginal notes, *try always to use your own words* instead of copying or abbreviating a phrase from the text. You will remember the point more easily if you have made the effort to express it yourself.

EXERCISE 1

Read the following passage carefully. Then reread it, underlining and circling key ideas and inserting annotations in the margins.

from ENCLOSED. ENCYCLOPEDIC. ENDURED
David Guterson

In our collective discourse the shopping mall appears with the tract house, the freeway, and the backyard barbecue as a product of the American postwar years, a testament to contemporary necessities and desires and an invention not only peculiarly American but peculiarly of our own era too. Yet the mall's varied and far-flung predecessors—the covered bazaars of the Middle East, the stately arcades of Victorian England, Italy's vaulted and skylit gallerias, Asia's monsoon-protected urban markets—all suggest that the rituals of indoor shopping, although in their nuances not often like our own, are nevertheless broadly known. The late twentieth-century American contribution has been to transform the enclosed bazaar into an economic institution that is vastly profitable yet socially enervated, one that redefines in fundamental ways the human relationship to the marketplace. At the Mall of America—an extreme example—we discover ourselves thoroughly lost among strangers in a marketplace intentionally designed to serve no community needs.

In the strict sense the Mall of America is not a marketplace at all—the soul of a community expressed as a *place*—but rather a tourist attraction. Its promoters have peddled it to the world at large as something more profound than a local mar-

1

2

ketplace and as a destination with deep implications. "I believe we can make Mall of America stand for all of America," asserted the mall's general manager, John Wheeler, in a promotional video entitled *There's a Place for Fun in Your Life.* "I believe there's a shopper in all of us," added the director of marketing, Maureen Hooley. The mall has memorialized its opening-day proceedings by producing a celebratory videotape: Ray Charles singing "America the Beautiful," a laser show followed by fireworks, "The Star-Spangled Banner" and "The Stars and Stripes Forever," the Gatlin Brothers, and Peter Graves. "Mall of America . . . ," its narrator intoned. "The name alone conjures up images of greatness, of a retail complex so magnificent it could only happen in America."

Indeed, on the day the mall opened, Miss America visited. The mall's logo—a   3
red, white, and blue star bisected by a red, white, and blue ribbon—decorated everything from the mall itself to coffee mugs and the flanks of buses. The idea, director of tourism Colleen Hayes told me, was to position America's largest mall as an institution on the scale of Disneyland or the Grand Canyon, a place simultaneously iconic and totemic, a revered symbol of the United States and a mecca to which the faithful would flock in pursuit of all things purchasable.

ASKING QUESTIONS

As you read actively and try to understand what you read, you will find yourself asking questions about your source. Sometimes you will want to write your answers down; sometimes answering your questions in your head is enough.

Questions to Aid Understanding

- What is the *meaning* of this word?
- How should I *understand* that phrase?
- Where do I have *difficulty understanding the text?* Why? Which passages are *easy* for me? Why?
- What does this passage *remind me of?*
- What is the *topic sentence* of the paragraph?
- What is the *connection* between these two points?
- What is the *transitional* word telling me?
- This concept is difficult: how would I *express* it *in my own words?*
- Is this point a *digression* from the main idea, or does it fit in with what I've already read?
- Can the whole page be *summarized* briefly?
- Does the essay have a main idea—a *thesis?* Is the writer trying to make a particular point?

On the previous page is a list of useful questions. You may have already used some of these questions when you annotated the passage in Exercise 1. And they are also the basis for the comprehension questions that follow "A Question of Degree" in the next few pages.

As these questions suggest, to understand what you read, your mind has to sweep back and forth between each sentence on the page and the larger context of the whole paragraph or essay. You can misunderstand the author's meaning if you interpret ideas *out of context*, ignoring the way in which they fit into the work as a whole.

Being a fast reader is not necessarily an advantage. Thorough comprehension takes time and careful reading. In fact, it is usually on the *second* reading, when you begin to understand the overall meaning and structure of the work, that questions begin to pop into your head and you begin to read more carefully.

Annotating and Asking Questions: "A Question of Degree"

Read "A Question of Degree" once, and then go over it more slowly a second time. During your second reading, as you read each paragraph:

A. *Underline* and *annotate* the text, while asking yourself *comprehension questions* based on the list of questions on p. 7.

B. *Compare your annotations* with the annotated version of the first two paragraphs on pp. 11–12.

C. *Compare your comprehension questions* with the list of sample questions starting on p. 12 (the paragraphs in the essay are numbered so that you can go back and forth from essay to list). Think of your own response to each question, and then compare your answers with the ones that are provided in the right-hand column.

Some of the sample questions may seem very subtle to you, and you may wonder whether you would have thought of all of them yourself. But they are model questions, to show you what you *could* ask if you wanted to gain an especially thorough understanding of the essay.

A QUESTION OF DEGREE
Blanche D. Blank

Perhaps we should rethink an idea fast becoming an undisputed premise of American life: that a college degree is a necessary (and perhaps even a sufficient) precondition for success. I do not wish to quarrel with the assumptions made about the benefits of orthodox education. I want only to expose its false god: the four-year, all-purpose, degree-granting college, aimed at the so-called college-age population and by now almost universally accepted as the stepping-stone to "meaningful" and "better" jobs.

What is wrong with the current college/work cycle can be seen in the following anomalies: we are selling college to the youth of America as a take-off pad for the material good life. College is literally advertised and packaged as a means for getting more money through "better" jobs at the same time that Harvard graduates are taking jobs as taxi drivers. This situation is a perversion of the true spirit of a university, a perversion of a humane social ethic and, at bottom, a patent fraud. To take the last point first, the economy simply is not geared to guaranteeing these presumptive "better" jobs; the colleges are not geared to training for such jobs; and the ethical propriety of the entire enterprise is very questionable. We are by definition (rather than by analysis) establishing two kinds of work: work labeled "better" because it has a degree requirement tagged to it and nondegree work, which, through this logic, becomes automatically "low level."

This process is also destroying our universities. The "practical curriculum" must become paramount; the students must become prisoners; the colleges must become servants of big business and big government. Under these conditions the university can no longer be an independent source of scientific and philosophic truth-seeking and moral criticism.

Finally, and most important, we are destroying the spirit of youth by making college compulsory at adolescence, when it may be least congruent with emotional and physical needs; and we are denying college as an optional and continuing experience later in life, when it might be most congruent with intellectual and recreational needs.

Let me propose an important step to reverse these trends and thus help restore freedom and dignity to both our colleges and our work-places. We should outlaw employment discrimination based on college degrees. This would simply be another facet of our "equal opportunity" policy and would add college degrees to sex, age, race, religion and ethnic group as inherently unfair bases for employment selection.

People would, wherever possible, demonstrate their capacities on the job. Where that proved impractical, outside tests could still serve. The medical boards, bar exams, mechanical, mathematical and verbal aptitude tests might still be used by various enterprises. The burden of proof of their legitimacy, however, would remain with the using agencies. So too would the costs. Where the colleges were best equipped to impart a necessary skill they would do so, but only where it would be natural to the main thrust of a university endeavor.

The need for this rethinking and for this type of legislation may best be illustrated by a case study. Joe V. is a typical liberal-arts graduate, fired by imaginative art and literature. He took a job with a large New York City bank, where he had the opportunity to enter the "assistant manager training program." The trainees rotated among different bank departments to gain technical know-how and experience and also received classroom instruction, including some sessions on "how to write a business letter." The program was virtually restricted to college graduates. At the end of the line, the trainees became assistant bank managers: a position consisting largely of giving simple advice to bank customers and a modest amount of

2

3

4

5

6

7

supervision of employees. Joe searched for some connection between his job and the training program, on the one hand, and his college-whetted appetites and skills on the other. He found none.

In giving Joe preference for the training program, the bank had bypassed a few enthusiastic aspirants already dedicated to a banking career and daily demonstrating their competence in closely related jobs. After questioning his superiors about the system, Joe could only conclude that the "top brass" had some very diffuse and not-too-well-researched or even well-thought-out conceptions about college men. The executives admitted that a college degree did not of itself ensure the motivation or the verbal or social skills needed. Nor were they clear about what skills were most desirable for their increasingly diverse branches. Yet, they clung to the college prerequisite.

Business allows the colleges to act as recruiting, screening and training agencies for them because it saves money and time. Why colleges allow themselves to act as servicing agents may not be as apparent. One reason may be that colleges are increasingly becoming conventional bureaucracies. It is inevitable, therefore, that they should respond to the first and unchallenged law of bureaucracy: Expand! The more that colleges can persuade outside institutions to restrict employment in favor of their clientele, the stronger is the college's hold and attraction. This rationale becomes even clearer when we understand that the budgets of public universities hang on the number of students "serviced." Seen from this perspective, then, it is perhaps easier to understand why such matters as "university independence," or "the propriety" of using the public bankroll to support enterprises that are expected to make private profits, can be dismissed. Conflict of interest is difficult to discern when the interests involved are your own. . . .

What is equally questionable is whether a college degree, as such, is proper evidence that those new skills that are truly needed will be delivered. A friend who works for the Manpower Training Program feels that there is a clear divide between actual job needs and college-degree requirements. One of her chief frustrations is the knowledge that many persons with the ability to do paraprofessional mental-health work are lost to jobs they could hold with pleasure and profit because the training program also requires a two-year associate arts degree.

Obviously, society can and does manipulate job status. I hope that we can manipulate it in favor of the greatest number of people. More energy should be spent in trying to upgrade the dignity of all socially useful work and to eliminate the use of human beings for any work that proves to be truly destructive of the human spirit. Outlawing the use of degrees as prerequisites for virtually every job that our media portray as "better" should carry us a long step toward a healthier society. Among other things, there is far more evidence that work can make college meaningful than that college can make work meaningful.

My concern about this degree/work cycle might be far less acute, however, if everyone caught up in the system were having a good time. But we seem to be generating a college population that oscillates between apathy and hostility. One of the major reasons for this joylessness in our university life is that the students see themselves as prisoners of economic necessity. They have bought the media messages about better jobs, and so they do their time. But the promised land of "better" jobs is, on the one hand, not materializing; and on the other hand the student is by now socialized to find such "better" jobs distasteful even if they were to materialize.

One of the major improvements that could result from the proposed legislation against degree requirements for employment would be a new stocktaking on the part of all our educational agencies. Compulsory schools, for example, would understand that the basic skills for work and family life in our society would have to be compressed into those years of schooling.　　　　13

Colleges and universities, on the other hand, might be encouraged to be as unrestricted, as continuous and as open as possible. They would be released from the pressures of ensuring economic survival through a practical curriculum. They might best be modeled after museums. Hours would be extensive, fees minimal, and services available to anyone ready to comply with course-by-course demands. Colleges under these circumstances would have a clearly understood focus, which might well be the traditional one of serving as a gathering place for those persons who want to search for philosophic and scientific "truths."　　　　14

This proposal should help our universities rid themselves of some strange and gratuitous practices. For example, the university would no longer have to organize itself into hierarchical levels: B.A., M.A., Ph.D. There would simply be courses of greater and lesser complexity in each of the disciplines. In this way graduate education might be more rationally understood and accepted for what it is—more education.　　　　15

The new freedom might also relieve colleges of the growing practice of instituting extensive "work programs," "internships" and "independent study" programs. The very names of these enterprises are tacit admissions that the campus itself is not necessary for many genuinely educational experiences. But, along with "external degree" programs, they seem to pronounce that whatever one has learned in life by whatever diverse and interesting routes cannot be recognized as increasing one's dignity, worth, usefulness or self-enjoyment until it is converted into degree credits.　　　　16

The legislation I propose would offer a more rational order of priorities. It would help recapture the genuine and variegated dignity of the workplace along with the genuine and more specialized dignity of the university. It should help restore to people of all ages and inclinations a sense of their own basic worth and offer them as many roads as possible to reach Rome.　　　　17

"A Question of Degree": Example of Annotations

everyone believes it

Perhaps we should rethink an idea fast becoming an undisputed premise of American life: that a college degree is a (necessary) (and perhaps even a (sufficient)) precondition for success. I do not wish to quarrel with the assumptions made about the benefits of (orthodox) education. I want only to expose its (false god) the four-year, all-purpose, degree-granting college, aimed at the (so-called) college-age population　　1

everyone thinks is a good education

necessary vs. sufficient?

=false idol

18 yrs old

B.B. doesn't agree

and by now almost universally accepted as the stepping-stone to "meaningful" and "better" jobs.

college leads to work

inconsistencies

What is wrong with the current college/work cycle can be seen in the following anomalies: we are selling college to the youth of America as a take-off pad for the material good life. College is literally advertised and packaged as a means for getting more money through "better" jobs at the same time that Harvard graduates are taking jobs as taxi drivers. This situation is a perversion of the true spirit of a university, a perversion of a humane social ethic and, at bottom, a patent fraud. To take the last point first, the economy simply is not geared to guaranteeing these presumptive "better" jobs; the colleges are not geared to training for such jobs; and the ethical propriety of the entire enterprise is very questionable. We are by definition (rather than by analysis) establishing two kinds of work: work labeled "better" because it has a degree requirement tagged to it and nondegree work, which, through this logic, becomes automatically "low level." *2 levels exist because of the convenience of these institutions.* [But surely the "better" v.s. "low level" work existed long before colleges saw profit in the difference!]

2

presented to the public

= corruption

= obvious

colleges can't deliver what they promise

Annotations (left margin):
high salary + expensive possessions
therefore, the premise is false
to reward good work
morality
definition = by saying so
analysis = by observing what's right and true

"A Question of Degree": Questions and Answers

Paragraph One

A. What does "false god" mean?

A. A false god is an idol that does not deserve to be worshiped.

B. In what context can a college degree be a false god?

B. Colleges are worshiped by students who believe that the degree will magically ensure a good career and a better life. Blank suggests that college degrees no longer have magic powers.

C. Why does Blank put "meaningful" and "better" in quotation marks?

C. Blank uses quotation marks around "meaningful" and "better" because she doesn't believe the adjectives are applicable; she is showing disagreement, disassociating herself through the quotation marks.

Paragraph Two

D. What is an anomaly?

D. An anomaly is anything that is inconsistent with ordinary rules and standards.

E. What conclusion can be drawn from the "Harvard graduates" sentence? (Note that the obvious conclusion is not stated.)

E. If Harvard graduates are driving taxis, a degree does not ensure a high-level job.

F. What does "perversion" mean? How many perversions does Blank mention? Can you distinguish between them?

F. Perversion means distortion or corruption of what is naturally good or normally done. If degrees are regarded as vocational qualifications, the university's proper purpose will be perverted, society's conception of proper qualifications for promotion and advancement will be perverted, and, by implication, young people's belief in the reliability of rewards promised by society will be perverted.

G. In the last two sentences, what are the two types of "fraud" that are described?

G. One kind of fraud is the deception practiced on young college students who won't get the good jobs that they expect. A second type of fraud is practiced on workers without degrees whose efforts and successes are undervalued because of the division into "better" and "worse" jobs.

Paragraph Three

H. What is the "practical curriculum"?

H. "Practical curriculum" refers to courses that will train college students for specific jobs; the term is probably being contrasted with "liberal arts."

I. What is the danger to the universities? (Use your own words.)

I. The emphasis on vocational training perverts the university's traditional pursuit of knowledge for its own sake, as it makes financing and curriculum very closely connected with the economic needs of the businesses and professions for which students will be trained.

J. What groups have suffered so far as a result of "compulsory" college?

J. Blank has so far referred to three groups: students in college; workers who have never been to college; and members of universities, both staff and students, interested in a liberal-arts curriculum.

Paragraph Four

K. What new group, not mentioned before, does Blank introduce in this paragraph?

K. Blank introduces the needs of older people who might want to return to college after a working career.

Paragraph Five

L. Can you explain "'equal-opportunity' policy" in your own words?

L. Equal-opportunity policy for employment means that the only prerequisite for hiring should be the applicant's ability to perform the job.

M. What is Blank's contribution to "our 'equal-opportunity' policy"?

M. Blank suggests that a college degree does not indicate suitability for employment and therefore should be classed as discriminatory, along with sex, age, etc.

Paragraph Six

N. What does "legitimacy" mean in this context?

N. If certain professions choose to test the qualifications of aspirants, professional organizations should prove that examinations are necessary and that the results will measure the applicant's suitability for the job. These organizations should be responsible for the arrangements and the financing; at present, colleges serve as a "free" testing service.

Paragraphs Seven and Eight

O. What point(s) does the example of Joe help to prove?

O. Joe V.'s experience supports Blank's argument that college training is not often needed in order to perform most kinds of work. Joe V.'s expectations were also pitched too high, as Blank has suggested, while the experience of other bank employees whose place was taken by Joe exemplifies the plight of those workers without college degrees whose experience is not sufficiently valued.

Paragraph Nine

P. What are the colleges' reasons for cooperating with business? (Explain in your own words.)

P. Colleges are competing for students in order to increase their enrollment; they therefore want to be able to assure applicants that many companies prefer to hire their graduates. Having become overorganized, with many levels of authority, the bureaucratic universities regard enrollment as an end in itself.

Q. What is the conflict of interest mentioned in the last sentence, and why is it hard to discern?

Q. The interests of an institution funded by the public might be said to be in conflict with the interests of a private, profit-making company; but the conflict is not apparent now that colleges choose to strengthen their connections with business.

Paragraph Eleven

R. Can you restate the third sentence in your own words?

R. Instead of discriminating between kinds of workers and kinds of work, we should distinguish between work that benefits everyone and should therefore be considered admirable, and work that is degrading and should, if possible, not be performed by people.

S. Is Blank recommending that everyone go to work before attending college (last sentence)?

S. Although Blanche Blank is not insisting that working is preferable to or should have priority over a college education, she implies that most people gain more significant knowledge from the work than from college.

Paragraph Twelve

T. Can you explain the meaning of "prisoners of economic necessity"?

T. Young people who believe that a degree will get them better jobs have no choice but to spend a four-year term in college, whether or not they are intellectually and temperamentally suited to the experience.

Paragraph Thirteen

U. What are the "compulsory schools" and how would their role change if Blank's proposal were adopted?

U. Compulsory schools are grade and high schools, which students must attend up to a set age. If students were not automatically expected to go on to college, the lower schools would have to offer a more comprehensive and complete education than they do now.

Paragraph Fourteen

V. What role does Blank envisage for the university in a healthier society? (Try not to use "museum" in your answer.)

V. Blanche Blank sees the colleges in a role quite apart from the mainstream of life. Colleges would be storehouses of tradition, to which people could go for cultural refreshment in their spare time, rather than training centers.

Paragraph Fifteen

W. What are the "strange and gratuitous" practices of the universities? What purpose do they serve?

W. The universities divide the process of education into a series of clearly defined levels of attainment. Blanche Blank finds these divisions "gratuitous" or unnecessary, perhaps because they are "hierarchical" and distinguish between those of greater or lesser achievements and status.

Paragraph Seventeen

X. What, according to Blank, would be a "rational order of priorities"? Does she see any connection at all between the work experience and the educational experience?

X. Blanche Blank's first priority is the self-respect of the average member of society who presently may be disappointed and frustrated at not being rewarded for his or her work, whether at the job or at college. Another priority is restoration of the university to its more purely intellectual role.

EXERCISE 2

Read "Thrice-Told Tales" twice, and then answer the comprehension questions that follow. You will notice that some of the "questions" resemble instructions, very much like examination questions, directing you to explain, define, or in other ways annotate the reading. *Answer in complete sentences,* and use your own words as much as you can.

THRICE-TOLD TALES
Owen Edwards

These are two of the lies I tell about myself: I say that while I was at the University of Virginia in the late 1950's, I attended classes taught by William Faulkner. If anyone asks what he was like, I mention his salty language, his wonderful offhand insights and his pronounced Southern accent. I also tell people that while in the Marine Corps I was a weapons instructor at Parris Island, playing a vengeful god in the much-storied style of the Marine drill instructor. 1

Neither of these stories is true, though neither is without some elements of truth. I never spent a minute in a class taught by Faulkner, but he and I were both at the University of Virginia at the same time, he as writer in residence, I as a faltering undergraduate. Though I did have a vague ambition to be a writer (having won a junior high school poetry contest), Faulkner's course was for promising upperclassmen, not struggling sophomores. I sometimes saw him walking past my fraternity house. One of my friends described the class to me. 2

As for the Marine story, in boot training I turned out to be, quite to my surprise, a good shot. I scored expert on the rifle range, and for a few days even held the recruit record with the .45-caliber pistol. I enjoyed shooting and no doubt could have signed on for duty at the rifle range. But I applied instead for a job as a reporter on the Parris Island newspaper, and spent the rest of my tour of duty covering recruit graduation ceremonies. 3

It has been said that when the writers of the Gospels injected falsifications into the accounts of historical events, they were simply telling the truth as it should have been. Both of those lies about myself, and others I tell, are not so much pure inventions as adjustments, so I tend to think of them less as lies than as the truth improved. 4

I've thought about this rather fine distinction during the last year because of the havoc that what is called "the character issue" has wrought in the careers of prominent men. Some of the damage has had to do with public disclosure of private misbehavior, but much stems from simple and seemingly inexplicable lies about the past. When someone like Joseph R. Biden Jr. misrepresents his academic record, or Douglas H. Ginsburg fails to mention pot smoking when asked if he had ever done anything that might prove compromising, or Pat Robertson remembers combat service that his military record doesn't bear out, we all react with astonishment. How could they do something so clumsy, so obvious, so easily discovered? 5

The answer, I suspect, is that these men have simply lost track of the ways things   6
actually were. They adjusted their lives to be what they preferred them to be, not
so much to deceive as to bring the past into line with the present. A rising young
politician—like Biden—with notable rhetorical skills ought to have done well in
college. So the past is enhanced a little, then perhaps a little more, until it is synchronized with the present. A self-proclaimed archpatriot who served in a war
zone might begin to think after some years that being close to combat is very much
the same thing as being in combat.

Perhaps this penchant for counterfeit self-improvement is a universal trait. Psy-   7
chologists have begun to suspect that some illusions about our worth may be essential to maintaining mental health. And not long ago I read about the wife of a
millionaire who had virtually invented her past. But I have a feeling that this adjustment is a thing men are particularly inclined to do. How can we resist? After all, we
are brought up on heroic tales, from Superman Comics to family legends about
Uncle Bill's football prowess. Not long ago there was a lot being said about changing the stereotypes that, critics declared, create in kids an artificial sense of who
they are. But hero worship in boys is a faith that can't be stamped out just because
it's out of tune with the times. You don't have to go much further than Saturday
television—"He-Man and Masters of the Universe"!—to know that nothing much
has changed.

John Updike wrote that American men are failed boys, and for most of us the   8
heart of failure is that we turned out to be less heroic than we once imagined we
would be, and possibly not heroic at all. Year by year, we come to realize that the
universe has mastered us, and we do what we can to obscure the unhappy fact.
Though few men weave fabulous careers out of whole cloth, when we've done
something we hoped would be remarkable but it didn't turn out that way, how
harmless it seems to tell the tale as we wish it had been. If being a Marine reporter
is too tame a reality, what harm is there in changing one's assignment into something a little more impressive? It could so easily have been that way, after all.

Early on in life, we learn that being seen in a favorable light has its rewards. Peo-   9
ple are impressed; attention is paid, and we are well liked. If, at the dinner table, we
can regale our parents with adventures from our day, our entertaining ways will
bring smiles and admiring laughter. In college, young men encounter upperclassmen
whose exploits are legendary, and however skeptical one might be about whether
everything happened as told, we want to believe, in the hope of becoming legends
ourselves. Thus, in college, high school achievements grow grander; starting out in
a career, a college reputation is burnished brighter.

When I applied for my first job in New York, and wrote my first résumé, I felt   10
that to acknowledge I hadn't finished college would mean not getting a job I desperately needed and felt sure I could do well. It didn't seem grandly fraudulent to
add a graduation year because, had life made sense, I would have graduated. That
résumé took me through three jobs, until I was confident enough to return my fictitious college degree.

I once interviewed a well-known artist who told me a dramatic story about his early childhood, involving his witnessing a fatal auto accident on a New York street. I had read the anecdote before, and knew that the artist considered the incident a signal influence on his work. But when I sat down and began to write about it, I realized that the timing was all wrong, that the scene couldn't have happened the way he'd described it to me. Though the extremely graphic encounter with death was a pivotal event in the artist's life, it seemed possible that it hadn't happened at all. Perhaps it was something that had been spoken of by someone at the dinner table, and that over the years had been grafted onto reality. It is by now so much a part of this man's life story that I'm sure he could pass a polygraph test while telling it. The fictional moment, or at least his fictional role in it, are part of his heroism, just as those invented classes with William Faulkner are part of mine. Fictional or not, they are facts of a sort, because who we wish to be is in some significant way who we really are. 11

Just for the record, I didn't actually win that poetry contest, I placed second. Or was I a runner-up? 12

Paragraphs One through Three

A. What do we learn about Edwards from these tales?

Paragraph Two

B. Why does Edwards take such pains to distinguish between truth and lies in the tales that he tells about himself?

Paragraph Four

C. Provide definitions for *invention* and *adjustment* in the sense that Edwards uses them. Then apply these definitions to the examples offered in the preceding paragraphs. Which definition is appropriate in each case?

D. Explain Edwards's reasons for embroidering the truth. In what sense is this a rationalization?

E. Why did Edwards initially describe his stories as "lies" in paragraph 1, and then merely as "adjustments" in paragraph 4?

Paragraph Five

F. Make explicit the relationship between "the character issue," "the careers of prominent men," and the "adjustments" to the past: why has "the character issue" "wrought havoc"?

G. Are the "inexplicable lies" of Biden, Ginsburg, and Robertson entirely comparable?

Paragraph Six

H. What does it mean "to bring the past into line with the present"?

I. How is this different from outright deception? Apply this distinction to the Biden and Robertson examples.

   J. What is the effect of the word *synchronized*?

   K. Do you accept the parallel between Edwards and the politicians with whom he compares himself?

Paragraph Seven

   L. Consider the function of this paragraph in the context of the essay as a whole. Is Edwards's intention to *defend* "counterfeit self-improvement," to *explain* how it comes about, or some combination of the two?

   M. Which purpose is served by each of the following examples that Edwards presents: the psychologists' theories; the millionaire's wife; Uncle Bill; and the "Masters of the Universe"? How do these examples relate to each other and to the development of the paragraph?

Paragraph Eight

   N. What does Edwards mean by "the universe has mastered us"?

   O. Does telling stories about oneself represent, in Edwards's view, a reasonable response to this situation?

   P. Again, Edwards distinguishes between telling such stories and "weaving fabulous careers out of whole cloth." How, in his view, is one justified and the other not?

   Q. How does he distinguish between "harm" and "harmless"?

Paragraph Nine

   R. Examine these examples according to the same criteria that you used for paragraph 8. Is there, at this point, a difference between defending and explaining "counterfeit self-improvement"?

   S. Explain the reference to skepticism (sentence 4).

Paragraph Ten

   T. How does Edwards use the phrase "had life made sense"?

   U. Does Edwards's use of the past tense (for example, "it didn't seem grandly fraudulent") suggest that he feels differently now?

Paragraph Eleven

   V. Is there a parallel between Edwards's fraudulent résumé and the artist's story about the fatal auto accident?

   W. Does Edwards change his attitude to self-embellishment when he is the audience, rather than the story teller?

   X. How has Edwards, in this paragraph, supported his contention that "who we wish to be is in some significant way who we are"?

   Y. Does he imply that fabrications can become a kind of supplementary reality if we believe them to be real? Examine the sequence of examples that Edwards uses throughout the essay. Do you see any relationship between the two opening examples and the two concluding ones?

Paragraph Twelve

Z. Is this ending effective? Is it too short? Why does it end with a question?

EXERCISE 3

Read "Migrations to Solitude" as many times as you need to gain a good understanding of the author's meaning, paragraph by paragraph. Then make up *a set of comprehension questions* that would help a reader to gain a better understanding of the essay. (Your instructor may ask you to work on questions for only one paragraph, but remember to become familiar with the entire essay, so your questions will fit into the context of the whole work.)

from MIGRATIONS TO SOLITUDE
Sue Halpern

Shortly after we were married my husband and I found ourselves outside New York City, driving against traffic, moving to a house on the rim of the wilderness. At the time, the percentage of Americans living in rural areas had never been lower; it's lower now. "Small towns and the countryside are in grave trouble. In an economic sense, a lot of these little places just aren't needed anymore," Calvin Beale, a demographer for the Agriculture Department, told the *New York Times* after the 1990 census revealed that less than a quarter of the population was rural, down from about half at mid-century. We were moving to one of those little places, where the skyline, shingled with granite and pine, and the sky itself, and the woods, deep as night, and night itself are reminders that we are even littler. By dusk, atop the mountain that is its cynosure, you can see that our town is described by two chains of light, and then there is nothing. That nothing is tamarack, birch, and hemlock, swamp maple and swamp and open field; that nothing is the tie that binds. 1

Recently a Gallup poll asked people, most of whom live in cities and suburbs and are going to stay there, where they would like to live. What they said most was small towns. This is more than a little wistful—they'd probably rather own a Model T, but they're going to buy the Taurus. What happens with that wistfulness, though, is that certain behavior and attitudes common to rural life become, to those who live elsewhere, values. And not only that, they become quaint values, values that one need not then incorporate into one's life because they belong to a different place and time. 2

I wasn't here then, but when the Crosses' house burned down a few years ago, the people in town got together and built them a new one. The men hammered and sawed; the women made sandwiches and lemonade. When Katie Cross died 3 last winter, I dressed to go to her funeral. It was bitter cold, and when I went to start the car, it wouldn't turn over. I called my nearest neighbor. He drove up a short while later, got out of his car, handed me his keys, and started to walk the mile and a half home.

If "good fences make good neighbors," distance is a kind of fence. It draws people in. A good illustration of this was given to me by a friend when he dropped off his rototiller. ("Are we renting the tiller from him?" I asked my husband. No, he informed me, we were borrowing.) My friend was talking about hitchhiking. "You go out on the highway, ten cars pass you a minute, and you can't get a ride," he said. "Out here maybe two people go by every twenty minutes, but chances are one or the other knows you and picks you up."

Still, there is a way in which we like to be bypassed, to be ignored, which is the allure of cities. The city relieves you of a past. Its promise of anonymity, its indifference to history, offer another kind of space, another kind of distance, one too vast for fencing. Here, no matter how far apart from each other we live, there is a way in which we are always on top of each other. Our general store rents movies. Every so often a mildly risqué film slips in among the Schwarzeneggers and the Stallones—something on the order of *Debbie Does Math*—and nobody rents it. How could they? The preacher might walk in just then, or the plumber, and then there is the man who owns the store, whom they'd have to face to sign it out, and this is not the way they'd like to be remembered. When one of the largest video rental chains in the country announced not long ago that it was inviting the preacher and the plumber over—that is, offering for sale lists of customer names and the movies they borrowed—there was a tremendous outcry from patrons, who had thought no one was looking. The desire to suppress the unedited version of ourselves is as strong, or stronger, than the desire to live it.

It's the unedited version of each other, though, that people seem so often to be after. It's Tom the tailor peeping through the shutter at Lady Godiva riding by in her glory. It's the tabloids, hiring a fleet of helicopters and a man in a llama suit to get a photograph of the wedding at a Vermont inn of the actors Michael J. Fox and Tracy Pollan. "Now bad reviews I can normally handle—you put your work out there and anybody can take their shot," Fox explained. "But Tracy and I had never conceived of our wedding as part of our oeuvre. That's why it hadn't occurred to us to invite the press." And so the value of the event increased. We know who you *say* you are, the readers of the *National Enquirer* must have said to themselves a few years later, when they handed over eighty-five cents for the cover story "Michael J. Fox Is a Jerk—Inside Story of 'Family Ties,'" but since I am not exactly who I say I am, you must not be who you say you are either, and I am going to find out the truth. The quest for these sorts of verities is not limited to Americans. The British tabloid industry is thriving, even after *The Sun* had to pay the singer Elton John $1.7 million for falsely claiming he hired a young male prostitute, and the editor of *The People* was fired for publishing photographs of seven-year-old Prince William urinating in a park.

4

5

6

It's not only the thrill of watching the mighty take a tumble that encourages people to polish their binoculars, though this is part of it. It's also that the insecurity that comes from realizing there is a difference between the world as it is presented and the world as it really is has led to the belief that somebody else, somebody who is richer or more famous or sexier, *does* actually know the score, which is why they are richer, more famous, or sexier. It's the belief that these people, or books by them or articles about them, or tracts with titles like "Wealth Without Risk," or dirty movies, or peeking through the shutters, are going to lead to this knowledge. It's the belief that there is just one piece of information remaining between you and your happiness. And so, curiosity becomes a spotlight rather than a lantern, and true mystery melts into the darkness at its edges, and the world is flattened by a single narrow beam.

True mystery is the hooded merganser on the pond behind our house, and what it took for her to get there. True mystery is the kindness of strangers, which is unwonted, and the kindness of neighbors, which is not. In our stretch of woods, you don't have to say much for news to travel, and sometimes you don't have to say anything at all. Once, when my husband was away, I was mailing a letter and the postmaster observed that it was almost time for him to be back from San Francisco. She was right, but I hadn't mentioned he was away, let alone where he was or when he was returning. Another time, the postmaster's assistant told me that she was sometimes accused of reading the postcards that passed through her hands. She said this indignantly, and of course she never would, but I could see why people might have thought it. Somehow, elliptically, we know things about each other.

In the beginning the mysterious intelligence that transformed private information into public knowledge left me feeling vulnerable and unsettled. After all, I came from a place where all natural predators had been extirpated and people looked upon each other with suspicion; where, because there were so many of us, we found safety, not in numbers but in statistics, in being a face in the crowd; where we made certain calculations about walking down this street or that, and talked about the odds of random violence.

Here, where nature still gangs up on people from time to time, where odds makers bet on the vagaries of weather and the power going out, there is no crowd to hide in, and hiding does no good. Cookies arrive on the doorsteps of the sick, and prayers are said, and the postmaster inquires after your absent husband.

EXERCISE 4

Read "The Hate Behind the Game" as many times as you need to gain a good understanding of the author's meaning, paragraph by paragraph. Then make up *a set of comprehension questions* that would help a reader to gain a better understanding of the essay. (Your instructor may ask you to work on questions for only one paragraph, but remember to become familiar with the entire essay, so your questions will fit into the context of the whole work.)

THE HATE BEHIND THE GAME
Bill Buford

What is it about football that makes its followers behave so badly?   1

By "football," I refer to the sport that people of all nations, except the U.S., un-   2
derstand by that name: the one you play with your feet. It is also the one that everyone, everywhere, except possibly in the U.S., will be watching tomorrow when the
World Cup begins. And by the bad behavior of its followers, I allude to the game's
century-long history of violence. Other sports, even the most brutal, do not regularly occasion riots. Other sports do not maintain a global death toll of their spectators. And as far as I know, no other sport has caused a war (the "Soccer War"
between Honduras and El Salvador erupted after a World Cup qualifying match in
1969).

I write as a student of the game's more hysterical manifestations. Twelve years   3
ago, I, an American resident in England, was about to board a train that was being
systematically taken to bits by fans from Liverpool inside it: tables, seats, a door, an
overhead coat rack, a toilet seat—all were being hurled out, item by item, as pan-
icky Britain Rail officials called for police reinforcements. An elementary instinct of
self-preservation prevented me from boarding the train—I took the next one, on
which only half the carriages were being torn apart.

But I had witnessed a revealing moment: While one part of English society might   4
satisfy Americans' notions of how the British are meant to behave—drinking Indian
tea with milk in china cups while eating cucumber sandwiches on a Saturday afternoon—another segment is rioting in the name of a sporting event. And I, anxious
that I was missing an important aspect of my hosts' culture, have been attending
games ever since.

The violence, of course, is not the preserve of the English alone. Over the last   5
10 years, there have been soccer riots in nearly every country participating in
World Cup. I offer an example from the 1988 European Championship in Germany.
The second week featured a game in Düsseldorf between England and the Netherlands. Both countries were, and still are, notorious for their violent followings, and
the prediction was that there would be trouble. The prediction turned out to be
largely correct, although the trouble was not between the English and the Dutch—
in my experience, amiable giants with blond hair and big bellies who seemed always
to be smiling (perhaps because, at the time, their team was always winning)—but
between the English and their German hosts.

I had never met a German hooligan, and I wanted to. During a lull in a small riot,   6
I crossed a police line and sought out a young man who had come from causing
trouble and was clearly on his way to engendering more. He was about 20 years
old, wiry and muscular and very alert. His muscles were taut, like an athlete's. He
was agile, primed for fight or flight.

There were some English supporters around the corner whom the German and   7
his mates intended to surprise. He was so preoccupied by this prospect that he

didn't notice me as I approached him and, to get his attention, actually had to tap him on the shoulder. There was then, across the features of his face, an intriguing metamorphosis: He turned, assuming I was a friend, saw that I was not, became puzzled, confused, until, slowly, he realized that I was an English speaker. His face, which was initially welcoming, snapped shut, became focused, sharp like a point, with a hatred so intense that it was exhilarating to behold—the kind of pure, un-complicated hatred that can free a person to do terrible things.

He cursed, spat into my face and dropped to the ground to pick up a stone that he clearly intended to crush into my forehead. I am not a nationalist, nor am I En-glish, and in the circumstances I did what any reasonable person in my position would have done: I ran. But I remained captivated by that instant, involuntary hatred—the purity of it. How do you learn to hate like that? What images were in his head and where did they come from? What movies or comic books or bits of overheard conversation? What shaped this view, with the power of an instinct, that to be an Englishman was such a bad thing that it required hurting any person who had the misfortune of being one? 8

Two years later I was in Sardinia for the 1990 World Cup. The occasion was an-other match between England and the Netherlands. Again, the prediction was that there would be terrible scenes of trouble. And again, there were terrible scenes of trouble, but not between the English and Dutch supporters—who were still blond, still fat, still insistently amiable (although their team was then usually losing)—but, again, between the English and their hosts, in this case the Italian police. 9

The police, in trying to contain the English fans, resorted to tear gas, then dogs and eventually guns. The fans, chased by hundreds of men in uniform, rampaged through the streets, breaking windows, kicking in car doors, throwing stones, smashing up shops and, in general, exhibiting that special kind of nationalistic pride with which the English male has so consistently distinguished himself in his global travels. This went on for a long time until, suddenly, something strange happened: the Italian police retreated. 10

It was a trick; the police were merely regrouping in order to ambush the trouble-makers. But none of the English fans understood. Instead, they thought that they had defeated the Italian police. In effect, they had defeated the Italian Army. In their collective fantasy, they had defeated Mussolini. 11

They began chanting "England!" over and over again. It was a celebration of vic-tory. That's when I understood what I was witnessing: these silly men—19 or 20 or 21 years old, despised at home, ridiculed in the press—badly wanted an England to defend. They didn't want Europe; they wanted war. They wanted a nation they could belong to and fight for, even if the fight was this absurd piece of street the-ater with the local Italian police. 12

What does any of this have to do with the sport? I still haven't found a gratify-ing one-line explanation. Maybe it doesn't exist. Instead I offer four inter-related observations. 13

- Being a supporter of any sport is an act of micro-nationalism. It satisfies an ap-   14
petite to belong to something—a team, a tribe, a nation—bigger than any of us.
- Soccer exaggerates this micro-nationalism because it is played at an interna-   15
tional level more often than other sports.
- Because it is organized around the principle of frustration, soccer exaggerates   16
a crowd's behavior—that quality of frenzy, the essential element in nationalism.
American sports—basketball, football and even baseball—are structured around
gratifying the spectator; points are scored with some regularity. Soccer is structured around deprivation; a fan's experience is to wait and wait for a goal that in
many games never comes. Frustration, deprivation, denial. They are the essential
features of the game whose greatest moment is when, against all odds, the ball, finally, hits the back of the net.
- The highly irrational, mindless little nationalist wars that I witnessed in Düssel-   17
dorf and Sardinia were, on some level, merely magnified versions of what takes
place among all supporters in a stadium.

Fanciful? Maybe. And as the World Cup organizers have repeatedly said, this   18
World Cup is unlikely to be as violent as previous ones, if only because the English—those charming ambassadors of civilized Europe—did not qualify for the
competition.

But I also recall when, in the 1990 World Cup, England lost to Germany in the   19
semifinals. I, by then a devoted follower of the game, was devastated, so miserable
that I can still recall every detail of that terrible day: the weather, the clothes I wore,
the food I ate, the conversations I had, including the one with a neighbor who
couldn't understand why I had taken it all so badly—after all, he pointed out, I'm
not even English. It was the only time I ever contemplated giving up my passport;
and it was all I could do not to bop him one in the nose.

DRAWING INFERENCES

When you are actively reading and annotating a text, you may sometimes
find yourself projecting your own thoughts and assumptions into what you
are reading. While you may intend to make a statement supported by information found in your source, your generalization may not accurately reflect the
factual evidence. After a while, it becomes difficult to differentiate between
your own ideas, inspired by what you have read, and the evidence found in
the source. Should such confusion occur, *you can easily attribute to your source
ideas that are not there at all.* When you generalize from specific facts—statistics,
for example—you have to be especially careful to make sure that your statement is based on a correct interpretation of the information. Otherwise, you
will be jumping to conclusions that may not be true.

There are several different ways to describe how your source uses evidence
and how you form conclusions from that evidence: *proving, stating, implying,*

and *inferring*. These terms will be explained and illustrated with excerpts from an article about patterns of marriage in America during the early 1980s.

Quoting a Census Bureau report, this 1984 *New York Times* article begins by *stating* that:

> More and more young Americans are putting off marriage, possibly to begin careers. . . .

At this point in the article, the *Times* is offering no specific evidence to support this conclusion. You probably accept the statement as true because you know that the *Times* is a newspaper of record, and you assume that the Census Bureau has provided statistics that justify the claim. And, in fact, several paragraphs later, we find evidence to *prove* the statement:

> The trend toward postponed marriage has been growing steadily in recent years. The study found that 74.8 percent of men aged 20 to 24 had never married, compared with 68.8 percent in 1980 and 54.7 percent in 1970. Among women aged 20 to 24, 56.9 percent were single in this year's survey, as against 50.2 percent in 1980 and 35.8 percent in 1970.

Here is an example of a statement (in italics) that is immediately followed by proof:

> *Traditional married couples continue to make up the majority of family households in the United States,* but the report documents the steady erosion of this group's dominance. The 50.1 million traditional families constitute 58.6 percent of American households, compared with 60.8 percent in 1980 and 70.5 percent in 1970.

Since the article is about postponing marriage and also refers to the increasing number of unmarried couples living together, you might jump to the conclusion that most households in the United States consist of unmarried couples or single-parent families. As the previous paragraph clearly indicates, that would be a *false conclusion*.

So far, we have been examining only what the article *explicitly states* or what it *proves*. But, in addition, most sources inform you indirectly, by *implying* obvious conclusions that are not stated in so many words. The implications of a statement can be easily found within the statement itself; they just are not directly expressed. For example, according to the Census Bureau report,

> Three-quarters of American men and more than half of American women under 25 are still single.

Although it does not say so, it *implies*—and it would be perfectly safe to conclude—that *more men than women are waiting until they are over 25 to marry.* The following paragraph also contains implication as well as statement:

"Many of these young adults may have postponed their entry into marriage in order to further their formal education, establish careers or pursue other goals that might conflict with assuming family responsibilities," said the bureau's study of households, families, marital status and living arrangements. The report also found that Americans are once again forming new households at high rates after a decline, apparently recession-induced, last year.

In addition to several *statements* about likely reasons for postponing marriage, the paragraph also provides you with an important *implication: Economic conditions seem to be a factor in predicting how many new households are formed in the United States.*

Finally, it is perfectly acceptable to draw a conclusion that is not implicit in the source, as long as you reach that conclusion through reasoning based on sound evidence. Unlike implication, *inference* requires the analysis of information—putting 2 and 2 together—for the hidden idea to be observed.

In the following brief and factual statement from the article, little of interest is *implied*, but important conclusions can be *inferred:*

A slight increase was noted in the number of unmarried couples living together; they totaled almost two million as of March and represent about 4 percent of the couples.

From this information, as well as previous evidence provided about postponement of marriage, it would be safe to *infer* that *one reason why people are marrying later may be that they are living together as unmarried couples first.*

It is perfectly correct to draw your own inferences from the sources that you are writing about, as long as you fulfill two conditions:

1. There must be a reasonable basis within the source for your inference.
2. The inferences should be clearly identified as yours, not the source's.

When in an essay you cite a specific work as the basis of an inference, your reader should be able to go to the source, locate the evidence there, and draw a similar inference.

What inferences can you draw from the following paragraph, when you put this information together with everything else that you have read in the article?

Though the report said that most young people are expected to marry eventually, it noted that the longer marriage was delayed the greater the chance that it would not occur. "Consequently, the percentage of today's young adults that do not ever marry may turn out to be higher than the corresponding percentage of their predecessors," the report speculated.

First, notice that the connection between delaying marriage and never marrying at all is *stated*, not *proved*. Assuming that the statement is correct, and realizing that the years of fertility are limited, it would be reasonable to *infer* that *the trend to marry later in life may be a factor in the declining birth rate.*

Because inferences are not totally rooted in the information provided by your source, they tend to be expressed in tentative terms. Both inferences cited above, for example, use "may be" to convey an appropriate degree of uncertainty. The following inference hedges in a different way: *If the trend toward later marriages continues at a steady rate, eventually there will be no more married couples in this country.* Here, the sweeping and improbable generalization—no more married couples—is put into some perspective through the conditional: "*if* this trend continues at a steady rate. . . ." However, given the variety of unpredictable influences affecting the decision to marry or not to marry, the negative trend is unlikely to continue at a steady rate. In fact, this inference is absurd.

As preparation for presenting your ideas and your source's, the following exercise gives you further practice in distinguishing between what an essay or book actually *proves*, what it *states*, what it *implies*, and what can be *inferred* from it.

EXERCISE 5

Read "Rate of Marriage Continues Decline" (1992) and note that the trend has, indeed, continued. Then decide which of the sentences that follow are *stated;* which are *implied* (or suggested by the essay); which can be *inferred* from the essay; and which are *false,* according to the information in the article.

RATE OF MARRIAGE CONTINUES DECLINE
Felicity Barringer

Even as "family values" have become a central theme in the 1992 Presidential campaign, newly released Government statistics show that the decadelong decline in American marriage rates accelerated sharply last year.   1

The figures, from the National Center for Health Statistics, were followed today by new Census Bureau data showing that in 1991, one in four Americans of ages 18 and older, about 41 million people, had never married. In 1970, that figure was about one in six adults.   2

Sociologists and statisticians speculated today that the most likely causes of the drop in marriage rates were economic hard times combined with demographic shifts that have reduced the number of young adults, the age group most likely to marry.   3

The proportion of Americans getting married in 1991 was lower than any year since 1965, a year when the oldest members of the post-World War II baby boom were just coming into prime marrying age.   4

While divorce rates peaked in the 1980's and have been leveling off, the drop in marriage rates was accompanied by continuing increases in single-parent families. Between 1970 and 1991, the Census Bureau reported, "the proportion of children living in two-parent living arrangements declined from 85 percent to 72 percent,   5 while the proportion living with one parent more than doubled, from 12 percent to 26 percent."

There were sharp differences in these statistics for whites and blacks. More than half the nation's black children, 58 percent, were living with one parent in 1991, compared with 20 percent of white children.   6

The statistics also showed more people postponing marriage, especially men. Last year, 17.6 percent of men in the 35-to-39 age group had never married, up from 7.8 percent in 1980. For women, the increase was almost as sharp: Never-married women, who were 6.2 percent of females in the 35-to-39 age group in 1980, accounted for 11.7 percent of the same group in 1991.   7

At all age levels, black men were disproportionately represented in the "never married" column. For instance, 31 percent of black men ages 35 to 39 had never been married in 1991, up from 18.5 percent in 1980 and 15.8 percent in 1970.   8

The Census Bureau data also showed that in almost all age groups from 25 to 74 more than a quarter of black men were not living with a spouse, a parent or with children. Only between the ages of 40 and 44 did the percentage of black men not in such family groups fall below 25 percent, to 23.7 percent.   9

For white men, the rate of those not living in a family group peaked between the ages of 25 and 29 at 28.3 percent, then declines rapidly. In the 40-to-44 age bracket, for example, 15.8 percent of white men do not live in family groups, and that rate drops to 12.9 percent between ages 55 to 64.   10

"This pattern is distinctively different for blacks and whites," said Robert J. Willis, who directs the economics research center of the University of Chicago's National Opinion Research Center. He said the differing patterns of marriage and family were evident not just in the less-educated segments of society but show up in surveys of high school graduates as well.   11

For the population as a whole, he said, "My own hunch is that the decline in marriage rates has something to do with the recession. Marriages tend to be accelerated or postponed depending on the state of the economy."   12

The median age at first marriage has also been increasing. It now stands at 26.3 years for men and 24.1 years for women, higher than at any time in the last century, and continuing long-established trends, he said. For women, he said, "there are two activities that are extremely time-intensive: bearing and raising children, and establishing yourself in a career."   13

"A lot of people are trying different ways of sequencing them—marriage first, then babies, then career, or getting established in a career first, then marriage or babies," he said. "It seems to me until people have found a right way to travel through this, it'll be very difficult to predict how these statistics are going to change."   14

1. Some women have chosen to establish their careers before getting married.
2. The U.S. economy declined in the 1970s and 1980s.
3. The proportion of children born out of wedlock has risen.
4. Deciding to postpone marriage is inconsistent with "family values."

5. Fewer people married in 1991 than in 1970.

6. Career opportunities for women have increased in the past ten years.

7. In 1991, there were more black children than white children living in single-parent families.

8. A higher proportion of men than women aged 35–39 are unmarried.

9. In the 40–44 age bracket, a higher proportion of black men than white men are unmarried.

10. The declining marriage rate is partly attributable to an increased number of young adults.

11. More people are establishing living arrangements other than those of the nuclear family.

12. Black men are likely to suffer disproportionately the effects of a poor economy.

13. The birthrate will influence future marriage rates.

14. White men are apparently postponing marriage, rather than rejecting it entirely.

Logic and Argumentation

When inferring an idea not explicitly expressed in a text, a reader *generalizes* or *draws a specific conclusion* from the available information, drawing on outside knowledge and experience to predict a likely conclusion or next step. For instance, if you look out a window and observe that the street and sidewalk are wet and the sky is overcast, you would most likely conclude that it had rained recently. You didn't directly observe the rain, but you can generalize from past experiences with the same evidence. Although this may seem like a simpleminded illustration, it is, in fact, a good example of the type of logical reasoning we all engage in every day.

There are two types of reasoning in formal logic—*deductive* reasoning and *inductive* reasoning, each a distinct process for arriving at defensible conclusions based on available evidence.

Deductive Reasoning

The classic format for deductive reasoning is the *syllogism,* which consists of a series of carefully limited statements, or premises, pursued to a circumscribed conclusion:

All reptiles are cold-blooded.	[premise]
Iguanas are reptiles.	[premise]
Therefore, iguanas are cold-blooded.	[conclusion]

This is a line of reasoning based on classification, that is, the creation of a generalized category based on shared traits. Members of the group we call "reptiles" have cold-bloodedness in common—in fact, cold-bloodedness is a defining trait of reptiles. Iguanas are members of the group reptiles, which means that they must also have that shared trait. Notice that the opening premise of a syllogism is a statement that the reader will be willing to grant as true without explicit proof. Deductive reasoning always begins with beliefs or knowledge that the writer and reader share, and the syllogism builds from that undisputed statement.

Deductive reasoning follows an almost mathematical rigor; provided the premises are true and the line of reasoning valid, the conclusion must necessarily be true.

Inductive Reasoning

In inductive reasoning, a conclusion or common principle is reached by generalizing from a body of evidence, as in the example of the wet street and overcast sky. The conclusions reached through inductive reasoning are always conditional to some extent—that is, there's always the possibility that some additional evidence may be introduced to suggest a different conclusion. Given the available evidence, you were perfectly justified in concluding that it had rained when you observed a wet street and overcast sky; but suppose you then turned on the radio and learned that a water main in the area had broken overnight. That overcast sky may be coincidental, and you should be prepared to revise your original conclusion based on the new information.

Inductive reasoning uses the available evidence to construct the most likely conclusion.

Logic in Argumentation

Elements of both deductive and inductive reasoning are employed in argumentative essays, one of the most common types of essays you'll encounter as you use sources. In argumentation, the writer attempts to prove some claim by carefully presenting the evidence and reasoning so that the reader can recreate the writer's logic. Because all argumentative writing revolves around some disputed viewpoint, there must be analysis and interpretation of evidence, as with inductive reasoning; in addition, argumentation must begin with beliefs or knowledge shared by writer and reader, as with deductive reasoning. For instance, few people would challenge you if you simply claimed that cruelty to animals is bad, but there is a wide range of opinion regarding exactly what constitutes cruelty, or whether certain specific activities (the use of animals in scientific research, for instance) are or are not cruel. Is inflicting pain, or even discomfort, "cruel" by definition? If inflicting pain serves some larger purpose, is it still cruel, or does "cruelty" refer only to *unnecessary* or *unjustifiable* pain? Before contesting the ethics of medical research practices, a persuasive argument about this issue would have to begin by establishing a premise—in this case, a definition of "cruelty"—that both the reader and the writer will find acceptable.

There are common patterns of logical reasoning familiar to all of us, even if we're not consciously aware of them:

- *Inferring a cause from observed effects*
  We've all had to reason backward from some observed phenomenon to its probable cause, as with the wet streets mentioned earlier.

- *Generalizing from a representative sample*
  Public opinion polls use limited evidence (the opinions of, say, 1,000 respondents) to predict the opinions of a much larger group—possibly the entire nation—by assuming that the opinions of the smaller group reflect proportionately the opinions of the larger. Here, for instance, is a report of a survey on attitudes towards health care taken in 1989:

  > American creativity made possible the heart-lung machine and the vaccines that conquered polio—but not a health-care system that satisfies. A survey shows the majority of U.S. respondents aren't happy with our system.
  >
  > The Harvard University School of Public Health and Louis Harris and Associates surveyed nearly 4,000 American, Canadian and British adults about their country's health care. . . . A full 89% of U.S. citizens feel our health-care system is fundamentally flawed. . . .

  You can readily see how the writer uses the responses of the 4,000 people surveyed to make larger claims about whole national groups ("A full 89% of U.S. citizens feel . . .").

- *Reasoning through analogies*
  A writer may compare a disputed idea or situation to some other, less controversial idea in order to reveal an inconsistency or to advocate a particular course of action. For instance, some might claim that the wide availability of foreign-made consumer products is analogous to an infection that threatens to destroy the health of the nation's economy. What similarities in the two situations in this writer exploiting? What parallels can be drawn between them?

nation	=	person
foreign-made consumer product • produced outside the nation • invades national economy	=	**infection** • originates outside the person • invades body of individual
harmful: threatens economic health of nation • workers laid off when American-made products aren't bought	=	**harmful:** threatens physical health of person • virus or infection destroys healthy cells, or otherwise weakens person
remedy: discourage imports	=	**remedy:** prevent invasive virus or infection; destroy existing virus or infection.

In both cases, some entity (in the first case a nation, and in the second a human being) is "invaded" by something potentially harmful (such as a Japanese VCR or German car in the case of the nation, and a virus or bacterial infection in the case of the person). Having suggested these similarities, the writer can extend the analogy: The undisputed remedy in the case of sickness—destroying or preventing the cause of the sickness—suggests the remedy for the economy's illness—discouraging the importation of foreign-made consumer products.

Analogies can provide vivid and persuasive images, but they are also easily distorted when pushed too far, and an alternative analogy may suggest itself to the reader. Foreign-made consumer products may have "invaded" the United States, but considering their popularity with U.S. consumers, they have also in some sense been "invited." To U.S. auto manufacturers or workers, foreign imports probably do seem very like opportunistic microbes, but consumers preparing to buy a new car are less likely to "destroy" them than to regard them as inexpensive generic medicines designed to heal ailing pocketbooks. Careful writers recognize the limits of their analogies.

Ineffective Arguments

Not every argument convinces us to accept the writer's conclusion. What undermines the credibility or persuasiveness of an inductive or deductive argument?

- *An argument may be based on an initial premise that is unconvincing.*
- *The line of reasoning that connects premise to premise may be flawed.*
- *The evidence itself may be misrepresented in some way that raises the reader's suspicions.*

It's easy to accept initial premises uncritically because they're generally expressed with confidence in the reader's agreement—remember, the writer assumes that the reader will grant the argument's opening premises without explicit proof. As you read, you should be careful to identify the assumptions a writer uses in constructing an argument. For example, look at the following opening premise, from the second paragraph of an unsigned editorial attacking the logic of a proposed ban on tobacco products. The editorial appeared in the magazine *National Review* in 1994.

> Even though nine-tenths of smokers don't die of lung cancer, there are clearly health dangers in cigarettes, dangers so constantly warned about that smokers are clearly aware that these dangers are the price they pay for the enjoyment and relaxation they get from smoking.

The writer claims here that because the health risks connected with smoking have been widely publicized, the decision to smoke is rational—that is, based on smokers' assessment of their desire for "enjoyment and relaxation" as against the potential health risks. You might grant the dangers of smoking have been well documented and publicized, but does it necessarily follow that knowing the risks involved ensures a rational decision? If, as has also been widely demonstrated, cigarettes are addictive, then the decision to smoke may *not* be entirely rational—that is, the decision to smoke may *not* be freely made after a careful consideration of the available data and the possible consequences.

Even if the premises of an argument are valid, there may be *fallacies* in the reasoning that holds the premises together. Logical fallacies are breakdowns in the reasoning that connects the premises of an argument; they occur when the writer makes *unjustifiable* generalizations or draws *unjustifiable* conclusions from the available evidence. Cause-and-effect reasoning, for example, can slide into before-and-after fallacies—the assumption that any event that precedes another must somehow *cause* the second event. It is often true that one event causes a second, later event, as in the case of rain causing the wet street you observe the next morning. But if you make that reasoning a universal rule, you might, for instance, conclude that because swimsuits habitually appear in your local clothing stores in May, and summer follows in June, swimsuits somehow *cause* summer. It may be perfectly true that swimsuits appear in stores in May and that summer usually begins in June, but this argument fails to consider *alternative explanations*—in this case, that the approach of summer actually causes manufactures to ship and retailers to display swimsuits in May, rather than the other way around; the swimsuits *anticipate,* rather than *cause,* summer.

For another type of logical fallacy, let's return to the editorial on the proposed tobacco ban from the *National Review.* Here's the entire paragraph.

> Even though nine-tenths of smokers don't die of lung cancer, there are clearly health dangers in cigarettes, dangers so constantly warned about that smokers are clearly aware that these dangers are the price they pay for the enjoyment and relaxation they get from smoking. As mortals we make all kinds of trade-offs between health and living. We drive automobiles knowing that forty thousand people die in them in the U.S. each year; we cross busy streets, tolerate potentially explosive gas in our homes, swim in fast-moving rivers, use electricity though it kills thousands, and eat meat and other foods that may clog our arteries and give us heart attacks and strokes. All the . . . demagoguery about the tobacco industry killing people could be applied with similar validity to the automobile industry, the electric utilities, aircraft manufacturers, the meat business, and more.

You probably recognize this as an argument based on analogies. Here, the reader is asked to compare the health risks associated with smoking with those of parallel but comparatively uncontroversial activities, such as crossing a busy street. According to the writer, the situations are comparable because both involve voluntarily engaging in activities known to be health risks, and that similarity is used to suggest that laws *prohibiting* smoking would be logically inconsistent because we don't prohibit other risky activities. If potential health risks justify regulation or even prohibition, then any number of modern activities should, by analogy, be regulated. Yet, in spite of the risks in crossing busy streets, no one ever suggests preventing people from doing so for their own good; smoking, however, is singled out for regulation and possible prohibition. The reader can further infer from this line of reasoning that, since we daily engage in all kinds of risky activities, individuals in all cases should be allowed to decide without government interference which risks to take.

In arguments based on analogy, logical fallacies often result from oversimplification. The reasoning can be attacked merely by demonstrating that the differences in the two situations are more significant than the similarities, and it's the differences that account for the apparent inconsistencies in their handling. In this case, we need to consider:

- if the decision to smoke and the decision to cross a busy street are *genuinely* comparable; and
- if there may be sound reasons for regulating smoking, and equally sound reasons for *not* regulating crossing the street.

Is the decision to smoke really comparable to the decision to cross a busy street? Most people could not live a normal life without crossing a busy street, but the same cannot be said of smoking. In addition, if a minimal amount of caution is exercised in crossing busy streets, most people will not be injured; when injuries do occur, they're the result of accidents or some other unexpected or unusual set of events. The same is true of the other "hazards" described in the editorial (driving automobiles, using gas appliances, and so on): injuries result from their *misuse*. By contrast, cigarettes pose a serious health threat when used exactly as intended by their manufacturers; no amount of caution will protect you from the risks associated with cigarettes.

You might also object to this argument on grounds that go beyond the logic of the reasoning to *the ways the evidence is presented*. The writer mentions, for instance, only that 9 in 10 smokers *don't die* of lung cancer, implying not only that a 10 percent death rate is insignificant but that death or lung cancer is the only potential health risk connected to smoking worth mentioning. The writer also states that "forty thousand people die" in automobiles each year in the United States, but because that number isn't presented as a percentage of all drivers on the road over the course of the year, it doesn't really address the *comparable* level of risk—those 40,000 may represent fewer than 1 percent of all

---

Guidelines for Assessing Arguments

1. Examine the writer's initial premises. Are you willing to grant those statements without explicit proof?
2. How is the writer assembling the evidence? How is the reasoning structured, and is it sound? Can you see acceptable alternatives to the conclusion the writer has drawn?
3. Is the writer manipulating the facts and their presentation to suit the purposes of the argument?

drivers, which would make driving considerably less risky than smoking. Misrepresenting the evidence in this way prods the careful reader to question the writer's trustworthiness and credibility. (For another discussion of distortion in argumentation, see Chapter 8, pp. 381–383.)

OUTLINING

In addition to making marginal notes and asking yourself comprehension questions, you can understand what you have read by *outlining the author's main ideas.* An outline can be much more clear and complete than marginal notes.

When you outline, you are identifying the main points of a chapter or an essay, leaving them in roughly the same order as the original.

Outlines are built around the major points that the author uses to support the main idea, or *thesis.* In a short essay, the major points will probably all be parallel or of the same kind: the *reasons* why *x* is true, or the *ways* in which *y* happens, or the *differences* between *x* and *y*, or the chief *characteristics* of *z*, and so on. In a longer, more complex essay, the author may use several different sets of major points in shifting from one argument to another, or from the description of a problem to its solution, and so on.

These major points are given the most prominent place in the outline, usually in a numbered list at the left-hand margin. Secondary material—the ideas, information, or examples being used as supporting evidence—appears directly under each major point and slightly to the right. If there are different kinds of evidence presented, or several examples, or both, each should be listed on a separate line and assigned numbers or letters of the alphabet to keep them in order.

To demonstrate the standard format, here is an outline of some of the points that have been made so far in this chapter.

   I. Underlining
      A. Important for active reading
         1. select what's important
            a. key generalizations and topic sentences
            b. useful examples
            c. transitional points
      B. Works best on second reading
         1. choose from alternative methods
            a. underline
            b. highlight
            c. circle
            d. bracket
            e. marginal checks

II.   Annotation
    A.   Helps you to understand what you read
        1.   interpret, evaluate, or question meaning
        2.   define difficult words or phrases
        3.   clarify confusing points
        4.   introduce ideas of your own
    B.   Involves participatory process
        1.   read slowly
        2.   write notes in the margin
        3.   use your own words

III.   Outlining
    A.   Clarifies the organization of an essay
        1.   identify main ideas
        2.   demonstrate the connection between related points
    B.   Based on parallel structure
        1.   group related ideas together
        2.   use similar syntax for related points
            a.   points on the same level of the outline should all be expressed in complete sentences or all be expressed in fragmentary phrases

For each of the three skills stated in the *first level* (I/II/III) this outline deals first with its purpose (in the *second level:* A) and then with ways of using the skill (in the *second level:* B). The *third level* (arabic numbers: 1/2/3) is reserved for examples, while the *fourth level* (small letters: a/b/c) contains more specific examples or explanations of points on the third level.

There is no fixed number of letters and numbers allocated for each section; whether you use only the four levels that you see in the preceding outline or include even more—the next two levels could be (1) and (a)—depends on the number and complexity of the supporting ideas that you find in your source.

The purpose of outlining is to show how the author has constructed the essay and to distinguish between main ideas and supporting material.

Multilevel numbering and lettering is not always necessary in an outline. It is possible to indicate the relationships between ideas simply by the way you place them on the page. However, the numbers and letters do provide an easy way of organizing and referring to a large number of points.

There are a few rules governing *the language used in outlining.* You may take the words of your outline directly from the original, or you may express the author's ideas in your own words. You may use complete sentences or fragmentary phrases, whichever is convenient. However, *consistency is important.* Try to make all points on the same level either fragments or complete sentences. For example, in the preceding outline, the points on the third level are consistently expressed as commands, while those on the second level are all sentence fragments.

Outlining Simple Essays

Outlining is the most effective way to record the main points of an essay whose structure is clear and straightforward. In "Must Doctors Serve Where They're Told?" for example, Harry Schwartz presents the arguments for both sides so clearly that underlining and numbering the key phrases in the essay would record its structure. (Each of the main points has been italicized in the essay.) However, since Schwartz moves back and forth from positive to negative reasons, it is helpful to outline the pairing of related arguments.

Read "Must Doctors Serve Where They're Told?" and then carefully examine the outline that follows.

MUST DOCTORS SERVE WHERE THEY'RE TOLD?

Harry Schwartz

Should young doctors be "drafted" and forced to serve some years in areas of 1 physician shortage? Or, less dramatically, should a portion of the places in the nation's medical schools be reserved for young people who promise that in return for government financial aid they will agree to serve where the government wants them to? These and related issues have been debated in Congress . . . and are still unresolved.

Currently, it costs an estimated average of about $13,000 a year to train a med- 2 ical student, but those students pay directly only about $1,000 to $6,000 in tuition. The remainder is paid by government funds, by return on endowments, by gifts and similar sources. Some lawmakers see a *compulsory service liability as a means of compensating the taxpayers for subsidizing the doctors' education.*

The specific proposals that have been debated in Congress have ranged from 3 Senator Edward M. Kennedy's suggestion for a universal draft for all medical school graduates to milder schemes that would give young doctors a choice between repaying the Federal Government or serving for several years in designated areas. In New York there is already a medical training program whose students have agreed to serve two years in doctor-short areas after graduating from medical school. Those who fail to meet this "service commitment" will be required to reimburse the city and state for up to $25,000 for their free undergraduate education.

Some conservative economists have argued that *physician incomes, which average* 4 *around $50,000, remove all excuse for government subsidy.* They would require medical students to pay the full costs, financing their way, if need be, by bank loans. Such an approach would remove the motive for any doctor draft, but many in Congress fear that this "solution" would close medical schools to children of the poor, the working class and minorities.

Proponents of some service requirements for young doctors usually base their 5 arguments on the *maldistribution of doctors in this country.* In 1973, for example, California had 265 doctors per 100,000 people, more than three times as many as South Dakota's 87 per 100,000. The actual disparities are even greater, because within each state physicians tend to congregate in metropolitan areas.

Opponents of forced service do not deny the existence of local shortages, but   6
they question the wisdom of *sending new physicians into shortage areas where they will
have little or no help* and consultation from older, more experienced doctors.

Opponents also ask *whether doctors serving in isolated areas against their will are*   7
likely to give satisfactory service. And they ask why young doctors and dentists should
be *singled out for coercion* when government helps finance the education of most
professionals and there are great inequalities in the current distribution of lawyers,
accountants, architects and engineers as well.

But more is involved in this debate than the allocation of physicians. The argu-   8
ment about young doctors is relevant to the broader national discussion about national economic planning and about the relative roles of government decision and
market forces in directing the American economy.

On one side are those who emphasize the *obligation of government to use all its re-*   9
sources to reach desirable goals for all Americans. If one assumes, as Mr. Kennedy and
others do, that every American has a "right" to health care, then it seems reasonable for government to take whatever actions are needed to make sure that doctors and related personnel and facilities are available everywhere. If market forces
do not produce the desired result, this school is prepared to use either government coercion or government financial persuasion. Moreover, this school of
thought wants to tailor the means to the end. Thus, instead of using government
money just to expand the number of doctors in general, they want to assure that
doctors are available wherever needed and available, moreover, in whatever distribution of specialities Congress or its servants decide is appropriate.

Opponents argue that such *regulation would be contrary to all American history and tra-*   10
dition, except for times of war or emergency when the military draft has been in effect.
The *American emphasis, these opponents hold, is primarily upon the freedom of the individ-*
ual and affords no warrant for infringing one person's freedom in order to benefit someone
else. The whole structure of publicly financed education in this country, from kindergarten to M.D. and Ph.D., it is pointed out, has developed over the decades without any related service requirement or repayment of any kind whatsoever. If doctors
are drafted, it will provide a precedent for drafting other categories of Americans.

The issue is not peculiarly American, of course, nor is the problem of physician   11
maldistribution confined to the United States. *In the Soviet Union and its associated*
Communist states, most graduates of higher educational institutions—not only physicians—are *assigned specific work locations* for the first few years after graduation.

Some non-Communist countries, like Mexico, have a requirement for compul-   12
sory service for a limited time by doctors before they can go into normal practice.
In Israel there is a universal service obligation for all young adults. *But in most coun-*
tries of Western Europe there is no draft of young doctors.

Most of the other democratic countries of the world are relatively small, both in   13
area and population . . . compared with the United States. So the advocates of a
doctor draft in the United States argue that the absence of such compulsion in
other countries is no conclusive argument against it here.

I. Obligations of young doctors: partial cost of education borne by public, which is entitled to compensation

    A. Debt to public can be repaid through service

        1. Kennedy plan

        2. New York two-year term of service

    B. Bank loan can be used for initial payment of medical school fees

        1. extremely high income will allow ultimate repayment

        2. possible difficulty in applying for initial loan

II. Needs of the public: not enough doctors to serve the country

    A. "Maldistribution" necessitates drafting: doctors tend to practice in certain populous states and cities

        1. California

        2. South Dakota

    B. Coercion would not ensure efficient service

        1. inexperienced doctors would be isolated from guidance

        2. unwilling doctors are inefficient

III. Powers of the government vs. the rights of the individual

    A. The government is empowered to satisfy everyone's right to health care

    B. Public policy shouldn't encourage coercion of individuals to benefit others; to draft doctors would be an unfortunate precedent

        1. other professions aren't subject to a draft

        2. other beneficiaries of public education aren't forced to repay costs

IV. Precedents in other countries

    A. Drafting doctors is routine in some countries

        1. Communist countries

        2. Mexico

        3. Israel

    B. Drafting doctors is not required in many countries with a democratic tradition similar to ours

        1. Western Europe

             a. these Western European countries are physically smaller than the United States and therefore have different requirements

Thesis: A decision to draft young doctors for service throughout the country will have to consider the obligations and rights of the doctors, as well as the responsibility of the government to serve the public.

This is a four-level outline, with the third and fourth levels (1,2,3/a) presenting either specific examples or more narrow statements than the broad ideas contained in the first and second levels. Notice how the language within each level remains relatively consistent: levels I through IV contain fragmentary phrases; levels A and B are written in complete sentences throughout; levels 1, 2, and 3 do vary, depending on whether the supporting material consists of examples (expressed as words or fragments) or narrow generalizations (complete sentences). The phrasing is parallel within each section; the clearest example is IV.A and IV.B, which use parallel participial constructions ("drafting doctors").

Outlining Complex Essays

Most essays are not as clearly organized as Harry Schwartz's. For example, the main ideas may not appear in the obvious place at the beginning of each paragraph. Some writers tend to put their topic sentences at the ends of paragraphs; others don't use topic sentences at all, or minimally. For example, Bill Buford's essay on sports violence (Exercise 4) is built around a series of extended examples; Buford does not always supply a generalization that sums up the point of the example, but leaves that job to the reader. To outline that essay, you would have to draw on a set of inferences Buford suggests toward the end that would serve as the main points of the outline.

Loosely organized essays are not bad essays or even badly constructed essays. They often deal with complex subjects, too complex to be easily contained in tightly constructed paragraphs. Experienced writers can afford to break the rules, for they know how to control the development of their ideas. Nevertheless, their essays do have a plan, a structure linking one idea with the next. And that plan means that these essays can be outlined.

Essays that deal with several main ideas simultaneously are especially difficult to outline, yet they usually require and repay careful, point-by-point outlining. Such an essay is Blanche Blank's "A Question of Degree" (see pp. 8–11).

Establishing a Thesis

The outline of Harry Schwartz's essay was followed by a statement of its *thesis*—the essay's central idea.

A thesis is usually a substantial generalization, written as a complete sentence, that can stand by itself as the basis of an essay's development.

A thesis should be broad enough and arguable enough to be worth defending in a work of at least several pages. In the Schwartz essay, the thesis does no more than suggest the underlying issues, since Schwartz himself does not decisively support one side of the argument or the other.

In contrast, Blanche Blank, in "A Question of Degree," *is* attempting to convince her readers to accept a specific point of view. An adequate thesis, then, should convey some of her distaste for the excessive value placed on college degrees. But even if you fully understand Blank's position, you may still write an incomplete or an inadequate thesis. What is wrong with each of these examples?

1. According to Blanche Blank, universities need to change their outlook and curricula and return to a more traditional role.

2. Blanche Blank suggests that our present ideology about the purpose of college should be reconsidered and redefined.

3. I agree with Blanche Blank's belief that college degrees have too much importance.

4. Blanche Blank argues that employment discrimination arises from an emphasis on college degrees.

5. Blanche Blank believes that a college education isn't necessary at an early age.

Remember that *a good thesis would be a generalization broad enough to cover most of Blank's argument without being so vague as to be meaningless.* Consider the following criticisms of the five theses:

- Thesis 1 accurately presents only one—and not the chief one—of Blank's points.
- Thesis 2 is uninformative: what is "our present ideology" and what sort of redefinition is in order?
- Thesis 3 is also vague: Blank may have convinced one reader, but which of her arguments did the reader find effective?
- Thesis 4 is much too broad: Blank does not argue that degrees are the only cause of employment discrimination, nor does she suggest that employment is the only area adversely affected by the importance attached to degrees.
- Thesis 5 is inaccurate and incomplete: Blank is not urging all would-be freshmen to bypass college.

The following thesis is somewhat better than the first five: it conveys something of Blank's central idea, but it says nothing about work and the self-respect of the worker, which are ideas crucial to the essay.

6. In Blanche Blank's view, acquiring a college degree immediately after high school should not be considered the best way to achieve a better life.

A satisfactory thesis would convey more precisely the dangers of overvaluing the college degree. Thesis 7 does so:

7. The possession of a college degree cannot automatically lead to a better life and better earnings for a college graduate; the universal practice of regarding the degree as an essential for getting a "good" job can only discourage a more just and efficient system of employment.

Both parts of Thesis 7 deal with the consequences of overvaluing the college degree: the first part is concerned with the effect on the individual, whose expectations may not be fulfilled; the second is concerned with the effect on social institutions and organizations, which may value credentials at the expense of merit. It is not accidental that Thesis 7 is the longest of the group; complex ideas often require complex means of expression.

An Outline Based on Categories

Because the paragraphs of "A Question of Degree" are crowded with ideas, constructing an outline is difficult. For example, within the following single paragraph, Blank mentions most of her main points, some more than once, and in varying order. (The numbers here are keyed to the outline on p. 45.)

What is wrong with the current college/work cycle can be seen in the following anomalies: we are selling college to the youth of America as a take-off pad for the material good life [I.A]. College is literally advertised and packaged as a means for getting more money through "better" jobs at the same time that Harvard graduates are taking jobs as taxi drivers[I.B]. This situation is a perversion of the true spirit of a university [III], a perversion of a humane social ethic [IV.A] and, at bottom, a patent fraud. To take the last point first, the economy simply is not geared to guaranteeing these presumptive "better" jobs [I.B]; the colleges are not geared to training for such jobs [III]; and the ethical propriety of the entire enterprise is very questionable [I and II]. We are by definition (rather than by analysis) establishing two kinds of work: work labeled "better" because it has a degree requirement tagged to it and nondegree work, which, through this logic, becomes automatically "low level" [IV.A].

When outlining a complex essay, you must look for organizing principles and categories of ideas as you read and reread it. *Experienced readers learn to watch for points that are repeated and emphasized to help them find a consistent way to organize and remember what they have read.* For this reason, the comprehension questions that analyzed "A Question of Degree" encouraged you to stop and review the points that Blanche Blank raised. Earlier, you were asked about the different groups of people who are affected by the unfortunate worship of college degrees. The easiest way to break down the mass of assertions in Blanche Blank's essay is to *use those groups as a way to establish categories:*

A. Students who are in college unwillingly
B. College graduates who work at frustrating jobs
C. Workers who have not been to college and are undervalued
D. True scholars who resent the decline in the quality of university life

If you combine the first two groups (both with career expectations and both disappointed by college), you have the basis for an outline with three major entries, plus a conclusion that sums up Blanche Blank's central ideas.

Thesis: The possession of a college degree cannot automatically lead to a better life and better earnings for a college graduate; the universal practice of regarding the degree as an essential for getting a "good" job can only discourage a more just and efficient system of employment.

I. The frustration of students with vocational expectations

    A. Whether or not they are suited to college, students believe that they must spend four years getting a degree to get a good job.

    B. Rewarding jobs are not necessarily available, even to those with degrees.

II. The frustration of working people without college degrees but with hopes for advancement

    A. Workers with experience and good qualifications are bypassed for promotion and denied their rightful status.

    B. Since college is considered the province of the young, it is unlikely that an experienced older person will seek a college education.

III. The frustration of students and teachers with traditional views of college

    A. Instead of continuing to emphasize the traditional pursuit of knowledge for its own sake, universities are trying to function as a service industry, preparing students for careers.

IV. The deterioration of human values

    A. People are encouraged to make invidious comparisons between less and more desirable kinds of work.

    B. One form of educational experience is being elevated at the expense of the others.

There are a few important points to notice about the format of this outline. First, in some ways, this is a traditional outline: *the main ideas are given Roman numerals and the secondary ideas are lettered.* As you have learned, this enables you to refer more easily to each of the items and, in the case of the lettered supporting arguments, to separate them clearly from one another. However, because the outline conforms to Blanche Blank's organization, the number of points included under each broad category varies. (For this reason, unlike some traditional outlines, it is permissible to have only one point [A] under III.)

Next, *the presentation need not be completely consistent, as long as it is consistent within each level.* In this outline, the main ideas are all written in sentence fragments and the supporting ideas are all complete sentences.

What is more important is that *all the entries are on roughly the same level of abstraction:* the main ideas are all very broad, while the secondary ideas suggest the more specific ways in which each paragraph in the essay will be developed. In contrast, here is an excerpt from an outline in which the main entries are both broad and specific:

I.   jobs aren't available

II.   Joe V. disappointed

III.   college students feel cheated

The example of Joe V. is used in the essay only to illustrate important ideas, not as an end in itself. Entry II is *evidence* in support of entries I and III, and therefore "Joe V." belongs in a more subordinate position:

I.   jobs aren't available

II.   college students feel cheated

   A.   Joe V. disappointed

All the entries in the complete Blank outline are *rewordings* of ideas taken from the essay and are *self-contained and self-explanatory.* Outlines that retain the wording of the original sometimes don't make sense by themselves. As a rule, phrases or sentences taken out of context cannot adequately represent main ideas. And, even if such fragmentary phrases serve as shorthand notes that you (and you alone) understand, they won't be very helpful if you want to communicate Blank's ideas to your reader in an essay of your own. Is this group of points easy to understand at a glance?

I.   Degree-granting colleges are like false gods.

II.   The college degree is regarded as a stepping-stone to "meaningful," "better" jobs.

III.   The ethical propriety of the entire system is in question.

IV.   Students see themselves as prisoners of economic necessity.

How these four points relate to each other or how they serve as arguments to support the essay's thesis is not immediately clear. Nor is it any more helpful to condense sentences into brief phrases.

I.   destruction of adolescents

II.   vocational schools instead of universities

III.   non-degree work menial

It would be impossible to understand and appreciate Blanche Blank's argument from reading an outline containing these entries.

EXERCISE 6

Select one of the essays listed below, establish its thesis, and construct an outline of its main ideas. The number of entries and the number of levels, main and subordinate, in the outline will depend on the structure of the essay that you select. (For example, you may or may not need a subsidiary level for the presentation of evidence.)

1. Excerpt from *The Overworked American*, by Juliet B. Schor. (Footnotes have been omitted.)
2. "Surplus of College Graduates Dims Job Outlook for Others," by Louis Uchitelle.

from THE OVERWORKED AMERICAN
Juliet B. Schor

In the last twenty years the amount of time Americans have spent at their jobs has risen steadily. Each year the change is small, amounting to about nine hours, or slightly more than one additional day of work. In any given year, such a small increment has probably been imperceptible. But the accumulated increase over two decades is substantial. When surveyed, Americans report that they have only sixteen and a half hours of leisure a week, after the obligations of job and household are taken care of. Working hours are already longer than they were forty years ago. If present trends continue, by the end of the century Americans will be spending as much time at their jobs as they did back in the nineteen twenties.

The rise of worktime was unexpected. For nearly a hundred years, hours had been declining. When this decline abruptly ended in the late 1940s, it marked the beginning of a new era in worktime. But the change was barely noticed. Equally surprising, but also hardly recognized, has been the deviation from Western Europe. After progressing in tandem for nearly a century, the United States veered off into a trajectory of declining leisure, while in Europe work has been disappearing. Forty years later, the differences are large. U.S. manufacturing employees currently work 320 more hours—the equivalent of over two months—than their counterparts in West Germany or France.

The decline in Americans' leisure time is in sharp contrast to the potential provided by the growth of productivity. Productivity measures the goods and services that result from each hour worked. When productivity rises, a worker can either produce the current output in less time, or remain at work the same number of hours and produce more. Every time productivity increases, we are presented with the possibility of either more free time or more money. That's the productivity dividend.

Since 1948, productivity has failed to rise in only five years. The level of productivity of the U.S. worker has more than doubled. In other words, we could now produce our 1948 standard of living (measured in terms of marketed goods and services) in less than half the time it took in that year. We actually could have chosen the four-hour day. Or a working year of six months. Or, *every worker in the United States could now be taking every other year off from work—with pay.* Incredible as it may sound, this is just the simple arithmetic of productivity growth in operation.   4

But between 1948 and the present we did not use any of the productivity dividend to reduce hours. In the first two decades after 1948, productivity grew rapidly, at about 3 percent a year. During that period, worktime did not fall appreciably. Annual hours per labor force participant fell only slightly. And on a per-capita (rather than a labor force) basis, they even rose a bit. Since then, productivity growth has been lower, but still positive, averaging just over 1 percent a year. Yet hours have risen steadily for two decades. In 1990, the average American owns and consumes more than twice as much as he or she did in 1948, but also has less free time.   5

How did this happen? Why has leisure been such a conspicuous casualty of prosperity? In part, the answer lies in the difference between the markets for consumer products and free time. Consider the former, the legendary American market. It is a veritable consumer's paradise, offering a dazzling array of products varying in style, design, quality, price, and country of origin. The consumer is treated to GM versus Toyota, Kenmore versus GE, Sony, or Magnavox, the Apple versus the IBM. We've got Calvin Klein, Anne Klein, Liz Claiborne, and Levi-Strauss; McDonald's, Burger King, and Colonel Sanders. Marketing experts and advertisers spend vast sums of money to make these choices appealing—even irresistible. And they have been successful. In cross-country comparisons, Americans have been found to spend more time shopping than anyone else. They also spend a higher fraction of the money they earn. And with the explosion of consumer debt, many are now spending what they haven't earned.   6

After four decades of this shopping spree, the American standard of living embodies a level of material comfort unprecedented in human history. The American home is more spacious and luxurious than the dwellings of any other nation. Food is cheap and abundant. The typical family owns a fantastic array of household and consumer appliances: we have machines to wash our clothes and dishes, mow our lawns, and blow away our snow. On a per-person basis, yearly income is nearly $22,000 a year—or sixty-five times the average income of half the world's population.   7

On the other hand, the "market" for free time hardly even exists in America.   8
With few exceptions, employers (the sellers) don't offer the chance to trade off income gains for a shorter work day or the occasional sabbatical. They just pass on income, in the form of annual pay raises or bonuses, or, if granting increased vacation or personal days, usually do so unilaterally. Employees rarely have the chance to exercise an actual choice about how they will spend their productivity dividend. The closest substitute for a "market in leisure" is the travel and other leisure industries that advertise products to occupy our free time. But this indirect effect

has been weak, as consumers crowd increasingly expensive leisure spending into smaller periods of time.

Nor has society provided a forum for deliberate choice. The growth of work-time did not occur as a result of public debate. There has been little attention from government, academia, or civic organizations. For the most part, the issue has been off the agenda, a nonchoice, a hidden trade off. It was not always so. As early as 1791, when Philadelphia carpenters went on strike for the ten-hour day, there was public awareness about hours of work. Throughout the nineteenth century, and well into the twentieth, the reduction of worktime was one of the nation's most pressing social issues. Employers and workers fought about the length of the work-ing day, social activists delivered lectures, academics wrote treatises, courts handed down decisions, and government legislated hours of work. Through the Depres-sion, hours remained a major social preoccupation. Today these debates and con-flicts are long forgotten. Since the 1930s, the choice between work and leisure has hardly been a choice at all, at least in any conscious sense. . . .

Contrary to the views of some researchers, the rise of work is not confined to a few, selective groups, but has affected the great majority of working Americans. Hours have risen for men as well as women, for those in the working class as well as professionals. They have grown for all marital statuses and income groups. The increase also spans a wide range of industries. Indeed, the shrinkage of leisure ex-perienced by nearly all types of Americans has created a profound structural crisis of time.

While academics have missed the decline of leisure time, ordinary Americans have not. And the media provide mounting evidence of "time poverty," overwork, and a squeeze on time. Nationwide, people report their leisure time has declined by as much as one third since the early 1970s. Predictably, they are spending less time on the basics, like sleeping and eating. Parents are devoting less attention to their children. Stress is on the rise, partly owing to the "balancing act" of reconcil-ing the demands of work and family life.

The experts were unable to predict or even see these trends. I suspect they were blinded by the power of technology—seduced by futuristic visions of automated fac-tories effortlessly churning out products. After all, they say, if we can build robots to do humans' work, what sense is there in doing it ourselves? Appealing as this opti-mism may be, it misses a central point about technology: the context is all important. Machines can just as easily be used to harness human labor as to free it. To under-stand why forty years of increasing productivity have failed to liberate us from work, I found that I had to abandon a naïve faith in technological potential and analyze the social, economic, and political context in which technology is put to use. Only then was I able to see that the experts' vision of our economic system is both analyti-cally mistaken, in ignoring powerful economic incentives to maintain long working hours, and historically inadequate, owing to a selective misreading of the past.

The experts' faith is based on their assumption that capitalism has already proved itself, by a hundred years of declining worktime. Before the market system, the majority of people are thought to have toiled from sunup to sundown, three hundred and sixty-five days a year. Today we are blessed with a forty-hour week, annual vacations, and extended years of schooling and retirement. The reigning conventional wisdom is that capitalism has created the world's first truly leisured societies.

Yet the claim that capitalism has delivered us from excessive toil can be sustained only if we take as our point of comparison eighteenth- and nineteenth-century Europe and America—a period that witnessed what were probably the longest and most arduous work schedules in the history of humankind. If we set our sights back a bit farther chronologically, . . . the comparison underlying the conventional wisdom fails to hold up.   14

The first step to a realistic comparison is to reject the idea that the medieval economy entailed continuous toil. It is unlikely that the workday was much above the standards of today. The medieval economy also provided ample opportunities for leisure within the year. And the medieval period appears not to have been exceptional, at least in Western history. Leisure time in Ancient Greece and Rome was also plentiful. Athenians had fifty to sixty holidays annually, while in Tarentum they apparently had half the year. In the old Roman calendar, 109 of 355 days were designated *nefasti,* or "unlawful for judicial and political business." By the mid-fourth century, the number of *feriae publicae* (public festival days) reached 175.   15

The lives of ordinary people in the Middle Ages or Ancient Greece and Rome may not have been easy, or even pleasant, but they certainly were leisurely. Initially, the growth of capitalism dramatically raised work effort. In the words of the anthropologist Marshall Sahlins, the market system handed down to human beings a sentence of "life at hard labor."   16

Once we realize that capitalism entailed an expansion of working time, the mid-nineteenth-century turn toward leisure no longer appears as a structural imperative of the market system, as proponents of the conventional wisdom believe. It occurred because workers struggled mightily *against* the normal processes that determined the length of working hours. In this sense, leisure exists *in spite of* rather than as a result of capitalism.   17

In its starkest terms, my argument is this: Key incentive structures of capitalist economies contain biases toward long working hours. As a result of these incentives, the development of capitalism led to the growth of what I call "long hour jobs." The eventual recovery of leisure came about because trade unions and social reformers waged a protracted struggle for shorter hours. Some time between the Depression and the end of the Second World War, that struggle collapsed. As the inevitable pressures toward long hours reasserted themselves, U.S. workers experienced a new decline that now, at the century's end, has created a crisis of leisure time. I am aware that these are strong claims which overturn most of what we have been taught to believe about the way our economy works. To make my case that the market system tends to create work, I compare it with the medieval economy preceding it.   18

Ironically, the tendency of capitalism to expand work is often associated with a   19
growth in joblessness. In recent years, as a majority have taken on the extra month
of work, nearly one-fifth of all participants in the labor force are unable to secure
as many hours as they want or need to make ends meet. While many employees
are subjected to mandatory overtime and are suffering from overwork, their co-
workers are put on involuntary part-time. In the context of my story, these irra-
tionalities seem to make sense. The rational, and humane, solution—reducing hours
to spread the work—has practically been ruled out of court.

In speaking of "long hour jobs" exclusively in terms of the capitalist marketplace,   20
I do not mean to overlook those women who perform their labor in the privacy of
their own homes. Until the late nineteenth century, large numbers of single and
married women did participate in the market economy, either in farm labor or
through various entrepreneurial activities (taking in boarders, sewing at home, and
so on). By the twentieth century, however, a significant percentage of married
women, particularly white women, spent all their time outside the market nexus,
as full-time "domestic laborers," providing goods and, increasingly, services for their
families. And they, too, have worked at "long hour jobs."

Studies of household labor beginning in the 1910s and continuing through to the   21
1970s show that the amount of time a full-time housewife devoted to her work remained virtually unchanged for over fifty years—despite dramatic changes in household technology. As homes, like factories, were "industrialized," refrigerators,
laundry machines, vacuum cleaners, and microwaves took up residence in the
American domicile. Ready-made clothes and processed food supplanted the home-
produced variety. Yet with all these labor-saving innovations, no labor has been
saved. Instead, housework expanded to fill the available time. Norms of cleanliness
rose. Standards of mothering grew more rigorous. Cooking and baking became
more complicated. At the same time, a variety of cheaper and more efficient ways
of providing household services failed in the market, and housewives continued to
do their own.

The stability of housewives' hours was due to a particular bias in the incentives   22
of what we may term the "labor market for housewives." Just as the capitalist labor
market contains structural biases toward long hours, so too has the housewife's
situation. . . . There are strong analogies between the two cases. And in neither
case has technology automatically saved labor. It has taken women's exodus from
the home itself to reduce their household labor. As women entered paid employment, they cut back their hours of domestic work significantly—but not by enough
to keep their total working time unchanged. According to my estimates, when a
woman takes a paying job, her schedule expands by at least twenty hours a week.
The overwork that plagues many Americans, especially married women, springs
from a combination of full-time male jobs, the expansion of housework to fill the
available hours, and the growth of employment among married women.

The biases of the household and the labor market have been powerful impedi-   23
ments to shorter hours. Yet Western Europe also has both capitalist labor markets

and full-time housewives and hours there have fallen substantially. A full explanation for longer hours in the United States involves specifically American factors. For one thing, trade unions are not as powerful here as they are in Europe, where they represent many more workers and have pushed hard for shorter hours. For another, there are the peculiarities of the American consumer.

Most economists regard the spending spree that Americans indulged in throughout the postwar decades as an unambiguous blessing, on the assumption that more is always better. And there is a certain sense in this approach. It's hard to imagine how having more of a desired good could make one worse off, especially since it is always possible to ignore the additional quantity. Relying on this little bit of common sense, economists have championed the closely related ideas that more goods yield more satisfaction, that desires are infinite, and that people act to satisfy those desires as fully as they can.   24

Now anyone with just a little bit of psychological sophistication (to go with this little bit of common sense) can spot the flaw in the economist's argument. Once our basic human needs are taken care of, the effect of consumption on well-being gets tricky. What if our desires keep pace with our incomes, so that getting richer doesn't make us more satisfied? Or what if satisfaction depends, not on absolute levels of consumption, but on one's level *relative* to others (such as the Joneses). Then no matter how much you possess, you won't feel well off if Jones next door possesses more.   25

How many of us thought the first car stereo a great luxury, and then, when it came time to buy a new car, considered it an absolute necessity? Or life before and after the microwave? And the fact that many of these commodities are bought on credit makes the cycle of income-consumption-more income-more consumption even more ominous. There is no doubt that some purchases permanently enhance our lives. But how much of what we consume merely keeps us moving on a stationary treadmill? The problem with the treadmill is not only that it is stationary, but also that we have to work long hours to stay on it. . . . The consumerist treadmill and long hour jobs have combined to form an insidious cycle of "work-and-spend." Employers ask for long hours. The pay creates a high level of consumption. People buy houses and go into debt; luxuries become necessities; Smiths keep up with Joneses. Each year, "progress," in the form of annual productivity increases, is doled out by employers as extra income rather than as time off. Work-and-spend has become a powerful dynamic keeping us from a more relaxed and leisure way of life.   26

Faith in progress is deep within our culture. We have been taught to believe that our lives are better than those who came before us. The ideology of modern economics suggests that material progress has yielded enhanced satisfaction and well-being. But much of our confidence about our own well-being comes from the assumption that our lives are easier than those of earlier generations or other cultures. I have already disputed the notion that we work less than medieval European peasants, however poor they may have been. The field research of anthropologists gives another view of the conventional wisdom.   27

The lives of so-called primitive peoples are commonly thought to be harsh—
their existence dominated by the "incessant quest for food." In fact, primitives do
little work. By contemporary standards, we'd have to judge them extremely lazy. If
the Kapauku of Papua work one day, they do no labor on the next. !Kung Bushmen
put in only two and a half days per week and six hours per day. In the Sandwich Islands of Hawaii, men work only four hours per day. And Australian aborigines have
similar schedules. The key to understanding why these "stone age peoples" fail to
act like us—increasing their work effort to get more things—is that they have limited desires. In the race between wanting and having, they have kept their wanting
low—and, in this way, ensure their own kind of satisfaction. They are materially
poor by contemporary standards, but in at least one dimension—time—we have
to count them richer.

I do not raise these issues to imply that we would be better off as Polynesian na-
tives or medieval peasants. Nor am I arguing that "progress" has made us worse
off. I am, instead, making a much simpler point. We have paid a price for prosperity.
Capitalism has brought a dramatically increased standard of living, but at the cost of
a much more demanding worklife. We are eating more, but we are burning up
those calories at work. We have color televisions and compact disc players, but we
need them to unwind after a stressful day at the office. We take vacations, but we
work so hard throughout the year that they become indispensable to our sanity.
The conventional wisdom that economic progress has given us more things *as well
as* more leisure is difficult to sustain.

However scarce academic research on the rising workload may be, what we do
know suggests it has contributed to a variety of social problems. For example,
work is implicated in the dramatic rise of "stress." Thirty percent of adults say that
they experience high stress nearly every day; even higher numbers report high
stress once or twice a week. A third of the population says that they are rushed to
do the things they have to do—up from a quarter in 1965. Stress-related diseases
have exploded, especially among women, and jobs are a major factor. Workers'
compensation claims related to stress tripled during just the first half of the 1980s.
Other evidence also suggests a rise in the demands placed on employees on the
job. According to a recent review of existing findings, Americans are literally working themselves to death—as jobs contribute to heart disease, hypertension, gastric
problems, depression, exhaustion, and a variety of other ailments. Surprisingly, the
high-powered jobs are not the most dangerous. The most stressful workplaces are
the "electronic sweatshops" and assembly lines where a demanding pace is coupled
with virtually no individual discretion.

Sleep has become another casualty of modern life. According to sleep researchers, studies point to a "sleep deficit" among Americans, a majority of whom are currently getting between 60 and 90 minutes less a night than they should for optimum
health and performance. The number of people showing up at sleep disorder clinics with serious problems has skyrocketed in the last decade. Shiftwork, long working hours, the growth of a global economy (with its attendant continent-hopping

28

29

30

31

and twenty-four-hour business culture), and the accelerating pace of life have all contributed to sleep deprivation. If you need an alarm clock, the experts warn, you're probably sleeping too little.

The juggling act between job and family is another problem area. Half the population now says they have too little time for their families. The problem is particularly acute for women: in one study, half of all employed mothers reported it caused either "a lot" or an "extreme" level of stress. The same proportion feel that "when I'm at home I try to make up to my family for being away at work, and as a result I rarely have any time for myself." This stress has placed tremendous burdens on marriages. Two-earner couples have less time together, which researchers have found reduces the happiness and satisfaction of a marriage. These couples often just don't have enough time to talk to each other. And growing numbers of husbands and wives are like ships passing in the night, working sequential schedules to manage their child care. Among young parents, the prevalence of at least one partner working outside regular daytime hours is now close to one half. But this "solution" is hardly a happy one. According to one parent: "I work 11–7 to accommodate my family—to eliminate the need for babysitters. However, the stress on myself is tremendous." 32

A decade of research by Berkeley sociologist Arlie Hochschild suggests that many marriages where women are doing the "second shift" are close to the breaking point. When job, children, and marriage have to be attended to, it's often the marriage that is neglected. The failure of many men to do their share at home creates further problems. A twenty-six-year-old legal secretary in California reports that her husband "does no cooking, no washing, no anything else. How do I feel? Furious. If our marriage ends, it will be on this issue. And it just might." 33

Serious as these problems are, the most alarming development may be the effect of the work explosion on the care of children. According to economist Sylvia Hewlett, "child neglect has become endemic to our society." A major problem is that children are increasingly left alone, to fend for themselves while their parents are at work. Nationwide, estimates of children in "self"—or, more accurately, "no"—care range up to seven million. Local studies have found figures of up to one-third of children caring for themselves. At least half a million preschoolers are thought to be left at home part of each day. One 911 operator reports large numbers of frightened callers: "It's not uncommon to hear from a child of six or seven who has been left in charge of even younger siblings." 34

Even when parents are at home, overwork may leave them with limited time, attention, or energy for their children. One working parent noted, "My child has severe emotional problems because I am too tired to listen to him. It is not quality time; it's bad quantity time that's destroying my family." Economist Victor Fuchs has found that between 1960 and 1986, the time parents actually had available to be with children fell ten hours a week for whites and twelve for blacks. Hewlett links the "parenting deficit" to a variety of problems plaguing the country's youth: poor performance in school, mental problems, drug and alcohol use, and teen suicide. 35

According to another expert, kids are being "cheated out of childhood. . . . There is a sense that adults don't care about them."

Of course, there's more going on here than lack of time. Child neglect, marital **36** distress, sleep deprivation, and stress-related illnesses all have other causes. But the growth of work has exacerbated each of these social ailments. Only by understanding why we work as much as we do, and how the demands of work affect family life, can we hope to solve these problems.

SURPLUS OF COLLEGE GRADUATES DIMS JOB OUTLOOK FOR OTHERS
Louis Uchitelle

Hundreds of thousands of jobs, once performed creditably without a college de- **1** gree, are going to college graduates today as employers take advantage of an oversupply of them.

College graduates are being found more and more among the nation's bakers, **2** traveling salespeople, secretaries, bookkeepers, clerks, data processors and factory supervisors. And they are shutting out qualified high school graduates from many jobs, according to Labor Department officials, corporate executives and economists.

There are several reasons why this is happening. One, of course, is the growing **3** complexity of many jobs that were once much simpler to perform. But more important is the current oversupply of college graduates.

More Graduates in Work Force

At roughly 25 percent of the work force—higher than in any other industrial na- **4** tion—college graduates outstrip the demand for their skills, the Labor Department reports. And the proportion of college graduates in the work force is continuing to increase.

Given this oversupply, many experts, including the authors of a report on the **5** American work force being released today, say that employers are reluctant to gamble on high school graduates. In an age when public schools are accused of turning out many illiterates, corporate America has come to rely on the college degree as the safest guarantee that an applicant has the skills, discipline and maturity to tackle a job.

"The college degree, or even the evidence of having participated in college, has **6** become the nation's major form of job certification," said William B. Johnston, a senior research fellow at the Hudson Institute. "It is a rather expensive and extravagant sorting mechanism, to send people off to schools to learn skills that might not be necessary for work, but it is all that we have right now."

The emphasis on hiring college graduates has helped to open a huge gap between **7** the incomes of the college educated and the high school educated. Many recent studies show that the standard of living of the high school graduate fell in the 1980's for the first time since World War II, while the college graduates' standard of living, or real wage, rose by nearly 8 percent. No other industrial nation has such a wide wage gap between the two groups.

That wage gap has helped to spur more high school graduates to go to college. 8 For decades only 50 percent had continued education after high school, but since 1982 the number has risen rapidly to nearly 59 percent, assuring the nation of a plentiful supply of college graduates for its job needs into the 21st century, according to Labor Department projections.

Russell Rumberger, a professor of education at the University of California at 9 Santa Barbara, estimates that the pool of college graduates exceeds by about 15 percent the need for their skills in professions that require college training, among them engineering, accounting, law and medicine.

The Uneducated Gain Skills Quickly

The wage inequity and the growing preference for college graduates have 10 prompted new studies to determine just how qualified high school-educated Americans are. Some case studies, among them several presented at a conference of labor economists and social scientists at Brown University this month, found that many uneducated workers can quickly acquire the necessary skills to man even the most modern and sophisticated factories. If those workers succeed, then the prospect of a drastic shortage of skilled workers may be far less realistic than many had thought.

"It is pretty consistently the finding of researchers that the training process in 11 state-of-the-art factories, with the most advanced technologies, is not that complicated," said Professor Clair Brown, an economist at the University of California at Berkeley, and co-author of studies involving half-a-dozen major companies.

Many companies agree. A panel of businessmen, union leaders and academics, the 12 Commission on the Skills of the American Work Force, in its report being released today, finds that 80 percent of the 400 employers interviewed said the appeal of educated workers lay not with specific skills they might have acquired at school.

Work skills can be taught on the job, they said, but education was associated 13 with the notion that having a degree meant a person also had such qualities as punctuality, good work habits and the ability to learn on the job. For many American employers the four-year college education has become the proxy for these qualities, said Curtis E. Plott, executive vice president of the American Society for Training and Development, whose members are mostly corporate officers.

All these new findings contradict some of the most widely held perceptions 14 about the American work force. One is that the United States has a shortage of skilled workers, making it unable to be competitive with other nations' industries, a shortage that is blamed primarily on public schools that turn out young people so poorly educated that they are untrainable.

In fact, according to Ronald Kutscher, a Labor Department official, the skill short- 15 age has yet to materialize, except in a few areas, like nursing and medical technicians. And some major corporations draw similar conclusions. The General Electric Company, for example, reports no problem in retraining older workers to operate complicated, computerized machinery or in staffing new, high technology appliance factories in Louisville, Ky., and Decatur, Ala., with applicants who had two years of vocational school training.

"Somehow, people find their way to vocational training for jobs that pay enough," said Frank Doyle, a company vice president. The appliance factory pay averages $16 to $18 an hour, including $4 to $5 in benefits.　16

Company Fails Half Taking Test

The New York Telephone Company contributed greatly to the perception of a nation of unschooled young people by reporting in 1987 that out of 90,000 applicants for jobs there, 84 percent had failed a basic literacy and math test. Unnoticed was that the people were mostly applying for low-wage, temporary jobs.　17

When the American Telephone and Telegraph Company gives a similar test to applicants for full-time clerical or operator jobs, positions that include health and pension benefits, the rate of passing is much higher, said Mary Tenopyr, the company's director of employee testing and selection.　18

"It has been our experience that when you offer a temporary job, you get a lesser quality person," Ms. Tenopyr said. What's more, the pool of applicants is so large that the company intentionally fails 50 percent of the test takers, qualifying only those who can score above average.　19

Motorola Inc. has found that even the poorly educated can be brought up to the standard fairly quickly and made ready for on-the-job training. In transferring workers from older factories to new, high technology plants that make cellular telephones, Motorola discovered that many could not pass a basic skills test that required an eighth-grade reading level, a knowledge of fractions and simple problem solving.　20

Most, however, mastered these skills after six months in the company's remedial training classes. "Those who have taken longer are usually immigrants who speak English as a second language and weren't literate in their native language," said Edward Bales, a director of education for Motorola.　21

Motorola is one of the few American companies that provides remedial training, and it resents having to do so. "We spent $5 million on this training last year, and that came right out of profits," Mr. Bales said. "The public schools should handle this task."　22

But students in the public schools have no reason to believe that taking courses like mathematics will get them jobs. In a survey involving 50 high schools across the country, Professor John Bishop of Cornell University's Center for Advanced Human Resources Studies asked thousands of students who were not bound for college what mathematics courses they needed to qualify for their first choice of jobs. Fewer than 30 percent checked any math course at all.　23

"They weren't displaying a resistance to study, but an awareness that the job market does not reward them for taking algebra or geometry or trigonometry," Mr. Bishop said.　24

Schools' Responses Worry Employers

The reason it does not is twofold: companies mistrust the caliber of the courses 25 given, even when students take them and the companies have trouble verifying exactly what courses high school-educated applicants actually took.

When they send to high schools for students' transcripts, fewer than two in 10 26 schools respond, surveys show. In one case, the Nationwide Mutual Insurance Company in Columbus, Ohio, where Mr. Bishop worked as a consultant, sent 1,200 letters requesting transcripts and received only 93.

The alternative is for a company to test high school-educated applicants, as do 27 Motorola, G.E. and the Ford Motor Company, among others. But smaller companies are reluctant to test because testing carries with it the risk that a rejected applicant will sue claiming discrimination. Smaller companies are not as willing as large ones to risk those legal costs, Mr. Bishop said.

Still, ad hoc ways are springing up among smaller companies to screen the high 28 school educated. One method popular among smaller companies is probation— telling a young person to first work on the job for six months, then there will be a spot on the permanent payroll. Another is to subject even the lowest-level applicant for a clerical or janitorial job to half a dozen or more interviews. "One object is to see if the person keeps showing up and gives consistent answers," said David Birch, president of Cognetics Inc., a consultant to small businesses.

Electronic Data System Corporation of Dallas, a subsidiary of the General Mo- 29 tors Corporation founded by Ross Perot, has made applicant screening into a high skill. The company hires non-college people as computer operators and for some positions usually given to college graduates, but only after the applicant has filled out an 8-page application and gone through a series of interviews.

"A degree, from high school or college, is not a substitute for E.D.S. screening," 30 said John Senderling, a company spokesman. "We are looking for elusive, almost ineffable character traits, for someone [who] tries hard and can succeed. Once we find that person, we assume we can teach them specific job skills."

WRITING A SUMMARY

When you underline and annotate a text, when you ask yourself questions about its contents, when you work out an outline of its structure, you are helping yourself to understand what you are reading. When you write a summary, you are *recording* your understanding for your own information; when you include the summary in an essay of your own, you are *reporting* your understanding to your reader.

A summary of a source is usually *a condensation of ideas or information.* It is neither necessary nor desirable to include every repetition and detail. Rather, you are to extract only those points that seem important—the main ideas, which in the original passage may have been interwoven with less important material. Thus, a summary of several pages can sometimes be as brief as one sentence.

In a brief summary, *you should add nothing new* to the material in the source, nor should you change the emphasis or provide any new interpretation or evaluation. For the sake of clarity and coherence, *you may rearrange the order of the ideas;* however, you should strive to remain in the background.

The brief summary is often used as part of a larger essay. You have probably summarized your own ideas in the topic sentence of a paragraph or in the conclusion of an essay. When you discuss another piece of writing, you generally summarize the contents briefly to establish for your reader the ideas that you intend to analyze. The writer of a research essay is especially dependent on the summary as a means of referring to source materials. Through summary, you can condense a broad range of information, and you can present and explain the relevance of a number of sources all dealing with the same subject.

Summarizing a Paragraph

Before you can begin to summarize a short reading—a paragraph, for example—you must, of course, read the passage carefully and understand the significance of each idea and the way it is linked to the other ideas. A good brief summary is never just a vague generalization, a spin-off loosely connected to the reading. The summary should above all be *comprehensive,* conveying as much as possible the totality of thought within the passage. Sometimes, you will find a single comprehensive sentence in the text itself, to be taken out verbatim and used as a summary. But, as a rule, you will find your summary in the text only when the passage is short and contains a particularly strong and comprehensive topic sentence.

The following paragraph *can* be summarized adequately by one of its own sentences. Which one?

It is often remarked that science has increasingly removed man from a position at the center of the universe. Once upon a time the earth was thought to be the center and the gods were thought to be in close touch with the daily actions of humans. It was not stupid to imagine the earth was at the center, because, one might think, if the earth were moving around the sun, and if you threw a ball vertically upward, it would seem the ball should come down a few feet away from you. Nevertheless, slowly, over many centuries, through the work of Copernicus, Galileo, and many others, we have mostly come to believe that we live on a typical planet orbiting a typical star in a typical galaxy, and indeed that no place in the universe is special.

GORDON KANE, from "Are We the Center of the Universe?"

Both the first and last sentences are possibilities, but the first is a broader generalization and a more comprehensive summary.

Usually, even when you find a strong sentence that suggests the main idea of the paragraph, you will still need to tinker with that sentence, expanding its meaning by giving the language a more general focus. Here, for example, is a paragraph in which no one sentence is broad enough to sum up the main idea, but which contains a scattering of useful phrases:

> In a discussion [with] a class of teachers, I once said that I liked some of the kids in my class much more than others and that, without saying which ones I liked best, I had told them so. After all, this is something that children know, whatever we tell them; it is futile to lie about it. Naturally, these teachers were horrified. "What a terrible thing to say!" one said. "I love all the children in my class exactly the same." Nonsense; a teacher who says this is lying, to herself or to others, and probably doesn't like any of the children very much. Not that there is anything wrong with that; plenty of adults don't like children, and there is no reason why they should. But the trouble is that they feel they should, which makes them feel guilty, which makes them feel resentful, which in turn makes them try to work off their guilt with indulgence and their resentment with subtle cruelties—cruelties of a kind that can be seen in many classrooms. Above all, it makes them put on the phony, syrupy, sickening voice and manner, and the fake smiles and forced, bright laughter that children see so much of in school, and rightly resent and hate.
>
> JOHN HOLT, from *How Children Fail*

Here, you might begin by combining key phrases: "a teacher who says" that she "loves all the children" "is lying to herself, or to others," and makes herself (and probably the children) "feel guilty" and "resentful." However, this kind of summarizing sentence resembles a patchwork, with the *words and phrasing pulled straight out of the original*. Even if you acknowledged the borrowings, by using quotation marks, as above, you would still be left with a weak sentence that is neither yours nor the author's. It is far better to construct an entirely new sentence of your own, such as this one:

> In Holt's view, although it is only natural for teachers to prefer some students to others, many teachers cannot accept their failure to like all equally well and express their inadequacy and dissatisfaction in ways that are harmful to the children.

Finally, some diffuse paragraphs give you no starting point at all for the summary and force you to write an entirely new generalization. How would you summarize this paragraph?

> To parents who wish to lead a quiet life, I would say: Tell your children that they are very naughty—much naughtier than most children. Point to the young people of some acquaintances as models of perfection and impress your own children with a deep sense of their own inferiority. You carry so many more guns than they do that they cannot fight you. This is called moral influence, and it will enable you to

bounce them as much as you please. They think you know and they will not have yet caught you lying often enough to suspect that you are not the unworldly and scrupulously truthful person which you represent yourself to be; nor yet will they know how great a coward you are, nor how soon you will run away, if they fight you with persistency and judgment. You keep the dice and throw them both for your children and yourself. Load them then, for you can easily manage to stop your children from examining them. Tell them how singularly indulgent you are; insist on the incalculable benefit you conferred on them, firstly in bringing them into the world at all, but more particularly in bringing them into it as your children rather than anyone else's. Say that you have their highest interests at stake whenever you are out of temper and wish to make yourself unpleasant by way of balm to your soul. Harp much upon these highest interests. Feed them spiritually upon such brimstone and treacle as the late Bishop of Winchester's Sunday stories. You hold all the trump cards, or if you do not you can filch them; if you play them with anything like judgment you will find yourselves heads of happy, united God-fearing families, even as did my old friend Mr. Pontifex. True, your children will probably find out all about it some day, but not until too late to be of much service to them or inconvenience to yourself.

SAMUEL BUTLER, from *The Way of All Flesh*

A summary of this paragraph would recommend that parents intimidate their children and thus put them in their place. However, although such a generalization sums up the series of examples contained in the paragraph, it does not convey the fact that, in his caricature of family life, Butler is exaggerating outrageously. *A comprehensive summary, then, would have to include not only the essence of Butler's recommendations, but also his implied point: that he does not expect anyone to follow his advice.* Irony is the term used to describe the conflict between Butler's real meaning—parents should not be monsters, but sometimes are—and the meaning apparently expressed by his words as he urges them to treat their children tyrannically. Here is one way to summarize the paragraph:

> When he ironically suggests that parents can gain tranquillity and domestic happiness by tyrannizing over their children and making them feel morally inferior, Butler seems to be urging parents to treat their children with respect and justice.

Guidelines for Summarizing a Brief Passage

1. Find a summarizing sentence within the passage (and, if you are using it in your own essay, put it in quotation marks); *or*
2. Combine elements within the passage into a new summarizing sentence; *or*
3. Write your own summarizing sentence.

Notice that this summarizing sentence includes Butler's name. *Mentioning the author's name effectively emphasizes that what you are summarizing is not your own work.* By making it clear who is responsible for what, you are avoiding any possibility of *plagiarizing*—borrowing from your source without acknowledgment.

EXERCISE 7

Read the following paragraph and decide which of the sentences following it provides the most comprehensive summary. (Only one answer is correct: state your reason for rejecting each of the other sentences.)

> Today, pornography attempts to make its audience focus their fantasies on specific people. The "Playmate of the Month" is a particular woman about whom the reader is meant to have particular fantasies. In my view, this has a more baneful effect on people—makes them demented, in fact, in a way that earlier pornography didn't. Today's pornography promises them that there exists, somewhere on this earth, a life of endlessly desirable and available women and endlessly potent men. The promise that this life is just around the corner—in Hugh Hefner's mansion, or even just in the next joint or the next snort—is maddening and disorienting. And in its futility, it makes for rage and self-hatred. The traditional argument against censorship—that "no one can be seduced by a book"—was probably valid when pornography was impersonal and anonymous, purely an aid to fantasizing about sexual utopia. Today, however, there is addiction and seduction in pornography.
>
> MIDGE DECTER

1. Pornography is responsible for all society's ills, including insanity, substance abuse, and violence.
2. Midge Decter points out that pornography today leads its readers into crime, violence, and delusion, while formerly it merely titillated the senses.
3. The explicit nature of pornography leads people to believe that available to them somewhere are others who exist only for sexual pleasure.
4. Pornography is dangerous because one can get addicted to fantasy.
5. According to Decter, the combination of pornography's explicit detail and its emphasis on fantasy can lead to a dangerous state of frustration where anything is possible.
6. Decter thinks that what is wrong with pornography is that it offers false promises.
7. Because pornography is more realistic now, using photographs of people with names and identities, Midge Decter thinks that it is more harmful to its readers and viewers, who can easily grow dissatisfied and frustrated with fantasies.

EXERCISE 8

Summarize each of the following paragraphs by doing *one* of three things:

A. Underline a sentence that will serve as a comprehensive summary; or

B. Combine existing phrases; then rewrite the sentence, based on these phrases, to create a comprehensive summary; or

C. Invent a new generalization to provide a comprehensive summary.

Be prepared to explain your summary in class discussion.

1. The neurotic individual may have had some special vulnerability as an infant. Perhaps he was ill a great deal and was given care that singled him out from other children. Perhaps he walked or talked much later—or earlier—than children were expected to, and this evoked unusual treatment. The child whose misshapen feet must be put in casts or the sickly little boy who never can play ball may get out of step with his age mates and with the expectations parents and other adults have about children. Or a child may be very unusually placed in his family. He may be the only boy with six sisters, or a tiny child born between two lusty sets of twins. Or the source of the child's difficulties may be a series of events that deeply affected his relations to people—the death of his mother at the birth of the next child or the prolonged illness or absence of his father. Or a series of coincidences—an accident to a parent, moving to a new town and a severe fright—taken together may alter the child's relationship to the world.

   MARGARET MEAD, from *Some Personal Views*

2. Suppose you fly in a plane. What is more important for you: the pilot's real competence or his papers that certify he is competent? Or suppose you get sick and need medical treatment. What is more important for you: your doctor's real competence or his diploma? Of course, in every case the real competence is more important. But last year I met a large group of people whose priorities were exactly the opposite: my students. Not all, but many. Their first priority was to get papers that certify that they are competent rather than to develop real competence. As soon as I started to explain to them something that was a little bit beyond the standard courses, they asked suspiciously: "Will this be on the test?" If I said "no," they did not listen any more and showed clearly that I was doing something inappropriate.

   ANDREI TOOM, from "A Russian Teacher in America"

3. I have no doubt that we will one day abolish the death penalty in America. It will come sooner if people like me who know the truth about executions do our work well and educate the public. It will come slowly if we do not. Because, finally, I know that it is not a question of malice or ill will or meanness of spirit that prompts our citizens to support executions. It is, quite simply, that people

don't know the truth of what is going on. That is not by accident. The secrecy surrounding executions makes it possible for executions to continue. I am convinced that if executions were made public, the torture and violence would be unmasked, and we would be shamed into abolishing executions. We would be embarrassed at the brutalization of the crowds that would gather to watch a man or woman being killed. And we would be humiliated to know that visitors from other countries—Japan, Russia, Latin America, Europe—were watching us kill our own citizens—we, who take pride in being the flagship of democracy in the world.

HELEN PREJEAN, from Dead Man Walking

4. In the storied old days a person invented something in the attic or basement, got a patent on it, began building and selling it, and made a pile of money, all pretty much alone. Today's inventor, with some isolated exceptions, is likely to be a salaried lab hand working in almost complete anonymity for a large corporation. If he or she gets any reward for building a better mousetrap, it may only be a smile and a pat on the back from the supervisor. Those few individual inventors who do make it big today—like Land, or Steve Wozniak of Apple Computer, or William Hewlett and David Packard of the company that bears their name—are all the more exceptional for being successful entrepreneurs and industrialists as well as inventors.

OLIVER E. ALLEN, from "The Power of Patents"

5. Holidays were once typically days of actual common celebration, of parades, ceremonies, feasts, songs, speeches, and marches. Today, most of this has been replaced by the public holiday's private competitor, the vacation. . . . The vacation is a relatively recent innovation, the product of bourgeois prosperity. The idea that wage earners could take paid vacations is an even more recent development; it only became widespread after World War I. It's fair to say that even in the 1930s and 1940s ordinary workers spent much more of their leisure time attending parades, carnivals, funerals, executions, and other communal events than they do today, and a good deal less time checking into motels. Today even solemn public holidays—holidays with as much contemporary meaning as Martin Luther King's birthday—are widely seen as simply more private leisure time, which is why we routinely fiddle with their dates to create three-day weekends.

MICKEY KAUS, from The End of Equality

6. There are many new terms and usages that seemed picky or unnecessary to conservatives when they appeared, but are now indispensable. What letter-writer, grateful for the coinage "Ms," which lets one formally address women without referring to their marital status, would willingly go back to choosing between "Mrs." and "Miss"? There is a case to be made for "African-American," though it seems to have no marked advantages over "black" beyond its length,

a quality of language many Americans mistake for dignity. Probably the term "Asian-American," vague as it is, is better than "Oriental," because it is at least decently neutral, without the cloud of disparaging imagery that still clings to the older word: "Oriental" suggests a foreignness so extreme that it cannot be assimilated, and raises the Fu-Manchu phantoms of 19th-century racist fiction— treacherous cunning, clouds of opium, glittering slit eyes. "Native American" for American Indian, or just plain Indian, sounds virtuous, except that it carries with it the absurd implication that whites whose forebears may have been here for three, five, or even the whole thirteen generations that have elapsed since 1776 are in some way still interlopers, not "native" to this country. By the time whites get guilty enough to call themselves "European-Americans" it will be time to junk the whole lingo of nervous divisionism; everyone, black, yellow, red and white, can revert to being plain "Americans" again, as well they might.

ROBERT HUGHES, from The Culture of Complaint

Summarizing an Article

When you want to summarize an essay in a few sentences, how do you judge which points are significant and which are not? Some essays, especially newspaper articles, have rambling structures and short paragraphs, so you don't even have fully developed paragraphs in which to search for summarizing topic sentences. Are there any standard procedures to help you decide which points to summarize?

> *Guidelines for Summarizing an Article*
>
> 1. Read the entire article more than once.
> 2. Ask yourself why the article was written and published.
> 3. Look for repetitions of and variations on the same idea.

Read "Holdup Man Tells Detectives How to Do It" from the *New York Times*, and, on the second reading, observe your own method of pinpointing the key ideas.

HOLDUP MAN TELLS DETECTIVES HOW TO DO IT
Selwyn Raab

His face hidden by a shabby tan coat, the career holdup man peeked out at his audience of detectives and then proceeded to lecture them on how easy it was to succeed at his trade in New York.

"I don't think there's much any individual police officer can do," the guest lec-   2
turer told 50 detectives yesterday at an unusual crime seminar sponsored by the
Police Department. "Once I knew what the police officer on the beat was up to I
wasn't much concerned about the cops."

The holdup man, who identified himself only as "Nick," is serving a prison term   3
of 6 to 13 years. He said his most serious arrest occurred after he was shot three
times by a supermarket manager—not in any encounter with the police.

When asked by a detective taking a course in robbery investigations what the best   4
deterrent would be against gunmen like himself, Nick replied crisply: "stiffer sentences."

After being seriously wounded in his last robbery attempt, Nick said he decided   5
it was time to retire.

"I'm close to 40 and not getting any younger," he explained. "I just don't want to   6
spend any more time in jail."

Nick also offered the detectives some tips on how robbers pick their targets and   7
make their getaways in the city.

Except for wearing a hat, Nick said he affected no disguise. "I usually picked a   8
store in a different neighborhood or in another borough where I was unknown."

Leads on places to hold up usually came from other criminals or from employ-   9
ees. There were no elaborate plannings or "casings," he said, adding:

"I liked supermarkets because there's always a lot of cash around. Uniformed   10
guards didn't deter me because they're not armed, they usually just have sticks. It's
better to pick a busy area rather than the suburbs. The chances of someone notic-
ing you are greater in residential or suburban areas."

The detectives, sitting at desks with notepaper in front of them, were rookies as   11
well as veterans. Besides city detectives, the audience included policemen from the
Transit Authority, the Housing Authority, the Yonkers Police Department and from
Seattle.

They listened carefully as Nick outlined how he or a confederate would inspect   12
the area for signs of uniformed or plainclothes police officers.

The retired robber said he had preferred supermarkets or stores with large win-   13
dow advertisements or displays because these materials prevented him from being
seen by passers-by on the street.

"I was always a little nervous or apprehensive before a job," he continued. "But   14
once you're inside and aware of the reaction of the people and you know the possibilities then your confidence comes back."

Nick said he always made his escape in a car and he preferred heavily trafficked   15
roads because it made the getaway vehicle less conspicuous than on little used side
streets.

In New York, cheap handguns were selling from $15 to $70, he told the detec-   16
tives. Such weapons as shotguns or automatic rifles, Nick said, could be rented for
about $100 an hour.

Nick said he had been a holdup man since the age of 20 and had committed about   17
30 "jobs," but was uncertain of the exact number. The biggest robbery he had par-

ticipated in netted a total of $8,000, and overall he got about $30,000 in his criminal activities.

Asked why he went back to robbing after his first arrest, Nick said: "I wanted whisky, women and big autos. Like most who rob I was not socially accepted. Big money elevates you above the people you think are looking down on you." 18

Short prison sentences, for first arrests, Nick asserted, probably do little to discourage holdup men. "I see them laying up in jail and it doesn't make any difference," he said. "They just go ahead planning the next one in a different way." 19

During his "on-and-off" criminal career, Nick said he had never fired any of the guns he carried. 20

After his one-hour appearance as guest lecturer, Nick, his face still covered by his coat, was escorted out of the classroom back to his cell at an undisclosed prison. 21

1. Read the entire article more than once.

This direction is not as simple as it sounds. Because you want to identify main ideas, you may underline what you regard as the key sentences on first reading, and, from then on, look only at the "boiled-down" parts. But *don't eliminate minor facts and interesting details too soon.* They do have a function in the article, supporting and illuminating the central ideas. For example, the fact that Nick chose to hide his face during and after his "lecture" hardly seems worth underlining and, in fact, would never by itself be regarded as crucial. But taken together with some of Nick's remarks, that minor fact helps you to recognize a key point of the article: The robber's reliance on *anonymity* enables him to commit a successful crime; Nick may at some point wish to resume his profession despite his "retirement." Although you should always underline your key points, remember to reread and consider every part of the article as you prepare your summary.

2. Ask yourself why the article was written and published.

What does the newspaper want its readers to learn? An inquiry into basic intention is especially important in analyzing a news article: the journal's and journalist's purpose is frequently twofold—to describe an event and to suggest the event's significance—and so it is easy for you to confuse the *facts* being recorded with the underlying *reasons* for recording them. Here are two one-sentence summaries of the article that are both off the mark because they concentrate too heavily on the event:

Nick, a convicted retired criminal, was guest speaker at a police seminar and told detectives how robbers pick their targets and make their getaways in New York.

Nick, after committing thirty robberies, suggested to detectives some possible methods of thwarting future robberies.

Both writers seem too concerned with Nick's colorful history and the peculiarity of his helping the police at all. They ignore the significance of what Nick was actually saying. The second summary—by emphasizing the phrase "thwarting future robberies"—is misleading and almost contradicts the point of the article; in fact, Nick is really suggesting that the police will continue to be ineffectual.

A news article can also mislead you into thinking that a headline is a summary: the headline "Holdup Man Tells Detectives How to Do It" does not summarize the material in the article, but because it is broad and vague, it "sounds" good. What, for example, is meant by the "it" of the headline—robbery or detection? What does Nick tell the detectives? Headlines are designed to include only as much as fits the column, and they are often written by people who do not have time to read the entire article.

3. Look for repetitions of and variations on the same idea.

There is one concrete point that Selwyn Raab and his readers and the police and Nick himself are all interested in: *ways of preventing criminals from committing crimes.* Not only are we told again and again about Nick's contempt for the police, but we are also given his flat statement that only fear of imprisonment ("stiffer sentences") will discourage a hardened criminal.

A brief summary of this article, then, would mention *tougher sentencing as a way of preventing crime.* But, in addition, the theme of *the criminal's need for anonymity* ought, if possible, to be incorporated into a complete summary. In Nick's opinion, his career has been relatively successful because he has managed to appear normal and blend into the crowd. The primary and secondary ideas can be joined in a summary like this one:

> Observing with contempt that the police have rarely been able to penetrate his "anonymous" disguise, Nick, the successful robber, argues that the presence of policemen will not deter most experienced criminals and that only "stiffer sentences" will prevent crime.

EXERCISE 9

Carefully read "In 'Minor' College Sports, Big Pressure" from the *New York Times*. Determine the article's purpose and pick out the ideas that the author emphasizes; then write a comprehensive summary in two or three sentences.

IN "MINOR" COLLEGE SPORTS, BIG PRESSURE
William C. Rhoden

College presidents and athletic directors gathering today in Dallas for the 84th   l
National Collegiate Athletic Association convention will once again wrestle with the excesses of big-time basketball and football.

But while they focus on those two high-profile sports, professionalization is also growing dramatically in less visible sports, with the potential for the same sort of abuses.

Athletes who once would go straight from high school to the pros are now using college baseball, hockey, tennis and golf programs as catapults into pro careers. As a result, the campus experience for all athletes in those sports has changed, becoming so intensive and time-consuming that even the most conscientious student-athlete finds it increasingly difficult to balance academics and athletics. Whether a player is a star or a third-stringer, the new and stringent, pro-style regimen must be followed.

"Sports have become year-around activities, and in those institutions where sports are serious, they are a year-around commitment," said Dr. David Goslin, the president of the American Institutes of Research, an independent, nonprofit research firm specializing in behavioral and social sciences.

"What we are asking kids to do is hold two full-time jobs: school is one, then they've got sports. It has become a tremendous burden."

Last year the institutes released the results of a five-part study on student-athletes at Division I schools, the N.C.A.A.'s top level. Among other things, the report concluded that intensive sports programs had become by far the greatest consumer of student-athletes' time, and in many cases had compromised their ability to take full advantage of their institutions.

The study found that football and basketball players spend an average of 30 hours a week on their sports, and about 13.7 in class. For other sports, the average given was 24.6 hours a week, but that figure includes a number of minor sports with minimal time requirements.

In golf, where players practice up to four hours a day and usually miss at least two classes a week during the season, participants spend more time on their sport than do football and basketball players. Tennis, hockey and baseball players spend as much time at practice, and can even spend more time traveling to and from competitions.

"The reason for all this is that the professional sports arena has expanded," Dr. Goslin said. "The professional opportunity is still only open to a small proportion of athletes in college, and the chances are small. But there are more teams. The slots have increased. At the same time, there's fiercer competition for those slots."

College athletic programs at the Division I level have increasingly become like finishing schools for the athletes trying to survive that competition, offering them year-round training, better coaching, top-flight facilities and pro-like schedules.

Martin Blackman, one of the top tennis players coming out of high school in 1987, had offers from U.C.L.A. and U.S.C. and accepted a scholarship to Stanford, one of the nation's dominant programs of the 1980's.

Stanford's men's team has won five national championships in this decade; its women's team has won five N.C.A.A. national championships since 1982, including consecutive championships from 1986 to 1989.

Blackman, following an increasingly typical pattern, dropped out of Stanford after two seasons and turned professional.   13

"I thought that I'd be able to improve my game for about at least two years, and I really wanted to experience college," Blackman said. "The advantage of going to a top college program is that, if you're not quite ready for the pros, you get the best coaches, you have other guys on the team you can practice with every day, you have time to work on your game, and you don't have the pressure of trying to make a living on the tour."   14

According to Richard Shultz, the executive director of the National Collegiate Athletic Association, the highest dropout rate among intercollegiate varsity sports is in tennis. He said he could not give the specific number.   15

College golf, with a season that runs from September to June and tournaments that last three or four days at a time, has become almost a prerequisite for making a living on the PGA Tour. Turning pro directly out of high school, which was common until about 15 years ago, has now become financially and competitively impractical.   16

"It would have been a lot harder to turn pro without going to college, because you'd have to work on it harder yourself and you wouldn't get a chance to play against the top people you play against in college," said Robert Gamez, an all-America golfer at the University of Arizona last season and the N.C.A.A. golfer of the year.   17

"Sure, you can play the mini-tours and stuff like that," he said, referring to the level below the PGA Tour that is used by those who do not qualify for the tour right away. "But mini-tours are real expensive; entry fees are high for the type of money they're playing for."   18

Gamez said that a drawback of college was that classes interfered with his golf regimen.   19

"I was kind of tired of the classroom," said Gamez, who dropped out last season after his junior year and earned his PGA Tour card. "There are a lot of guys on the tour that never finished school. Some guys don't want to go to school, or are not there to graduate, not there to become rocket scientists. They're in there to play golf."   20

The sport with the most dramatic change in status on campus is baseball, where professional teams are now literally recruiting against top college programs for the best high school seniors. Traditionally, talented high school players went straight to the minor leagues and incubated there until the parent club felt they were ready to move up. College was considered a waste of time for a player with pro aspirations and talent.   21

But the dwindling number of minor league teams, down to a low of 132 in 1973 after reaching a high of 448 in 1949, and the higher caliber of college baseball has made college an attractive option. The better programs offer a 60-to-70-game schedule, often with coaching provided by former pro players and managers.   22

Last summer, Jeff Hammonds, a talented center fielder from Scotch Plains High School in New Jersey, turned down a $250,000 offer from the Toronto Blue Jays and accepted a baseball scholarship to Stanford. The year before, Alex Fernandez of Pace High School in Miami, one of the nation's top pitching prospects, turned   23 down an offer of $130,000 by the Milwaukee Brewers to attend the University of Miami.

One of Hammonds's teammates, Mike Mancini, a pitcher, was drafted by the Baltimore Orioles out of high school but turned down their contract offer to accept Stanford's scholarship. 24

"The minor leagues just weren't for me," said Mancini, now a sophomore. "Right out of high school, you're 18 years old, you're used to being at home, then all of a sudden, bam! you're on the road. You're in a van or bus every day, traveling four or five or six hours. I didn't see that I was mature enough to handle that at the time." 25

His counterparts 10 or 15 years ago would have had to handle it, whether they felt mature enough or not, because the level of college competition was so low. But Mancini and the prospects of today have a competitive alternative. Stanford, for example, will play a 61-game schedule that begins Jan. 26 and ends May 20 (later if the Cardinals, who have won two consecutive national championships, participate in post-season play). 26

College hockey, which is the third-largest college revenue-producing sport after basketball and football, now offers advantages similar to those found in those sports. 27

As recently as 1980, most high school hockey players with aspirations of playing professionally went through the Major Junior Hockey League in Canada, where they began an apprenticeship in one of three divisions. The better players then joined a professional team in a minor league or the National Hockey League. It was rare for a college player to become an N.H.L. success, because college programs lacked the quality or intensity to prepare a player for the pros. 28

Today, while 70 percent of drafted players continue to come out of the Canadian Major Junior Hockey League, college is a legitimate alternative. Increasing numbers of the better high school players, both Canadian and American, are accepting scholarships to American college hockey programs, for two main reasons. 29

"I thought I would need an education because I didn't have a clear-cut opportunity for professional hockey," said Warren Sharples, a goalie at the University of Michigan who was a ninth-round draft choice of the Calgary Flames out of high school. "Now I know I can stop at any time. I don't have to play hockey somewhere where I don't want to play. I can stop if I want to. A lot of players don't have that option because they didn't get the education." 30

One of his teammates, Ryan Pardowski, said he decided on college because he was too small physically to survive the rigors of pro hockey, even at the major-junior level. He wanted time to grow and to refine his game, and a scholarship gave him the opportunity to do so at little expense. 31

The paradox of the athletic scholarship is that the time demands of today's Division I sports programs, and the athlete's own single-minded focus on meeting them, often make it impossible for him or her to exploit fully the academic and extracurricular resources of the school. 32

"It's the hours that they put in, but it's also that those are heavy work kinds of hours," said Mary Ann Swain, an assistant dean of admissions at the University of 33

Michigan. "They work really, really hard for four, five or six hours a day, and then we expect them to sit down, focus and concentrate their energies on studying. It's not only that they're running out of hours in the day, they're tired. Just downright physically tired."

A fundamental issue is whether the rigors of balancing education and athletics have become too great for athletes at this level. Those who are less confident in their academic abilities, or more single-minded about athletics, often choose a path of least resistance and take less demanding courses.   34

"I wanted to be an accountant," said Gamez, the former Arizona golfer. "But it's really hard to take that much time to do your accounting and get good grades."   35

Some student-athletes have resolved to try to do well in class, but with the understanding that they cannot compete at a championship level athletically and also compete for A's with their more academically-minded peers.   36

"You have to make some sacrifices in the classroom to be the best you can be in the sport you're doing," said Jennifer Azziz, an all-America basketball guard at Stanford. "I find that people here will put their whole heart into their athletics, at least equal to schoolwork, if not a little before it."   37

Others find athletics so consuming that it is a struggle simply to stay eligible to play.   38

"My first semester I got by with just over a 2.0," said Pardowski of Michigan's hockey team, referring to his grade-point average. "Last semester I didn't do well. I went below a 2.0 but my cumulative stayed above it. This semester, if I go below a 2.0, I'm gone."   39

Pardowski said that between classes, practice, and getting dinner after practice, he usually doesn't get home until 9 P.M., and is often too distracted to study.   40

"And you're trying so hard to fit in with hockey, and to make it there," he said, "that you lose your focus that you're here for school. You just kind of go through the motions."   41

Warde Manuel, who had to stop playing football for Michigan this year because of a degenerative nerve condition, now questions the extent to which high-level competition and academic performance are compatible.   42

"Athletics takes away some of your ambition for academics," he said. "More now I feel like a student, because I don't have to go to the football building; I don't have to go to practice.   43

"I never really realized that education could be as fun, that it could be as demanding," he added. "Now I see why people talk about athletics being a challenge in college, because it's so much easier now for me to focus. I'm not as tired, mentally or physically."   44

Another of the frequent complaints among student-athletes at Division I schools, according to the American Institutes of Research surveys, was that athletes had little time to play a role in the student life of their universities.   45

"I feel cheated in a way," said Tim Williams, a senior linebacker for Michigan, who received the team's scholar-athlete award this season and will graduate next spring with a degree in business. "When I was younger, I felt that college would be   46 full of symposiums, guest speakers, getting involved in groups like Amnesty International. I envisioned letter-writing, being politically active, being wild and crazy, taking more classes and taking advantage of more educational opportunities.

"The reality is that you don't have time for that. I'm upset about it, I guess. But on the other hand I've had an experience that only a handful of people will ever experience." 47

Another troublesome side effect of more intense college sports programs is the widening social gap between students and student-athletes, and a greater ambivalence in their attitude toward each other. 48

The impression of many students is that scholarship athletes, even those who perform outside the glare of a national spotlight, are not harder workers than students who work at jobs and attend class. 49

"Some argue that student-athletes get as much as they do because they work so hard," said Paige Oliver, editor of the Auburn student newspaper. "But what about students that have to work full time and put themselves through school? Don't they put in just as many hours working? 50

"They're not on the field, but they spend just as many hours working at Burger King, or just as many hours working at the mall, or anywhere, pumping gas. They have to live in the dorms or live in an efficiency, and just take what they can get. I feel that's where the students have a problem and that's where the sour grapes come in." 51

Perhaps the significant difference is that the scholarship athlete holds two full-time jobs and to a greater extent is chained to them both, and is under great pressure to do well in both. 52

For the tennis player from Sweden, the hockey player from Canada or the golfer from Arizona, the stakes in intercollegiate athletics have intensified across the board. 53

"You have to have a professional attitude about it," said Sharples, the Michigan goalie. "They treat you as a professional here. The school puts a lot of money into the athletic programs, and they expect something in return. It's very intense and you'd be naïve to not believe that it was a business. It's a professional atmosphere even at the university level. We have fun, but there is a lot of responsibility. 54

"The most fun I have playing these days is when I go home at Christmas and I can skate on the outdoor ice out on the lagoon, and just skate around for the pure joy of it. Here, there is a lot of responsibility and unless you're winning, it's no fun at all." 55

Summarizing a Complex Essay

When you are asked to summarize a reading containing a number of complex and abstract ideas, a reading that may be disorganized and therefore difficult to comprehend and condense, *the best way to prepare for your summary is to isolate each important point and note it down in a list.*

Here are some guidelines for summarizing a complex essay:

1. The summary must be comprehensive.
2. The summary must be concise.
3. The summary must be coherent.
4. The summary must be independent.

Here is an essay by Bertrand Russell, followed by a preliminary list of notes, a statement of Russell's thesis, and the final summary. (The numbers in the margin are keyed to the preliminary list of notes on pp. 76–77.) Russell's essay is difficult, so be sure to read it slowly, and more than once. If you get confused at any point, try referring to the list of notes that follows; but be sure to *go back to the essay* after you have identified and understood each numbered point.

THE SOCIAL RESPONSIBILITY OF SCIENTISTS
Bertrand Russell

Science, ever since it first existed, has had important effects in matters that lie outside the purview of pure science. Men of science have differed as to their re- [1] sponsibility for such effects. Some have said that the function of the scientist in so- [2] ciety is to supply knowledge, and that he need not concern himself with the use to which this knowledge is put. I do not think that this view is tenable, especially in our age. The scientist is also a citizen; and citizens who have any special skill have a public duty to see, as far as they can, that their skill is utilized in accordance with [3] the public interest. Historically, the functions of the scientist in public life have generally been recognized. The Royal Society was founded by Charles II as an antidote to "fanaticism" which had plunged England into a long period of civil strife. The scientists of that time did not hesitate to speak out on public issues, such as religious [4] toleration and the folly of prosecutions for witchcraft. But although science has, in various ways at various times, favored what may be called a humanitarian outlook, it has from the first had an intimate and sinister connection with war. Archimedes sold his skill to the Tyrant of Syracuse for use against the Romans; Leonardo secured a salary from the Duke of Milan for his skill in the art of fortification; and Galileo got employment under the Grand Duke of Tuscany because he could calculate the trajectories of projectiles. In the French Revolution the scientists who were not guillotined were set to making new explosives, but Lavoisier was not spared, because he was only discovering hydrogen which, in those days, was not a weapon of war. There have been some honorable exceptions to the subservience of scientists to warmongers. During the Crimean War the British government consulted Faraday as to the feasibility of attack by poisonous gases. Faraday replied that it was entirely feasible, but that it was inhuman and he would have nothing to do with it.

Modern democracy and modern methods of publicity have made the problem of [5] affecting public opinion quite different from what it used to be. The knowledge that

the public possesses on any important issue is derived from vast and powerful organizations: the press, radio, and, above all, television. The knowledge that governments possess is more limited. They are too busy to search out the facts for
themselves, and consequently they know only what their underlings think good for
them unless there is such a powerful movement in a different sense that politicians
cannot ignore it. Facts which ought to guide the decisions of statesmen—for instance, as to the possible lethal qualities of fallout—do not acquire their due importance if they remain buried in scientific journals. They acquire their due
importance only when they become known to so many voters that they affect the
course of the elections. In general, there is an opposition to widespread publicity
for such facts. This opposition springs from various sources, some sinister, some
comparatively respectable. At the bottom of the moral scale there is the financial
interest of the various industries connected with armaments. Then there are various effects of a somewhat thoughtless patriotism, which believes in secrecy and in
what is called "toughness." But perhaps more important than either of these is the
unpleasantness of the facts, which makes the general public turn aside to pleasan-
ter topics such as divorces and murders. The consequence is that what ought to be
known widely throughout the general public will not be known unless great efforts
are made by disinterested persons to see that the information reaches the minds
and hearts of vast numbers of people. I do not think this work can be successfully
accomplished except by the help of men of science. They, alone, can speak with
the authority that is necessary to combat the misleading statements of those scientists who have permitted themselves to become merchants of death. If disinterested scientists do not speak out, the others will succeed in conveying a distorted
impression, not only to the public but also to the politicians.

It must be admitted that there are obstacles to individual action in our age
which did not exist at earlier times. Galileo could make his own telescope. But
once when I was talking with a very famous astronomer he explained that the telescope upon which his work depended owed its existence to the benefaction of
enormously rich men, and, if he had not stood well with them, his astronomical
discoveries would have been impossible. More frequently, a scientist only acquires
access to enormously expensive equipment if he stands well with the government
of his country. He knows that if he adopts a rebellious attitude he and his family
are likely to perish along with the rest of civilized mankind. It is a tragic dilemma,
and I do not think that one should censure a man whatever his decision; but I do
think—and I think men of science should realize—that unless something rather
drastic is done under the leadership or through the inspiration of some part of the
scientific world, the human race, like the Gadarene swine, will rush down a steep
place to destruction in blind ignorance of the fate that scientific skill has prepared
for it.

It is impossible in the modern world for a man of science to say with any honesty, "My business is to provide knowledge, and what use is made of the knowledge is not my responsibility." The knowledge that a man of science provides may

6

7

8

9

10

fall into the hands of men or institutions devoted to utterly unworthy objects. I do not suggest that a man of science, or even a large body of men of science, can altogether prevent this, but they can diminish the magnitude of the evil.

There is another direction in which men of science can attempt to provide leadership. They can suggest and urge in many ways the value of those branches of science of which the important and practical uses are beneficial and not harmful. Consider what might be done if the money at present spent on armaments were spent on increasing and distributing the food supply of the world and diminishing the population pressure. In a few decades, poverty and malnutrition, which now afflict more than half the population of the globe, could be ended. But at present almost all the governments of great states consider that it is better to spend money on killing foreigners than on keeping their own subjects alive. Possibilities of a hopeful sort in whatever field can best be worked out and stated authoritatively by men of science; and, since they can do this work better than others, it is part of their duty to do it.   11

As the world becomes more technically unified, life in an ivory tower becomes increasingly impossible. Not only so; the man who stands out against the powerful organizations which control most of human activity is apt to find himself no longer in the ivory tower, with a wide outlook over a sunny landscape, but in the dark and subterranean dungeon upon which the ivory tower was erected. To risk such a habitation demands courage. It will not be necessary to inhabit the dungeon if there are many who are willing to risk it, for everybody knows that the modern world depends upon scientists, and, if they are insistent, they must be listened to. We have it in our power to make a good world; and, therefore, with whatever labor and risk, we must make it.   12

First Stage: List of Notes and Establishing a Thesis

1. Should scientists try to influence the way their discoveries are used?

2. One point of view: the scientist's role is to make the discovery; what happens afterward is not his concern.

3. Russell's point of view: scientists are like any other knowledgeable and public-spirited people; they must make sure that the products of their knowledge work for, not against, society.

4. In the past, some scientists have made public their views on controversial issues like freedom of religion; others have been servants of the war machine.

5. The power to inform and influence the public is now controlled by the news media.

6. Government officials are too busy to be well informed; subordinates feed them only enough information to get them reelected.

7. It is in the interests of various groups, ranging from weapons makers to patriots, to limit the amount of scientific information that the public receives.

8. The public is reluctant to listen to distasteful news.

9. Since the public deserves to hear the truth, scientists, who are respected for their knowledge and who belong to no party or faction, ought to do more to provide the public with information about the potentially lethal consequences of their discoveries. By doing so, they will correct the distortions of those scientists who have allied themselves with warmongers.

10. It is very difficult for scientists to speak out since they depend on government and business interests to finance their work.

11. While scientists cannot entirely stop others from using some of their discoveries for antisocial purposes, they can support other, more constructive kinds of research.

12. Speaking out is worth the risk of incurring the displeasure of powerful people; since the work of scientists is so vital, the risk isn't too great, especially if they act together.

Russell's Thesis: Contrary to the self-interested arguments of many scientists and other groups, scientists have a social responsibility to make sure that their work is used for, not against, the benefit of humanity.

Second Stage: Summary

Some scientists, as well as other groups, consider that they need not influence the way in which their discoveries are used. However, Bertrand Russell, in "The Social Responsibility of Scientists," believes that scientists have a responsibility to make sure that their work is used for, not against, the benefit of humanity. In modern times, he argues, it has been especially difficult for concerned scientists to speak out because many powerful groups prefer to limit and distort what the public is told, because government officials are too busy to be thoroughly informed, because scientists depend on the financial support of business and government, and because the public itself is reluctant to hear distasteful news. Nevertheless, Russell maintains that scientists have the knowledge and the prestige to command public attention, and their work is too vital for their voices to be suppressed. If they act together, they can warn us if their work is likely to be used for an antisocial purpose and, at least, they can propose less destructive alternatives.

This summary of Russell's essay is not a simple compilation of phrases taken from the text, nor a collection of topic sentences, one from each paragraph. Rather, it is a clear, coherent, and unified summary of Russell's ideas, expressed in the writer's own voice and words.

A *framework* is immediately established in the first two sentences of the summary, which present *the two alternative views of the scientist's responsibility*. The next sentence, which describes the four obstacles to scientific freedom of speech, illustrates the rearrangement of ideas that is characteristic of summary. While reviewing the list of notes, the summarizer has noticed that points 6, 7, 8, and 10 each refers to a different way in which scientific truth is often suppressed; she has therefore brought them together and lined them up in a par-

---

Guidelines for Summarizing a Complex Essay

1. *The summary must be comprehensive.* You should review all the notes on your list, and include in your summary all those ideas that are essential to the author's development of the thesis.

2. *The summary must be concise.* Eliminate repetitions in your list, even if the author restates the same points. Your summary should be considerably shorter than the source.

3. *The summary must be coherent.* It should make sense as a paragraph in its own right; it should not be taken directly from your list of notes and sound like a list of sentences that happen to be strung together in a paragraph format.

4. *The summary must be independent.* You are not being asked to imitate or identify yourself with the author whom you are writing about. On the contrary, you are expected to maintain your own voice throughout the summary. Even as you are jotting down your list of notes, you should try to use your own words. Nevertheless, while you want to make it clear that *you* are writing the summary, you should be careful not to create any misrepresentation or distortion by introducing comments or criticisms of your own. (Such distortion is most likely to occur when you strongly disagree with the material that you are summarizing.) You must make it clear to your reader when you are summarizing directly from the text and when you are commenting on, inferring from, or explaining what is being summarized.

allel construction based on the repeated word "because." Finally, the last two sentences contain *a restatement of Russell's thesis* and point out that the obstacles to action are not as formidable as they seem.

Notice that the Russell summary excludes points 1, 4, and 5 on the list of notes: point 1 is included in the presentation of points 2 and 3; point 4 is an example, one which is not essential to an understanding of the essay; and point 5 is not directly related to Russell's argument.

In summarizing Russell's essay, it would not be acceptable to include extraneous points, such as the dangers of making scientific secrets public, for that would be arguing with Russell. Such ideas should be reserved for a full-length essay whose purpose is to develop an idea of your own, not just to summarize Russell's. Within limits, however, it is acceptable to go beyond point-by-point summary, to *suggest the author's implied intention,* and, in a sense, to *interpret the work's meaning for your reader.* You might state, for example, that ours is an age that encourages interdependence and discourages independent action. *Such an interpretation would have to be supported by evidence from the reading.* While Russell does not say so specifically, in so many words, the assertion about interdependence is certainly substantiated by the material in the last two paragraphs. For further discussion of interpreting as you summarize, see pp. 161–186 in Chapter 3.

ASSIGNMENT 1

Summarize one of the following three passages in a few sentences. Before you begin your summary (on your second reading), underline and annotate key ideas, and make a preliminary list of points.

from THE WAY WE NEVER WERE:
AMERICAN FAMILIES AND THE NOSTALGIA TRAP
Stephanie Coontz *about Amer. Idea of Independence*

The Anglo-American notion that dependence on others is immature, weak, 1
shameful, or uniquely feminine is foreign to most cultures. In the world view of these societies, independence is antisocial; expressing one's neediness, even codifying it, is the route to social harmony and personal satisfaction for both men and women. The Japanese, for example, have a noun *amae,* which means reliance on the goodwill or indulgence of another, and a verb *amaru,* which means essentially to ask for such indulgence. Although increasingly there is a disapproving connotation attached to these words, it is not culturally stigmatized to emphasize one's dependence on others. Modern American parents teach their children that they can be anything they want to be; in ancient Greece, such overweening confidence in the individual's ability to shape his or her own fate was the sin of hubris, and it brought the protagonists of many Greek tragedies to bitter ends.

In most precapitalist societies, economic, social, and political interactions were   2
not separable from personal relations. No individual operated independently of the
kin group or the local community. Consequently, definitions of self were always
contextual, because the self did not pick and choose relations with others; it emerged
out of these relations and remained dependent on them. Independence was feared,
not cherished. A person's entitlements and obligations, similarly, were not deduced
from abstract principles of equal rights but from highly particularistic personal relationships. (It is striking how many of these descriptions still apply to women. Some
psychologists argue that women's moral standards differ from men's in precisely this
regard, since those standards are derived from personal relationships and concrete
responsibilities rather than from abstract rights. This probably has less to do with
intrinsically female "ways of knowing" than with the fact that women's lives have remained far more rooted in personalistic, nonmarket interactions than have men's.)

The notion that love was, or should be, a purely personal relationship between   3
two individuals, and the primary source of sustained commitments, was equally
foreign to most precapitalist cultures. Social customs recognized both the inevitability of dependence and the necessity of dispersing it across society, beyond separate
couples or even extended-family networks. Gift giving was one such custom; it established a relationship that was alternately one-sided and therefore more permanent
than an "even" relationship in which accounts are always settled so that one party
can leave at any time.

Our values tell us to "even things up" as quickly as possible, to discharge our   4
debts and obligations, and to recover the "natural" state of individual independence.
Once Americans pass the age of childhood, there are few things that distress us
more than receiving a holiday gift, however small, from someone for whom we do
not have a gift in return. We find it equally disturbing to give or receive a gift that is
"worth" less than that of the other party in the exchange. Our notions of fairness
and justice revolve around giving as good as we get and getting as much as we give.

Among the San people of the Kalahari Desert in Africa, by contrast, giving an im-   5
mediate return for any offering implies a profound insult, for such an act suggests
that one is unwilling to be indebted to others, uninterested in bearing the burden
of obligation that helps a relationship last. Rather, the recipient waits a decent
amount of time and eventually returns a gift that is slightly larger, putting the original donor under future obligation. Elsewhere, institutions such as the Kula exchange
networks of the Trobriand Islanders in the Pacific and the funeral ceremonies of
early Native Americans extended this reciprocity over much greater distances and
periods of time. As the Melanesians put it: "Our feasts are the movement of a needle which sews together the parts of our reed roofs, making of them a single roof,
a single word."

In these societies, gift giving is not an individual act of love or even an outcome   6
of family solidarity; it is a social and political way of establishing ties and duties that
extend beyond family borders. Acceptance of a gift does not impugn one's manhood or confirm one's femininity. The obligation and responsibility involved in re-

ceiving any gift are recognized by all, yet bestowal of a gift is emphatically not a personal bargain. Among the Trobrianders, for example, a man suspected of giving gifts to his Kula partner in order to force a comparable return is "labeled with the vile phrase: he barters."

Organizing social relations through reciprocity involves a delicate balance. It is unacceptable to give a gift with the sole motive of getting something in return, yet it is unthinkable to accept a gift without understanding that it sets up conditions for future behavior; it is an equally antisocial act to refuse a gift and the obligation that gift entails. The difficulty of maintaining this balance may explain why some languages—German, for example—came to refer to gifts and poison with the same word. Personal relations of dependency, deference, and commitment may be stable and humane in some cultures, but they have produced tremendous abuses in others.

7

from **THE DANCING MATRIX**
Robin Marantz Henig

Science oriented about viruses

An emerging virus isn't necessarily a new virus; it's just new to the community that is threatened by it. When a virus mutates spontaneously, or crosses species or geographic borders, it imperils a population that was never before exposed. And it's in the first wave of an emerging virus epidemic that the most damage is done—as occurred with the rabbit virus, deliberately introduced into Australia in 1950 to wipe out an imported rabbit population that had grown totally out of control. A British gentleman had first imported a few dozen rabbits from England "for sport" in the 1850s, but within twenty years they had reproduced so wildly—the rabbit has no natural predators in Australia—that it was a threat to crops, pastures, and the survival of less prolific species. So in 1950, a highly virulent strain of a rabbit virus known as myxomatosis was brought to Australia from Brazil, where it was a relatively harmless tumor-causing agent.

1

For a while, it looked as if myxomatosis would do the trick. In the first weeks after the virus was released, myxomatosis killed Australian rabbits with a fatality rate of 99.8 percent. But just one year later, the fatality rate was down to 90 percent; by 1958, it was a mere 25 percent. Rapid evolutionary changes in both the myxomatosis virus and the Australian rabbits had led to adaptations that allowed pathogen and host to coexist in relative equilibrium. "We now see a fascinating interplay between genetic changes in host and virus," wrote Frank Fenner, a prominent Australian virologist, more than thirty years after the myxomatosis introduction, which he had helped coordinate. "It is to be hoped that observations can be continued, at intervals of perhaps a decade, to examine this unique model of the continuing evolution of an infectious disease."

2

Myxomatosis qualifies as an emerging virus disease for Australian rabbits. But it did not just generate spontaneously. Scientists found the virus in a laboratory in Brazil, where it was killing rabbits imported from Europe for experimentation but sparing

3

native rabbits in the surrounding woods near São Paulo. They isolated the virus from the rabbits that died, grew it in the laboratory, and brought it into Australia to inject it into rabbits living in warrens near the upper Murray River. On river flats twenty miles away, rabbits began dying of myxomatosis—not because of the inoculations alone, but because an important vector of the virus, the mosquito, also existed in the region. (A vector is an insect or animal that can bite a viral victim, take in some of the virus, and allow the virus to grow in its own body and be passed on later through another bite.) So human intervention was necessary, but not sufficient, for touching off the Australian plague of myxomatosis. The introduction of the virus was stunning in its early success—indeed, in three short months the myxomatosis plague had spread across a geographic area the size of western Europe—but human actions also required one critical natural condition: the prior existence of the vector mosquito.

The pattern of the myxomatosis plague is probably followed in other emerging   4
virus diseases, animal and human alike. When a new population is hit, the immediate effect is almost total devastation. Within a few years, though, the animal host evolves to become collectively less vulnerable. Those not killed in the first wave either are genetically resistant or have become resistant after developing antibodies against an initial infection. And while the animal host evolves, the virus is evolving too. The most lethal strains kill their hosts so rapidly that they themselves die out; they are unable to infect a second host before the first host dies. This gives an advantage to strains of virus that kill more slowly. After the host animal has gone through about six generations, this coevolution usually works its way to a state approaching equilibrium: one with a virus that is less virulent, so its host stays healthy enough to pass it around, and with a host that is less vulnerable, so it survives despite this native infection. To reach this equilibrium usually takes about six generations—no time at all for fast-breeding rabbits, which become parents by the age of six to ten months, but at least 125 years for human beings.

Similarly, emerging viruses that infect humans have generally been in nature, per-   5
colating beneath the surface, for quite some time. Something about the virus then changes: its actual genetic configuration, its position in the ecological balance, or its proximity to a species not previously encountered. When a virus "emerges," it slides out of its original niche and begins infecting a new population. This usually occurs as a result of an actual mutation in one of the virus's genes, which changes its ability to infect; of changes in the environment, including patterns of rainfall and temperature, which interfere with the balance between certain predators and their prey and give an unchanged virus a new niche in which to thrive; or of the things people do—building roads into the rain forest, transporting microbes from one region to another, erecting housing on the edge of woodland—that change man's relationship to the environment and expose new populations of people to viruses they'd never seen before.

These last two mechanisms—in which either man or nature shifts sufficiently to   6
change the balance between the two—are not inherently as interesting as the first.

It seems we would much rather imagine weird microbes arising out of the blue than think about the more mundane matter of how our actions affect our health. From the best-selling *Andromeda Strain*—Michael Crichton's 1969 novel about a new infectious agent falling from outer space—to inflamed political rhetoric about a new microbe getting loose from a gene-splicing laboratory, mutations have taken center stage in our collective nightmare. But mutations are almost never responsible for emerging viruses, which makes one wonder why we are so captivated by the image of man as hapless victim of nature, rather than the other way around. The fact is, as far as nature is concerned, human beings are not at the center of things, and nowhere is this more in evidence than in the study of new viruses. Occasionally, we bumble into some virus's way, and we encounter catastrophe. But that is not what the virus was doing there originally. We created the mishap, and our suffering is of no consequence to the virus itself. As the essayist Lewis Thomas has put it, "We have always been a relatively minor interest of the vast microbial world. . . . Disease usually results from inconclusive negotiations for symbiosis, and an overstepping of the line by one side or the other, a biologic misinterpretation of borders."

7 Viruses and their natural hosts—which are almost always *not* human beings— could go on quite happily without our interference. But interfere we do, over and over again. And it's when this happens that we get ourselves in trouble, as we have been doing for at least five hundred years, ever since Columbus—and probably for many hundreds of years before that. The causes of the great diseases of antiquity still remain mysteries to modern epidemiologists, but the health effects of the discovery of the New World have been clearly documented. When European explorers first came to the Americas, they brought along in their bodies and their baggage deadly viruses that the Native Americans had never before seen. The epidemics that resulted helped shape the course of history.

8 Cortés's small band of warriors, for instance, probably would never have been able to conquer Mexico in 1521 had it not been for smallpox. The disease killed more than one-third of the Aztecs that year; the tribespeople considered such massive devastation to be the gods' punishment for some unintentional transgression. This was confirmed, in the Aztecs' mind, by the bizarre pattern of death in the wake of this hideous pestilence: none of the Spaniards died of smallpox. There was of course a simple biological explanation for this—the Spaniards had all been exposed to the virus in childhood, so they were immune—but the Aztecs thought it was a kind of holy magic. They were dying, they believed, because they deserved to die, and the white men were living because they somehow had earned favor with the gods. As William McNeill put it in his classic historical work *Plagues and Peoples,* "From the Amerindian point of view, stunned acquiescence in Spanish superiority was the only possible response."

9 As ships continued to crisscross the oceans over the centuries, viruses continued to stow away on board. Sometimes, as with measles and smallpox, the virus took up residence in the sailors themselves. When the sick sailors got off at the port of call, their very presence in the new city was enough to start spreading disease.

But not every virus is passed directly from one person to another. Many of them   10
involve an intermediate insect or animal carrier—a vector—that can harbor the
virus with no ill effect and, when it bites its next victim, pass on the virus as effi-
ciently as would a hypodermic syringe filled with viral fluid. Vector-borne diseases
can never be transmitted by people breathing on each other, as measles and smallpox can. They can never be passed on by people having sex with each other, as
most of the herpesviruses can. They are contagious only through an intermediary.
So for these diseases to be introduced into a new geographic location, two separate events must occur in close succession: the virus must be imported (usually inside a human patient), and the vector (usually an arthropod, but occasionally a small
rodent) must be imported too, or must already be present on native soil.

The slave ships of the seventeenth century turned out to offer the ideal con-   11
veyance for bringing one type of virus vector, the notorious *Aedes aegypti* mosquito, from its native West Africa to the rest of the world. *Aedes aegypti* can carry
and transmit the virus of yellow fever, a debilitating disease that causes high fever,
headache, nausea and vomiting, and, in the worst cases, jaundice (a sign of liver failure), proteinuria (protein in the urine, a sign of kidney failure), and so-called black
vomit (which indicates internal bleeding). The yellow fever mosquito is highly do-
mesticated and will breed only in artificial containers; it won't lay its eggs in water
with a muddy or sandy bottom. When ships began transporting Africans to the
Caribbean, where they were sold as slaves, the open water barrels on board were
propitious breeding grounds for *Aedes aegypti* larvae. And once the boats docked in
the Caribbean, the warm climate proved quite hospitable for this tropical Old
World mosquito.

The mosquito vector was one of the two critical ingredients needed for yellow   12
fever to take hold. The other one was the virus itself. That came to the Caribbean
in the 1640s, when sailors on a slave ship took ill during the long voyage from West
Africa to Havana. They were suffering from "yellow jack," so called because an infected ship was required to fly a yellow flag, or jack, as a warning to those onshore.
As more and more European sailors died, mosquitoes continued to breed in the
water casks; new, nonimmune mosquitoes continued to hatch, and as they bit the
infected sailors, the pernicious cycle dragged on. When the boat finally docked in
Cuba, it released dozens of sick men and bucketloads of young mosquitoes, some
of which were already viremic (carrying virus in their blood). When the viruses in
these carrier mosquitoes migrated into the salivary glands—as infectious agents do
in all mosquito-borne diseases—and the mosquitoes bit the nonimmune Cuban na-
tives, yellow fever virus was passed directly into the Cubans' bloodstreams. So in
1648, the hemisphere's first cases of yellow fever were reported in the port cities
of Cuba and Yucatán, thus establishing in the New World a disease that had already
ravaged the Old.

In recent years, another mosquito, known informally as the Asian tiger mosquito,   13
seems to be replacing the *Aedes aegypti* in both Latin America and the southern
United States. (Its made-for-tabloids nickname comes from its coloration—white

and black stripes—as well as from its big-cat tendency to attack and bite with abandon.) The tiger mosquito arrived in 1985 on a boat traveling from Japan that was carrying a shipment of used automobile tires to a dock in Texas. Stowed away on board were mosquito larvae, which are always hatched in wet areas. The rainwater that had accumulated in the tire hulls was just wet enough for the purpose. Beginning with this Texas importation, tiger mosquitoes have since spread to eighteen states, mostly in the southwestern United States. In many states, the new mosquitoes have almost wiped out the population of the native *Aedes aegypti*. That may sound comforting, but it's not: the tiger mosquito can carry the yellow fever virus too. (Not every mosquito can serve as a vector for every virus.) And in addition, the tiger mosquito, more properly called *Aedes albopictus,* can carry the virus that causes two related diseases: dengue (pronounced *deng*-ee) fever, which is relatively mild, and the more virulent dengue hemorrhagic fever.

Many experts consider dengue fever to be the most likely candidate for the next 14 American plague. No native cases have yet arisen in the United States, but it seems only a matter of time. Now that the mosquito vector has arrived, we need only a few sick people for dengue to take hold. Once the mosquito bites an infected person, the virus passes to the mosquito's salivary glands for an important stop in its life cycle—a chance to replicate logarithmically. Then the mosquito bites an uninfected person, and the endless cycle begins.

from THE CULTURE OF PAIN
David B. Morris

We can better grasp the dilemma facing people with chronic pain—especially 1 their sense of dislocation—if we consider the ways in which our culture teaches us to confront pain with silence and denial. Americans today probably belong to the first generation on earth that looks at a pain-free life as something like a constitutional right. Pain is a scandal. Leonardo da Vinci in his notebooks wrote that "the chief evil is bodily pain." Leonardo and his age, however, also knew something about how to live in a world where evil cannot be routinely exorcised with a bottle of pills. We are not well equipped for what happens when our pills fail. Suppose the pain simply will not go away. Suppose it follows us and takes up residence in our bones so that nothing we buy or swallow or rub on our skin will make it vanish. What then?

Silence is among the most frequent responses to chronic pain. We tend to think, 2 with good reason, that pain almost instantly finds a voice. All newborn infants cry, and their cries (as all parents know) come in distinctively different tones. Yet this apparently natural response to pain—although not itself learned—is swiftly *unlearned* and *relearned*. We very soon replace our earliest natural responses to pain with carefully calibrated understandings about how much crying is permitted, about when and where you can cry, about who can cry and for what reasons. The truth is that we learn almost everything we know about pain, including the need to deny it and to smother it in silence.

Ronald Melzack, one of the major figures in modern pain research, early in his   3
career designed an experiment in which he raised dogs from birth in the laboratory equivalent of padded cells. They were isolated from other dogs and completely sheltered from painful stimuli. When full grown, these dogs proved deficient in the ability to perceive and respond to pain. Melzack reports that one dog, observed in a room with low-lying water pipes, knocked its head on the pipes more than thirty times in an hour without showing any evidence of pain behavior. Such experiments strongly suggest that an understanding of pain is something we learn in the course of our normal growth. ("People were taught to bear necessary pain in my day," says a sixty-year-old man in an 1899 play by Shaw.) As soon as we are born, we are educated day and night in the school of pain. But it is mostly acute pain that we learn about. No one teaches us what to do with a pain that never stops.

Nevertheless we learn. Patients with chronic pain soon discover that their com-   4
plaints (potentially endless, like their pain) often exhaust, frustrate, and finally alienate family and friends and physicians. Many patients thus learn to retreat into a defensive isolation. They keep to themselves. They experience firsthand the failure of words in the face of suffering. Virginia Woolf wrote: "The merest schoolgirl, when she falls in love, has Shakespeare or Keats to speak her mind for her; but let a sufferer try to describe a pain in his head to a doctor and language at once runs dry." The normal failure of language under the assault of acute pain, which Woolf describes, is a common but not devastating experience. A pain that lasts for months or years, however, begins to wear out everyone's patience and goodwill; it constitutes a radical assault on language and on human communication. There is simply nothing that can be said.

It is not entirely clear why language should run dry or crumble under the influ-   5
ence of pain. Love is no less mysterious, yet it fills thousands of songs, poems, and novels with its apparently inexhaustible speech. Even the inventive McGill-Melzack Pain Questionnaire reduces the patient's experience of pain to a mere seventy-eight words. Love, of course, draws people together, creating an intimacy that bypasses and transcends normal communication. The understanding between lovers is deep, instant, and unspoken. Chronic pain, in contrast, most often seems to build up walls of separation. It breaks down understanding. It places people in utterly different worlds of feeling. It surrounds them with silence. In many ways, the person in chronic pain might as well be standing on the moon.

"Pain," wrote Aristotle, "upsets and destroys the nature of the person who feels   6
it." Notice how even a minor irritant—a passing headache, say, or stiffness in the neck—tends to change your mood. Pain makes most of us irritable and cranky. The composed face with which we greet the world begins to look slightly pinched or haggard. A stronger pain can succeed in driving out every erotic impulse. ("Not tonight, dear.") It can turn a normally imperturbable man suddenly mean and hostile, as if replacing him with his savage twin. A scream, which we might think of as

speech unraveled, seems to be the natural language of intense acute pain. Yet all these instances are somehow familiar. Even a scream manages to communicate something, if only the presence of a nameless terror. The shift from acute to chronic pain, however, initiates a difference of kind, not degree. Prolonged chronic pain threatens to unravel the self.

There is much to be said for the view that silence is the natural language of chronic pain. Everyone responds to acute pain with more or less distinctive but related cries: in English, *ow!* in French, *aie!* in German, *ach!* in Yiddish, *oy!* These hollow monosyllables, however, are eminently social. Like a scream, they communicate instantly and quite often constitute an implicit request for help. Chronic pain opens on an unsocial, wordless terrain where all communication threatens to come to a halt. Cries for help prove mostly useless. Indeed, at its most intense or most protracted, chronic pain may push us toward an area of human life we know almost nothing about. Its inarticulate silences serve as the expression of an otherness so alien that we have no words and no language with which to comprehend it.

7

▪2▪

Presenting Sources to Others

I hate quotations. Tell me what you know.

Ralph Waldo Emerson (1849)

By necessity, by proclivity, and by delight, we all quote.

Ralph Waldo Emerson (1876)

These quotations appear to be contradictory, but they merely represent the development of one writer's understanding of his craft. Like Emerson in 1849, most writers hope to rely entirely on what they know and to express their knowledge in their own words. But, as Emerson realized later, one rarely writes about ideas that no one has ever explored. Someone has usually gone part of the way before, so it makes sense to build on that person's discoveries.

Because most of your writing in college will be based directly or indirectly on what you have read, you will need a working knowledge of two more methods of presenting other people's ideas to your readers: *quotation* and *paraphrase*.

REASONS FOR QUOTING

In academic writing, presenting the words of another writer through *quotation* is the most basic way to support your own ideas. Quotation is a pivotal skill. Writers who know how to quote understand the need to give credit to their sources for both borrowed ideas and borrowed words.

- *Correct quotation* tells your reader that you respect your sources, that you know how to distinguish between your own work and theirs, and that you will not *plagiarize*—make unacknowledged use of another writer's words and ideas.

- *Appropriate quotation* tells your reader that you know when to quote and that you are not allowing your sources' words to dominate your writing.

88

Quotations are not a substitute for summary or paraphrase. Experienced writers hold quotation marks in reserve for those times when they think it essential to present the source's exact words.

> ### *Reasons to Use Quotation*
>
> 1. For support
> 2. To preserve vivid or technical language
> 3. To comment on the quotation
> 4. To distance yourself from the quotation

1. Quoting for Support

You will most often refer to another writer's work as evidence in support of one of your own points. To ensure that the evidence retains its full meaning and impact, you retain the author's original language, instead of putting the sentences in your own words. Very often, quoted material appears in an essay as an *appeal to authority;* the source being quoted is important enough or familiar enough with the subject (as in an eyewitness account) to make the original words worth quoting. For example, the only quotation in a *New York Times* article describing political and economic chaos in Bolivia presents the opinion of a government official:

> Even the Government acknowledges its shaky position. "The polity is unstable, capricious and chaotic," Adolfo Linares Arraya, Minister of Planning and Coordination, said. "The predominance of crisis situations has made the future unforeseeable."

The minister's words in themselves seem vague and glib, and therefore not especially quotable. (Indeed, they may not even be true.) But his position as representative of the government makes the minister's exact words necessary evidence for the reporter's presentation of the Bolivian crisis.

2. Quoting Vivid or Technical Language

The wording of the source material may be so ingenious that the point will be lost if you express it in your own words. *You will want to quote a sentence that is very compact or that relies on a striking image to make its point.* For example, here is a paragraph from a review of a book about Vietnamese history:

> Not many nations have had such a history of scrapping: against Mongols and Chinese seeking to dominate them from the north, and to the south against weaker and more innocent peoples who stood in the way of the Vietnamese march to the rich Mekong Delta and the underpopulated land of Cambodia. Mr. Hodgkin [the author] quotes from a poem by a medieval Vietnamese hero: "By its tradition of defending the country / the army is so powerful it can swallow the evening star."

The quotation adds authentic evidence to the reviewer's discussion and provides a memorable image for the reader.

It is also important to retain the precise terminology of a *technical or legal document*. Changing one word of the text can significantly change its meaning. Here is a sentence from the final paragraph of a Supreme Court decision upholding the civil rights of three tenth-graders who had been suspended by school officials for "spiking" the punch at a meeting of an extracurricular club:

> We hold that a school board member is not immune from liability for damages if he knew or reasonably should have known that the action he took within his sphere of official responsibility would violate the constitutional rights of the student affected, or if he took the action with the malicious intention to cause a deprivation of constitutional rights or other injury to the student.

Virtually every word of the sentence has potential impact on the way this decision will be interpreted in subsequent legal suits. Note, for example, the distinction between "knew" and "reasonably should have known" and the way in which "intention" is qualified by "malicious."

3. Quoting Another Writer to Comment on the Quotation

In your essay, you may want to analyze or comment on a statement made by another writer. Your readers should have that writer's exact words in front of them if they are to get the full benefit of your commentary; *you have to quote it in order to talk about it.* Thus, when a writer reviewing Philip Norman's biography of the Beatles wants to criticize the biographer's style, he must supply a sample quotation so that his readers can make up their own minds.

> Worst of all is the overwritten prologue, about John Lennon's death and its impact in Liverpool: "The ruined imperial city, its abandoned river, its tormented suburban plain, knew an anguish greater than the recession and unemployment which have laid Merseyside waste under bombardments more deadly than Hitler's blitz." A moment's thought should have made Norman and his publishers realize that this sort of thing, dashed off in the heat of the moment, would quickly come to seem very embarrassing indeed.

4. Gaining Distance through Quotation

Writers generally use quotation to distinguish between the writer of the essay and the writer being cited in the essay. There are, however, a few less important reasons for using quotation marks—reasons that also involve this concept of *the distance between the writer and his or her sources of information.*

For example, you may want to use quotation marks to indicate that a word or phrase is not in common or standard use. A phrase may be *obsolete,* no longer in current usage:

Many "flower children" gathered at the rock festivals of the late 1960s.

Or a phrase may be *slang*, not yet having been absorbed into standard English:

She tried to "cop out" of doing her share of the work.

In effect, you want to use the phrase and at the same time "cover" yourself by signaling your awareness that the phrase is not quite right: you are distancing yourself from your own vocabulary. *It is usually better to take full responsibility for your choice of words and to avoid using slang or obsolete vocabulary, with or without quotation marks.* But if the context requires such phrasing, you may use quotation marks to gain the necessary distance.

You can achieve a different kind of distance when you use quotation marks to suggest *irony*:

Gaining Distance

The actor was joined by his "constant companion."

The quoted phrase is a familiar *euphemism*, a bland expression substituted for a more blunt term. Again, by placing it in quotation marks, the author is both *calling attention to* and *distancing him- or herself from* the euphemism.

Quotation marks also serve as a means of *disassociation* for journalists who wish to avoid taking sides on an issue or making editorial comments.

A fire that roared through a 120-year-old hotel and took at least 11 lives was the work of a "sick arsonist," the county coroner said today. Robert Jennings, the Wayne County coroner, said that he had told county officials that the building was a "fire trap."

The author of this article did not want the responsibility of attributing the fire to a "sick arsonist" or labeling the building a "fire trap"—at any rate, not until the findings of an investigation or a trial make the terminology unquestionably true. Thus, he is careful not only to use quotation marks around certain phrases, but also to cite the precise source of the statement.

USING QUOTATIONS

The apparatus for quotation is twofold:

1. By *inserting quotation marks,* you indicate that you are borrowing certain words, as well as certain ideas, that appear in your writing.
2. By *inserting a citation* containing the source's name, you give credit for both ideas and words to the author.

Citation

Theodore Roosevelt said,

Quotation

"Speak softly and carry a big stick;

you will go far."

Combine citation written by you with the words you are quoting.

Direct Quotation: Separating Quotations from Your Own Writing

when you are quoting someone (but you want to keep a distance)

The simplest way to quote is to combine the citation (written by you) with the words you are quoting (*exactly as they were said or written by your source*). This method of quotation joins together two separate statements, with punctuation—comma or colon—bridging the gap and a capital letter beginning the quoted phrase.

St. Paul declared, "It is better to marry than to burn."

In his first epistle to the Corinthians, St. Paul commented on lust: "It is better to marry than to burn."

In both these forms of direct quotation, the quoted words are *not* fully integrated into the grammatical structure of your sentence. The *comma or colon* and the *capital letter* at the beginning of the quoted sentence separate the two parts, making it clear that *two voices appear in the sentence: yours and your source's.* In general, you should choose this kind of direct quotation when you want to differentiate between yourself and the quoted words. There are many reasons for wanting to emphasize this difference; an obvious example would be your own disagreement with the quotation.

The *colon* is used less frequently than the comma: It usually follows an introductory phrase that is more formal than a short citation. In fact, the colon often follows a clause that can stand alone as a complete sentence. As such, the colon separates a complete idea of your own from a complementary or supporting idea taken from your source.

Direct Quotation: Integrating Quotations into Your Sentences

In an alternative kind of direct quotation, *only the quotation marks indicate that you are using someone else's words.*

St. Paul declared that "it is better to marry than to burn."

Alvin Toffler defined future shock as "the shattering stress and disorientation that we induce in individuals by subjecting them to too much change in too short a time."

There is no signal for the reader that separates citation from quotation—no comma or colon, no capital letter. The first word of the quoted material, in this second type of direct quotation, is *not* capitalized, even if it was capitalized in the source.

Original

Beware of all enterprises that require new clothes.

HENRY DAVID THOREAU

Quotation

Thoreau warned his readers to "beware of all enterprises that require new clothes."

The effect is very smooth, and the reader's attention is not distracted from the flow of sentences.

The Two Kinds of Direct Quotation

Separated

- Comma or colon and quotation marks separate citation and quotation.
- The first letter of the quotation is capitalized.
- You are distinguishing between your ideas and those of your source.

Integrated

- No punctuation (but quotation marks) separates citation and quotation.
- The first letter of the quotation is not capitalized.
- You are integrating your ideas with those of your source.

Because integrating the quotation tends to blur the distinction between writer and source, you must be careful to avoid confusion. Look, for example, at the various ways of quoting this first-person sentence, which was originally spoken by a motorist: "I hate all pedestrians."

Separated Quotation

The motorist said, "I hate all pedestrians."

Integrated Quotation

The motorist said that "I hate all pedestrians."

The first method, quoting with separation by punctuation, requires no alteration in the original sentence. But in the second version, quoting with integration, the original wording does not quite fit.

- The first-person "I" conflicts with the third-person "motorist" (the reader may wonder who "I" is—the motorist or the writer!).
- The present-tense "hate" conflicts with the past-tense "said," so "hate" must be turned into "hated."

But once the person [I] and the tense [hate] of the original statement have been altered for clarity and consistency, only two words—"all pedestrians"—are actually being quoted:

Direct Quotation

The motorist said that she hated "all pedestrians."

You may even prefer not to put quotations around the remaining two words taken from the original source. If so, you are not quoting anything directly; you are using indirect quotation. *In indirect quotation, you report rather than quote what has been said.*

Indirect Quotation

The motorist said that she hated all pedestrians.

However, the absence of quotation marks in the indirect quotation could be confusing. If you were collecting evidence for a legal suit, quotation marks would indicate that the motorist was responsible for the precise wording. Therefore, direct quotation, separated by punctuation, is probably the most appropriate method of presenting the motorist's opinion of pedestrians.

As a rule, the writer has the obligation to insert quotation marks when using a source's exact words, whether written or oral.

Direct Quotation

Robert Ingersoll condemned those who deny others their civil liberties: "I am the inferior of any man whose rights I trample underfoot."

Indirect Quotation

Robert Ingersoll proclaimed that he was the inferior of any man whose rights he trampled underfoot.

The indirect quotation does not indicate exactly who wrote this sentence. Even if you changed "I" to "he" and the present to the past tense, *you are still not using your own words;* the basic phrasing of the sentence remains Ingersoll's. *To imply, as this indirect quotation could, that the wording is yours, not Ingersoll's, would be plagiarism.*

For this reason, *writers should use indirect quotation with great care.* If one of the two forms of direct quotation does not seem appropriate, you should invent your own phrasing—called *paraphrase*—to express the source's original statement.

The Historical Present Tense

Certain ideas and statements remain true long after their creators have died. By convention, or general agreement, writers often refer to these statements in the present tense.

Shakespeare states, "This above all: to thine own self be true."

When you are devoting part of your own essay to a "discussion" with another writer, you may prefer to conduct the discussion on a common ground of time and use the present tense, called the *historical present*. The historical present is also useful to *place a variety of different sources on equal terms, especially when they are from different eras.* In the following example, the introductory verbs, all in the present tense, are underlined:

Probably not on exam.

> While Shelley <u>acknowledges</u> that poets are creators of language and music and art, he also <u>asserts</u> that they have a civic role: "They are the institutors of laws, and the founders of civil society, and the inventors of the arts of life." Writing one hundred years later, Benedetto Croce <u>affirms</u> Shelley's insistence upon the social and spiritual responsibilities of the poet. According to Croce, Shelley <u>sees</u> poetry "as the eternal source of all intellectual, moral, and civil vitality."

Finally, the historical present is almost always used when you refer to *important documents* (often written by a group of people, rather than a single author) that remain in force long after they were created. Obvious examples include the Constitution, the Declaration of Independence, the laws of Congress, Supreme Court decisions, the charter of your state government, and the bylaws governing your college or university.

> The Constitution guarantees that women—and, indeed, all citizens—shall have the vote in elections; Amendment XIX states that the right to vote "shall not be denied or abridged by the United States or by any State on account of sex."

Punctuating Direct Quotations

You have already learned about punctuating *the beginning of the quotation:*

1. In a separated direct quotation, the citation is followed by a comma or a colon.
2. In an integrated direct quotation, the citation is followed by no punctuation at all.

Some writers tend to forget this second point and include an unnecessary comma:

Incorrect Quotation

Ernest Hemingway believed that, "what is moral is what you feel good after and what is immoral is what you feel bad after."

Remember that *an integrated quotation should have no barriers between citation and quotation:*

Correct Quotation

Ernest Hemingway believed that "what is moral is what you feel good after and what is immoral is what you feel bad after."

In the integrated direct quotation, note that the first letter of the quotation is not capitalized.

There is no easy way of remembering the proper sequence of punctuation for *closing a quotation*. The procedure has been determined by conventional and arbitrary agreement, originally for the convenience of printers. Although other countries abide by different conventions, in the United States the following rules apply—and *there are no exceptions.*

1. All periods and commas are placed inside the terminal quotation marks.

It does not matter whether the period belongs to *your* sentence or to the quoted sentence: it goes *inside* the marks. This is the most important rule and the one most often ignored. Don't resort to ambiguous devices such as placing the quotes directly over the period (.").

P. T. Barnum is reputed to have said that "there's a sucker born every minute."

P. T. Barnum is reputed to have said that "there's a sucker born every minute," and Barnum's circuses undertook to entertain each and every one.

Notice that, in the second example, the comma at the end of the quotation really belongs to the framework sentence, not to the quotation itself; nevertheless, it goes *inside* the marks.

2. All semicolons, colons, and dashes are placed outside the terminal quotation marks.

They should be regarded as the punctuation for *your* sentence, and not for the quotation.

George Santayana wrote that "those who cannot remember the past are condemned to repeat it"; today, we are in danger of forgetting the lessons of history.

Occasionally, when a semicolon, colon, or (most likely) a dash appears at the end of the material to be quoted, you will decide to include the punctuation in the quotation; in that case, the punctuation should be placed inside the marks. In the following example, the dash appears in Lucretia Mott's original statement, so it is placed inside the quotation marks.

Lucretia Mott argued urgently for women's rights: "Let woman then go on—not asking favors, but claiming as a right the removal of all hindrances to her elevation in the scale of being—" so that, as a result, she might "enter profitably into the active business of man."

3. Question marks and exclamation points are sometimes placed inside the quotation marks and sometimes placed outside.

- If the quotation is itself a question or an exclamation, the mark or point goes *inside* the quotation marks.
- If your own sentence is a question or an exclamation, the mark or point goes *outside* a quotation placed at the *very end* of your sentence.

> In 1864, General Sherman signaled the arrival of his reinforcements: "Hold the fort! I am coming!"

The exclamation is General Sherman's; the exclamation point goes inside the quotation.

> Can anyone in the 1980s agree with Dumas that "woman inspires us to great things and prevents us from achieving them"?

Dumas was *not* asking a question; the question mark goes at the very end of the sentence, after the quotation marks.

> Sigmund Freud's writings occasionally reveal a remarkable lack of insight: "The great question that has never been answered, and which I have not yet been able to answer despite my thirty years of research into the feminine soul, is: What does a woman want?"

Freud himself asked this famous question; the question mark goes inside the quotation.

> Freud was demonstrating remarkably little insight when he wrote, "What does a woman want?" citing his "thirty years of research into the feminine soul"!

The exclamation is the writer's, not Freud's; the exclamation point goes outside the quotation marks.

It is possible to construct a sentence that ends logically in two question marks (or exclamation points): one for the quotation and one for your own sentence. In such cases, you need include only one—and, by convention, it should be placed *inside* the marks:

> What did Freud mean when he asked, "What does a woman want?"

These rules apply only to the quotation of complete sentences or reasonably long phrases. *Whether it is a quotation or an obsolete, slang, or ironic reference, a single word or a brief phrase should be fully integrated into your sentence, without being preceded or followed by commas.*

> Winston Churchill's reference to "blood, sweat and tears" rallied the English to prepare for war.

Be careful not to quote words or phrases excessively. Even though the quotation marks make it clear that you are borrowing the words, using more than one quotation, however brief, in a sentence or quoting sentence after sentence creates the impression that you cannot express your thoughts in your own words.

Interrupting Quotations

Sometimes it is desirable to break up a long quotation or to vary the way you quote your sources by interrupting a quotation *and placing the citation in the middle.*

"I do not mind lying," wrote Samuel Butler, "but I hate inaccuracy."

Butler's statement is divided into two separate parts, and therefore you need to use *four* sets of quotation marks: two introductory and two terminal. The citation is joined to the quotation by a comma on either side. There are two danger points:

- If you forget to use the marks at the beginning of the second half of the quotation, you are failing to distinguish your words from Butler's.
- You must also put the first comma *inside* the terminal quotation marks (because terminal commas *always* go inside the quotation marks) and put the comma that concludes the citation *before* the quotation marks (because it is *your* comma, not Butler's).

Quoting inside a Quotation

Sometimes a statement that you want to quote already contains a quotation. In that case, you must use *two sets of quotation marks, double and single,* to help your reader to distinguish between the two separate sources.

- *Single quotation* marks are used for the words already quoted by your source (and this is the *only* time when it is appropriate to use single quotation marks).
- *Double quotation* marks are used around the words that you are quoting.

Goethe at times expressed a notable lack of self-confidence: "'Know thyself?' If I knew myself, I'd run away."

At the beginning of World War I, Winston Churchill observed that "the maxim of the British people is 'Business as usual.'"

The same single/double procedure is used even when there is no author's name to be cited.

A Yiddish proverb states that "'for example' is not proof."

Very occasionally, you may need to use triple quotation marks, usually to quote a source who is quoting another source who is using a quoted word or phrase. An article about the author Muriel Spark included the following statement by that novelist:

I draw the line at "forever."

Victoria Glendinning, the author of the article, quoted Spark's statement using single and double quotation marks.

Eternally inquiring and curious about places and people, "I draw the line at 'forever.'"

To quote that sentence in your essay, you would need to distinguish yourself from Victoria Glendinning and Muriel Spark.

In her recent profile, Victoria Glendinning emphasizes Muriel Spark's search for variety: "Eternally inquiring and curious about places and people, 'I draw the line at "forever."'"

Notice that you would deliberately plan the quotation marks so that the double marks are used for the framework quotation.

EXERCISE 10

A. Correct the errors in the following sentences:

1. Almost 6,000 years ago, a citizen of Lagash, in the Middle East, lamented that "You can have a Lord", "You can have a King", but the man to fear is the tax collector".

2. Baron de Montesquieu, a philosopher of the eighteenth-century Enlightenment, sympathized with the needs of the masses, "The real wants of the people," he wrote, ought never to give way to the imaginary wants of the state".

3. Oscar Wilde recognized the irony of romance, concluding that "there are two great tragedies in life, losing the one you love and winning the one you love.

4. According to Andreas Capellanus, who lived in twelfth-century France; "love is a certain inborn suffering derived from the sight of and excessive meditation upon the beauty of the opposite sex, which causes each one to wish above all things the embraces of the other"

5. Robert F. Wagner, former mayor of New York, believed in keeping a low profile and offered this advice—"When in danger, ponder; when in trouble, delegate" when in doubt, mumble"

6. The candidate said that, "He was not able to comment at this time."

7. When he said "It is not work that men object to, but the element of drudgery, Henry Ford understood the monotony of most factory

routine. We shall never be wholly civilized, Ford continued "until we remove the treadmill from the daily job.

8. Before the Revolutionary War, Patrick Henry made a passionate speech, "is life so dear or peace so sweet, as to be purchased at the price of chains and slavery"? "Forbid it, Almighty God"! I know not what course others may take, but as for me, give me liberty or give me death."!

9. In *Invisible Man*, Ralph Ellison noted that the fate of America, Is to become one, and yet many."

10. In his biography of George Bernard Shaw, Hesketh Pearson writes about "A strange lady giving an address in Zurich who wrote him a proposal thus: "You have the greatest brain in the world, and I have the most beautiful body; so we ought to produce the most perfect child." "Shaw asked: '"What if the child inherits my body and your brains'?"'

B. Use quotations from the following group as directed:

- Choose one quotation and write a sentence that introduces a direct quotation with separation.

- Choose a second quotation and write a sentence that introduces a direct quotation with integration.

- Choose a third quotation and write a sentence that interrupts a quotation with a citation in the middle.

1. Who said you should be happy? Do your work. (Colette)

2. I must say acting was good training for the political life which lay ahead for us. (Nancy Reagan)

3. Children's talent to endure stems from their ignorance of alternatives. (Maya Angelou)

4. We call schools free because we are not free to stay away from them until we are sixteen years of age. (Robert Frost)

5. That man is not truly brave who is afraid either to seem or to be, when it suits him, a coward. (Edgar Allan Poe)

6. People want economy and they will pay any price to get it. (Lee Iacocca)

7. Beggars should be abolished. It annoys one to give to them, and it annoys one not to give to them. (Friedrich Nietzsche)

8. I have now come to the conclusion never again to think of marrying, and for this reason: I can never be satisfied with anyone who would be blockhead enough to have me. (Abraham Lincoln)

Quoting Accurately   *Be careful about that*

Quoting is not a collaboration in which you try to improve on your source's writing. If you value a writer's words enough to want to quote them, you should respect the integrity of the sentence.

Unless you are applying the conventional methods of presenting quotations, don't make minor changes or carelessly leave words out, but faithfully transcribe the exact words, the exact spelling, and the exact punctuation that you find in the original.

Original

Those who corrupt the public mind are just as evil as those who steal from the public purse.

ADLAI STEVENSON

Inexact Quotation

Adlai Stevenson believed that "those who act against the public interest are just as evil as those who steal from the public purse."

Exact Quotation

Adlai Stevenson believed that "those who corrupt the public mind are just as evil as those who steal from the public purse."

Even if you notice an error (or what you regard as an error), you still must copy the original wording. For example, old-fashioned spelling should be retained, as well as regional or national dialect and spelling conventions:

One of Heywood's Proverbes tells us that "a new brome swepeth clean."

In one of his humorous stories, Colonel Davy Crockett predicted the reactions to his own death: "It war a great loss to the country and the world, and to ole Kaintuck in particklar. Thar were never known such a member of Congress as Crockett, and never will be agin. The painters and bears will miss him, for he never missed them."

Standards of acceptable punctuation have also changed; if a comma or semi-colon looks incorrect, remember that it may be correct for the *author's* era or locality.

Dr. Johnson believed that "it is better to live rich, than to die rich."

To our eyes, the comma breaking into the flow of such a short sentence is intrusive and incorrect, but it is not our job to edit Dr. Johnson's eighteenth-century prose.

The need to include the precise punctuation of the original, however, applies only to the material placed *inside* quotation marks. The punctuation immediately preceding or following the quoted words in the original text may be omitted and, indeed, should be omitted if it will help the quotation to fit more smoothly into your sentence.

Original

It is better to be making the news than taking it; to be an actor than a critic.

WINSTON CHURCHILL

Incorrect Quotation

Churchill observed, "It is better to be making the news than taking it;"

Correct Quotation

Churchill observed, "It is better to be making the news than taking it."

You do not have to assume the blame if the material that you are quoting contains errors of syntax, punctuation, or spelling. You can use a conventional way to point out such errors and inform the reader that the mistake was made, not by you, but by the author whom you are quoting. *The Latin word* sic *(meaning "thus") is placed in square brackets and inserted immediately after the error.* The [sic] signals that the quotation was "thus" and that you, the writer, were aware of the error, which was not the result of your own carelessness in transcribing the quotation.

In the following example, [sic] calls attention to an error in subject-verb agreement:

Richard Farson points out that "increased understanding and concern has [sic] not been coupled with increased rights."

You may also want to use [sic] to indicate that the source used archaic spelling:

In describing Elizabeth Billington, an early nineteenth-century singer, W. Clark Russell observed that "her voice was powerful, and resembled the tone of a clarionet [sic]."

It would be tedious, however, to use [sic] to indicate each misspelling in the Davy Crockett quotation; in your essay about Crockett, you could, instead, explain his use of dialect as you discuss his life and writing.

TAILORING QUOTATIONS TO FIT YOUR WRITING

There are several ways to change quotations to fit the quoted material naturally into your own sentences. Like [sic], these devices are *conventions*, established by generally accepted agreement: *you cannot improvise; you must follow these rules.* Usually, the conventional rules require you to inform your reader that a change is being made; in other words, they make clear the distinction between your wording and the author's.

Changing Capital and Small Letters

The first way of altering quotations depends entirely on how and where the quotation fits into your sentence.

- When a quotation is *integrated* completely into your sentence (usually when your citation ends in "that"), the first letter of the quotation will be small, whether or not it is a capital in the original. (Two exceptions are the pronoun "I" and proper nouns, which are always capitalized.)
- When a quotation is *separated* from your sentence, and your citation ends in a comma or a colon, the first letter of the quotation will be large, whether or not it is a capital in the original.

Integrated Quotation

The poet Frost wrote that "good fences make good neighbors."

Separated Quotation

The poet Frost wrote, "Good fences make good neighbors."

As a rule, it is not necessary to indicate to your readers that you have altered the first letter of your quotation from small to capital or from capital to small. Naturally, if you change the capitalization of any word (other than the first one), you must indicate this change to your reader, usually by using brackets, which are explained in a later section.

Using Ellipses

It is permissible to *delete* words from a quotation, provided that you indicate to the reader that something has been omitted. Your condensed version is as accurate as the original; it is just shorter. But you must remember to insert the conventional symbol for deletion, *three spaced dots,* called an *ellipsis.* Once made aware by the three dots that your version differs from the original, any reader who wants to see the omitted portion can consult the original source.

Original

It is not true that suffering ennobles the character; happiness does that sometimes, but suffering, for the most part, makes men petty and vindictive.

W. SOMERSET MAUGHAM

Quotation with Ellipsis

Maugham does not believe that "suffering ennobles the character; . . . suffering, for the most part, makes men petty and vindictive."

Notice that:

- The three dots are spaced equally.
- The dots *must* be three—not two or a dozen.
- The semicolon is retained, to provide terminal punctuation for the first part of the quotation.

If you wish to delete the end of a quotation, and the ellipsis coincides with the end of your sentence, you must use the three dots, plus a fourth to signify the sentence's end.

Quotation with Terminal Ellipsis

Maugham does not believe that "suffering ennobles the character; happiness does that sometimes. . . . "

Here, you'll note:

- There are four dots, three to indicate a deletion and a fourth to indicate the period at the end of the sentence.
- The first dot is placed immediately after the last letter.
- The sentence ends with quotation marks, as usual, with the marks placed *after* the dots, not before.

You can also use the three dots to link two separate quotations from the same paragraph in your source; the ellipsis will indicate the deletion of one or more sentences, but *only* if the two sentences that you are quoting are fairly near each other in the original. *An ellipsis cannot cover a gap of more than a few sentences.* When you use an ellipsis to bridge one or more sentences, use only *one* set of quotation marks. Your full quotation, with an ellipsis in the middle, is still continuous—a single quotation—even though there is a gap.

When an ellipsis is used following a quoted complete sentence, the period of the quoted sentence is retained so that a total of four dots is used, as in the following example.

Original

In one sense there is no death. The life of a soul on earth lasts beyond his departure. You will always feel that life touching yours, that voice speaking to you, that spirit looking out of other eyes, talking to you in the familiar things he touched, worked with, loved as familiar friends. He lives on in your life and in the lives of all others that knew him.

ANGELO PATRI

Quotation with Ellipsis

Patri states that "in one sense there is no death. The life of a soul on earth lasts beyond his departure. . . . He lives on in your life and in the lives of all others that knew him."

An ellipsis should be used to make a quotation fit more smoothly into your own sentence. It is especially convenient when you are working with a long passage that contains several separate points that you wish to quote. But ellipses should *not* be used to condense long, tedious quotations or to replace summary and paraphrase. If you only want to quote a brief extract from a lengthy passage, then simply quote that portion and ignore the surrounding material. An ellipsis is poorly used when it is used too often. Reading a paragraph full of dots can be very distracting.

The meaning of the original quotation must always be exactly preserved, despite the deletion represented by the ellipsis.

Original

As long as there are sovereign nations possessing great power, war is inevitable.

ALBERT EINSTEIN

Inexact Quotation

Einstein believes that " . . . war is inevitable."

It would not be accurate to suggest that Einstein believed in the inevitability of war, under all circumstances, without qualifications. *To extract only a portion of this statement with ellipsis is to oversimplify and thus to falsify the evidence.*

Another common consequence of misused ellipses is a mangled sentence. *Deleting words from a quotation can distort and destroy its syntax and structure.*

Original

In some sort of crude sense which no vulgarity, no humor, no overstatement can quite extinguish, the physicists have known sin; and this is a knowledge which they cannot lose.

J. ROBERT OPPENHEIMER

Inexact Quotation

J. Robert Oppenheimer thought that "in some sort of crude sense . . . the physicists have . . . a knowledge which they cannot lose."

Using Brackets

[   ] *your words*

Brackets have an opposite function: ellipsis signifies deletion; *brackets signify addition or alteration.* Brackets are not the same as parentheses. Parentheses would be confusing for this purpose, for the quotation might itself include a parenthetical statement, and the reader could not be sure whether the parentheses contained the author's insertion or yours. Instead, brackets, a relatively unusual form of punctuation, are used as a conventional way of informing the reader that material has been inserted. (You have already seen how to use

---

✳ *Reasons to Use Brackets*

- To explain a vague word
- To replace a confusing phrase
- To suggest an antecedent ← *word refers back to use pronoun.*
- To correct an error in a quotation
- To adjust a quotation to fit your own writing

---

brackets with [sic], which enables you to comment on the material that you are quoting.) You simply insert the information *inside* the quotation, placing it in square brackets.

The most common reason for using brackets is to clarify a vague word. You may, for example, choose to quote only the last portion of a passage, omitting an important antecedent:

Original

Man lives *by* habits, indeed, but what he lives *for* is thrills and excitement.

WILLIAM JAMES

Quotation with Brackets

William James argues that "what he [man] lives <u>for</u> is thrills and excitement."

William James argues that "what [man] lives <u>for</u> is thrills and excitement."

In the second example, the vague word "he" has been deleted entirely; the brackets themselves indicate that there has been a substitution, but the reader doesn't know what was originally there. For that reason, unless the presentation of both wordings seems very awkward, *it is better to follow the first example: quote the original and also provide the clarification in brackets.* This way, you will leave your reader in no doubt about your source's words.

Brackets can also be used to complete a thought that has been obscured by the omission (often through ellipsis) of an earlier sentence:

Original

A well-trained sensible family doctor is one of the most valuable assets in a community. . . . Few men live lives of more devoted self-sacrifice.

SIR WILLIAM OSLER

Quotation with Brackets

The great surgeon Sir William Osler had enormous respect for his less famous colleagues: "Few men live lives of more devoted self-sacrifice [than good family doctors]."

In addition to his warnings about the dangers of majority rule, which were cited earlier in the discussion of public opinion, John Stuart Mill also expresses concern about "the functions of police; how far liberty may legitimately be invaded for the prevention of crime, or of accident."

- Avoid referring to the author twice in the same citation, once by name and once by pronoun. In the following citation, we really can't be sure who "he" is:

  In John Stuart Mill's *On Liberty*, he writes . . .

- Finally, unless you genuinely do not know the author's name, use it! There is no point in being coy, even for the sake of variety:

  A famous man once made an ironic observation about child-rearing: "If you strike a child, take care that you strike it in anger. . . . A blow in cold blood neither can nor should be forgiven."

Your guessing game will only irritate readers who are not aware that this famous man was George Bernard Shaw.

Choosing the Introductory Verb

The citation provides an important link between your thoughts and those of your source. The introductory verb can tell your reader something about your reasons for presenting the quotation and its context in the work that you are quoting. Will you choose "J. S. Mill says," or "J. S. Mill writes," or "J. S. Mill thinks," or "J. S. Mill feels"? Those are the most common introductory verbs— so common that they have become boring! Whenever appropriate, select less stereotyped verbs. As the senses are not directly involved in writing, avoid "feels" entirely. And, unless you are quoting someone's spoken words, substitute a more accurate verb for "says."

Here are some introductory verbs:

argues	adds	concludes
establishes	explains	agrees
emphasizes	believes	insists
finds	continues	maintains
points out	declares	disagrees
notes	observes	states
suggests	proposes	compares

Of course, once you stop using the all-purpose "says" or "writes," you have to remember that verbs are not interchangeable and that you should choose the verb that best suits your purpose.

The citation should suggest the relationship between your own ideas (in the previous sentence) and the statement that you are about to quote.

You should examine the quotation before writing the citation to define the way in which the author makes a point:

- Is it being asserted forcefully?
  Use "argues" or "declares" or "insists."
- Is the statement being offered only as a possibility?
  Use "suggests" or "proposes" or "finds."
- Does the statement immediately follow a previous reference?
  Use "continues" or "adds."

For clarity, the introductory verb may be expanded:

X is aware that . . .
X stresses the opposite view
X provides one answer to the question
X makes the same point as Y
X erroneously assumes . . .

But make sure that the antecedent for the "view" or the "question" or the "point" can be found in the previous sentences of your essay. Finally, all the examples of introductory verbs are given in the *present tense*, which is the conventional way of introducing most quotations.

Varying Your Sentence Patterns

Even if you choose a different verb for each quotation, the combination of the author's name, introductory verb, and quotation can become repetitious and tiresome. One way to vary the citations is occasionally to place the name of the source in a less prominent position, tucked into the quotation instead of calling attention to itself at the beginning.

1. You can interrupt the quotation by placing the citation in the middle.

"I made my mistakes," acknowledged Richard Nixon, "but in all my years of public service, I have never profited from public service. I have earned every cent."

The verb and the name may be placed in reverse order (instead of "Richard Nixon acknowledged") when the citation appears in the middle of the quotation. Remember to include two commas: one at the end of the first portion of the quotation (*inside* the quotation marks), one at the end of the citation.

One citation is quite enough. There is no need to inform your reader back to back, as in this repetitive example:

"The only prize much cared for by the powerful is power," states Oliver Wendell Holmes. He concludes, "The prize of the general . . . is command."

Nor can you interrupt the quotation at just any point. The citation in the following sentence should be placed at a more logical break in the sentence, preferably the beginning:

Awkward Citation

"The only prize much cared for," states Oliver Wendell Holmes, "by the powerful is power."

Clear Citation

Oliver Wendell Holmes states that "the only prize much cared for by the powerful is power."

2. You can avoid the monotonous "X says that . . ." pattern by phrasing the citation as a subordinate clause or a phrase.

In Henry Kissinger's opinion, "Power is 'the great aphrodisiac.'"

As John F. Kennedy declares, "Mankind must put an end to war or war will put an end to mankind."

3. In your quest for variety, avoid placing the citation after the quotation.

The author's name at the end may weaken the statement, especially if the citation is pretentiously or awkwardly phrased:

Awkward Citation

"I am the inferior of any man whose rights I trample underfoot," as quoted from the writings of Robert Ingersoll.

Clear Citation

A champion of civil liberties, Robert Ingersoll insisted, "I am the inferior of any man whose rights I trample underfoot."

Two rules should govern your choice of citation:

1. Don't be too fancy.
2. Be both precise and varied in your phrasing.

Presenting an Extended Quotation

Occasionally, you may have reason to present *an extended quotation*, a single extract from the same source that runs *more than four printed or typewritten lines*. For extended quotations, you must, by conventional rule, set off the quoted passage by *indenting the entire quotation on the left*.

- Introduce an extended quotation with a colon.
- Start each line of the quotation *10* spaces from the left-hand margin; stop each line at your normal right-hand margin.
- Some instructors prefer single-spacing within extended quotations; some prefer double-spacing. If possible, consult your instructor about the style appropriate for your course or discipline. If you are given no guidelines, use double-spacing.
- Omit quotation marks at the beginning and end of the quoted passage; the indented margin (and the introductory citation) will tell your readers that you are quoting.

Here is an example of an extended quotation:

Although he worked "hard as hell" all winter, Fitzgerald had difficulty finishing The Great Gatsby. On April 10, 1924, he wrote to Maxwell Perkins, his editor at Scribner's:

> While I have every hope & plan of finishing my novel in June . . . even [if] it takes me 10 times that long I cannot let it go unless it has the very best I'm capable of in it or even as I feel sometimes better than I'm ca- pable of. It is only in the last four months that I've realized how much I've—well, almost deteriorated. . . . What I'm trying to say is just that . . . at last, or at least for the first time in years, I'm doing the best I can.

INTEGRATING QUOTATIONS INTO YOUR PARAGRAPHS

You have learned how to present the words of others with accuracy and ap- propriate acknowledgment; now, you must learn to make the quotation serve the larger purpose of your paragraph or essay. Here are some suggestions for integrating quotations into your writing:

1. **Use quotation sparingly.**

   If quotation seems to be your primary purpose in writing, your reader will assume that you have nothing of your own to say. *Quote only when you have a clear reason for doing so:* when you are intending to analyze a quotation, when you are sure that the wording of the quotation is essen- tial to your argument, or when you simply cannot say it in your own words.

2. **Quotations generally belong in the body of your paragraph, not at the very beginning as a replacement for the topic sentence.**

   The topic sentence should establish—in your own words—what you are about to explain or prove. The quotation should appear later in the paragraph, as supporting evidence.

3. **Let the quotation make its point; your job is to explain or interpret its meaning, not to translate it word for word.**

Once you have presented a quotation, it is usually not necessary to provide an exact repetition of the same idea in your own words, making the same point twice. Instead, follow up a quotation with an *explanation* of its relevance to your paragraph or an *interpretation* of its meaning; but make sure that your commentary does more than echo the quotation.

In the following student example, the quotation used in the development of the paragraph is no more or less important than any of the other supporting sentences. The quotation adds interest to the paragraph because of the shift in tone and the shift to a sharper, narrower focus.

Some parents insist on allowing their children to learn through experience. Once a child has actually performed a dangerous action and realized its consequences, he will always remember the circumstances and the possible ill effects. Yvonne Realle illustrates the adage that experience is the best teacher by describing a boy who was slapped just as he reached for a hot iron. The child, not realizing that he might have been burned, had no idea why he had been slapped. An observer noted that "if he had learned by experience, if he'd suffered some discomfort in the process, then he'd know enough to avoid the iron next time." In the view of parents like Yvonne Realle, letting a child experiment with his environment will result in a stronger lesson than slapping or scolding the child for trying to explore his surroundings.

EXERCISE 12

1. The following student paragraph is taken from an essay, "Moral Prejudices in the 90s." The second passage comes from *Rethinking Social Policy* by Christopher Jencks.

Choose one appropriate supporting quotation from the Jencks passage, decide where to place it in the student paragraph, and insert the quotation correctly and smoothly into the paragraph. Remember to lead into the quotation by citing the source.

Student Paragraph

For the past three decades, public attitudes toward single parenthood have become less and less rigid. Today, many unmarried women who find themselves pregnant prefer to bring up their babies alone, rather than resorting to the "shotgun marriages" that used to be the rule. These women are less concerned about possible societal disapproval than they are about the freedom to pursue their own career and personal goals. Parents are increasingly becoming sympathetic to their daughters who make this choice, and are willing to help them out financially. The negative term "unwed mother" has changed into the more neutral "single parent."

Source

As having babies out of wedlock and getting divorced became more socially acceptable, couples' self-interest began to assert itself. Instead of assuming that they had to get married if they were expecting a baby, prospective parents began to ask themselves whether they wanted to get married. And instead of assuming that they had to stay married, unhappy spouses began to wonder if it was worthwhile to stay married. For a growing minority, the answer was no. The men often wanted freedom. The women often thought they could do without, or do better than, the lout who made them pregnant. Improved job opportunities for women also encouraged them to look at their potential mates more critically.

2. The following student paragraph is taken from an essay entitled "Anorexia and Bulimia: The Danger for Teenage Girls." The second passage comes from *Anorexia and Bulimia* by Richard A. Gordon.

    Choose one appropriate supporting quotation from the article, decide where to place it in the paragraph, and insert the quotation correctly and smoothly into the paragraph. Remember to lead into the quotation by citing the source.

Student Paragraph

Bulimia is a disease that tends to affect young girls who are determined to be as thin as possible. Losing a great deal of weight and then maintaining that loss is, of course, extremely difficult and forces them to an abstinence from food that is really unnatural. With bulimia, the teenager engages in what is called the "binge and purge" syndrome. What happens is that she suddenly decides to eat and eat and eat. Then, after stuffing herself, she feels guilty and determines to rid herself of all the food that she has consumed, so she induces vomiting or uses laxatives, and the food disappears. Through the whole process, the girl is really indulging and then punishing herself for having allowed herself to have a good time.

Source

What is usually not stated is the extent to which the characteristic experiences and problems of anorexic [and bulimic] patients mirror and magnify common problems of female identity, problems that are typically encountered in especially acute form during adolescence. For the intense sense of ineffectiveness and exclusive focus on external expectations is the extreme version of a common developmental pattern among girls in Western societies. Studies of normal female development, which have a certain degree of cross-cultural consistency, show that despite changes in public ideology about sex roles, girls are still socialized to be pleasers and are given far less encouragement than boys to develop self-initiated and autonomous behaviors.

ASSIGNMENT 2

1. Choose one of the following topics. Each is a specific question that can be answered adequately in a single paragraph.
   A. Question: Should children be spanked?
   B. Question: Should children wear school uniforms?
   C. Question: What is the best way to deal with sibling rivalry?
2. Ask someone you know to comment briefly on the question you have chosen, offering a suggestion or an example. Write down any part of the comment that you think might be worth quoting, transcribe the words accurately, and show the statement to your source to confirm its accuracy. Make sure that you have the name properly spelled. If the first person you ask does not provide you with a suitable quotation, try someone else.
3. Answer your own question in a single paragraph of four to eight sentences, limiting the paragraph to ideas that can be clearly developed in such a brief space. The paragraph as a whole should express *your* views, not those of your source. Choose a *single* quotation from your source and integrate it into the development of your paragraph, using proper punctuation, citation, and (if necessary) ellipses and brackets. If your source agrees with you, use the quotation as support. If your source disagrees, answer the objection in your own way. Try not to quote in the first or second sentence of your paragraph. Hand in both your paragraph and the sheet on which you originally wrote down the quotation.

responsible for test

AVOIDING PLAGIARISM

Quoting without quotation marks is called plagiarism. Even if you cite the source's name somewhere on your page, a word-for-word quotation without marks would still be considered a plagiarism.

Plagiarism is the unacknowledged use of another writer's words or ideas. The only way to acknowledge that you are using someone else's actual words is through citation and quotation marks.

Chapter 9 discusses plagiarism in detail. At this point, you should understand that:

- If you plagiarize, you will never learn to write.
- Literate people consider plagiarism to be equivalent to theft.
- Plagiarists eventually get caught!

It is easy for an experienced reader to detect plagiarism. Every writer, professional or amateur, has a characteristic style or voice that readers quickly learn to recognize. In a few paragraphs or pages, the writer's voice becomes familiar enough for the reader to notice that the style has changed and that, suddenly, there is a new, unfamiliar voice. When there are frequent acknowledged quotations, the reader simply adjusts to a series of new voices. *When there are unacknowledged quotations, the absence of quotation marks and the change of voices usually suggest to an experienced reader that the work is poorly integrated and probably plagiarized.* Plagiarized essays are often identified in this way.

Instructors are well aware of style and are trained to recognize inconsistencies and awkward transitions. A revealing clue is the patched-together, mosaic effect. The next exercise will improve your own perception of shifting voices and encourage you to rely on your own characteristic style as the dominant voice in everything that you write.

EXERCISE 13

The following paragraphs contain several plagiarized sentences. Examine the language and tone of each sentence, as well as the continuity of the entire paragraph. Then underline the plagiarized sentences.

A.   The Beatles' music in the early years was just plain melodic. It had a nice beat to it. The Beatles were simple lads, writing simple songs simply to play to screaming fans on one-night stands. There was no deep, inner meaning to the lyrics. Their songs included many words like I, and me, and you. As the years went by, the Beatles' music became more poetic. Sergeant Pepper is a stupefying collage of music, words, background noises, cryptic utterances, orchestral effects, hallucinogenic bells, farmyard sounds, dream sequences, social observations, and apocalyptic vision, all masterfully blended together on a four-track tape machine over nine agonizing and expensive months. Their music was beginning to be more philosophical, with a deep, inner, more secret meaning. After it was known that they took drugs, references to drugs were seen in many songs. The "help" in Ringo's "A Little Help From My Friends" was said to have meant pot. The songs were poetic, mystical; they emerged from a self-contained world of bizarre carnival colors; they spoke in a language and a musical idiom all their own.

B.   Before the Civil War, minstrelsy spread quickly across America. Americans all over the country enjoyed minstrelsy because it reflected something of their own point of view. For instance, Negro plantation hands, played usually by white actors in blackface, were portrayed as devil-may-care outcasts and minstrelmen played them with an air of comic triumph, irreverent wisdom, and an underlying note of rebellion, which had a special appeal to citizens of a young country. Minstrelsy was ironically the beginning of black involvement in the American theater. The American people learned to identify with certain aspects of the black people. The Negro became a sympathetic symbol for a pioneer people who required resilience as a prime trait.

PARAPHRASING

Some passages are worth quoting for the sake of their precise or elegant style or their distinguished author. But many sources that you will use in your college essays are written in more ordinary language. Indeed, some of your sources may be written in the jargon of an academic discipline or the bureaucratic prose of a government agency. (There are few examples of jargon in this book; however, look at Excerpt 6 on p. 133 to sample the kind of prose you probably would not want to quote.) You will gain nothing by quoting such material; rather, you have a positive duty to help your readers by providing them with a clear paraphrase.

Paraphrase is the point-by-point recapitulation of another person's ideas, expressed in your own words.

Through paraphrase, you are both informing your reader and proving that you understand what you are writing about. When you paraphrase, you retain everything about the original writing but the words. The primary differences between *paraphrase* and *summary* are length and emphasis. See the box on the next page for a comparison of paraphrase and summary.

Using Paraphrase in Your Essays

Your paraphrased explanations help your readers to gain a detailed understanding of sources that they may never have read and, indirectly, to accept your own thesis as valid. There are two major reasons for using paraphrase in your essays.

Comparing Paraphrase and Summary

Paraphrase	Summary
■ Reports your understanding to your reader	■ Reports your understanding to your reader
■ Records a relatively short passage	■ Records a passage of any length
■ Records every point in the passage	■ Selects and condenses, recording only the main ideas
■ Records these points consecutively	■ Changes the order of ideas when necessary
■ Includes no interpretation	■ Explains and (if the writer wishes) interprets

1. Use paraphrase to present ideas or evidence whenever there is no special reason for using a direct quotation.

Many of your sources will not have sufficient authority or a distinctive enough style to justify your quoting their words. The following illustration, taken from a *New York Times* article, paraphrases a report written by an anonymous group of "municipal auditors" whose writing merits only paraphrase, not quotation:

> A city warehouse in Middle Village, Queens, stocked with such things as snow shovels, light bulbs, sponges, waxed paper, laundry soap and tinned herring, has been found to be vastly overstocked with some items and lacking in others. Municipal auditors, in a report issued yesterday, said that security was fine and that the warehouse was quicker in delivering goods to city agencies than it was when the auditors made their last check, in August, 1976. But in one corner of the warehouse, they said, nearly 59,000 paper binders, the 8½-by-11 size, are gathering dust, enough to meet the city's needs for nearly seven years. Nearby, there is a 10½-year supply of cotton coveralls.
>
> Both the overstock and shortages cost the city money, the auditors said. They estimated that by reducing warehouse inventories, the city could save $1.4 million, plus $112,000 in interest. . . .

2. Use paraphrase to give your readers an accurate and comprehensive account of ideas taken from a source—ideas that you intend to explain, interpret, or disagree with in your essay.

The first illustration comes from a *Times* article about the data and photographs provided by *Voyager 2* as it explored the farthest reaches of the solar system. In summarizing a press conference, the article paraphrases various scientists' descriptions of what *Voyager* had achieved during its journey near Triton, one of the moons of the planet Neptune. Note the limited use of carefully selected quotations within the paraphrase.

> Out of the fissures [on Triton], roughly analogous to faults in the Earth's crust, flowed mushy ice. There was no eruption in the sense of the usual terrestrial volcanism or the geyser-like activity discovered on Io, one of Jupiter's moons. It was more of an extrusion through cracks in the surface ice.
>
> Although scientists classify such a process as volcanism, Dr. Miner said it could better be described as a "slow-flow volcanic activity." A somewhat comparable process, he said, seemed to have shaped some of the surface features of Ariel, one of the moons of Uranus.
>
> Dr. Soderblom said Triton's surface appeared to be geologically young or "millions to hundreds of millions of years old." The absence of many impact craters was the main evidence for the relatively recent resurfacing of the terrain with new ice.

The next example shows how paraphrase can be used more briefly, to present another writer's point of view as the basis for discussion. Again, the writer of this description of a conference on nuclear deterrence has reserved quotation to express the precise point of potential dispute:

> Scientists engaged in research on the effects of nuclear war may be "wasting their time" studying a phenomenon that is far less dangerous than the natural explosions that have periodically produced widespread extinctions of plant and animal life in the past, a University of Chicago scientist said last week. Joseph V. Smith, a professor of geophysical sciences, told a conference on nuclear deterrence here that such natural catastrophes as exploding volcanoes, violent earthquakes, and collisions with comets or asteroids could produce more immediate and destructive explosions than any nuclear war.

Using Paraphrase as Preparation for Reading and Writing Essays

Paraphrase is sometimes undertaken as *an end in itself*. Paraphrasing difficult passages can help you to improve your understanding of a complex essay or chapter. When you grasp an essay at first reading, when its ideas are clearly stated in familiar terms, then you can be satisfied with annotating it or writing a brief outline or summary. But when you find an essay hard to understand, writing down each sentence in your own words forces you to stop and make sense of what you have read, so that you can succeed in working out ideas that at first seem beyond your comprehension.

Paraphrase can also be *a means to an end*, a preparation for writing an essay of your own. Assume that you are taking notes for an essay based on one or more sources. If you write down nothing but exact quotations, you will not only be doing a good deal of unnecessary transcription, but you may also be tempted to quote excessively in your essay.

When you take notes, paraphrase; quote only when recording phrases or sentences that, in your opinion, merit quotation.

All academic writers are expected to be scrupulously accurate in their presentation of material taken from their sources. All quotable phrases and sentences should be transcribed accurately in your notes, with quotation marks clearly separating the paraphrase from the quotation.

Paraphrase and Outlining

In some respects, a paraphrase resembles an outline, but there are some important distinctions.

Comparing Paraphrase and Outline

Paraphrase	*Outline*
■ Presents ideas in the same order as the original.	■ Presents ideas in the same order as the original.
■ Doesn't emphasize any one point more than another (unless the original writer does so).	■ Doesn't emphasize any one point more than another (unless the original writer does so).
■ Suggests the scope and reasoning of the original passage, and specifies the main ideas.	■ Lists the main ideas, but doesn't attempt to present all the reasoning leading up to them.
■ Can be as long as necessary—as long as the original text or even longer if there are complex ideas to be explained; *it is a full presentation of the text.*	■ Can be as short and condensed as you wish, provided that you include all the main ideas; *it is a memorandum for future reference.*

Writing a Good Paraphrase

The paraphraser is like a translator. As if the text were in a foreign language, you are trying to recreate its meaning in your own words and style. Like the translator, you use your own idiom, and within the scope of that idiom, you often must rewrite the text.

In a good paraphrase, the sentences and the vocabulary do not duplicate those of the original. *You cannot merely substitute synonyms for key words and leave the sentences otherwise unchanged; that is plagiarism in spirit, if not in fact;* nor does word-for-word substitution really demonstrate that you have understood the ideas.

The level of abstraction within your paraphrase should resemble that of the original: It should be neither more general nor more specific. If you do not understand a sentence, do not try to guess or cover it up with a vague phrase that slides over the idea. Instead:

- Look up difficult words.
- Think of what they mean and how they are used together.
- Consider how the sentences are formed and how they fit into the context of the entire paragraph.
- Then, to test your understanding, write it all out.

Remember that a good paraphrase makes sense by itself; it is coherent and readable, without requiring reference to the original essay.

Guidelines for a Successful Paraphrase

- A paraphrase must be accurate.
- A paraphrase must be complete.
- A paraphrase must be written in your own voice.
- A paraphrase must make sense by itself.

Free Paraphrase

When a paraphrase moves completely away from the words and sentence structure of the original text and presents ideas in the paraphraser's own style and idiom, then it is said to be "free." A free paraphrase is not only challenging to write but can be as interesting to read as the original—provided that the substance of the source has not been altered, disguised, or substantially condensed. Because a free paraphrase can summarize repetitious parts of the original text, it may be somewhat briefer than the original, but it will present ideas in much the same order.

Here, side by side with the original, is a free paraphrase of an excerpt from Machiavelli's *The Prince*. This passage exemplifies the kind of text—very famous, very difficult—that really benefits from a comprehensive paraphrase. *The Prince* was written in 1513. Even though the translation from the Italian used here was revised in this century, the paraphraser has to bridge a tremendous gap in time and in style to present Machiavelli in an idiom suitable for modern readers.

Original Version

It is not, therefore, necessary for a prince to have [good faith and integrity], but it is very necessary to seem to have them. I would even be bold to say that to possess them and always to observe them is dangerous, but to appear to possess them is useful. Thus it is well to seem merciful, faithful, humane, sincere, religious, and also to be so; but you must have the mind so disposed that when it is needful to be otherwise you may be able to change to the opposite qualities. And it must be understood that a prince, and especially a new prince, cannot observe all those things which are considered good in men, being often obliged, in order to maintain the state, to act against faith, against charity, against humanity, and against religion. And therefore, he must have a mind disposed to adapt itself according to the wind, and as the variations of fortune dictate, and . . . not deviate from what is good, if possible, but be able to do evil if constrained.

A prince must take great care that nothing goes out of his mouth which is not full of the above-mentioned five qualities, and to see and hear him, he should seem to be all mercy, faith, integrity, humanity, and religion. . . . Everyone sees what you appear to be, few feel what you are, and those few will not dare to oppose themselves to the many, who have the majesty of the state to defend them; and in the actions of men, and especially of princes, from which there is no appeal, the end justifies the means. Let a prince therefore aim at con-

Paraphrase

It is more important for a ruler to give the impression of goodness than to be good. In fact, real goodness can be a liability, but the pretense is always very effective. It is all very well to be virtuous, but it is vital to be able to shift in the other direction whenever circumstances require it. After all, rulers, especially recently elevated ones, have a duty to perform which may absolutely require them to act against the dictates of faith and compassion and kindness. One must act as circumstances require and, while it's good to be virtuous if you can, it's better to be bad if you must.

In public, however, the ruler should appear to be entirely virtuous, and if his pretense is successful with the majority of people, then those who do see through the act will be outnumbered and impotent, especially since the ruler has the authority of government on his side. In the case of rulers, even more than for most men, "the end justifies the means." If the ruler is able to assume power and administer it successfully, his methods will always be judged proper and satisfactory; for the common people will accept the pretense of virtue and the reality of success, and the astute will find no one is listening to their warnings.

Original Version (continued)

quering and maintaining the state, and
the means will always be judged honorable and praised by every one, for
the vulgar are always taken by appearances and the issue of the event; and
the world consists only of the vulgar,
and the few who are not vulgar are
isolated when the many have a rallying point in the prince.

Paraphrase and Summary

To clarify the difference between paraphrase and summary, here is a paragraph that *summarizes* the excerpt from *The Prince*.

According to Machiavelli, perpetuating power is a more important goal
for a ruler than achieving personal goodness or integrity. Although he should act
virtuously if he can, and always appear to do so, it is more important for him to
adapt quickly to changing circumstances. The masses will be so swayed by his
pretended virtue and by his success that any opposition will be ineffective. The
wise ruler's maxim is that "the end justifies the means."

To make the distinction between summary and paraphrase entirely clear,
here is a recapitulation of the guidelines for writing a brief summary:

1. *A summary is comprehensive.* Like the paraphrase, the summary of *The
   Prince* says more than "the end justifies the means." While that is probably the most important idea in the passage, it does not by itself convey
   Machiavelli's full meaning. For one thing, it contains no reference at all to
   princes and how they should rule—and that, after all, is Machiavelli's
   subject.
2. *A summary is concise.* It should say exactly as much as you need—and no
   more. The summary of *The Prince* is considerably shorter than the paraphrase.
3. *A summary is coherent.* The ideas are not presented in the same sequence
   as that of the original passage, as they are in the paraphrase; nor are the
   language and tone at all reminiscent of the original. Rather, the summary
   includes only the passage's most important points, linking them together
   in a unified paragraph.
4. *A summary is independent.* What is most striking about the summary, compared with the paraphrase, is the writer's attitude toward the original

text. While the paraphraser has to follow closely Machiavelli's ideas and point of view, the summarizer does not. Characteristically, Machiavelli's name is cited in the summary, calling attention to the fact that it is based on another person's ideas.

Either summary or paraphrase should enable you to refer to this passage quite easily in an essay. Which you would choose to use depends on your topic, on the way you are developing your essay, and on the extent to which you wish to discuss Machiavelli.

- In an essay citing Machiavelli as only one among many political theorists, you might use the brief four-sentence summary; then you might briefly comment upon Machiavelli's ideas before going on to summarize (and perhaps compare them with) another writer's theories.

- In an essay about a contemporary politician, you might analyze the way in which your subject does or does not carry out Machiavelli's strategies; then you probably would want to familiarize your readers with *The Prince* in some detail through paraphrase. You might include the full paraphrase, interspersed, perhaps, with an analysis of your present-day "prince."

Writing an Accurate Paraphrase

The basic purpose of paraphrase is to present the main ideas contained in the original text. Without this essential coverage, a paraphrase is worthless. When paraphrase fails to convey the substance of the source, there are three possible explanations:

1. *Misreading:* The writer genuinely misunderstood the text.
2. *Projecting:* The writer insisted on reading his or her own ideas into the text.
3. *Guessing:* The writer had a spark of understanding and constructed a paraphrase centered around that spark, but ignored too much of the original text.

Read Christopher Lasch's analysis of the changing role of the child in family life. Then examine each of the three paraphrases that follow, deciding whether it conveys Lasch's principal ideas and, if not, why it has gone astray. Compare your reactions with the analysis that follows each paraphrase.

Original

The family by its very nature is a means of raising children, but this fact should not blind us to the important change that occurred when child-rearing ceased to be simply one of many activities and became the central concern—one is tempted to say the central obsession—of family life. This development had to wait for the recognition of the child as a distinctive kind of person, more impressionable and hence more vulnerable than adults, to be treated in a special manner befitting his peculiar requirements. Again, we take these things for granted and find it hard to imagine anything else. Earlier, children had been clothed, fed, spoken to, and educated as little adults; more specifically, as servants, the difference between child-hood and servitude having been remarkably obscure throughout much of Western history. . . . It was only in the seventeenth century in certain classes that childhood came to be seen as a special category of experience. When that happened, people recognized the enormous formative influence of family life, and the family became above all an agency for building character, for consciously and deliberately forming the child from birth to adulthood.

"Divorce and the Family in America," *Atlantic Monthly*

Paraphrase A

The average family wants to raise children with a good education and to encourage, for example, the ability to read and write well. They must be taught to practice and learn on their own. Children can be treated well without being pampered. They must be treated as adults as they get older and experience more of life. A parent must build character and the feeling of independence in a child. No longer should children be treated as kids or servants, for that can cause conflict in a family relationship.

This paraphrase has very little in common with the original passage. True, it is about child-rearing, but the writer chooses to give advice to parents, rather than present the contrast between early and modern attitudes toward children, as Lasch does. Since the only clear connection between Lasch and this paragraph is the reference to servants, the writer was probably confused by the passage, and (instead of slowing down the process and paraphrasing it sentence by sentence) guessed—mistakenly—at its meaning. There is also some projection of the writer's ideas about family life. Notice how assertive the tone is; the writer seems to be admonishing parents rather than presenting Lasch's detached analysis.

Paraphrase B

When two people get married, they usually produce a child. They get married because they want a family. Raising a family is now different from the way it used to be. The child is looked upon as a human being, with feelings and thoughts of his own. Centuries ago, children were treated like robots, little more than hired help. Now, children are seen as people who need a strong, dependable family background to grow into persons of good character. Parents are needed to get children ready to be the adults of tomorrow.

This paragraph also seems to combine guessing (beginning) and projection (end). The middle sentences do present Lasch's basic point, but the beginning and the end move so far away from the main ideas that the paraphrase as a whole does not bear much resemblance to the original text. It also includes an exaggeration: are servants "robots"?

Paraphrase C

Though the family has always been an important institution, its child-rearing function has only in recent centuries become its most important activity. This change has resulted from the relatively new idea that children have a special, unique personality. In the past, there was little difference seen between childhood and adulthood. But today people realize the importance of family life, especially the family unit as a means of molding the personalities of children from childhood to adulthood.

Although this paraphrase is certainly the most accurate of the three, it is too brief to be a complete paraphrase. In fact, the writer seems to be summarizing, not paraphrasing. Lasch's main idea is there, but the following points are missing:

1. There is a tremendous difference between pre-seventeenth-century and twentieth-century perceptions of childhood.
2. Before the seventeenth century, it was difficult to distinguish between the status and treatment of children and that of servants.
3. Child-rearing has now become of overriding ("obsessive") importance to the family.
4. Children are different from adults in that they are less hardened and less experienced.

The author of Paraphrase C has done a thorough job of the beginning and the end of Lasch's passage, and evidently left the middle to take care of itself. But a paraphrase cannot be considered a reliable "translation" of the original text unless all the supporting ideas are given appropriate emphasis. The omission of Point 2 is particularly important.

Here is a more comprehensive paraphrase of the passage:

Though the family has always been the institution responsible for bringing up children, only in recent times has its child-raising function become the family's overriding purpose and its reason for being. This striking shift to the child-centered family has resulted from the gradual realization that children have a special, unique personality, easy to influence and easy to hurt, and that they must be treated accordingly. Special treatment for children is the norm in our time; but hundreds of years ago, people saw little or no difference between childhood and adulthood, and, in fact, the child's role in the family resembled that of a servant. It was not until the seventeenth century that people began to regard childhood as a distinctive stage of growth. That recognition led them to understand what a powerful influence the family environment must have on the child and to define "family" as the chief instrument for molding the child's personality and moral attitudes.

EXERCISE 14

The next passage is followed by a group of paraphrases. Examine each one and identify those which conform to the guidelines for paraphrasing. Ask yourself whether the paraphrase contains any point that is not in the original passage and whether the key points of the original are *all* clearly presented in the paraphrase.

from TO DEFLATE GRADE INFLATION, SIMPLIFY THE SYSTEM
Arthur Levine

Reports of grade inflation tend to elicit cries of outrage, encouraging critics to lambaste academe for its loss of integrity and causing academics to long for days gone by. Certainly it is tempting to turn grade inflation into a morality play. One can point to grade-grubbing students who sniff out gut or Mickey Mouse courses. It is also true that some professors pump up the enrollment in their courses by giving out sky-high grades. And, of course, some administrators worry about the lost tuition money if students flunk out. 1

It is easy to conclude that colleges and universities are going to hell in a hand basket. But the problem of grade inflation is more educational than moral: When GPAs are artificially high, evaluation of student performance loses its meaning. Considering grade inflation as a moral issue turns a concrete problem with potential solutions into a vague abstraction that can too easily be ignored. 2

Grades serve two purposes beyond indicating whether a student has passed or failed a course and is making progress toward a degree. The first is providing students with information about their performance, individually and relative to that of their classmates. The second purpose is informing a variety of publics—employers, graduate schools, and others—about students' performance as individuals and relative to other applicants. Grade inflation, however, frustrates both those purposes, since artificially high grades provide minimal information to anyone. 3

1. Rumors about grade inflation make people angry and lead some of them to think that people in the academic world are no longer straightforward and moral. They also blame students who take easy courses about Mickey Mouse, and they blame professors who inflate their classes by awarding astronomical grades. If students don't pass, they won't stay in school.

   This is a no-win situation, and colleges are not in good shape. If you inflate grades, no one knows whether a student is doing well. Even though this is a moral issue, the problem can be solved.

We need to have grades so that students can tell if they are doing well and will pass and will graduate. Other people are also interested in how well they do. Grade inflation is frustrating to everyone, because there isn't enough information provided.

2. One problem with grade inflation is moral. Students try to do well and take easy courses, and faculty help them by giving easy grades. This is not a good thing for colleges and universities. Inflated grades mean that grades have no real meaning anymore, and the whole idea of an honest evaluation of someone's effort loses its meaning. This is not only a moral problem, but an educational problem. Students deserve to know about their progress, and faculty should give them honest grades. Otherwise, they may have problems getting jobs and getting into graduate school. It is very frustrating for everyone concerned since you don't learn anything from grades that are inflated.

3. We hear a lot about grade inflation these days and some people tend to blame our colleges for past times when that didn't happen. These people make too much of a moral issue about grade inflation. Sure, there are students who try to get into courses that will give them a certain "A," and there are professors who want to look good and get their courses filled and so give out higher grades than other faculty do, and there are administrators concerned about the possibility that students will flunk out and they'll have to return tuition.

This problem should be looked at purely educationally. Grades don't just tell whether students are doing well in their courses and moving toward their degree. They are also used to judge whether students trying for jobs and graduate school places are better than the other applicants. Inflated grades aren't helpful because they don't provide enough information.

PARAPHRASING IN TWO STAGES

Since translating another writer's idiom into your own can be difficult, a paraphrase is often written in two stages.

- In your first version, you work out a *word-for-word substitution*, staying close to the sentence structure of the original, as if, indeed, you are writing a translation. This is the *literal paraphrase.*
- In your second version, you work from your own literal paraphrase, turning it into a *free paraphrase* by reconstructing and rephrasing the sentences to make them more natural and more characteristic of *your own writing style.*

Writing a Literal Paraphrase

To write a paraphrase that is faithful to the original text is impossible if you are uncertain of the meaning of any of the words. To write a literal paraphrase of a difficult passage:

- Use a dictionary, especially if the passage contains obsolete or archaic language.
- Write down a few possible synonyms for each difficult word, making sure that you understand the connotations of each synonym.
- Choose the most precise substitute that best fits the context of your literal paraphrase.

Too often, the writer of a paraphrase forgets that there *is* a choice and quickly substitutes the first synonym in the dictionary. Even when appropriate synonyms have been carefully chosen, the literal paraphrase can look peculiar and sound dreadful. While the old sentence structure has been retained, the key words have been yanked out and new ones plugged in. Still, at the beginning this process may be necessary to work out the exact meaning of each sentence.

To illustrate the pitfalls of this process, here is a short excerpt from Francis Bacon's essay "Of Marriage and Single Life," written around 1600. Some of the phrasing and word combinations are archaic and may sound unnatural, but nothing in the passage is too difficult for modern understanding *if* the sentences are read slowly and carefully.

> He that hath wife and children hath given hostages to fortune; for they are impediments to great enterprises, either of virtue or mischief. Certainly, the best works and of greatest merit for the public have proceeded from the unmarried or childless men: which both in affection and means have endowed the public.

The passage's main idea is not too difficult to establish: *Unmarried men, without the burden of a family, can afford to contribute to the public good.* But by now you must realize that such a brief summary is not the same as a paraphrase, for it does not fully present Bacon's reasoning. In contract, look at these two very different *literal paraphrases* of Bacon's first sentence. (The key words have been underlined.)

Paraphrase A

He who has a wife and children has <u>bestowed</u> <u>prisoners</u> to <u>riches</u>; for they are <u>defects</u> in huge <u>business</u> <u>organizations</u> either for <u>morality</u> or <u>damage</u>.

Paraphrase B

He who has a wife and children has <u>given</u> a <u>pledge</u> to <u>destiny</u>; for they are <u>hindrances</u> to large <u>endeavor</u>, either for <u>good</u> or for <u>ill</u>.

Neither sentence sounds very normal or very clear; but the second has potential, while the first makes no sense. Yet, in *both* cases, the inserted words *are* synonyms for the original vocabulary. In Paraphrase A the words do not fit Bacon's context; in Paraphrase B they do. For example, it is misleading to choose "business organizations" as a synonym for "enterprises," since the passage doesn't actually concern business, but refers to any sort of undertaking requiring freedom from responsibility. "Impediment" can mean either "defect" (as in speech impediment) or "hindrance" (as in impediment to learning); but—again, given the context—it is the latter meaning that Bacon has in mind. You will choose the correct connotation or nuance only if you think carefully about the synonyms and use your judgment: the process cannot be hurried.

A phrase like "hostage to fortune" offers special difficulty, since it is a powerful image expressing a highly abstract idea. No paraphraser can improve on the original wording or even find an equivalent phrase. However, expressing the idea is useful: a bargain made with life—the renunciation of future independent action in exchange for a family. Wife and children become a kind of bond ("hostage") to ensure one's future social conformity. The aptness and singularity of Bacon's original phrase are measured by the difficulty of paraphrasing three words in less than two sentences!

Writing a Free Version of the Literal Paraphrase

Correct though the synonyms may be, the passage from Bacon cannot be left as it is in Paraphrase B, for no reader could readily understand this stilted, artificial sentence. It is necessary to rephrase the paraphrase, ensuring that the meaning of the words is retained, but making the sentence sound more natural. The first attempt at "freeing up" the paraphrase stays as close as possible to the literal version, leaving everything in the same sequence, but using a more modern idiom:

Paraphrase C

Married men with children are hindered from embarking on any important undertaking, good or bad. Indeed, unmarried and childless men are the ones who have done the most for society and have dedicated their love and their money to the public good.

The second sentence (which is simpler to paraphrase than the first) has been inverted here, but the paraphrase is still a point-by-point recapitulation of Bacon. Paraphrase C is acceptable, but can be improved, both to clarify Bacon's meaning and to introduce a more personal voice. What exactly *are* these unmarried men dedicating to the public good? "Affection and means." And what is the modern equivalent of means? Money? Effort? Time? Energy?

Paraphrase D

A man with a family has obligations that prevent him from devoting himself to any activity that pleases him. On the other hand, a single man or a man without children has a greater opportunity to be a philanthropist. That's why most great contributions of energy and resources to the good of society are made by single men.

The writer of Paraphrase D has not supplied a synonym for "affection," assuming perhaps that the expenditure of energy and resources result from interest and concern; affection is almost too weak a motivation for the philanthropist as he is described here.

Paraphrase E

The responsibility of a wife and children prevents a man from taking risks with his money, time, and energy. The greatest social benefactors have been men who have adopted the public as their family.

The second sentence here is the only one of the five versions that approaches Bacon's economy of style. "Adopted the public" is not quite the same as "endowed the public" with one's "affection and means"; but nevertheless, this paraphrase is successful because it speaks for itself. It has a life and an importance of its own, independent of Bacon's original passage, yet it makes the same point that Bacon does.

Guidelines for Paraphrasing a Difficult Passage

1. Look up in a dictionary the meanings of all the words of which you are uncertain. Pay special attention to the difficult words, considering the context of the whole passage.

2. Write a literal paraphrase of each passage by substituting appropriate synonyms within the original sentence structure.

3. Revise your literal paraphrase, keeping roughly to the same length and number of sentences as the original, but using your own sentence style and phrasing throughout. You may prefer to put the original passage aside at this point, and work entirely from your own version.

4. Read your free paraphrase aloud to make sure that it makes sense.

ASSIGNMENT 3

Paraphrase one of the following passages, using the guidelines in the box above. (Your instructor may assign a specific paragraph for the entire class to paraphrase; you may be asked to work together with one or more of your classmates.)

1. Organized professional baseball was a 19th-century innovation. Its mechanics are about open fields, and its ethos is agrarian, about reaping what you sow. It

lent itself to the postwar suburban frontier, where city met country and baseball was the only game in town. Now the dynamic has shifted to basketball and hockey, intensely paced urban sports played out on spaces sandwiched between buildings. Offense switches to defense in the flick of a wrist; a player about to go in for the kill is unmanned in a flash, and the action moves deep into his home turf. It makes sense on the court or the rink because it makes sense in the city— and in the pace of the nation, as regulated by the thermostat of television and cable TV.

HARLAN JACOBSON, from "Take Me Out to the Movies"

2. Because we are frightened by violence and find it hard to comprehend, whether the gratuitous violence of the streets or a more abstract act of terrorism, we are prone to the idea that violence is some kind of epidemic, a pestilence sweeping through society like the Black Death. By the same manner of thought we imagine some earlier Golden Age in which the streets were safe. . . . Yet it seems that each generation in its turn imagines itself to be afflicted by an unprecedented plague of violence. Our belief that we live in a mounting wave of crime and juvenile delinquency, and the similar beliefs of previous generations, is more likely to do with changes in the reporting of crime, in rates of detecting or the attitudes of the courts.

PETER JENKINS, from "It Depends
What You Mean by Violence"

3. As a writing instrument, the computer is not so much a better pencil as a better eraser. Although it serves well enough to put words on the page, where it really excels is in wiping them out again. Writing with a computer affords you the luxury of changing your mind, again and again, without penalty. The excised word leaves no scar; the page never becomes gray or tattered from rubbing; the margins do not fill up with afterthoughts; there is no tangle of arrows showing how sentences are to be rearranged. When you write on the glass screen, the world need never know how you labored to achieve that easygoing prose style. Indeed, this very paragraph conceals the tortured history of its own composition: you the reader cannot see in the space between the lines how I have revised it, a dozen times or more, until hardly a word of the first draft survives.

BRIAN HAYES, from "The Electronic Palimpsest"

4. The American citizen lives in a world where fantasy is more real than reality, where the image has more dignity than its original. We hardly dare face our bewilderment, because our ambiguous experience is so pleasantly iridescent, and the solace of belief in contrived reality is so thoroughly real. We have become eager accessories to the great hoaxes of the age. These are the hoaxes we play on ourselves.

DANIEL J. BOORSTIN, from The Image

5. Historically, war has been seen as the primal archetype for masculine activity, the supreme example of what men can do better than women. War created the ultimate challenge for the manly virtues of physical prowess, strength, and courage. But today the viability of these traditional virtues is questionable, and the idea that the battlefield provides an appropriate arena for initiations cannot be logically sustained. Modern warfare—even in the "good war," World War II—is exceedingly impersonal, and this impersonal style of warfare fails to fulfill the most fundamental function of an initiation ritual: to provide a structured path towards the achievement of manhood. Since there are no built-in programs that ensure success for those with the talent and the will to succeed, modern warfare can break a man's will as readily as it can strengthen it. In more primitive forms of warfare, in single, man-to-man combat, a warrior was encouraged to develop his strength, power, and courage for good and practical reasons—these virtues were directly correlated with his prospects for survival and victory. Now, the relationship between manly virtue and success is indirect, almost random. Survival depends less on personal ability than on politics or fate. Artillery fired from a distant enemy might or might not blow a soldier to pieces, regardless of his courage or cowardice, his strength or weakness. A warhead on a computerized missile might or might not destroy a man and his family and his entire city, regardless of whether the fellow ever had any aspirations to prove himself as a warrior.

RAY RAPHAEL, from *The Men from the Boys*

6. It is somewhat ironic to note that grading *systems* evolved in part because of [problems in evaluating performance]. In situations where reward and recognition often depended more on who you knew than on what you knew, and lineage was more important than ability, the cause of justice seemed to demand a method whereby the individual could demonstrate specific abilities on the basis of objective criteria. This led to the establishment of specific standards and public criteria as ways of reducing prejudicial treatment and, in cases where appropriate standards could not be specified in advance, to the normal curve system of establishing levels on the basis of group performance. The imperfect achievement of the goals of such systems in no way negates the importance of the underlying purposes.

WAYNE MOELLENBERG, from "To Grade or
Not to Grade—Is That the Question?"

INCORPORATING PARAPHRASE INTO YOUR ESSAY

The paraphrased ideas of other writers should never take control of your essay, but should always be subordinate to *your* ideas. When you insert a paraphrased sentence or a brief paraphrased passage (rather than a quotation) into one of your paragraphs, you minimize the risk that the source material will dominate your writing. However, whatever you paraphrase, whether short or long, must still contain an accurate and fair representation of the source's ideas.

Most academic writers rely on a combination of quotation, paraphrase, and summary to present their sources.

To illustrate the way in which these three techniques of presentation can be successfully combined, here is an extract from an article by Conor Cruise O'Brien that depends on a careful mixture of paraphrase, summary, and quotation. In "Violence—And Two Schools of Thought," O'Brien gives an account of a medical conference concerned with the origins of violence. Specifically, he undertakes to present and (at the end) comment on the ideas of two speakers at the conference.

VIOLENCE—AND TWO SCHOOLS OF THOUGHT*
Conor Cruise O'Brien

Summary   The opening speakers were fairly representative of the main schools of thought which almost always declare themselves when violence is discussed. The first school sees a propensity to aggression as biological but capable of being socially conditioned into patterns of acceptable behavior. The second sees it as essentially created by social conditions and therefore capable of being removed by benign social change.   1

Quotation   The first speaker held that violence was "a bio-social phenomenon." He rejected the notion that human beings were blank paper "on which the environment can write whatever it likes." He de-   2

Paraphrase   scribed how a puppy could be conditioned to choose a dog food it did not like and to reject one it did like. This was the creation of conscience in the puppy. It was done by mild punishment. If human beings were acting more aggressively and anti-socially, despite the advent of better social conditions and better housing, this might be because permissiveness, in school and home, had checked the process of social conditioning, and therefore of conscience-building. He favored the reinstatement of conscience-building, through the use

Quotation   of mild punishment and token rewards. "We cannot eliminate violence," he said, "but we can do a great deal to reduce it."

Summary   The second speaker thought that violence was the result of stress;   3
in almost all the examples he cited it was stress from overcrowding.

*In its original format in *The Observer,* the article's paragraphing, in accordance with usual journalistic practice, occurs with distracting frequency; the number of paragraphs has been reduced here, without any alteration of the text.

The behavior of apes and monkeys in zoos was "totally different" from the way they behaved in "the completely relaxed conditions in the wild." In crowded zoos the most aggressive males became leaders and a general reign of terror set in; in the relaxed wild, on the other hand, the least aggressive males ruled benevolently. Space was all: "If we could eliminate population pressures, violence would vanish."

Paraphrase/ Quotation

Paraphrase Quotation

Summary

4

The student [reacting to the argument of the two speakers] preferred the second speaker. He [the second speaker] spoke with ebullient confidence, fast but clear, and at one point ran across the vast platform, in a lively imitation of the behavior of a charging ape. Also, his message was simple and hopeful. Speaker one, in contrast, looked sad, and his message sounded faintly sinister. Such impressions, rather than the weight of argument, determine the reception of papers read in such circumstances.

Author's Comment

Summary/ Paraphrase

Nonetheless, a student queried speaker two's "relaxed wild." He seemed to recall a case in which a troop of chimpanzees had completely wiped out another troop. The speaker was glad the student had raised that question because it proved the point. You see, where that had occurred, there had been an overcrowding in the jungle, just as happens in zoos, and this was a response to overcrowding. Conditions in the wild, it seems, are not always "completely relaxed." And when they attain that attributed condition—through the absence of overcrowding—this surely has to be due to the "natural controls," including the predators, whose attentions can hardly be all that relaxing, or, indeed, all that demonstrative of the validity of the proposition that violence is not a part of nature. Speaker two did not allude to predators. Nonetheless, they are still around, on two legs as well as on four.

Author's Comment

5

Selecting Quotations When You Paraphrase

Although we do not have the texts of the original papers given at the conference to compare with O'Brien's description, this article seems to present a clear and comprehensive account of a complex discussion. In the first paragraph, O'Brien uses brief summaries to help us distinguish between the two speakers; next, he provides us with two separate, noncommittal descriptions of the two main points of view.

The ratio of quotation to paraphrase to summary works very effectively. O'Brien quotes for two reasons: *aptness of expression* and *the desire to distance himself from the statement.* For example, he chooses to quote the vivid image of the blank paper "on which the environment can write whatever it likes." And he also selects points for quotation that he regards as open to dispute—"totally different"; "completely relaxed"; "violence would vanish." Such strong or sweeping statements are often quoted so that writers can disassociate themselves from the implications of their source material; this way, they cannot be accused of either toning down or exaggerating the meaning in their paraphrases.

Reasons to Use Quotation

- You can find no words to convey the economy and aptness of phrasing of the original text.
- A paraphrase might alter the statement's meaning.
- A paraphrase would not clearly distinguish between your views and the author's.

Reasons to Avoid Quotation

- Lack of understanding
- Awe for the authority of the source
- Feelings of inadequacy
- Laziness

Avoiding Plagiarism: Citing Your Paraphrased Sources

The one possible source of confusion in O'Brien's article occurs when he begins his own commentary. In the last two paragraphs, it is not always easy to determine where O'Brien's paraphrase of the speakers' ideas ends and his own opinions begin. In Paragraph 4, his description of the student's reactions to the two speakers appears objective. At the end of the paragraph, however, we learn that O'Brien is scornful of the criteria that the student is using to evaluate these ideas. But at first we cannot be sure whether O'Brien is describing the *student's observation* or giving *his own account* of the speaker's platform maneuvers. It would be clearer to us if the sentence began: "According to the responding student, the second speaker spoke with ebullient confidence. . . . " Similarly, the last sentence of Paragraph 4 is undoubtedly O'Brien's opinion, yet there is nothing to indicate the transition from the student to O'Brien as the source of commentary.

This *confusion of point of view* is especially deceptive in Paragraph 5 as O'Brien moves from his paraphrased and neutral account of the dialogue between student and speaker to his own opinion that certain predators influence behavior in civilization as well as in the wild. It takes two readings to notice the point at which O'Brien is no longer paraphrasing but beginning to speak in his own voice. Such confusions could have been clarified by inserting citations—the name of the source or an appropriate pronoun—in the appropriate places.

In academic writing the clear acknowledgment of the source is not merely a matter of courtesy or clarity; it is an assurance of the writer's honesty.

> *When you paraphrase another person's ideas, you must cite the author's name, as you do when you quote, or else risk being charged with plagiarism. Borrowing ideas is just as much theft as borrowing words.*

You omit the quotation marks when you paraphrase, but you must not omit the citation. Of course, the citation of the name should be smoothly integrated into your sentence, following the guidelines used for citation of quotations. The source's name need not appear at the beginning of the sentence, but it should signal the beginning of the paraphrase:

> Not everyone enjoys working, but most people would agree with Jones's belief that work is an essential experience of life.

The writer of the essay is responsible for the declaration that "not everyone enjoys working" and that most people would agree with Jones's views; but the belief that "work is an essential experience of life" is attributed to Jones. Here, the citation is well and unobtrusively placed; there are no quotation marks, so presumably Jones used a different wording.

Here, then, are additional guidelines for the proper citation of sources:

- When you *quote*, there can never be any doubt about where the borrowed material begins and where it ends: the quotation marks provide a clear indication of the boundaries.

- When you *paraphrase*, although the citation may signal the *beginning* of the source material, your reader may not be sure exactly where the paraphrase *ends*.

There is no easy method of indicating the termination of paraphrased material. (As you will see in Chapter 9, the author's name in parentheses works well if you are using that method of documentation.) It is possible to signal the end of a paraphrase simply by starting a new paragraph. However, you may need to incorporate more than one person's ideas into a single paragraph. *When you present several points of view in succession, be careful to acknowledge the change of source by citing names.*

In some kinds of essays, it may be appropriate to signal the shift from paraphrased material to your own opinions by using the first person. Instructors' attitudes toward the first person vary, but some find it acceptable to use "I" in certain kinds of writing as long as it is not inserted excessively or monotonously. A carefully placed "I" can leave your reader in no doubt as to whose voice is being heard. Make sure, however, that using "I" is consistent with the tone and point of view of your essay. If you are presenting sources through a narrative in which you otherwise remain in the background, the sudden appearance of "I" would mean a sharp break in the overall tone and would therefore be inappropriate.

EXERCISE 15

1. Read "'Retirement Pregnancies' Spur a Wide Ethical Debate," by William E. Schmidt.

2. In the margin, indicate where the author uses quotation (Q), paraphrase (P), summary (S), and commentary (C).

3. In class discussion, be prepared to evaluate the use of quotation, paraphrase, and summary, and to indicate those places in the article where, in your opinion, one of the techniques is inappropriately or unnecessarily used, or where the transition from one technique to the other is not clearly identified.

"RETIREMENT PREGNANCIES" SPUR A WIDE ETHICAL DEBATE

William E. Schmidt

This week, after a 59-year-old woman gave birth to twins in a London hospital, doctors and politicians here have become snarled in a thickening ethical debate. Should governments and organized medicine consider limits on the age at which a woman can seek to become pregnant as a result of human fertility treatments?

The London woman, who has not been identified but is described as wealthy, gave birth after eggs donated by a younger woman and fertilized by the older woman's husband were implanted into her at a private fertility clinic in Rome. Doctors in London had earlier refused to perform the same procedure because they believed she was too old to face the emotional stress of being a mother.

Coupled with news from Italy on Tuesday that a 61-year-old woman treated at the same clinic may soon become one of the oldest women ever to give birth, startled physicians and health ministers are raising the possibility of more such "retirement pregnancies."

It has been technically possible for a postmenopausal woman to become pregnant with donor eggs since 1990, but the number of such pregnancies is still small. Most in-vitro-fertilization clinics in the United States will not accept women who are older than their early 40s because of the low success rate.

While such pregnancies are now rare, Stuart Horner, the chairman of the British Medical Association's ethics committee, said the problem might grow over the next decade as the procedure becomes more common. *The Times* of London reported that at least 13 women between the ages of 50 and 52 have already undergone similar treatment in the last year at fertility clinics in Britain. At least two have given birth, the newspaper said.

A similar situation took place in the United States when a 53-year-old woman, whose daughter was infertile, gave birth to her own grandchild earlier this year. The ethical issues in that case were muted, however, by its altruistic nature.

"Women do not have the right to have a child," said Virginia Bottomley, the British secretary of health. "The child has a right to a suitable home."

Most of the objections raised by ministers and physicians in the debate are ethical ones, based on the strong belief that it is best for a child to have active, able parents. In addition, critics have argued on medical grounds that such late pregnancies pose grave medical risks to the mother. And because donor eggs are in such short supply, some physicians make the public-health argument that they should be reserved for younger women, where the success rate is higher. 8

In a few cases, the National Health Service, which provides medical care without charge to all Britons, perform[s] in-vitro, or "test tube," fertilizations. But such cases are based on the physician's determination of relative medical and clinical need and the likelihood of a satisfactory outcome. 9

Critics say that such procedures for older women should not be paid for by the National Health Service. 10

But even as Mrs. Bottomley proposed a joint effort among European health ministers to explore what she described as "ethical controls" to deal with potential abuses of the medical technology that has stretched a woman's child-bearing years, others said it was wrong to tell a woman she had no right to give birth because she is too old. 11

Such proposals to limit pregnancy on the basis of age not only are unfair to older women, but suggest a sexual bias as well, Ian Craft, the director of the London Fertility Center, said in a London newspaper. While it was his clinic that refused to treat the woman who later sought help in Rome, he still said it was not right to impose age barriers for women "when there is no age limit for men." 12

Peter Bromwich, the director of a private fertility clinic in London, was among several physicians who said he would treat a woman in her 50s as long as he was convinced she was healthy, financially secure and had a supportive family. In that regard, the mother of twins was a suitable subject, Dr. Bromwich said, as she is described as a wealthy businesswoman who has a 45-year-old husband. 13

The woman had been impregnated in the Rome clinic with eggs fertilized by her husband. The eggs had been donated by an Italian woman in her 20s. 14

In a column in *The Times* of London, Sandy MacAra, chairman of the Council of the British Medical Association, sharply disagreed with those who say without qualification that a mother in her 60s or 70s cannot provide a suitable home and family life for a young child. 15

"Relative youth is no guarantee of parental function or competence, as repeated reports of abandoned and neglected children forcibly remind us," Dr. MacAra wrote. "Better, it may be argued, a fit, healthy 59-year-old than an unfit, unhealthy 19-year-old." Dr. MacAra argued the final decision should be left to the physician. 16

At the center of the debate is Severino Antinori, the Italian gynecologist and a former veterinarian who claims to have helped more than 40 women in their 50s become mothers. 17

Over the years, Dr. Antinori has become a familiar face in Italian newspapers. In the late 1980s, he was condemned by the Vatican following reports that he had helped a 53-year-old woman to have a child by implanting one of her eggs, fertilized 18 by her partner, in the womb of her own daughter. The physician later denied being responsible for the procedure.

Last summer in *The Independent on Sunday*, he defended his work with older women, saying there was no reason a woman in her 50s should not have a child. "A man can have a child at that age and everyone says, 'Isn't he clever?'" Dr. Antinori said. "But those same people say that a woman of 55 is a dishrag." 19

Another of his patients, Rossana Dalla Corte, 61, told *Il Messaggero*, the Rome daily, that the doctor implanted a donor's fertilized eggs in her uterus three months ago. She said she and her husband wanted a child after their only son was killed in an automobile accident last year. He was 19. 20

In the sharpest criticism, John Marks, the former chairman of the Council of the British Medical Association, said such cases "bordered on the Frankenstein syndrome." 21

EXERCISE 16

All the quotations in the following paragraph come from a single source: "Grading Students: A Failure to Communicate," by Reed G. Williams and Harry G. Miller. The student quoting from this article has carefully put opening and closing quotation marks around all the sentences, but has made no effort to write a continuous paragraph. Make the paragraph coherent by reducing the number of quotations through paraphrase (the finished paragraph should contain only *one* quotation, if any). Remember to acknowledge the authors, making clear how much of the paragraph is taken from their essay.

A minority of faculty members in colleges would prefer to solve the problem of grades by eliminating them. "A strategy sometimes adopted by those who wish to abolish grades, but who are unable to muster enough support among colleagues to obtain the necessary changes in policy, is that of blanket grading or the awarding of very high grades." "Such strategies sometimes are adopted with the deliberate intent of sabotaging the grading system, while others use them to avoid the unpleasant task of giving low grades." "Whatever the purpose, however, high grades which are not based on superior achievement have negative consequences for both students and institutions." "In many ways the awarding of unjustified high grades has consequences for the academic system which are comparable to the effects of counterfeit currency on a monetary system." "In both cases, the ones who suffer most are those who struggle hard under noninflationary conditions to accumulate the legitimate currency, which then loses its value because of the inflation caused by the bogus issues which have no real meaning in the standard system." "Finally, in both cases, the breakdown of the standardized medium of exchange leaves a vacuum which permits frauds to flourish and makes legitimate transactions difficult."

PRESENTING SOURCES: A SUMMARY OF PRELIMINARY WRITING SKILLS

1. **Annotation: underlining the text and inserting marginal comments on the page.**

   The notes can explain points that are unclear, define difficult words, emphasize key ideas, point out connections to previous or subsequent paragraphs, or suggest the reader's own reactions to what is being discussed.

2. **Outlining: constructing a systematic list of ideas that reflects the basic structure of an essay or book, with major and minor points distributed on different levels.**

   Outlining is a reductive skill that suggests the bones of a work, but little of its flesh or outward appearance. Outlining is especially useful for covering a long sequence of material containing ideas whose relationship is easy to grasp. Densely written passages that rely on frequent and subtle distinctions and dexterous use of language are not easily condensed into an outline.

3. **Paraphrasing: recapitulating, point by point, using your own words.**

   A paraphrase is a faithful and complete rendition of the original, following much the same order of ideas. Although full-length paraphrase is practical only with relatively brief passages, it is the most reliable way to make sense out of a difficult text. Paraphrasing a sentence or two, together with a citation of the author's name, is the best method of presenting another person's ideas within your own essay.

4. **Quotation: including another person's exact words within your own writing.**

   Although quotation requires the least amount of invention, it is the most technical of all these skills, demanding an understanding of conventional and complex punctuation. In your notes and in your essays, quotation should be a last resort. If the phrasing is unique, if the presentation is subtle, if the point at issue is easily misunderstood or hotly debated, quotation may be appropriate. When in doubt, paraphrase.

5. **Summary: condensing a paragraph or an essay or a chapter into a relatively brief presentation of the main ideas.**

   Unlike annotation, a summary should make sense as an independent, coherent piece of writing. Unlike paraphrase, a summary includes only main ideas. However, the summary should be complete in the sense that it provides a fair representation of the work and its parts. Summary is the all-purpose skill; it is neither crude nor overly detailed.

EXERCISE 17

Consider each of the following situations, and (in preparation for class discussion) decide which of the five skills summarized would be an appropriate method of preparation. (More than one skill may be applicable to each situation, but try to write them down in order of probable usefulness.)

1. You are about to take a closed-book exam based on materials from six different sources—about a hundred pages in all.
2. You are a social worker who has had a client transferred to you; you have a long case history to absorb before the next staff meeting.
3. You are preparing to participate in a debate on foreign policy, for which you have read two books; you will be given twenty-five minutes to present your point of view.
4. You are preparing to debate a controversial book in a roundtable discussion; the format will be conversational.
5. You have been given access to archives containing irreplaceable historic letters, too fragile to be photocopied.
6. You are about to take an open-book exam based on a single text.
7. You are a law student looking up a crucial court decision that will be a precedent for a mock trial in which you are the prosecutor.
8. You are taking notes at a one-hour lecture in your field of specialization.
9. You are interviewing an important official who has suddenly begun to talk about his political intentions.
10. You are being given verbal instructions in the working of complex scientific apparatus that, if misused, may blow up.

Part II

WRITING FROM SOURCES

The previous two chapters have described some basic ways to understand another writer's ideas and present them accurately and naturally, as part of your own writing. Until now, however, you have been working with forms of writing that are brief and limited—the sentence and the paragraph. Now you can use the skills that you practiced in Part I to develop your own ideas in a full-length essay based on sources.

When you write at length from sources, you must work with *two points of view—your own* and *those of the authors you're writing about.* You therefore have a dual responsibility: You must do justice to yourself by developing your own ideas, and you must do justice to each source by fairly representing its author's ideas. But blending the ideas of two or more people within the same essay can create confusion: Who should dominate? How much of yourself should you include? How much of your source? Moreover, in academic and professional writing you may have to consider a third voice—that of your teacher or supervisor, who may assign a topic or otherwise set limits and goals for your work.

Chapter 3 discusses three approaches to writing based on a single source. Each demonstrates a way to reconcile the competing influences on your writing and blend the voices that your reader ought to hear:

- You can distinguish between your source and yourself by writing about the two separately, first the source and then yourself.
- You can help your reader to understand a difficult and confusing source by presenting your own interpretation of the author's ideas.
- You can use your source as the basis for the development of your own ideas by writing an essay on a similar or related topic.

In the end, *your voice should dominate.* It is you who will choose the thesis and control the essay's structure and direction; it is your understanding and judgment that will interpret the source materials for your reader. When you and your classmates are asked to write about the same reading, your teacher hopes to receive, not an identical set of essays, but rather a series of individual interpretations with a common starting point in the same source.

Combining your own ideas with those of others inevitably becomes more difficult when you begin to work with *a group of sources* and must represent several authors. This is the subject of Chapter 4. It is more than ever vital that your own voice dominate your essay and that you do not simply summarize first one source and then the next, without any perspective of your own.

Blending together a variety of sources is usually called *synthesis*. You try to look beyond each separate assertion and, instead, develop a broad generalization that will encompass your source material. Your own generalized conclusions become the basis for your essay's thesis and organization, while the ideas of your sources serve as the evidence that supports those conclusions.

Chapter 4 emphasizes the standard methods of presenting multiple sources:

- The analysis of each source in a search for common themes.
- The establishment of common denominators or categories that cut across the separate sources and provide the structure for your essay.
- The evaluation of each source's relative significance as you decide which to emphasize.
- The citation of a group of references from several different sources in support of a single point.

These skills are closely related to some of the most common and useful strategies for constructing an essay: *definition, classification,* and *comparison.* Chapter 4 also includes some specialized practice in the selection, arrangement, and presentation of sources.

▪3▪

The Single-Source Essay

When you write from a source, you must understand another writer's ideas as thoroughly as you understand your own. The first step in carrying out each of the strategies described in this chapter is to *read carefully through the source essay,* using the skills for comprehension that you learned about in Chapters 1 and 2: annotation, outlining, paraphrase, and summary. Once you are able to explain to your reader what the source is all about, you can begin to plan your *rebuttal, interpretation,* or *analysis* of the author's ideas; or you can write your own essay on a similar topic.

You will work with three strategies in this chapter:

1. Separating source and self
2. Interpreting what you summarize
3. Using a source as the starting point for your own essay

STRATEGY ONE:
SEPARATING SOURCE AND SELF

The simplest way to write about someone else's ideas is *complete separation.*

The structure of your essay breaks into two parts, with the source's views presented first, and your own reactions given equal (or greater) space immediately afterward.

This strategy works best when you are writing about an author with whom you totally or partially disagree. Instead of treating the reading as evidence in support of your point of view and blending it with your own ideas, you write an essay that *first analyzes and then refutes your source's basic themes.* Look, for example, at Roger Sipher's "So That Nobody Has to Go to School If They Don't Want To."

SO THAT NOBODY HAS TO GO TO SCHOOL IF THEY DON'T WANT TO

Roger Sipher

A decline in standardized test scores is but the most recent indicator that American education is in trouble.   1

One reason for the crisis is that present mandatory-attendance laws force many to attend school who have no wish to be there. Such children have little desire to learn and are so antagonistic to school that neither they nor more highly motivated students receive the quality education that is the birthright of every American.   2

The solution to this problem is simple: Abolish compulsory-attendance laws and allow only those who are committed to getting an education to attend.   3

This will not end public education. Contrary to conventional belief, legislators enacted compulsory-attendance laws to legalize what already existed. William Landes and Lewis Solomon, economists, found little evidence that mandatory-attendance laws increased the number of children in school. They found, too, that school systems have never effectively enforced such laws, usually because of the expense involved.   4

There is no contradiction between the assertion that compulsory attendance has had little effect on the number of children attending school and the argument that repeal would be a positive step toward improving education. Most parents want a high school education for their children. Unfortunately, compulsory attendance hampers the ability of public school officials to enforce legitimate educational and disciplinary policies and thereby make the education a good one.   5

Private schools have no such problem. They can fail or dismiss students, knowing such students can attend public school. Without compulsory attendance, public schools would be freer to oust students whose academic or personal behavior undermines the educational mission of the institution.   6

Has not the noble experiment of a formal education for everyone failed? While we pay homage to the homily, "You can lead a horse to water but you can't make him drink," we have pretended it is not true in education.   7

Ask high school teachers if recalcitrant students learn anything of value. Ask teachers if these students do any homework. Quite the contrary, these students know they will be passed from grade to grade until they are old enough to quit or until, as is more likely, they receive a high school diploma. At the point when stu-   8 dents could legally quit, most choose to remain since they know they are likely to be allowed to graduate whether they do acceptable work or not.

Abolition of archaic attendance laws would produce enormous dividends. 9

First, it would alert everyone that school is a serious place where one goes to 10 learn. Schools are neither day-care centers nor indoor street corners. Young people who resist learning should stay away; indeed, an end to compulsory schooling would require them to stay away.

Second, students opposed to learning would not be able to pollute the educa- 11 tional atmosphere for those who want to learn. Teachers could stop policing recalcitrant students and start educating.

Third, grades would show what they are supposed to: how well a student is learn- 12 ing. Parents could again read report cards and know if their children were making progress.

Fourth, public esteem for schools would increase. People would stop regarding 13 them as way stations for adolescents and start thinking of them as institutions for educating America's youth.

Fifth, elementary schools would change because students would find out early 14 that they had better learn something or risk flunking out later. Elementary teachers would no longer have to pass their failures on to junior high and high school.

Sixth, the cost of enforcing compulsory education would be eliminated. Despite 15 enforcement efforts, nearly 15 percent of the school-age children in our largest cities are almost permanently absent from school.

Communities could use these savings to support institutions to deal with young 16 people not in school. If, in the long run, these institutions prove more costly, at least we would not confuse their mission with that of schools.

Schools should be for education. At present, they are only tangentially so. They 17 have attempted to serve an all-encompassing social function, trying to be all things to all people. In the process they have failed miserably at what they were originally formed to accomplish.

Presenting Your Source's Point of View

Sipher opposes compulsory attendance laws. On the other hand, suppose that you can see advantages in imposing a very strict rule for attendance. In order to challenge Sipher convincingly, you will have to incorporate both his point of view and yours within a single short essay.

Since your objective is to *respond* to Sipher, you begin by *presenting his ideas to your readers*. State them as fairly as you can, without pausing to argue with him or to offer your own point of view about mandatory attendance. Even though you seem to be giving the first round to your opponent, his ideas need not dominate your essay.

At first it may seem easiest to follow Sipher's sequence of ideas (especially since his points are so clearly numbered). But Sipher is more likely to dominate if you follow the structure of his essay, presenting and answering each of his points one by one; for you will be arguing on *his* terms, according to *his* conception of the issue rather than yours. Instead, make sure that your reader understands what Sipher is actually saying before you begin with your rebuttal. To do so, carry out *both* of the following steps:

1. Briefly summarize the issue and the reasons that prompted the author to write the essay.

You do this by writing a brief summary, as explained in Chapter 1. Here is a summary of Sipher's article:

> Roger Sipher argues that the presence in the classroom of unwilling students who are indifferent to learning can explain why public school students as a whole are learning less and less. Sipher therefore recommends that public schools discontinue the policy of mandatory attendance. Instead, students would be allowed to drop out if they wished, and faculty would be able to expel students whose behavior made it difficult for serious students to do their work. Once unwilling students were no longer forced to attend, schools would once again be able to maintain high standards of achievement; they could devote money and energy to education, rather than custodial care.

You can make such a summary more detailed by paraphrasing some of the author's arguments and, if you wish, quoting once or twice.

2. Analyze and present some of the basic principles that underlie the author's position on this issue. .

In debating the issue with the author, you will need to do more than just contradict his main ideas: Sipher says mandatory attendance is bad, and you say it is good; Sipher says difficult students don't learn anything, and you say all students learn something useful; and so on. This point-by-point rebuttal shows that you disagree, but it provides no context so that readers can decide who is right and who is wrong. You have no starting point for your counterarguments and no choice but to sound arbitrary.

Instead, *ask yourself why the author has taken this position,* one which you find so easy to reject.

- What are the foundations of his arguments?
- What larger principles do they suggest?
- What policies is he objecting to? Why?
- What values is he determined to defend?
- Can these values or principles be applied to issues other than attendance?

You are now examining Sipher's specific responses to the practical problem of attendance in order to *infer some broad generalizations* about his philosophy of education.

Although Sipher does not specifically state such generalizations in this article, you would be safe in concluding that Sipher's views on attendance derive from a *conflict of two principles:*

1. The belief that education is a right that may not be denied under any circumstances, and

2. The belief that education is a privilege to be earned.

Sipher advocates the second position. Thus, after your summary of the article, you should analyze Sipher's implicit position in a separate paragraph.

> Sipher's argument implies that there is no such thing as the right to an education. A successful education can only depend on the student's willing presence and active participation. Passive or rebellious students cannot be educated and should not be forced to stay in school. Although everyone has the right to an opportunity for education, its acquisition is actually the privilege of those who choose to work for it.

Through this analysis of Sipher's position, you have not only found out more about the issue being argued, but you have also established a common context—*eligibility for education*—within which you and he disagree. Provided with a clear understanding of the differences between you, your reader now has a real basis for choosing between your opposing views. At the same time, your reader is being assured that this point and no other is the essential point for debate; thus, you will be fighting on ground that *you* have chosen.

Presenting Your Point of View

3. *Present your reasons for disagreeing with your source.*

Once you have established your opponent's position, you may then plan your own counterarguments by writing down your reactions and pinpointing the exact reasons for your disagreement. (All the statements analyzed in this section are taken from such preliminary responses; they are *not* excerpts from finished essays.) Your reasons for disagreeing with Sipher might fit into one of three categories:

- You believe that his basic principle is not valid (Student B).
- You decide that his principle, although valid, cannot be strictly applied to the practical situation under discussion (Student C).
- You accept Sipher's principle, but you are aware of other, stronger influences that diminish its importance (Student E).

Whichever line of argument you follow, it is impossible to present your case successfully if you *wholly ignore Sipher's basic principle,* as Student A does:

Student A

Sipher's isn't a constructive solution. Without strict attendance laws, many students wouldn't come to school at all.

Nonattendance is exactly what Sipher wants: he argues that indifferent students should be permitted to stay away, that their absence would benefit everyone. Student A makes no effort to refute Sipher's point; he is, in effect, saying to his source, "You're wrong!" without explaining why.

Student B, however, tries to *establish a basis for disagreement:*

Student B

If mandatory attendance were to be abolished, how would children acquire the skills to survive in an educated society such as ours?

According to Student B, the practical uses of education have become so important that a student's very survival may one day depend on having been well educated. *Implied here is the principle, in opposition to Sipher's, that receiving an education cannot be a matter of choice or a privilege to be earned.* What children learn in school is so important to their future lives that they should be forced to attend classes, even against their will, for their own good.

But this response is still superficial. Student B is confusing the desired object—*getting an education*—with one of the means of achieving that object—*being present in the classroom; attendance, the means, has become an end in itself.* Since students who attend but do not participate will not learn, mandatory attendance cannot by itself create an educated population.

On the other hand, although attendance may not be the *only* condition for getting an education, the student's physical presence in the classroom is certainly important. In that case, should the decision about attendance, a decision likely to affect much of their future lives, be placed in the hands of those too young to understand the consequences?

Student C

The absence of attendance laws would be too tempting for students and might create a generation of semi-illiterates. Consider the marginal student who, despite general indifference and occasional bad behavior, shows some promise and capacity for learning. Without a policy of mandatory attendance, he might choose the easy way out instead of trying to develop his abilities. As a society, we owe these students, at whatever cost, a chance at a good and sound education.

Notice that Student C specifies a "chance" at education. In a sense, there is no basic conflict between Student C's views and Sipher's. *Both agree in principle that society can provide the opportunity, but not the certainty, of being educated.* The distinction here lies in the way in which the principle is applied. Sipher feels no need to make allowances or exceptions: there are limits to the opportunities that society is obliged to provide. Student C, however, believes that society must act in the best interests of those too young to make such decisions; for their sake, the principle of education as a privilege should be less rigorously applied. Students should be exposed to the conditions for (if not the fact of) education, whether they like it or not, until they become adults, capable of choice.

Student D goes even further, suggesting that not only is society obliged to provide the student with educational opportunities, but schools are responsible for making the experience as attractive as possible.

Student D

Maybe the reason for a decrease in attendance and an unwillingness to learn is not that students do not want an education, but that the whole system of discipline and learning is ineffective. If schools concentrated on making classes more appealing, the result would be better attendance.

In Student D's analysis, passive students are like consumers who need to be encouraged to take advantage of an excellent product that is not selling well. To encourage good attendance, the schools ought to consider using more attractive marketing methods. *Implicit in this view is a transferral of blame from the student to the school.* Other arguments of this sort might blame the parents, rather than the schools, for not teaching their children to understand that it is in their own best interests to get an education.

Finally, Student E accepts the validity of Sipher's view of education, but finds that the whole issue has become subordinate to a more important problem.

Student E

We already have a problem with youths roaming the street, getting into serious trouble. Just multiply the current number of unruly kids by five or ten, and you will come up with the number of potential delinquents that will be hanging around the streets if we do away with the attendance laws that keep them in school. Sipher may be right when he argues that the quality of education would improve if unwilling students were permitted to drop out, but he would be wise to remember that those remaining inside school will have to deal with those on the outside sooner or later.

In this perspective, *security becomes more important than education.* Student E implicitly accepts and gives some social value to the image (rejected by Sipher) of school as a prison, with students sentenced to mandatory confinement.

A reasonably full response, like those of Students C and E, can provide the material for a series of paragraphs that argue against Sipher's position. Here, for example, is Student E's statement analyzed into the basic topics for a four-paragraph rebuttal within the essay. (The topics are on the left.)

Student E

danger from dropouts if Sipher's plan is adopted (3)

custodial function of school (2)

concession that Sipher is right about education (1)

interests of law and order outweigh interests of education (4)

We already have a problem with youths roaming the street, getting into serious trouble. Just multiply the current number of unruly kids by five or ten, and you will come up with the number of potential delinquents that will be hanging around the streets if we do away with the attendance laws that keep them in school. Sipher may be right when he argues that the quality of education would improve if unwilling students were permitted to drop out, but he would be wise to remember that those remaining inside school will have to deal with those on the outside sooner or later.

And here are Student E's four topics, with the sequence reordered, in outline format. Notice that the student's basic agreement with Sipher has become the starting point.

I. Sipher is right about education.
   A. It is possible that the quality of education would improve if unwilling students were allowed to drop out.
II. School, however, has taken on a custodial function.
   A. It is attendance laws that keep students in school.
III. If Sipher's plan is adopted, dropouts might be a problem.
   A. Youths are already roaming the streets getting into trouble.
   B. An increase in the number of unruly kids hanging out in the streets means even greater possibility of disorder.
IV. The interests of law and order outweigh the interests of education.
   A. Educators will not be able to remain aloof from the problems that will develop outside the schools if students are permitted to drop out at will.

Guidelines for Separating Source and Self

■ Present your source's point of view
   1. Briefly summarize the issue and the reasons that prompted the author to write the essay.
   2. Analyze and present some of the basic principles that underlie the author's position on this issue.
■ Present your point of view
   3. Present your reasons for disagreeing with your source.

Student E can now develop four full-length paragraphs by explaining each point and offering supporting evidence and illustrative examples.

ASSIGNMENT 4

Read "What Our Education System Needs Is More F's," "Someone Is Stealing Your Life," and "Appearances Are Destructive." As the starting point for a summary-and-response, select the essay with which you disagree most. (Or, with your instructor's permission, bring in an essay that you are certain that you disagree with, and have your instructor approve your choice.)

1. Write a two-part summary of the essay, the first part describing the author's position and explicitly stated arguments, the second analyzing the principles underlying that position.
2. Then present your own rebuttal of the author's point of view.

The length of your essay will depend on the number and complexity of the ideas that you find in the source and the number of counterarguments that you can assemble. The minimum acceptable length for the entire assignment is two typewritten pages (approximately 500–600 words).

WHAT OUR EDUCATION SYSTEM
NEEDS IS MORE F's

Carl Singleton

I suggest that instituting merit raises, getting back to basics, marrying the university to industry, and the other recommendations will not achieve measurable success [in restoring quality to American education] until something even more basic is returned to practice. The immediate need for our educational system from pre-kindergarten through post-Ph.D. is not more money or better teaching but simply a widespread giving of F's.

Before hastily dismissing the idea as banal and simplistic, think for a moment about the implications of a massive dispensing of failing grades. It would dramatically, emphatically, and immediately force into the open every major issue related to the inadequacies of American education.

Let me make it clear that I recommend giving those F's—by the dozens, hundreds, thousands, even millions—only to students who haven't learned the required material. The basic problem of our educational system is the common practice of giving credit where none has been earned, a practice that has resulted in the sundry faults delineated by all the reports and studies over recent years. Illiteracy among high-school graduates is growing because those students have been passed rather than flunked; we have low-quality teaching because of low-quality teachers who never should have been certified in the first place; college students have to take basic reading, writing, and mathematics courses because they never learned those skills in classrooms from which they never should have been granted egress.

School systems have contributed to massive ignorance by issuing unearned passing grades over a period of some 20 years. At first there was a tolerance of students who did not fully measure up (giving D's to students who should have received firm F's); then our grading system continued to deteriorate (D's became C's, and B became the average grade); finally we arrived at total accommodation (come to class and get your C's, laugh at my jokes and take home B's).

Higher salaries, more stringent certification procedures, getting back to basics will have little or no effect on the problem of quality education unless and until we insist, as a profession, on giving F's whenever students fail to master the material.

Sending students home with final grades of F would force most parents to deal with the realities of their children's failure while it is happening and when it is yet possible to do something about it (less time on TV, and more time on homework, perhaps?). As long as it is the practice of teachers to pass students who should not be passed, the responsibility will not go home to the parents, where, I hope, it belongs. (I am tempted to make an analogy to then Gov. Lester Maddox's statement some years ago about prison conditions in Georgia—"We'll get a better grade of prisons when we get a better grade of prisoners"—but I shall refrain.)

Giving an F where it is deserved would force concerned parents to get themselves away from the TV set, too, and take an active part in their children's education. I realize, of course, that some parents would not help; some cannot help. However, Johnny does not deserve to pass just because Daddy doesn't care or is ignorant. Johnny should pass only when and if he knows the required material.

Giving an F whenever and wherever it is the only appropriate grade would force principals, school boards, and voters to come to terms with cost as a factor in improving our educational system. As the numbers of students at various levels were increased by those not being passed, more money would have to be spent to accommodate them. We could not be accommodating them in the old sense of passing them on, but by keeping them at one level until they did in time, one way or another, learn the material.

Insisting on respecting the line between passing and failing would also require us to demand as much of ourselves as of our students. As every teacher knows, a failed student can be the product of a failed teacher.

Teaching methods, classroom presentations, and testing procedures would have to be of a very high standard—we could not, after all, conscionably give F's if we have to go home at night thinking it might somehow be our own fault.

The results of giving an F where it is deserved would be immediately evident. There would be no illiterate college graduates next spring—none. The same would be true of high-school graduates, and consequently next year's college freshmen—all of them—would be able to read.

I don't claim that giving F's will solve all of the problems, but I do argue that unless and until we start failing those students who should be failed, other suggested solutions will make little progress toward improving education. Students in our schools and colleges should be permitted to pass only after they have fully met established standards; borderline cases should be retained.

The single most important requirement for solving the problems of education in America today is the big fat F, written decisively in red ink millions of times in schools and colleges across the country.

13

SOMEONE IS STEALING YOUR LIFE
Michael Ventura

Most American adults wake around 6 or 7 in the morning. Get to work at 8 or 9. Knock off around 5. Home again, 6-ish. Fifty weeks a year. For about 45 years.

1

Most are glad to have the work, but don't really choose it. They may dream, they may study and even train for work they intensely want; but sooner or later, for most, that doesn't pan out. Then they take what they can and make do. Most have families to support, so they need their jobs more than their jobs admit to needing them. They're employees. And, as employees, most have no say whatsoever about much of anything on the job. The purpose and standards of the product or service, the short- and long-term goals of the company, are considered quite literally "none of their business"—though these issues drastically influence every aspect of their lives. No matter that they've given years to the day-to-day survival of the business; employees (even when they're called "managers") mostly take orders. Or else. It seems an odd way to structure a free society: Most people have little or no authority over what they do five days a week for 45 years. Doesn't sound much like "life, liberty, and the pursuit of happiness." Sounds like a nation of drones.

2

It used to be that one's compensation for being an American drone was the freedom to live in one's own little house, in one's own quirky way, in a clean and safe community in which your children had the chance to be happier, richer drones than you. But working stiffs can't afford houses now, fewer communities are clean, none are safe, and your kid's prospects are worse. (This condition *may* be because for five days a week, for 45 years, you had no say—while other people have been making decisions that haven't been good for you.) I'm not sure whose happiness we've been pursuing lately, but one thing is clear: It's not the happiness of those who've done our society's work.

3

On the other hand—or so they say—you're free, and if you don't like your job you can pursue happiness by starting a business of your very own, by becoming an "independent" entrepreneur. But you're only as independent as your credit rating. And to compete in the business community, you'll find yourself having to treat others—*your* employees—as much like slaves as you can get away with. Pay them as little as they'll tolerate and give them no say in anything, because that's what's most efficient and profitable. Money is the absolute standard. Freedom, and the

4

dignity and well-being of one's fellow creatures, simply don't figure in the basic formula.

This may seem a fairly harsh way to state the rules America now lives by. But if I sound radical, it's not from doing a lot of reading in some cozy university, then dashing off to dispense opinion as a prima donna of the alternative press. I learned about drones by droning. From ages 18 to 29 (minus a few distracted months at college when I was 24) I worked the sort of jobs that I expected to have all my life: typesetter for two years, tape transcriber for three, proofreader (a grossly incompetent one) for a few weeks, messenger for a few months, and secretary (yes, secretary) for a year and a half. Then I stopped working steadily and the jobs got funkier: hospital orderly, vacuum-cleaner salesman, Jack-in-the-Box counterperson, waiter, nail hammerer, cement mixer, toilet scrubber, driver.

It was during the years of office work that I caught on: I got two weeks' paid vacation per year. A year has 52 weeks. Even a comparatively unskilled, uneducated worker like me, who couldn't (still can't) do fractions or long division—even I had enough math to figure that two goes into 52 . . . how many times? Twenty-six. Meaning it would take me 26 years on the job to accumulate one year for myself. And I could only have that year in 26 pieces, so it wouldn't even feel like a year. In other words, no time was truly mine. My boss merely allowed me an illusion of freedom, a little space in which to catch my breath, in between the 50 weeks that I lived but *he* owned. My employer uses 26 years of my life for every year I get to keep. And what do I get in return for this enormous thing I am giving? What do I get in return for my *life*?

A paycheck that's as skimpy as they can get away with. If I'm lucky, some health insurance. (If I'm *really* lucky, the employer's definition of "health" will include my teeth and my eyes—maybe even my mind.) And, in a truly enlightened workplace, just enough pension or "profit-sharing" to keep me sweet but not enough to make life different. And that's it.

Compare that to what my employer gets: If the company is successful, he (it's usually a he) gets a standard of living beyond my wildest dreams, including what I would consider fantastic protection for his family, and a world of access that I can only pitifully mimic by changing the channels on my TV. His standard of living wouldn't be possible without the labor of people like me—but my employer doesn't think that's a very significant fact. He certainly doesn't think that this fact entitles me to any say about the business. Not to mention a significant share in ownership. Oh no. The business is his to do with as he pleases, and he owns my work. Period.

I don't mean that bosses don't work. Most work hard, and have the satisfaction of knowing that what they do is *theirs*. Great. The problem is: What I do is theirs too. Yet if my companion workers and I didn't do what we do—then nobody would be anybody's. So how come what we do is hardly ours? How come he can get rich while we're lucky to break even? How come he can do anything he wants with the company without consulting us, yet we do the bulk of the work and take the brunt of the consequences?

The only answer provided is that the employer came up with the money to start the enterprise in the first place; hence, he and his money people decide everything and get all the benefits. 10

Excuse me, but that seems a little unbalanced. It doesn't take into account that nothing happens unless work is done. Shouldn't it follow that, work being so important, the doers of that work deserve a more just formula for measuring who gets what? There's no doubt that the people who risked or raised the money to form a company, or bail it out of trouble, deserve a fair return on their investment—but is it fair that they get *everything*? It takes more than investment and management to make a company live. It takes the labor, skill, and talent of the people who do the company's work. Isn't *that* an investment? Doesn't it deserve a fair return, a voice, a share of the power? 11

I know this sounds awfully simplistic, but no school ever taught me anything about the ways of economics and power (perhaps because they didn't want me to know), so I had to figure it out slowly, based on what I saw around me every day. And I saw: 12

That it didn't matter how long I worked or what a good job I did. I could get incremental raises, perhaps even medical benefits and a few bonuses, but I would not be allowed power over my own life—no power over the fundamental decisions my company makes, decisions on which my *life* depends. My future is in the hands of people whose names I often don't know and whom I never meet. Their investment is the only factor taken seriously. They feed on my work, on my life, but reserve for themselves all power, prerogative, and profit. 13

Slowly, very slowly, I came to a conclusion that for me was fundamental: My employers are stealing my life. 14

They. Are. Stealing. My. Life. 15

If the people who do the work don't own some part of the product, and don't have any power over what happens to *their* enterprise—they are being robbed. *You* are being robbed. And don't think for a minute that those who are robbing you don't know they are robbing you. They know how much they get from you and how little they give back. They are thieves. They are stealing your life. 16

The assembly-line worker isn't responsible for the decimation of the American auto industry, for instance. Those responsible are those who've been hurt least, executives and stockholders who, according to the *Los Angeles Times,* make 50 to 500 times what the assembly-line worker makes, but who've done a miserable job of managing. Yet it's the workers who suffer most. Layoffs, plant closings, and such are no doubt necessary—like the bumper stickers say, shit happens—but it is not necessary that workers have no power in the fundamental management decisions involved. 17

As a worker, I am not an "operating cost." I am how the job gets done. I *am* the job. I am the company. Without me and my companion workers, there's nothing. I'm willing to take my lumps in a world in which little is certain, but I deserve a say. Not just some cosmetic "input," but significant power in good times or bad. A place 18 at the table where the decisions are made. Nothing less is fair. So nothing less is moral.

And if you, as owners or management or government, deny me this—then you are choosing not to be moral, and you are committing a crime against me. Do you expect me not to struggle?   19

Do you expect us to be forever passive while you get rich by stealing our lives?   20

APPEARANCES ARE DESTRUCTIVE

Mark Mathabane

As public schools reopen for the new year, strategies to curb school violence will once again be hotly debated. Installing metal detectors and hiring security guards will help, but the experience of my two sisters makes a compelling case for greater use of dress codes as a way to protect students and promote learning.   1

Shortly after my sisters arrived here from South Africa I enrolled them at the local public school. I had great expectations for their educational experience. Compared with black schools under apartheid, American schools are Shangri-Las, with modern textbooks, school buses, computers, libraries, lunch programs and dedicated teachers.   2

But despite these benefits, which students in many parts of the world only dream about, my sisters' efforts at learning were almost derailed. They were constantly taunted for their homely outfits. A couple of times they came home in tears. In South Africa students were required to wear uniforms, so my sisters had never been preoccupied with clothes and jewelry.   3

They became so distraught that they insisted on transferring to different schools, despite my reassurances that there was nothing wrong with them because of what they wore.   4

I have visited enough public schools around the country to know that my sisters' experiences are not unique. In schools in many areas, Nike, Calvin Klein, Adidas, Reebok and Gucci are more familiar names to students than Zora Neale Hurston, Shakespeare and Faulkner. Many students seem to pay more attention to what's on their bodies than in their minds.   5

Teachers have shared their frustrations with me at being unable to teach those students willing to learn because classes are frequently disrupted by other students ogling themselves in mirrors, painting their fingernails, combing their hair, shining their gigantic shoes or comparing designer labels on jackets, caps and jewelry.   6

The fiercest competition among students is often not over academic achievements, but over who dresses most expensively. And many students now measure parental love by how willing their mothers and fathers are to pamper them with money for the latest fads in clothes, sneakers and jewelry.   7

Those parents without the money to waste on such meretricious extravagances are considered uncaring and cruel. They often watch in dismay and helplessness as their children become involved with gangs and peddle drugs to raise the money.   8

When students are asked why they attach so much importance to clothing, they frequently reply that it's the cool thing to do, that it gives them status and earns them respect. And clothes are also used to send sexual messages, with girls thinking that the only things that make them attractive to boys are skimpy dresses and gaudy looks, rather than intelligence and academic excellence. 9

The argument by civil libertarians that dress codes infringe on freedom of expression is misleading. We observe dress codes in nearly every aspect of our lives without any diminution of our freedoms—as demonstrated by flight attendants, bus drivers, postal employees, high school bands, military personnel, sports teams, Girl and Boy Scouts, employees of fast-food chains, restaurants and hotels. 10

In many countries where students outperform their American counterparts academically, school dress codes are observed as part of creating the proper learning environment. Their students tend to be neater, less disruptive in class and more disciplined, mainly because their minds are focused more on learning and less on materialism. 11

It's time Americans realized that the benefits of safe and effective schools far outweigh any perceived curtailment of freedom of expression brought on by dress codes. 12

STRATEGY TWO: INTERPRETING WHAT YOU SUMMARIZE

Interpretation means the explanation or clarification of something that has been read, seen, or heard. The interpreter serves as a link between the author and the reader or audience. Actors interpret roles; at the United Nations, interpreters translate speeches into other languages so that all the delegates can understand them. You interpret a source by "translating" the author's ideas into terms that readers may find more understandable and more meaningful.

In daily life, you interpret ideas and information for yourself and for others whenever you try to explain an action or event or situation. Suppose that a friend has asked you to explain why the drugstore on the next corner has gone bankrupt. One easy way to explain it might be to *list the reasons in chronological order,* year by year, month by month. For example, two years ago, the owner of the Best Pharmacy fell ill and was unable to supervise the store; shortly afterward, the zoning laws changed and the neighborhood became less residential; next, the chief pharmacist decided to move to the south; meanwhile, an outbreak of vandalism and petty thefts had begun; then a discount store opened a block away; only two months ago, the overworked owner had his second heart attack; and so on. Without stressing any one event, you could elaborate on each reason, providing exact dates and details to form a chronological account of the store's gradual decline.

But if your friend only wanted a brief account of the long story, you would need to emphasize one (or more) of the reasons, probably removing it from its place in the chronological order. *As soon as you make that choice and decide which piece of information to take out of the original time-sequence, you have begun to interpret the event.* Of course, you must be familiar with all the stages in **order** to pull out one fact and confidently state that *this* was the primary reason for the pharmacy's bankruptcy. But, after weighing each fact against the others, you might finally conclude that the drugstore failed because of *a shift in residential patterns in that area of town.* Then (you might add) this shift led to outbreaks of crime, the pharmacist's move to Florida, and the worries that brought about the owner's heart attack.

The chronological summary was a factual list, with no attempt to stress one idea more than the next; therefore, there was little possibility of dispute. But as soon as you stress one major reason for the drugstore's bankruptcy, another informed observer might reject your interpretation of events. Instead, she might claim that, in *her* view, the success of a neighborhood store always depends on *the diligence of the owner and the quality of service;* therefore, the illness of the owner and, to a lesser extent, the departure of the pharmacist were chiefly responsible for the loss of business.

Given the conflict between these two interpretations—*declining residential population versus declining service*—each of you might wish to supply some supporting evidence to reinforce your main point. The second observer might offer *personal experiences* to back up her interpretation: after several of the substitute employees had been rude and neglectful, she and her neighbors began to shop at the discount store up the street. You, on the other hand, might cite *statistics* about the effect of the new zoning laws on all small businesses in the neighborhood.

The point is that both interpretations may be equally valid. Each is based on personal judgment as well as factual evidence. Each person has employed particular values and preconceptions in interpreting the actual events, which are common knowledge. (There is less opportunity for speculation and disagreement when one is interpreting a *written* source.) In fact, a third interpretation of the same event might emphasize a quite different idea. A stranger, who has listened to both versions, might later conclude that "there are *two* main reasons why that drugstore failed. . . ." Or, by now quite familiar with all the events (and more objective than either of the first two interpreters), he might try to incorporate *all* the reasons into a new interpretive summary: "*Conditions of modern urban life do not favor the small, owner-operated business.*" Notice that, in order to encompass everything that has come before, this final summary is more general than the first two.

EXERCISE 18

Reviews of films, plays, television programs, and books generally serve a dual purpose: they explain what the work is about (*summary* and *interpretation*) and they assess its value for an audience (*evaluation*). It is important to be able to distinguish between:

- *Interpretation,* which does not explicitly pass judgment on the worth of a work, and

- *Evaluation,* which contains the reviewer's opinion of the work as well as the standards which, according to the reviewer, the work should meet.

Read "Old Miser Bringing Up the Cute Girl Is (a) Marner (b) Martin?" and, in preparation for class discussion, use different symbols to mark:

1. Passages and phrases where the reviewer *summarizes* the program; include and identify quotation and paraphrase.

2. Passages and phrases where she *interprets* (or provides additional background for) the ideas and themes of the program.

3. Passages and phrases where she *evaluates* the program.

Are there any passages that do not fall into one of these three categories? What is their function in the review?

OLD MISER BRINGING UP THE CUTE GIRL IS (A) MARNER (B) MARTIN?

Janet Maslin

It's safe to surmise that nobody but Steve Martin thinks Mr. Martin needed to   1
appear in a lighthearted, contemporary screen version of "Silas Marner," casting
himself in the role of George Eliot's lonely miser. But Mr. Martin was doubtless
searching for another "Roxanne" and a role with a poignancy to match Cyrano's.
So he has adapted this tale in contemporary terms, to the point where a horse in
the 1861 version is now a Mercedes-Benz.

"A Simple Twist of Fate" borrows the not-so-simple twists of a novel that has   2
been the bane of many a high school English class, and that even its author was
known to denigrate. "Indeed, I should not have believed that anyone would have
been interested in it but myself (since Wordsworth is dead)," she once wrote to
her publisher. But what interests Mr. Martin is the redemptive love experienced by
Silas Marner, a k a Michael McCann, once he stops caring about money and lets an
orphaned little girl into his life.

"Silas Marner," in brief: A disgraced weaver, romantically spurned and wrongly ac-   3
cused of a crime, leaves the town he lives in and moves to a tiny village. Living nearby
is a wealthy squire whose supposedly upright son is secretly married to an opium
addict. Another, no-good son has tried to blackmail his brother about this. This
son also happens to rob Silas, who is known to hoard money in his cottage.

Silas is heartbroken. Time passes. Then, miraculously, Silas spies something golden   4
in his cottage, which turns out to be the flaxen hair of a little lost girl. She is the
daughter of the Squire's son and the opium addict, and she provides Silas with a
chance at happiness. Not knowing her parentage, he raises the girl lovingly until,
years later, her natural father tries to claim her as his own.

Melodramatic as it is, this story also has a strain of realism, which was naturally   5
the first thing lost in translation. The social currents of 19th-century England are
not easily adapted to the Virginia countryside, which is where the film takes place.

And many a strange adjustment becomes necessary. One of the film's daffier choices is making the baby's natural father a local politician named John Newland, and assigning the role to Gabriel Byrne, an Irish actor struggling mightily to wrap his vowels around a thick Virginia accent. Mr. Martin, as Michael, has no accent at all.

What's craziest about "A Simple Twist of Fate" is its tone: warm and comic, with frequent dashes of fate-twisting pathos. Even allowing for the fact that this has become principally a Steve Martin vehicle, it's hard to reconcile the story's heart-wrenching moments with the scene where Michael and Mathilda, his adopted daughter, dance and pantomime to the tune of "Running Bear." This is strictly a Steve Martin "King Tut" moment, and there weren't many of those in Silas Marner's life.

The best to be said for "A Simple Twist of Fate" is that it's gentle and lively enough to hold the interest during even its rockiest moments, and that it could have been so much worse. The smartest choice made here is that of the director, Gillies MacKinnon, the Scottish film maker known for the enormous charm of "The Playboys."

That film's story was also about a strong-willed single person struggling to raise a child. And it had a pleasing, colorful sense of small-town life that is echoed here. If there was anyone who could make even partial sense of this material, it was Mr. MacKinnon, and he does his considerable best.

Mr. Martin tries hard, too, but he tries too many different modes. His comic moments, with little Mathilda playing straight man, interfere with the story's dramatic weight, while the drama bogs down the humor. In a tacked-on courtroom ending that George Eliot never imagined, he even manages to offset the tension of the moment with a practical joke. At least one preview audience seemed to be watching this film avidly but bewilderedly, never quite knowing when it was time for Mr. Martin to start clowning and do what he does best.

Also in the film is Catherine O'Hara, adding comic relief and playing a modest small-town memorabilia dealer who happens to sell Michael some very valuable gold coins. (The shadow of "Silas Marner" makes for endless farfetched touches like that one.) Stephen Baldwin disappears very quickly as Mr. Byrne's bad-boy brother, and Laura Linney makes a glamorous impression as Mr. Byrne's picture-perfect wife. Six little girls play Mathilda at ages 1 through 10, among them two talented sisters, Alana and Alyssa Austin. To his credit, and to make some sense of why this film was made at all, Mr. Martin shows off a lovely, playful rapport with these young girls.

Writing an Interpretive Summary

When you write about a long and complex essay, one with many ideas woven together, you often have to interpret and recast its contents. In such cases, you present your interpretation of the source through a long summary:

- through the ideas and information that you choose to emphasize
- through your explanations of ambiguous or contradictory ideas

- through the connections that you make between apparently unrelated ideas
- through the gaps or deficiencies in the author's argument that you may point out

While giving credit to the source and remaining faithful to its ideas, *you will be presenting those ideas in a new and clearer light,* enabling your reader to understand them more easily.

Because your purpose is summary as well as interpretation, you will condense the original material, using selection and emphasis to convey to the reader what is important and what is not. Nevertheless, your version may run almost as long as the original essay. Its contents will be organized according to *your* interpretation of the source's ideas, and the readers will be hearing *your* characteristic voice, not the author's. For these reasons, *the interpretive summary may be regarded as a separate essay in its own right.*

An interpretive summary would be an appropriate strategy in any or all of the following circumstances:

- An essay contains a great many major ideas interwoven together.
- An essay presents a lengthy argument with a step-by-step sequence so complex that, if any stage is omitted, the reader will miss something vital.
- An essay is very disorganized and would benefit from reordering.
- An essay is ambiguous and needs to have certain contradictions pointed out, if not resolved.

When all four of these conditions appear in a single essay, the summarizer would indeed be performing a service by clarifying what is obscure.

Guidelines for Writing an Interpretive Summary

1. After reading the essay once, go through it again slowly, listing each separate idea; as you read each sentence and paragraph, ask yourself whether the new point is individual enough, important enough, and pertinent enough to the essay's main themes to be an entry on your list.

2. Rearrange your list of points into an outline of the essay, following the author's basic strategy.

3. Using your outline of the essay, designate each major entry as a separate paragraph in *your* summary.

4. Plan an introductory paragraph that contains a clear statement of the author's thesis and scope; if you can, include some reference to the author's strategy.

5. As you write each paragraph, include related minor points and a few key details from the original essay, which are to be subordinated to the paragraph's central topic.

When you have studied the five guidelines, read "The Corruption of Sports" and then consider how these guidelines might be applied to Christopher Lasch's essay.

THE CORRUPTION OF SPORTS
Christopher Lasch

Among the activities through which men seek release from everyday life, games offer in many ways the purest form of escape. Like sex, drugs, and drink, they obliterate awareness of everyday reality, not by dimming that awareness but by raising it to a new intensity of concentration. Moreover, games have no side-effects, produce no hangovers or emotional complications. Games satisfy the need for free fantasy and the search for gratuitous difficulty simultaneously; they combine childlike exuberance with deliberately created complications.

By establishing conditions of equality among the players, Roger Caillois says, games attempt to substitute ideal conditions for "the normal confusion of everyday life." They re-create the freedom, the remembered perfection of childhood and mark it off from ordinary life with artificial boundaries, within which the only constraints are the rules to which the players freely submit. Games enlist skill and intelligence, the utmost concentration of purpose, on behalf of utterly useless activities, which make no contribution to the struggle of man against nature, to the wealth or comfort of the community, or to its physical survival.

In communist and fascist countries sports have been organized and promoted by the state. In capitalist countries the uselessness of games make them offensive to social reformers, improvers of public morals, or functionalist critics of society like Veblen, who saw in the futility of upper-class sports anachronistic survivals of militarism and tests of prowess. Yet the "futility" of play, and nothing else, explains its appeal—its artificiality, the arbitrary obstacles it sets up for no other purpose than to challenge the players to surmount them, the absence of any utilitarian or uplifting object. Games quickly lose part of their charm when pressed into the service of education, character development, or social improvement.

Modern industry having reduced most jobs to a routine, games in our society take on added meaning. Men seek in play the difficulties and demands—both intellectual and physical—which they no longer find in work. The history of culture, as Huizinga showed in his classic study of play, Homo Ludens, appears from one perspective to consist of the gradual eradication of the elements of play from all cultural forms—from religion, from the law, from warfare, above all from productive labor. The rationalization of these activities leaves little room for the spirit of arbitrary invention or the disposition to leave things to chance. Risk, daring, and uncertainty, important components of play, have little place in industry or in activities infiltrated by industrial methods, which are intended precisely to predict and control the future and to eliminate risk. Games accordingly have assumed an importance unprecedented even in ancient Greece, where so much of social life revolved around contests. Sports, which satisfy also the starved need for physical exertion—for a renewal of the sense of the physical basis of life—have become an obsession not just of the masses but of those who set themselves up as a cultural elite.

The rise of spectator sports to their present importance coincides historically   5
with the rise of mass production, which intensifies the needs sport satisfies while at the same time creating the technical capacity to promote and market athletic contests to a vast audience. But according to a common criticism of modern sport, these same developments have destroyed the value of athletics. Commercialized play has turned to work, subordinated the athlete's pleasure to the spectator's, and reduced the spectator himself to a state of passivity—the very antithesis of the health and vigor sport ideally promotes. The mania for winning has encouraged an exaggerated emphasis on the competitive side of sport, to the exclusion of the more modest but more satisfying experiences of cooperation and competence. The cult of victory, loudly proclaimed by such football coaches as Vince Lombardi and George Allen, has made savages of the players and rabid chauvinists of their followers. The violence and partisanship of modern sports lead some critics to insist that athletics impart militaristic values to the young, irrationally inculcate local and national pride in the spectator, and serve as one of the strongest bastions of male chauvinism.

Huizinga himself, who anticipated some of these arguments and stated them far   6
more persuasively, argued that modern games and sports had been ruined by a "fatal shift toward over-seriousness." At the same time, he maintained that play had lost its element of ritual, had become "profane," and consequently had ceased to have any "organic connection whatever with the structure of society." The masses now crave "trivial recreation and crude sensationalism" and throw themselves into these pursuits with an intensity far beyond their intrinsic merit. Instead of playing with the freedom and intensity of children, they play with the "blend of adolescence and barbarity" that Huizinga calls puerilism, investing games with patriotic and martial fervor while treating serious pursuits as if they were games. "A far-reaching contamination of play and serious activity has taken place," according to Huizinga:

> The two spheres are getting mixed. In the activities of an outwardly serious nature hides an element of play. Recognized play, on the other hand, is no longer able to maintain its true play-character as a result of being taken too seriously and being technically over-organised. The indispensable qualities of detachment, artlessness, and gladness are thus lost.

An analysis of the criticism of modern sport, in its vulgar form as well as in Hui-   7
zinga's more refined version, brings to light a number of common misconceptions about modern society. A large amount of writing on sports has accumulated in recent years, and the sociology of sport has even entrenched itself as a minor branch of social science. Much of this commentary has no higher purpose than to promote

athletics or to exploit the journalistic market they have created, but some of it aspires to social criticism. Those who have formulated the now familiar indictment of organized sport include the sociologist Harry Edwards; the psychologist and former tennis player Dorcas Susan Butt, who thinks sports should promote "competence" instead of competition; disillusioned professional athletes like Dave Meggyesy and Chip Oliver; and radical critics of culture and society, notably Paul Hoch and Jack Scott.

Critics of sport, in their eagerness to uncover evidence of corruption and decline, attack intrinsic elements of athletics, elements essential to their appeal in all periods and places, on the erroneous assumption that spectatorship, violence, and competition reflect conditions peculiar to modern times. On the other hand, they overlook the distinctive contribution of contemporary society to the degradation of sport and therefore misconceive the nature of that degradation. They concentrate on issues, such as "over-seriousness," that are fundamental to an understanding of sports, indeed to the very definition of play, but that are peripheral or irrelevant to the ways they have changed in recent history.   8

Take the common complaint that modern sports are "spectator-oriented rather than participant-oriented." Spectators, in this view, are irrelevant to the success of the game. What a naive theory of human motivation this implies! The attainment of certain skills unavoidably gives rise to an urge to show them off. At a higher level of mastery, the performer no longer wishes merely to display his virtuosity—for the true connoisseur can easily distinguish between the performer who plays to the crowd and the superior artist who matches himself against the full rigor of his art itself—but to ratify a supremely difficult accomplishment; to give pleasure; to forge a bond between himself and his audience, a shared appreciation of a ritual executed not only flawlessly but with much feeling and with a sense of style and proportion.   9

In all games, particularly in athletic contexts, the central importance of display and representation serves as a reminder of the ancient connections between play, ritual, and drama. The players not only compete, they enact a familiar ceremony that reaffirms common values. Ceremony requires witnesses: enthusiastic spectators conversant with the rules of the performance and its underlying meaning. Far from destroying the value of sports, the attendance of spectators is often necessary to them. Indeed one of the virtues of contemporary sports lies in their resistance to the erosion of standards and their capacity to appeal to a knowledgeable audience. Norman Podhoretz has argued that the sports public remains more discriminating than the public for the arts and that in sports "excellence is relatively uncontroversial as a judgment of performance." The public for sports still consists largely of men who took part in sports during boyhood and thus acquired a sense of the game and a capacity to make discriminating judgments.   10

The same can hardly be said for the audience of an artistic performance, even though amateur musicians, dancers, actors, and painters may still comprise a small nucleus of the audience. Constant experimentation in the arts, in any case, has cre-   11 ated so much confusion about standards that the only surviving measure of excellence, for many, is novelty and shock-value, which in a jaded time often resides in a work's sheer ugliness or banality. In sport, on the other hand, novelty and rapid shifts of fashion play only a small part in its appeal to a discriminating audience.

Yet even here, the contamination of standards has already begun. Faced with rising costs, owners seek to increase attendance at sporting events by installing exploding scoreboards, broadcasting recorded cavalry charges, giving away helmets and bats, and surrounding the spectator with cheerleaders, usherettes, and ball girls. Television has enlarged the audience for sports while lowering the quality of that audience's understanding; at least this is the assumption of sports commentators, who direct at the audience an interminable stream of tutelage in the basics of the game, and of the promoters, who reshape one game after another to conform to the tastes of an audience supposedly incapable of grasping their finer points. 12

The American League's adoption of the designated hitter rule, which relieves pitchers of the need to bat and diminishes the importance of managerial strategy, provides an especially blatant example of the dilution of sports by the requirements of mass promotion. Another example is the "Devil-Take-the-Hindmost Mile," a track event invented by the San Francisco Examiner, in which the last runner in the early stages of the race has to drop out—a rule that encourages an early scramble to avoid disqualification but lowers the general quality of the event. When the television networks discovered surfing, they insisted that events be held according to a prearranged schedule, without regard to weather conditions. A surfer complained, "Television is destroying our sport. The TV producers are turning a sport and an art form into a circus." The same practices produce the same effects on other sports, forcing baseball players, for example, to play World Series games on freezing October evenings. Substituting artificial surfaces for grass in tennis, which has slowed the pace of the game, placed a premium on reliability and patience, and reduced the element of tactical brilliance and overpowering speed, commends itself to television producers because it makes tennis an all-weather game and even permits it to be played indoors, in sanctuaries of sport like Caesar's Palace in Las Vegas. 13

As spectators become less knowledgeable about the games they watch, they become more sensation-minded and bloodthirsty. The rise of violence in ice hockey, far beyond the point where it plays any functional part in the game, coincided with the expansion of professional hockey into cities without any traditional attachment to the sport—cities in which weather conditions, indeed, had always precluded any such tradition of local play. But the significance of such changes is not, as such critics as Jack Scott and Paul Hoch imagine, that sports ought to be organized solely for the edification of the players and that corruption sets in when sports begin to be played to spectators for a profit. It is often true that sport at this point ceases to be enjoyable and becomes a business. Recent critics go astray, however, in supposing that organized athletics ever serve the interests of the players alone or that "professionalization" inevitably corrupts all who take part in it. 14

In glorifying amateurism, equating spectatorship with passivity, and deploring   15
competition, recent criticism of sport echoes the fake radicalism of the counter-
culture, from which so much of it derives. It shows its contempt for excellence by
proposing to break down the "elitist" distinction between players and spectators. It
proposes to replace competitive professional sports, which notwithstanding their
shortcomings uphold standards of competence and bravery that might otherwise
become extinct, with a bland regimen of cooperative diversions in which everyone
can join in, regardless of age or ability—"new sports for the noncompetitive," having "no object, really," according to a typical effusion, except to bring "people together to enjoy each other." In its eagerness to strip from sport the elements that
have always explained its imaginative appeal, the staged rivalry of superior ability,
this "radicalism" proposes merely to complete the degradation already begun by
the very society the cultural radicals profess to criticize and subvert.

What corrupts an athletic performance, as it does any other performance, is not   16
professionalism or competition but the presence of an unappreciative, ignorant
audience and the need to divert it with sensations extrinsic to the performance.
It is at this point that ritual, drama, and sports all degenerate into spectacle. Huizinga's analysis of the secularization of sport helps to clarify this issue. In the degree to which athletic events lose the element of ritual and public festivity,
according to Huizinga, they deteriorate into "trivial recreation and crude sensationalism." But even Huizinga misunderstands the cause of this development. It
hardly lies in the "fatal shift toward over-seriousness." Huizinga himself, when he is
writing about the theory of play rather than the collapse of "genuine play" in our
own time, understands very well that play at its best is always serious; indeed that
the essence of play lies in taking seriously activities that have no purpose, serve no
utilitarian ends. He reminds us that "the majority of Greek contests were fought
out in deadly earnest" and discusses, under the category of play, duels in which
contestants fight to the death, water sports in which the goal is to drown your opponent, and tournaments for which the training and preparation consume the athletes' entire existence.

The degradation of sport, then, consists not in its being taken too seriously but   17
in its subjection to some ulterior purpose, such as profit-making, patriotism, moral
training, or the pursuit of health. Sport may give rise to these things in abundance,
but ideally it produces them only as by-products having no essential connection
with the game. When the game itself, on the other hand, comes to be regarded as
incidental to the benefits it supposedly confers on participants, spectators, or promoters, it loses its peculiar capacity to transport both participant and spectator
beyond everyday experience—to provide a glimpse of perfect order uncontami-
nated by commonplace calculations of advantage or even by ordinary considerations of survival.

*1. After reading the essay once, go through it again slowly, listing each
separate idea. As you read each sentence and paragraph, ask yourself*

whether the new point is individual enough, important enough, and pertinent enough to the essay's main themes to be an entry on your list.

Since "The Corruption of Sports" is a very complex essay, the listing of ideas becomes an especially crucial step. A preliminary reading suggests that Christopher Lasch is chiefly concerned with the contrast between *the original life-enhancing purpose of sports* and *the commercialization and sensationalism that characterize sports today.*

To prepare for your summary, you must exclude (or list separately) any points, interesting in themselves, that are only loosely connected to Lasch's central themes. The numerous references to Huizinga are a good example: while Huizinga's classic work certainly provides an excellent background for understanding Lasch, he cites Huizinga only to provide evidence in support of his own points. The excerpts from Huizinga are not intended to be central ideas in their own right, so they can be excluded from your list.

As you write the list of ideas, *try to make each entry a complete sentence in your own words.* When you retain the original wording, you may be including phrases that sound good but do not actually stand for coherent ideas. Remember also that you will not necessarily find a new idea in every paragraph, and some paragraphs will contain more than one idea worth listing. Here is one student's summary list in the order of appearance in the essay (with each relevant paragraph number cited):

a. One of the functions of sports is to provide escape. (1)

b. Sports heighten the mind and the senses; they are activities that require concentration, yet are relaxing. (1)

c. Sports provide an opportunity to live out one's fantasies. (1)

d. It is a characteristic of games that they should be played in artificial, almost ideal circumstances, in which the players are theoretically equal. (2)

e. Games should be essentially purposeless, lacking reality and with no connection to the real world or usefulness to society. (2) (3)

f. Games provide an artificial challenge not found in modern working life, a sense of controlled risk and danger. (4)

g. Sports give people an opportunity to exercise, to regain contact with their physical selves. (4)

h. Sports have been commercialized and are now more like work than play. (5)

i. The need to make sports profitable has made it vital to gather together the largest possible audience; spectators now tend to be passive, rather than interested participants. (5)

j. Sports now emphasize victory at all costs, which encourages violence and unsportsmanlike tactics, and competition at the expense of teamwork and skill. (5)

k. Spectators now tend to be partisans and regard players and teams as "my side" and "the other side," something that can have unpleasant militaristic overtones. (5) (6)

l. Spectators have always been essential to the success of sport, as audiences appreciate the players' skill and artistry. (9)

m. Sports have a social function as the ritual enactment of shared beliefs and values, which is why audience participation is so important. (10)

n. A knowledgeable audience can be used to maintain high standards of playing. (10)

o. To attract the largest possible audience, organizers need to satisfy people in the quickest, easiest way; audiences these days are very unsophisticated and have not been encouraged to expect a high standard of play. (12)

p. The present emphasis on victory and lethal competition results from the belief that only an appeal to primitive emotions will ensure spectator interest. (13) (14)

q. Some people suggest that a return to amateur sports would solve the problem, since there would be less commercialization and less need for violent competition, but the loss of the competitive spirit would be just as corrupting to sports as commercialization has been. (15)

r. The importance of sports in our lives is related to their ability to be played as an end in itself, apart from the everyday concerns of the world; when they are used to fulfill a social, political, or economic function, then it gets corrupted. (17)

2. Rearrange your list of points into an outline of the essay, following the author's basic strategy.

3. Using your outline of the essay, designate each major entry as a separate paragraph in your summary.

The outlining of the source essay and the paragraphing of your own essay are actually part of the same process. (To review the procedure for outlining a complex essay, see Chapter 1, pp. 42–47.) After reviewing your list of central ideas, you should realize that the essay breaks into *two overlapping parts.*

- The first six paragraphs contain a description of the original purposes of sports, emphasizing the degree to which games provide a safe and relaxing means of escaping from the realities of daily life;
- The next eight paragraphs contain an analysis of the ways in which these purposes have been commercialized and corrupted. Toward the end, in paragraphs 15 and 17, Lasch considers how sports might be restored to their original wholesome and therapeutic functions.

Essentially, Lasch is working with *two strategies.* First, he is presenting a contrast between sports in the past and sports in the present, *a before-and-after comparison.* As an experiment, you might try to organize an interpretation around this strategy by selecting and rearranging certain items on your list.

Sports: Original Function	Sports: Present Function
a. One of the functions of sports is to provide escape.	h. Sports have been commercialized and are now more like work than play.
b. Sports heighten the mind and the senses; they are activities that require concentration, yet are relaxing.	
c. Sports provide an opportunity to live out one's fantasies.	
e. Games should be essentially purposeless, lacking in reality and with no connection to the real world of usefulness in society.	j. Sports now emphasize victory at all costs, which encourages violence and unsportsmanlike tactics.
f. Games provide an artificial challenge not found in modern working life, a sense of controlled risk and danger.	
d. It is characteristic of games that they should be played in artificial, almost ideal circumstances, in which the players are theoretically equal.	k. Spectators now tend to be partisans.
m. Sports have a social function as the ritual enactment of shared values.	i. Spectators now tend to be passive.

When you look at these lists, you immediately notice that *the comparison is not well-balanced:* you have many more items on the "original function" side than you have on the "present function" side. This imbalance does not result from lack of interest, for Lasch devotes more than half his essay (and the title) to describing how corrupt sports have become. Indeed, *what really occurs halfway through the essay is that Lasch switches his strategy.*

After starting with a straightforward description of the purposes of sport, focusing on the players, he shifts to an analysis of the reasons why these purposes can no longer be carried out. That shift results in a *parallel change of focus from the players to the spectators.* In Lasch's view, the corruption of the spectators, primarily for economic reasons, has brought about the corruption of the players and of the various sports themselves. At the end of the essay, he suggests educating a more active and knowledgeable audience, one composed of participants rather than mere spectators.

To present this *second strategy* in your essay, you have to rearrange your list again, selecting only those items that contribute to an understanding of the *problem and its possible solution.* In this outline, the numbers in parentheses again represent paragraphs in the original essay.

I.   Ideal: Sports as they should be

    A.   One function of sports is to provide escape. (1)

        1.   Sports provide an opportunity to live out one's fantasies. (1)

    B.   Games should be essentially purposeless, lacking reality and with no connection to the real world or usefulness to society. (2) (3)

        1.   Games provide an artificial challenge not found in modern working life, a sense of controlled risk and danger. (4)

        2.   It is a characteristic of games that they should be played in artificial, almost ideal circumstances, in which the players are theoretically equal. (2)

    C.   Sports have a social function as the ritual enactment of shared beliefs and values, which is why audience participation is so important. (10)

        1.   Spectators have always been essential to the success of sports, as audiences appreciate the players' skill and artistry. (9)

II. Problem: Sports as they are today

    A.   The need to make sports profitable has made it vital to gather together the largest possible audience; spectators now tend to be passive, rather than interested participants. (5)

    B.   To attract the largest possible audience, organizers need to satisfy people in the quickest, easiest way; audiences these days are very unsophisticated and have not been encouraged to expect a high standard of play. (12)

1. The present emphasis on victory and lethal competition results from the belief that only an appeal to primitive emotions will ensure spectator interest. (13) (14)

2. Sports now emphasize victory at all costs, which encourages violence and unsportsmanlike tactics, and competition at the expense of teamwork and skill. (5)

C. Spectators now tend to be partisans and regard players and teams as "my side" and "the other side," something that can have unpleasant militaristic overtones. (5) (6)

III. Solution: Making sports "free" again

A. Some people suggest that a return to amateur sports would solve the problem, since there would be less commercialization and less need for violent competition, but the loss of the competitive spirit would be just as corrupting to sport as commercialization has been. (15)

B. A knowledgeable audience can be used to maintain high standards of playing. (10)

C. The importance of sports in our lives is related to their ability to be played as ends in themselves, apart from everyday concerns of the world; when they are used to fulfill a social, political, or economic function, sports are corrupted. (17)

You will observe that two points on the original list (b and g) have been omitted from this outline; physical relaxation as a reason for participating in sports does not really belong in an interpretation that emphasizes spectators as well as players. Also, related points have been grouped together for inclusion in individual paragraphs.

4. Plan an introductory paragraph that contains a clear statement of the author's thesis and scope; if you can, include some reference to the author's strategy.

Make sure that your introduction provides a fair account of Lasch's purpose. Some summarizers go beyond their legitimate function as interpreters of the original essay and wander off into digressions that the author did not include or intend. Here is the beginning of an introduction in which *the summarizer's own views are attributed to Christopher Lasch:*

> According to Christopher Lasch, it is no longer worthwhile for a spectator to attend sports events because the players and teams are interested only in profit. The average baseball, football, or tennis star is eager to become a millionaire as quickly as possible. Lasch thinks that these greedy individuals are corrupting sports and providing audiences with a poor show.

This writer is manipulating Lasch's ideas in order to write an argumentative essay of her own. She starts out by changing Lasch's emphasis and attributing the problem to the players rather than the organizers. Later in the essay, it might be appropriate to disagree with the author, provided that it is made clear who is responsible for which point of view. But in an introduction, such a statement can only create an initial false impression for the reader.

Here is an introduction in which the scope, purpose, and strategy of Lasch's essay are described more objectively:

> In "The Corruption of Sports," Christopher Lasch sets out to explore the reasons why so many sports and games have become unpleasant, even violent confrontations, with bloodthirsty spectators cheering on players and teams that try to pulverize the opposition, not just win the game. After describing the traditional spirit of sports, with participants appreciating skill as well as power, Lasch analyzes the ways in which the emphasis on profits has resulted in a new kind of audience and a new kind of player. This problem of corruption in sports can be solved, he concludes, only if games are once again played purely for their own sake, rather than to serve an economic or social function.

5. As you write each paragraph, include related minor points and a few key details from the original essay, which are to be subordinated to the paragraph's central topic.

You need to convey to your reader some sense of the supporting materials that were provided in the original text. Although the actual writing of the summary's paragraphs ought to be relatively easy once the strategy and outline have been established, there are a few pitfalls to avoid. For example, *you may pull a minor point out of the context of accompanying ideas and misinterpret it.* One summarizer cites the rising incidence of violence in ice hockey, which Lasch discusses in Paragraph 14:

> Lasch thinks that ice hockey should be played only in the cold-weather cities where it originated; in other places, more violent kinds of playing are encouraged.

In fact, Lasch does not favor restricting the locations for playing ice hockey; he is merely commenting on the higher quality of play that occurs in places where the audiences are more knowledgeable. By all means *use the examples that the author provides, but be careful to interpret them correctly.* And *do not hesitate to include illustrations of your own.* You might, for example, raise the issue of the Olympics and the way in which television coverage tends to encourage support for national teams rather than admiration for fine athletes of all nations.

Other equally serious problems can arise from a confusion between the author and his sources. Since Lasch generally agrees with Huizinga and frequently cites the latter's theories as evidence for his own ideas, you might be tempted to attribute to Lasch Huizinga's argument (in Paragraph 6) that sports have become excessively serious and are no longer sufficiently linked to the fabric of society. However, Lasch recognizes this as a point of disagreement between himself and Huizinga—and says so later in the essay, in Paragraph 16.

While they may not all be equally important, there are three points of view represented in your essay—Lasch's, Huizinga's, and your own. The reader must be made aware of the boundary lines dividing these three points of view. Writers of successful interpretive summaries will integrate but not confuse their own opinions, those of the original authors, and those of the sources cited by the original authors.

ASSIGNMENT 5

Write an interpretive summary of "The New Sovereignty." Before taking the first step and writing a list of ideas, consider why this essay needs and deserves to be interpreted at length.

THE NEW SOVEREIGNTY
Shelby Steele

Toward the end of a talk I gave recently at a large midwestern university, I noticed a distinct tension in the audience. All respectful audiences are quiet, but I've come to understand that when there is disagreement with what's being said at the podium the silence can become pure enough to constitute a statement. Fidgeting and whispering cease, pencils stay still in notetakers' hands—you sense the quiet filling your pauses as a sign of disquiet, even resistance. A speaker can feel ganged-up on by such a silence. 1

I had gotten myself into this spot by challenging the orthodoxy of diversity that is now so common on university campuses—not the *notion* of diversity, which I wholly subscribe to, but the rigid means by which it is pursued. I had told the students and faculty members on hand that in the late 1960s, without much public debate but with many good intentions, America had embarked upon one of the most dramatic social experiments in its history. The federal government, radically and officially, began to alter and expand the concept of entitlement in America. Rights to justice and to government benefits were henceforth to be extended not simply to individuals but to racial, ethnic, and other groups. Moreover, the essential basis of all entitlement in America—the guarantees of the Constitution—had apparently been found wanting; there was to be redress and reparation of past grievances, and the Constitution had nothing to say about that. 2

I went on to explain that Martin Luther King and the early civil rights leaders had demanded only constitutional rights; they had been found wanting, too. By the late sixties, among a new set of black leaders, there had developed a presumption of collective entitlement (based on the redress of past grievances) that made blacks eligible for rights beyond those provided for in the Constitution, and thus beyond those afforded the nation's non-black citizens. Thanks to the civil rights movement, 3 a young black citizen as well as a young white citizen could not be turned away from a college because of the color of his or her skin; by the early seventies a young black citizen, poor or wealthy, now qualified for certain grants and scholarships—might even be accepted for admission—simply *because* of the color of his or her skin. I made the point that this new and rather unexamined principle of collective entitlement had led America to pursue a democracy of groups as well as of individuals—that collective entitlement enfranchised groups just as the Constitution enfranchised individuals.

It was when I introduced a concept I call the New Sovereignty that my audience's   4
silence became most audible. In America today, I said, sovereignty—that is, power to act autonomously—is bestowed upon any group that is able to construct itself around a perceived grievance. With the concept of collective entitlement now accepted not only at the federal level but casually at all levels of society, any aggrieved group—and, for that matter, any assemblage of citizens that might or might not have previously been thought of as such a group—could make its case, attract attention and funding, and build a constituency that, in turn, would increase attention and funding. Soon this organized group of aggrieved citizens would achieve sovereignty, functioning within our long-sovereign nation and negotiating with that nation for a separate, exclusive set of entitlements. And here I pointed to America's university campuses, where, in the name of their grievances, blacks, women, Hispanics, Asians, Native Americans, gays, and lesbians had hardened into sovereign constituencies that vied for the entitlements of sovereignty—separate "studies" departments for each group, "ethnic" theme dorms, preferential admissions and financial aid policies, a proportionate number of faculty of their own group, separate student lounges and campus centers, and so on. This push for equality among groups, I said, necessarily made for an inequality among individuals that prepared the ground for precisely the racial, gender, and ethnic divisiveness that, back in the sixties, we all said we wanted to move beyond.

At the reception that followed the talk I was approached by a tall, elegant woman   5
who introduced herself as the chairperson of the women's studies department. Anger and the will to be polite were at war in her face so that her courteous smile at times became a leer. She wanted to "inform" me that she was proud of the fact that women's studies was a separate department at her university. I asked her what could be studied in this department that could not be studied in other departments. Take the case of, say, Virginia Woolf: in what way would a female academic teaching in a women's studies department have a different approach to Woolf's writing than a woman professor in the English department? Above her determined smile her eyes became fierce. "You must know as a black that they won't accept us"—meaning women, blacks, presumably others—"in the English department. It's an oppressive environment for women scholars. We're not taken seriously there." I asked her if that wasn't all the more reason to be there, to fight the good fight, and to work to have the contributions of women broaden the entire discipline of literary studies. She said I was naive. I said her strategy left the oppressiveness she

talked about unchallenged. She said it was a waste of valuable energy to spend time fighting "old white males." I said that if women were oppressed, there was nothing to do *but* fight.

We each held tiny paper plates with celery sticks and little bricks of cheese, and I'm sure much body language was subdued by the tea party postures these plates imposed on us. But her last word was not actually a word. It was a look. She parodied an epiphany of disappointment in herself, as if she'd caught herself in a bizarre foolishness. *Of course, this guy is the enemy. He is the very oppressiveness I'm talking about. How could I have missed it?* And so, suddenly comfortable in the understanding that I was hopeless, she let her smile become gracious. Grace was something she could afford now. An excuse was made, a hand extended, and then she was gone. Holding my little plate, I watched her disappear into the crowd.

Today there are more than five hundred separate women's studies departments or programs in American colleges and universities. There are nearly four hundred independent black studies departments or programs, and hundreds of Hispanic, Asian, and Native American programs. Given this degree of entrenchment, it is no wonder this woman found our little debate a waste of time. She would have had urgent administrative tasks awaiting her attention—grant proposals to write, budget requests to work up, personnel matters to attend to. And suppose I had won the debate? Would she have rushed back to her office and begun to dismantle the women's studies department by doling out its courses and faculty to long-standing departments like English and history? Would she have given her secretary notice and relinquished her office equipment? I don't think so.

I do think I know how it all came to this—how what began as an attempt to address the very real grievances of women wound up creating newly sovereign fiefdoms like this women's studies department. First there was collective entitlement to redress the grievances, which in turn implied a sovereignty for the grievance group, since sovereignty is only the formalization of collective entitlement. Then, since sovereignty requires autonomy, there had to be a demand for separate and independent stature within the university (or some other institution of society). There would have to be a separate territory, with the trappings that certify sovereignty and are concrete recognition of the grievance identity—a building or suite of offices, a budget, faculty, staff, office supplies, letterhead, et cetera.

And so the justification for separate women's and ethnic studies programs has virtually nothing to do with strictly academic matters and everything to do with the kind of group-identity politics in which the principle of collective entitlement has resulted. My feeling is that there can be no full redress of the woeful neglect of women's intellectual contributions until those contributions are entirely integrated into the very departments that neglected them in the first place. The same is true for America's minorities. Only inclusion answers history's exclusion. But now the sovereignty of grievance-group identities has confused all this.

It was the sovereignty issue that squelched my talk with the women's studies chairperson. She came to see me as an enemy not because I denied that women

6

7

8

9

10

writers had been neglected historically; I was the enemy because my questions challenged the territorial sovereignty of her department and of the larger grievance identity of women. It was not a matter of fairness—of justice—but of power. She would not put it that way, of course. For in order to rule over her sovereign fiefdom it remains important that she seem to represent the powerless, the aggrieved. It remains important, too, that my objection to the New Sovereignty can be interpreted by her as sexist. When I failed to concede sovereignty, I became an enemy of women.

In our age of the New Sovereignty the original grievances—those having to do with fundamental questions such as basic rights—have in large measure been addressed, if not entirely redressed. But that is of little matter now. The sovereign fiefdoms are ends in themselves—providing career tracks and bases of power. This power tends to be used now mostly to defend and extend the fiefdom, often by exaggerating and exploiting secondary, amorphous, or largely symbolic complaints. In this way, America has increasingly become an uneasy federation of newly sovereign nations.   11

In *The True Believer,* Eric Hoffer wrote presciently of this phenomenon I have come to call the New Sovereignty: "When a mass movement begins to attract people who are interested in their individual careers, it is a sign that it has passed its vigorous stage; that it is no longer engaged in molding a new world but in possessing and preserving the present. It ceases then to be a movement and becomes an enterprise."   12

If it is true that great mass movements begin as spontaneous eruptions of long-smoldering discontent, it is also true that after significant reform is achieved they do not like to pass away or even modify their grievance posture. The redressing of the movement's grievances wins legitimacy for the movement. Reform, in this way, also means recognition for those who struggled for it. The movement's leaders are quoted in the papers, appear on TV, meet with elected officials, write books—they come to embody the movement. Over time, they and they alone speak for the aggrieved; and, of course, they continue to speak *of* the aggrieved, adding fresh grievances to the original complaint. It is their vocation now, and their means to status and power. The idealistic reformers thus become professional spokespersons for the seemingly permanently aggrieved. In the civil rights movement, suits and briefcases replaced the sharecropper's denim of the early years, and $500-a-plate fundraisers for the National Association for the Advancement of Colored People replaced volunteers and picket signs. The raucous bra burning of late sixties feminism gave way to women's studies departments and direct-mail campaigns by the National Organization of Women.   13

This sort of evolution, however natural it may appear, is not without problems for the new grievance-group executive class. The winning of reform will have dissipated much of the explosive urgency that started the movement; yet the new institutionalized movement cannot justify its existence without this urgency. The problem   14 becomes one of maintaining a reformist organization after considerable reforms have been won.

To keep alive the urgency needed to justify itself, the grievance organization will do three things. First, it will work to inspire a perpetual sense of grievance in its constituency so that grievance becomes the very centerpiece of the group itself. To be black, or a woman, or gay, is, in the eyes of the NAACP, NOW, or Act Up, to be essentially threatened, victimized, apart from the rest of America. Second, these organizations will up the ante on what constitutes a grievance by making support of sovereignty itself the new test of grievance. If the women's studies program has not been made autonomous, this constitutes a grievance. If the National Council of La Raza hasn't been consulted, Hispanics have been ignored. The third strategy of grievance organizations is to arrange their priorities in a way that will maximize their grievance profile. Often their agendas will be established more for their grievance potential than for the actual betterment of the group. Those points at which there is resistance in the larger society to the group's entitlement demands will usually be made into top-priority issues, thereby emphasizing the status of victim and outsider necessary to sustain the sovereign organization.

Thus, at its 1989 convention, the NAACP put affirmative action at the very top of its agenda. Never mind the fact that studies conducted by both proponents and opponents of affirmative action indicate the practice has very little real impact on the employment and advancement of blacks. Never mind, too, that surveys show most black Americans do not consider racial preferences *their* priority. In its wisdom the NAACP thought (and continues to think) that the national mood against affirmative action programs is a bigger problem for black men and women than teen pregnancy, or the disintegrating black family, or black-on-black crime. Why? Because the very resistance affirmative action meets from the larger society makes it an issue of high grievance potential. Affirmative action can generate the urgency that justifies black sovereignty far more than issues like teen pregnancy or high dropout rates, which carry no load of collective entitlement and which the *entire* society sees as serious problems.

In the women's movement, too, the top-priority issues have been those with the highest grievance potential. I think so much effort and resources went into the now-failed Equal Rights Amendment because, in large part, it carried a tremendous load of collective entitlement (a constitutional amendment for a specific group rather than for all citizens) and because it faced great resistance from the larger society. It was a win-win venture for the women's movement. If it succeeded there would be a great bounty of collective entitlement; if it failed, as it did, the failure could be embraced as a grievance—an indication of America's continuing unwillingness to assure equality for women. *America does not want to allow us in!*—that is how the defeat of the ERA could be interpreted by NOW executives and by female English professors eager to run their own departments; the defeat of the ERA was a boon for the New Sovereignty.

I also believe this quest for sovereignty at least partially explains the leap of abortion rights to the very top of the feminist agenda on the heels of the ERA's failure. Abortion has always been an extremely divisive, complex, and emotionally charged issue. And for this reason it is also an issue of enormous grievance potential for the women's movement—assuming it can be framed solely in terms of female grievance. My own belief is that abortion is a valid and important issue for the women's movement to take up, and I completely support the pro-choice position the movement advocates. However, I think women's organizations like NOW have framed the issue in territorial terms in order to maximize its grievance potential. When they make women's control of their own bodies the very centerpiece of their argument for choice, they are making the fact of pregnancy the *exclusive* terrain of women, despite the obvious role of men in conception and despite the fact that the vast majority of married women deciding to have abortions reach their decisions with their husbands. Framed exclusively as a woman's right, abortion becomes not a societal issue or even a family issue but a grievance issue in the ongoing struggle of the women's movement. Can women's organizations continue to frame pro-choice as a grievance issue—a question of a right—and expect to garner the votes in Congress or in the state legislatures, which is where the abortion question is headed? 18

I don't think this framing of the issue as a right is as much about abortion as it is about the sovereignty and permanency of women's organizations. The trick is exclusivity. If you can make the issue exclusively yours—within your territory of final authority—then all who do not capitulate are aggrieving you. And then, of course, you must rally and expand your organization to meet all this potential grievance. 19

But this is a pattern that ultimately puts grievance organizations out of touch with their presumed constituencies, who grow tired of the hyperbole. I think it partially explains why so many young women today resist the feminist label and why the membership rolls of the NAACP have fallen so sharply in recent years, particularly among the young. The high grievance profile is being seen for what it mostly is—a staying-in-business strategy. 20

How did America evolve its now rather formalized notion that groups of its citizens could be entitled collectively? I think it goes back to the most fundamental contradiction in American life. From the beginning America has been a pluralistic society, and one drawn to a radical form of democracy—emphasizing the freedom and equality of *individuals*—that could meld such diversity into a coherent nation. In this new nation no group would lord it over any other. But, of course, beneath this America of its ideals there was from the start a much meaner reality, one whose very existence mocked the notion of a nation made singular by the equality of its individuals. By limiting democracy to their own kind—white, male landowners—the Founding Fathers collectively entitled themselves and banished all others to the edges and underside of American life. There, individual entitlement was either curtailed or—in the case of slavery—extinguished. 21

The genius of the civil rights movement that changed the fabric of American life   22
in the late 1950s and early 1960s was its profound understanding that the enemy of
black Americans was not the ideal America but the unspoken principle of collective
entitlement that had always put the lie to true democracy. This movement, which
came to center stage from America's underside and margins, had as its single, overriding goal the eradication of white entitlement. And, correspondingly, it exhibited
a belief in democratic principles at least as strong as that of the Founding Fathers,
who themselves had emerged from the (less harsh) margins of English society. In
this sense the civil rights movement reenacted the American Revolution, and its
paramount leader, Martin Luther King, spoke as twentieth-century America's greatest democratic voice.

All of this was made clear to me for the umpteenth time by my father on a very   23
cold Saturday afternoon in 1959. There was a national campaign under way to integrate the lunch counters at Woolworth stores, and my father, who was more a
persuader than an intimidator, had made it a point of honor that I join him on the
picket line, civil rights being nothing less than the religion of our household. By this
time, age twelve or so, I was sick of it. I'd had enough of watching my parents heading off to still another meeting or march; I'd heard too many tedious discussions on
everything from the philosophy of passive resistance to the symbolism of going to
jail. Added to this, my own experience of picket lines and peace marches had impressed upon me what so many people who've partaken of these activities know:
that in themselves they can be crushingly boring—around and around and around
holding a sign, watching one's own feet fall, feeling the minutes like hours. All that
Saturday morning I hid from my father and tried to convince myself of what I longed
for—that he would get so busy that if he didn't forget the march he would at least
forget me.

He forgot nothing. I did my time on the picket line, but not without building up   24
enough resentment to start a fight on the way home. What was so important about
integration? We had never even wanted to eat at Woolworth's. I told him the truth,
that he never took us to *any* restaurants anyway, claiming always that they charged
too much money for bad food. But he said calmly that he was proud of me for
marching and that he knew *I* knew food wasn't the point.

My father—forty years a truck driver, with the urges of an intellectual—went on   25
to use my little rebellion as the occasion for a discourse, in this case on the concept of integration. Integration had little to do with merely rubbing shoulders with
white people, eating bad food beside them. It was about the right to go absolutely
anywhere white people could go being the test of freedom and equality. To be anywhere they could be and do anything they could do was the point. Like it or not,
white people defined the horizon of freedom in America, and if you couldn't touch
their shoulder you weren't free. For him integration was the *evidence* of freedom
and equality.

My father was a product of America's margins, as were all the blacks in the early   26
civil rights movement, leaders and foot soldiers alike. For them integration was a

way of moving from the margins into the mainstream. Today there is considerable ambivalence about integration, but in that day it was nothing less than democracy itself. Integration is also certainly about racial harmony, but it is more fundamentally about the ultimate extension of democracy—beyond the racial entitlements that contradict it. The idea of racial integration is quite simply the most democratic principle America has evolved, since all other such principles depend on its reality and are diminished by its absence.

But the civil rights movement did not account for one thing: the tremendous release of black anger that would follow its victories. The 1964 Civil Rights Act and the 1965 Voting Rights Act were, on one level, admissions of guilt by American society that it had practiced white entitlement at the expense of all others. When the oppressors admit their crimes, the oppressed can give full vent to their long repressed rage because now there is a moral consensus between oppressor and oppressed that a wrong was done. This consensus gave blacks the license to release a rage that was three centuries deep, a rage that is still today everywhere visible, a rage that—in the wake of the Rodney King verdict, a verdict a vast majority of all Americans thought unfair—fueled the worst rioting in recent American history.   27

By the mid-sixties, the democratic goal of integration was no longer enough to appease black anger. Suddenly for blacks there was a sense that far more was owed, that a huge bill was due. And for many whites there was also the feeling that some kind of repayment was truly in order. This was the moral logic that followed inevitably from the new consensus. But it led to an even simpler logic: if blacks had been oppressed collectively, that oppression would now be redressed by entitling them collectively. So here we were again, in the name of a thousand good intentions, falling away from the hard challenge of a democracy of individuals and embracing the principle of collective entitlement that had so corrupted the American ideal in the first place. Now this old sin would be applied in the name of uplift. And this made an easy sort of sense. If it was good enough for whites for three hundred years, why not let blacks have a little of it to get ahead? In the context of the sixties—black outrage and white guilt—a principle we had just decided was evil for whites was redefined as a social good for blacks. And once the formula was in place for blacks, it could be applied to other groups with similar grievances. By the 1970s more than 60 percent of the American population—not only blacks but Hispanics, women, Asians—would come under the collective entitlement of affirmative action.   28

In the early days of the civil rights movement, the concept of solidarity was essentially a moral one. That is, all people who believed in human freedom, fairness, and equality were asked to form a solid front against white entitlement. But after the collaboration of black outrage and white guilt made collective entitlement a social remedy, the nature of solidarity changed. It was no longer the rallying of diverse peoples to breach an oppressive group entitlement. It was the very opposite: a rallying of people within a grievance group to pursue their own group entitlement. As   29 early as the mid-sixties, whites were made unwelcome in the civil rights movement, just as, by the mid-seventies, men were no longer welcome in the women's movement. Eventually, collective entitlement *always* requires separatism. And the irony is obvious: those who once had been the victims of separatism, who had sacrificed so dearly to overcome their being at the margins, would later create an ethos of their own separatism. After the sixties, solidarity became essentially a separatist concept, an exclusionary principle. One no longer heard words like "integration" or "harmony"; one heard about "anger" and "power." Integration is anathema to grievance groups for precisely the same reason it was anathema to racist whites in the civil rights era: because it threatens their collective entitlement by insisting that no group be entitled over another. Power is where it's at today—power to set up the organization, attract the following, run the fiefdom.

But it must also be said that this could not have come to pass without the cooperation of the society at large and its institutions. Why did the government, the public and private institutions, the corporations and foundations, end up supporting principles that had the effect of turning causes into sovereign fiefdoms? I think the answer is that those in charge of America's institutions saw the institutionalization and bureaucratization of the protest movements as ultimately desirable, at least in the short term, and the funding of group entitlements as ultimately a less costly way to redress grievances. The leaders of the newly sovereign fiefdoms were backing off from earlier demands that America live up to its ideals. Gone was the moral indictment. Gone was the call for difficult, soulful transformation. The language of entitlements is essentially the old, comforting language of power politics, and in the halls of power it went down easily enough. 30

With regard to civil rights, the moral voice of Dr. King gave way to the demands and cajolings of poverty program moguls, class action lawyers, and community organizers. The compromise that satisfied both political parties was to shift the focus from democracy, integration, and developmental uplift to collective entitlements. This satisfied the institutions because entitlements were cheaper in every way than real change. Better to set up black studies and women's studies departments than to have wrenching debates within existing departments. Better to fund these new institutions clamoring for money because who knows what kind of fuss they'll make if we turn down their proposals. Better to pass laws permitting Hispanic students to get preferred treatment in college admission—it costs less than improving kindergartens in East Los Angeles. 31

And this way to uplift satisfied the grievance-group "experts" because it laid the ground for their sovereignty and permanency: You negotiated with *us*. You funded *us*. You shared power, at least a bit of it, with *us*. 32

This negotiation was carried out in a kind of quasi-secrecy. Quotas, set-asides, and other entitlements were not debated in Congress or on the campaign trail. They were implemented by executive orders and Equal Employment Opportunity Commission guidelines without much public scrutiny. Also the courts played a quiet but persistent role in supporting these orders and guidelines and in further spelling 33 out their application. Universities, corporations, and foundations implemented their own grievance entitlements, the workings of which are often kept from the public.

Now, it should surprise no one that all this entitlement has most helped those who least need it—white middle-class women and the black middle class. Poor blacks do not guide the black grievance groups. Working-class women do not set NOW's agenda. Poor Hispanics do not clamor for bilingualism. Perhaps there is nothing wrong with middle-class people being helped, but their demands for entitlements are most often in the name of those less well off than themselves. The negotiations that settled on entitlements as the primary form of redress after the sixties have generated a legalistic grievance industry that argues the interstices of entitlements and does very little to help those truly in need.   34

In a liberal democracy, collective entitlements based upon race, gender, ethnicity, or some other group grievance are always undemocratic expedients. Integration, on the other hand, is the most difficult and inexpedient expansion of the democratic ideal; for in opting for integration, a citizen denies his or her impulse to use our most arbitrary characteristics—race, ethnicity, gender, sexual preference—as the basis for identity, as a key to status, or for claims to entitlement. Integration is twentieth-century America's elaboration of democracy. It eliminates such things as race and gender as oppressive barriers to freedom, as democrats of an earlier epoch eliminated religion and property. Our mistake has been to think of integration only as a utopian vision of perfect racial harmony. I think it is better to see integration as the inclusion of all citizens into the same sphere of rights, the same range of opportunities and possibilities that our Founding Fathers themselves enjoyed. Integration is not social engineering or group entitlements; it is a fundamental *absence* of arbitrary barriers to freedom.   35

If we can understand integration as an absence of barriers that has the effect of integrating all citizens into the same sphere of rights, then it can serve as a principle of democratic conduct. Anything that pushes anybody out of this sphere is undemocratic and must be checked, no matter the good intentions that seem to justify it. Understood in this light, collective entitlements are as undemocratic as racial and gender discrimination, and a group grievance is no more a justification for entitlement than the notion of white supremacy was at an earlier time. We are wrong to think of democracy as a gift of freedom; it is really a kind of discipline that avails freedom. Sometimes its enemy is racism and sexism; other times the enemy is our expedient attempts to correct these ills.   36

I think it is time for those who seek identity and power through grievance groups to fashion identities apart from grievance, to grant themselves the widest range of freedom, and to assume responsibility for that freedom. Victimhood lasts only as long as it is accepted, and to exploit it for an empty sovereignty is to accept it. The New Sovereignty is ultimately about vanity. It is the narcissism of victims, and it brings only a negligible power at the exorbitant price of continued victimhood. And all the while integration remains the real work.   37

STRATEGY THREE:
USING A SOURCE AS THE STARTING POINT
FOR YOUR OWN ESSAY

This third strategy gives you the freedom to develop your own ideas and present your own point of view in an essay that is only loosely linked to the source. Reading an assigned essay helps you to generate ideas and topics and provides you with evidence or information to cite in your own essay; but *the thesis, scope, and organization of your essay are entirely your own.*

As always, you begin by studying the assigned essay carefully, establishing its thesis and main ideas.

- As you read, start *noting ideas of your own* that might be worth developing. You need not cover exactly the same material as the source essay. What you want is a *spin-off* from the original reading, not a summary.

- If you read the essay a few times without thinking of a topic, *test some standard strategies* for developing an essay, applying them to the source essay in ways that might not have occurred to the original author.

Here, for example, are some strategies that generate topics for an essay based on Blanche Blank's "A Question of Degree." (Blank's essay can be found on pp. 8–11.) You will notice that the proposed topics and the source are not always closely connected and that some of the final suggestions will result in essays almost entirely independent of Blanche Blank's.

Argumentation

You can argue for Blanche Blank's assertions or against them. If you disagree with her conclusions, if you do not believe that the role of college has been overemphasized, then you can follow the first strategy described in this chapter and refute her arguments, disproving her evidence or casting doubt on her interpretation of the evidence. On the other hand, it is just as acceptable to agree with Blanche Blank and to support and confirm her thesis by suggesting new lines of argument or citing new sources of evidence. The resulting essay would be a combination of her basic ideas and yours.

It is not always possible to argue for or against an author's thesis; not all source essays provide clearcut assertions for you to support or refute. Several readings in this book explain and analyze a topic rather than attempt to convince the reader of a specific point of view. To understand the difference, compare "A Question of Degree" with the essay "Beer Commercials" by Lance Strate (pp. 197–207). Both essays are concerned with the negative impact of certain of our institutions, but Strate makes his point by analyzing the evidence rather than persuading his readers to accept a point of view.

Process

You might examine in detail one of the processes that Blank describes only generally. For example, you could write about your own experience to explain the ways in which teenagers are encouraged to believe that a college degree is essential, citing high school counseling and college catalogues and analyzing the unrealistic expectations that young students are encouraged to have. Or, if you have sufficient knowledge, you might describe the unjust manipulation of hiring procedures that favor college graduates or the process by which a college's liberal arts curriculum gradually becomes "practical."

Illustration

If you focused on a single discouraged employee, showing in what ways ambition for increased status and salary have been frustrated, or a single disillusioned college graduate, showing how career prospects have failed to measure up to training and expectations, your strategy would be an illustration proving one of Blank's themes.

Definition

Definition often emerges from a discussion of the background of an issue. What should the work experience be like? What is the function of a university? What is a good education? By attempting to define one of the components of Blank's theme in terms of the ideal, you are helping your reader to understand her arguments and evaluate her conclusions more rationally.

Cause and Effect

You can examine one or more of the reasons why a college degree has become a necessary credential for employment. You can also suggest a wider context for discussing Blank's views by describing the kind of society that encourages this set of values. In either case, you will be accounting for, but not necessarily justifying, the nation's obsession with degrees. Or you can predict the consequences, good or bad, that might result if Blank's suggested legislation were passed. Or you might explore some hypothetical possibilities and focus on the circumstances and causes of a situation different from the one that Blank describes. What if everyone in the United States earned a college degree? What if education after the eighth grade were abolished? By taking this approach, you are radically changing the circumstances that Blank depicts, but still sharing her concerns and exploring the principles discussed in her essay.

Comparison

You can alter the reader's perspective by moving the theme of Blank's essay to another time or place. Did our present obsession with education exist a hundred years ago? Is it a problem outside the United States at this moment? Will it probably continue into the twenty-first century? Or, focusing on late-twentieth-century America, how do contemporary trends in education and employment compare with trends in other areas of life—housing, finance, recreation, child-rearing, or communications? With all these approaches, you begin with a description of Blank's issue and contrast it with another set of circumstances, past or present, real or hypothetical.

Before choosing any of these speculative topics, you must first decide:

- What is practical
- Whether it requires research
- Whether, when fully developed, it will retain some connection with the source essay

For example, there may be some value in comparing the current emphasis on higher education with monastic education in the Middle Ages. Can you write such an essay? How much research will it require? Will a discussion of monastic education help your reader better to understand Blank's ideas? Or will you immediately move away from your starting point—and find no opportunity to return to it? Do you have a serious objective, or are you simply making the comparison "because it's there"?

PLANNING A SINGLE-SOURCE ESSAY

Consider how you might develop an essay based on one of the topics suggested in the previous section. Notice that the chosen topic is expressed as a question.

Topic: What is the function of a university in the 1990s?

1. Taking Notes and Writing a Thesis

- After thinking about your topic, start your list of notes *before* you reread the essay, to make sure that you are not overly influenced by the author's point of view and to enable you to include some ideas of your own in your notes.
- Next, review the essay and add any relevant ideas to your list, *remembering to indicate when an idea originated with the source and not with you.*

Here is a complete list of notes for an essay defining the function of a university in the 1990s. The paragraph references, added later, indicate which points were made by Blank and where in her essay they can be found. The thesis, which follows the notes, was written after the list was complete.

WHAT THE UNIVERSITY SHOULD DO

1. to increase students' understanding of the world around them

   e.g., to become more observant and aware of natural phenomena

   (weather, for example) and social systems (like family relationships)

2. to help students to live more fulfilling lives

   to enable them to test their powers and know more and become more versatile; to speak with authority on topics that they didn't understand before

3. to help students live more productive lives

   to increase their working credentials and qualify for more interesting and well-paying jobs (B.B., Paragraphs 3–9)

4. to serve society by creating better informed, more rational citizens

   not only through college courses (like political science) but through the increased ability to observe and analyze and argue (B.B., Paragraphs 3, 14)

5. to contribute to research that will help to solve scientific and social problems (not a teaching function) (B.B., Paragraphs 3, 14)

6. to serve as a center for debate to clarify the issues of the day

   people should regard the university as a source of unbiased information and counsel; notable people should come to lecture (B.B., Paragraphs 3, 14)

7. to serve as a gathering place for great teachers

   students should be able to regard their teachers as worth emulating

8. to allow students to examine the opportunities for personal change and growth

   this includes vocational goals, e.g., career changes (B.B., Paragraph 4)

WHAT THE UNIVERSITY SHOULD NOT DO

9. it should not divide the haves from the have-nots

   college should not be considered essential; it should be possible to be successful without a college degree (B.B., Paragraphs 8, 10)

10. it should not use marketing techniques to appeal to the greatest number

    what the university teaches should be determined primarily by the faculty and to a lesser extent by the students; standards of achievement should not be determined by students who haven't learned anything yet

11. it should not ignore the needs of its students and its community by clinging to outdated courses and programs

12. it should not cooperate with business and government to the extent that it loses its autonomy (B.B., Paragraphs 6, 9)

13. it should not be an employment agency and vocational center to the exclusion of its more important functions (B.B., Paragraphs 6, 9, 16)

<u>Thesis</u>: As Blanche Blank points out, a university education is not a commodity to be marketed and sold; a university should be a resource center for those who want the opportunity to develop their intellectual powers and lead more productive, useful, and fulfilling lives.

2. Deciding on a Strategy

As a rule, you would consider strategies for your essay as soon as you have established your thesis. In this case, however, the choice of strategy—definition—was made earlier when you chose your topic and considered several possible strategies. *The notes, divided into what a university should and should not do, already follow a definition strategy, with its emphasis on differentiation.*

3. Constructing an Outline

Having made all the preliminary decisions, you are ready to plan the structure of your essay.

- Mark those portions of the reading that you will need to use in support of your thesis. Your essay will be based on both your own ideas and the ideas of your source.
- Check whether your notes accurately paraphrase the source, and decide how many source references you intend to make so that you can write a balanced outline.
- Double-check to make sure that you are giving the source credit for all paraphrased ideas.
- Organize your notes in groups or categories, each of which will be developed as a separate paragraph or sequence of related paragraphs.
- Decide the order of your categories (or paragraphs).
- Incorporate in your outline some of the points from Blanche Blank's essay that you intend to use as support (or possibly to argue against). Cite the paragraph number of the relevant material with your outline entry. If the source paragraph contains several references that you expect to place in different parts of your outline, use a sentence number or a set of symbols or a brief quotation for differentiation.

Here is one section of the completed outline for an essay on "Defining a University for the 1990s." This outline incorporates notes 3, 13, 9, and 8 from the list on pp. 189–190.

I.   The university should help students to live more productive lives, to increase their working credentials, and to qualify for more interesting and well-paying jobs. (Paragraph 6—last sentence)

   A.   But it should not be an employment agency and vocational center to the exclusion of its more important functions. (Paragraph 9—"servicing agents"; Paragraph 12—"joylessness in our university life"; Paragraph 16)

   B.   It should not divide the haves from the have-nots; success without a college degree should be possible. (Paragraph 2—"two kinds of work"; Paragraph 17)

II. The university should allow students to examine the opportunities for personal growth and change; this includes vocational goals, e.g., career changes. (Paragraph 4—"an optional and continuing experience later in life")

WRITING A SINGLE-SOURCE ESSAY

When you write from sources, you are engaged in a kind of partnership. *You strive for an appropriate balance between your own ideas and those of your source.* By reading your source carefully and using annotation, outlining, and paraphrase, you familiarize yourself with the source's main ideas and reasoning and prepare to put those ideas in your essay. But *it is your voice that should dominate the essay.* You, after all, are writing it; you are responsible for its contents and its effect on the reader. For this reason, *all the important "positions" in the structure of your essay should be filled by you.* The topic sentences, as well as the introduction, should be written in your own words and, if possible, should certainly stress your views, not those of your author. On the other hand, your reader should not be allowed to lose sight of the source essay; it should be treated as a form of evidence and cited whenever it is relevant, but always as a context in which to develop your own strategy and assert your own thesis.

Many students find it helpful to work with a step-by-step list, especially when they have not yet had much experience in writing about sources. On the facing page are some steps to follow when you write a single-source essay.

ASSIGNMENT 6

A.   Read "From Hero to Celebrity: The Human Pseudo-Event," "Beer Commercials: A Manual on Masculinity," and "Measures of Life." One of these three essays will serve as the starting point for an essay of your own. Assume that the essay you are planning will be approximately three pages long, or 600–900 words. Using steps one and two, think of *three* possible

Guidelines for Writing a Single-Source Essay

1. Identify the source essay's thesis; analyze its underlying themes, if any, and its strategy; and construct a rough outline of its main ideas.

2. Decide on two or three possible essay topics based on your work in Step 1, and narrow down one of them. (Be prepared to submit your topics for your teacher's approval and, in conference, to choose the most suitable one.)

3. Write down a list of notes about your own ideas on the topic, being careful to distinguish between points that are yours and points that are derived from the source.

4. Write a thesis of your own that fairly represents your list of ideas. Mention the source in your thesis if appropriate.

5. If you have not done so already, choose a strategy that will best carry out your thesis; it need not be the same strategy as that of the source essay.

6. Mark (by brackets or underlining) those paragraphs or sentences in the source that will help to develop your topic.

7. Draw up an outline for your essay. Combine repetitious points; bring together similar and related points. Decide on the best sequence for your paragraphs.

8. Decide which parts of the reading should be cited as evidence or refuted; place paragraph or page references to the source in the appropriate sections of your outline. Then decide which sentences of the reading to quote and which to paraphrase.

9. Write the rough draft, making sure that, whenever possible, your topic sentences express your views, introduce the material that you intend to present in that paragraph, and are written in your voice. Later in the paragraph, incorporate references to the source, and link your paragraphs together with transitions. Do not be concerned about a bibliography for this single-source essay. Cite the author's full name and the exact title of the work early in your essay. (See pp. 108–112 for a review of citations.)

10. Write an introduction that contains a clear statement of your thesis, as well as a reference to the source essay and its role in the development of your ideas. You may also decide to draft a conclusion.

11. Review your first draft to note problems with organization, transitions, or language. Proofread your first draft very carefully to correct errors of grammar, style, reference, and spelling.

12. Using standard-size paper and leaving adequate margins and spacing, prepare the final draft. Proofread once again to catch careless errors in copying.

topics for such an essay, and submit the most promising (or, if your teacher suggests it, all three) for approval.

B. Plan your essay by working from notes to an outline. Be prepared to submit your thesis and outline of paragraphs (with indications of relevant references to the source) to your teacher for approval.

C. Write a rough draft after deciding which parts of the essay should be cited as evidence or refuted, distributing references to the source among appropriate sections of your outline, and determining which parts of the reading should be quoted and which should be paraphrased.

D. Write a final draft of your essay.

from FROM HERO TO CELEBRITY: THE HUMAN PSEUDO-EVENT
Daniel J. Boorstin

The hero was distinguished by his achievement; the celebrity by his image or trademark. The hero created himself; the celebrity is created by the media. The hero was a big man; the celebrity is a big name.   1

Formerly, a public man needed a *private* secretary for a barrier between himself and the public. Nowadays he has a *press* secretary, to keep him properly in the public eye. Before the Graphic Revolution (and still in countries which have not undergone that revolution) it was a mark of solid distinction in a man or a family to keep out of the news. A lady of aristocratic pretensions was supposed to get her name in the papers only three times: when she was born, when she married, and when she died. Now the families who are Society are by definition those always appearing in the papers. The man of truly heroic stature was once supposed to be marked by scorn for publicity. He quietly relied on the power of his character or his achievement.   2

In the South, where the media developed more slowly than elsewhere in the country, where cities appeared later, and where life was dominated by rural ways, the celebrity grew more slowly. The old-fashioned hero was romanticized. In this as in many other ways, the Confederate General Robert E. Lee was one of the last surviving American models of the older type. Among his many admirable qualities, Southern compatriots admired none more than his retirement from public view. He had the reputation for never having given a newspaper interview. He steadfastly refused to write his memoirs. "I should be trading on the blood of my men," he said. General George C. Marshall (1880–1959) is a more recent and more anachronistic example. He, too, shunned publicity and refused to write his memoirs, even while other generals were serializing theirs in the newspapers. But by his time, few people any longer considered this reticence a virtue. His old-fashioned unwillingness to enter the publicity arena finally left him a victim of the slanders of Senator Joseph McCarthy and others.   3

The hero was born of time: his gestation required at least a generation. As the saying went, he had "stood the test of time." A maker of tradition, he was himself   4 made by tradition. He grew over the generations as people found new virtues in him and attributed to him new exploits. Receding into the misty past he became more, and not less, heroic. It was not necessary that his face or figure have a sharp, well-delineated outline, nor that his life be footnoted. Of course there could not have been any photographs of him, and often there was not even a likeness. Men of the last century were more heroic than those of today; men of antiquity were still more heroic; and those of pre-history became demigods. The hero was always some-how ranked among the ancients.

The celebrity, on the contrary, is always a contemporary. The hero is made by   5
folklore, sacred texts, and history books, but the celebrity is the creature of gossip, of public opinion, of magazines, newspapers, and the ephemeral images of movie and television screen. The passage of time, which creates and establishes the hero, destroys the celebrity. One is made, the other unmade, by repetition. The celebrity is born in the daily papers and never loses the mark of his fleeting origin.

The very agency which first makes the celebrity in the long run inevitably de-   6
stroys him. He will be destroyed, as he was made, by publicity. The newspapers make him, and they unmake him—not by murder but by suffocation or starvation. No one is more forgotten than the last generation's celebrity. This fact explains the newspaper feature "Whatever Became Of . . . ?" which amuses us by accounts of the present obscurity of former celebrities. One can always get a laugh by referring knowingly to the once-household names which have lost their celebrity in the last few decades: Mae Bush, William S. Hart, Clara Bow. A woman reveals her age by the celebrities she knows.

There is not even any tragedy in the celebrity's fall, for he is a man returned to   7
his proper anonymous station. The tragic hero, in Aristotle's familiar definition, was a man fallen from great estate, a great man with a tragic flaw. He had somehow be-come the victim of his own greatness. Yesterday's celebrity, however, is a common-place man who has been fitted back into his proper commonplaceness not by any fault of his own, but by time itself.

The dead hero becomes immortal. He becomes more vital with the passage of   8
time. The celebrity even in his lifetime becomes passé: he passes out of the picture. The white glare of publicity, which first gave him his specious brilliance, soon melts him away. This was so even when the only vehicles of publicity were the magazine and the newspaper. Still more now with our vivid round-the-clock media, with ra-dio and television. Now when it is possible, by bringing their voices and images daily into our living rooms, to make celebrities more quickly than ever before, they die more quickly than ever. This has been widely recognized by entertainment celebri-ties and politicians. President Franklin Delano Roosevelt was careful to space out his fireside chats so the citizenry would not tire of him. Some comedians (for ex-ample, Jackie Gleason in the mid-1950's) have found that when they have weekly programs they reap quick and remunerative notoriety, but that they soon wear out their images. To extend their celebrity-lives, they offer their images more spar-ingly—once a month or once every two months instead of once a week.

There is a subtler difference between the personality of the hero and that of the   9
celebrity. The figures in each of the two classes become assimilated to one another,
but in two rather different ways. Heroes standing for greatness in the traditional
mold tend to become colorless and cliché. The greatest heroes have the least distinctiveness of face or figure. We may show our reverence for them, as we do for
God, by giving them beards. Yet we find it hard to imagine that Moses or Jesus could
have had other special facial characteristics. The hero while being thus idealized
and generalized loses his individuality. The fact that George Washington is not a
vivid personality actually helps him serve as the heroic Father of Our Country. Perhaps Emerson meant just this when he said that finally every great hero becomes a
great bore. To be a great hero is actually to become lifeless; to become a face on a
coin or a postage stamp. It is to become a Gilbert Stuart's Washington. Contemporaries, however, and the celebrities made of them, suffer from idiosyncrasy. They
are too vivid, too individual to be polished into a symmetrical Greek statue. The
Graphic Revolution, with its klieg lights on face and figure, makes the images of different men more distinctive. This itself disqualifies them from becoming heroes or
demigods.

While heroes are assimilated to one another by the great simple virtues of their   10
character, celebrities are differentiated mainly by trivia of personality. To be known
for your personality actually proves you a celebrity. Thus a synonym for "a
celebrity" is "a personality." Entertainers, then, are best qualified to become celebrities because they are skilled in the marginal differentiation of their personalities.
They succeed by skillfully distinguishing themselves from others essentially like
them. They do this by minutiae of grimace, gesture, language, and voice. We identify Jimmy ("Schnozzola") Durante by his nose, Bob Hope by his fixed smile, Jack
Benny by his stinginess, Jack Paar by his rudeness, Jackie Gleason by his waddle,
Imogene Coca by her bangs.

With the mushroom-fertility of all pseudo-events, celebrities tend to breed more   11
celebrities. They help make and celebrate and publicize one another. Being known
primarily for their well-knownness, celebrities intensify their celebrity images simply by becoming widely known for relations among themselves. By a kind of symbiosis, celebrities live off one another. One becomes better known by being the
habitual butt of another's jokes, by being another's paramour or ex-wife, by being
the subject of another's gossip, or even by being ignored by another celebrity. Elizabeth Taylor's celebrity appeal has consisted less perhaps in her own talents as an
actress than in her connection with other celebrities—Nick Hilton, Mike Todd, and
Eddie Fisher. Arthur Miller, the playwright, became a "real" celebrity by his marriage to Marilyn Monroe. When we talk or read or write about celebrities, our
emphasis on their marital relations and sexual habits, on their tastes in smoking,
drinking, dress, sports cars, and interior decoration is our desperate effort to distinguish among the indistinguishable. How can those commonplace people like us
(who, by the grace of the media, happened to become celebrities) be made to seem
more interesting or bolder than we are?

BEER COMMERCIALS:
A MANUAL ON MASCULINITY
Lance Strate

Jocks, rock stars, and pick-up artists; cowboys, construction workers, and comedians; these are some of the major "social types" (Klapp, 1962) found in contemporary American beer commercials. The characters may vary in occupation, race, and age, but they all exemplify traditional conceptions of the masculine role. Clearly, the beer industry relies on stereotypes of the man's man to appeal to a mainstream, predominantly male target audience. That is why alternate social types, such as sensitive men, gay men, and househusbands, scholars, poets, and political activists, are noticeably absent from beer advertising. The manifest function of beer advertising is to promote a particular brand, but collectively the commercials provide a clear and consistent image of the masculine role; in a sense, they constitute a guide for becoming a man, a rulebook for appropriate male behavior, in short, a manual on masculinity. . . .

Myths, according to semioticians such as Roland Barthes (1972), are not falsehoods or fairy tales, but uncontested and generally unconscious assumptions that are so widely shared within a culture that they are considered natural, instead of recognized as products of unique historical circumstances. Biology determines whether we are male or female; culture determines what it *means* to be male or female, and what sorts of behaviors and personality attributes are appropriate for each gender role. In other words, masculinity is a social construction (Fejes, 1989; Kimmel, 1987a). The foundation may be biological, but the structure is manmade; it is also flexible, subject to change over time and differing significantly from culture to culture. Myth, as a form of cultural communication, is the material out of which such structures are built, and through myth, the role of human beings in inventing and reinventing masculinity is disguised and therefore naturalized (and "biologicized"). The myth of masculinity is manifested in myriad forms of mediated and nonmediated communication; beer commercials are only one such form, and to a large extent, the ads merely reflect preexisting cultural conceptions of the man's man. But in reflecting the myth, the commercials also reinforce it. Moreover, since each individual expression of a myth varies, beer ads also reshape the myth of masculinity, and in this sense, take part in its continuing construction.

Myths provide ready-made answers to universal human questions about ourselves, our relationships with others and with our environment. Thus, the myth of masculinity answers the question: What does it mean to be a man? This can be broken down into five separate questions: What kinds of things do men do? What kinds of settings do men prefer? How do boys become men? How do men relate to each other? How do men relate to women? Let us now consider the ways in which beer commercials answer these questions.

What kinds of things do men do? Although advertisers are prevented from actually showing an individual drinking beer in a television commercial, there is no question that drinking is presented as a central masculine activity, and beer as the beverage of choice. Drinking, however, is rarely presented as an isolated activity, but rather is associated with a variety of occupational and leisure pursuits, all of which, in one way or another, involve overcoming challenges. In the world of beer commercials, men work hard and they play hard.

Physical labor is often emphasized in these ads, both on and off the job. Busch   5
beer features cowboys riding horses, driving cattle, and performing in rodeos. Budweiser presents a variety of blue-collar types, including construction workers, lumberjacks, and soldiers (as well as skilled laborers and a few white-collar workers). Miller Genuine Draft shows men working as farm hands and piano movers. But the key to work is the challenge it poses, whether to physical strength and endurance, to skill, patience, and craftsmanship, or to wit and competitive drive in the business world. The ads do associate hard work with the American dream of economic success (this theme is particularly strong in Budweiser's campaign), but it is also presented as its own end, reflecting the Puritan work ethic. Men do not labor primarily out of economic necessity nor for financial gain, but rather for the pride of accomplishment provided by a difficult job well done; for the respect and camaraderie of other men (few women are visible in the beer commercial workplace); for the benefit of family, community, and nation; and for the opportunity to demonstrate masculinity by triumphing over the challenges work provides. In short, work is an integral part of a man's identity.

Beer is integrated with the work world in three ways. *First,* it is represented in   6
some commercials as the product of patient, skillful craftsmanship, thus partaking of the virtues associated with the labor that produced it; this is particularly apparent in the Miller beer commercials in which former football player Ed Marinaro takes us on a tour of the Miller brewery. In effect, an identity relationship between beer and labor is established, although this is overshadowed by the identification between beer and nature discussed below. *Second,* beer serves as a reward for a job well done, and receiving a beer from one's peers acts as a symbol of other men's respect for the worker's accomplishment—"For all you do, this Bud's for you." Beer is seen as an appropriate reward not just because drinking is pleasurable, but because it is identified with labor, and therefore can act as a substitute for labor. Thus, drinking beer at the end of the day is a symbolic reenactment of the successful completion of a day's work. And *third,* beer acts as a marker of the end of the work day, the signal of quitting time ("Miller time"), the means for making the transition from work to leisure ("If you've got the time, we've got the beer"). In the commercials, the celebration of work completed takes on a ritualistic quality, much like saying grace and breaking bread signal the beginning of meal time; opening the can represents the opening of leisure time.

The men of beer commercials fill their leisure time in two ways: in active pursuits   7
usually conducted in outdoor settings (e.g., car and boat racing, fishing, camping, and sports; often symbolized by the presence of sports stars, especially in Miller Lite ads) and in "hanging out," usually in bars. As it is in work, the key to men's active

play is the challenge it provides to physical and emotional strength, endurance, and daring. Some element of danger is usually present in the challenge, for danger magnifies the risks of failure and the significance of success. Movement and speed are often a part of the challenge, not only for the increased risk they pose, but also because they require immediate and decisive action and fine control over one's own responses. Thus, Budweiser spots feature automobile racing; Michelob's music video-like ads show cars moving in fast-motion and include lyrics like "I'm overheating, I'm ready to burn, got dirt on my wheels, they're ready to turn"; Old Milwaukee and Budweiser commercials include images of powerboat, sailboat, and canoe racing; Busch beer features cowboys on galloping horses; and Coors uses the slogan, "The Silver Bullet won't slow you down." Activities that include movement and speed, along with displays of coordination, are particularly troubling when associated with beer, in light of social problems such as drinking and driving. Moreover, beer commercials portray men as unmindful of risks, laughing off danger. For example, in two Miller Genuine Draft commercials, a group of young men are drinking and reminiscing; in one they recall the time when they worked as farm hands, loading bales of hay onto a truck, and the large stack fell over. In the other, the memory is of moving a piano, raising it up by rope on the outside of a building to get it into a third-story apartment; the rope breaks and the piano crashes to the ground. The falling bales and falling piano both appear dangerous, but in the ads the men merely joke about the incidents; this attitude is reinforced visually as, in both cases, there is a cut from the past scene to the present one just before the crash actually occurs.

When they are not engaged in physical activity, the men of beer commercials 8
frequently seek out symbolic challenges and dangers by playing games such as poker and pool, and by watching professional sports. The games pose particular challenges to self-control, while spectator sports allow for vicarious participation in the drama of challenge, risk, and triumph. Even when they are merely hanging out together, men engage in verbal jousts that contain a strong element of challenge, either in the form of good-natured arguments (such as Miller-Lite's ongoing "tastes great—less filling" conflict) or in ribbing one another, which tests self-control and the ability to "take it." A sense of proportion and humor is required to overcome such challenges, which is why jokers and comedians are a valued social type in the myth of masculinity. Women may also pose a challenge to the man's ability to attract the opposite sex and, more important, to his self-control.

[The central theme of masculine leisure activity in beer commercials, then, is 9
challenge, risk, and mastery—mastery over nature, over technology, over others in good-natured "combat," and over oneself.] And beer is integrated into this theme in two ways: one obvious, the other far more subtle. At the overt level, beer functions in leisure activities as it does in work: as a reward for challenges successfully overcome (the race completed, the big fish landed, the ribbing returned). But it also serves another function, never explicitly alluded to in commercials. In several ways drinking, in itself, is a test of mastery. Because alcohol affects judgment and slows reaction time, it intensifies the risks inherent in movement and speed, and

thereby increases the challenge they represent. And because it threatens self-control, drinking poses heightened opportunities for demonstrating self-mastery. Thus beer is not merely a reward for the successful meeting of a challenge in masculine work and leisure, but is itself an occasion for demonstrating mastery, and thus, masculinity. Beer is an appropriate reward for overcoming challenge because it is a challenge itself, and thereby allows a man to symbolically reenact his feat. It would be all but suicidal for advertisers to present drinking as a challenge by which the masculine role can be acted out; instead, they associate beer with other forms of challenge related to the myth of masculinity.

What kinds of settings do men prefer? In beer commercials, the settings most closely 10 associated with masculinity are the outdoors, generally the natural environment, and the self-contained world of the bar. The outdoors is featured prominently as both a workplace and a setting for leisure activity in ads for Busch beer, Old Milwaukee, Miller Genuine Draft, and Budweiser. As a workplace, the natural environment provides suitable challenge and danger for demonstrating masculinity, and the separation from civilization forces men to rely only on themselves. The height of masculinity can be attained when the natural environment and the work environment coincide, that is, when men have to overcome nature in order to survive. That is why the cowboy or frontiersman is the archetypical man's man in our culture. Other work environments, such as the farm, factory, and office, offer their own form of challenge, but physical danger is usually downplayed and the major risk is economic. Challenge and danger are also reduced, but still present, when nature is presented as a leisure environment; male bonding receives greater emphasis, and freedom from civilization becomes freedom for men to behave in a boyish manner.

In the ads, nature is closely associated with both masculinity and beer, as beer is 11 presented as equivalent to nature. Often, beer is shown to be a product that is natural and pure, implying that its consumption is not harmful, and perhaps even healthy. Moreover, a number of beers, including Rolling Rock, Heileman's Old Style, and Molson's Golden, are identified with natural sources of water. This identification is taken even further in one Busch beer commercial: We see a cowboy on horseback, herding cattle across a river. A small calf is overcome by the current, but the cowboy is able to withstand the force of the river and come to the rescue. The voice-over says, "Sometimes a simple river crossing isn't so simple. And when you've got him back, it's your turn. Head for the beer brewed natural as a mountain stream." We then see a six-pack pulled out of clear running water, as if by magic. The raging water represents the power and danger of nature, while the mountain stream stands for nature's gentler aspect. Through the voice-over and the image of the hand pulling the six-pack from the water, beer is presented as identical with the stream, as bottled nature. Drinking beer, then, is a relatively safe way of facing the challenge of raging rivers, of symbolically reenacting the taming of the frontier.

Beer is identified with nature in a more general way in the ads for Old Milwau- 12 kee, which are usually set in wilderness environments that feature water, such as the Florida Everglades, and Snake River, Wyoming. In each ad, a group of men is engaged in recreational activities such as high-speed air-boating, flat-bottom boat racing, or fishing. Each commercial begins with a voice-over saying something like, "The Florida Everglades and Old Milwaukee both mean something great to these guys." Each ad includes a jingle, which says, "There's nothing like the flavor of a special place and Old Milwaukee beer." In other words, Old Milwaukee is equivalent to the special place. The place is special because it is untouched by civilization, allowing men to engage in forms of recreation not available elsewhere. It therefore must be fairly inaccessible, but since beer is presented as identical to the place, drinking may act as a substitute for actually going there.

Beer is also identified with nature through animals. For example, the symbol of Busch beer, found on its label and in its commercials, is a horse rearing on its hind legs, a phallic symbol that also evokes the idea of the untamed. And in another Busch ad, a young rodeo rider is quickly thrown from his mount; trying to cheer him up, an older cowboy hands him a beer and says, "Here. This one don't buck so hard." Thus, the identification of beer and nature is made via the horse. Drinking beer is like rodeo-riding, only less strenuous. It is a challenge that the rider can easily overcome, allowing him to save face and reaffirm masculinity. Budweiser beer also uses horses as a symbol: the Budweiser Clydesdales, a breed of "draft" horse. Whereas the Busch Stallion represents the frontier wilderness, the Clydesdales stand for the pastoral. Also, Colt 45 malt liquor, by its very name, invokes images of the Old West, horses, and of course guns, another phallic symbol. Another way in which beer is identified with nature and animals is through Budweiser's "Spuds McKenzie" and Stroh's "Alex," both dogs that behave like humans; both are in turn identified with masculinity as they are male characters, and canines are the animals most closely associated with masculinity. 13

As a setting for masculine activity, the bar runs a close second to nature, and many commercials seem to advertise bar patronage as much as they do a particular brand of beer. Of course, the drinking hall has a venerable history in Western culture as a center for male socializing and tests of skill, strength, and drinking ability. It is a setting featured prominently in the myths and legends of ancient Greece, and in Norse and Old English sagas. The pub is a popular setting in British literature, as is the saloon in the American Western genre. Like its predecessors, the bar of the beer commercial is presented as a male-dominated environment, although it sometimes serves as a setting for male-female interaction. And it is generally portrayed as a relaxed and comfortable context for male socializing, as well as a place where a man can find entertainment and excitement. The bars are immaculate and smokeless, and the waitresses and bartenders are always friendly; thus, along with nature, bars are the ideal male leisure environment. The only exception is the Bud Light bar, where men who are so uninformed as to ask for "a light" rather than a specific brand are subjected to pranks by the bartenders; still, even in this case the practical jokes are taken in stride, reaffirming the customer's masculinity. 14

It is worth noting that in the romanticized barroom of beer commercials, no one ever pays for his drinks, either literally or in terms of alcohol's effects. In other 15 words, there are no consequences to the men's actions, which is consistent with the myth of masculinity's tendency to ignore or downplay risk and danger. The bar is shown as a self-contained environment, one that, like the outdoors, frees men from the constraints of civilization, allowing them to behave irresponsibly. Moreover, most settings featured as drinking-places in beer commercials are probably places that people would drive to—and drive home from. Because the action is confined to these settings, however, the question of how people arrived and how they will get home never comes up.

How do boys become men? In the world of beer commercials, boys become men   16 by earning acceptance from those who are already full-fledged members of the community of men. Adult men are identified by their age, their size, their celebrity, and their positions of authority in the work world and/or status in a bar. To earn acceptance, the younger man must demonstrate that he can do the things that men do: take risks, meet challenges, face danger courageously, and dominate his environment. In the workplace, he demonstrates this by seizing opportunities to work, taking pride in his labor, proving his ability, persisting in the face of uncertainty, and learning to accept failure with equanimity. Having proven that he can act out the masculine role, the initiate is rewarded with beer. As a reward, beer symbolizes the overcoming of a challenge, the fulfilling of the requirements for group membership. The gift of beer also allows the adult male to show his acceptance of the initiate without becoming emotional. Beer then functions as a symbol of initiation and group membership.

For example, one of Budweiser's most frequently aired commercials during the   17 1980s features a young Polish immigrant and an older foreman and dispatcher. In the first scene, the dispatcher is reading names from a clipboard, giving workers their assignments. Arriving late, which earns him a look of displeasure from the foreman, the nervous young man takes a seat in the back. When he is finally called, the dispatcher stumbles over the immigrant's foreign name. The young man walks up to the front of the room, corrects the dispatcher's mispronunciation—a risky move, given his neophyte status, but one that demonstrates his pride and self-confidence. He receives his assignment, and the scene then shifts to a montage of the day's work. At the beginning, he drops a toolbox, spilling its contents, a mishap noted by the foreman; by the end of the day, however, he has demonstrated his ability and has earned the respect of his co-workers. The final scene is in a crowded tavern; the young man walks through the door, making his way to the bar, looking around nervously. He hears his name called, turns around, and the foreman, sitting at the bar, hands him a beer. In both the first and final scene, the immigrant begins at the back of the room, highlighting his outsider status, and moves to the front as he is given a chance to prove himself. The commercial's parallelism is not just an aesthetic device, but a mythic one as well. Having mastered the challenge of work, the neophyte receives the reward of a beer, which is both a symbol of that mastery and an invitation to symbolically reenact his feat. By working hard and well, he gains acceptance in the work world; by drinking the beer, he can also gain acceptance into the social world of the bar. The foreman, by virtue of his age, his position of authority, and his position sitting at the bar in the center of the tavern, holds the power of confirmation in both worlds.

The theme of initiation is also present in a subtle way in the Bud Light ads in which someone orders "a light," is given a substitute such as lamp or torch, and then corrects himself, asking for a "Bud Light." As one of the commercials revealed, the bartenders play these pranks because they are fed up with uninformed customers. The bizarre substitutions are a form of hazing, an initiation into proper barroom etiquette. The mature male is familiar with brands of beer, knows what he wants, and shows decisiveness in ordering it. Clearly, the individuals who ask for "a light" are inexperienced drinkers, and it is important to keep in mind that, to the barroom novice (and especially to the underage drinker), bars and bartenders can seem very threatening. While the substitute "lights" come as a surprise to the patrons, and thus threaten their composure, they are a relatively mild threat. The customers are able to overcome this challenge to their self-control, correct their order, and thereby gain entry into barroom society. 18

The biological transition from childhood to adulthood is a gradual one, but in traditional cultures, it is symbolized by formal rituals of initiation, rites of passage which mark the boundary between childhood and adulthood, clearly separating these two social positions. In our own culture, there are no initiation rites, and therefore the adolescent's social position is an ambiguous one. A number of events and activities do serve as symbols of adulthood, however. The commercials emphasize entry into the work world as one such step; financial independence brings the freedom of adulthood, while work is an integral part of the adult male's identity. As a symbol of initiation into the work world, beer also functions as a symbol of adulthood. And although this is never dealt with in the commercials, drinking in and of itself is a symbol of adulthood in our culture, as is driving, particularly in the eyes of underage males. Bars are seen as exclusively adult environments, and so acceptance in bars is a further sign of manhood. In the commercials, bars and workplaces complement each other as environments in which initiation into adulthood can be consummated. 19

How do men relate to each other? In beer commercials, men are rarely found in solitary pursuits (and never drink alone), and only occasionally in one-to-one relationships, usually involving father-son or mentor-protégé transactions. The dominant social context for male interaction is the group, and teamwork and group loyalty rank high in the list of masculine values. Individualism and competition, by contrast, are downplayed, and are acceptable only as long as they foster the cohesiveness of the group as a whole. Although differences in status may exist between members of the group and outsiders, within the group equality is the rule, and elitism and intellectualism are disdained. This reflects the American value of egalitarianism and solidifies the importance of the group over individual members. The concept of group loyalty is extended to community and to country, so that patriotism is also presented as an important value for men. 20

The emotional tenor of relationships among men in beer commercials is characterized by self-restraint. Generally, strong emotions are eschewed, especially overt displays of affection. In the workplace, mutual respect is exhibited, but respect must be earned through ability and attitude. In leisure situations, humor is a major element in male interactions. Conversations among men emphasize joking, bragging, storytelling, and good-natured insults. The insults are a form of symbolic challenge; taking a ribbing in good spirit is a demonstration of emotional strength and self-mastery. By providing a controlled social context for the exchange of challenges and demonstrations of ego strength and self-control, the group provides continuous reinforcement of the members' masculinity. Moreover, gathering in groups provides men with the freedom to act irresponsibly; that is, it allows men to act like boys. This is particularly the case in the Miller Lite ads that feature retired sports stars, comedians, and other celebrities.

In beer commercials, drinking serves several important functions in promoting group solidarity. Beer is frequently the shared activity that brings the group together, and in the ads for Miller Genuine Draft, sharing beer acts as a reminder of the group's identity and history. Thus, beer becomes a symbol of group membership. It also serves as a means for demonstrating the group's egalitarian values. When one man gives a beer to another, it is a sign of acceptance, friendship, or gratitude. In this role, beer is also a substitute for overt display of affection. Although the commercials never deal with why beer takes on this role, the answer lies in the effects of alcohol. Certainly, its function as mood enhancer can have a positive influence on group interaction. And, as previously discussed, alcohol itself constitutes a challenge, so that drinking allows each member of the group to publicly demonstrate his masculinity. Alcohol also lowers inhibitions, making it easier for men to show their affection for one another. The well-known saying that you cannot trust a man who does not drink reflects the popular conception that under the influence of alcohol, men become more open and honest. Moreover, the effects of drinking on physical coordination make a man less of an immediate threat. All these properties contribute to beer's role as a medium of male bonding and a facilitator of group solidarity.

In general, men are not portrayed as loners in beer commercials, and in this respect the ads differ markedly from other expressions of the myth of masculinity. There are no isolated Marlboro men in the Busch frontier, for example. When he saves the calf from being swept away by the river, the Busch cowboy appears to be on his own, but by the time he is ready for his reward, another cowboy has appeared out of nowhere to share his beer. In another Busch ad, a jingle with the following lyrics is heard: "There's no place on earth that I'd rather be, than out in the open where it's all plain to see, if it's going to get done it's up to you and me." In this way, the ideal of individual self-reliance that is so central to the American myth of the frontier is transformed into group self-reliance. In the world of beer commercials, demonstrating one's masculinity requires an audience to judge one's performance and confirm one's status. Moreover, the emphasis the ads place on beer

21

22

23

drinking as a group activity undermines the idea that it is in any way problematic. One of the most widespread stereotypes of problem drinkers is that they are solitary and secretive loners. The emphasis on the group in beer commercials plays on the common misconception that drinking, when it is done socially and publicly, cannot be harmful.

How do men relate to women? Although the world of beer commercials is often 24 monopolized by men, some of the ads do feature male-female interaction in the form of courtship, as well as in more established relationships. When courtship is the focus, the image of the man's man gives way to that of the ladies' man, for whom seduction is the highest form of challenge. And while the obvious risk in courtship is rejection by the opposite sex, the more significant danger in beer ads is loss of emotional self-control. The ladies' man must remain cool, confident, and detached when faced with the object of his desires. This social type is exemplified by Billy Dee Williams, who plays on his romantic image in Colt 45 commercials. Strangely enough, Spuds McKenzie, Budweiser's "party animal," also fits into this category, insofar as he, like Alex, is treated like a human being. In his ads, Spuds is surrounded by the Spudettes, three beautiful young women who dance with him, serve him, even bathe him. The women are attractive enough to make most males salivate like Pavlov's dogs, but Spuds receives their attentions with casual indifference (and never betrays the insecurities that haunt his cousin Snoopy when the *Peanuts* dog assumes his "Joe Cool" persona). While the commercials do not go so far as to suggest bestiality, there is no question that Spuds is a stud.

Emotional control is also demonstrated by the male's ability to divide his atten- 25 tion. For example, in one Michelob commercial, a young woman is shown leaning over a jukebox and selecting a song; her expression is one of pure pleasure, and she seems lost in thought. Other scenes, presumably her memories, show her dancing in the arms of a handsome young man. His arms are around her neck, and he is holding in one hand, behind her back, a bottle of beer. This image emphasizes the difference between the myths of masculinity and femininity; her attention is focused entirely on him, while his interests extend to the beer as well as the woman. According to the myth of masculinity, the man who loses control of his emotions in a relationship is a man who loses his independence, and ultimately, his masculinity; dividing attention is one way to demonstrate self-control. Michelob also presents images of ladies' men in the form of popular musicians, such as the rock group Genesis, rock star Eric Clapton, and popular vocalist Frank Sinatra. Many male pop stars have reputations as sexual athletes surrounded by groupies; in the ads, however, they function as modern troubadours, providing a romantic backdrop for lovers and facilitating social interaction. Acting, like Spuds McKenzie, as mascots for the beer companies, they imply that the beer they are identified with serves the same functions.

By far the most sexist of beer commercials, almost to the point of farce, are the 26 Colt 45 ads featuring Billy Dee Williams. One of these, which is divided into three segments, begins with Williams saying: "There are two rules to remember if you want to have a good time: Rule number one, never run out of Colt 45. Rule number two, never forget rule number one." In the next segment, Williams continues: "You want to know why you should keep plenty of Colt 45 on hand? You never know when friends might show up." As he says this, he opens a can and a woman's hand reaches out and takes it. In the third segment, he concludes, "I don't claim you can have a better time with Colt 45 than without it, but why take chances?" As he says this, the camera pulls back to reveal Williams standing, and an attractive woman sitting next to him. The ad ends with a picture of a Colt 45 can and the slogan, "The power of Colt 45: It works every time." There are a number of ways to interpret this pitch. First, malt liquor has a higher alcohol content than beer or ale, and therefore is a more *powerful* beverage. Second, the ad alludes to alcohol's image as an aphrodisiac, despite the fact that it actually reduces male potency. As noted, the Colt 45 pistol is a phallic symbol, while the slogan can be read as a guarantee against impotency—"it works every time." Third, it can be seen as referring to alcohol's ability to make men feel more confident about themselves and more interested in the opposite sex. And fourth, it plays on the popular notion that getting a woman drunk increases her desire for and willingness to engage in sex. Williams keeps Colt 45 on hand not just for himself, but for "friends," meaning "women." His secret of seduction is getting women to drink. In the ad, the woman is eager to drink Colt 45, implying that she will be just as eager to make love. The idea that a woman who drinks is "looking for it" is even clearer in a second ad.

This commercial begins with the title "Billy Dee Williams on Body Language." 27 Moving through an outdoor party, Williams says, "You know, body language tells you a lot about what a person is thinking. For instance, that means she has an interest in the finer things in life." As he says this, the camera plans to show an attractive women sitting at a bar alone, holding her necklace. She shifts her position and strokes her hair, and Williams says, "That means she also wants a little fun in her life, but only with the right man." At this point, the woman fills her glass with Colt 45, as Williams says, "And now she's pouring Colt 45 and we all know what that means." He then goes over to her and asks if she would mind if he joined her, and she replies, "You must have read my mind." Williams responds, "Something like that," and the ad ends with the same slogan as the first. What is implied in this commercial is that any woman who would sit by herself and drink must be looking to get picked up; she is sending out signals and preparing herself to be seduced. And although she is making herself approachable, she must wait for Williams to make the first move. At the same time, the woman appears to be vain, fondling her jewelry and hair. And in both ads, the women are seated while Williams stands. This portrayal of the woman's woman, based on the myth of femininity, is the perfect counterpart to Williams' image as a ladies' man.

When the commercials depict more established relationships, the emphasis shifts 28 from romance and seduction to male activities in which women are reduced largely to the role of admiring onlookers. Men appear to value their group of friends over their female partners, and the women accept this. Women tend to be passive, not participating but merely watching as men perform physical tasks. In other words, they become the audience for whom men perform. For the most part, women know their place and do not interfere with male bonding. They may, however, act as emotional catalysts for male interaction, bringing men together. Occasionally, a woman may be found together with a group of men, presumably as the girlfriend or wife of one of the group members. Here, the presence of women, and their noninterference, indicates their approval of masculine activity and male bonding, and their approval of the role of beer in these situations. Even when a group of men acts irresponsibly and/or boyishly, the presence of a woman shows that this behavior is socially sanctioned.

Alternate images of femininity can be found in beer commercials, but they are generally relegated to the background; for the most part, the traditional roles of masculinity and femininity are upheld. One exception is a Michelob Light ad that features Madeline Kahn. Introduced by a male voice-over, "Madeline Kahn on having it all," she is lying on her side on a couch, wearing an expensive-looking gown and necklace, and holding a bottle of beer. Kahn does a short humorous monologue in which she acknowledges her wealth and glamour, and the scene shifts to a shot of the beer, as the male voice-over says, "Michelob Light. You *can* have it all." While this represents something of a concession to changing conceptions of femininity, the advertisers hedge their bets. The male voice-over frames, and in a sense controls, Kahn's monologue, while Kahn's position, lying on her side, is a passive and seductive one. To male viewers, the commercial can easily imply that "having it all" includes having a woman like her.   29

Conclusion

In the world of beer commercials, masculinity revolves around the theme of challenge, an association that is particularly alarming, given the social problems stemming from alcohol abuse. For the most part beer commercials present traditional, stereotypical images of men, and uphold the myths of masculinity and femininity. Thus, in promoting beer, advertisers also promote and perpetuate these images and myths. Although targeted at an adult audience, beer commercials are highly accessible to children; between the ages of 2 and 18, American children may see as many as 100,000 of these ads (Postman et al., 1987). They are also extremely attractive to children: humorous, exciting, and offering answers to questions about gender and adulthood. And they do have an impact, playing a role in social learning and attitude formation (Wallack, Cassady, & Grube, 1990). As Postman (1979) argues, television constitutes a curriculum, one that children spend more time with than in schoolrooms. Beer commercials are a prominent subject in television's curriculum, a subject that is ultimately hazardous to the intellectual as well as the physical health of the young. The myth of masculinity *does* have a number of redeeming features (facing challenges and taking risks are valuable activities in many contexts), but the unrelenting one-dimensionality of masculinity as presented by beer commercials is clearly anachronistic, possibly laughable, but without a doubt sobering.   30

Francisco José de Goya, *The Executions of May 3, 1808, in Madrid,* 1814

MEASURES OF LIFE
Robert M. Sapolsky

It is one of the most riveting paintings ever made. In 1808 the populace of Madrid rose up against an occupying French army, an uprising that was soon crushed; the painting records the mass executions of insurgent Spaniards that began before dawn on the third day of May. Goya captures the appalling, machine-like process of the slaughter, implied by the piled-up bodies and the waiting line—those men in the light, seconds away from death, who have time only for a single burst of emotion: mute terror, fervent prayer to an indifferent god, or a final bellow affirming life and existence. And then they too are dead. It is impossible not to think of their dying and impossible not to imagine oneself in that circumstance. One wonders: How would I react? Would I be brave? Again and again one's eyes return to the men in that circle of final light.

It is only later that the mind returns to the other men in the picture. The face-less ones, automatons with guns, the members of the firing squad. Although their pull on the viewer is more gradual than that of the doomed men in the light, it is just as powerful. For those French soldiers were the agents of one of the most magnetic of human dramas, the taking of life. How could they do it? What did they

feel? *Did* they feel? Perhaps they were evil, or perhaps they were coerced. Or perhaps they truly believed in the necessity of their actions.

One of the great horrors of a world that provides its Goyas with endless such   3
scenes to paint is the possibility that after the smoke clears and the corpses are removed, the executioners give the executions no thought whatever. More likely,
though, at least some of those faceless men do reflect on their work, and do feel
guilt over it—or at least fear that others will someday judge them as well. In fact,
such remorse seems pervasive enough that firing squads have evolved in a way that,
in some circumstances, accommodates it. Central to that evolution are some sub-
tly distorting aspects of human cognition that have much to do with how people go
about killing people, how they judge people and how they set priorities for their
resources. And oddly, such cognitive distortions may have something to do with
how some of us feel about doing science.

Underpinning those suggestions is work done over the past twenty years, princi-   4
pally by the psychologists Amos N. Tversky of Stanford University and Daniel Kahneman of the University of California at Berkeley. Tversky and Kahneman have shown
that one can present people with two choices that, in terms of formal logic, are
equivalent—yet one choice may be strongly and consistently preferred and may
carry an emotional weight altogether different from that of the other choice. On
the other hand, one can offer people two logically disparate choices, yet the people may see them as equivalent. Such apparent contradictions could come about in
several ways: they could be caused by some commonly held cognitive biases identified by Tversky and Kahneman; they could be the outcome of the way the choices
are presented; or they could be a reflection of the makeup of each individual.

Consider this scenario: You are told about a young woman who in college was   5
much involved in leftist and progressive causes, a true social activist, committed
and concerned. You are then told that the young woman has since gone on to one
of four careers, and you are asked to rate the likelihood of her having pursued each
one: (1) an organizer of farmworkers (good chance, you say); (2) an environmental
activist (again, good chance); (3) a bank teller (seems highly unlikely); and (4) a bank
teller who is active in the feminist movement (well, surely that is much more likely
than her having become a mere bank teller; at least she's politically involved some
of the time). Thus you rate choice 4 as being more likely than choice 3. Logically,
however, it is impossible for choice 4, which features two constraints, to be more
likely than choice 3, which has only one.

Much of Tversky and Kahneman's work has gone into figuring out why people   6
sometimes make that distortion, embedding something more likely inside something less likely. Another aspect of their work identifies ways people regard scenarios as unequal when in fact they are formally equivalent:

> You are a physician and you have a hundred sick people on your hands. If you
> perform treatment A, twenty people will die. If you opt for treatment B, every-
> one has a 20 percent chance of dying. Which one do you choose?

The alternative scenario runs like this:

> You have a hundred sick people. If you perform treatment A, eighty people will live. If you opt for treatment B, everyone has an 80 percent chance of living. Which one do you choose?

The two scenarios are formally identical; they are merely framed differently. But it turns out that for the first scenario, which states things in terms of death, people will prefer option B, whereas for the second scenario, stated in terms of survivorship, people prefer option A. Thus when thinking about life, people prefer certainty; when thinking about death, they prefer odds, because it is always conceivable the odds can be beaten.   7

What if Tversky and Kahneman's scheme were applied to an early-nineteenth-century militia bent upon taking fatal revenge on some prisoners? At the time, a single shot fired from a moderate distance was often not enough to kill a person. Thus, some options: one man could stand at a distance and shoot at the prisoner five times; or five men could stand at the same distance and shoot at the prisoner once each.   8

Five-times-one or one-times-five are formally equivalent. So why did the firing squad evolve? I suspect it had something to do with a logical distortion it allowed each participant: if it takes one shot from each of five people to kill a man, each participant has killed one-fifth of a man. And on some cognitive level, it is far easier to decide then that you have not *really* killed someone or, if you possess extraordinary powers of denial, that you have not even contributed to killing someone.   9

Why do I think the firing squad was an accommodation to guilt, to the perception of guilt and to guilty consciences? Because of an even more intriguing refinement in the art of killing people. By the middle of the nineteenth century, when a firing squad assembled, it was often the case that one man would randomly be given a blank bullet. Whether each member of the firing squad could tell if he had the blank or not—by the presence or absence of a recoil at the time of the shooting—was irrelevant. Each man could go home that night with the certainty that he could never be accused, for sure, of having played a role in the killing.   10

Of course, the firing squad wasn't always the chosen method of execution, and that is where Tversky and Kahneman's work says something about the emotional weight of particular killings. If civilians were being killed—members of an unruly urban populace rising up in threatening protest—a single close-range shot to the head, a bayoneting or any such technique would be suitable. If the victim was some nondescript member of the enemy army, a firing squad was assembled in which there was rarely a random blank. But if, by the addled etiquette of nineteenth-century warfare, the victim was someone who mattered, an accomplished and brave officer of the enemy or an ex-comrade turned traitor, the execution would be a ceremony filled with honorifics and ambivalence.   11

For example, military law for the Union army during the American Civil War specified the rules of executing a traitor or deserter. Explicit instructions were   12 given to cover a range of details: how the enlisted men in attendance should be lined up, to ensure that everyone would see the shooting; the order in which the execution party marched in; the music to be played at various points by the band of the prisoner's regiment—and exactly when the provost marshal was supposed to put a blank into one of the guns, out of sight of the firing squad.

It all seems so quaint. But the same traditions persist today. In the states in the U.S. that allow executions, lethal injection is fast becoming the method of choice. In states more "backward" about the technology of execution, execution is done manually. But among the cutting-edge states, a $30,000 lethal-injection machine is used. Its benefits, extolled by its inventor at the wardens' conventions he frequents, include dual sets of syringes and dual stations with switches for two people to throw at the same time. A computer with a binary-number generator randomizes which syringe is injected into the prisoner and which ends up in a collection vial—then erases the decision. The state of New Jersey even *stipulates* the use of execution technology with multiple stations and a means of randomization. No one will ever know who really did it—not even the computer. 13

Such rites of execution are part of a subtle cognitive game. The formal set of circumstances exemplified by the multiple executioners who contribute to a singular execution has challenged societies in other forms. If five people must shoot to kill a man, then on some logical level no one of the shooters is a murderer. A different version of that principle is central to the idea of causation as taught in the law schools. Suppose two men start fires simultaneously, at opposite ends of a property. The fires merge and burn down the property. Who is responsible for the damage? The logic adopted by nineteenth-century American courts would have given solace to any participant in a firing squad. Each of the two arsonous defendants can correctly make the same point: If I had not set the fire, the property would still have burned. So how can I be guilty? Both of them would have walked free. 14

By 1927 a different interpretation rose out of a landmark court decision, *Kingston v. Chicago and NW Railroad*. The case did indeed begin with two fires—one caused by a locomotive and the other of unknown origin; the fires then joined to burn down the plaintiff's property. Before *Kingston*, judges would have ruled that the guilt of the singular burning of a property could not be distributed among multiple parties. But in the *Kingston* case, the courts declared for the first time that guilt for a singular burning, a singular injury, a singular killing, could be distributed among contributing parties. The decision prompted an almost abashed disclaimer from the judge: were the railroad able to get off free, he said, "the injustice of such a doctrine sufficiently impeaches the logic upon which it is founded." It was as if he had to apologize for being compassionate instead of logical. 15

His decision, however, was no more or less logical than the earlier ones that would have freed the railroad of wrongdoing. Again, it is a matter of Tverskian and Kahnemanesque framing: two fires join and burn down a property. The issue of guilt depends on whether the judges are more emotionally responsive to the defendants ("If I hadn't been there, the place would still have burned. How could I be 16 guilty?"), or more responsive to the plaintiff ("My home was burned by these people"). Daniel J. H. Greenwood of the University of Utah College of Law, who has thought long and hard about the 1927 philosophical transition, thinks the change reflects the general social progressiveness of the time: it shed some vestiges of the legal thought that had reflected the interests of robber barons and trusts. Judges began to frame cases logically in a way that would make them think first of the individual and damaged plaintiff, and that made it more difficult for anyone to hide behind corporate aggregateness. Suddenly it was possible for a number of people to be statistically guilty for a singular event.

The act of placing a blank among the bullets for the firing squad is even subtler in its cognitive implications. For example, on what occasions are people allowed the comfort of a metaphorical blank? Criminal law in the United States requires the unanimity of twelve jurors in a decision. You can bet that when the all-white jury acquitted the police in the first Rodney King trial, the jurors desperately wished for a system that would have allowed them to vote eleven-to-one for acquittal. Each one could then have hinted to the enraged world that he or she had been the innocent in the travesty. Yet the system does not allow such blanks, probably because the desire for perceived unanimity when the state forces its citizens to judge one another outweighs the desire of the state to protect the citizens who do the judging. 17

An even more intriguing aspect of the metaphorical blank is what one does with it cognitively. When a member of the two-man lethal-injection team goes home the night after the execution—and assuming he has a twinge of conscience—he does not think, "I am a murderer," or, "Today, I contributed to a murder," or even, "I have a 50 percent chance of having helped murder someone today." More likely, he would frame the same logic in terms of statistical innocence: "I have a 50 percent chance of *not* having helped kill someone." Or he might even find a way of rationalizing a fraction of innocence into an integer: "One of us didn't really do it. Why shouldn't it be me?" Or: "I know what the dummy button feels like. It was mine." Given the duality of perceiving the event as one of fractional guilt or fractional innocence, people not only bias toward the latter; they also are replete with clever rationalizations that distort the matter further, until it is the certain integer of innocence. 18

In other circumstances the bias goes the other way. An archetypally villainous industrialist, bloated and venal, contemplates a new profitable venture for his factory. His minions of advisers, on the basis of their calculations, tell him that the pollution his factory will dump into the drinking water will probably lead to three cancer deaths in his town of 100,000. Naturally he decides to go ahead with his remunerative plans. But that night he surely doesn't think in integers: "Today, for profit, I have consigned three innocents to their deaths." Instead, all his cognitive biases lead him to frame the matter in terms of statistical guilt: "All it does is increase the cancer risk .003 percent for each person. Trivial. Charles, you may serve me my dinner." 19

Tversky uses the term *tendencies* to describe the practice of conceiving guilt and innocence in fractions. He reserves the term *frequencies* to describe the bias toward viewing the same facts in integers. If one has done something bad, it is no ac- 20 cident that one thinks fractionally—or, statistically speaking, in terms of distributed tendencies, a world without complete faces. If one has done something good, the pull is toward frequencies and integers.

Thinking in frequencies is also the easiest way of getting someone to consider 21 another person's pains. It is overwhelmingly likely that if it is ever decided in the courts to hold tobacco companies responsible for killing endless numbers of people, the decision will not be a result of a class action suit, with claims of distributed pain. Rather, it will be because a jury will understand the pain of one personifying individual killed by cigarettes. "People think less extensionally when they think of tendencies than when they think of frequencies," says Tversky. In other words, as every journalist knows, empathy is grounded in a face, a whole number of vulnerability.

The work of Tversky and Kahneman teaches scientists all kinds of lessons about 22 cognitive pitfalls—including the fairly obvious ones people confront as they struggle with problems that invariably have multiple causes. For example, is the causality distributed among so many agents that people cannot perceive it? Do people distort their work with a cognitive bias toward finding a single magic bullet? We who do science all could learn a thing or two from Tversky and Kahneman. But there is an aspect of their work that tugs at my emotions. It comes from another of their scenarios:

> In a population, all the deaths are attributable to two diseases, each accounting for half the deaths. You have a choice. You can discover something that cures all the known cases of one disease, or you can discover something that cures half the cases of each disease.

By now it should be clear that the two options are formally equivalent: $1 \times \frac{1}{2}$ is 23 equal to $(\frac{1}{2} \times \frac{1}{2}) + (\frac{1}{2} \times \frac{1}{2})$. Yet people show a strong bias toward curing all the cases of one disease. It closes the books on that disease, enables one category to be crossed off. That kind of integer satisfies a sense of closure. In spite of our poetry and theorems and dreams, our cognitive pull is toward being concrete and tangible. And as a scientist, that is what plagues me emotionally.

In 1977 a group of biomedical scientists from the World Health Organization in- 24 oculated the populace of a town called Merca, in the hinterlands of Somalia, and thereby accomplished something extraordinary: they eradicated the last known case of smallpox on this planet. I think of that moment often, and always with the envy of knowing I will never accomplish something like that. When I was a postdoctoral fellow at the Salk Institute for Biological Studies, I would occasionally see Jonas Salk at seminars and feel a sense of awe, a scientist who knows an extraordinary closure.

I will never achieve that sense, not just because I am not as skillful a biomedical 25 scientist, but also because of the way science is typically done these days. Now the scientific arena is one in which a coherent picture of a problem emerges from the work of teams of people in dozens of laboratories, in which diseases often have multiple causes, in which biological messengers have multiple effects; in which a long, meandering route of basic research might eventually lead to clinical trials. The chances that one person can single-handedly bring closure to a biological research problem become ever more remote.

My own research is at an extreme of distributed causality. I study how stress, and a class of hormones secreted during stress, can endanger neurons in the brain and make those cells less likely to survive neurological disasters such as cardiac arrest and seizure. In other words, I do not study so much how stress can damage the brain as much as how it may exacerbate the toxicity of neurological insults. It is by no means clear yet whether things really work that way, let alone how important a variable stress is. But if every scientific fantasy of mine comes true—if, inconceivably, every experiment I go near works perfectly—I will be able to demonstrate that stress is an exacerbating factor in modulating the neurological damage that affects hundreds of thousands of people each year. And if every half-baked therapeutic idea I have works, the new knowledge will lead to a way of decreasing the brain damage, at least a little bit, in each of those people.   **26**

But even in my fantasy world, stress would be only one of many statistical villains. It may be a factor in many diseases that cause brain damage, but, at best, it is only a small factor; its importance would be distributed over the vast number of cases. And with deep knowledge of the problem, the best I could hope for is to bring about statistical good—in effect, to save a hundredth or a thousandth of a life here and there. That would be wonderful, indeed. Still there is the pull of integers.   **27**

Few scientists will ever save or solve in integers rather than in fractions. Saving in integers is the realm of clinical medicine; there one deals with one person at a time. Moreover, saving lives in integers is the realm of an era of science that for the most part is past, when the lone investigator could conceivably vanquish a disease. Instead, in the present world we scientists have *factors* that modulate and synergize and influence and interact, but, oh, so rarely *cause*. It is abundantly true that $1 \times \frac{1}{2}$ is equal to $(\frac{1}{2} \times \frac{1}{2}) + (\frac{1}{2} \times \frac{1}{2})$. We have a cognitive bias toward the former, and we are in a profession that must exalt extreme versions of the latter.   **28**

That bias must plague us scientists when we try to justify why we do the work we do. I don't mean *justify* in the sense in which we use the term when we come up with our nonsense rationalizations in the last paragraphs of our grant proposals, hoping the National Institutes of Health will bless us for another five years. I mean the justifications we come up with at night, when we think about being in a profession that requires us to pour radiation down a sink or to kill animals, that calls on us to work so hard that the rest of our selves wither. We must battle distributed villains, charge them with statistical guilt, do the groundwork that will lead to minute fractional victories somewhere down the line. Such is the nature of our progress. But I wish the demands of our profession were not so at odds with our fundamental cognitive bias. I wish they were not so at odds with the desire to see the face of someone we helped.   **29**

▪4▪

The Multiple-Source Essay

Until now, most of your writing assignments have been based on information derived from a *single* source. You have learned to paraphrase, summarize, re-arrange, and unify your evidence without sacrificing accuracy or completeness.

Now, as you begin to work with *many* different sources, you will need to un-derstand and organize a wider range of materials. You will want to present the ideas of your sources in all their variety while at the same time maintaining your own perspective, encompassing all the shades of opinion.

- How can you describe each author's ideas without taking up too much space for each one?
- How can you fit all your sources smoothly into your essay without allow-ing one to dominate?
- How can you transform a group of disparate sources into an essay that is yours?

To help you learn to work with multiple sources, most of the examples, ex-ercises, and writing assignments in this chapter will use materials that are brief and easy to experiment with. Most come from notes taken by students during informal interviews or written responses to a topic or an article. In the writing assignments, you may be asked to collect your own materials by doing a series of interviews or by joining your classmates in writing your reactions to a gen-eral question.

The statements that you will work with in this chapter not only provide useful practice for library research, but also have their equivalents in professional writing. Lawyers, doctors, engineers, social workers, and other professionals regularly consult written sources and engage in various kinds of library research; but, equally often, they work from notes taken at interviews to prepare case notes, case studies, legal testimony, reports, and market research.

SELECTING INFORMATION FOR A MULTIPLE-SOURCE ESSAY

In academic writing, you do not usually find the materials for an essay in a neatly assembled package. On the contrary, before beginning an essay, you must find and select your materials. The first stage of a research project is traditionally the trip to the library with a topic to explore and questions to ask, a search for information that will later be interpreted, sifted, and synthesized into a finished essay.

To demonstrate this process, assume that you have been assigned the following project, which calls for a *narrow range of research:*

Read an entire newspaper or news magazine published on a day of your choice during this century (such as your birthday), and write a summary describing what life was like on that day. Your sources are the articles and advertisements in that day's paper.

Given the amount and variety of information contained in the average newspaper, you must first decide what and how much to include. You would look for two kinds of evidence—major events that might have altered the fabric of most people's lives, and more ordinary happenings that might suggest how people typically spent their days. While these events may have taken place before your birth, your not having been there may give you the advantage of perspective: as an outsider, you can more easily distinguish between stories of lasting historic importance and those that simply reflect their era.

To begin this project, follow these steps:

1. Read rapidly through the entire newspaper. Then read the same issue again more slowly, jotting down your impressions of important *kinds* of events or *characteristics* of daily life. Search for a pattern, a thesis that sums up what you have read.

2. Review your notes, and isolate a few main ideas that seem worth developing. Then read the issue a third time, making sure that there really is sufficient evidence for the points that you wish to make. Note any additional information that you expect to use, and write down the page number next to each reference in your notes. Remember that you are not trying to "use up" all the available information.

3. Plan a series of paragraphs, each focusing on a somewhat different theme that is either significant in itself or typical of the day that you are describing. Spend some time choosing a strategy for a sequence of paragraphs that will not only introduce your reader to the world that you are describing, but also make apparent the pattern of events—the thesis—that seems to characterize that day.

Drawing Conclusions from Your Information

Through your essay, you should help your readers to form conclusions about the significance of the information it contains. *The evidence should not be expected to speak for itself.* Consider the following paragraph:

> Some popular books in the first week of 1945 were Brave Men by Ernie Pyle, Forever Amber, by Kathleen Winsor, and The Time for Decision by Sumner Welles. The average price of these new, hard-cover books was about three dollars each. The price of the daily Times was three cents, and Life magazine was ten cents.

What is probably most interesting to your reader is how little the reading material cost. This evidence would be very informative in a paragraph devoted to the cost of living or the accessibility of information through the media. Here, however, the emphasis is on the books. Can you tell why they were popular? Do they seem typical of 1945's best-seller list? If you don't have sufficient knowledge to answer questions like these, you will do better to focus on some other aspect of daily life that the paper describes in greater detail. *Unexplained information is of no value to your reader,* who cannot be assumed to know more than—or even as much as—you do.

In contrast, another student, writing about a day shortly after the end of World War II, built a paragraph around a casualty list in the *New York Times.* What seemed significant about the list was the fact that, by the end of the war, casualties had become so routine that they assumed a relatively minor place in daily life. Notice that the paragraph begins with a topic sentence that establishes the context and draws its conclusion at the end.

> For much of the civilian population, the worst part of the war had been the separation from their loved ones, who had gone off to fight in Europe, Africa, and the Pacific. Even after the end of the war, they still had to wait for the safe arrival home of the troops. In order to inform the public, the New York Times ran a daily list of troop arrivals. However, not everyone was destined to return, and the Times also ran a list of casualties. On September 4, that list appeared at the very bottom of page 2, a place where it would be easily overlooked except by those interested in finding a particular name.

Another paragraph about May 6, 1946, informs the reader that the postwar mid-forties were a transitional period.

> The process of switching over from a wartime to a peacetime economy was not without its pains. Then, as now, there was a high rate of unemployment. The Times featured a story about the million women production workers who had recently lost their jobs in war industries. Returning male and female veterans were also flooding the job market. Some working wives were waiting to see how their husbands readjusted to postwar jobs. If their ex-GI husbands could bring home enough money to support the family, they could return to their roles as housewives. If their husbands chose to continue their education or vocational training under the GI Bill, they would expect to stay on the job as long as they could.

This paragraph appears to be a straightforward account of the transition from a wartime economy, as expressed in the topic sentence; but the writer is, in fact, summarizing information taken from *several* articles in that day's newspaper. (Notice that, while the source of the information—the *Times*—is cited, the names of the reporters are not considered significant in this very general summary.) The suggestion of a personal comment—unemployment, one gathers, is a recurring problem—adds immediacy and significance to a topic that might otherwise be remote to today's readers.

Finally, it is not always necessary to present your conclusion in a topic sentence at the *beginning* of your paragraph. Here is one in which the evidence is presented first:

> The July 30, 1945, issue of Newsweek lists three bills that were going before Congress. The first, the Burton-Ball-Hatch Bill, proposed that all industries institute a labor management mediation system. The second, the Kilgore Bill, proposed providing $25 a week in unemployment for a period of 26 weeks. And the third, the Mead Bill, proposed raising the minimum wage from 40 cents to 65 cents. It is obvious from these three bills that a great deal of attention was being focused on employment, or the lack of it. Here we have another clue about the life-style of 1945. The majority of the working class must have been greatly dissatisfied with economic conditions for their congressmen to have proposed these improvements. These bills were also in keeping with the late President Roosevelt's New Deal policy, which was primarily directed toward the improvement of economic conditions. From these bills, it is safe to assume that the cost of living may have been rising, that unemployment was still something of a problem, and that strikes by workers were becoming so prevalent that a mediation system seemed necessary.

This paragraph explicitly links together three related points, suggests their possible significance, and provides a historical context (the New Deal) in which to understand them.

EXERCISE 19

Read the following student essay, a description of life taken from the *New York Times* of September 21, 1967. Analyze each paragraph and be prepared to discuss the following questions:

1. What are the writer's reasons for building a paragraph around that piece of information? (Use your own knowledge of the contents of the average newspaper today to estimate the range of choices that the writer might have had.)
2. How clear and complete is the presentation of the information?
3. How do the topic sentences interpret the information and suggest its significance for the reader?
4. How is the essay organized: the relationship between paragraphs; the sequence of paragraphs; the unity within each paragraph; the transitions between paragraphs?
5. What is the thesis and how well does the author characterize September 21, 1967, as typical of its era and as a contrast to her own era?

According to the New York Times, on September 21, 1967, there was considerable violence and unrest in the United States, much of it in response to the United States' involvement in the Vietnam War. The United States had increased its bombing of Vietnam in an attempt to cut off the port of Haiphong from contact with the rest of the world. As a result, a group opposed to President Johnson's Vietnam policy began an "anti-Johnson" campaign. They were a coalition of Democrats who hoped to block his reelection. Meanwhile, seventy female antiwar demonstrators were arrested outside the White House. Later, to protest their arrest, 500 members of Women Strike for Peace marched to the White House and clashed with police.

There was not only civil unrest on this day, but also a conflict between President Johnson and the House Ways and Means Committee over the President's proposed tax increase. The committee would not approve the increase without a 5 billion dollar cut in spending. The Senate proposed the following cuts: a 2 billion dollar decrease in defense spending; a 1 billion dollar decrease in "long-range research"; and a 2 billion dollar decrease in other civilian services. However, aid to the poor and to cities was not to be cut. In defense of the president's request, Secretary of Commerce Trowbridge said that a tax increase would be necessary because of inflation.

Throughout the rest of the country, there was much racial tension and violence. There had been days of fighting in Dayton, Ohio's West Side, which had a large black population. A rally took place there to protest the killing of a black Social Security Administration field-worker. There was also a supermarket fire in Dayton, which resulted in $20,000 of damage. In the end, twenty teenagers were arrested. In the Casa Central Outpost, a Puerto Rican neighborhood in Chicago, Governor Romney of Michigan, a would-be presidential candidate, was given a hostile welcome. His visit to the Outpost was blocked by its director, Luis Cuza, who handed him a two-page press release claiming that the Governor was only touring these poor neighborhoods for political gain. Governor Romney expressed outrage at the accusation and the fact that the Outpost had not informed him earlier that he would not be welcome. In the meantime, the streets of Hartford, Connecticut's North End were quiet after three days of racial violence. Civil rights demonstrators were marching against housing discrimination in the South End, a predominantly middle-class Italian neighborhood. There were 66 arrests, mainly of young blacks. To control the violence, five to ten policemen were posted at every intersection, and the mayor asked for a voluntary curfew.

On the local level, a protest against traffic conditions took place in the Bronx, at 149th Street and Courtlandt Avenue. The protesters, four clergymen and dozens of neighbors, wanted Courtlandt Avenue to be one way. Two men refused to leave after police tried to disperse the crowd.

There was not only racial unrest in the country on this day, but also many labor disputes and strikes. Seventeen thousand Prudential Insurance Company of America agents threatened to strike if no contract was agreed on in four days. They could not accept any of the proposals previously given to them. Also, the steelhaulers' strike in Chicago was spreading east, and had already resulted in a violent confrontation in Pittsburgh. Finally, on strike were the 59,500 New York public school teachers, whose refusal to enter the classrooms had kept more than a million students out of school for eight days. The teachers' slogan was "no contract, no work."

Even the weather was in turmoil. Hurricane Beulah, in Texas, had winds estimated at 80 miles per hour at the center of the storm and 120-150 miles per hour at its peak. Eighty-five percent of Port Isabel, a town at the southern tip of Texas, was destroyed, and four people were killed by the record number of twenty-seven tornadoes spawned by Beulah. All the Gulf states experienced heavy rain in Beulah's aftermath. Meanwhile, rain and thunderstorms also battered the east coast.

GENERALIZING FROM EXAMPLES

Summarizing the contents of a newspaper can cause problems for the writer because newspaper stories often have little in common except that they all happened on the same day. Academic writing is rarely so arbitrary: *a common theme often links apparently dissimilar ideas or facts.* The writer should observe this common theme and construct generalizations that cover several items in the sources.

Assume that you have been asked to consider and react to *seven different but related situations,* and then formulate *two generalizations.*

A. In a sentence or two, write down your probable reaction if you found yourself in each of the following situations.* Write quickly; this exercise calls for immediate, instinctive responses.

1. You are walking behind someone. You see him take out a cigarette pack, pull out the last cigarette, put the cigarette in his mouth, crumple the package, and nonchalantly toss it over his shoulder onto the sidewalk. What would you do?

2. You are sitting on a train and you notice a person (same age, sex, and type as yourself) lighting up a cigarette, despite the no smoking sign. No one in authority is around. What would you do?

3. You are pushing a shopping cart in a supermarket and you hear the thunderous crash of cans. As you round the corner, you see a two-year-old child being beaten, quite severely, by his mother, apparently for pulling out the bottom can of the pile. What would you do?

4. You see a teenager that you recognize shoplifting at the local discount store. You're concerned that she'll get into serious trouble if the store detective catches her. What would you do?

5. You're driving on a two-lane road behind another car. You notice that one of its wheels is wobbling more and more. It looks as if the lugs are coming off one by one. There's no way to pass, because cars are coming from the other direction in a steady stream. What would you do?

6. You've been waiting in line (at a supermarket or gas station) for longer than you expected and you're irritated at the delay. Suddenly, you notice that someone very much like yourself has sneaked in ahead of you in the line. There are a couple of people before you. What would you do?

7. You've raised your son not to play with guns. Your rich uncle comes for a long-awaited visit and he brings your son a .22 rifle with lots of ammunition. What would you do?

B. Read over your responses to the seven situations and try to form two general statements (in one or two sentences each), one about *the circumstances in which you would take action* and a second about *the circumstances in which you would choose to do nothing.* Do *not* simply list the incidents, one after the other, divided in two groups.

*Adapted from "Strategy 24" in Sidney B. Simon et al., *Values Clarification* (New York: Hart, 1972).

You form your generalizations by examining the group of situations in which you *do* choose to take action and determining *what they have in common.* (It is also important to examine the "leftovers," and to understand why these incidents did *not* warrant your interference.) As a first step, you might try looking at each situation in terms of either its *causes* or its *consequences.* For example, in each case there is someone to blame, someone who is responsible for creating the problem—except for number five, where fate (or poor auto maintenance) threatens to cause an accident.

As for consequences, in some of the situations (littering, for example), there is *little potential danger,* either to you or to the public. Do these circumstances discourage action? In others, however, the possible victim is oneself or a member of one's family. Does self-interest alone drive one to act? Do adults tend to intervene in defense of children—even someone else's child—since they cannot stand up for themselves? Or, instead of calculating the consequences of *not* intervening, perhaps you should imagine *the possible consequences of interference.* In which situations can you expect to receive abuse for failing to mind your own business? Would this prevent you from intervening? As always, *only by examining the evidence can you discover the basis for a generalization.*

The list of examples has two characteristics worth noting:

1. Each item is intended to illustrate a specific and very different situation. Thus, although it does not include every possible example, the list as a whole constitutes a *set* of public occasions for interfering with a stranger's conduct.

2. Since you probably would not choose to act in every situation, you cannot use the entire list as the basis for your generalization. Rather, you must *establish a boundary line,* dividing those occasions when you would intervene from those times when you would decide not to act. The exact boundary between intervention and nonintervention will probably differ from person to person, as will the exact composition of the list of occasions justifying intervention. Thus, there is no one correct generalization.

This exercise results in a set of guidelines for justifiably minding other people's business. *You formulate the guidelines by applying your own standards to a sampling of possible examples.*

Broad concepts offer a great deal of room for disagreement and ambiguity and therefore allow a great many interpretations. You can clarify your ideas and opinions about any important abstract issue by inventing a set of illustrations, marking off a subgroup, and then constructing a generalization that describes what is *inside* the boundary: the common characteristics of the contents of the subgroup. Thus, in the previous problem, one person might consider the set of seven examples and then decide to intervene only in Situations 3 (the child beaten in a supermarket), 5 (the wobbly wheel), and 7 (the gift of a gun). What makes these three cases different from the others? They and they alone involve protecting some person from physical harm.

This process of *differentiation*, followed by *generalized description*, is usually called "definition"; it can serve as an essay strategy in its own right or form the basis for a comparison, classification, argumentation, or evaluation essay.

ANALYZING MULTIPLE SOURCES

When you write from sources, your object is not to establish a single "right" conclusion but rather to present a thesis statement of your own that is based on your examination of a variety of views. Some of these views may conflict with your own and with each other. Because of this diversity, organizing multiple sources is more difficult than working with a series of examples, with the contents of a newspaper, or with even a highly complex single essay.

The writing process for multiple sources begins with the *analysis of ideas*.

Analysis is first breaking down a mass of information into individual pieces and then examining the pieces.

As you underline and annotate your sources, you look for similarities and distinctions in meaning, as well as the basic principles underlying what you read. Only when you have taken apart the evidence of each source to see how it works can you begin to find ways of putting everything back together again in your own essay.

To illustrate the analysis of sources, assume that you have asked five people what the word *foreign* means. You want to provide a reasonably complete definition of the word by exploring all the shades of meaning (or connotations) that the five sources suggest. If each one of the five gives you a completely different answer, then you will not have much choice in the organization of your definition. In that case, you would probably present each separate definition of *foreign* in a separate paragraph, citing a different person as the source for each one. But *responses from multiple sources almost always overlap*, as these do. Notice the common meanings in this condensed list of the five sources' responses:

John Brown: "Foreign" means unfamiliar and exotic.

Lynne Williams: "Foreign" means strange and unusual.

Bill White: "Foreign" means strange and alien (as in "foreign body").

Mary Green: "Foreign" means exciting and exotic.

Bob Friedman: "Foreign" means difficult and incomprehensible (as in "foreign language").

Planning your essay depends on finding common meanings, not writing down the names of the five sources. That is why the one-source-per-paragraph method should hardly ever be used (except on those rare occasions when all the sources completely disagree.)

When you organize ideas taken from multiple sources, you should reject the idea of devoting one paragraph to each page of your notes, simply because all the ideas on that page happen to have come from the same person.

If you did so, each paragraph would have a topic sentence that might read, "Then I asked John Brown for his definition," as if John Brown were the topic for discussion, instead of his views on "foreign." And if John Brown and Mary Green each get a separate paragraph, there will be some repetition because both think that one of the meanings of "foreign" is "exotic." "Exotic" should be the topic of one of your paragraphs, not the person (or people) who suggested that meaning.

Analyzing Shades of Meaning

Here is a set of notes, summarizing the ideas of four different people about the meaning of the word *individualist*. How would you analyze these notes?

Richard Becker: an "individualist" is a person who is unique and does not "fall into the common mode of doing things"; would not follow a pattern set by society. "A youngster who is not involved in the drug scene just because his friends are." A good word; it would be insulting only if it referred to a troublemaker.

Simon Jackson: doing things on your own, by yourself. "She's such an individualist that she insisted on answering the question in her own way." Sometimes the word is good, but mostly it has a bad connotation: someone who rebels against society or authority.

Lois Asher: one who doesn't "follow the flock." The word refers to someone who is very independent. "I respect Jane because she is an individualist and her own person." Usually very complimentary.

Vera Lewis: an extremely independent person. "An individualist is a person who does not want to contribute to society." Bad meaning: usually antisocial. She first heard the word in psych class, describing the characteristics of the individualist and "how he reacts to society."

At first glance, all the sources seem to say much the same thing: the individualist is different and "independent." However, it is worthwhile to examine the context in which the four sources are defining this word. First, *all the responses define the individualist in terms of other people,* either the "group," or the "flock," or "society." Oddly enough, it is not easy to describe the individualist as an individual, even though it is that person's isolation that each source is emphasizing. Whatever is "unique" about the individualist—what is described as "independent"—is defined by *the gap between that person and everyone else.* (Notice that both "unique" and "independent" are words that also suggest a larger group in the background; after all, one has to be independent *of* something!)

Having found a meaning that is common to all four sources ("independence") and, just as important, having established the context for a definition ("from the group"), you must now look for differences. Obviously, Lois Asher thinks that to be an individualist is a good thing; Vera Lewis believes that individualism is bad; and the other two suggest that both connotations are possible. But simply describing the reactions of the four sources stops short of defining the word according to those reactions.

Richard Becker and Lois Asher, two people who suggest a favorable meaning, describe the group from which the individual is set apart in similar and somewhat disapproving terms: "common"; "pattern set by society"; "follow the flock." Becker and Asher both seem to suggest *a degree of conformity or sameness which the individualist is right to reject*, as Becker's youngster rejects his friends' drugs. But Vera Lewis, who thinks that the word's connotation is bad, sees the individualist in a more benign society, with which the individual ought to identify himself and to which he ought to contribute. To be antisocial is to be an undesirable person—from the point of view of Lewis and society. Simon Jackson (who is ambivalent about the word) uses the phrases "by yourself" and "on your own," which suggest the isolation and the lack of support, as well as the admirable independence, of the individualist. In Jackson's view, the individualist's self-assertion becomes threatening to all of us in society ("antisocial") only when the person begins to rebel against authority. Probably for Jackson, and certainly for Vera Lewis, the ultimate authority should rest with society as a whole, not with the individualist. Even Richard Becker, who admires independence, draws the line at allowing the individualist complete autonomy: when reliance on one's own authority leads to "troublemaking," the term becomes an insult.

EXERCISE 20

Analyze the following set of notes for a definition of the word *luxury*. Then explore some ways to organize these notes by following these steps:

A. Find the important terms or concepts that can lead to a context for defining *luxury*.

B. Write two generalizations that might serve as topic sentences for a two-paragraph essay. (Do not use "favorable" and "unfavorable" as your two topics.)

Sabrina Bryant: describing something of unusually high quality or refinement; it refers to an object that exceeds ordinary standards of value. "BMWs are luxury cars because of the quality of the engineering and the attention to all details in their assembly."

Cynthia Martin: an elitist commodity beyond the reach of most people; something that serves only to mark someone's social or economic status, but is otherwise impractical. "Gold-plated faucets and marble sinks are luxuries."

John St. Clair: something non-essential, but which makes life more pleasant. A treat most people allow themselves only occasionally. "Caviar or champagne are luxuries for most people."

Regina Torres: anything that contributes to a life of self-absorption and seclusion; an object that shields people from the difficulties of the "real world." "The wealthy live behind a wall of luxuries that protect them from the harsh realities most people suffer."

Margaret Williams: profligacy, excess, physical overindulgence that leads to dissipation. "People who surrender to a life of luxury lose their moral bearings."

SYNTHESIZING MULTIPLE SOURCES

Once you have analyzed each of your sources and discovered their similarities and differences, you then reassemble these parts into a more coherent whole. This process is called *synthesis*. Although at first you may regard analysis and synthesis as contradictory operations, *they are actually overlapping stages of a single, larger process.*

To illustrate the way in which analysis and synthesis work together, let us examine a set of answers to the question: "Would you buy a lottery ticket? Why?" First, read through these summaries of all seven responses.

Mary Smith: She thinks that lottery tickets were made for people to enjoy and win. It's fun to try your luck. She looks forward to buying her ticket, because she feels that, for one dollar, you have a chance to win a lot more. It's also fun scratching off the numbers to see what you've won. Some people don't buy tickets because they think the lottery is a big rip-off; but "a dollar can't buy that much today, so why not spend it and have a good time?"

John Jones: He would buy a lottery ticket for three reasons. The first reason is that he would love to win. The odds are like a challenge, and he likes to take a chance. The second reason is just for fun. When he has two matching tickets, he really feels happy, especially when he thinks that dollars can be multiplied into hundreds or thousands. "It's like Russian roulette." The third reason is that part of the money from the lottery goes toward his education. The only problem, he says, is that they are always sold out!

Michael Green: He has never bought a lottery ticket in his life because he doesn't want to lose money. He wants to be sure of winning. Also, he says that he isn't patient enough. The buyer of a lottery ticket has to be very patient to wait for his chance to win. He thinks that people who buy tickets all the time must enjoy "living dangerously."

Anne White: Buying a lottery ticket gives her a sense of excitement. She regards herself as a gambler. "When you win two dollars or five dollars you get a thrill of victory, and when you see that you haven't, you feel the agony of defeat." She thinks that people who don't buy tickets must be very cautious and noncompetitive, since the lottery brings "a sense of competition with you against millions of other people." She also knows that the money she spends on tickets goes toward education.

Margaret Brown: She feels that people who buy tickets are wasting their money. The dollars spent on the lottery could be in the bank, getting interest. Those people who buy tickets should expect to have thrown out their money, and should take their losses philosophically, instead of jumping up and down and screaming about their disappointment. Finally, even if she could afford the risk, the laws of her religion forbid her to participate in "any sort of game that is a form of gambling."

William Black: He would buy a lottery ticket, because he thinks it can be fun, but he wouldn't buy too many, because he thinks it's easy for people to get carried away and obsessed by the lottery. He enjoys the anticipation of wanting to win and maybe winning. "I think that you should participate, but in proportion to your budget; after all, one day you might just be a winner."

Elizabeth Watson: She wouldn't buy a lottery ticket because she considers them a rip-off. The odds are too much against you, 240,000 to 1. Also, it is much too expensive, "and I don't have the money to be throwing away on such foolishness." She thinks that people who indulge themselves with lottery tickets become gamblers, and she's against all kinds of gambling. Such people have no sense or self-control. Finally, "I'm a sore loser, so buying lottery tickets just isn't for me."

Making a Chart of Common Ideas

Since you are working with seven sources with varying opinions, you need a way to record the process of analysis. One effective way is to make a *chart of commonly held views*. To do so, follow these two steps, which should be carried out *simultaneously*:

1. Read each statement carefully, and identify each separate reason that is being cited for and against playing the lottery by writing a number above or next to the relevant comment. When a similar comment is made by another person, use *the same number* to provide a key to the final list of common reasons. In this step, you are analyzing your sources. Here is what the first two sets of notes might look like once the topic numbers have been inserted:

Mary Smith: She thinks that lottery tickets were made for people to enjoy and win. It's fun to try your luck. She looks forward to buying her ticket, because she feels that, for one dollar, you have a chance to win a lot more. It's also fun scratching off the numbers to see what you've won. Some people don't buy tickets because they think the lottery is a big rip-off; but "a dollar can't buy that much today, so why not spend it and have a good time?"

John Jones: He would buy a lottery ticket for three reasons. The first reason is that he would love to win. The odds are like a challenge, and he likes to take a chance. The second reason is just for fun. When he has two matching tickets, he really feels happy, especially when he thinks that dollars can be multiplied into hundreds or thousands. "It's like Russian roulette." The third reason is that part of the money from the lottery goes toward his education. The only problem, he says, is that they are always sold out!

2. At the same time as you number each of your reasons, also write a list or chart of reasons on a separate sheet of paper. Each reason should be assigned *the same number* you wrote next to it in the original statement. Don't make a new entry when the same reason is repeated by a second source. Next to each entry on your chart, put the names of the people who have mentioned that reason. You are now beginning to synthesize your sources.

Here's what your completed list of reasons might look like:

Reason	Sources
1. People play the lottery because it's fun.	Smith; Jones
2. People play the lottery because they like the excitement of taking a chance and winning.	Smith; Jones; Green; White; Black
3. People don't play the lottery because they think it's a rip-off.	Smith; Watson
4. People play the lottery because they are contributing to education.	Jones; White
5. People don't play the lottery because they have better things to do with their money.	Green; Brown; Watson
6. People play the lottery because they like to gamble.	White; Brown; Watson
7. People who play the lottery and those who refuse to play worry about the emotional reactions of the players.	Green; White; Brown; Black; Watson

The process of synthesis starts as soon as you start to make your list. The list of common reasons represents the reworking of seven separate sources into a single new pattern that can serve as the basis for a new essay.

Distinguishing between Reasons

One of the biggest problems in synthesis is deciding, in cases of overlapping, whether you actually have one reason or two. Since overlapping reasons were deliberately not combined, the preceding list may be unnecessarily long.

For example, Reasons 1 and 2 reflect *the difference between the experiences of having fun and feeling the thrill of excitement*—a difference in sensation that most people would understand. You might ask yourself, "Would someone play the lottery just for fun without the anticipation of winning? Or would someone experience a thrill of excitement without any sense of fun at all?" If one sensation can exist without the other, you have sufficient reason for putting both items on your chart. Later on, the similarities, not the differences, might make you want to combine the two; but, *at the beginning, it is important to note down exactly what ideas and information are available to you.*

The distinction between the thrill of excitement (2) and the pleasure of gambling (6) is more difficult to perceive. The former is, perhaps, more innocent than the latter and does not carry with it any of the obsessive overtones of gambling.

Resenting the lottery because it is a rip-off (3) and resenting the lottery because the players are wasting their money (5) appear at first glance to be similar reactions. However, references to the rip-off tend to emphasize the "injured victim" whose money is being whisked away by a public agency. In other words, Reason 3 emphasizes *self-protection from robbery;* Reason 5 emphasizes *the personal virtue of thrift.*

Reason 7 is not really a reason at all. Some comments in the notes do not fit into a tidy list of reasons for playing, yet they provide a valuable insight into human motivation and behavior as expressed in lottery-playing. An exploration of the emotions that characterize the player and the nonplayer (always allowing for the lottery preference of the source) might be an interesting way to conclude an essay.

Deciding on a Sequence of Topics

The topics in your chart appear in the same random order as your notes. Once the chart is completed, you should decide on a more logical sequence of topics by ordering the entries in the list. You can make an indirect impact on your reader by choosing a logical sequence that supports the pattern that you discovered in analyzing your sources.

Here are two possible ways to arrange the "lottery" reasons. Which sequence do you prefer? Why?

1. fun	1. fun
2. excitement	2. rip-off
3. gambling	3. excitement and gambling
4. education	4. misuse of money
5. rip-off	5. education
6. misuse of money	6. personality of the gambler
7. personality of the gambler	

The right-hand sequence *contrasts the advantages and disadvantages* of playing the lottery. Moving back and forth between paired reasons calls attention to the relation between opposites and, through constant contrast, makes
the material interesting for the reader. The left-hand sequence places all
the advantages and disadvantages together, providing an opportunity to *explore positive and negative reactions to the lottery separately* without interruption, therefore encouraging more complex development. Both sequences are
acceptable.

EXERCISE 21

This exercise is based on a set of interview notes, answering the question "Would
you give money to a beggar?"

A. Read through the notes. 1) Identify distinct and different reasons by placing numbers next to the relevant sentences. 2) As you number each new
   reason, add an entry to the chart. (The first reason is already filled in.)

Reason	Sources
1. I can afford to give to beggars.	
2.	
3.	
4.	
5.	
6.	
7.	
8.	
9.	
10.	

B. Arrange the numbered reasons in a logical sequence. If it makes sense to
   you, combine those reasons that belong together. Be prepared to explain
   the logic behind your sequence of points. If you can find two possible sequences, include both, explaining the advantages of each.

Would You Give Money to a Beggar? Responses

Jonathan Cohen: When asked for money on the street, I often apply a maxim of a friend of mine. He takes the question, "Have you got any spare change?" literally: if he has any loose change, he hands it over, without regard for his impression of what the money's for, since he doesn't think ulterior motives are any of his business. Since I can always afford the kind of contribution that's usually asked for—fifty cents or a dollar—or am at least less likely to miss it than the person asking me for it, I usually take the request as the only qualification of "need." I'm more likely to give out money if I don't have to go into my billfold for it, however, and would rather give out transit tokens or food, if I have them. But I want to be sympathetic; I often think, "There but for the grace of God go I."

Jennifer Sharone: I hate to think about what people who beg have to undergo; it makes me feel so fortunate to be well dressed and to have good food to eat and a home and a job. Begging seems kind of horrifying to me—that in this country there are people actually relying on the moods of strangers just to stay alive. I give to people who seem to have fallen on hard times, who aren't too brazen, who seem embarrassed to be asking me for money. I guess I do identify with them a lot.

Michael Aldrich: If a person meets my eye and asks plainly and forthrightly (and isn't falling-down drunk), I try to empty my pocket, or at least come up with a quarter or two. If the person has an unusually witty spiel—even if it's outlandish—I give more freely. I don't mind giving small change; it's quick and easy. I try not to think about whether or not the person really "needs" the money—how could you ever know? On some level, I think that if someone's begging, they need the money. Period. There's an old guy who stands on my corner—he's been there for years. I always give him money, if I have the change. If I don't have it, he says a smile will do. I would hate to think of him going without a meal for a long time or having to sleep out in the rain. He reminds me of my father and my uncle.

Marianne Lauro: I used to give people money, but frankly, I'm too embarrassed by the whole process. It seems to me that folks who really couldn't be all that grateful for somebody's pocket change still make an effort to appear grateful, and then I'm supposed to get to feel magnanimous when I really feel ridiculous telling them they're welcome to a couple of coins that don't even amount to carfare. So the whole transaction seems vaguely humiliating for everyone concerned. Really, the city or the state or the federal government should be doing something about this—not expecting ordinary people, going home from work, or whatever, to support people who have mental or physical impairments or addictions, especially when you're never sure what their money will be used for. But maybe I'm just rationalizing now—maybe the most "humane" thing about these kinds of transactions is the mutual embarrassment.

Donald Garder: I try, when possible, to respond to the person approaching me, by looking at them, perhaps even making eye contact, which frequently lends some dignity to the moment. But then I don't always reach into my pocket. I often give to people with visible physical handicaps, but rarely to someone who's "young and able-bodied." Sometimes I feel guilty, but I'm never sure if the person is for real or not—I've known people who swindled people out of money by pretending to be homeless, so I have a nagging doubt about whether or not a beggar is legitimate.

Darrin Johnson: I never give on the subway—I hate the feeling of entrapment, of being held hostage. The "O.K., so I have you until the next stop so I'm going to wear you down with guilt until I get the money out of you." I really resent that. I flatly refuse to give under those circumstances because it just pisses me off. I might give to somebody just sitting on the street, with a sign and a cup or something—someone who isn't making a big scene, who leaves it up to me whether I give or not. But I hate feeling coerced.

Jenny Nagel: I never give to people on the streets anymore—there are places where people who are really in need can go if they're really starving or need drug treatment or something. Someone once told me, after I'd given money to some derelict looking guy, that he'd probably buy rubbing alcohol or boot polish and melt it down for the alcohol content—that my money was just helping him kill himself. After that I never gave to anyone on the street. I'd rather make a contribution to a social agency.

Paul O'Rourke: I used to give money or if asked I'd give a cigarette. But one day a beggar let loose with a stream of obscenities after I gave him some money. A lot of these people are really messed up—the government should be looking after them, doing more to help them; if they keep getting money from people off the street, they'll just keep on begging. So now I volunteer once a month at a food shelf, and give to charitable organizations, rather than hand out money on the street.

ORGANIZING MULTIPLE SOURCES

Playing the lottery is not a subject that lends itself to lengthy or abstract discussion; therefore, charting reasons for and against playing the lottery is not difficult. The article that follows defines a social, political, and humanitarian problem and suggests two methods of dealing with it, without favoring either "solution" or the values on which each is based. The reporter's sources, quoted in the article, simply cite aspects of the problem and the hope that the courts will deal with it.

Fifteen students were asked to read the article and to offer their opinions; these are presented following the article. As you read the article and the student opinions, assume that you plan to address the issue and synthesize the opinions in an essay of your own.

CITY LAYOFFS HURT MINORITIES MOST
Francis X. Clines

City officials reported yesterday that layoffs resulting from the fiscal crisis were having "devastating" effects on minority employment in government.

In the last 18 months, they disclosed, the city lost half of its Spanish-speaking workers, 40 percent of the black males on the payroll and almost a third of its female workers.

"You are close to wiping out the minority work force in the City of New York," said Eleanor Holmes Norton, the chairman of the Commission on Human Rights, after releasing the data in response to a request.

The dwindling employment, in turn, has put the city in "serious jeopardy" of losing various kinds of Federal aid, according to Deputy Mayor Paul Gibson, Jr.

The city's fiscal failure and the resultant layoffs have worsened the situation in such predominantly male, white agencies as the Police Department, where, after some limited gains in recent years, the ranks of women police officers have been reduced by 55 percent because of the budget crisis, according to the city's latest data.

Meanwhile, a Federal appeals court declared that Civil Service seniority was not immune from legal challenge by women police officers who were dismissed because of the city's fiscal crisis.

Scores of complaints alleging discrimination have been filed by laid-off workers, both as class members and individuals, squeezing the city between the pressures of the traditional primacy of union seniority protections and Federal equal-employment requirements.

Federal officials said yesterday they were processing the complaints, which could result in a cut-off of funds. They added that they were hoping for guidance from the United States Supreme Court this year on the clash between the seniority principle, which tends to protect male white workers, and the Federal minority employment guidelines of Federal law.

The data on dismissals, which had been quietly compiled by city officials in recent weeks, were a further indication of the price the city is paying in the campaign to balance the budget and come to grips with its huge legacy of excessive debt.

Inevitably, the requirements of the austerity drive interfere, too, with attempts to soften the layoff effects on minority-group workers and women.

For example, Commissioner Norton emphasized that the levying of budget cuts on an even percentage basis in city agencies was the best way to protect equal opportunity. But various fiscal experts intent on improving the city's management say across-the-board cutting is the worst way of economizing because it ignores the relative quality of programs.

"We had begun to make an effort," Commissioner Norton said, "But one recession takes it all out in an instant."

Since the budget crisis surfaced in the summer of 1974, the city payroll has been reduced by 40,000 jobs—two-thirds of them reported as layoffs. This was a total cut of 13 percent to the current level of about 255,000 workers, according to city records.

A maxim of the seniority system that the last hired should be the first dismissed is the chief factor preventing an even 13 percent sharing of the layoff burden without regard to race or sex, city officials say.   14

The austerity drive, in which the city must try to cut its spending by $1 billion in less than three years, is forcing the conflict between what Commissioner Norton describes as "two competing and legitimate interests"—seniority and equal opportunity.   15

Federal and city civil rights officials were reluctant to discuss the scope of the complaints that have been filed. Werner H. Kramarsky, the state's Commissioner of Human Rights, described the issues raised as "very thorny" and extending to such questions as whether provisional, or temporary, employees should be credited with time on the job in determining relative seniority.   16

The available public records indicate that the state commission is handling at least 35 cases, some of them class complaints, and has sent 98 cases involving former city welfare workers to Federal officials of the Equal Employment Opportunity Commission, which already has received about 160 complaints from welfare workers alone.   17

The complaints are being pressed not only by women and minority group members, but also by a group of a half dozen disabled persons who contend that they were unfairly victimized in the layoff drive, according to state records.   18

There have been various court challenges in recent years of the seniority protections, which generally have been unsuccessful. One recent ruling threw out a racial quota program for city school principals. Federal civil rights officials emphasize that the Supreme Court is considering the issue at present and the hope is that some definitive standard will be set.   19

According to Deputy Mayor Gibson, minorities represented 31 percent of the payroll, but suffered 44 percent of the cuts. Males, he said, were 70 percent of the payroll and were affected by 63 percent of the cuts.   20

Commissioner Norton said that even before the layoffs, Federal officials had warned the city from time to time that financing for various programs would be cut off because of noncompliance with equal opportunity standards. She said that Mayor Beame had signed an executive order in 1974 committing city agencies to specific improvement programs.   21

Thus far there have been no Federal threats of cutoffs during the fiscal crisis, she said, apparently because the city is on record as pledging to seek a more equitable system in the event it ever resumes full-scale hiring.   22

But Deputy Mayor Gibson feels the situation is becoming critical. "We're losing ground," he said.   23

Student Opinions

Lydia Allen: The performance of a job must be the primary focus in deciding layoffs. I feel that, as a whole, people with more seniority in a job would perform that job best. Therefore, seniority, not minority, rights must be the deciding vote.

Grace Burrows: I believe that both sides have validity. I do feel that because minorities have been held back for so long *some* concessions should be made in their favor. Minorities were just beginning to make progress and now they will be set back once again. A person who's been on the job for a number of years shouldn't be made to suffer either.

Marion J. Buskin: I believe that an individual should be dismissed according to his ability to produce. A person with more seniority should not be allowed to keep his job if someone with less time on the job is capable of performing it better.

Robert Fuhst: I believe in seniority for job protection. If seniority doesn't prevail, then your job is based on how well you are liked and your freedom to express yourself is hampered.

John Giannini: Minorities should have a say in matters of layoffs, especially when a large percentage of the minority is affected. Minorities and senior personnel should share layoffs equally.

Dorothy Humphrey: I think there should be equal employment in this country. If an individual is senior in a field and satisfactorily functioning, he should remain employed. On the other hand, if a member of a minority can function even better, why not employ him instead? Production of work is what counts, not who performs it.

Rosemary McAleer: I favor seniority in employment because it is a system that does not permit discrimination. Regardless of race, color, or creed, if you have acquired more time than another employee, your job should be secure.

Marc Page: The longer a man is yoked to a job and its connected financial position, the more severe are the effects of being sundered from it. Seniority is the overriding consideration.

Megan Phillips: I feel seniority of employment is important in the job crisis because it is the only way of ensuring good and efficient services. Second, I feel the more mature one is in a job, the more the job becomes a part of one's welfare, as opposed to a younger person or a novice in the job, who only performs the job for the money.

Alice Reich: I think seniority in employment is an important consideration for the major reason that the benefits of seniority are hard-earned over the years. It seems unjust for a person who has given perhaps seven-eighths of his working lifetime to a job to find himself "out in the cold." Worse yet, the time of life when seniority would count is the time, very often, when other employment is unobtainable.

Robert Rivera: I feel that minority groups should be protected from job cutbacks. The reason is that the minorities that were hired were hired to fulfill the employment clauses set up through government laws. This law deals with equal opportunity for sexes and minorities to hold jobs and offices. Since this law has been recently enforced (in the last five or six years), why should minorities then hired be affected so tremendously by unemployment?

Jesse Rogers: I feel that minority workers for the city government should be protected, because it does not seem fair that, after waiting so long to get in, they are so easily kicked out by the unions.

Peter Rossi: I believe the federal government should compensate the minority people who were fired because of budget cuts and lack of seniority. The compensation should be the creation of new jobs and not unemployment insurance.

John Seeback: Most jobs run on the idea that the last hired are the first fired, even if the jobs held by senior workers are costing the business millions of dollars. Also, the white majority of senior workers feels superior to the minority workers on a racial basis rather than on a performance basis. Many employers also feel the minority workers are expendable: they had to hire them because of the law; now they have a good reason to fire them.

Nancy Vitale: Men and women, after putting their time and effort (not to mention their skills) into a job for a great number of years, deserve the protection of their jobs in accordance with seniority. It is unfair to dismiss a person from a longstanding position to make a position for a minority member.

When you prepare to explore a variety of opinions about a complex and perhaps controversial subject, follow these steps:

1. *Summarize the facts of the issue.*

Write a brief, objective summary of the issue under discussion (in this case, the problem described in the article). Your summary of this article should convey both the situation and the two key ideas that are stressed. Try structuring your paragraph to contrast the conflicting opinions.

2. *Establish your own point of view.*

End your summary with a statement of your own reaction to suggest a possible direction for your essay.

The second step is more important than it might at first seem. Once you begin to analyze a mass of contradictory opinion, you may find yourself being completely convinced by first one source and then another, or you may try so hard to stay neutral that you end up with no point of view of your own at all. You need to find a vantage point for yourself from which to judge the validity of the statements that you read. Of course, you can (and probably will) adjust your point of view as you become more familiar with all the arguments and evidence that your sources raise. *Do not regard your initial statement of opinion as a thesis to be proven, but rather as a hypothesis to be tested, modified, or even abandoned.*

3. *Synthesize your evidence.*

Label your set of opinions and establish categories. The statements follow-ing the article are all personal reactions to job layoffs and the issue of seniority protection versus equal employment opportunity. For each statement, follow these steps:

A. *Read each statement carefully and think about its exact meaning.* First, get a rough idea of what each statement says—do a mental paraphrase, if you like. You will naturally notice which "side" the author of each statement is on. There is a tendency to want to stop there, as if the authors' posi-tions are all that one needs to know. But your object is not only to find out which side of an issue each person prefers, but also to understand *why* that side was chosen.

B. *Try to pick out the chief reason put forth by each person, or, even better, the prin-ciple that lies behind each argument.* Sum up the reasoning of each person in a word or two, a phrase—invent a label, as if for a scientific specimen.

C. When you have labeled the statements, the final stage of synthesis be-comes easier. *Review your summarizing phrases to see if there is an abstract idea, used to describe several statements, that might serve as a category title.* (Some change in the wording may be necessary.) Once two or three cate-gories become obvious, consider their relationship to each other. Are they parallel? Are they contrasting? Then attempt to see how the smaller categories fit into the pattern that is beginning to form.

How the Three Steps Work

Following is one student's exploration of the article on New York City lay-offs and the fifteen student opinions.

1. **Summarizing.** Here the student identifies the article to which he and his sources are responding, summarizing the issue and the nature of the conflict.

> In the New York Times, Francis X. Clines reported that the budget crisis had substantially reduced the number of minorities—blacks, women, and His-panics—on New York City's payroll. The minority members laid off were the em-ployees most recently hired by the city to meet federal minority employment requirements. Eleanor Holmes Norton, chairman of the Commission on Human Rights, described the situation as a conflict between "two competing and legiti-mate interests"—the traditional principle of union seniority protection and equal opportunity employment.

2. **Hypothesizing** (stating your own point of view). Here the student ex-presses an opinion that suggests the possible direction for an essay. At

this point, the student has not studied the group of opinions that accompanies the article.

Both the competing interests are right in their claims, but there is a third principle that goes beyond both: in the name of fairness, the city should take the trouble to evaluate the performance of all its employees and dismiss those whose performance is inferior. Where a senior employee and a minority employee share the same performance rating but are competing for a single position, the city should help both employees and wait for retirements to make room for both.

3. **Labeling your set of opinions and establishing categories.** In this step, the student moves away from the article to examine the opinions of others who have read the article, determining first the position of each respondent and then the reasoning behind the position. Here, the statements of the fifteen respondents are repeated, with a summarizing label following each statement.

Lydia Allen: The performance of a job must be the primary focus in deciding layoffs. I feel that, as a whole, people with more seniority in a job would perform that job best. Therefore, seniority, not minority, rights must be the deciding vote.

Allen: seniority ensures performance

Grace Burrows: I believe that both sides have validity. I do feel that because minorities have been held back for so long *some* concessions should be made in their favor. Minorities were just beginning to make progress and now they will be set back once again. A person who's been on a job for a number of years shouldn't be made to suffer either.

Burrows: evades the issue—both approaches unfortunate

Marion J. Buskin: I believe that an individual should be dismissed according to his ability to produce. A person with more seniority should not be allowed to keep his job if someone with less time on the job is capable of performing it better.

Buskin: performance should be the only criterion

Robert Fuhst: I believe in seniority for job protection. If seniority doesn't prevail, then your job is based on how well you are liked and your freedom to express yourself is hampered.

Fuhst: seniority deserves protection (without it employment becomes a popularity contest)

John Giannini: Minorities should have a say in matters of layoffs, especially when a large percentage of the minority is affected. Minorities and senior personnel should share layoffs equally.

Giannini: minorities and senior personnel should share burden equally

Dorothy Humphrey: I think there should be equal employment in this country. If an individual is senior in a field and satisfactorily functioning, he should remain employed. On the other hand, if a member of a minority can function even better, why not employ him instead? Production of work is what counts, not who performs it.

Humphrey: performance should be the prevailing criterion

Rosemary McAleer: I favor seniority in employment because it is a system that does not permit discrimination. Regardless of race, color, or creed, if you have acquired more time than another employee, your job should be secure.

McAleer: seniority protection is fundamentally the only nondiscriminatory criterion

Marc Page: The longer a man is yoked to a job and its connected financial position, the more severe are the effects of being sundered from it. Seniority is the overriding consideration.

Page: seniority protection is the more humane policy

Megan Phillips: I feel seniority of employment is important in the job crisis because it is the only way of ensuring good and efficient services. Second, I feel the more mature one is in a job, the more the job becomes a part of one's welfare, as opposed to a younger person or a novice in the job, who performs the job only for the money.

Phillips: seniority protection leads to greater efficiency, i.e., performance

Alice Reich: I think seniority in employment is an important consideration for the major reason that the benefits of seniority are hard-earned over the years. It seems unjust for a person who has given perhaps seven-eighths of his working lifetime to a job to find himself "out in the cold." Worse yet, the time of life when seniority would count is the time, very often, when other employment is unobtainable.

Reich: seniority protection is the more humane policy (other employment often impossible for those laid off)

Robert Rivera: I feel that minority groups should be protected from job cutbacks. The reason is that the minorities that were hired were hired to fulfill the employment clauses set up through government laws. This law deals with equal opportunity for sexes and minorities to hold jobs and offices. Since this law has been recently enforced (in the last five or six years), why should minorities then hired be affected so tremendously by unemployment?

Rivera: the law requires that minorities be protected

Jesse Rogers: I feel that minority workers for the city government should be protected, because it does not seem fair that, after waiting so long to get in, they are so easily kicked out by the unions.

Rogers: minority protection is the more humane policy in the light of history

Peter Rossi: I believe the federal government should compensate the minority people who were fired because of budget cuts and lack of seniority. The compensation should be the creation of new jobs and not unemployment insurance.

Rossi: compensate laid-off minority employees with new jobs (implication that city should not lay off senior employees in order to accommodate minority employees)

John Seeback: Most jobs run on the idea that the last hired are the first fired, even if the jobs held by senior workers are costing the business millions of dollars. Also, the white majority of senior workers feels superior to the minority workers on a racial basis rather than on a performance basis. Many employers also feel the minority workers are expendable: they had to hire them because of the law; now they have a good reason to fire them.

Seeback: (implies that) minorities, as victims of union and employer prejudice, deserve protection

Nancy Vitale: Men and women, after putting their time and effort (not to mention their skills) into a job for a great number of years, deserve the protection of their jobs in accordance with seniority. It is unfair to dismiss a person from a long-standing position to make a position for a minority member.

Vitale: seniority protection is the more humane policy

From this list, the student can establish five categories that cover the range of answers. Here is the list of categories:

Category	Source	Note
1. Seniority ensures good performance.	Allen; Phillips	——

Category	Source	Note
2. Performance = vital criterion	Buskin; Humphrey	——
3. Seniority protection = vital criterion	Page	Financial and emotional hardship greatest for laid-off senior employees
	Reich; Vitale	——
	Fuhst	Employment would be popularity contest without it
	McAleer	Truly nondiscriminatory policy
4. Minority protection = vital criterion	Rivera	Legally
	Seeback	Compensation for past and present injustices
	Rogers	——
5. Each group should share the burden.	(Burrows); Giannini; Rossi	Federal gov't should hire laid-off minorities Senior employees should retain city jobs

EVALUATING SOURCES

Although you are obliged to give each of your sources serious and objective consideration and a fair presentation, synthesis also requires a certain amount of selection. Certainly, no one's statement should be immediately dismissed as trivial or crazy; include them all in your chart. But do not assume that all opinions are equally convincing and deserve equal representation in your essay.

The weight of a group of similar opinions can add authority to an idea. If most of your sources hold a similar view, you will probably give that idea appropriate prominence in your essay. However, *majority rule should not govern the structure of your essay.* Your own perspective determines the thesis of your essay, and you must use your understanding of the topic—which is likely to be more thorough and detached than that of any of your sources—to evaluate your materials:

- Review the hypothesis that you formulated before you begin to analyze the sources. *Decide whether that hypothesis is still valid* or whether, as a result of your full exploration of the subject, you wish to change it or abandon it entirely.

■ Sift through all the statements and *decide which ones seem thoughtful and well-balanced, supported by convincing reasons and examples, and which seem to be thoughtless assertions that rely on stereotypes, catch phrases, and unsupported references.* Your evaluation of the sources may differ from someone else's, but you must assert your own point of view and assess each source in the context of your background, knowledge, and experience.

You owe it to your reader to evaluate the evidence that you are presenting, partly through what you choose to emphasize and partly through your explicit comments about flawed and unconvincing statements.

In synthesis, your basic task is to present the range of opinion on a complex subject. You need not draw firm conclusions in your essay or provide definitive answers to the questions that have been raised. But you must have a valid thesis, an overall view of the competing arguments to present to your reader. Your original hypothesis, either confirmed or altered in the light of your increased understanding, becomes the *thesis* of your essay.

WRITING A SYNTHESIS ESSAY

Although synthesizing ideas is certainly a most difficult stage in working with multiple sources, don't neglect the actual writing of your essay. Spend some time planning your sequence of ideas and considering possible arrangements and strategies. Do your topic and materials lend themselves to a cause-and-effect structure, or definition, or problem and solution, or comparison, or argument?

Next, before starting to write each paragraph, review your sources' statements. By now, you should be fully aware of the reasoning underlying each point of view and the pattern connecting them all. But because your reader does not know as much as you do, *you need to explain your main ideas in enough detail to make all the complex points clear.* Remember that your reader has neither made a list nor even read the original sources. It is therefore important to include some explanation in your own voice, in addition to quoting and paraphrasing specific statements.

If possible, you should present your sources by using all three methods of reference: *summary, paraphrase,* and *quotation.* Remember that, as a rule, paraphrase is far more effective than quotation. When you paraphrase someone's reaction in your own voice, you are underlining the fact that you are in charge, that the opinion you are citing is only one of a larger group, and that a full exploration of the topic will emerge from your presentation of *all* the evidence, not from any one source's quoted opinion. *The first sentence presenting any new idea (whether the topic sentence of a new paragraph or a shift of thought within a paragraph) should be written entirely in your own voice,* as a generalization, without any reference to your sources.

To summarize, each paragraph of your essay should use some or all of the following elements:

- *Topic sentence:* Introduce the category or theme of the paragraph, and state the idea that is the common element tying this group of opinions together.
- *Explanation:* Support or explain the topic sentence. Later in the paragraph, if you are dealing with a complex group of statements, you may need a connecting sentence or two, showing your reader how one reason is connected to the next. For example, an explanation might be needed in the middle of the "seniority protects the worker" paragraph, as the writer moves from financial and emotional hardship for laid-off senior employees to the prevention of discriminatory job conditions.
- *Paraphrase or summary:* Present specific ideas from your sources in your own words. In these cases, you must of course *acknowledge your sources* by citing names in your sentence.
- *Quotation:* Quote from your sources when the content or phrasing of the original statement justifies word-for-word inclusion. In some groups of statements, there may be several possible candidates for quotation; in others, there may be only one; often you may find no source worth quoting. For example, read the statements made by Page, Reich, and Vitale once again. Could you reasonably quote any of them? Although Reich and Vitale both take strong positions well worth presenting, there is no reason to quote them and every reason to use paraphrase. On the other hand, Page's briefer statement might be quoted, since the contrast between "yoked" and "sundered" is effective and difficult to paraphrase.

EXERCISE 22

Read the following paragraph and decide which sentences (or parts of sentences) belong to each of the categories in the preceding list. Insert the appropriate category name in the left margin, and bracket the sentence or phrase illustrating the term. Be prepared to explain the components of the paragraph in class discussion.

Those who emphasize the upgrading of minority employment have pointed out that, since the hiring of minorities has been encouraged by governmental legislation only for the last few years, the seniority system will of necessity operate against those minorities. Thus, in the opinion of Robert Rivera, it is only fair that, during the present budget crisis, workers from minority groups be protected from cutbacks. One statement, by John Seeback, even suggests the possibility of a return to racial discrimination by white workers who have seniority and by employers, if equal opportunity laws are not enforced: "Many employers feel the minority workers are expendable: they had to hire them because of the law; now they have a good reason to fire them." In a related argument, Jesse Rogers points out that, since minorities have waited such a long time for decent job opportunities, a certain amount of preferential treatment might serve as a concrete measure of compensation. Neither Seeback nor Rogers emphasizes the abstract principle of equal opportunity implemented by the law. Peter Rossi advocates a practical solution: the federal government should undertake "the creation of new jobs," so that, presumably, there would be enough to satisfy both groups.

Guidelines for Citing Sources for Synthesis

- *Cite the source's full name,* whether you are quoting or not.

- *Try not to begin every sentence with a name,* nor should you introduce every paraphrase or quotation with "says."

- *Each sentence should do more than name a person;* don't include sentences without content: "Mary Smith agrees with this point."

- If possible, *support your general points with references from several different sources,* so that you will have more than one person's opinion or authority to cite.

- When you have several relevant comments to include within a single paragraph, *consider carefully which one should get cited first—and why.*

- You need not name every person who has mentioned a point (especially if you have several almost identical statements); however, *you may find it useful to sum up two people's views at the same time,* citing two sources for a single paraphrased statement:

  "Mary Smith and John Jones agree that playing the lottery can be very enjoyable. She finds a particular pleasure in scratching off the numbers to see if she has won."

- *Cite only one source for a quotation,* unless both have used exactly the same wording. In the example above, the first sentence would not make sense if you *quoted* "very enjoyable."

- If an idea under discussion is frequently mentioned in your sources, *convey the relative weight of support* by citing "five people" or "several commentators." Then, after summarizing the common response, cite one or two specific opinions, with names. But try not to *begin* a paragraph with "several people"; remember that, whenever possible, the topic sentence should be a generalization of your own, without reference to the supporting evidence.

- *Discuss opposing views within a single paragraph as long as the two points of view have something in common.* Radically different ideas should, of course, be explained separately. Use transitions to indicate the relationship between contrasting opinions.

CITING SOURCES

Throughout your essay, it is essential that you refer to your sources by name, for they serve as authorities for your explanations and conclusions.

Here is an example of a paragraph that follows these guidelines. Notice that it is based on contrasting views, with a turn of thought at the word *but*. The two transitional words are circled.

> Most people would agree that children need money to buy the things that they want: candy, small toys, games, ice cream. A regular allowance will prevent children from having to go to their parents whenever they need money for small purchases. Edward Andrews thinks that a child needs money when he goes out to buy things with his friends; otherwise, he'll feel left out. (Similarly,) Edna Rogers believes in giving an allowance because the child will always have money when she needs it. (But) those who oppose giving allowances argue that parents usually start such a routine to keep children from bothering them all the time. According to Barbara Lewis, an allowance can easily become a means for the neglectful parent to avoid responsibility.

THE LIMITS OF SYNTHESIS

In synthesis, you take several separate sources of information—a group of statements, a collection of essays—and you analyze each individual point of view and each way of looking at the topic. In the long run, however, your object is not to present individual summaries of every source, but rather to incorporate them all in a new essay that is designed to represent a variety of opinion as well as your own point of view. *Your thorough presentation of the topic counts more than the contribution of any single author.* If the process of synthesis has been complete, coherent, and impartial, your readers can learn just as much about the overall topic—and learn it more quickly—than they would by reading each of the source materials.

The danger is that the sources may lose much of their distinctiveness and individuality. *Synthesis depends not so much on distinguishing between your materials as on recognizing their similarities.* The terminology of synthesis includes such instructions as "break down into categories" and "reduce to common denominators." "Reduction," however, has a double implication: it suggests distillation through the elimination of impurities, but it also leads to a loss of substance.

> *Do not be so intent on making your material conform to your synthesis categories that you ignore the awkward but interesting bits of information— the impurities—that are being "reduced" from your notes. Synthesis is a method, not an end in itself.*

The academic writer should be able to distinguish between material that is appropriate for synthesis and material whose individuality should be recognized and preserved. One example of the latter is fiction; another is autobiography. Assume that three writers are reminiscing about their first jobs: one was a clerk in a drugstore, the second a telephone operator, and the third plowed his father's fields. In their recollections, the reader can find several similar themes: accepting increased responsibility; sticking to the job; learning appropriate behavior; living up to the boss's or customers' or father's expectations. But, just as important, the three autobiographical accounts *differ* sharply in their context and circumstances, in their point of view and style. You cannot lump them together in the same way that you might categorize statements about the lottery or opinions about school uniforms, for they cannot be reduced to a single common experience. The three are not *interchangeable;* rather, *they are comparable.*

SYNTHESIS AND COMPARISON

Since *synthesis* does not always do justice to individual works, *comparison* can be a more effective strategy for writing about several full-length essays with a common theme. In many ways, comparison resembles synthesis. Both involve analyzing the ideas of several sources and searching for a single vantage point from which to view these separate sources. However, there is an important difference. *The writer of a synthesis constructs a new work out of the materials of the old; the writer of a comparison tries to leave the sources intact throughout the organizational process, so that each retains its individuality.*

The functions of synthesis and comparison rarely overlap.

In academic and professional writing, you will use synthesis to assimilate assorted facts and ideas into a coherent body of information.

When you are assigned an essay topic, and when you assemble several sources, you are not likely to want to *compare* the information that you have recorded in your notes; rather, you will *synthesize* that material into a complete presentation of the topic. One of your sources may be an encyclopedia; another a massive survey of the entire subject; a third may devote several chapters to a scrutiny of that one small topic. In fact, these three sources are really not comparable, nor is your primary purpose to distinguish between them or to understand how they approach the subject differently. You are only interested in the results that you can achieve by using and building on this information. In contrast, the appropriate conditions for comparison are more specific and rare.

For comparison, you must have two or more works of similar length and complexity that deal with the same subject and that merit individual examination.

Point-to-Point Comparison

Point-to-point comparison resembles synthesis. You select certain major ideas that are discussed in all the works being compared and then, to support conclusions about these ideas, describe the full range of opinion concerning *each* point, one at a time.

Because point-to-point comparison cuts across the source essays, as synthesis does, you must work hard to avoid oversimplification. If you are focusing on one idea, trying to relate it to a comparable reaction in another essay, don't forget that the two works are separate and whole interpretations of the topic. Otherwise, you may end up emphasizing similarities just to make your point.

Here is a paragraph taken from a *point-to-point comparison* of three movie reviews:

> None of the three reviewers regards Lady and the Tramp as a first-rate product of the Walt Disney studio. Their chief object of criticism is the sugary sentimentality, so characteristic of Disney cartoons, which has been injected into Lady in excessive quantities. Both John McCarten in the New Yorker and the Time reviewer point out that, for the first time, the anthropomorphic presentation of animals does not succeed because the "human" situations are far too broadly presented. Lady and the Tramp are a "painfully arch pair," says McCarten. He finds the dialogue given to the movie's human characters even more embarrassing than the clichés exchanged by the animals. Even Bosley Crowther of the Times, who seems less dismissive of feature cartoons, finds that Lady and the Tramp lacks Disney's usual "literate originality." Crowther suggests that its oppressive sentimentality is probably made more obvious by the film's use of the wide screen. McCarten also comments on the collision between the winsome characters and the magnified production: "Obviously determined to tug all heartstrings," Disney presents the birth of Lady's puppy "while all the stereophonic loudspeakers let loose with overwhelming barrages of cooings and gurglings." All the reviewers agree that the audience for this film will be restricted to dog lovers, and lapdog lovers at that.

Whole-to-Whole Comparison

In whole-to-whole comparison, you discuss each work, one at a time. This method is more likely to give the reader a sense of each source's individual qualities. But unless your sources are fairly short and simple, this method can be far more unwieldy than point-to-point. If you compare a series of long and complex works, and if you complete your entire analysis of one before you move on to the next, the reader may get no sense of a comparison and forget that you are relating several sources to each other. *Without careful structuring, whole-to-whole comparison becomes a series of loosely related summaries,* in which readers must discover for themselves all the connections, parallels, and contrasts.

There are two ways to make the structure of whole-to-whole comparison clear to the reader:

1. **Although each work is discussed separately and presented as a whole, you should nevertheless try to present common ideas *in the same order,* an order that will carry out the development of your thesis about the works being compared.**

   Thus, whichever topic you choose as the starting point for your discussion of the first work should also be used as the starting point for your treatment of each of the others. The reader should be able to find the same general idea discussed in (roughly) the same place in each section of a whole-to-whole comparison.

2. **Remind the reader that this is a comparison by frequent *cross-cutting* to works already discussed; you should make frequent use of standard transitional phrases to establish such cross-references.**

   Initially, you have to decide which work to begin with. The best choice is usually a relatively simple work that nonetheless touches on all the major points of comparison and that enables you to begin establishing your own point of view. Beginning with the second work, you should refer back to what you have said about the first writer's ideas, showing how they differ from those of the second. This process can become extremely complex when you are analyzing a large number of essays, which is one reason that whole-to-whole comparison is rarely used to compare more than three works.

Here is the second major paragraph of a *whole-to-whole comparison* that deals with critical reaction to the film *West Side Story*:

> Like the author of the Time review, Pauline Kael criticizes West Side Story for its lack of realism and its unconvincing portrayal of social tensions. She points out that the distinction between the ethnic groups is achieved through cosmetics and hair dye, not dialogue and actions. In her view, the characters are like Munchkins, stock figures without individual identities and recognizable motives. Natalie Wood as the heroine, Maria, is unfavorably compared to a mechanical robot and to the Princess telephone. Just as the Time reviewer accuses the film of oversentimentalizing its teenage characters at society's expense, so Kael condemns the movie's division of its characters into stereotypical good guys and bad guys. In fact, Kael finds it hard to account for the popularity of West Side Story's "frenzied hokum." She concludes that many may have been overwhelmed by the film's sheer size and technical achieve-

ments. The audience is persuaded to believe that bigger, louder, and faster has to be better. Her disapproval extends even to the widely praised dancing; like the rest of the movie, the choreography tries too hard to be impressive. In short, Pauline Kael agrees with the Time reviewer: West Side Story never rises above its "hyped-up, slam-bang production."

Listing Points for Comparison

Whether you choose point-to-point or whole-to-whole comparison depends on your sources. Whichever you choose, begin planning your comparison (as you would begin synthesis) by *listing the important ideas discussed by several of your sources.*

- If you eventually choose to write a *point-to-point* essay, then your list can become the basis for your paragraph outline.
- If you decide to compare each of your essays *whole-to-whole*, your list can suggest what to emphasize and can help you to decide the order of topics within the discussion of each work.

These lists can never be more than primitive guidelines; but unless you establish the primary points of similarity or difference among your sources, your essay will end up as a series of unrelated comments, not a comparison.

SUPPLEMENTARY EXERCISES AND ASSIGNMENTS

This section contains a variety of assignments to give you practice in writing from multiple sources. Your instructor will select a few of these exercises and assignments for your class to work on.

ASSIGNMENT 7

Choose *one* of the following:

1. At the library, examine the issue of the *New York Times* that was published on the day that your mother or father was born. Most libraries keep complete microfilms of the *New York Times*. Ask your librarian how to locate and use these microfilms. (Alternatively, locate an issue of a news magazine that covers that week.) Select the articles that seem most interesting and typical of the period, and use them as evidence for an account of what it was like to live on that day. *This essay should not merely be a collection of facts; you should suggest the overall significance of the information that you include.* Remember that your reader was almost certainly not born on that date, and that your job is to arouse that reader's interest. If you like, draw some parallels with the present time, but don't strain the comparison. The essay should not run much more than 1,000 words: select carefully and refer briefly to the evidence.

2. Use a newspaper or magazine published this week and try to construct a partial portrait of what it is like to live in America (or in your city or town) right now. Don't rely entirely on news stories, but, instead, draw your evidence as much as possible from advertisements and features (like TV listings, classifieds, announcements of all sorts). Try, if you can, to disregard personal knowledge; pretend you are a Martian if that will enable you to become detached from your familiar environment. Don't offer conclusions that the evidence does not substantiate, and don't try to say *everything* that could possibly be said. The essay should not run much more than 1,000 words: select carefully and refer briefly to the evidence.

EXERCISE 23

A. In each of the following situations, would you give money to the person who is begging? Write yes or no.

1. A man is sitting on the sidewalk, dressed in clean-looking rags, with no visible legs and a box of pencils. There is a sign: "There but for the grace of God go I."

2. A middle-aged businessman approaches you, says that he is renovating the brownstone on the next block and has been locked out, and asks for the fare to get to his home where there is a spare key.

3. A woman, very untidy, but not visibly unclean, is standing quite straight on the sidewalk, entertaining passersby by singing (very badly) at the top of her voice. It is not possible to determine whether she is drunk.

4. A small, adorable, smudged-looking child is selling small, untidy bunches of dandelions for 50 cents.

5. A man with a cane is tapping his way through a crowded subway car, politely thanking each person who drops change into his cup.

6. A man with a dirty rag is wiping the windshields of cars stopping for red lights. Clearly drunk, he is arguing with some of the drivers and might prove to be a nuisance if he continues to cling to the car after the light changes.

7. A young boy is wiping the windshields of cars stopping for red lights. He is smiling and polishing carefully.

8. A sweet old lady approaches you at the cash register of a coffee shop and, saying that she has forgotten her purse, timidly asks if you would lend her the money to pay for her meal.

9. A huge old woman, looking like a rag pile, is crouching on the steps leading to a subway train, monotonously repeating, "Give me a quarter."

10. In a stationery store, a small boy needs an extra quarter to buy a piece of oaktag. He says that the store is closing in five minutes and that, if he doesn't get it, his teacher will kill him.

11. A young woman in her twenties, neatly dressed in ordinary clothes (jeans and sneakers), indistinguishable from the other passengers, walks through a subway train, politely and pleasantly asking for change.

12. Leaving a theatrical performance at the first intermission, you are approached by an ordinary-looking man who asks if he can have your ticket stub to see the remainder of the program.

13. A drunken woman asks for change for a beer.

14. A dirty little boy leads a slumped man, presumably his father, to the bus stop and asks for money to get on the bus.

15. A man dressed in a Santa Claus costume rings a bell at Christmas time; the name of the charitable organization is clearly displayed on a sign next to him.

16. A blind man holds a sign that says: "Help me to get a seeing-eye dog."

17. A young woman in religious habit approaches you at the airport, blocks your way, and asks for a contribution.

18. Two young musicians, clean and neatly dressed, play music professionally and pleasantly, with a sign saying: "Help us complete our studies."

19. Your cousin is participating in a walkathon for a local charity and asks you to give money by sponsoring her.

20. A man in faded army fatigues with a sign, "I am a Viet Vet," asks you for money.

21. Chanting, a group of young people with shaven heads, wearing strange orange clothes, dances up to you, hands outstretched.

22. A man and woman, carrying clipboards and wearing identification cards, approach people on a busy street corner and ask for contributions to an obscure ecological organization.

23. After a well-publicized natural disaster, you stop at a small-town convenience store where a large jar by the cash register is hand-labeled "Donations to Aid Flood Victims."

24. A young, bearded man in tee-shirt and jeans asks for a donation in return for a one-page photocopy of his poems.

25. On Veterans' Day, an elderly man affixes an artificial poppy to your collar and then asks for a contribution to a veterans' organization.

26. A twelve-year-old boy approaches you outside a department store and asks if you'd like to buy a raffle ticket to help support his school's athletic programs.

27. Two men sit at a folding table strewn with photocopied brochures and photos of a deteriorating building, soliciting contributions to support the private, alternative high school they've created for homeless teenagers.

B. Consider your motives for giving or refusing charity in each case. Under what circumstances do you give money to beggars? Without mentioning any of these specific situations, write—in a sentence or two—your personal definition of *charity*.

EXERCISE 24

Make up a set of materials for a definition exercise, like the set used in Exercise 23. Invent a representative group of examples illustrating *one* of the following situations:

1. Several possible occasions for parents interfering in the affairs of their children (i.e., *private* intervention).
2. Several possible occasions for complaining to authority about another person's conduct (consider ethics of the classroom and office environments).
3. Examples of *heroism* or *prejudice* or *innocence*.

Remember that your list of illustrations should not be restricted to those that would satisfy your own personal definition; try to provide the broadest possible base. For that reason, if your teacher approves, it may be helpful to work on this exercise with a group of students in your class.

EXERCISE 25

Read the following story.

Jack is in his third year of college and doing passing but below-average work. His mother has been insisting that he plan to enroll in law school and become an attorney, like his father. Angry at him for not receiving better grades, she has told him that under no circumstances will he get the car or the trip that he has been promised unless his average goes up one full grade. Although Jack has done slightly better work this term, he has been having trouble with his sociology course, especially with the term paper. Twice he has asked for a conference with his teacher, but Professor Brown has told him that he isn't being paid to run a private tutoring service. So Jack has postponed writing the paper and finally puts it together hastily the night before it is due. Then, Professor Brown calls him in and tells him that the paper is disgraceful and that he has no chance of getting a passing grade or even an incomplete unless he submits a more acceptable essay by 9 a.m. the next day. Jack tries to explain his situation and his mother's demands, and he asks for some more time to revise the paper, but his teacher is inflexible and says, "You probably don't belong in college anyway." Since there is no way that Jack is going to be able to produce the revised essay in time, he decides to salvage the car and trip by getting somebody to write it for him. He has heard about Victor, a recent graduate who always needs money. Victor agrees and, after some haggling about the fee, he writes an acceptable paper overnight. A few days after Professor Brown has accepted the paper and given Jack his grade, Jack gets a call from Victor, who says that, unless he gets double the original fee, he will reveal the entire transaction to Professor Brown and the Dean. Jack doesn't have the money and cannot tell his parents.

1. In your opinion, which character's actions are the worst among the group? Write a brief statement explaining your reasons.
2. Here are some statements containing frequently expressed reasons for disliking each of the characters. Consider why each person considers his or her choice the worst person in the story. Then try to generalize about the ethical principles that lie behind each group of responses.

     The people who consider Jack (for example) worse than Victor are employing a particular set of values. What principles or beliefs are most important to each group? Remember to consider whether the respondents are reacting logically, based on their own principles of conduct, or emotionally, based on a personal reaction that you cannot analyze. Give weight to those responses that appear to have a logical basis, whether or not you agree with the logic of the respondent(s).

     You are being asked to describe a set of *negative* opinions in terms of the underlying *positive* beliefs. Therefore, stress positive values. Try not to say, "The people who condemn Jack's mother strongly believe that she is too ambitious."

Jack's Mother

Barbara Bailey: Jack's mother is trying to run his life. He is old enough to decide what he wants to do. But she is trying to make him be just like his father. She hasn't bothered to ask him whether he wants to be a lawyer. He might not even be smart enough to get through law school. She is forcing him to live up to her expectations; she is trying to live through him. Even if Jack eventually becomes successful, he will be unhappy and dissatisfied, like his mother.

Gina Britton: She is forcing her son past his natural abilities. She does not see him as a separate individual with separate needs. She should be happy that Jack is attending college and trying to get an education. But she doesn't seem to care about his feelings or his future. She is too ambitious.

Wallace Humphrey: Jack's mother should have understood that her son was trying hard to pass. If she had shown more patience and sympathy, he might have done well. She hasn't done her part as a mother, so Jack can't be a good son.

Kathy Harris: Jack's mother is threatening to punish him, not because she honestly wants him to succeed, but because she is so angry with him. In a way, she is forcing him into a desperate act. It is her demands which cause Jack eventually to become the victim of blackmail.

Mohammed Taylor: Jack's mother is very unreasonable. She expects her son to be like her husband, but they are two different people, and Jack should be treated as an individual. She is encouraging him to cheat. By bribing him, she is encouraging him to use bribery himself to get his paper written. How can he do well in his studies with a mother like her?

Summary: The people who condemn Jack's mother strongly believe

_____

_____

Jack

Chris Bennett: Jack is the worst person because he is not doing the work for its own sake, but for the gain he will receive from his mother. Although his teacher refused to see him, Jack shouldn't have waited to write his paper. He could have sought help from another teacher or from the tutoring center.

Dona Morrow: Jack regards college as a bargaining institution. First he bargains with his mother over his material reward; then he bargains with his teacher as to how much time he'll have for an assignment; last, he bargains with his college acquaintance over money. Jack is too greedy to enjoy life, and he doesn't want to do any work.

Josephine Navarre: Jack allows himself to be placed in this pressure chamber by trying to avoid his responsibilities, by his use of deception, by not standing up for his rights, by his unwillingness to be held accountable for his actions or lack thereof.

Bernice Richards: As a junior in college, Jack should already know how to write a paper. He sought only one source of (unwilling) help—his professor. There's no reason for Jack to get so negative about Professor Brown; he should have realized that his teacher was inflexible, and he should have tried to write a good paper the first time. Jack expects everyone to oblige him without making any effort. He just waits around to be bailed out by someone else.

John Suarez: School is a responsibility, just as a job is, and Jack does not live up to his responsibility. He is now in college, not high school, so we have to assume that he chose to take the course that he's failing. What will happen when he gets to law school? Who will do his work when he's defending a client? Jack is just a helpless whiner.

Summary: The people who condemn Jack strongly believe

_____

_____

Professor Brown

Jack Dougherty: Professor Brown is the worst character because he could have listened to Jack's complaints and pleas for help. He isn't doing his job. He's not getting paid to tutor, but he is getting paid to teach, and helping students is part of teaching.

Andrea Notare: This story shows that some teachers don't give a damn about their students. Professor Brown is not only offensive to Jack, with no justification, but he makes impossible demands. If he'd helped Jack with his paper in the first place, maybe Jack would have received a passing grade. To expect Jack to hand in an acceptable paper in twenty-four hours is impossible and unjust.

Mary Ann Smith: Professor Brown has placed Jack in a situation which has no reasonable answer. He did not want to help Jack and yet demanded a better paper. Trapped, Jack must resort to cheating. This is ironic, since a teacher is supposed to represent learning.

Raphael Alvarez: Professor Brown appears as a person who doesn't care for his students or his profession and who teaches only for the money. His attitude is as mercenary as Victor's, but since he's a teacher, his attitude is more hypocritical.

Summary: The people who condemn Professor Brown strongly believe

_____

_____

Victor

Margo Drohan: Since he had already agreed on a fee, it is not right for Victor to exploit the situation and ask Jack for double the amount. He is using another person's unfortunate position for personal gain. Victor is a greedy blackmailer, and there's nothing worse than that.

Denise Generale: Victor shouldn't have agreed to help Jack with the paper. Though he is not breaking the law by writing the paper, he is helping Jack to violate the rules of the college and, unlike Jack, he has no desperate need to do so. If he's such a good writer, he should turn his talent to a legitimate business and get a decent job.

Chris Pappas: Victor has made a deal with Jack and has reneged on this arrangement in an underhanded way. He is a shakedown artist.

Harry Murphy: Victor makes his final ultimatum to Jack of his own free will; he doesn't have to do it. Unlike the other characters, he has no emotional involvement in the situation. He is intentionally mean and cruel when he asks for that money.

Tom Natoli: Victor is a criminal. He has agreed to do the work for a set fee through a verbal contract with Jack. He goes back on his word in the end, all for money (which, as everyone knows, is the root of all evil anyway), when he blackmails Jack.

Summary: The people who condemn Victor strongly believe

_____

_____

ASSIGNMENT 8

All the words in the following list are in common use and have either more than one usual meaning or a meaning that can be interpreted both favorably and unfavorably. Choose one word from the list as the topic for a definition essay. (Or, if your teacher asks you to do so, select a word from the dictionary or the thesaurus.)

shrewd	clever	self-interest
curiosity	ordinary	respectable
capitalism	power	conservative
bias	flamboyant	polite
progress	eccentric	obedience
habit	politician	ambition
credit	genius	duty
ladylike	failure	poverty
royalty	competition	sophisticated
masculine	peace	humility
cautious	welfare	solitude
bias	immature	spiritual
dominance	culture	sentimental
revolution	aggression	glamorous
passive	failure	self-confidence
influential	feminine	passionate
criticism	imagination	impetuous
jealousy	romantic	successful
small	workman	smooth
cheap	privilege	intrigue
fashion	enthusiast	smart
pompous	mercenary	criticize
obligation	shame	freedom
control	idealistic	artificial
ambition	ethical	perfection

1. Clarify your own definition of the word by writing down your ideas about its meaning.
2. Interview five or six people, or as many as you need, to get a variety of reactions. Your purpose is to become aware of several ways of using your word. Take careful and complete notes of each reaction that you receive.
3. Each person should be asked the following questions:

   ■ What do you think X means? Has it any other meanings that you know of?

   ■ How would you use this word in a sentence? (Pay special attention to the way in which the word is used, and note down the differences. Two people might say that a word means the same thing and yet use it differently.)

   ■ Is this a positive word or a negative word? In what situation could it possibly have a favorable or unfavorable connotation?

In listening to the answers to these questions, do not hesitate to ask, "What do you mean?" It may be necessary to make people think hard about a word that they use casually.

4. As you note reactions, consider how the meaning of the word changes and try to identify the different circumstances and usages that cause these variations. Be alert, for example, for a difference between the *ideal* meaning of the word and its *practical* application in daily life.

5. If one person's reaction is merely an echo of something that you already have in your notes, you may summarize the second response more briefly, but keep an accurate record of who (and how many) said what.

6. Although your notes for each source may run only a few sentences, plan to use a separate sheet for each person.

7. Your notes should include not only a summary of each reaction, but also, if possible, a few quotations. If someone suggests a good definition or uses the word in an interesting way, try to record the exact words; read the quotation back to the speaker to make sure that what you have quoted is accurate; put quotation marks around the direct quotation.

8. Make sure that the names of all your sources are accurately spelled.

9. Analyze your notes and make an outline of possible meanings and contexts.

10. Write a series of paragraphs, first explaining *the most common meaning attributed to the word*, according to your sources. Be sure to cite different examples of this common usage. Then, in successive paragraphs, review the other connotations, favorable and unfavorable, always trying to trace the relationships and common contexts among the different meanings. With your overview of all the variations of meaning, you are in an excellent position to observe and explain what the worst and the best connotations of the word have in common.

There is no set length for this essay. Contents and organization are governed entirely by the kind and extent of the material in your notes. *Your notes should be handed in with your completed essay.*

ASSIGNMENT 9

Choose a topic from the list below; or think of a question that might stimulate a wide range of responses, and submit the question for your teacher's approval. Try to avoid political issues and very controversial subjects that may make it difficult for you to control the interview and prevent you from getting a well-balanced set of notes. You want a topic in which everyone you interview can take an interest, without becoming intensely partisan.

Suggestions for Topics

Should wives get paid for housework?

Is jealousy a healthy sign in a relationship, or is it always destructive?

Should boys play with dolls?

Is "traditional" dating still desirable today?

If you could be reborn, would you change your sex?

Does it matter whether an elementary school child has a male or female teacher?

Is there a right age to get married?

What are the ingredients for a lasting marriage?

Should children be given the same first names as their parents?

Is it better to keep a friend by not speaking your mind or risk losing a friend by honesty?

What should a child of (pick an age) be told about death?

Should English be made the official language of the United States?

Are laws requiring the wearing of seat belts an infringement of individual rights?

Is graffiti vandalism?

Should animals be used in laboratory research?

Is it alienating to live in a large city?

How should ethics be taught in the schools?

How should the commandment "honor thy parents" be put into practice today?

What, if anything, is wrong with the nuclear family?

Are students forced to specialize too soon in their college experience?

Should schools stay in session all year round?

Should citizens have to pay a fine for not voting?

Should movies have a rating system?

Should grade-school students be left back?

Should children's TV time be rationed?

Should parents be held legally or financially responsible for damage done by their children?

At what age is it acceptable for children to work (outside the family)?

Should high school students be tested for drug use?

Should hosts who serve alcohol be held responsible if their guests later are involved in auto accidents?

Should students have to maintain passing grades in order to participate in school athletics?

How should society deal with homeless people?

When should parents cease to be financially responsible for their children?

1. Once your topic is decided (and, if necessary, approved), interview at least six people, or as many as you need to get a variety of reactions. (Some of your sources should be students in your class.) Your purpose is to learn

about several ways of looking at the topic, not to argue, but to exchange views. If you wish, use the following format for conducting each interview:

Name: (first and last: check the spelling!)

Do you think . . . . ?

Why do you think so? What are some of your reasons? (later) Are there any other reasons?

Why do you think people who take the opposite view would do so?

Do any examples come to your mind to illustrate your point?

Quotation:

2. Take careful and complete notes of the comments that you receive. (*You will be expected to hand in all your notes, in their original form, with your completed essay.*) Keep a separate sheet for each person. If one of your sources says something worth quoting, write down the exact words; read them back to make sure that what you have quoted is what the speaker meant to say; then put quotation marks around the direct quotation. Otherwise use summary or paraphrase. Do not hesitate to ask, "What do you mean?" or "Is this what I heard you say?" or "How does that fit in with what you said just before?"

3. List the ideas from your notes and arrange the points in a sequence of your choice. Then write an essay that presents the full range of opinion, paraphrasing and (occasionally) quoting from representative sources.

ASSIGNMENT 10

Read the following paragraph by Christopher Jencks on white-collar crime.

1. Write a summary of the point at issue, and then a brief explanation of your opinion of this issue.

2. Use the statements that follow as a basis for a synthesis essay. These statements were written in response to the question: How should white-collar criminals be punished? Analyze each statement, label each kind of reason, and organize all the categories in a chart. Then write an essay that presents the full range of opinion, paraphrasing and, if desirable, quoting from representative sources.

from RE-THINKING SOCIAL POLICY

Christopher Jencks

Public concern about crime is obviously selective. The mere fact that some behavior is illegal does not worry most Americans much. Every year millions of Americans defraud the Internal Revenue Service by underreporting their income or overstating their deductions. The amounts stolen in this way almost certainly exceed the amounts stolen by muggers on the streets. Yet very few Americans view tax fraud as a serious threat to themselves or to the republic. The reason seems obvious. Unlike robbery, tax evasion has no individual victims. It forces the rest of us to pay higher taxes than we otherwise would, but it does not create the same kind of fear or the same sense of personal violation as being raped or even having your house burgled. We react to most other white-collar crimes with equal indifference. Given a choice, almost everyone would rather be robbed by computer than at gunpoint. This does not make white-collar crime morally preferable to blue-collar crime, but it does explain why white-collar crime is not a major political issue.

Statements

Donald Bach: White-collar criminals usually don't steal anything of great value, just a little something extra to help them get by. For many, the temptation is great. These people work and pay taxes (which is more than most criminals do). It really isn't fair to treat them the same as the guy who holds up a grocery store. Although the amount of money taken may be the same, a corporation or the government will be more likely to absorb the loss without being put into a financial bind as a small store owner would.

Brian Byers: As long as lenient sentences are given for certain kinds of crimes, the same crimes will be repeated again and again by more and more people. A tough jail sentence is a good deterrent.

Sonia Cyzinsky: Judges should look at the whole individual and especially find out if this is a first offense. Many will have a clean record. Some of them receive a very low salary. Without them, their families would have no food and place to live.

Sally DeSantos: Most people who commit white-collar crimes cannot plead extreme poverty. They are people who have gone to college and become professionals. They are generally earning a good living. They don't really deserve our sympathy.

Margaret Jones: A person caught for a white-collar crime should only get a taste of punishment. He might be put in jail for the weekend, to see what jail is all about. He probably wouldn't commit another crime after that. Throwing white-collar criminals into jail for a long sentence is pointless since it is likely the family will go on welfare and the state will have to support them.

John Kearney: Corruption is everywhere; you aren't going to get anywhere putting everyone in jail who tries to get away with a white-collar crime. Giving stiff sentences to white-collar criminals would just take up more jail space, which would result in potentially worse criminals out in our streets.

Ana Khan: Putting a white-collar criminal in jail just results in defaming his reputation and making it difficult for him to start over again when he is released. Is it worth it for someone who hasn't done any bodily harm to anyone? His innocent wife and children, who had nothing to do with the robbery, would be suffering greatly.

Wally Kim: One argument for leniency for white-collar criminals is that the crime is not as serious as it could be. These are not violent crimes, like murder or rape, which are truly against society's interests. A traffic cop taking a bribe from someone getting a ticket hasn't really hurt anyone permanently. Putting the white-collar criminal in jail with other criminals would brutalize him, making him a greater threat to society when he is set free.

Iris Levine: In the constitution it says that all people shall be treated equally under the law. Why are white-collar criminals given a special break? What kind of an example does this set for others? If a criminal deserves to go to jail for five years, send him. Don't look at his responsibilities to his family; look at the responsibility that he owes to the public.

Lori Lieberman: When white-collar crime is not dealt with firmly, then people begin to lose respect for the law. If crime is not stopped in its tracks, it seems to grow. If one person gets caught but is let off lightly, others will look upon that as a sign that they, too, can take a chance because they won't get caught or, if they do, they won't face a tough punishment.

Kenneth Matos: If a man does take one or two hundred dollars to help feed his family, I don't think that he should be punished harshly. The courts should understand that the man did not do it to enjoy himself or to use the money wrongly, e.g., to buy drugs. The man uses the money to help his poor family, to feed his little children. They need their father at home, not in jail. The white-collar criminal deserves a second chance.

Felix Medina: Any crime is wrong, no matter how small or big. Every crime should be punished. Nobody should have the right to take another person's property. If you show too much sympathy, people will begin to think that these crimes are a joke. The person who steals two hundred dollars will try again and take five hundred dollars. The sad part is that there's a very good chance of getting away with it because of the understaffed police force and the court system.

Maria Morgan: Everyone should be treated equally when it comes to sentencing for a crime. No one should receive a sentence based upon his professional background. This would be discrimination against people with less important jobs.

Glenn Nicotinis: White-collar criminals are not usually hard, vicious people who go around killing others. The crimes that they commit really don't harm people directly. If you cheat on your taxes or withhold some kind of payment due to the city, you can still be a fairly decent person. But, if you are lenient, this should be a one-time-only option. The next time, the criminal should go to jail for a long time.

Danny Olivera: A lenient sentence allows the white-collar criminal to look forward towards the future, to see his children growing up. That a white-collar criminal pays a fine, serves some kind of sentence, and loses his job is enough punishment. He can look forward to becoming a better person, more decent, more respectful, and more careful.

Larry Pannerini: Many people feel that white-collar crimes are not so bad because they only affect the city or big companies. This is not true because when these organizations start losing money, they don't just accept it; they pass it right along to us. Then taxes and prices go up, not only because of inflation, but because of shoplifting and embezzlement.

Rosa Prewitt: If some store clerk steals some money from the cash register or some goods from the stock room, he should be given a light sentence the first time. I could almost guarantee that, after experiencing a trial, he will not pull another stunt like that again. Giving them a good scare is enough.

Carlos Rivera: Most white-collar workers hold positions of trust; they are trusted by the public, and some were even elected by the public. When such an official commits a criminal act, he should be punished to the fullest extent of the law and should be denied any effort to retrieve his position. A crime committed by such a person is not only a crime against the law but also against the public.

Kenny Rodriguez: White-collar crime is an important issue because if officials working for city governments commit crimes, corruption increases and the city's reputation really goes downhill. Such crimes also cost the city great amounts of money, usually in taxes from people like me, to restore things back. Also, people lose respect for the law.

Saisi Wabuge: It doesn't matter that these people have families. Many murderers have families, yet they get life sentences.

Elizabeth Wilson: It is enough that these criminals will be embarrassed, even humiliated, by having their actions made public. These are not giants of crime. To put them in jail means they will be in contact with murderers, rapists, and other vicious immoral people. Many will be corrupted by the time they end their sentence.

ASSIGNMENT 11

Read about the case of Herbert Buriel from *Ethics on Call.*

1. Write a brief summary of the issue raised by Nancy N. Dubler and David Nimmons.
2. Consider the arguments for and against forcing Mr. Buriel to accept dialysis.
3. Write a paragraph of three to five sentences in which you argue for or against allowing patients such as Herbert Buriel to refuse treatment.
4. Submit your summary and paragraph to your instructor, who will distribute copies of all the statements by members of your class.
5. Read, label, and categorize each person's response.
6. Write a synthesis essay presenting a complete examination of the issue and its implications.

from ETHICS ON CALL
Nancy N. Dubler and David Nimmons

Herbert Buriel . . . was an eighty-eight-year-old man, slightly confused, forgetful, and disoriented. He had been in a nursing home for three years, placed there when he became too difficult for his family to manage at home. From all reports, he was a nasty, disagreeable sort at the best of times, and had not improved with age. For a year or so, he had been receiving kidney dialysis in various outpatient centers, but had grown increasingly fractious and disruptive. Finally, all of the outpatient units refused to treat him and he was brought into the hospital. He was facing imminent uremic coma and was in urgent need of dialysis to save his life.

But at this juncture, he dug in his heels, categorically refusing to be dialyzed. Although his verbal communications were less than clear, his actions spoke loudly: he regularly fought off his nurses and doctors, ripping out his dialysis and intravenous tubes, and generally did his best to thwart care. The week before, he had torn out an intravenous needle and almost bled to death.

The options were stark: objectively, he was not doing well on dialysis and was experiencing enormous pain and discomfort. If the dialysis team didn't dialyze him, he would slip into a coma and die of uremic poisoning in a matter of weeks. But to do so would require the nurses to "snow and snug" him—sedating, then bodily restraining him for twice-weekly dialysis treatments. As grim a prospect as that would be for Herbert, it would be devastating for his care team. They were tremendously conflicted about feeling like medical thugs, tying down and drugging this patient as he struggled and kicked—all to save a life he didn't seem to want saved.

Stymied, the care team called in risk management, who called the Law and Ethics Consultation team. That afternoon, about a dozen of us met on the dialysis unit: several of the unit's specialist nurses, two physicians who were caring for Herbert, and various members of the hospital's administration staff, including an attorney.

We began, as usual, with the facts about his condition and his prognosis. Seeking to anchor the discussion in his life pattern of wishes and behavior, I asked who else could help us know more about Mr. Buriel. Unfortunately, the primary physician who had treated him for several years was out of town. Mr. Buriel's own family was both uninvolved and divided. In short, nobody in this discussion had a track record with Herbert or his family over time. Clearly, we lacked some important tools.

Given the family's absence and division, risk management was understandably concerned. If the hospital doesn't treat a treatable condition, it, and the responsible physicians, could be sued for negligence. The risk of suit, everyone knew, is especially acute when there is family conflict. Herbert might not want dialysis, but not treating was riskier for the hospital—and the job of the hospital administration, after all, is to avoid that risk. They recommended we go to court for an order to compel care. That way, at least, they knew someone else with proper legal authority would make the hard decision. Other staff members argued that it was wrong not to treat him when treatment would prolong his life and when it was not crystal clear that he was capable of making decisions. Nor did everyone agree that his disagreeable behavior amounted to a clear refusal.

I argued that he should have the right to determine his care—if he was of sound   7
mind. While Herbert was cantankerous and somewhat confused, disoriented, and forgetful, his wishes seemed clear and consistent. He was not telling us in the "appropriate" formal way what he wanted, although he always said, "No, no more." But this feisty old gentleman was speaking with his fists, fighting off doctors and nurses at every turn. When we asked what he was doing, he would occasionally say, "I'm ready to die—I don't want this." In Herbert's own way, as refractory as he was, with whatever capacities he possessed, he knew what he did—and didn't—want. Moreover, he was letting us know it in no uncertain terms, as the many scratches on the nurses' arms could attest.

ASSIGNMENT 12

The following situations briefly describe different ways in which information can be censored or suppressed.

1. An act of censorship that may be justifiable is one which censors the obscenities that people sometimes say on television talk shows. Is it really necessary to curse in order to make a joke funny?

2. The friends and relatives of an extremely sick man might wish to remove all medical encyclopedias from the household to prevent the patient from learning about his disease before the doctors are ready to inform him.

3. Preventing jurors from discussing a case that is being tried before them is usually considered justifiable because they might otherwise be influenced by the opinions of others, which might result in prejudgment of the defendant.

4. During World War II, a commonly heard phrase was "a slip of the lip can sink a ship." Letters from sailors overseas were read to eliminate any trace of location or dates. If the enemy had no knowledge of where or when a military ship was going, the chances of the ship arriving at its destination were more certain.

5. Aware that certain stock market figures (or company reports) do not look promising, one person attempts to suppress that information so that a friend will not dispose of his holdings, and the first person can therefore sell at a profit.

6. The ratings of all movies are examples of a kind of censorship designed to protect children from listening to profane and vulgar language and from seeing explicit sex and violence.

7. When the *New York Times* obtained copies of the secret Pentagon Papers, an account of the U.S. involvement in Indochina, and began to publish them, the Justice Department obtained a temporary restraining order against fur-

ther publication, arguing that the interests of the country would suffer "immediate and irreparable harm."

8. In Spain, actors were prevented from putting on a scene from the play *Equus* in which there is a naked couple. Although no one in the audience would have been forced to see the play, the government nevertheless cut that scene from local performances.

9. A college prohibits its student newspaper from printing articles that contain negative remarks, without documentation, about some campus and local administrators.

10. A mother thinks it best for her young son to become a doctor, despite the boy's preference for athletics. She prevents her son from reading the sports pages at home and forbids him to play on school teams. She believes that medicine is a more worthwhile and prestigious career than sports.

11. A cigarette company tries to persuade a magazine not to publish a new survey documenting the ill effects of smoking.

12. Some groups are lobbying to prevent the showing of X-rated films on cable television; they argue that small children might watch these movies without their parents' knowledge.

13. A woman whose husband has been brutally murdered tries to prevent any newspapers from coming into the house so that her small children will think that their father died peacefully.

14. A woman whose husband has been found guilty of tax evasion and required to pay a large fine tries to prevent any newspapers from coming into the house so that her small children will not know that their father has committed a crime.

15. Administrators prohibit the placement of pamphlets about birth control in the reception room of a high school counseling center.

16. A TV network removes from a news magazine show a story about a former president's alleged sexual affairs.

17. A third-world country forbids TV journalists to film incidents of unrest in its capital city, saying that such films give a false view of the attitudes of its citizens.

18. After members of Congress express concern about awarding federal grants to artists whose work may offend certain standards of good taste, a museum chooses not to show an exhibit containing some erotic photographs.

19. A school board bans the teaching of Mark Twain's *Huckleberry Finn* and Shakespeare's *The Merchant of Venice* on the grounds that racial and religious stereotypes might disturb some of the students.

20. A newspaper omits all references to AIDS in its obituaries.

21. The owners of a large shopping mall prohibit the distribution of any literature on the mall's premises without prior approval.

22. After members of a minority group complain about an offensive lecture at a local university, a legislator introduces a bill banning "incendiary speakers " from lecturing at state-supported institutions.

Write an essay that attempts to establish *appropriate limits for the public and private distribution of information*. Can certain facts, performances, and programs be censored without excessively curtailing the liberties of each citizen?

In planning your essay, do not settle for dividing the examples into justifiable and unjustifiable forms of censorship. Instead, ask yourself these questions about each situation on the list:

- Who will benefit?
- Who is being protected and from what?
- What are the political consequences of suppressing information?
- Do we invariably have a right to freedom of choice?
- Should we ever be deprived of the freedom to form opinions, communicate information, and watch the entertainment that we prefer? When and why?

Choose the questions that you wish to ask, and then ask them *consistently* as you think about and analyze each example on the list.

As you explore each example, decide whether, in your opinion, suppressing this information or imposing this kind of censorship is justified—and why. Take notes to record your decision and your reasons in each case or to indicate your doubt if you cannot decide. As you analyze each instance, you will be engaging in *three* overlapping operations:

- *interpreting* each situation
- establishing some common denominators for *categorizing* the entire group
- *evaluating* the various examples in order to develop your own definition of acceptable censorship and suppression of information

Before beginning to write, make a list of your categories. *The paragraphs in your essay should form a series of generalizations characterizing acceptable and unacceptable systems of censorship.* Remember that your reader has not seen the list of examples that you have been working from, and briefly paraphrase—not just refer to or quote from—each situation that you discuss. (If you wish, add your own examples to those already on the list.) Use your paraphrased descriptions to support the topic sentences of your paragraphs.

ASSIGNMENT 13

Write a comparison of three reviews of a film. Your first concern should be the reactions of the critics, not your own opinion of the work; you are not expected to write a review yourself, but to analyze and contrast each critic's view of the film. Try to describe the distinctive way in which each reacts to the film; each will have seen a somewhat different film and will have a different understanding of what it signifies.

Use the *Readers' Guide to Periodical Literature* and the *New York Times Index* to locate possible reviews. For films before 1970, consult James Salem's *A Guide to*

Critical Reviews. Don't commit yourself to a specific film until you have seen a sampling of reviews; if they are all very similar in their criticisms or all very short, choose a different film. If you have doubts about the reviews' suitability, let your teacher see a set of copies. *Be prepared to hand in a full set of the reviews with your completed essay.*

Part III

WRITING THE RESEARCH ESSAY

Most long essays and term papers in college courses are based on library research. Sometimes, an instructor will expect you to develop and present a topic entirely through synthesizing preassigned sources; but for many other assignments, you will be asked to formulate your own opinion and then to validate and support that opinion by citing authorities. Whether your essay is to be wholly or partly substantiated through research, you will still have to start your essay by choosing sources at the library.

Your research essay (or extended multiple-source essay) will present you with several new problems, contradictions, and decisions. On the one hand, you will probably be starting out with no sources, no thesis, and only a broad topic to work with. Yet as soon as you go to the library and start your research, you will probably find yourself with too many sources—shelf after shelf of books and articles from which you will have to make your own selection of readings. Locating and evaluating sources are complex skills, calling for quick comprehension and rapid decision-making.

- At the *indexes* and *on-line computer catalogs,* you have to judge which books are worth locating.
- At the *shelves,* you have to skim a variety of materials rapidly to choose the ones that may be worth reading at length.
- At the *library table* and *computer terminal,* you have to decide which facts and information should go into your notes and which pages should be duplicated in their entirety.

In Chapters 5, 6, and 7, you will be given explicit guidelines for using the library, choosing sources, and taking notes.

As you have learned, in order to write a multiple-source essay, you have to establish a coherent structure that builds on your reading and blends together your ideas and those of your sources. In Chapter 8, you will find a stage-by-stage description of the best ways to organize and write an essay based on complex sources. But here, again, is a contradiction.

Even as you gather your materials and synthesize them into a unified essay, you should also keep in mind the greatest responsibility of the researcher—*accountability. From your first visit to the library, you must carefully keep track of the precise source of each of the ideas and facts that you may use in your essay.* You already know how to distinguish between your ideas and those of your sources and to make that distinction clear to your readers.

Now, you also have to make clear which source is responsible for which idea and on which page of which book that information can be found—without losing the shape and coherence of your own paragraphs.

To resolve this contradiction between writing a coherent essay and accounting for your sources, you will use a system that includes the familiar skills of *quotation, paraphrase,* and *citation of authors,* as well as the skills of *documentation* and *compiling a bibliography.* This system is explained in Chapter 9.

Finally, in Chapter 10, you will be able to examine the product of all these research, writing, and documenting techniques: three essays that demonstrate, respectively, how to write a successful persuasive, narrative, and analytical research essay.

▪5▪

Gathering Materials at the Library: Bibliography

Knowing exactly what you want to write about is a great advantage when you are beginning your research. Your instructor may give you that advantage by assigning a precise topic. On the other hand, you may be asked to *narrow a broad subject* or to *develop a topic of your own choosing*, perhaps an idea that you wrote about in your single- or multiple-source essay to give you a head start.

Topic-narrowing should be a *practical* process. Here are some of the questions that you should ask yourself before you go to the library:

- How much time do I have?
- What resources are available to me?
- How long an essay am I being asked to write?
- How complex a project am I ready to undertake?

Choosing a good topic requires some familiarity with the subject and with the available resources, which is why topic-narrowing should continue all through the early stages of your research. Even before you start work at the library, you should invest some time in analyzing your subject and considering your options. Here are some approaches to topic-narrowing that have worked well for students starting their first research project.

> ## Guidelines for Narrowing Your Topic
>
> 1. Whether your instructor assigns a broad topic for your research paper or you are permitted to choose your own topic, do some *preliminary reading* to get more background information.
> 2. As you start your reading, begin to *break down the broad topic into its components:* try thinking about a specific point in time or the influence of a particular event or person if your topic is *historical or biographical;* try applying the standard strategies for planning an essay if you're going to write about a *contemporary issue.*
> 3. Consider *your own perspective* and what interests you about the person, event, or issue.
> 4. *Formulate a few questions* that might help you to structure your reading and research.
> 5. Think about the possible answers to these questions as you read, especially those questions and answers that might develop into a *thesis* for your essay.

FOCUSING THE TOPIC: BIOGRAPHICAL AND HISTORICAL SUBJECTS

Biographical and historical topics have an immediate advantage: they can be defined and limited by space and time. Events and lives have clear beginnings, middles, and ends, as well as many identifiable intermediate stages. You are probably not ready to undertake the full span of a biography or a complete historical event, but you could select *a specific point in time as the focus for your essay.* You can choose to examine as broad or as narrow a period as you wish. At the same time, both the scope of the project and the amount of research will become more manageable.

Assume, for example, that by choice or assignment your broad subject is *Franklin Delano Roosevelt,* who was president of the United States for fourteen years—an unparalleled term of office—between 1932 and 1945. You begin by reading *a brief overview of FDR's life.* An encyclopedia article of several pages might be a starting point. This should give you enough basic information to decide which events in FDR's life interest you enough to sustain you through the long process of research. You might also read a few articles about the major events that formed the background to FDR's career: the Great Depression, the New Deal, the changing role of the president.

Now, instead of tracing *all* the incidents and related events in which he participated during his sixty-three years, you might decide to describe FDR at the point when his political career was apparently ruined by polio. Your focus would be the man in 1921, and your essay might develop a thesis drawing on any or all of the following topics—his personality, his style of life, his experiences, his idea of government—at *that* point in time. Everything that happened to FDR after 1921 would be relatively unimportant to your chosen perspective. Another student might choose a different point in time and describe *the new president in 1933 against the background of the depression.* Yet another might focus on an intermediate point in FDR's presidency and construct *a profile of the man as he was in 1940, when he decided to run for an unprecedented third term in office.*

The topic might be made even more specific by focusing on *a single event and its causes.* For example, the atomic bomb was developed during FDR's presidency and was used in Japan shortly after his death:

- What was FDR's attitude toward atomic research?
- Did he advocate using the bomb?
- Did he anticipate its consequences?

Or you might want to study Roosevelt in the context of an important political tradition:

- How did he influence the Democratic party?
- How did the party influence his personal and political decisions?
- What role did Roosevelt play in the establishment of the United States as a "welfare state"?

This kind of profile attempts to describe the subject and explore his or her motives and experiences. In effect, *your overriding impression of character or intention serves as the thesis, the controlling idea of the biographical profile.* You undertake to determine whether the available evidence supports your thesis, and present that thesis—if valid—to your readers, supported by facts and details.

You can also view a *historical event* from a similar specific vantage point. Your broad subject might be the Civil War, which lasted more than four years, or the Berlin Olympics of 1936, which lasted a few weeks, or the Los Angeles riots of 1991, which lasted a few days. To cover a long span of time, you might focus on an intermediate point or stage, which can serve to illuminate and characterize the entire event. The Battle of Gettysburg, for example, is a broad topic often chosen by those interested in the even broader topic of the Civil War. Since the three-day battle, with its complex maneuvers, can hardly be described in a brief narrative, you would want to narrow the focus even more. You might describe the battlefield and the disposition of the troops, as a journalist would, at a single moment in the course of the battle. In this case, your thesis might demonstrate that the disposition of the troops at this point was typical (or atypical) of tactics used throughout the battle, or that this moment did (or did not) foreshadow the battle's conclusion. In fact, always assuming that sufficient material is available, *you will find that it makes sense to narrow your focus as much as you can.*

In writing about history, you also have to consider your own point of view. If, for example, you set out to recount an episode from the Civil War, you first need to establish your perspective: Are you describing the Union's point of view? the Confederacy's? the point of view of the politicians of either side? the generals? the civilians? industrialists? hospital workers? slaves in the South? black freedmen in the North? If you tried to deal with *all* these reactions to a chosen event, you might have difficulty in settling on a thesis and, in the long run, would only confuse and misinform your reader.

The "day in the life" approach can also be applied to *events that had no specific date.*

- When and under what circumstances were primitive guns first used in battle?
- What was the psychological effect of gunfire on the opposing troops?
- What was the reaction when the first automobile drove down a village street?

Or, rather than describe the effects of a new invention, you might focus on *a social institution that has changed radically.*

- What was it like to shop for food in Paris in 1810?
- In Chicago in 1870?
- In any large American city in 1945?

Instead of attempting to write a complete history of the circus from Rome to Ringling, try portraying *the particular experience of a single person.*

- What was it like to be an equestrian performer in Astley's Circus in eighteenth-century London?
- A chariot racer in Pompeii's Circus Maximus in 61 B.C.?

Setting a tentative target date helps you to focus your research, giving you a practical way to judge the relevance and the usefulness of each of your sources. As you narrow your topic and begin your reading, *watch for your emerging thesis—a single, clear impression of the person or event that you wish your reader to receive.* Whether you are writing about a sequence of events, like a battle or a flood, or a single event or issue affecting the life of a well-known person, you will still need both a *thesis* and a *strategy* to shape the direction of your essay. *A common strategy for biographical and historical topics is the cause-and-effect sequence*—why a certain decision was made or an event turned out one way and not another.

Finally, do not allow your historical or biographical portrait to become an exercise in creative writing. Your evidence must be derived from and supported by well-documented sources, not just your imagination. The "Napoleon might have said" or "Stalin must have thought" in some biographies and historical novels is often a theory or an educated guess that is firmly rooted in research—and the author should provide documentation and a bibliography to substantiate it.

FOCUSING THE TOPIC: CONTEMPORARY ISSUES

When you write about a historical or biographical topic, you can use the perspective of time to achieve a narrow focus. But when you work with a more abstract topic, the multiplicity of possible applications and examples may make it difficult for you to find a focus. If you chose to write about the early history of the circus, you would find an assortment of books describing many traditional kinds of circus activity, from the Roman arena to the turn-of-the-century Barnum and Bailey big top. But there has been an enormous increase in the amount of information published in this half of the twentieth century; reviews and features are printed—and preserved for the researcher—every time Ringling Brothers opens in a new city. Your research for an essay about the circus today might be endless and the results unmanageable unless, quite early, you focus your approach.

If your topic cannot be defined and narrowed through the perspective of time, you can analyze its component parts and select *a single aspect* as the tentative focus of your essay. If you do a computer search for information, you will scan a large number of "descriptors" for your broad topic. Reviewing all these subtopics may help you to find a narrow focus for your topic.

You will find that many of the guides, indexes, and on-line databases in the reference room contain not only lists of sources but also a useful breakdown of subtopics, suggesting possibilities for the direction of your essay. You will automatically narrow your perspective if you begin to ask questions about and apply different strategies to possible topics. Here are some sample questions:

- How does this actually operate? What procedures does it use?
- What are its benefits? its dangers?
- Is there a better way of doing it?
- Which groups of people does it especially affect?
- How is it to be compared with this or that variation on the same topic?

For example, suppose that *food* is your broad topic. Your approach might be *descriptive*, analyzing *causes and effects*: you could write about some aspect of nutrition, discussing what we ought to eat and the way in which our nutritional needs are best satisfied. Or you could deal with the production and distribution of food—or, more likely, a specific kind of food—and use *process description* as your approach. Or you could analyze a different set of *causes*: Why don't we eat what we ought to? Why do so many people have to diet, and why aren't diets effective? Or you could plan a *problem-solution* essay: What would be the best way to educate the public in proper nutrition? By building your topic on a controversial point, you could *argue* the virtues or defects of food additives, or junk foods, or convenience cooking. Within the narrower focus of *food additives*, there are numerous ways to develop the topic:

- To what degree are additives dangerous?
- What was the original purpose of the Food and Drug Act of 1906?
- Would individual rights be threatened if additives like Nutrasweet were banned?
- Can the dangers of food additives be compared with the dangers of alcohol?

On the other hand, your starting point could be *a concrete object*, rather than *an abstract idea*: you might decide to write about the Big Mac. You could describe its contents and nutritional value; or recount its origins and first appearance on the food scene; or compare it to best-selling foods of past eras; or evaluate its relative popularity in different parts of the world. All of these topics require *research*.

It is desirable to have a few possible narrow topics in mind before you begin intensive reading. Then, as you start to compile your preliminary bibliography, you can begin to distinguish between sources that are potentially useful and sources that will probably be irrelevant. What you *cannot* do at this stage is formulate a definite thesis. *Your thesis will probably answer the question that you asked at the beginning of your research.* Although, from the first, you may have your own theories about the answer, you cannot be sure that your research will confirm your hypotheses. Your thesis should remain tentative until your reading has given your essay content and direction.

EXERCISE 26

The following topic proposals were submitted by students who had already spent two sessions at the library focusing their topics for an eight- to ten-page research essay. Consider the scope and focus of each proposal, and decide which ones suggest *practical* topics for an essay of this length. If the proposal is too broad, be prepared to offer suggestions for narrowing the focus.

Student A

Much of the interest in World War II has been focused on the battlefield, but the war years were also a trying period for the public at home. I intend to write about civilian morale during the war, emphasizing press campaigns to increase the war effort. I will also include a description of the way people coped with brown-outs, shortages, and rationing, with a section on the victory garden.

Student B

I intend to deal with the role of women in feudal life, especially the legal rights of medieval women. I would also like to discuss the theory of chivalry and its effects on women, as well as the influence of medieval literature on society. My specific focus will be the ideal image of the medieval lady.

Student C

I have chosen the Lindbergh kidnapping case as the subject of my essay. I intend to concentrate on the kidnapping itself, rather than going into details about the lives of the Lindberghs. What interests me is the planning of the crime, including the way in which the house was designed and the kidnapping was carried out. I also hope to include an account of the investigation and courtroom scenes.

Student D

I would like to explore methods of travel one hundred and fifty years ago, and compare the difficulties of traveling then with the conveniences of traveling now. I intend to stress the economic and social background of the average traveler. My focus will be the Grand Tour that young men used to take.

Student E

I intend to explore certain kinds of revivalist religions in America today, to describe typical experiences, and to try to explain their interest and attraction for so many young people.

Student F

I'd like to explore different definitions of quality in television programs. Specifically, I'd like to contrast popular and critically acclaimed TV shows of today with comparable programs ten and twenty years ago, in an effort to determine whether there really has been a decline in popular taste. It may be necessary to restrict my topic to one kind of television show—situation comedies, for example, or coverage of sports events.

Student G

I would like to do research on several aspects of adolescent peer groups, trying to determine whether the overall effects of peer groups on adolescents are beneficial or destructive. I intend to include the following topics: the need for peer acceptance; conformity; personal and social adjustment; and peer competition. I'm not sure that I can form a conclusive argument, since most of the information available on this subject is purely descriptive; but I'll try to present an informed opinion.

EXERCISE 27

A. Here are ten different ways of approaching the broad topic of *poverty in America*. Decide which questions would make good starting points for an eight- to ten-page research essay. Consider the practicality and the clarity of each question, the probable availability of research materials, and the likelihood of being able to answer the question in approximately nine pages. Try rewriting two of the questions that seem too broad, narrowing the focus.

1. How should the nation deal with poverty in its communities?

2. What problems does your city or town encounter in its efforts to make sure that its citizens live above the poverty level?

3. What are the primary causes of poverty today?

4. Whose responsibility is it to deal with the poor?

5. What effects does a life of poverty have on a family?

6. What can be done to protect children and the aged, groups that make up the largest proportion of the poor?

7. Does everyone have the right to freedom from fear of poverty?

8. Which programs for alleviating poverty have been particularly successful, and why?

9. Should all those receiving welfare funds be required to work?

10. What nations have effectively solved the problem of poverty, and how?

B. Make up several questions that would help you to develop the broad topic of *health care in America* for an eight- to ten-page research essay.

COMPILING A WORKING BIBLIOGRAPHY: LOCATING SOURCES

> ### *Preliminary Research in the Library: Three Overlapping Stages*
>
> 1. Discovering and locating the titles of some possible sources.
> 2. Recording basic facts about each source.
> 3. Noting each source's potential usefulness—or lack of usefulness—to your topic.

These three stages usually form a *continuous cycle*. You probably will not be able to locate *all* your sources at once, and then record *all* your basic information, and lastly take notes about *all* your sources. Rather, you will have to move back and forth from computer terminal to stacks to reference room. Even after you begin to plan and write your essay, you will probably find yourself back at the library, checking another potentially useful source.

Because you may be looking at a great many titles and because, in any one session at the library, you may be at a different stage of research with each of several different books and articles, you should thoroughly familiarize yourself with the three steps.

The Library

Even before your research essay is assigned, you should become acquainted with your college library. Every library has a different layout, with a different on-line (computerized) catalog, and stacks that use various kinds of numbering systems. *Find out how your library is organized, how the on-line catalog works, and what it contains.* Most libraries provide guided tours for groups of interested students. Ask the reference librarian about tour schedules; in fact, the librarian will probably provide you with pamphlets about the library, a map, and almost any other information you're likely to need.

If a tour is not available, make your own exploratory visit. Ask yourself some of the following questions:

- How are the books arranged?
- Are the collections for the different disciplines housed in separate buildings?
- Do you have access to all the stacks of books?
- Is there a map of the reference room on the wall?
- How are the guides and indexes arranged in the reference room? Do you have access to these on-line?
- Is there a list of all the periodicals owned by the library? Is this list on-line?
- What kinds of sources are available on microfilm and microcards? Where are the microfilm and microcard readers, and how do you locate and sign out the cards and spools of film?
- Is there a computerized database, and how do you get access to it?
- Does your library have a consortial arrangement with neighboring libraries, and do you have access to materials at these libraries, via a delivery system (interlibrary loan) or computer print-out?
- Does your library provide access to the Internet? What special research services are available?

Get these questions answered before you start your research; then you will not lose time and impetus because of interruptions later on.

Online Databases

Until recently, libraries listed all their holdings on cards—one card per book—contained in narrow drawers: the *card catalog.* Sometimes, instead of cards in drawers, libraries used a series of bound volumes, with forty or more entries per page. Now, most libraries are converting to *on-line databases,* often called On-Line Public Access Catalogs (OPACs). These computerized catalogs enable you to sit at a computer terminal and, using a menu that appears on your screen, call up information about a topic or an author or a book. This information can consist of:

- the holdings of your library
- the holdings of other libraries that are part of a local group
- general and specialized indexes and bibliographies that list the names of sources—books and periodicals—some of which may be owned by the library

- certain journals that are on-line—that is, that you can call up and read on your computer screen—and from which you can obtain print-outs of specific articles

Some libraries have databases of electronic information sources available on CD-ROM (compact disk read only memory). This means that the database is stored on a computer disk, periodically updated, which can be borrowed from the reference librarian. Once the disk is inserted in the reference room computer, the process of searching for sources is much the same whether the database is on-line or CD-ROM.

Each library system with its own on-line database has a set of commands—slightly different at each library—that students can type in order to access information about the library's collections on the screen. You will usually find a clear set of instructions posted by each terminal, indicating the basic steps to follow in order to find what you are looking for or even to find out what you want to look for.

Figure 5-1 shows a sample—one screen—of what's available on-line to students on the twenty campuses of The City University of New York (CUNY).

Using a database is, in many ways, easier than using a card catalog. To check a number of possible topics or authors in the card catalog, you would have to move from drawer to drawer, pulling one out, thumbing through the cards, making notes, returning the drawer, and moving to a different section of the catalog for your next reference. It is physically easier to remain at a terminal,

```
                                                                    N002
          CITY UNIVERSITY OF NEW YORK LIBRARIES INFORMATION SYSTEM
                            CUNY+PLUS




     DPAC        CUNY Online Catalog

                 Periodical and Newspaper Indexes
     *DPER        Periodical Index
     *DUMI        Newspaper Index
      ABII        ABI/Inform




                                      * Databases that require Sign-On.
     -------------------------------------------- + Page 1 of 3 ---------
     HELp            Select a database label from above      <F8> FORward
                     NEWs (Library System News)


     Database Selection:
     4-©                   Sess-A                        0011    NET3270
```

Figure 5-1

locating potential sources by making choices from a menu and typing in key words so that the information you want appears on the screen. What you see on the screen is probably not much different from what you would find in the card catalog. But the process is faster and, once you become familiar with the steps, much less tedious.

On-line databases can have their limitations. Your library's basic database may be restricted to its own holdings (or, if your college is part of a system or a consortium, the combined holdings of all the libraries in the system). But some are now linked to university holdings across the state or even the nation. If you want to examine a range of all the possible sources on a particular topic, you will have to consult a specialized database that will undoubtedly include some titles that your library doesn't own. (See below for information about conducting a computerized search in a specialized database.)

For decades, researchers have had access to a number of general and specialized indexes and bibliographies that they use to find articles (and sometimes books) related to their research topics. For example, *Applied Science and Technology Index* contains brief summaries of a large number of journal articles about topics in science and technology, while *Human Resources Abstracts* lists articles about areas such as poverty, the workforce, and the distribution of human services. Until a few years ago, the listings in indexes such as *Applied Science and Technology Index* or the *Human Resources Abstracts* were contained in large volumes on the reference room shelf. Now, however, an increasingly large number of these reference works can be obtained on-line. Appendix A contains an extensive listing of these reference sources (and the asterisks next to the entries in Appendix A indicate which of them have been computerized). Although they contain essentially the same information, one important advantage of the on-line databases over printed indexes is that bound volumes are restricted to single years; you may have to look at several before you find articles that are appropriate to your topic, while a single computer search will provide you with all relevant sources for the past several years.

Because your library has to pay to subscribe to most of these databases, you may be asked to pay a fee—sometimes sizable—for the search to take place. Increasingly, however, OPACs provide access to an amazing variety of research materials, including periodical indexes (and some periodical articles), government documents, sound recordings, and gateways to other systems that can expand your information horizon even more.

The Electronic Network: Internet

In addition to those resources already mentioned, the computer terminal in your library (or in your dormitory room) can provide you with access to many other powerful tools that will produce information in incredible range and depth. This access to information generally depends upon a gigantic electronic network—or, rather, an enormous web of many thousands of smaller networks—that is called the *Internet*. Commercial services that exist for this purpose collect specific categories of data, put that information on-line, revise and add to it regularly, and sell access to that information to individuals, businesses, agencies, and educational institutions that are interested in using it.

Several million people use the Internet all across the world, and the number increases daily. Individuals can participate in the Internet services by paying a fee and establishing an account; students and faculty at universities frequently have access to the Internet at minimal or no charge as part of the information systems available to the college community. Your librarian or your computer services technicians can tell you about what's available at your campus—and whether it will cost you any money.

Using the Internet enables you to carry out all kinds of activities, starting with sending and receiving messages through electronic mail (see below) and tapping into databases in specialized fields. The Internet is the generic parent of the smaller network that (for a fee) provides your campus library with its on-line databases and with the thousands of reference works, newspapers, magazines, and journals that can now be accessed and read at your terminal. These on-line databases are accessible *only* through a computer and only by subscribing to the service (which is generally called "having an account").

Independent database services that may be obtainable through the Internet at your library include:

- *Nexis*, allowing you to search for, review, and print out newspaper and magazine articles related to a given person or topic
- *Dow Jones News/Retrieval*, specializing in newspapers and business publications
- *Lexis*, providing access to legal citations, case law, and statutes
- *DIALOG*, containing professional and corporate information
- *LOCIS*, providing information from the Library of Congress on federal legislation

Figure 5.2 shows only two of the basic menus available from a Library of Congress database called *LC Marvel*. If you ask the menu to provide you with the second item on the second screen—"Historical Documents of the U.S."—a new menu will appear (Figure 5.3) offering you a choice of primary documents relevant to historical research.

Electronic mail: E-mail is a facet of the Internet that is used by millions of people who may have very little interest in the technology of computers and information systems, but who simply want an easy way of instantly communicating with people—friends and strangers, singly and in groups—all over the world. In its simplest form, E-mail helps people to talk to each other and exchange information without the unwieldy process of writing or typing a letter, mailing it, and sending it to a far-off destination. It is as quick and easy as a telephone conversation, but expands the impact of a conference call involving no more than half dozen people to an audience of hundreds of thousands—with the added advantage of obtaining a print-out of everything that has been said just by pressing a button.

```
Rice CMS Gopher 2.4.0                              marvel.loc.gov
1/13
                     Library of Congress (LC MARVEL)
<menu>      About LC MARVEL
<menu>      Events, Facilities, Programs, and Services
<menu>      Research and Reference (Public Services)
<menu>      Libraries and Publishers (Technical Services)
<menu>      Copyright
<menu>      Library of Congress Online Systems
<menu>      Employee Information
<menu>      U.S. Congress
<menu>      Government Information
<menu>      Global Electronic Library (by Subject)
<menu>      Internet Resources
<menu>      What's New on LC MARVEL
<menu>      Search LC MARVEL Menus




1= Help      2=           3= Return     4= Print      5= Receive   6= Find
7= Backward  8= Forward   9= Bookmark   10= Booklist  11=          12= Quit
4-©                  Sess-A                           0011    NET3270
```

Figure 5-2A

```
Rice CMS Gopher 2.4.0                              marvel.loc.gov
19/27
                     General Information Resources
<document>  Guide to Internet Government Resources in Bus. and Econ. (2/94)
<menu>      Historical Documents of the U.S.
<menu>      Job Openings in the Federal Government
<telnet>    Monthly Catalog (Govt. Pubs. Via CARL:  choose PAC, 1, 22, 83)
<menu>      National Performance Review Report
<menu>      National Social Statistics:  Surveys, Census (Via UPenn)
<menu>      Open Source Solutions, Inc. (OSS Gopher)
<menu>      The Legal Domain Network
<menu>      Wiretap Gopher






1= Help      2=           3= Return     4= Print      5= Receive   6= Find
7= Backward  8= Forward   9= Bookmark   10= Booklist  11=          12= Quit
4-©                  Sess-A                           0011    NET3270
```

Figure 5-2B

```
Rice CMS Gopher 2.4.0                                    wiretap.Spies.COM
1/27
                         Historical Documents of the U.S.
<document>   Declaration of Arms, 1775
<document>   Declaration of Independence
<document>   Emancipation Proclamation
<document>   Federalist Papers #10
<document>   Federalist Papers #51
<document>   First Open Door Note, September 1899
<document>   Freedom of Information Act Request Package
<document>   Fundamental Orders of 1639
<document>   Letter of Transmittal of US Constitution
<document>   Mayflower Compact
<document>   Monroe Doctrine
<menu>       Naval Fighting Ships
<document>   Northwest Ordinance
<menu>       Pre World War II Documents
<document>   Procalamtion of Neutrality, 1793
<document>   Resolves of the Continental Congress
<document>   Treaty of Greenville
<document>   Treaty of Paris, 1793
<document>   U2 Shootdown Incident of 1960

1= Help      2=           3= Return    4= Print     5= Receive   6= Find
7= Backward  8= Forward   9= Bookmark  10= Booklist 11=          12= Quit
4-©                   Sess-A                         0011   NET3270
```

Figure 5-3

For the researcher, this exchange of information is invaluable, since a request for assistance in exploring a particular topic—when broadcast over E-mail—can reach a vast number of people, many of whom will send messages back with offers of data and materials, all of which can also be transmitted through E-mail. Remember that any information obtained through E-mail that is subsequently used in an essay must be documented. (See Appendix B for the appropriate format.)

Gophers: The Internet provides such a huge number of resources that some organizing software is necessary to provide users with orderly access to information. Put simply, a "gopher" is an electronic search tool—and there are more than a thousand of them—that, through menus, helps people to determine which of the available databases on Internet is likely to have the information they want. Once you have logged on to a specific gopher, you use the menu, as well as key words that will call up the right kind of information, and you will be automatically passed from one gopher site to the next until you reach a database that has that information. Powerful gophers called VERONICA (since it searches through *archives*) or WAIS (Wide Area Information Servers) carry out the search and help you to navigate through the Internet's databases.

Technology—through the Internet—offers opportunities for you to pursue your research with the help of one or more databases. Because the computer is programmed according to logical principles, it will help you to make connections between the topic that you have in mind when you start your research and the topic that you will eventually write about. The information on the screen often includes suggestions that will help you to narrow your topic and find useful sources. In many cases, the terminal will have a printer that will provide you with a list of these suggestions—a miniature database of your own.

Cross-Referencing

To use virtually all on-line databases—OPACs, gophers, standard research indexes, and databases provided by commercial services—you have to carry out a computer search, based on the principle of *cross-referencing*. A single source—book, article, document, recording, set of statistics—may be useful for research on dozens of different topics, but not for *every* topic in the database. When a new source—a book, for example—is being entered into a database, it would be foolish to include a separate entry for that book under every possible subject heading; that would create an overflowing database and an unmanageable system. Instead, just as libraries have done for decades in organizing their card catalogs, most on-line databases today use cross-referencing. First, *a standardized set of subject headings* is created to index information in the database. Then, the newly acquired book is scanned, and an entry for that book is placed *only* under those subject headings that are relevant to its content. On-line databases generally use a set of subject headings for cross-referencing. The most commonly used is the three-volume *Library of Congress Subject Headings* (LCSH), containing the standard set of cross-references found in all libraries using the Library of Congress system. Or a database may have a special list of descriptors relevant to its subject that can be found in a separate "thesaurus." Libraries generally have LCSH lists or other thesauruses available on-line or in books near the computer terminals.

Computer Searches

Suppose that you come to the library with a broad topic in mind: you plan to write an essay about *Prohibition*, the period between 1920 and 1933 when the Eighteenth Amendment to the U.S. Constitution prohibited the manufacture and sale of all alcoholic beverages in the United States. How would you determine the sources that were available? How would you begin your search through all these databases that contain more information than you need or want?

A computer search usually begins by consulting the LCSH or other thesaurus to identify the appropriate *key words* (called *subject headings* or *descriptors*)—that describe your topic. The object is to find a group of descriptors that you can use, separately or together, to narrow down your topic. (This process is sometimes called *Boolean searching*, a term derived from mathematics, referring to questions limited in scope by combining two descriptors—for example, greater than, less than, x *and* y, x *and not* y—in order to narrow down a topic.) Figure 5-4 shows a listing of LCSH topics that you could look up in addition to Prohibition.

Many other subject headings might lead to useful information about Prohibition, yet they don't appear on the cross-referencing list. Some preliminary

```
                        PROHIBITION

                          see also

                     LICENSE SYSTEMS
                     LIQUOR LAWS
                     LIQUOR PROBLEMS
                     LOCAL OPTIONS
                     PROHIBITIONISTS
                     TEMPERANCE
```

Figure 5-4. Listing of Library of Congress Subject Heading Topics

reading on the topic might encourage you to look up "Organized Crime," for example, or "Smuggling of Illegal Substances."

If you can't find appropriate key words in LCSH, and your on-line catalog has the capacity to do a Keyword or Boolean search, you would consult the menu for Keyword Searching and then type in combinations of possible key words. Figure 5-5 shows two of the Help Screens, in sequence, in the CUNY Online Catalog that give students a choice of appropriate commands to do a Keyword Search.

If you wanted to do a Keyword Search for the topic "Prohibition," using the AND search, you would choose another appropriate term ("Temperance," for example), and, at the K= prompt, you would type in: Prohibition and Temperance.

Here is the result of a computer search in the ERIC database using a combination of *three* key words: the student typed in a request for articles about PRO-HIBITION and ALCOHOL and the UNITED STATES. Only two articles fulfilled those three descriptors. Figures 5-6 and 5-7 show the summaries of those two articles that appeared on the computer screen (and could, later on, be printed).

Either of these two articles might be interesting material for an essay on Pro-hibition in the United States. The Rorabaugh article seems to provide general background (but note that it is only three pages long), and the last section of the Wasserman article explicitly describes the period immediately before the passage of the Eighteenth Amendment. The printout contains information about the journal, volume, and date of publication, but does not use MLA or any other standard method of documentation.

The student tried another computer search, using the same three descrip-tors, this time in a database called DPAC (a book catalog database). The search resulted in the titles of one book and one book review. Unlike ERIC, DPAC provides no summaries, but does include a set of additional descriptors that might prompt you to enter a different combination of commands and produce a different group of titles from the database. In Figure 5-8, the information about the Blocker book review tells you the name of the work being reviewed,

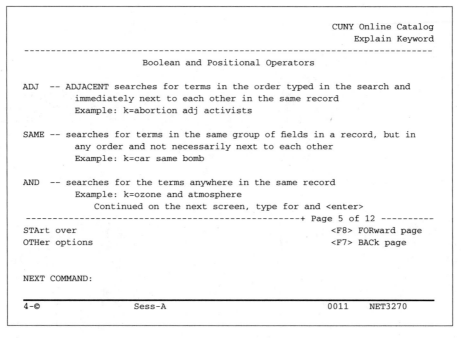

```
                                                        CUNY Online Catalog
                                                        Explain Keyword
   -----------------------------------------------------------------------
                     Boolean and Positional Operators

   ADJ  -- ADJACENT searches for terms in the order typed in the search and
             immediately next to each other in the same record
             Example: k=abortion adj activists

   SAME -- searches for terms in the same group of fields in a record, but in
             any order and not necessarily next to each other
             Example: k=car same bomb

   AND  -- searches for the terms anywhere in the same record
             Example: k=ozone and atmosphere
                 Continued on the next screen, type for and <enter>
   -------------------------------------------------+ Page 5 of 12 ----------
   STArt over                                           <F8> FORward page
   OTHer options                                        <F7> BACk page


   NEXT COMMAND:

   _____
   4-©              Sess-A                         0011    NET3270
```

Figure 5-5A

```
                                                        CUNY Online Catalog
                                                        Explain Keyword
   -----------------------------------------------------------------------
                 Boolean and Positional Operators - continued

   NOT  -- Searches for occurrences of the first term and will match only if
             the second term is NOT in the same record
             Example: k=haymarket not riot

   NEAR -- Searches for the two terms next to each other, but in any order
             Example: k=mexico near trade

   OR   -- Searches for the first term or second term or both
             Example: k=hurricanes or typhoons


            For information on qualifying search terms press <enter>
   -------------------------------------------------+ Page 6 of 12 ----------
   STArt over                                           <F8> FORward page
   OTHer options                                        <F7> BACk page


   NEXT COMMAND:

   _____
   4-©              Sess-A                         0011    NET3270
```

Figure 5-5B

1 of 2
Marked in Search: #6

AN ACCESSION NUMBER: EJ449332
AU PERSONAL AUTHOR: Rorabaugh, -W.-J.
TI TITLE: Alcohol in America.
PY PUBLICATION YEAR: 1991
JN JOURNAL CITATION: OAH-Magazine-of-History; v6 n2 p17-19 Fall 1991
AB ABSTRACT: Traces the history of alcohol use in the United States from the colonial period to the present. Discusses changes in public attitudes toward drinking. Explores attempts at prohibition, alcohol preferences, the relationship between alcohol consumption and economic prosperity, and the dichotomy of alcohol as a part of a European heritage that is also a destructive substance. (DK)

Figure 5-6

2 of 2
Marked in Search: #6

AN ACCESSION NUMBER: EJ448301
AU PERSONAL AUTHOR: Wasserman,-Ira-M.
TI TITLE: The Impact of Epidemic, War, Prohibition and Media on Suicide: United States, 1910-1920.
PY PUBLICATION YEAR: 1992
JN JOURNAL CITATION: Suicide-and-Life-Threatening-Behavior; v22 n2 p240-54 Sum 1992
AV AVAILABILITY: UMI
AB ABSTRACT: Estimated impact of exogenous social and political events on suicide behavior in the United States between 1910 and 1920. Concluded that World War I did not influence suicide; Great Influenza Epidemic caused suicide to increase; and continuing decline in alcohol consumption from 1910 to 1920 depressed national suicide rates. (Author/NB)

Figure 5-7

```
DPER [Periodical Database]
Sample Computer Screen entry
From search: k= prohibition and alcohol and United States

AUTHOR:       Blocker, Jack S. Jr.

ARTICLE TITLE: Book Reviews: Profits, Power, and Prohibition

SOURCE
DATE:         Journal of American History. Dec. 1990,
              v77n3, P.1010-1011

ABSTRACT:     J.S. Blocker, Jr. reviews "Profits, Power, and Prohibition:
              Alcohol Reform and the Industrializing of America,
              1800-1930," by John H. Rumbarger.

SUBJECT
DESCRIPTORS:  Nonfiction
              History
              Prohibition era
              Reforms
              United States

LENGTH:       Medium (10-30 col inches)

ARTICLE
TYPE:         Book Review Favorable


AUTHOR:       Rumbarger, John J.

TITLE:        PROFITS, POWER, AND PROHIBITION: ALCOHOL REFORM AND THE
              INDUSTRIALIZING OF AMERICA, 1800-1930.

PUBLISHER:    Albany: SUNY Press, 1989.

SUBJECTS:     Prohibition—United States—History
              Temperance—United States—History
              United States—Industries—History
```

Figure 5-8

suggests that the length of the review is "medium," and assures you that the review is "favorable."

Specialized Indexes

In addition to the larger on-line databases available through the Internet, a number of smaller indexes of periodicals and journals intended for research in specific disciplines are available on-line or through CD-ROM disks that you can access yourself at a terminal. (Appendix A has a comprehensive listing.) Most library information systems have the most frequently used periodical indexes right in their on-line system as separate databases (usually limited to the last ten years). To continue your research on Prohibition, you might want to consult the *Social Sciences Index*, the *Readers' Guide to Periodical Literature*, or the *Times Index*.

The *Readers' Guide to Periodical Literature* is especially useful for research on contemporary issues. It contains listings of a number of popular magazines, but very few scholarly journals, so it should not be the *only* index that you consult in preparing an academic paper. For your essay on Prohibition, you would look at the *Readers' Guide* for the 1920s and early 1930s, and find titles such as "Why Repeal Will Be Coming Soon." Here is what a *Readers' Guide* entry for a 1932 article looks like:

After Prohibition, what? L. Rogers. New Repub. 73:91–99   D7 '32
[title]   [author]   [magazine]   [volume; pages]   [date]

As you can see, the title of the article comes first; then L. Rogers, the author's name, with the first name indicated only by the initial; then the title of the periodical (often abbreviated); then the volume number, followed by a colon and the pages (91–99) on which the article appears; then the month, day, and year (December 7, 1932) of publication. *Be aware that this citation is not the appropriate format for your bibliography.* It is merely the sequence of information used by *this* index.

Another popular source of information on contemporary life is the *Times Index*, which contains topical news articles from the *New York Times* on Prohibition, such as "Rise in Gangland Murders Linked to Bootlegging." Here is a typical *Times Index* listing for 1933:

25 Buffalo speakeasies and stills raided, S 24,   IV,   6:6
                            [date] [section] [page: column]

The title of the article is followed by the date (24 September), the section of the newspaper (IV, indicated in Roman numerals to avoid confusion), the page (6), and the column (the sixth from left). Again, the format of this citation is peculiar to this index and is not to be used as a model for your bibliography.

Since these indexes have to cram a great deal of information into a relatively small space, they include only one entry for each book or article, and make extensive use of cross-referencing. In the *Readers' Guide* for 1932–1933, for example, you would find four columns of articles about Prohibition, first divided into regions and then into a series of headings that include "Economic Aspects," "Enforcement," "Political Aspects," "Repeal," and "Results." But at the very beginning of the list, the reader is referred to other subject headings to be found elsewhere in the *Guide:*

See *also*
alcohol
liquor problem
liquor traffic
liquor

It is your job to check any of the other headings that seem relevant to your topic, and include some of them in your list of key words for additional computer searches in the larger databases.

Some indexes do not provide "See also" lists. In one year's listings of the *Social Sciences Index,* for example, the subject headings do not include "Prohibition," but under the broad heading of "Alcohol," you would find "Social Interaction in the Speakeasy of 1930." The Library of Congress Subject Headings can help you to identify possible topics for checking, but you also need to use your ingenuity and imagination to cross-reference your topic.

Using Your Library's On-line Periodicals Database

Many campus libraries provide students with access to a *periodicals database* listing all the articles in all the newspapers, magazines, and journals available in *that* library (or group of libraries). A student searching the CUNY database—using the key word "Prohibition"—accessed the screen shown in Figure 5-9, which contains the first fourteen entries on that topic in the database.

The student wanted to know more about the first article and typed in #1 at the prompt to get a detailed description of "Carry from Kansas Became a Nation All Unto Herself." As Figure 5-10 shows, the article (which appeared in *Smithsonian*) deals with the more bizarre aspects of Carry Nation's life. Moreover, the temperance crusader died more than eight years before Prohibition became law. Before deciding whether to read the article, you should consider whether you want to limit your topic and your research to the 1920s or whether you are interested in exploring the historical background of the temperance movement, which was instrumental in bringing about Prohibition.

```
Search Request: S=PROHIBITION                          General Periodical Ind
Search Results: 52 Entries Found                              Subject Index
--------------------------------------------------------------------------
        PROHIBITION
   1    CARRY FROM KANSAS BECAME A NATION ALL UNTO H <1989> (RG)
   2    DRINKING IN AMERICA <1990> (RG)
   3    FISH DRY AND VOTE WET <1987> (RG)
   4    GOOD BYE WHISKEY GOOD BYE GIN <1992> (RG)
   5    LAST UNTOUCHABLE <1987> (RG)
   6    LESSONS OF PROHIBITION <1988> (RG)
   7    PROHIBITIONS FAILURE LESSONS FOR TODAY <1992> (RG)
   8    REAL ELIOT NESS <1987> (RG)
   9    REAL MCCOY <1987> (RG)
  10    REFLECTIONS ON THE DRY SEASON <1990> (RG)
  11    SHOULD WE LEGALIZE DRUGS HISTORY ANSWERS <1993> (RG)
  12    SHOULD WE LEGALIZE DRUGS HISTORY ANSWERS <1993> (RG)
  13    WANTED CONSENSUS ON ABORTION <1989> (RG)
  14    WHAT HAPPENED IN HINTON <1988> (RG)
-------------------------------------------------- CONTINUED on next page  ---
STArt over       Type number to display record         <F8> FORward page
HELp             GUIde
OTHer options


NEXT COMMAND:
4-©               Sess-A                        0011    NET3270
```

Figure 5-9

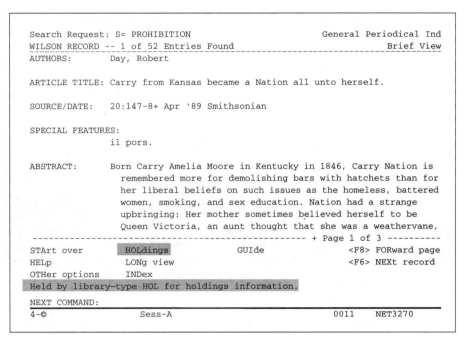

```
Search Request: S= PROHIBITION                    General Periodical Ind
WILSON RECORD -- 1 of 52 Entries Found                        Brief View
AUTHORS:       Day, Robert

ARTICLE TITLE: Carry from Kansas became a Nation all unto herself.

SOURCE/DATE:   20:147-8+ Apr '89 Smithsonian

SPECIAL FEATURES:
               il pors.

ABSTRACT:      Born Carry Amelia Moore in Kentucky in 1846, Carry Nation is
               remembered more for demolishing bars with hatchets than for
               her liberal beliefs on such issues as the homeless, battered
               women, smoking, and sex education. Nation had a strange
               upbringing: Her mother sometimes believed herself to be
               Queen Victoria, an aunt thought that she was a weathervane,
-------------------------------------------------- + Page 1 of 3 ----------
STArt over        HOLdings           GUIde              <F8> FORward page
HELp              LONg view                             <F6> NEXt record
OTHer options     INDex
Held by library-type HOL for holdings information.

NEXT COMMAND:
4-©                    Sess-A                        0011     NET3270
```

Figure 5-10

Selecting Sources for Examination

Perhaps the most obvious source of information for an essay on Prohibition is the on-line catalog of the books available for borrowing in your library system. Using key words to search that catalog should be relatively simple and should turn up a list of several possible books. Figure 5-11 shows reproductions of three different computer screens accessed in response to such a subject search. How would you decide which book to examine first?

The first two titles in Figure 5-11 are both relevant to your paper topic; the third is probably not.

- *Ardent Spirits:* The topics at the bottom of the *Ardent Spirits* screen are listed in order of their importance in the book. Accordingly, Kobler's main emphasis is on Prohibition and its relation to American history; you would almost certainly find some useful information there. There is a sixteen-page bibliography.

- *Repealing National Prohibition:* Since there is only one topic listed under "Subject," *Repealing National Prohibition* is evidently concerned only with Prohibition. Judging from its title, the book focuses on the end of the period you would be concerned with. So you can conclude that its treatment of the topic will probably be more detailed than the first book's. It also has a longer bibliography—twenty pages—than *Ardent Spirits* does. However, for a broad overview of the subject, you might begin with *Ardent Spirits.*

```
CALL #      HV 5089.K67  Location: 7th floor stacks   Status: not checked out
AUTHOR      Kobler, John.
TITLE       Ardent spirits : the rise and fall of prohibition / by John
              Kobler.
EDITION     1st Da Capo Press ed.
IMPRINT     New York : Da Capo Press, 1993.
DESCRIPT    386 p. : ill. ; 21 cm.
NOTE        Originally published: New York : Putnam, 1973.
            Includes bibliographical references (p. [358]-[373]) and index.
SUBJECT     Prohibition Party (U.S.)
            Prohibition--United States--History.
            Temperance--United States--History.
```

```
CALL #      HV 5089.K95  Location: 7th floor stacks   Status: not checked out
AUTHOR      Kyvig, David E.
TITLE       Repealing national prohibition / David E. Kyvig.
IMPRINT     Chicago : University of Chicago Press, 1979.
DESCRIPT    xix, 274 p. : ill. ; 24 cm.
NOTE        Bibliography: p. 245-266.
            Includes index.
SUBJECT     Prohibition--United States.
```

```
CALL #      JF 848.P3    Location: 7th floor stacks   Status: not checked out
AUTHOR      Paulson, Ross E.
TITLE       Women's suffrage and prohibition: a comparative study of
              equality and social control [by] Ross Evans Paulson.
IMPRINT     Glenview, Ill., Scott, Foresman [1973]
DESCRIPT    212 p. front. 23 cm.
NOTE        Includes bibliographical references.
SUBJECT     Woman--Suffrage--Case studies.
            Prohibition--Case studies.
            Equality--Case studies.
            Social control--Case studies.
```

Figure 5-11

■ *Women's Suffrage and Prohibition:* If you were interested in the connection between the women's suffrage movement and the temperance movement, you might want to consult the third title. But Prohibition is not Paulson's primary subject; it is highlighted on the screen only because the book has been cross-referenced under that broad topic. Moreover, *Women's Suffrage and Prohibition* seems to consist largely of case studies; your interest would depend on what cases Paulson chooses to examine at length.

Figure 5-12 is not a reproduction of a computer screen, but a facsimile of the entry for *Ardent Spirits* found in a subject card catalog. Notice that the information about Kobler's book is almost identical to that on the computer screen and that it is organized in much the same way. Both the card and the screen provide you with a call number so that, if you wish, you can retrieve the book from the stacks. Unless your database provides you with a printout of the entire entry, remember to copy the book's call number from the screen or card, as well as other important information such as author, title, and the book's probable focus. If the stacks of your library are open to students, explore them until you find the books that you need. Otherwise, use the procedure for having the library staff find these books for you.

Using Bibliographies

Once you locate *Ardent Spirits* or *Repealing National Prohibition,* you check either book's bibliography for other books relevant to your project. This step allows you to add to your own bibliography some of the titles that these authorities used in researching and developing their studies of Prohibition. Of course, you will have to find and examine these other titles before you can decide whether to use them. Again, check the author or title database or catalog, record their call numbers, and then find them in the stacks. If your library does not own these titles, you will have to decide whether any look interesting enough to warrant a visit to another library.

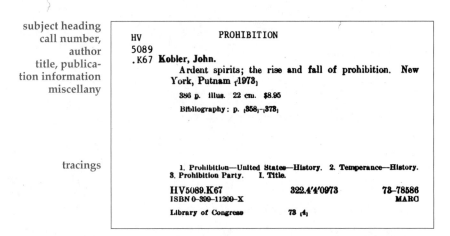

Figure 5-12. A Bibliographic Entry in a Card Catalog

If you are unable to locate a vital source in any of the local libraries, you might consult your college librarian about the possibility of an *interlibrary loan*, in which books or copies of articles are sent to your library from the library that owns the source that you need. But remember that interlibrary loans may take some time, and allow for that as you plan your research schedule. Finally, some libraries have "shared systems" that facilitate the delivery of documents. If you want a printed copy of an article in a periodical index, you press a button at your terminal and then pick up the hard copy at a central desk. There may be a charge for this service.

Using Databases to Focus Your Topic

- Become familiar with your library's information system.
- Use computer searches in the databases/indexes to help you to narrow the focus of your broad topic and to identify possible sources.
- Use your library's on-line databases to get information about available books and articles that might be worth exploring; on the basis of that information, decide which ones to obtain from the library.
- Examine the bibliography at the back of each book that you obtain at the library and note down information about other titles that seem useful to your topic.
- Throughout all the stages of this process, take *complete* notes about the books and articles you may be working with (unless the system provides you with a computer print-out of information about each one).
- Exploring a topic at the library is an assisted form of brainstorming. The screen or card will provide you with ideas about your topic, and that will prompt you to come up with ideas of your own. Make sure that you note down interesting directions for your research as they occur to you.

Focusing Your Topic

After you look in catalogs, bibliographies, and indexes, you will probably have listed and located the following *kinds* of sources for an essay on Prohibition:

- Economic and social histories for a general background of the period
- Congressional reports, political analyses, and legal studies of the Eighteenth Amendment
- Contemporary newspaper accounts, magazine articles, and memoirs describing the everyday effects of the ban on liquor
- Exposés of bootlegging and other criminal activities associated with Prohibition

- Biographies of prominent people in the Prohibition party
- Philosophy and psychology books and articles dealing with recurring forms of Puritanism

At the beginning, uncertain about the precise scope and focus of your essay, you may find it difficult to decide which of these sources will ultimately be useful to you. What are you going to write about?

- Will you stress the reasons for the movement toward Prohibition?
- The religious influence?
- The economic background?
- Prohibition as a consequence of social changes in the era after World War I?
- The link between Prohibition and organized crime?
- The effects of Prohibition on recreation and leisure?
- The constitutionality of the Eighteenth Amendment?
- The rituals of illegal drinking?
- The relationship between the prohibition of alcohol in the 1920s and the prohibition of marijuana decades later?
- The convivial scene in bars all over the nation on the day Prohibition was repealed?

Unless you know what interests you, you cannot afford to ignore too many of the titles that you see listed. Nor can you afford to stop the search for titles in order to examine each source in detail. First, you need to estimate the *amount of material that is available* and the approximate *amount of time that you will need to spend on library research.*

1. At the beginning, if you have an hour or two to spend in the library, you should spend that time at the terminal or in the reference room, rounding out your list of possible sources and narrowing down your topic. At this stage, you should not start to read extensively (and take notes) in any single work.
2. Later on, after you have compiled a working bibliography, you will begin the reading part of your research, starting with the most comprehensive source.

Certainly, you will want to find out if the most likely titles are available in the stacks and, if they are, to check them out and take them home. *But, at this point, don't spend too much time with each book.* At the most, you will want to look at a book's table of contents, index, and bibliography, or flip through an article in order to gain a rough idea of its scope and relevance.

Writing a successful research essay depends on your doing your research thoroughly and checking a reasonable number of reference works, bibliographies, indexes, and other sources. If you wonder how many is a "reasonable" number, report your progress to your instructor or a librarian, and ask for comments.

COMPILING A WORKING BIBLIOGRAPHY: RECORDING BASIC INFORMATION

A *bibliography* is loosely defined as *a complete list of all the works that you use in preparing your essay*. In practice, however, there are really two kinds of bibliography, corresponding to the stages of your research.

Your **preliminary** or **working bibliography** consists of all the sources that you learn about and perhaps examine as you discover what material is available and as you develop your ideas about the topic.

Your **final bibliography** (sometimes called "Works Cited") consists of the material that you will actually use in the writing of your essay. (For a discussion of the final bibliography, see Chapter 9, pp. 422–425.)

You need to have very precise information for all the entries in your bibliography. If you have consistently used a computer database that has printed out lists of books or articles, then you may be able to work from those lists when you prepare your final bibliography. (On the other hand, it can be awkward to rely on separate pieces of paper—in no particular order, some containing several entries, some containing one—when you are trying to assemble an alphabetical list of works cited.) If you are working with a database that doesn't have a printer, or if you are relying entirely or partly on a card catalog and printed indexes from the reference room, you should, from the very beginning of your research, carefully copy down all facts that you may need later on in order to construct a complete and correct final bibliography. These notes can be written either on *index cards* or in a separate section of your notebook. The major advantage of index cards is that, with one entry per card, the stack can be easily organized and alphabetized when you are assembling your final bibliography.

It really does not matter which method you use; what is important is that your records be *accurate, readable, and reasonably consistent*. Several weeks later, when you are working on your list of "works cited" for submission with your essay, you should be able to transform your notes into the correct format without difficulty. (Some software programs, like Nota Bene, allow you to enter data about each source and then automatically prepare correct bibliographic entries in any of the standard formats.) In your early sessions at the library, even though you are at the beginning of your research and cannot be sure which sources will actually become important, *make your notes legible* and *do not abbreviate* unless you are aware of the significance of each symbol. If you cannot read your writing, you will have to return to the library to check your references, probably when you can least spare the time.

As you work from the computer screen or the catalog or from one of the indexes or from a bibliography, start a fresh card or a fresh place on the page for each new item. It may help to assign a number to each new source. Since some indexes do not always provide complete information, indicate gaps in your notes that you can later fill when you are examining the article itself. If you are using a notebook page, remember to leave enough space for comments about the work's potential usefulness.

More likely than not, you will be using MLA style to document your essay. (See Chapter 9, pp. 403–412, for an explanation.) To prepare a final bibliography in MLA style, you should include the following facts in your preliminary notes:

For Books

- the author's full name
- the exact title, underlined
- the name of the editor(s) (for an anthology) or the name of the translator (for a work first written in a foreign language)
- the date and place of publication and the name of the publisher
- the original date of publication and the date of the new edition or reprint, if the book has been reissued
- the inclusive page numbers if you are planning to use only a single chapter or section of the book
- the call number, so that you will not need to return to the database/catalog if you decide to locate the book

For Articles

- the author's full name
- the title of the article, in quotation marks
- the exact title of the periodical, underlined
- the volume number and the date of the issue
- the inclusive page numbers of the article
- the call number of the periodical, so that you will not need to return to the database/catalog if you decide to locate the article

Later, when you locate the book or article itself, remember to check all these facts and supply missing information by examining the front and back of the title page of the book or the first page of the article and the title page of the periodical or newspaper. The *Readers' Guide* does not always include the author's name in its entries (especially the first name), so remember to note it down. Check the spelling of the author's name; find out if the book had an editor; find out whether the place of publication was, for example, Cambridge, Massachusetts, or Cambridge, England.

Figure 5-13 shows two sample note cards, each containing basic information about one of the works on Prohibition mentioned earlier in this chapter. Since these notes are part of a preliminary bibliography, prepared in the library under time pressure, the information is jotted down as a list, using no particular style of documentation. Notice that the first card contains a note questioning the book's relevance to the topic, and the second specifies the *Readers' Guide to Periodical Literature* as the source of the article.

To show you what information looks like when it is placed in the standard format, here is a *bibliography* for the Prohibition essay, with some of the works listed so far:

Ross E. Paulson   JF
                                     848
                                     .P3

Women's Suffrage and Prohibition:
a comparative study of equality
and social control

Glenview, Illinois / Scott, Foresman

1973

212 pp.
              Prohibition = Secondary Subject

L. Rogers

"After Prohibition, what ?"

New Republic 7 Dec. 1932

pp. 91-9

(Readers' Guide)

Figure 5-13. Two Sample Note Cards for Bibliography

LIST OF WORKS CITED

Kobler, John. Ardent Spirits: The Rise and Fall of Prohibition. New York: Putnam, 1973.

Kyvig, David E. Repealing National Prohibition. Chicago: U of Chicago P, 1979.

Paulson, Ross E. Women's Suffrage and Prohibition: A Comparative Study of Equality and Social Control. Glenview: Scott, 1973.

Rogers, L. "After Prohibition, What?" New Republic 7 Dec. 1932: 91–99.

"25 Buffalo Speakeasies and Stills Raided." New York Times 24 Sept. 1933, sec. 4:6.

Research is open-ended. You cannot judge in advance how many sources will provide adequate documentation for your topic. *You need to include enough sources to support your thesis convincingly, yet not so many that you treat them superficially.* Your instructor may stipulate that you consult at least five authorities, or ten, or fifteen; but that recommendation is probably an artificial (though realistic) one, intended to make sure that each student in the class does a reasonable and roughly equal amount of research. Certainly, without guidelines, your preliminary list of sources could conceivably reach and exceed the dozens, even the hundreds. If you wished, you could copy whole sections of a database, or whole pages of an index, or whole rows of titles on the shelves; but you would have little knowledge of the contents or the relevance of your "Works Cited." An endless list of sources does not automatically demonstrate your competence in research. What is important is not quantity, but usefulness for your purpose.

> *A good grade for a research essay is likely to depend on the inclusion of a few crucial sources, the works of well-known authorities, whose evidence or points of view must be considered if your essay is to be thoroughly documented.*

In Chapter 6, you will start learning how to distinguish those useful sources from the irrelevant ones.

It is not enough to have compiled the suggested number of source materials if the works on your list are minor or trivial or peripheral to the topic. *Never settle for the first five sources that come into your hands.* Your research must continue until you are satisfied that you have consulted all those worth reading that are available to you.

TAKING NOTES ABOUT THE USEFULNESS OF EACH SOURCE

In addition to the factual information that you will need for your bibliography, you should also write down a few preliminary notes about the probable usefulness of each work. This step takes place *after* you have *located* and briefly *examined* a source. These are not notes that you will use later in writing your essay, but, rather, comments indicating which sources merit closer examination and note-taking at a later stage of your research. You simply jot down your initial assessment of the work's scope and contents, strong or weak points, and possible relevance to your topic, as well as any rough impressions about the author's reliability as a source. Often, you can write down such comments just by examining the table of contents and leafing through the pages. *Don't trust your memory.* If you forget to note your reaction, weeks later you may find yourself wondering whether to return to the library to check what seems to be a likely looking title.

Your preliminary comments also enable you to review the progress of your research. You can glance through your notes after each trip to the library to decide whether your sources are going to be numerous and thorough enough to support your essay or whether you should return to the computer terminal and reference room to add a few new authors to your list.

Finally, your preliminary notes will be useful when you assemble your final bibliography, especially if you are expected to *annotate* it.

Annotation means that you insert a short comment after each item in your bibliography, describing the work's scope and specific focus and suggesting its relevance and usefulness to the development of your topic.

This is a more formal variation on annotating a text, which was the first topic in this book. The annotations in a bibliography are usually only a sentence or two, just enough to help your reader judge the importance of each source.

In the following annotated bibliography for an essay on politics and the Olympics, the notes for each entry were taken, with few changes, from the earlier working bibliography.

AN ANNOTATED LIST OF SOURCES CONSULTED

Espey, Richard. The Politics of the Olympic Games. Berkeley: U of
  California P, 1979. Espey spends 8 or so pages on each of the modern Olympics up to 1976, with an emphasis on political motivation
  and the shift of emphasis from the athlete to the nation.

Kieran, John, Arthur Daley, and Pat Jordan. The Story of the Olympic
  Games 776 B.C.–1960. Rev. ed. Philadelphia: Lippincott, 1977.
  Approximately 12 pages on each of the games up to 1976, with a
  concise and interesting narrative, but little interest in politics. The
  authors assume that the Olympics will always continue as they have.

Ludwig, Jack. Five Ring Circus. Toronto: Doubleday Canada, 1976. A
  lengthy account of the Montreal 1976 Olympics, with anecdotes.
  Most interesting on the Canadian commercial and political role in
  staging the Olympics.

Mandell, Richard D. The First Modern Olympics. Berkeley: U of
  California P, 1976. A detailed account of the reasons and
  preparations for reviving the Olympics in Athens in 1896, with
  an emphasis on Coubertin's personality and philosophy.

---. The Olympics of 1972: A Munich Diary. Chapel Hill: U of North
  Carolina P, 1991. Written in the form of a literary diary, provides an
  insider's views on the terrorist attacks during the 1972 Olympics.
  Examines the political context and ramifications of terrorism and
  sports.

Shaw, Russell. "Whistling Dixie: Professionalism and Politics Lure '96
  Olympics to Atlanta." Sporting News 1 Oct. 1990: 8–10. An account

of Atlanta's campaign to court the International Olympic
Committee in order to host the 1996 games. Analyzes Atlanta's
political image.

Williams, Roger M. "Moscow '80, Playing for Political Points." Saturday
Review 1 Sept. 1979: 12–16. A detailed analysis of political and
nationalistic interests in the Moscow Olympics, with emphasis on
Soviet motivation.

EXERCISE 28

Some entries from the *Readers' Guide to Periodical Literature* (1992) under the
comprehensive heading "Education" are reproduced in this section.

1. Select one article that appears to relate directly to the topic "How can the
   nation begin to reform its public school system?"
2. Locate and examine the article in your college library.
3. Prepare an index card containing all the information necessary for a bibliographical entry.
4. Add a few sentences describing the article's scope, focus, difficulty, and usefulness for this topic.

Remember that, although the information is the same, the form used for entries in the *Readers' Guide* is *not* the form used in the standard bibliography of a
research essay; do not simply copy out the entry from the *Guide,* but list the
facts, indicating what each number or abbreviation signifies. See p. 301 for two
sample note cards.

EDUCATION

What we need to fix U.S. schools [Fortune education summit; special section] il
   Fortune 126:132-4+ N 16 '92

Aims and Objectives

See also
Educational sociology

An appraisal of Secretary of Education Lamar Alexander's first year in office [Amer-
   ica 2000 strategy] T. H. Bell and D. L. Elmquist. *Phi Delta Kappan* 73:757-9 Je '92

As long as we're talking about goals for education . . . how about some national
   goals for business people and politicians, too? W. J. Banach. il *The Education Digest* 58:28-30 O '92

The challenge, the opportunity [school reform] D. P. Doyle. il *Phi Delta Kappan*
   73:512-16+ Mr '92

The changing look of education's policy networks. G. R. Kaplan and M. D. Usdan. bibl f il *Phi Delta Kappan* 73:664-8+ My '92

The Clinton plan for excellence in education. B. Clinton. il por *Phi Delta Kappan* 74:131+ O '92

The federal reform of schools: looking for the silver bullet. E. W. Eisner, *Phi Delta Kappan* 73:722-3 My '92

Lamar Alexander and the politics of school reform [America 2000 strategy] G. R. Kaplan. bibl f il *Phi Delta Kappan* 73:753-6 Je '92

On taking school reform seriously [America 2000] J. I. Goodlad, bibl f *Phi Delta Kappan* 74:232+ N '92

A revolution to achieve excellence in education. G. Bush. il por *Phi Delta Kappan* 74:130+ O '92

"Schools for the 21st century" [G. Bush's address on America 2000 plan, January 1992] J. C. Szabo. il por *Nation's Business* 80:22 F '92

Sins of omission in "America 2000". H. Howe, II. *The Education Digest* 57:29-32 F '92

Some direction for our schools: our politicians' educational priorities are out of touch with students' needs. K. Ferrell. il *Omni (New York, N.Y.)* 14:8 Je '92

St. John's educational policy for a "living community". E. T. H. Brann. il *Change* 24:36-43 S/O '92

Technology and choice: educational opportunity [school reform] D. P. Doyle. *Current (Washington, D.C.)* 343:22-9 Je '92

Transitioning toward educational futures [school reform] D. Glines and K. Long. bibl f il *Phi Delta Kappan* 73:557-60 Mr '92

Why do American kids learn so little? E. Van den Haag. *National Review* 44:34-6 Ag 3 '92

Bibliography

The activist library: a symposium. *The Nation* 255:293-304 S 21 '92

New materials. See issues of The Education Digest beginning September 1986

Conferences

Calendar. See issues of The Education Digest beginning September 1986

Of many things [National Summit of Independent Higher Education] T. H. Stahel. *America* 166:182 Mr 7 '92

Evaluation

See also
Accountability (Education)
International Assessment of Educational Progress

The 24th annual Gallup/Phi Delta Kappa poll of the public's attitudes toward the public schools. S. M. Elam and others. il *Phi Delta Kappan* 74:41-53 S '92

Adam Smith meets Albert Shanker [incentive schools concept] A. S. Blinder. il *Business Week* p20 D 14 '92

Better teaching or "Just the facts, ma'am"? [flaws in reform agenda] L. Cuban. *The Education Digest* 58:40-2 S '92

Competitive ignorance [address, November 21-22, 1991] R. B. McKenzie. *Vital Speeches of the Day* 58:271-7 F 15 '92

The corporate myth of reforming public schools. L. Cuban. il *Phi Delta Kappan* 74:157-9 O '92

The "education crisis": more rhetoric than reality. G. W. Bracey. *The Education Digest* 57:39-42 F '92

Getting reform right: what works and what doesn't [cover story] M. Fullan and M. B. Miles. bibl f il *Phi Delta Kappan* 73:744-52 Je '92

Give me an A [interview with A. Shanker] K. L. Adelman. il por *Washingtonian* 27:31-4 S '92

Help wanted [address, November 9, 1991] D. M. Blandin. *Vital Speeches of the Day* 58:281-4 F 15 '92

If it looks like manure . . . [school reform] M. N. Riley. *Phi Delta Kappan* 74:239-41 N '92

Look who's ahead of the learning curve. T. Segal. il *Business Week* Reinventing America Special Issue:92+ '92

Pinpointing the failures in American education. H. L. Hodgkinson. *The Education Digest* 57:36-8 F '92

Reform school confidential. K. Boo. il *The Washington Monthly* 24:17-24 O '92

Reform versus the status quo. C. Pipho. il *Phi Delta Kappan* 73:430-1 F '92

Reinventing teaching [Central Park East School in Harlem; views of Deborah Meier] G. W. Bracey. il *Phi Delta Kappan* 74:264-5 N '92

Saving our schools [with Business week/Harris poll; cover story] il *Business Week* p70-4+ S 14 '92

School reform: what's missing [cover story] T. R. Sizer. il por *World Monitor* 5:20-4+ N '92

The second Bracey report on the condition of public education [cover story] G. W. Bracey. bibl f il *Phi Delta Kappan* 74:104-8+ O '92

Small education. J. Fail, Jr. *BioScience* 42:243 Ap '92

The state role in school reform. A. C. Ornstein. il *The Education Digest* 57:48-51 Mr '92

Students must come first in education policy [school reform] D. K. Lipsky. il *Utne Reader* p76-7 N/D '92

The three Rs—again [Economic Council of Canada report] T. Fennell. il *Maclean's* 105:46 My 11 '92

Up from mediocrity [adaptation of address] C. E. Finn. *Policy Review* no61:80-3 Summ '92

What do we get for our school dollars? [cover story] J. Novack. il *Forbes* 150:92-6
    O 12 '92

What's right with America? B. J. Wattenberg. il *The Education Digest* 58:34-6 O '92

Federal Aid

$30.4 billion education budget goes to Congress. H. Fields. *Publishers Weekly* 239:9
    F 3 '92

Previews of Chapter 1 changes? A. C. Lewis. *Phi Delta Kappan* 73:740-1 Je '92

The slow track [women's sports after twenty years of Title IX] A. Wolff. il *Sports Il-
    lustrated* 77:52-64 S 28 '92

The style and substance of an education president. A. C. Lewis. il *Phi Delta Kappan*
    74:4-5 S '92

What to do about Chapter 1: an alternative view from the street. S. Pogrow. bibl f
    il *Phi Delta Kappan* 73:624-30 Ap '92

Finance

See also
Church schools—Finance
Colleges and universities—Finance
Education—Federal aid
Education—State aid
Foundations, Charitable and educational
Voucher plan in education

Are we spending enough on America's schools? il *Reader's Digest* 140:109 F '92

The business of education [profit motive as incentive for effective education]
    P. Wallich. *Scientific American* 267:117 O '92

A coordinated development program for K-12 schools. G. P. White and N. H. Mor-
    gan. bibl f *Phi Delta Kappan* 74:260-2 N '92

Desperate measures? Urban education: should the wealthy pay for city schools?
    K. Monagle. *Scholastic Update (Teachers' edition)* 124:12-13 Ja 10 '92

Everything's up to date [Kansas City and Westboro, Mo.] B. Hurst. *Reason* 23:47
    Mr '92

If money doesn't matter, why all the Savage inequalities? [New Jersey] J. Kozol. *The
    Education Digest* 57:32-6 Mr '92

It's time to stop this savage neglect [views of J. Kozol] R. E. Burns. *U.S. Catholic* 57:2
    Mr '92

Lazarus' schools [views of J. Kozol] J. W. Donohue. *America* 166:301-3 Ap 11 '92

Money in the schools [special section] il *The Education Digest* 57:3-22 Ap '92

School finance in the 1990s. A. Odden. bibl f il *Phi Delta Kappan* 73:455-61 F '92

Separate and savagely unequal [interview with J. Kozol] N. Chiles. il por *Essence*
    23:60-2+ Ag '92

What do we get for our school dollars? [cover story] J. Novack. il *Forbes* 150:92-6 O 12 '92

History

See also
Adult education—History
Colleges and universities—History

Myths, lies and public schools. D. Meier. *The Nation* 255:271-2 S 21 '92

'Top school problems' are myths [1940 vs. today] M. Males. il *Phi Delta Kappan* 74:54-5 S '92

Historiography

Lawrence A. Cremin. D. Ravitch. *The American Scholar* 61:83-9 Wint '92

International Aspects

Focus: international education [special section] *The Education Digest* 57:3-27 Mr '92

The knowledge bearers [cover story; special issue; with editorial comment by Federico Mayor and introd. by Bahgni Elnadi and Adel Rifaat] il *The Unesco Courier* 45:8-22+ S '92

Laws and Regulations

See Educational laws and regulations

Philosophy

See also
College education—Philosophy

Research

See Educational research

Social Aspects

See Educational sociology

Standards

See also
Colleges and universities—Standards
National Council on Education Standards and Testing (U.S.)

House bill includes school delivery standards. A. C. Lewis. il *Phi Delta Kappan* 74:100-1 O '92

How Shakespeare can save our kids [national book requirement instead of national curriculum] B. Lerner. il *National Review* 44:30-2+ Ja 20 '92

One nation, one curriculum? B. Kantrowitz and P. Wingert. il *Newsweek* 119:59-60 Ap 6 '92

Outcomes or 'edubabble'? [outcomes-based assessment] C. Pipho. il *Phi Delta Kappan* 73:662-3 My '92

The politics of policy making. A. C. Lewis. il *Phi Delta Kappan* 73:508-9 Mr '92

Raising the stakes: how colleges could really improve the schools [raising entry standards] C. E. Finn. il *Change* 24:8-11 My/Je '92

Unwillingly to school [discussion of January 20, 1992 article, How Shakespeare can save our kids] B. Lerner. *National Review* 44:45-6+ Mr 2 '92

What our kids must learn. K. Labich. il *Fortune* 125:64-6 Ja 27 '92

EXERCISE 29

The following is a list of four different topics for a research essay dealing with the broad subject of *advertising,* followed by a bibliography of twenty articles, arranged in order of their publication dates. Each item in the bibliography is followed by a note giving a brief description of its contents.

Examine the bibliography carefully and choose a set of appropriate sources for each of the four essay topics. You are not expected to locate and read these articles; use the notes to help you make your decisions.

The bibliography is numbered to make the distribution process easier. List the numbers of the articles that you select underneath each topic. You will notice that many of the articles can be used for more than one topic.

Topics

A. What is an appropriate role for advertising in our society? What are the advertiser's responsibilities?

B. Feminists have argued that the image of women created by the advertising industry remains a false and objectionable one. Is that claim valid?

C. How do advertising agencies go about manipulating the reactions of consumers?

D. To what extent does advertising serve the public? harm the public?

1. "Advertising in Disguise." *Consumer Reports* Mar. 1986: 179–181. This article is a thorough critical examination of the practice, prevalent in many print and broadcast media, of incorporating "planted plugs" of advertising material in news or editorial features.

2. Blotnick, S. "We Just Want to Help People." *Forbes* 28 Apr. 1986: 226. This describes how unscrupulous advertisers adopt talk-show formats on local and cable television to sell real estate, baldness cures, and diet plans. The author raises questions about Americans' susceptibility to manipulation by televised media.

3. Trachtenberg, J. A. "Beyond the Hidden Persuaders." *Forbes* 23 Mar. 1987: 134–135. This extensive article, sympathetic to the advertising industry, is

about the development of advertising campaigns. It emphasizes the psychological research underlying the design of product images and the selection of celebrity spokespersons.

4. Marquardt, D. "A Thinly Disguised Message." *Ms.* May 1987: 33. This article asserts a connection between eating disorders in women and the unrealistic image of the "ideal" female body presented in advertisements.

5. Foote, J. "The Ad World's New Bimbos." *Newsweek* 25 Jan. 1988: 44–45. This brief article examines the trend toward reversal of traditional stereotypical sex roles in several current advertising campaigns where men are portrayed in domestic situations or are presented as helpless, incompetent, or sexually passive.

6. Caputi, J. "Seeing Elephants: The Myths of Phallotechnology." *Feminist Studies* Feb. 1988: 487–524. This is a radical feminist critique of sexist, militaristic imagery in advertising and some other media forms.

7. Sullivan, J. L., and P. J. O'Connor. "Women's Role Portrayals in Magazine Advertising: 1958–1983." *Sex Roles* Feb. 1988: 181–188. This scholarly but accessible article reports an increasing realism and diversity in the roles assigned to women in advertisements and a decline in the use of sex to sell products to men.

8. Laver, R. M. "Evaluating Sex in Advertising." *Humanist* May/June 1988: 25–26. This is a sophisticated, fairly intellectual article on issues related to censorship, personal judgment, and the conditionability of human response. The tone is critical of the advertising industry's techniques and ethics.

9. Miller, A., and D. Tiantsar. "Psyching Out Consumers." *Newsweek* 27 Feb. 1989: 46–47. This piece assesses the effect of psychological and social science research methods on the advertising industry. It provides valuable insights into the decision-making mechanics of large advertising firms.

10. "The Sexism Watch." *US News & World Report* 27 Mar. 1989: 12. This short but informative piece describes public reaction to sexism in advertising and the advertising industry's responses to public attitudes with regard to campaign design.

11. Eller, J. "The Era of the Big Blur." *Newsweek* 22 May 1989: 73. The author of this article presents a highly critical analysis of the increasing "blurring" of advertising and editorial content prevalent in many print media.

12. Kanner, B. "Mind Games." *New York* 8 May 1989: 34–40. This article is an overview of the psychological testing and research methods used by advertising firms to maximize the effectiveness of their campaigns.

13. Eder, Peter F. "Advertising and Mass Marketing: The Threat and the Promise." *The Futurist* May/June 1990: 38–40. This article describes alterations in mass media research techniques as advertisers employ market research to determine what consumers want. The shift considers the change from mass marketing to micro-marketing in order to better affect consumers' purchasing habits.

14. Landler, Mark. "Madison Avenue Is Getting a Lot Less Madcap." *Business Week* 29 Oct. 1990: 78+. This article examines the relationship between a decline in flamboyant advertising campaigns and shrinking marketing budgets. The new advertising style attempts to conjure links between images and values and the product in the minds of consumers.

15. Rudman, William J., and Verdi, Patty. "Exploitation: Comparing Sexual and Violent Imagery of Females and Males in Advertising." *Woman & Health.* 20 no 4 (1993): 1–14. This article attempts to trace the depiction of women in the mass media and link it to sexual violence to determine if advertising and sexual depictions can affect social interactions. The article raises the question of the responsibility of advertisers when they create images of women.

16. Madden, Patricia A. "The Frequency and Nature of Alcohol and Tobacco Advertising in Televised Sports, 1990 Through 1992." *American Journal of Public Health* Feb. 1994: 297–9. This article traces the advertising industry's attempts to link cigarettes and beer to television sports in the minds of sports viewers, so as to create an association of them with healthy activities.

17. Jolley, Reed. "The Condom War on Children." *Christianity Today* 7 Mar. 1994: 38. This article charges that the Clinton administration's public service ad campaign designed to prevent the spread of AIDS promotes casual sex between young unmarried couples, and it criticizes the manipulation of the young through advertising.

18. Ingrassia, Michele. "Going One Step Ogle the Line? (Diet Coke Ads Depict Ogling of Men by Women)." *Newsweek* 14 Mar. 1994. This article contends that gender depiction role reversal signifies a shift in the public's increasing resistance to the objectification of women.

19. Rich, Frank. "Gay Shopping Spree. (Reactions to IKEA Television Ad Featuring a Gay Male Couple; Op-Ed)." *New York Times* 3 Apr. 1994, sec. 4: 11. This

article praises the first mainstream commercial featuring a gay couple, which marked a breakthrough in advertisers' depictions of society, possibly signalling a service to the audience by expanding the normal scope of images they are presented with.

20. Signorielli, Nancy. "Gender Stereotypes in MTV Commercials: The Beat Goes On." *Journal of Broadcasting & Electronic Media* Winter 1994: 91–101. This long article examines the presentation of gender roles through commercials to the typically adolescent viewer of MTV. The depiction of women as linked primarily to sexuality is also discussed.

ASSIGNMENT 14

A. Choose a broad topic that, for the next few weeks, you will research and develop into an extended essay of eight or more pages.

- If you have a *person or an event* in mind, but do not have sufficiently detailed knowledge to decide on a focus and target date, wait until you have done some preliminary reading. Start with an encyclopedia article or an entry in a biographical dictionary; then use the on-line catalog and any databases and bibliographies that you find along the way. Decide whether your topic is recent enough to have been featured in available newspapers and periodicals, and consult the appropriate indexes.

- If you select a *contemporary issue*, examine some of the entries dealing with that topic in recent volumes of the *Readers' Guide* or the *New York Times Index*; then formulate a few questions that you might try to answer in your essay.

B. Compile a preliminary bibliography, consulting the relevant indexes and databases. At this point, you need not examine all the sources, take notes, or plan the organization of your essay. Your purpose is to assess the *amount* and, as much as possible, the *quality* of the material that is available. Whether or not your instructor asks you to hand in your preliminary bibliography, make sure that the publication information that you record is accurate and legible. Indicate which sources your library has available and which may be difficult to obtain.

C. Submit a topic proposal to your instructor, describing the probable scope and focus of your essay. (If you are considering more than one topic, suggest a few possibilities.) Be prepared to change the specifics of your proposal as you learn more about the number and availability of your sources.

·6·

Gathering Materials at the Library: Evaluating Sources

While compiling a preliminary bibliography, a student has located several promising sources. Her topic is *high school dropouts:* specifically, she wants to discuss the age at which adolescents should be allowed to leave school.

At the library, the student has consulted indexes and bibliographies, and has found a number of books and articles, all of which, judging by their titles, might be relevant. Some of these authors have a better claim to being cited as authorities than others. Since all the names are unfamiliar to her, which should she read first? How can she weigh one source of evidence against another and decide whose ideas she should emphasize in her essay?

First of all, the student can try to find out something about each author's credentials. Is the writer a *teacher*? an *administrator*? an *educator*? a *journalist*, presenting secondhand information? Are the writer's qualifications appropriate for the subject? A *kindergarten teacher* may not be the best person to offer opinions about sixteen-year-olds. On the other hand, you might not think that an *economist* would be worth consulting on the topic of high school dropouts; yet, if one has made a study of the job market and the career prospects of workers without high school diplomas, then an economist's evidence and recommendations should be worth including in a research essay. Would a *social psychologist* be a useful source? That would depend on the nature of the work: a study of abnormal social behavior in adolescents might be unrelated to the problem of determining the minimum age for leaving high school; but a study

313

of juvenile delinquency might suggest connections between teenage crime and teenage dropouts.

Chapter 3 included an article about strict attendance policies in grade school. What *are* Roger Sipher's qualifications for making such tough recommendations? Consider also "A Question of Degree" in Chapter 1. Who *is* Blanche Blank, and why should we believe her claim that we have grossly inflated the value of a college degree? Is Blank an employee denied promotion because she lacks a B.A.? Or is she a college graduate seeking a more interesting job? a homemaker eager to return to college? a college teacher who specialized in education (as, in fact, she is)? What difference would this information make to your understanding of her essay?

On the other hand, you may be asked to write about a writer or a group of writers (in an anthology, perhaps) whose names are all familiar to you. Why would you need to find out more about these authors? Would they have been chosen for inclusion in an anthology if their authority were questionable? Once again, how can information about the source help in the writing of your research essay?

LEARNING MORE ABOUT YOUR SOURCES

It is useful to know something about the mind, personality, and experience of the authors that you cite (as well as the times in which they lived), if only to provide a context for understanding their purpose and meaning. There may be some significant connection between an author's background—education, previous writings, professional interests, political leanings, life experience—and the ideas in the book or article that you may write about. Finding out about an author's credentials and background not only helps you to decide whether the source is trustworthy, but also enables you to make allowances for an individual approach to the subject and, occasionally, for bias.

In this sense, "bias" is not a bad word, nor is it quite the same thing as "prejudice." *Bias means special interest or personal angle: the line of thought that this person would be expected to pursue, which might affect his or her opinion about the subject that interests you.* Few knowledgeable people are entirely detached or objective, whether about their pet interests or about the area of learning that has been their life's work. The awareness of bias may weaken your belief in the author's credibility; it is the person who is both knowledgeable and with minimal bias whose opinions tend to carry the most weight. Nevertheless, you shouldn't discount a good idea just because you believe that the writer's ideas may reflect a special interest. Once you have identified a possible bias, you can either disregard it as harmless or adjust your judgment to allow for its influence.

Learning about an author's background does not always permit you to make assumptions about that person's probable point of view. For example, one of the authors whose writings are included in this book is an academic writer whose interests are intellectual rather than popular. Yet, on the basis of that information, it would be foolish to try to trace a cause-and-effect connection between his academic background and the negative attitudes toward sports expressed in his essay. *In general, the purpose of inquiring about the author's life and work is to understand more about the wider context of the work that you are reading.* Then, the small area on which you are focusing—a single essay, a chapter in a book, even a brief quotation—will open up, expand, and become more revealing and interesting.

Authors

Where do you go to find out about a writer's background? Possibly to the book itself. The *preface* may contain biographical information, and the *blurb* on the cover will probably describe the author (but frequently in such laudatory terms that you may have to discount much of the information). Periodicals may provide a *thumbnail biography* of an article's author at the bottom of its first page, or at the end of the article, or in a group of authors' biographies at the beginning or end of an issue.

What you should look for are details about the author's education, professional experience, and published works. These facts can tell you quite a bit about the writer's probable approach to the subject of your research. Look out for vague descriptions: "a freelance writer who frequently writes about this topic" can describe a recognized authority or an inexperienced amateur. You can also consult one of the many *biographical dictionaries, encyclopedias,* and *indexes.* Some of them are more informative than others. *Who's Who,* for example, provides some basic facts about positions held and works published; but you may need to know a good deal about the academic world to interpret this information, and you may not find out very much about the author's characteristic activities or interests. Good indexes to consult are *Biographical Index* and *Current Biography.*

To illustrate this evaluating process, let us look more closely at the author of one of the paragraphs in Exercise 8 on p. 63. Margaret Mead's name is very famous, yet you may have often read and heard that name without really knowing why she is famous. To find out something about her achievements and her credentials for writing about family relationships, you stop in the library and check one of the biographical reference works. (If you know where these books are shelved or you can call up the text on a computer terminal, this step can take less than ten minutes.) In the index to *Current Biography,* you find a listing for Margaret Mead's obituary in the 1978 volume; to supplement that brief paragraph, you can also look up the complete article on Mead in the 1951 volume. Here is the obituary, followed by a few excerpts from the much longer 1951 article (which ends with references to twelve other sources of information about Margaret Mead).

1978 Volume

MEAD, MARGARET Dec. 16, 1901–Nov. 15, 1978. One of world's foremost anthropologists; pioneered in research methods that helped to turn social anthropology into a major science; curator emeritus (from 1969) of American Museum of Natural History, with which she had been associated since 1926; taught at Fordham,

Columbia, and other universities; made many expeditions, to Samoa, New Guinea, Bali, and other parts of South Pacific; author of hundreds of articles and more than a score of books, including all-time best-seller *Coming of Age in Samoa* (1928); commented on American institutions in such books as *And Keep Your Powder Dry* (1942) and *Male and Female* (1949); promoted environmentalism, women's rights, racial harmony, and other causes; died in New York City. See *Current Biography* (May) 1951.

Obituary

NY Times A pl + N 16 '78

1951 Volume

Before leaving [on her second field trip to the West Pacific], Miss Mead completed her now well-known book *Coming of Age in Samoa* (1928). The work was praised in the *New York Times* as "sympathetic throughout . . . but never sentimental" and as "a remarkable contribution to our knowledge of humanity"; it went into five printings within two years and has been twice reissued. . . .

. . . [Mead] published *And Keep Your Powder Dry* (1942), subtitled *An Anthropologist Looks at America* and described in the *Library Journal* as "American character outlined against the background of the seven other cultures" the author had studied.

Dr. Mead during World War II "wrote OWI pamphlets and interpreted GI's to the British" *(Saturday Review of Literature)* and also served (1942–5) as executive secretary of the committee on food habits, the National Research Council. She was a visiting lecturer at Teacher's College (1945–51) and has further served as consultant on mental health, as a member of the committee on research of the mental health division of the National Advisory Mental Health Council of the United States Public Health Service and as a member of the interim governing board of the International Mental Health Congress. . . .

What do you learn from this information?

- Margaret Mead was a *scientist,* thoroughly familiar with the rigorous methods and the complexities of scientific research; therefore, she is unlikely to be casual in her analysis of the sources of neurosis in children.

- Margaret Mead was a *social scientist,* specifically, an *anthropologist;* she was accustomed to studying the whole of a community or society, assessing its customs, its stability, its morale, its probable responses to challenges and emergencies; this training would make her acutely sensitive to and objective about the dynamics within the American family.

- Margaret Mead did not restrict her writing to anthropological studies of remote tribes; the article quoted in Exercise 8 is by no means her first comment on the American scene, and so her analysis and predictions gain the credibility that comes with *repeated observation.*

- Family relationships were among Margaret Mead's special concerns; thus, one can understand the *context* for her analysis of the neurotic child.

- Finally, the *popularity* of her best-selling scientific work suggests that her readers would be more likely to accept her conclusions than they would the ideas of an author who was less well known and whose background was exclusively academic.

On the other hand, the fact that Mead was a *popularizer*—one who takes dry and difficult ideas and makes them understandable to a wide public—helps to explain why her presentation may seem facile, with many of its assertions unsupported. In fact, the paragraph on p. 63 comes from an article written for *Redbook,* not for a scholarly journal; it can be important to consider the audience for which an author is writing. *The writings of Margaret Mead, the anthropologist, clearly differ from those of Margaret Mead, the social commentator.*

Finding out about your sources can enhance your understanding of what you read; however, getting this information should not dominate the research process. If your preliminary bibliography contains twenty books, and you are writing an essay in which no single source will be emphasized, don't waste your time looking up each author at length in the reference room.

But if you are building a paper around a subject for which there are clearly going to be only a few highly important sources, and if you feel uneasy about your ignorance of their qualifications, invest some time in reading a few articles about these authors and their writings.

Check the *Book Review Index* and read reviews of the books that you intend to cite, or look at articles cited in *Biographical Index.* If no other information is available, check the catalog and indexes to see what other books and articles these authors have published. In the end, however, you may have to rely on your research instincts, which will become remarkably accurate after you spend some time comparing the content and style of the sources that you find.

Dates of Publication

One indication of a work's usefulness for your purpose is its *date.* In your essay on high school dropouts, to survey past and present policy, you want to choose some representative works published over the last few decades. However, if you are focusing only on the present, using only material published in the fifties or sixties would be pointless (unless you wanted to include some predictions that might or might not have come true). An article about outdated school attendance laws or social conditions (like the draft) that have changed would be of little value in preparing an essay about contemporary dropouts. However, you may find older sources with theoretical content that is not dated, such as discussions of the role of education in the formation of personality.

Primary and Secondary Sources

To judge the usefulness of a work, you should know the difference between *primary* and *secondary sources.*

A primary source is a work that is itself the subject of your essay or (if you are writing a historical research essay) a work written during the period that you are writing about that gives you direct or primary knowledge of that period.

"Primary source" is frequently used to describe an original document—such as the Constitution—or memoirs and diaries of historical interest, or a work of literature that, over the years, has been the subject of much written commentary.

A secondary source can be any commentary written both after and about the primary source. Thus, a history textbook is a secondary source.

While you generally study a primary source for its own sake, the secondary source is important—often, it only exists—because of its primary source.

- If you are asked to write an essay about *Huckleberry Finn* and your instructor tells you not to use any *secondary sources,* you are to read *only* Mark Twain's novel and not consult any commentaries.
- Carl Sandburg's biography of Abraham Lincoln is a *secondary source* if you are interested in Lincoln, but a *primary source* if you are studying Sandburg.
- And if you read the *New York Times* in order to acquire information about life in America on a certain date, you are using the newspaper as a *primary source,* since it is your direct object of study; but when you look up a *Times* review of a book or a movie you want to write about, then you are locating a *secondary source* in order to learn more about your primary subject.

In the sciences and social sciences, the most recent secondary sources usually replace earlier ones. However, that rule does not always apply to secondary sources written about historical and biographical subjects. For example, Forster's biography of Charles Dickens, written in the nineteenth century, is still considered an interesting work, in part because Forster knew Dickens and could provide much firsthand information. Nevertheless, because research is always unearthing new facts about people's lives, Forster's work has been superseded by new biographies that feature the latest information. In fact, for a biographical or historical essay, you should consult some primary sources, a few secondary sources written at the time of the event or during the subject's lifetime, and the most recent and reliable secondary sources. It is the sources in the middle—written a few years after your target date, without the perspective of distance—that often lack authenticity or objectivity.

If you are in doubt about the credibility of a source, check to see whether the author has included documentation and a bibliography; *well-documented works tend to be the most reliable sources.* But the absence of documentation is not the only reason for distrusting a source. You can decide not to take a book seriously just by glancing through it. If it is written in a superficial, frivolous, or overly dramatic style, then you may be right to suspect its claim to authority.

Finally, try dividing the available sources into *three* groups: those you are sure that you will want to use, those you rejected on sight, and those you are doubtful about. *Indicate the reasons for your doubts in the notes for your bibliography.* Later in your research, you can check the qualifications of those sources with your instructor or (with the help of the reference librarian) in reference works; or you can simply annotate your bibliography to make your reader aware of your reasons for proceeding with caution.

SELECTING SOURCES THAT WORK WELL TOGETHER

In Chapter 4, when you learned how to work with multiple sources, the process was simplified to make your assignments easier: the sources were all of the same kind, homogeneous, and therefore relatively easy to synthesize. The statements in each group all came from students who had roughly the same skills and experience, and whose opinions were therefore comparable. But in research at the library, the sources that you find may have nothing at all in common but their subject.

Periodicals provide a clear example, for most are published for specific audiences with well-defined interests, reading habits, and (in some cases) social and political views. Since readership varies so greatly, articles on the same subject in two different periodicals are likely to vary widely in their point of view and development. An article on dropouts in a well-known women's magazine is likely to be reassuring and helpful, filled with concrete advice to parents. It will not have the same purpose, nor cite the same kinds of evidence, nor be expressed in the same kind of vocabulary as an article of comparable length published the same year in *Psychology Today*. And that, in turn, will probably not resemble a scholarly essay on dropouts in the *Journal of the American Psychological Association* or the *American Journal of Sociology*. An equivalent article in *Newsweek* or *Time* will be shorter and livelier, filled with vivid, concrete illustrations.

Because of these differences, these periodicals will not be equally valuable as evidence for your essay:

- News magazines provide factual information.
- Periodicals like *Psychology Today* popularize ideas in the social sciences, presenting them in a readable form for a wide audience.
- Scholarly journals usually contain a depth of analysis and a breadth of research that makes them comprehensive and convincing.

On the other hand, articles in scholarly journals are often written in a dense style, with a vocabulary comprehensible only to someone familiar with the discipline. Someone writing a freshman essay on a general topic may find these articles difficult to read and understand. Books can be even more difficult to synthesize since they vary so greatly in length, purpose, and presentation.

Suppose that in researching your paper on high school dropouts you have found three very different sources:

- The first is exclusively about dropouts; chapter after chapter is filled with statistical studies and case histories presented in dense detail and in an abstract language that requires concentration to absorb.

- The second book is a comprehensive study of decision-making in education; there is one lengthy chapter about the reasons why students may choose to drop out.

- The third source is a stirring speech, directed at educators and business-people, with one section devoted to the importance of making students stay in school. The issue is presented broadly and rhetorically.

Here are the excerpts from these three sources:

1. At the secondary school level the question of the impact of increased time requirements on student achievement has been examined through a series of studies regarding the relationship between time spent on homework, a readily apprehendible form of student effort, and achievement. Coleman, Hoffer, and Kilgore, using data from the nationally representative sample of students in the High School and Beyond Survey found that differences in the time spent on homework by high school students accounted for a small but consistent part of the differences in achievement test scores between public and private sector schools. Using this same data set, Keith showed that the amount of time that students spent on homework contributed significantly and positively to their grades. A meta-analysis of 15 empirical studies of the relationship of time spent on homework to learning found a modest, positive effect of homework on learning.

EDWARD L. MCDILL, GARY NATRIELLO, and
AARON M. PALLAS, "A Population at Risk: Potential
Consequences of Tougher School Standards for Student
Dropouts," from *School Dropouts: Patterns and Policies*

2. There is indeed quite a high correlation between failure at school and the probability of dropping out. . . . (In one of the surveys analyzed here, 71 percent of the dropouts had at least one failure as opposed to an average of 44 percent over the whole sample.) There are, however, certain considerations which prevent one from concluding that dropping out is not a decision at all. First there is the fact that the correlation between repeating and dropping out is far from perfect and that more than one-quarter of those who left during high school had never been kept down. Moreover, only half of them declared that they had left as consequence of a failure.

DIEGO GAMBETTA, from *Were They Pushed or Did They Jump:
Individual Decision Mechanisms in Education*

3. In my parents' day, a child of thirteen more often than not would leave school to help support the family during the hard times of the "Great Depression." Getting a high school education ran a distant second to helping the family survive.

Today, I believe many students—and even some bitter educators—view dropping out as a viable alternative to completing school. The pressure to drop out isn't always economic any more. After all, there are many avenues of public assistance. . . .

As a citizen, I'm appalled that we'll waste the potential of so many of our young people. As a business leader, I'm shocked. We have to rely on the public schools to produce the people who will lead our businesses and our society. There are no "spare" people. Society needs us all.

ANTON J. CAMPANELLA,

from "Public Education Is Turning the Corner"

Can these three sources be integrated into the same essay? All three are relevant to the topic, and each may be interesting and useful in itself. But the difference in *depth* and *level of detail* among them is so great that it is hard to see how the three can be used together in a single essay. And, indeed, the only thing that you should not do is to plunk down excerpts from these three sources side by side, in adjoining sentences. If they are to be integrated at all, you must first recognize and then communicate to your reader that *the three sources are not equivalent or even similar.*

This does not mean that all of your sources should cover the same range of ideas, be roughly the same length, and employ the same vocabulary and depth of evidence. And certainly *you should avoid using a single book or journal as the sole source of supporting evidence for your essay.* Working with materials of the same order of difficulty may be convenient, but developing a balanced bibliography offering a variety of approaches to your topic is more important. The key is to become sensitive to the *kinds of sources* that you find in your research. As you glance through an article or a chapter in a book, ask yourself:

- Is the content primarily theoretical or practical?
- How often does the author offer evidence to support conclusions? What kind of evidence?
- Does the book's thesis depend on a series of broad propositions, linked together into an argument?
- What is the scope of the book?
- Is the focus narrow, with the entire work centered around one person's experience? Or does it sum up the work of others?

Finally, be alert to the kind of language that the author is using and make mental or written notes about its difficulty and your ability to understand it.

Understanding the differences among your sources will help you to determine your *research priorities.* You would not begin your research by taking notes from the book on dropouts; much of its contents would be irrelevant to your eventual thesis. Instead, you might begin with the single comprehensive chapter from the second source to give you an overview of the subject and help you to establish your own approach to the topic and your thesis. Once you have a list of specific points that you want to develop, you may not need to read every chapter of the first source; you could look up items of interest in the table of contents and the index. And don't forget the third work; the speech might provide you with a broader understanding of your topic, as well as provide you with an excellent quotation or two.

Guidelines for Choosing Sources

As you choose sources for your essay, consider the following:

- the author's background and qualifications to write on that subject;
- the date of the work, whether it is a primary or secondary source, and (if secondary) whether its information is still timely;
- the scope of the work and the extent to which it deals with your topic;
- the depth of detail, the amount and kind of evidence presented, and the level of analysis and theory—these three don't necessarily go together;
- the degree to which you understand and feel comfortable with the author's language and style; and
- the way in which possible sources could be used together in your essay.

INTEGRATING YOUR SELECTED SOURCES

Once you have become familiar with your main sources, their differences, and their relative usefulness, how do you integrate them into your essay? You may simply decide to exclude those that do not mesh easily with the others. You may not want to confuse your reader by moving back and forth from extremely broad statements of policy to detailed citations of case studies or statistical evidence, especially if the different sources are expressed in a completely different vocabulary and style. The following excerpt comes from a paper in which the three sources on dropouts are lumped together through quotation. It's not clear that the writer understood the purpose of the "correlation" presented in Excerpt 1 or the relationship between higher academic standards and the decision to drop out. The writer tries to disguise this by working very hard on the transitions between quotations, leaving the reader to figure out what it all means. The transitional phrase "on the other hand" is not really contrasting anything.

Educators find it difficult to solve the problem of dropouts. Diego Gambetta points out the "high correlation between failure at school and the probability of dropping out." On the other hand, higher standards, such as giving students more homework, can help students to achieve, not fail: "A meta-analysis of 15 empirical studies of the relationship of time spent on homework to learning found a modest, positive effect of homework on learning." It is important for efforts to be made to keep students in school because, as Anton Campanella has said, "we have to rely on the public schools to produce the people who will lead our businesses and society."

Even if you use your own style to integrate your sources through paraphrase, it would still be difficult to combine these three sources in a single paragraph. *In a short essay of less than ten pages, you would be wise to limit your sources to those that blend well together because they are of the same order of difficulty.* The writers you cite do not have to agree with each other; rather, their scope and approach should be roughly similar.

For a short essay, you would have to decide in the early stages of your research which kind of source would help develop your thesis. How sophisticated is your argument? Does it require support from complex case studies? If you intend to prove that dropouts come from a specific kind of family environment, you will probably need to cite such scholarly sources as the dropout book. On the other hand, you might want to argue that the dropout rate can be linked to a general decline in standards of education, drawing to some extent on your own high school experience. This thesis would be more "popular" in its approach to the subject and would require less rigorous sources. Remember that *a popularization is a simplification of a difficult subject; popular essays could not exist without the evidence found in longer and more complex works.* In a sense, a college research essay has to be "popular" since it is intended to be evidence of the student's understanding of the subject, rather than a contribution to scholarly knowledge.

In deciding whether or not to use the popular approach, remember to consider the level of your course. In an *introductory course,* you are expected only to grasp the broad concepts that are basic to the discipline; so your instructor will probably not expect you to go out of your depth in hunting scholarly sources for your essay. On the other hand, in an *advanced course,* you are preparing to do your own research; and so you need to demonstrate your understanding of the work of others as well as the methods that are commonly used in that field. In an advanced course, the popular approach can be regarded as superficial.

In a longer essay of ten pages or more, you should have much less trouble blending ill-assorted sources. With the opportunity for leisurely development, you can position each source in the place where it is most appropriate and where it will have the most convincing effect. Thus, for the dropout essay the quotations that you select from the speech might be placed in the introduction or conclusion of your essay; the theories relating students' decisions to drop out could be included in your preliminary presentation of your argument; and the detailed evidence of the longest source could be cited in support of your own ideas or as part of your survey of the work already done in this field. In short, these very different sources can be used together successfully, provided that you do not give your reader the impression that they are interchangeable in their usefulness. Unfortunately, a single paragraph cannot be included here to demonstrate the successful incorporation of the three excerpts on pp. 320–321 into a research essay; you would need to read the entire paper to see how each of the three sources was deployed.

Finally, in your search for a well-balanced bibliography, include only what you yourself understand. By all means, consult your instructor or librarian, or the staff of the writing center on your campus, to clarify the meaning of difficult sources that nevertheless seem important enough to include in your essay. However, *if you cite sources whose writing makes no sense to you, no matter how eminent and qualified these authorities may be, your essay will be a failure; for you will be pretending a mastery of the subject that you do not actually have.*

EXERCISE 30

Examine the following preliminary bibliography of articles for a research essay on the broad topic of *education*.

A. Make up two *narrow* topics, one focused on an issue in education that is presently being debated, the other suggesting a more historical approach that might include articles published during the last few decades. (Your instructor may ask the entire class to work on the same two topics.)

B. Carefully read the preliminary bibliography, and consider the probable contents of each article, as suggested by the *title*; the *kind of periodical* it appears in; the *length;* and the *date* of publication. What can you conclude about each article?

C. Determine your research priorities for each of your two topics by choosing a list of five articles that you believe ought to be located and consulted first. Record your two lists, and be prepared to explain your choices.

Akande, B. "Six Ways to Save Our Schools." *USA Today* 122 Nov. 1993: 62–63.

"America's Schools: A Panorama of Excellence." *Today's Education* 1984–1985 Annual: 3–35.

"Are High-School Standards Too Low?" *Ladies Home Journal* Sept. 1956: 86–88.

"Are Schools Changing Too Much Too Fast?" *Changing Times* Sept. 1966: 6–10.

"Back to Basics in the Schoolhouse." *Readers Digest* Feb. 1975: 149–52.

Bailey, S. K. "Educational Planning: Purposes and Promise." *Public Administration Review* May 1971: 345–52.

Barber, B. R. "America Skips School." *Harper's* 287 Nov. 1993: 39–46.

Bracey, G. W. "The 'Education Crisis': More Rhetoric than Reality." *The Education Digest* 57 (Fall 1992): 39–42.

Broudy, H. S. "Demand for Accountability: Can Society Exercise Control over Education?" *Education and Urban Society* Feb. 1977: 235–50.

Burris, V. "Social and Political Consequences of Overeducation." *American Sociology Review* Aug. 1983: 454–67.

Cuban, L. "Better Teaching or 'Just the Facts Ma'am'? [Flaws in Reform Agenda]." *The Education Digest* 58 (Spring 1992): 40–42.

Doyle, D. P. "The Challenge, the Opportunity [School Reform]." *Phi Delta Kappan* 73 Mar. 1992: 512–16+.

Drucker, P. F. "How Schools Must Change." *Psychology Today* May 1989: 18–20.

Eisner, E. W. "The Federal Reform of Schools: Looking for the Silver Bullet." *Phi Delta Kappan* 73 May 1992: 722–23.

Frazier, K. "'Perspectives on Education in America': Sandia Study Challenges Misconceptions." *Skeptical Inquirer* 18 (Fall 1993): 26–31.

Frazier, M. "Inner City Schools that Work." *Readers Digest* June 1980: 24–28.

Handl, J. "Educational Chances and Occupational Attitudes of Women: A Sociohistorical Analysis." *Journal of Social History* 17 (Spring 1984): 463–87.

Hechinger, Grace, and Fred M. Hechinger. "Report Card on Education." *Ladies Home Journal* Sept. 1985: 96.

Hershey, J. A. "How Schools Sabotage a Creative Work Force." *Business Week* 13 July 1987: 16.

Hillson, M. "Reorganization in the School: Bringing About a Remission of the Problems Faced by Minority Children." *Phylon* 28 (Fall 1967): 230–45.

Hodgkinson, H. L. "Pinpointing the Failures in American Education." *The Education Digest* 57 (Fall 1992): 36–38.

Holcomb, J. H. "Can We—Should We Save the Public Schools?" *American Educator* June 1983: 34–37.

"Johnny Is Doing a Lot Better." *Life* Apr. 1961: 32.

Kantrowitz, B. "A Nation Still at Risk [10th Anniversary of 'A Nation at Risk']." *Newsweek* 121 Apr. 1993: 46–49.

"Keeping God Out of the Classroom." *Newsweek* 29 June 1987: 23–24.

Kirst, M. W. "How to Improve Schools without Spending Money." *Phi Delta Kappan* Sept. 1982: 6–8.

Klitgaard, R. E., and G. R. Hall. "Are There Unusually Effective Schools?" *Journal of Human Resources* 10 (Winter 1975): 90–106.

Lanier, H. B., and J. Byrne. "How High School Students View Women: The Relationship Between Perceived Attractiveness, Occupation, and Education." *Sex Roles* 7 (1981): 145–48.

Leonard, G. E. "The Great School Reform Hoax." *Esquire* Apr. 1984: 47–52.

Liazos, A. "School Alienation and Delinquency." *Crime and Delinquency* July 1978: 355–70.

Lieberman, M. "Why School Reform Isn't Working." *Fortune* 17 February 1986: 135–36.

Linton, C. D. "In Defense of a Liberal Arts Education." *Christianity Today* May 1974: 5–8.

"Low Marks for U.S. Education." *Saturday Evening Post* 20 Oct. 1962: 96.

Martin, J. R. "Becoming Educated: A Journey of Alienation or Integration?" *Educational Digest* May 1986: 26–29.

Melby, E. O. "Education Is the Ultimate Weapon." *Educational Forum* Nov. 1956: 45–54.

Miles, C. G. "Do Boys and Girls Need Different Schooling?" *Educational Digest* Apr. 1981: 23–25.

Morris, J. P. "Principles of Education for a Free Society." *Bulletin of the National Association of Secondary School Principals* Dec. 1954: 99–100.

Petrie, M. A. "Education Without Schools." *Nation* 15 November 1971: 505–506.

Pipho, C. "Gridlock on the Road to Reform." *Phi Delta Kappan* 74 June 1993: 750–51.

Poplin, M., and J. Weeres. "Listening at the Learner's Level: Voices from Inside the Schoolhouse." *The Education Digest* 59 (Spring 1993): 9–13.

Riesman, D. "Quixotic Ideas for Education Reform." *Society* 30 Mar./Apr. 1993: 17–24.

Rohlen, T. P. "Japanese Education: If They Can Do It, Should We?" *American Scholar* (Winter 1985–86): 29–43.

Rossides, D. W. "What Is the Purpose of Education? The Worthless Debate Continues." *Change* Apr. 1984: 14–21.

Scully, M. A. "Some Hope for the Schools." *National Review* 9 March 1984: 47.

Silber, J. R. "Need for Elite Education." *Harper's* June 1977: 22–24.

Spock, B. "Coercion in the Classroom Won't Work." *Atlantic* Apr. 1984: 28–31.

Szabo, J. C. "'Schools for the 21st Century' [G. Bush's Address on America 2000 Plan, January 1992]." *Nation's Business* 80 (Fall 1992): 22.

"Teacher Quality Is a National Crisis." *U.S. News & World Report* 7 January 1985: 80.

Tevis, C. "Why Local Schools Aren't Good Enough." *Successful Farming* Dec. 1986: 18N–18O.

Van den Haag, E. "Why Do American Kids Learn So Little?" *National Review* 44 Aug. 1992: 34–36.

"Why Our Schools Went Wrong." *Changing Times* May 1978: 25–28.

Will, George F. "D Is for Dodo: Grade Inflation." *Newsweek* 19 February 1976: 84.

EXERCISE 31

Each of the following passages has been extracted from a longer article or book on the general subjects of *anorexia* and *bulimia*. Most of these excerpts deal specifically with the causes and symptoms of these adolescent diseases, and some are especially concerned with teenage anorexics and bulimics.

A. Carefully examine the distinctive way in which each passage presents its information, noting especially:

- the amount and kind of evidence that is cited
- the expectations of the reader's knowledge and understanding
- the relative emphasis on generalizations and abstract thinking
- the characteristic tone and vocabulary
- the date of publication.

B. Take into consideration what you may already know about these publications and the audience for each. Then decide how—or whether—you would use these sources together in a single research essay on anorexia and bulimia.

C. Write a thesis for such an essay, and then decide which three sources you would definitely use in writing your essay. Be prepared to justify your choice.

1. ANOREXIA NERVOSA, an-ə-rek' sē-ə nər-vō' sə, a psychosomatic illness in which self-inflicted starvation leads to a devastating loss of weight. It occurs chiefly among well-to-do high school and college girls, affecting about one out of every 200 girls in that group. Girls affected with this disorder have a pathological fear of being fat, which leads to a relentless pursuit of excessive slimness coupled with an intense interest in food. Severe personality problems are common. The typical patient is overcompliant in childhood, and thus inadequately prepared for adolescence and independence. Excessive control over weight—to the point of starvation—represents an effort to establish a sense of selfhood and autonomy. Starvation, in turn, creates its own physiological and psychological symptoms and complications.

from *Encyclopedia Americana* (1994)

2. Bulimia, an appetite disorder, has been recognized as a significant problem with college-age females. Has this disorder filtered down to the high school level as have other collegiate life styles? This research clearly answers the question in the affirmative.

   Bulimia is a newly documented appetite disorder characterized by an uncontrollable urge to eat, consideration of oneself as a binge eater, feelings of guilt coupled with self-deprecating thoughts, actual binging on food, and a fear of not being able to stop eating. The third edition of the *Diagnostic and Statistical Manual* of the American Psychiatric Association (DSM-III, 1980) has recognized bulimia as a distinct disorder when three of these characteristics are present.

   This research project, among the first to be conducted with a high school population, surveyed the entire female population of a mid-western suburban high school; 1093 students responded to the Eating Disorder Inventory (EDI). Students identified as Probably Bulimic were present in all age groups (14–18), and all ethnic groups.

Thus it would appear that there is, indeed, a new adolescent problem which   4
needs to be recognized by people who work with adolescents.

There was an interest in bulimia even before the symptoms were first de-   5
scribed in the DSM-III. In 1976, Marlene Boskind-Lodahl's study defined buli-
marexia as a cyclical eating disorder characterized by binging/purging behaviors
and abnormally low self-esteem. In this study, the low self-esteem which affected
women was hypothesized to be caused by a society which teaches women to be
responsive to the needs of men and to feel the need to be attractive to them.
Stangler and Printz (1980) used the DSM-III to diagnose a college population
and found that bulimia was frequently present in this age group:

> The emergence of bulimia as a diagnostic entity and its striking frequency in
> our sample serves as one example of the complicated sociocultural issues
> surrounding femininity.

Thirty-four case studies were reported by Pyle et al. (1981), all of which met   6
the criteria set by DSM-III for bulimia. All were white females with a median age
of twenty-four; the median age of onset was eighteen; and most had suffered
from bulimia for several years without treatment. These patients stated that
they had not told anyone of their problem because they feared they would be
considered weird.

MARY DEANNA VAN THORRE and FRANCES X. VOGEL,
from "The Presence of Bulimia in High School Females,"
Adolescence (1985)

3. So central are issues of female identity in anorexia nervosa that it is difficult to   1
see why more has not been made of this issue in previous formulations. Most
cultural interpretations of anorexia have stressed the fashion of female slender-
ness, which is undoubtedly of central importance in understanding the eating
disorders. But few have addressed the more complex issue of *why* the emphasis
on thinness is so important to contemporary women, and particularly to those
who develop eating disorders. More detailed study of the psychological conflicts
that lead certain women to develop anorexia lead centrally to the underlying issues of identity and self-worth that lead the single-minded pursuit of thinness to
be "chosen" as the principal symptom.

A central feature of anorexic patients emphasized by Hilde Bruch is that these   2
are girls or women who grow up with a profound sense of ineffectiveness, a
sense of deficiency in their ability to influence their environment and determine
their own fate. This lacuna in the sense of the self is a consequence of growing
up in a family which places intense emphasis on achievement and performance,
but simultaneously deprives the child of opportunities for self-initiated behavior
or for the development of her own unique possibilities. When such a child becomes an adolescent, therefore, she is not well equipped to cope with the typi-

cal developmental demands of that period, which require a greater degree of independent functioning and autonomous choice. The events that typically trigger the onset of anorexic dieting are typically just those experiences that challenge the adolescent's sense of independence and power: the first heterosexual relationship, the loss of a friendship, an illness or death of a valued family member, or moving away from home. For those whose sense of autonomy is deficient, these "normal" developmental stresses precipitate a crisis in self-confidence. Dieting and weight loss, which not only bring about positive comments from others but also give the individual an experience of power that she has never before known, become quickly reinforced and then entrenched as a source of pride and perhaps even superiority.

This description of the typical developmental course of anorexia nervosa is now widely accepted, and is well borne out by clinical experience. What is usually not stated is the extent to which the characteristic experiences and problems of anorexic patients mirror and magnify common problems of female identity, problems that are typically encountered in especially acute form during adolescence. For the intense sense of ineffectiveness and exclusive focus on external expectations is the extreme version of a common developmental pattern among girls in Western societies. Studies of normal female development, which have a certain degree of cross-cultural consistency, show that despite changes in public ideology about sex roles, girls are still socialized to be pleasers and are given far less encouragement than boys to develop self-initiated and autonomous behaviors. Bruch's suggestion that the mothers of anorexic patients fail to respond to their daughter's self-initiated activities and signals actually reflects a more general pattern, established by developmental research, of providing girls with significantly less "response-contingent stimulation" than is typically given to boys. The orientation toward pleasing others and the intense sensitivity and responsiveness to external demands is of course consistent with girls' socialization to be nurturers, a pattern which persists, despite the changes brought about by feminism. Jean Baker Miller, in her pioneering book about female identity, suggests that women's self-worth is still determined by the requirement to help and assist others, a project that requires the subordination of one's own needs to the needs and expectations of another. Such a formulation is directly applicable to the core experiences of those who develop anorexia nervosa, although the latter is an extreme version of the norm.

RICHARD A. GORDON, from *Anorexia and Bulimia* (1990)

4. The larger world never gives girls the message that their bodies are valuable simply because they are inside them. Until our culture tells young girls that they are welcome in any shape—that women are valuable to it with or without the excuse of "beauty"—girls will continue to starve. And institutional messages

then reward young women's education in hunger. But when the lesson has been taken too dangerously to heart, they ignore the consequences, reinforcing the disease. Anorexics want to be saved; but they cannot trust individual counselors, family members, or friends; that is too uncertain. They are walking question marks challenging—pleading—with schools, universities, and the other mouth-pieces that transmit what is culturally acceptable in women, to tell them un-equivocally: This is intolerable. This is unacceptable. We don't starve women here. We value women. By turning an indifferent eye to the ravages of the back-lash among their young women, schools and universities are killing off America's daughters; and Europe is learning to do the same to its own. You don't need to die to count as a casualty. An anorexic cannot properly be called alive. To be anorexic is to keep a close daily tally of a slow death; to be a member of the walking undead.

Since institutions are treating this epidemic as one of those embarrassing fem-inine things imported into the cloister like tampon dispensers or commoner's gowns worn over skirts, there is no formal mourning. Women students are kept from openly recognizing what they privately know is going on around them. They are not permitted to claim this epidemic as real, and deadly, and taking place beside and inside them. So they have to repress horrifying knowledge, or trivialize it, or blame the sufferer. Another one sickens. Another disappears. An-other one bites the dust.   2

In college, we never had a chance to mourn for Sally. Dressed like a tatty rag doll, in faded ginghams and eyelet lace, she wore a peacock feather in an old hat. She kept her round kwashiorkor belly politely hidden and her vicious intelligence sheathed, but she was able to shred an argument into so much cotton wool and negligently hold up a conclusion sharp as quartz. Her small voice would come to a flat halt and her lips press whitely together. At parties she'd lean back her flossy head, so much too big for her body, to get the leverage to bang it again and again into the nearest wall; her brain loosened for comfort, she would dance like a Halloween creepie, waving her disjointed limbs. It was a campus set piece: "Play something good for Sally to dance to."   3

She left suddenly. Her roommates had to pack her things up after her: the postage scales for weighing the day's half bread roll; the fifteen-pound hand weights; the essay of devastating clarity left on her desk half-finished.   4

When I was told her strength had run out, I remembered one bright blue afternoon in autumn, when a group of students came out of a classroom, ar-guing, high on words. She dropped her books with a crash. Flinging back her shoulders, from which her sweater hung letting in great pockets of icy air, she turned in a slow pirouette, and leaped right up into the knot of the group. A boy caught her before she fell, and offered her to me, wriggling like a trouble-some baby.   5

I held her between my forearms without strain. She'd made it. She had es-caped gravity. Her limbs were as light as hollow birch branches, the scrolls of   6 their bark whole, but the marrow crumbled, the sap gone brittle. I folded her up easily, because there was nothing to her.

Bundles of twigs, bones in worn-soled Nikes, slapping forward into a relentless weather; the young women cast shadows of Javanese stick-puppets, huge-headed, disappearing in a sideways light. Dry-mouthed like the old, unsteady, they head home on swollen knees while it is still morning.

Nothing justifies comparison with the Holocaust; but when confronted with a vast number of emaciated bodies starved not by nature but by men, one must notice a certain resemblance. The starving body cannot know it is middle-class. The imprisoned body cannot tell that it is considered free. The experience of living in a severely anorexic body, even if that body is housed in an affluent suburb, is the experience of a body living in Bergen-Belsen—if we imagine for the Belsen inmate a 40-percent chance of imprisonment forever and a 15-percent chance of death. These experiences are closer to one another than either is to that of a middle-class body that is not in prison in the affluent First World. Though I am trying to avoid the imagery of death camps, it returns. These young women weigh no more than the bodies documented in the archives of what is legitimately called Hell. They have, at their sickest, no more to eat; and they have no choice. For an unknown reason that must be physiological, at a certain point in their starvation they lose the ability to stop starving, the choice to eat. Finally—as is seldom acknowledged—they are hungry; I was hungry every conscious moment; I was hungry in my sleep.

Women must claim anorexia as political damage done to us by a social order that considers our destruction insignificant because of what we are—less. We should identify it as Jews identify the death camps, as homosexuals identify AIDS: as a disgrace that is not our own, but that of an inhumane social order.

Anorexia is a prison camp. One fifth of well-educated American young women are inmates. Susie Orbach compared anorexia to the hunger strikes of political prisoners, particularly the suffragists. But the time for metaphors is behind us. To be anorexic or bulimic *is* to be a political prisoner.

NAOMI WOLF, from *The Beauty Myth* (1991)

5. Anorexia nervosa patients are often portrayed in clinical observations as competent, accomplished, and even overachieving, yet they lack an awareness of their resources and a confidence in their initiative. They appear unable to recognize their own accomplishments and capabilities or feel are on their own. Bruch (1962, 1975, 1978) identified in these patients a paralyzing underlying sense of ineffectiveness that pervades their thinking and activities. She suggested that the overall sense of ineffectiveness might be more basic than their other disturbances in body image and the interpretation of internal stimuli, such as hunger. The excessive concern with the body and its size and the rigid overeating, Bruch thought, were late symptoms in the development of youngsters who have been engaged in a desperate fight against feeling enslaved and exploited,

not competent to lead a life of their own. Strober (1981) demonstrated empirically that personality features associated with autonomy deficits characterize anorexic patients compared with control patients; and Garner and Bemis (1985) discussed the possible origin and reinforcement of self-concept deficits in the anorexic's family environment.

SUSAN A. BERS and DONALD M. QUINLAN,
from "Perceived-Competence Deficit in Anorexia
Nervosa," *Journal of Abnormal Psychology* (1992)

6. In November 1992 I signed myself into a psychiatric hospital that had an eating disorders treatment program.

Once I had heard an inpatient eating-disorders program described as "boot camp for bulimics." The description was accurate. In the hospital I was awakened at 6:30 A.M. three times a week to be weighed, my back to the scale. Breakfast was at 8:00 sharp, lunch at noon, afternoon snack at 2:00, dinner at 5:00, evening snack at 8:00. Meals lasted a half hour, snacks, 15 minutes. At all other times the cafeteria was off-limits. The rule was, absolutely no talk about food or weight while eating. After meals and snacks I was "on 45s," which meant I could not go anywhere for 45 minutes without staff accompaniment. If I had to go to the bathroom during that time, a staff person would stand outside the door to make sure I didn't purge.

I was required to eat whatever was put before me—all 1,500 or more calories of it. That included desserts: cookies, ice cream, cake, pie. The point was to learn to eat everything in moderation, the nutritionist explained. Amazingly, I lost five pounds during the three weeks I spent in the hospital.

I was being deprogrammed.

Between meals the days were packed with individual and group therapy sessions: body-image group, intimacy group, cognitive-therapy group, nutrition group, coping-strategies group and half a dozen others.

When uncomfortable situations or memories arose, I couldn't eat my way past them; I had to talk about them, cry about them, face them instead. There was simply no way for me to escape myself.

My hospital stay was short but effective. It didn't cure me, but it put me ten steps ahead in my recovery. I have not purged since leaving the hospital. I'm more relaxed about my food; I know I don't have to deprive myself to return to a normal weight. I still overeat at times. But today I can eat just a few cookies or potato chips. Forbidding myself those foods had given them extraordinary power over me. Giving myself permission to eat them has broken their spell.

JUDITH ANDERSON, from "Battling Bulimia:
My War Story," *Glamour* (1993)

EVALUATING TEN SOURCES: AN EXAMPLE

Assume that you are gathering information for an essay about *Ernest Hemingway's life in Paris in 1924 and 1925.* From your introductory reading, you have already become familiar with some of the basic facts. You know that the novelist Hemingway and his wife, Hadley, traveled to Paris with their infant son, Bumby; that the Hemingways had very little money; that they associated with many of the literary figures who lived in Paris at the time; that they took occasional trips to Spain for the bull-running and to Austria for the skiing; and that Hemingway was working on a novel called *The Sun Also Rises.* Now, through research, you intend to fill in the details that will enable you to construct a portrait of Hemingway and his Paris experiences. You have selected a preliminary bibliography of ten books. Here is the *annotated preliminary bibliography*; the comments are based on a rapid examination of each book and are intended for your own use in completing research and organizing the essay.

Baker, Carlos. *Hemingway: A Life Story.* New York: Scribner's, 1969. 563 pages of biography, with 100 pages of footnotes. Everything seems to be here, presented in great detail.

Donaldson, Scott. *Hemingway: By Force of Will.* New York: Viking, 1977. The material isn't organized chronologically; instead, the chapters are thematic, with titles like "Money," "Sex," and "War." Episodes from Hemingway's life are presented within each chapter. The introduction calls this "a mosaic of [Hemingway's] mind and personality." Lots of footnotes.

Griffin, Peter. *Less Than a Treason: Hemingway in Paris.* New York: Oxford UP, 1990. Part of a multivolume biography. Covers Hemingway's life from 1921–1927, exclusively. Griffin says in the preface that his goal is not to "analyze this well examined life" but "to recreate it." Reads like a novel. A little bit choppy and anecdotal, and documentation format is unwieldy. Should probably be cautious about Griffin's preoccupation with EH's stories as autobiographical/psychological documents, but could be useful for speculations on connections between personal life and work.

Gurko, Leo. *Ernest Hemingway and the Pursuit of Heroism.* New York: Crowell, 1968. This book is part of a series called "Twentieth-Century American Writers": a brief introduction to the man and his work. After fifty pages of straight biography, Gurko discusses Hemingway's writing, novel by novel. There's an index and a short bibliography, but no notes. The biographical part is clear and easy to read, but it sounds too much like a summary.

Hemingway, Ernest. *A Moveable Feast.* New York: Scribner's, 1964. This is Hemingway's own version of his life in Paris. It sounds authentic, but there's also a very strongly nostalgic tone, so I'm not sure how trustworthy it is.

Hemingway, Leicester. *My Brother, Ernest Hemingway.* Cleveland: World, 1962. It doesn't sound as if the family was very close. For 1924–1925, he's using information from Ernest's letters (as well as commonly known facts). The book reads like a thirdhand report, very remote; but L. H. sounds honest, not as if he were making up things that he doesn't know about.

Hotchner, A. E. *Papa Hemingway.* New York: Random House, 1955. This book is called a "personal memoir." Hotchner met Hemingway in 1948, and evidently hero-worshiped him. Hemingway rambled on about his past, and Hotchner tape-recorded much of it. The book is their dialogue (mostly Hemingway's monologue). No index or bibliography. Hotchner's adoring tone is annoying, and the material resembles that of *A Moveable Feast,* which is better written.

Meyers, Jeffrey. *Hemingway: A Biography.* New York: Harper, 1985. 572 pages of bio. Includes several maps, and two chronologies: illnesses and accidents, and travel. Book organized chronologically, with every year accounted for, according to table of contents. Well documented, and seems less gossipy than Griffin.

Reynolds, Michael. *Hemingway: The Paris Years.* Cambridge, Mass.: Blackwell, 1989. Second of three-volume biography. Includes a chronology covering December 1921–February 1926, five very basic outline maps ("Hemingway's Europe 1922–26," "France," "Switzerland," "Italy," and "Key points for Hemingway's several trips through France and Spain"). Chapters grouped into sections by single years, from "Part One: 1922," to "Part Four: 1925."

Sokoloff, Alice Hunt. *Hadley, the First Mrs. Hemingway.* New York: Dodd, 1973. This is the Paris experience from Hadley's point of view, most of it taken from her recollections and from the standard biographies. (Baker is acknowledged.) It's a very slight book—102 pages—but there's an index and footnotes, citing letters and interviews that some of the other biographers might not have been able to use.

Examining the Sources

The preliminary notes describing these ten sources seem to be the outgrowth of two separate processes. In the first place, the student is noting basic facts about each biography—the *length* of the book, the amount of *documentation*, the potential *bias* of the writer (if it is easily recognized), and the *organization* of the material. But there are also several comments on *tone*, impressions of the way in which the information is being presented: "sounds like . . ." or "reads like. . . ." How were these impressions formed?

Let's begin with the biography, which, according to the annotations, may be the most thorough and complete of the ten. Here is Carlos Baker's account of Ernest and Hadley Hemingway immediately after their arrival in Paris:

The first problem in Paris was to find an apartment. Ezra's pavillon in the rue Notre Dame des Champs was too cold and damp for the baby, but there was another available flat on the second floor of a building farther up the hill. It was a pleasant street sloping down from the corner of the Avenue de l'Observatoire and the Boulevard du Montparnasse, an easy stroll from the Luxembourg Gardens, where Hadley could air the baby, a stone's throw from an unspoiled café called La Closerie des Lilas, and much closer to Gertrude Stein's than the former walk-up apartment in the rue du Cardinal Lemoine. The whole neighborhood was a good deal prettier and more polite than that of the Montagne Ste.-Geneviève, though not much quieter. The Hemingways' windows at Number 113 looked down upon a sawmill and lumberyard. It was owned and operated by Pierre Chautard, who lived with his wife and a small dog on the ground floor. The whine of the circular saw, the chuff of the donkey-engine that drove it, the hollow boom of newly sawn planks being laid in piles, and the clatter of the ancient camions that carried the lumber away made such a medley that Ernest was often driven to the haven of the Closerie des Lilas to do his writing.

In the apartment itself, a dark tunnel of a hall led to a kitchen with a stone sink and a two-ring gas burner for cooking. There was a dining room, mostly filled by a large table, and a small bedroom where Ernest sometimes worked. The master bedroom held a stove and double bed, with a small dressing room large enough for the baby's crib. Hadley quickly rehired the *femme de ménage*, Madame Henri Rohrback, who had worked for her off and on before. Marie was a sturdy peasant from Mur-de-Bretagne. She and her husband, who was called Ton-Ton, lived at 10 bis, Avenue des Gobelins. Her own nickname was Marie Cocotte, from her method of calling the chickens at home on the farm in Brittany. She took at once to the child and often bore him away in a carriage lent by the Straters to see Ton-Ton, who was a retired soldier with time on his hands. Madame Chautard, the wife of the owner of the sawmill, was a plump and childless woman with brassy hair and a voice so harsh that it made the baby cry. She seemed to be envious of Hadley's motherhood. Watching the child drink his daily ration of orange juice she could only say scornfully, "*Il sera un poivrot comme sa mère.*"* Of the baby's many nicknames—Gallito, Matt, and Joe—the one that stuck was Bumby, which Hadley invented to signify his warm, plump, teddy-bearish, arm-filling solidity which both parents admired and enjoyed.

*"He'll become a lush like his mother."

(CARLOS BAKER)

What makes Baker's description so effective is the *impressive amount of detail.* You cannot help believing a biographer who offers so much specific information about everyone and everything with even the remotest connection to his subject. You expect to be told what Hemingway ate for dinner and, indeed, in reporting the novelist's skiing trip to Schruns, Baker writes that the cook prepared "great roasts of beef, with potatoes browned in gravy, jugged hare with wine sauce, venison chops, a special omelette soufflé, and homemade plum pudding." On the other hand, you are sometimes told more than you want to know. There's a house-that-Jack-built effect in the sentences about the Hemingways' nursemaid who was a "sturdy peasant from Mur-de-Bretagne," who had a husband named Ton-Ton, who lived in the Avenue des Gobelins, whose nickname was the result of . . . and so on. Nevertheless, Baker tells a good story and his description of the apartment is effective: notice the description of the sounds that Hemingway must have heard from his windows.

Next, in sharp contrast to all this detail, we have a comparable passage from the biography by Leo Gurko (which the bibliography described as "a summary"). *Gurko* is dealing with the same material as *Baker,* in less than one-tenth the space, and naturally offers much less detail.

Paris in the 1920s was everyone's catalyst. It was the experimental and fermenting center of every art. It was highly sophisticated, yet broke up naturally into small intimate quartiers. Its cafés were hotbeds of intellectual and social energy, pent up during the war and now released. Young people from all over the world flocked to Paris, drawn not only by the city's intrinsic attractions but by the devaluation of the franc.

The young Hemingways settled on the Left Bank, and since they were short of money, rented modest rooms in an ancient walkup. They moved several times, taking flats that were usually on the top floor, five or six flights up, commanding good views of the roofs of Paris. This was somehow in tune with a passion to absorb the city. Hemingway did much of his writing in cafés, where he would sit for hours over a beer or *Pernod* with paper spread before him. He took long walks through the streets and gardens, lingered over the Cézannes in the Luxembourg Museum, and let the great city permeate his senses.

(LEO GURKO)

Baker was trying as much as possible to draw the reader into the scene and to share the Hemingways' own experience of Paris. In contrast, *Gurko* is outside the scene, describing what he, the observer, has seen over the distance of time. He does not hesitate to tell his reader what to think—about Paris, about its expatriate population, and about the Hemingways. Notice in this short passage how *Gurko* moves from verifiable facts to his own hypotheses:

The Hemingways put themselves on short rations, ate, drank, and entertained as little as possible, pounced eagerly on the small checks that arrived in the mail as payment for accepted stories, and were intensely conscious of being poor. The sensation was not altogether unpleasant. Their extreme youth, the excitement of living abroad, the sense of making a fresh start, even the unexpected joy of parent-hood, gave their poverty a romantic flavor.

(LEO GURKO)

Gurko's book does not document his sources; the reader is asked to accept Gurko's assertion that being poor in Paris was "not altogether unpleasant" for Hemingway, because of its romantic connotations. Other biographers, however, may not agree with this statement. Remember that Gurko's hypothesis is one person's opinion and is not to be confused with fact or presented as such in a research essay. Acceptance of his opinion depends on Gurko's credentials as an authority on Hemingway and on what other established authorities have to say.

Here's a final excerpt from Gurko's biography, as a starting point for a second group of comparisons. Notice his tendency to generalize and summarize and, especially, to speak for Hemingway. Then contrast *Gurko's* approach with that of *Alice Sokoloff:*

He was becoming increasingly devoted to imaginative writing, to the point where his newspaper assignments and the need to grind out journalistic pieces were growing more and more irksome. Another threat to his work was the "arty" atmosphere of Paris. The cafés of the city, he soon recognized, were filled with aesthetes of one kind or another who wanted to be artists, talked incessantly and even knowledgeably about art, but never really produced anything. There were a hundred of these clever loafers and dilettantes for every real writer. Hemingway developed a contempt and even fear of them, perhaps because there was in him, as in most genuine artists, a feeling of uncertainty about his own talent. He drove himself to hard work and avoided the café crowd as much as he could.

(LEO GURKO)

It was a worldly crowd, full of intellectual and artistic ferment, some of it real, some of it bogus, some of them obsessed with their own egos, a few of them deeply and sincerely interested in Ernest's talent. The Hemingways' finances were as restricted as ever, but these people "could offer them all the amenities, could take them anywhere for gorgeous meals," could produce any kind of entertainment and diversion. Although Ernest accepted it all, Hadley thought that he resented it and always kept "a very stiff upper front to satisfy himself." He did not want "simply to sink back and take all this," but the success and admiration was heady stuff and he could not help but enjoy it.[1] Hadley used to be wryly amused when Ernest and Gertrude Stein would talk about worldly success and how it did not mean anything to them.[2] The fact that this was true for a part of him, and that he despised anything false or pretentious, was a source of inner conflict which sometimes expressed itself in malice.

[1] John Dos Passos. *The Best Times* (New York: New American Library, 1966), p. 143.
[2] Interview with Hadley Richardson Hemingway Mowrer, January 18, 1972.

(ALICE SOKOLOFF)

Sokoloff's conclusions differ from *Gurko*'s: she points to a conflict in Hemingway's reaction to his Paris acquaintances, and offers *footnotes* to support her suggestion. In another sense, Sokoloff's commentary is limited: because the subject of her biography is Hadley Hemingway, she is describing events from Hadley's point of view. On the other hand, Sokoloff's presentation makes it fairly easy to figure out where Hadley's version leaves off and the biographer's account begins, and the story is told coherently.

Leicester Hemingway's account of his brother's life is far more confusing; most of his information comes from letters, and he makes little attempt to sort out the contents into a form that the average reader can follow easily:

> Things were going very well for Ernest, with his home life as well as with his writing. Bumby was beginning to talk and Ernest was learning that a child could be more fun than fret. With wife and son he took off for Schruns in the Vorarlberg when good skiing weather set in. For months they were deep in the snow up there, working and enjoying the sports, before returning to Paris in mid-March.
>
> Ernest wrote the family that when they camped in the mountains, up above 2,000 meters, there had been lots of ptarmigan and foxes, too. The deer and chamois were lower down.
>
> He said Bumby weighed twenty-nine pounds, played in a sand pile with shovel and pail, and was always jolly. His own writing was going very well. *In Our Time* was out of print and bringing high prices, he said, while his stories were being translated into Russian and German. . . .
>
> Hadley added other details, thanking the family for the Christmas box which had been delayed more than two months in customs, but had arrived without damage to the fruit cake—Mother's one culinary triumph besides meat loaf. She wrote that Bumby had a wonderful nurse who had taken care of him while she and Ernest spent days at a stretch in mountain huts to be near good snow.
>
> (LEICESTER HEMINGWAY)

Ernest's writing is mixed up with Bumby's pail and shovel and fruitcakes for Christmas. This is certainly raw material. The biography offers no interpretation at all for the reader to discount or accept. The material is stitched together so crudely that one has to spend time sorting out important details from trivia. Certainly, this biography would be a poor choice for the student who was beginning research on this topic; but the details might provide interesting background once the events of 1924–1925 were made more familiar by other biographies.

Next, here are three more recent biographies of Hemingway. How do they describe the apartment near the lumberyard?

> "Hemingway had then and has always a very good instinct for finding apartments in strange but pleasant localities," wrote Gertrude Stein, "and good femmes de menage and good food." They arrived in France on January 29, 1924, and soon found a flat above a noisy sawmill, near Pound's old studio, at 113 rue Notre Dame des Champs, where the street curves parallel to the Boulevard Montparnasse.

But the flat had more character than comfort. American friends, who were used to living well in France, were shocked by the squalor. Kitty Cannell said: "The Hemingways lived in a cold-water apartment that gave on[to] a lumber yard in the Montparnasse quarter. It had neither gas nor electric light." And the journalist Burton Rascoe wrote: "They lived, at the time, in an incredibly bare hovel, without toilet or running water, and with a mattress spread on the floor for a bed; it was in the court of a lumber yard, on the second floor, to which one climbed by a flight of rickety steps."

(JEFFREY MEYERS)

Meyers attempts to give some idea of what the Hemingways themselves were experiencing, not by piling on physical details, but by providing a kaleidoscope of eyewitness impressions, rather like interviews in a documentary film or the accumulation of evidence at a trial. An explicit interrogation of the testimony here and the speakers might be helpful, and reminiscences aren't always reliable (the other biographers mention the lack of electricity, but no one else says there was no running water), but this passage does alert us to some of the issues of class that colored Hemingway's experience of Paris, and words like "squalor" and "hovel" offer a contrast to the romantic picture drawn by Baker.

Just before he'd left New York, Ernest had heard from Ford Madox Ford. Ford had written that, since the Pounds were traveling, the Hemingways could spend a few weeks in the Pounds' flat at 70 Rue Notre Dames des Champs. But Ford had made a mistake. When Ernest arrived at Pound's apartment, he learned that, although Ezra was, as Ford said, traveling, he had left no key. Ernest, exhausted and desperate, trudged through the wet snow toward the noise of a band saw, a few buildings down the street. In a small square of black, dripping trees and narrow old wooden houses, he found Pierre Chautard, a carpenter.

When Ernest asked if the carpenter knew of a place to stay, Chautard showed him a five-room flat over the sawmill. The kitchen had a slimy slate sink and a gas stove, with piles of burnt matches beneath the two burners. The place was furnished, Chautard said. But Ernest saw little more than a big bed in one room and a big table in another. Still, there was the pleasant smell of fresh-cut lumber, and windows all around. Madame Chautard, a foulmouthed, henna-haired harridan, sneered at the young couple and suggested she was doing them a favor—especially with the baby. Though he wanted to, Ernest did not haggle over the rent. For himself, his wife, and his son, nothing mattered more than a good night's sleep.

(PETER GRIFFIN)

Griffin's entire book is devoted to Hemingway's experiences in Paris, so we should expect a level of detail to at least rival that of Baker. Griffin acknowledges in his preface his indebtedness to Baker, and we recognize here some of the same details we learned in Baker: the slate sink, the gas stove, the big table.

Baker passed over why, specifically, the Hemingways were in the Montparnasse district; Griffin gives us some sense of how professional and personal
lives were entangled, with messages from Pound being relayed by another literary luminary, Ford Madox Ford. Is this additional information useful?

On February 8, after much shopping, Ernest leased a second-floor apartment at
113 rue Notre-Dame-des-Champs, a stone's throw from Ezra's studio and directly
behind Montparnasse. A month's rent was 650 francs, almost three times their
Cardinal Lemoine rent, but the space was better, the location closer to their friends,
and with the franc fluctuating at twenty-one to the dollar, the real cost was about
$30 monthly. The apartment had no electricity, and the lumberyard buzz saw in the
courtyard below whined steadily during working hours, but their old *femme de
menage*, Marie Rohrbach, returned to help with the baby. As February rain mixed
with snow, Hadley, sick and physically worn out, watched her furniture move once
more into new quarters. "We have the whole second story," she told mother-in-law
Grace, "tiny kitchen, small dining room, toilet, small bedroom, medium size sitting
room with stove, dining room where John Hadley sleeps and the linen and his and
our bath things are kept and a very comfortable bedroom . . . you're conscious all the
time from 7 a.m. to 5 p.m. of a very gentle buzzing noise. They make door and window frames and picture frames. The yard is full of dogs and workmen[,] and rammed
right up against the funny front door covered with tarpaulin is the baby's buggy."
Despite the lumberyard's noise, the new apartment was an improvement over
their first Paris home. Here they were only a few minutes walk from the Notre-
Dame-des-Champs Metro station, the Luxembourg Gardens, Sylvia's bookshop and
Gertrude Stein's place on the rue de Fleurus. The neighborhood was less working class, less down at the heels. At one end of the street stood the Clinique
d'Accouchement, for which both Ernest and Hadley hoped they would have no
use. (In his 1924 day book, mostly blank, Ernest was keeping careful track of Hadley's
monthly periods.) Nearby, on the Boulevard Montparnasse, in good weather and
bad, their American friends gathered to drink and talk at the Select, the Rotonde
and the Dome where one could gossip, leave messages, borrow money, repay debts
and keep generally abreast of local news.

(MICHAEL REYNOLDS)

Here is another full-length work devoted to the Paris years. Like *Griffin*,
Reynolds professes his debt to Carlos Baker, and he sees the significance of the
new flat in much the same light as did Baker: better, more convenient location,
with the disadvantages of the apartment minimized. Like *Meyers*, Reynolds relies on eyewitness reports, in this case a letter written by Hadley, giving her
own impressions of the new apartment and directly contradicting Burton Rascoe's assertion that there was no toilet (although in writing to her mother-in-
law she might have minimized the "squalor").

Finally, here are five descriptions of Hemingway as a baby sitter, odd-job
man, and scavenger, all dealing with similar experiences:

Ernest was working fairly hard. He awoke early in the spring mornings, "boiled the rubber nipples and the bottles, made the formula, finished the bottling, gave Mr. Bumby a bottle," and wrote for a time at the dining-room table before Hadley got up. Chautard had not begun his sawing at that hour, the street was quiet, and Ernest's only companions were Mr. Bumby and Mr. Feather Puss, a large cat given them by Kitty Cannell and named with one of Hadley's nicknames. But Ernest was truly domestic only in the early mornings. He took the freedom of Paris as his personal prerogative, roving as widely as he chose. There was a gymnasium in the rue Pontoise where he often went to earn ten francs a round by sparring with professional heavyweights. The job called for a nice blend of skill and forbearance, since hirelings must be polite while fighting back just enough to engage, without enraging, the emotions of the fighters. Ernest had befriended a waiter at the Closerie des Lilas and sometimes helped him weed a small vegetable garden near the Porte d'Orléans. The waiter knew that he was a writer and warned him that the boxing might jar his brains. But Ernest was glad enough to earn the extra money. He had already begun to save up to buy pesetas for another trip to Spain in July.

(CARLOS BAKER)

When there were the three of us instead of just the two, it was the cold and the weather that finally drove us out of Paris in the winter time. Alone there was no problem when you got used to it. I could always go to a café to write and could work all morning over a café crème while the waiters cleaned and swept out the café and it gradually grew warmer. My wife could go to work at the piano in a cold place and with enough sweaters keep warm playing and come home to nurse Bumby. It was wrong to take a baby to a café in the winter though; even a baby that never cried and watched everything that happened and was never bored. There were no baby-sitters then and Bumby would stay happy in his tall cage bed with his big, loving cat named F. Puss. There were people who said that it was dangerous to leave a cat with a baby. The most ignorant and prejudiced said that a cat would suck a baby's breath and kill him. Others said that a cat would lie on a baby and the cat's weight would smother him. F. Puss lay beside Bumby in the tall cage bed and watched the door with his big yellow eyes, and would let no one come near him when we were out and Marie, the *femme de ménage,* had to be away. There was no need for baby-sitters. F. Puss was the baby-sitter.

(ERNEST HEMINGWAY)

Ernest wanted me to see the neighborhood where he had first lived; we started on Rue Notre-Dame-des-Champs, where he had lived over a sawmill, and slowly worked our way past familiar restaurants, bars and stores, to the Jardin du Luxembourg and its museum, where, Ernest said, he fell in love with certain paintings that taught him how to write. "Am also fond of the Jardin," Ernest said, "because it kept us from starvation. On days when the dinner pot was absolutely devoid of content,

I would put Bumby, then about a year old, into the baby carriage and wheel him over here to the Jardin. There was always a *gendarme* on duty, but I knew that around four o'clock he would go to a bar across from the park to have a glass of wine. That's when I would appear with Mr. Bumby—and a pocketful of corn for the pigeons. I would sit on a bench, in my guise of buggy-pushing pigeon-lover, casing the flock for clarity of eye and plumpness. The Luxembourg was well known for the classiness of its pigeons. Once my selection was made, it was a simple matter to entice my victim with the corn, snatch him, wring his neck, and flip his carcass under Mr. Bumby's blanket. We got a little tired of pigeon that winter, but they filled many a void. What a kid that Bumby was—played it straight—and never once put the finger on me."

(A. E. HOTCHNER)

. . . As he grew older (and *A Moveable Feast* was the last book he finished), Hemingway laid increasing stress on the poverty he suffered in Paris. Without question, Ernest and Hadley Hemingway lived on a relatively scant income during those years, but they were never so badly off as the writer, in retrospect, liked to believe.

In any case, poverty is virtually apotheosized in *A Moveable Feast*. As the title hints, a gnawing hunger for food and drink symbolizes Hemingway's indigence. According to the legend constructed in this book, Hemingway worked all day in his unheated garret, too poor to buy firewood or afford lunch. At least he does not tell here the unlikely yarn that appears in A. E. Hotchner's biography: the one about Hemingway catching pigeons in the Luxembourg Gardens in order to satisfy a rumbling stomach. But poverty, and its symbolic hunger, are nonetheless celebrated. "You got very hungry when you did not eat enough in Paris," Hemingway writes, because of the good things on display in the *pâtisseries* and at the outdoor restaurants. Mostly he and Hadley survived on leeks *(poireaux),* but at least so frugal a diet enabled one to savor, truly, the joys of eating well when an unexpected windfall made it possible for them to dine out.

(SCOTT DONALDSON)

In the late spring of 1925, when the cold rains that ended the winter had come and gone and the warmth of the sun increased each day, Ernest loved to take his son in the stroller, "a cheap, very light, folding carriage, down the streets to the Closerie des Lilas." They would each have brioche and cafe au lait, Ernest pouring some of the hot coffee into the saucer to cool it, and to let Bumby dip his brioche before eating. Ernest would read the papers, now and then looking up to see his son attentive to everything that passed on the boulevard. After breakfast, Ernest would wheel Bumby across the street from the cafe and past the Place de l'Observatoire. Bumby loved to see the bronze horses rearing in the fountain spray that made the June air smell so clean.

(PETER GRIFFIN)

Characteristically, *Baker* describes exactly how the father tended his son, pausing to explain the full name and the origins of their cat. *Griffin* pays the same attention to detail, without being so exhaustive. *Hemingway* himself, years after the event, describes much the same relationship, but with a completely different emphasis and set of details. These three passages are not in conflict; but they are not at all the same kind of writing and, in fact, they provide an excellent illustration of the difficulties of combining sources written in different modes for different kinds of audience. The Hemingway who reminisced for *A. E. Hotchner* offers a somewhat different version of the same experience, a version criticized in *Donaldson*'s extract, which tries to distinguish between nostalgia and truth. Unlike *Gurko*'s, *Donaldson*'s presentation is detailed; unlike *Baker* and *Griffin*, he has an outsider's perspective, and the combination, backed up by documentation, is quite convincing.

In what order, then, would you consult these ten books for full-scale research? You might begin with Gurko's brief account, to establish the sequence of events, and then fill in the details by reading Baker's longer version or the more recent, comprehensive biographies by Meyers or Reynolds, which depend so much on Baker's earlier work. Donaldson gets pushed down the list to third or fourth, primarily because his biography is not chronological; gathering the scattered references to 1924 will be easier once the overall chronology has been made clear by Gurko, Baker, Meyers, or Reynolds. Now, you can also draw on the details to be found in the works by "interested" parties: wife, brother, friend, and the author himself. And, at intervals, you should stop reading and note-taking to compare these various versions of one life and determine which of the sources was in a position to know the truth—the man himself thirty years later? his correspondence at the time? records left by his wife (whom, in fact, he divorced in 1929)? his biographers, whose information is presented secondhand? a combination of all the sources?

EXERCISE 32

Each of the following authors is represented by an essay or paragraph in this book. Choose one of the authors and:

A. Find out some information about the author's background and write a paragraph describing his or her qualifications for writing about this subject.

B. Think about the suggested research topics that accompany the references. Would you use this passage if you were writing an essay on that topic?

Bertrand Russell: "The Social Responsibility of Scientists" (Chapter 1, pp. 74–76)
  a) The arms race
  b) The power of the media

Daniel Boorstin: excerpt from *The Image, or What Happened to the American Dream* (Chapter 3, pp. 194–196)
  a) The popularity of supermarket tabloids
  b) The disappearance of heroes from American culture

Shelby Steele: excerpt from "The New Sovereignty" (Chapter 3, pp. 177–186)
a) Are affirmative action programs justified?
b) Should our curriculums be "politically correct"?

Margaret Mead: excerpt from *Some Personal Views* (Chapter 1, p. 63)
a) Origins of neurosis
b) Problems of the handicapped child

EXERCISE 33

In the middle of the night of November 29, 1942, a Boston nightclub called the Cocoanut Grove burned down, resulting in the deaths of at least 300 people. Read the following three accounts of this disaster, and be prepared to discuss the differences in content, organization, tone, purpose, and point of view. What is the thesis of each article? Consider how you would use the three articles in a single research essay dealing with the Cocoanut Grove disaster. Are these three variations interchangeable?

NEW YORK TIMES, 30 NOVEMBER 1942

300 KILLED BY FIRE, SMOKE AND PANIC IN BOSTON RESORT—DEAD CLOG EXITS—Terror Piles Up Victims as Flames Suddenly Engulf Nightclub—Service Men to Rescue—Many of Them Perish—Girls of Chorus Leap to Safety—150 Are Injured

BOSTON, Sunday, Nov. 29—More than 300 persons had perished early this morning in flames, smoke and panic in the Cocoanut Grove Night Club in the midtown theatre district.   1

The estimate of the dead came at 2 A.M. from William Arthur Reilly, Fire Commissioner, as firemen and riggers searched the ruins for additional bodies. It was a disaster unprecedented in this city.   2

The chief loss of life resulted from the screaming, clawing crowds that were wedged in the entrance of the club. Smoke took a terrific toll of life and scores were burned to death.   3

At the Boston City Hospital officials said there were so many bodies lined up in corridors that they would attempt no identifications before daybreak.   4

Commissioner Reilly stated that an eyewitness inside the club said the fire started when an artificial palm near the main entrance was set afire.   5

Martial law was clamped on the entire fire area at 1:35 A.M. Sailors, Coast Guardsmen, shore patrolmen and naval officers dared death time and again trying to get at bodies that were heaped six feet high by one of the entrances.   6

Firemen said that many bodies were believed to have fallen into the basement after the main floor collapsed.   7

A chorus boy, Marshall Cook, aged 19, of South Boston, led three co-workers, eight chorus girls and other floor show performers totaling thirty-five to an adjoining roof from the second-floor dressing rooms and from there they dropped to the ground from a ladder. 8

Scores of ambulances from nearby cities, the Charlestown Navy Yard and the Chelsea Naval Hospital poured into the area, but the need for ambulances became so great that even railway express trucks were pressed into service to carry away victims. At one time victims, many of them dead, lay two deep in an adjoining garage. 9

Many of the victims were soldiers, sailors, marines and Coast Guardsmen, some of them junior officers, visiting Boston for a weekend of merrymaking. In the throng were persons who had attended the Holy Cross–Boston College football game. 10

Scores of dead were piled up in the lobbies of the various hospitals as the doctors and nurses gave all their attention to the 150 injured. 11

A "flash" fire, believed to have started in the basement, spread like lightning through the dance floor area, and the panic was on. All available nurses and priests were being called into the disaster area. 12

Among the dead were a marine and one who appeared to be a fireman. Casualties were arriving at hospitals so rapidly that they were being placed in the corridors wherever a suitable place could be found. 13

It appeared probable that the greatest loss of life was in the newly opened lounge of the night club in Broadway. Here, one policeman said, burned and suffocated persons were heaped to the top of the doors, wedged in death. 14

The night club was a one-and-a-half story building with a stucco exterior. The blaze was said to have broken out in the basement kitchen at 10:17 P.M. just as the floor show performers were preparing for their next performance. Performers on the second floor were met by terrific smoke and flame as they started downstairs. Their stories were the only ones available, as those who had escaped the dance floor and tables were too hysterical to talk. 15

A temporary morgue and hospital were set up in the garage of the Film Exchange Transfer Company at the rear of the club in Shawmut Street. At least fourteen persons, suffocated and lying in grotesque positions, were lying on the garage floor at one time, while scores of injuries were cared for by garage workers and others. 16

The city's Civilian Defense Workers were called to the scene to maintain order and to give first aid to those suffering from burns and smoke inhalation. Every hospital in the area soon was loaded with the victims. 17

At least thirty-five performers and their friends were rescued by the quick actions of Marshall Cook, a South Boston boy. He was met by a blast of flame as he started down stairs, went back to the dressing room and organized those caught there. 18

He then smashed his way through a window, carrying away the casing. Through this opening he led a group to an adjoining room, where a small ladder was found. The ladder was not long enough to reach the street, but Cook and several other male performers held the top end over the roof's edge and guided the women over the side. They had to jump about 6 feet to reach the ground. 19

At the City Hospital bodies were piled on the floors, many so burned that there was no attempt to identify them immediately. Many service men were among the victims, many of whom were partly identified through their uniforms.   20

Buck Jones, the film star, was believed to be one of the victims.   21

Among the first at the scene was the Rev. Joseph A. Marcus of Cranwell School, Lenox, who administered the last rites for at least fifty persons. In the meantime, thirty or forty ambulances rushed to the fire, these coming from Lynn, Newton, and Brookline. Despite the hindrances caused by automobiles parked in the streets, some of the dead and injured were taken from nearby buildings, where they had been left covered only by newspapers.   22

Abraham Levy, a cashier at the Cocoanut Grove, said there were about 400 in the place, including many sailors.   23

Sailors saved many lives, pulling people through the doors and out of danger. A fireman said that he saw at least thirty bodies lying on the floor, and that he believed some of them were firemen.   24

Among the spectacular escapes were those of two of the eight chorus girls, who leaped from the second floor and were caught by two of the male dancers. They were Lottie Christie of Park Drive, Boston, and Claudia Boyle. They jumped into the arms of Andrew Louzan and Robert Gilbert. Louzan and Gilbert had climbed out of a window of their dressing room to an adjoining roof and then descended by ladder.   25

TIME, 7 DECEMBER 1942
CATASTROPHE: BOSTON'S WORST

Holy Cross had just beaten Boston College: downtown Boston was full of men & women eager to celebrate or console. Many of them wound up at Cocoanut Grove: they stood crowded around the dimly lighted downstairs bar, filled the tables around the dance floor upstairs. With them mingled the usual Saturday night crowd: soldiers & sailors, a wedding party, a few boys being sent off to Army camps.   1

At 10 o'clock Bridegroom John O'Neil, who had planned to take his bride to their new apartment at the stroke of the hour, lingered on a little longer. The floor show was about to start. Through the big revolving door, couples moved in & out.   2

At the downstairs bar, a 16-year-old busboy stood on a bench to replace a light bulb that a prankish customer had removed. He lit a match. It touched one of the artificial palm trees that gave the Cocoanut Grove its atmosphere; a few flames shot up. A girl named Joyce Spector sauntered toward the checkroom because she was worried about her new fur coat.   3

Panic's Start

Before Joyce Spector reached the cloakroom, the Cocoanut Grove was a screaming shambles. The fire quickly ate away the palm tree, raced along silk draperies, was sucked upstairs through the stairway, leaped along ceiling and wall. The silk hangings, turned to balloons of flame, fell on table and floor.   4

Men & women fought their way toward the revolving door; the push of bodies jammed it. Nearby was another door; it was locked tight. There were other exits, but few Cocoanut Grove patrons knew about them. The lights went out. There was nothing to see now except flame, smoke and weird moving torches that were men & women with clothing and hair afire. 5

The 800 Cocoanut Grove patrons pushed and shoved, fell and were trampled. Joyce Spector was knocked under a table, crawled on hands & knees, somehow was pushed through an open doorway into the street. A chorus boy herded a dozen people downstairs into a refrigerator. A few men & women crawled out windows; a few escaped by knocking out a glass brick wall. But most of them, including Bridegroom John O'Neil, were trapped. 6

Panic's Sequel

Firemen broke down the revolving door, found it blocked by bodies of the dead, six deep. They tried to pull a man out through a side window; his legs were held tight by the mass of struggling people behind him. In an hour the fire was out and firemen began untangling the piles of bodies. One hard bitten fireman went in to hysterics when he picked up a body and a foot came off in his hand. They found a girl dead in a telephone booth, a bartender still standing behind his bar. 7

At hospitals and improvised morgues which were turned into charnel houses for the night, 484 dead were counted; it was the most disastrous U.S. fire since 571 people were killed in Chicago's Iroquois Theater holocaust in 1903. One Boston newspaper ran a two-word banner line: BUSBOY BLAMED. But the busboy had not put up the Cocoanut Grove's tinderbox decorations, nor was he responsible for the fact that Boston's laws do not require nightclubs to have fireproof fixtures, sprinkler systems or exit markers. 8

HARPER'S, FEBRUARY 1943
Bernard DeVoto

On the last Sunday morning of November, 1942, most inhabitants of greater Boston learned from their newspapers that at about the time they had gone to bed the night before the most terrible fire in the history of their city had occurred. The decorations of a crowded night club had got ignited, the crowd had stampeded, the exits had jammed, and in a few minutes hundreds of people had died of burns or suffocation. Two weeks later the list of dead had reached almost exactly five hundred, and the war news was only beginning to come back to Boston front pages. While the Allied invasion of North Africa stalled, while news was released that several transports engaged in it had been sunk, while the Russians and the Germans fought monstrously west of Stalingrad and Moscow, while the Americans bombed Naples and the RAF obliterated Turin and conducted the war's most widespread raids over western Europe, while the Japs tried again in the Solomons and mowed down their attackers in New Guinea, while a grave conflict of civilian opinion over 1

the use of Admiral Darlan developed in America and Great Britain, while the anniversary of Pearl Harbor passed almost unnoticed—while all this was going on the
Boston papers reported it in stickfuls in order to devote hundreds of columns to
the fire at the Cocoanut Grove. And the papers did right, for the community has
experienced an angry horror surpassing anything that it can remember. For weeks
few Bostonians were able to feel strongly about anything but their civic disaster.

There is irony in such preoccupation with a minute carnage. In the same fort-   2
night thousands of men were killed in battle. Every day, doubtless, more than five
hundred were burned to death, seared by powder or gasoline from bombed dumps,
in buildings fired from the sky, or in blazing airplanes and sinking ships. If these are
thought of as combatants meeting death in the line of duty, far more than five hundred civilians were killed by military action in Germany, Italy, France, Great Britain,
Russia, China, Australia, and the islands of the Pacific. Meanwhile in two-thirds of
the world civilians died of torture and disease and starvation, in prison camps and
wire stockades and the rubble of their homes—they simply came to their last
breath and died, by the thousand. At a moment when violent death is common-
place, when it is inevitable for hundreds of thousands, there is something grotesque
in being shocked by a mere five hundred deaths which are distinguished from the
day's routine only by the fact that they were not inevitable. When hundreds of
towns are bombed repeatedly, when cities the size of Boston are overrun by invad-
ing armies, when many hundreds of Boston's own citizens will surely be killed in
battle in the next few weeks, why should a solitary fire, a truly inconsiderable
slaughter, so oppress the spirit?

That oppression provides perspective on our era. We have been so conditioned   3
to horror that horror must explode in our own backyard before we can genuinely
feel it. At the start of the decade our nerves responded to Hitler's murdering the
German Jews with the outrage properly felt in the presence of cruelty and pain.
Seven years later our nerves had been so overloaded that they felt no such outrage
at the beginning of a systematic effort to exterminate an entire nation, such as
Poland. By progressive steps we had come to strike a truce with the intolerable,
precisely as the body develops immunity to poisons and bacteria. Since then three
years of war have made the intolerable our daily bread, and every one of us has
comfortably adapted to things which fifteen years ago would have driven him insane. The extinction of a nation now seems merely an integral part of the job in
hand. But the needless death of five hundred people in our home town strikes
through the immunity and horrifies us.

The fire at the Cocoanut Grove was a single, limited disaster, but it exhausted   4
Boston's capacity to deal with an emergency. Hospital facilities were strained to the
limit and somewhat beyond it. If a second emergency had had to be dealt with at
the same time its victims would have had to wait some hours for transportation
and a good many hours for treatment. If there had been three such fires at once,
two-thirds of the victims would have got no treatment whatever in time to do them
any good. Boston is an inflammable city and it has now had instruction in what to

expect if a dozen hostile planes should come over and succeed in dropping incendiary bombs. The civilian defense agencies which were called on justified themselves and vindicated their training. The Nurses' Aid in particular did a memorable job; within a few hours there was a trained person at the bed of every victim, many other Aids worked to exhaustion helping hospital staffs do their jobs, and in fact more were available than could be put to use. Nevertheless it was clearly demonstrated that the civilian agencies are nowhere near large enough to take care of bombings if bombings should come. There were simply not enough ambulances; Railway Express Company trucks had to be called on to take the injured to hospitals and the dead to morgues. The dead had to be stacked like cord wood in garages because the morgues could take no more; the dying had to be laid in rows in the corridors of hospitals because the emergency wards were full. The drainage of doctors into the military service had left Boston just about enough to care for as many victims as this single fire supplied. Six months from now there will be too few to handle an equal emergency; there are far too few now for one twice as serious. One planeload of incendiaries would start more fires than the fire department and its civilian assistants could put out. There would be more injured than there are even the most casually trained first-aiders to care for. Hundreds would be abandoned to the ignorant assistance of untrained persons, in streets so blocked by rubble and so jammed with military vehicles that trained crews could not reach them even when trained crews should be free. Boston has learned that it is not prepared to take care of itself. One doubts if any community in the United States is.

Deeper implications of the disaster have no direct connection with the war. An outraged city has been confronting certain matters which it ordinarily disregards. As a place of entertainment the Cocoanut Grove was garish but innocuous and on the whole useful. It has been called "the poor man's Ritz"; for years people had been going there to have a good time and had got what they were looking for. With the naive shock customary in such cases, the city has now discovered that these people were not receiving the minimum protection in their pleasures to which they were entitled and which they supposed they were receiving.

The name of the night club suggests the kind of decorations that cluttered it; the public supposed that the law required them to be fireproof; actually they burned like so much celluloid. The laws relating to them were ambiguous and full of loopholes; such as they were, they were not enforced. The public supposed that an adequate number of exits were required and that periodic inspections were made; they were not. There were too few exits for the customary crowds, one was concealed, another could not be opened, and panic-stricken people piled up before the rest and died there by the score. The public supposed that laws forbidding overcrowding were applied to night clubs and were enforced; on the night of the fire the place was packed so full that movement was almost impossible, and it had been just as crowded at least once a week throughout the years of its existence. The public supposed that laws requiring safe practice in electric wiring and machinery were enforced; the official investigations have shown that the wiring was installed by unlicensed electricians, that a number of people had suspected it was faulty, and that in fact officials had notified the club that it was violating the law and had threatened to take action—but had not carried out the threat. Above all, the public supposed that an adequate building code taking into account the realities of modern architecture and modern metropolitan life established certain basic measures of protection. It has now learned that the Boston building code is a patched makeshift based on the conditions of 1907, and that though a revision which would modernize it was made in 1937, various reasons have held up the adoption of that revision for five years.

These facts have been established by five official investigations, one of them made by the Commonwealth of Massachusetts in an obvious expectation that the municipal authorities of Boston would find convincing reasons to deal gently with themselves. They have turned up other suggestive facts. The Cocoanut Grove was once owned by a local racketeer, who was murdered in the routine of business. The present owners were so expertly concealed behind a facade of legal figureheads that for twenty-four hours after the fire the authorities were not sure that they knew who even one of them was and two weeks later were not sure that they knew them all. An intimation that financial responsibility was avoided by a technically contrived bankruptcy has not yet been followed up as I write this, and other financial details are still lost in a maze of subterfuges. It is supposed that some of the club's employees had their wagescale established by terrorism. Investigators have encountered, but so far have not published, the customary free-list and lists of those entitled to discounts. Presumably such lists contemplated the usual returns in publicity and business favors; presumably also they found a use in the amenities of regulation. Names and business practices of the underworld have kept cropping up in all the investigations, and it is whispered that the reason why the national government has been conducting one of them is the presence at the club of a large amount of liquor on which the latest increase in revenue taxes ought to have been paid but somehow had not been.

In short, Boston has been reminded, hardly for the first time, that laxity in municipal responsibility can be made to pay a profit and that there can be a remunerative partnership between the amusement business and the underworld. A great many Bostonians, now writing passionate letters to their newspapers and urging on their legislators innumerable measures of reform, have gone farther than that. They conclude that one of the reasons why the modernized building code has not been adopted is the fact that there are ways of making money from the looser provisions of the old code. They suppose that one reason why gaps and loopholes in safety regulations are maintained is that they are profitable. They suppose that one reason why laws and regulations can be disregarded with impunity is that some of those charged with the duty of enforcing them make a living from not enforcing them. They suppose that some proprietors of night clubs find that buying immunity is cheaper than obeying safety regulations and that they are able to find enforcement agents who will sell it. They suppose that civil irresponsibility in Boston can be related to the fact that a lot of people make money from it.

7

8

But the responsibility cannot be shouldered off on a few small grafters and a few 9
underworld characters who have established business relations with them, and it
would be civic fatuousness to seek expiation for the murder of five hundred citizens in the passage of some more laws. The trouble is not lack of laws but public
acquiescence; the damaging alliance is not with the underworld but with a communal reverence of what is probably good for business. Five hundred deaths in a single
hour seem intolerable, but the city has never dissented at all to a working alliance
between its financial interests and its political governors—a partnership which daily
endangers not five hundred but many thousand citizens. Through Boston, as through
every other metropolis, run many chains of interests which might suffer loss if regulations for the protection of the public's health and life were rigorously enforced.
They are sound and enlightened regulations, but if they should be enforced then
retail sales, bank clearings, and investment balances might possibly fall off. The corner grocery and the downtown department store, the banks and the business
houses, the labor unions and the suburban housewife are all consenting partners in
a closely calculated disregard of public safety.

Since the system is closely calculated it usually works, it kills only a few at a time, 10
mostly it kills gradually over a period of years. Sometimes however it runs into another mathematical certainty and then it has to be paid for in blocks of five hundred lives. At such times the community experiences just such an excess of guilt as
Boston is feeling now, uncomfortably realizing that the community itself is the per-
petrator of wanton murder. For the responsibility is the public's all along and the
certain safeguard—a small amount of alertness, civic courage, and willingness to
lose some money—is always in the public's hands. That means not the mayor's
hands, but yours and mine.

It is an interesting thing to hold up to the light at a moment when millions of 11
Americans are fighting to preserve, among other things, the civic responsibility of a
self-governing people. It suggests that civilians who are not engaged in the war effort, and who feel intolerably abased because they are not, could find serviceable
ways to employ their energies. They can get to work chipping rust and rot from
the mechanisms of local government. The rust and rot are increasing because people who can profit from their increase count on our looking toward the war, not
toward them. Your town may have a police force of no more than four and its
amusement business may be confined to half a dozen juke joints, but some percentage of both may have formed a partnership against your interests under cover
of the war.

Certainly the town has a sewage system, a garbage dump, fire traps, a rudimen- 12
tary public health code, ordinances designed to protect life, and a number of Joe
Doakes who can make money by juggling the relationship among them. Meanwhile
the ordinary hazards of peace are multiplied by the conditions of war, carelessness
and preoccupation increase, and the inevitable war pestilence is gathering to spring.
The end-products do not look pleasant when they are seen clearly, especially when
a community realizes that it has killed five hundred people who did not need to die.

▪ 7 ▪

Gathering Materials at the Library: Taking Notes

Have copying machines and computers put an end to note-taking? Some sources, such as newspaper articles, are difficult to copy clearly; others contain only one or two useful sentences and are not worth the expense of copying. Still, there are other reasons why taking notes remains an important skill.

When you have found and copied some useful sources, what do you do with the stack of photocopied pages or the excerpts typed into your laptop computer? So far, you have only moved the raw materials from the library to your desk. How do you turn them into an essay? In order to take inventory and start working on your *essay* (as distinguished from your *research*), you must find the important points and discard the irrelevancies that surround them. Of course, you could plan the organization of your essay by cutting up each page and sorting the vital passages into separate piles; but unless you identify each source clearly on each bit of cut-up paper, you can easily lose track of its origin.

It therefore makes sense to *take notes as part of the research process* and to express as much of the information as you can *in your own words*. At the same time, you should make copies of the most important passages, so that you will have the originals to refer to if your notes let you down. *There is no substitute for good notes.*

352

TAKING GOOD NOTES

The following guidelines should help your note-taking:

1. **Try to complete your survey of the library's resources and work out a preliminary bibliography before you start to make copies or take notes.**

   You will get a good idea of what materials are available and the probable extent of your research, and you will also make sure that your preferred topic is a practical one. If you start taking notes before you are certain of your precise focus, you may waste a good deal of time. You may discover, for example, that there is very little documented information about the gunfight at the O.K. Corral, and decide to shift your focus to Wyatt Earp. Or the amount of technical material about Lindbergh's flight in the *Spirit of St. Louis* might overwhelm you, with the result that you switch to Lindbergh's opposition to America's entry into World War II.

2. **Use paraphrase and summary rather than quotation.**

   If you copy down sentence after sentence, word for word from your source onto index cards or a pad, or into a computer, you might as well save time and photocopy the page. Remember that using the language of the original author will make it more difficult for you to shift to your own writing style. If your first draft reads like an anthology of cannibalized quotations, then you will find it hard to make your final essay coherent and intelligible. The pasted-together sources will still be in control. Take the trouble *now* to master each new idea by putting it in your own words.

3. **Make sure that your notes make sense.**

   Remember that you will have read a vast number of similar pages by the time you begin to organize your essay and that you won't remember everything. In your notes, spell out the author's exact meaning.

4. **Include a certain number of facts to serve as your supporting evidence.**

   It is not enough to say that "X's father lost his job." What was his job? Why did he lose it? What did he do instead? Later, you may find that these details are irrelevant and will not fit into the shape of your essay; but if you do need supporting evidence, you will find it easier to look in your notes than to go back to the library.

5. **Differentiate your own ideas from those that you are paraphrasing.**

   Taking notes is often an intellectually stimulating experience, probably because it requires so much concentration and because your reading rate is slowed down. You may have plenty of comments about the source that you are paraphrasing. As you develop your own ideas and include them in your notes, be careful to separate them from those of your sources. Later, you will want to know exactly which ideas were yours and which were your source's. Using square brackets [like these] around your own ideas is a good way of making this distinction.

6. **Keep a running record of page references.**

In your essay, you will have to cite the correct page number for *each* reference, not an approximate guess. It is not enough to write "pp. 285–91" at the top of the note card or page. Three weeks later, or three hours later, how will you remember on *which* pages you found the point that you want to cite in your essay? If you are writing a lengthy set of notes that paraphrase your source, make a slash and insert a new page number to indicate exactly where you turned the page. Recording page numbers is especially important for *quotations*. Of course, it is vital that you immediately put quotation marks around all quotations.

7. **Keep a master list of the sources in your preliminary bibliography, assigning a code number or symbol to each one.**

As you take notes, use an abbreviation or code number to identify each new source. When you begin a new card or sheet, you won't have to repeat all the basic information.

Guidelines for Taking Good Notes

1. Try to complete your survey of the library's resources and work out a preliminary bibliography before you start to make copies or take notes.

2. Use paraphrase and summary rather than quotation.

3. Make sure that your notes make sense.

4. Include a certain number of facts to serve as your supporting evidence.

5. Differentiate your own ideas from those that you are paraphrasing.

6. Keep a running record of page references.

7. Keep a master list of the sources in your preliminary bibliography, assigning a code number or symbol to each one.

Using Note Cards—One Fact per Card

The traditional method of taking notes is to write *a single fact or piece of information on one three-by-five-inch index card.* These single-note cards are easily organized by topic into stacks; they can also be left at home when you go back to the library. Index cards, however, can stray from the pile and become lost. A stack of cards should be kept under control with a sturdy rubber band.

Certain topics lend themselves to note cards, topics that require the collection of small, fragmentary bits of information, like facts or brief descriptions, which fit easily on an index card. Eight-by-ten-inch cards or sheets of paper (written by hand or on the computer) may be more practical for an ab-

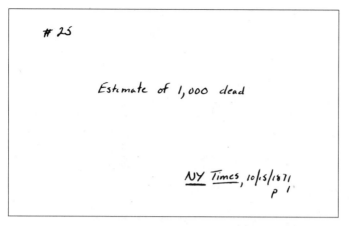

 # 25

Estimate of 1,000 dead

NY Times, 10/15/1871 p 1

Figure 7-1. The One-Fact-per-Card Method

stract topic that depends on complex sources, with each one discussed at length. If you are typing notes into a computer, put a page break between each fact or each topic, so you can print out a separate sheet for each piece of information.

> *Whether you write on small cards or long sheets, make sure that you write on one side only. Whether you write by hand or use a computer, be careful to label each separate unit of information with its exact source and page number, using abbreviations, symbols, or numbers.*

One student, taking notes for an essay describing the 1871 fire that devastated Chicago, used the one-fact-per-card method shown in Figure 7-1. The empty space left on this card may seem wasteful, but the method enables the writer, later on, to place all the cards that refer to the category *casualties* in a single pile. If the card contained information relating to two different categories—like *casualties* and *looting*—the same card would have to be placed in two separate piles, which would defeat the purpose of the organizational system. Notice that, to keep track of all the notes, the writer has assigned a number (#25) to the card. Of course, the source *and* page number are included.

Notes Grouped by Topic

A second student used a more sophisticated system combining note-taking and preliminary organization. Early in the note-taking process, the student decided that at least one card would be devoted only to notes about *fire-fighting*. Thereafter, every time the student came across a new point about fire-fighting—no matter what the source—it was added to that card. Students who take notes using a computer can start a new file for each topic or simply establish several topics within the same file, and scroll through searching

 # 10

fire-fighting

all engines and hose carts in city came (NYT, 10/8, p 3)

*water station on fire, with no water to put out
small fires (Hall, p. 228)*

*all engines out There; fire too big to stop(NYT, 10/8
p 5)*

*fire department "demoralized"; bad fire previous
night ; men were drinking afterwards ; fire
marshal "habitually drunk " (NYT, 10/23, p 2)*

Figure 7-2. Notes Grouped by Topic

for the topic name as each new piece of information is added. Such organization depends on making a list, either written or mental, of possible categories or note topics.

Because the notes in Figure 7-2 are grouped according to topic, this student will find organizing an outline easier than will the first student. But preliminary categorizing during the note-taking stage is practical only with relatively short items. A lengthy presentation of a theory can ruin this tidy system by forcing the note-taker to devote card after card to a single idea from a single source. (Notice that none of the sources on the "fire-fighting" card seems to offer any lengthy opinions about the fire.) For this reason, when you organize notes by topic, you may prefer to use long sheets of paper or a computer, in order to be prepared for any kind of material and to have enough space.

Notes Grouped by Source

Instead of putting one point on each card or one topic on each card, a third student chose to use *one source per sheet*. This system, shown in Figure 7-3, "uses up" one source at a time and produces a long sheet of notes in which the information is presented in the order of its appearance in the source.

The disadvantage of this method is that it doesn't encourage you to start categorizing. This student, however, *numbered each item* on the sheet and also gave each sheet *a code letter*. When the time comes to synthesize these notes into paragraph topics, the student can establish a category dealing with, say, *food supplies*, find the relevant references to that topic, and place the code numbers under that heading. While writing the first draft, the writer will find H-11 under the heading *food supplies* and have immediate access to information about the price of bread after the fire. (For further explanation of this process, see Chapter 8, p. 368).

Source H

NY Times, 10/15/1871, p. 1

1. city normal again
2. still martial rule; Gen. Sheridan in charge
3. citizens working at night to watch for new outbreak of fire
4. newspapers moved to other locations
5. estimate 1,000 dead
6. earlier reports of looting and loss of life not exaggerated
7. waterworks won't open till next day
8. two-thirds of city still using candlelight
9. suffering mostly among "humbler classes"
10. businessmen are "buoyant"
11. bread is 8¢
12. Saloons are closed at 9:00 P.M. for one week

Figure 7-3. Notes Grouped by Source

TAKING NOTES FROM ABSTRACT SOURCES

As the sample notes suggest, research on the Chicago fire uncovered mostly factual information about incidents that occurred during and after the catastrophe. The notes are therefore brief, factual summaries. When the source consists of generalizations and evidence used to develop complex ideas, the note-taker must often struggle to understand and paraphrase abstract thinking.

To illustrate the difficulties, here is a brief extract from *Victorian Cities*, by Asa Briggs. Assume that the book is being consulted for an essay on "The City One Hundred Years Ago."

> The industrial city was bound to be a place of problems. Economic individualism and common civic purpose were difficult to reconcile. The priority of industrial discipline in shaping all human relations was bound to make other aspects of life seem secondary. A high rate of industrial investment might mean not only a low rate of consumption and a paucity of social investment but a total indifference to social costs. Overcrowding was one problem: displacement was another. There were parts of Liverpool with a density of 1,200 persons to the acre in 1884: rebuilding might entail the kind of difficulties which were set out in a verse in *The Builder* of 1851:
>
> Who builds? Who builds? Alas, ye poor!
> If London day by day "improves,"
> Where shall ye find a friendly door,
> When every day a home removes?

The paragraph may seem hard to understand on first reading because Briggs is developing his image of the industrial city through *a series of abstract words combined into phrases*—"economic individualism," "common civic purpose," "industrial discipline," and "low rate of consumption."

These difficult abstractions, typical of the social sciences, are included in the paragraph as if everyone could easily understand them. Fortunately, the essential point is repeated in several different ways and supported by some straightforward facts about the density of population in Liverpool. The passage ends with quite a different kind of evidence: a verse-quotation suggesting that, earlier in the century, people were already aware of the dangers of unlimited expansion.

The following figures show a few attempts at note-taking based on Briggs's paragraph.

In Figure 7-4, the researcher has made a point of paraphrasing, rather than copying the original phrasing, and thus has avoided the danger of quoting the author's words without acknowledgment. The researcher's brief comments in square brackets, clearly distinguished from the notes on Briggs, suggest some points for development in the research essay.

If you don't expect to refer to Briggs in any detail, making a note that summarizes his basic point more briefly would be sufficient, as in Figure 7-5.

In taking good notes, everything depends on achieving a clear understanding of the author's meaning. Figure 7-6, however, suggests that the researcher did not bother to puzzle out the complexities of the paragraph and, instead, tried a few wild guesses. With the possible exception of the first sentence, none of these points can be correctly attributed to Briggs, whose meaning has been entirely distorted. On the other hand, in Figure 7-7, the attempt to play it safe by copying out the phrases verbatim is equally unsuccessful. Although this information is beautifully laid out in outline form, with quotation marks carefully inserted, there is no evidence that the researcher has understood a word of Briggs's paragraph. Moreover, the outline format makes it hard to understand the relationship among these concepts. When the time comes to include a reference to Briggs in the research essay, this student will have no idea how the phrases fit together.

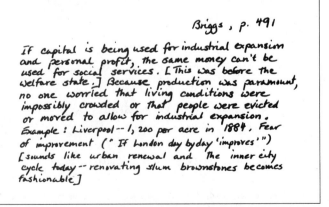

Figure 7-4. **Note A: Effective Summary, Using Paraphrase**

Briggs, p. 491

Danger of industrialization: profit becomes more important than social values, Expansion results in a highly dense population and the need for relocating existing neighborhoods,

Figure 7-5. Note B: Effective Short Summary

Briggs, p. 491

A city of crowded business brings chaos. People couldn't find a job. Your rights meant nothing. Industries didn't respect peoples real needs, The cities were overcrowded because industrial investments were poor.

Figure 7-6. Note C: Distortion of the Source

Briggs, p 491

Problems of the industrial city:

1. "economic individualism"
2. "common civic purpose" difficult to reconcile
3. "industrial discipline" takes priority over "all human relations"
4. "high rate of social investment" and "total indifference to social costs"
5. "over-crowding"
6. "displacement"

Figure 7-7. Note D: Meaningless List

Even when a reading is much less abstract and densely argued than the excerpt from Briggs, it is possible to distort the author's meaning by selecting the wrong points to emphasize in your notes. Here are two paragraphs from *Shakespeare of London*, by Marchette Chute, followed by sample notes for an essay on "Shakespeare's Education as a Playwright."

> Apart from teaching him Latin, Stratford grammar school taught Shakespeare nothing at all. It did not teach him mathematics or any of the natural sciences. It did not teach him history, unless a few pieces of information about ancient events strayed in through Latin quotations. It did not teach him geography, for the first (and most inadequate) textbook on geography did not appear until the end of the century, and maps and atlases were rare even in university circles. It did not teach him modern languages, for when a second language was taught at a grammar school it was invariably Greek.
>
> What Shakespeare learned about any of these subjects he learned for himself later, in London. London was the one great storehouse in England of living, contemporary knowledge and in that city an alert and intelligent man could find out almost anything he wanted to know. It was in London, for instance, that Shakespeare learned French; and French was taught by Frenchmen who worked in competition with each other and used oral conversational methods that were designed to get colloquial French into the student's head as quickly as possible.

In Figure 7-8, the note-taker has made the essential contrast between Stratford and London, and the generalization is clearly distinguished from the evidence that Chute cites to support it. In Figure 7-9, the focus shifts from what Shakespeare did or did not learn to the deficiencies of schools in sixteenth-century England.

What the student is missing in Note F is the contrast between an ordinary, unsophisticated school in rural England and the resources available to an in-

> Chute, p.17
>
> Most of the basic knowledge that Shakespeare needed to write his plays was learned in London, not in school.
>
> Evidence: grammar school taught no math, natural science, history, geography, modern languages

Figure 7-8. Note E: Summarizing the Main Point, with Supporting Facts

Chute, p.17

Elizabethan schools were no good; taught only useless subjects.

Figure 7-9. Note F: False Emphasis/Context Disregarded

quiring young man (no longer a school boy) in the capital city. The note-taker has ignored the *context* of the two paragraphs and the material that surrounds them in the original source. Chute has previously explained the advantages that Shakespeare derived from learning Latin at school, and is now listing what he was unable to learn (partly because books and other teaching materials had not yet been developed). Chute is *not* condemning Stratford grammar school, but preparing the reader for the burst of learning that would occur when Shakespeare arrived in London. The context for the paper—Shakespeare's development—is ignored in favor of a narrower focus on the inaccurate statement that he was taught nothing at all.

EXERCISE 34

In 1937, the German airship *Hindenburg* caught fire near Lakehurst, New Jersey, killing thirty-six people. Two of the many eyewitness accounts were by Leonhard Adelt and Margaret Mather, both passengers on the ship. Read these two passages (which begin on p. 362) and then evaluate the sets of notes that follow them prepared by students writing about the *Hindenburg* disaster. Consider the following criteria:

1. Does one get a good sense of the experience from reading the notes?
2. Which sets of notes are reliable? complete?
3. Do any of the notes omit anything important?
4. Which notes quote excessively?
5. Does the note-taker recognize that the two sources often confirm each other's testimony, and indicate when they agree?
6. Would the notes make sense to someone who had not read the original?
7. Which sets of notes would you prefer to work from if you were writing an essay on the *Hindenburg*?

Leonhard Adelt's Account

With my wife I was leaning out of a window on the promenade deck. Suddenly there occurred a remarkable stillness. The motors were silent, and it seemed as though the whole world was holding its breath. One heard no command, no call, no cry. The people we saw seemed suddenly stiffened.

I could not account for this. Then I heard a light, dull detonation from above, no louder than the sound of a beer bottle being opened. I turned my gaze toward the bow and noticed a delicate rose glow, as though the sun were about to rise. I understood immediately that the airship was aflame. There was but one chance for safety—to jump out. The distance from the ground at that moment may have been 120 feet. For a moment I thought of getting bed linen from the corridor in order to soften our leap, but in the same instant, the airship crashed to the ground with terrific force. Its impact threw us from the window to the stair corridor. The tables and chairs of the reading room crashed about and jammed us in like a barricade.

"Through the window!" I shouted to my fellow passengers, and dragged my wife with me to our observation window.

Reality ceased with one stroke, as though fate in its cruelty was yet compassionate enough to withdraw from its victims the consciousness of their horror. I do not know, and my wife does not know, how we leaped from the airship. The distance from the ground may have been 12 or 15 feet. I distinctly felt my feet touch the soft sand and grass. We collapsed to our knees, and the impenetrable darkness of black oil clouds, shot through with flames, enveloped us. We had to let go of each other's hands in order to make our way through the confusion of hot metal pieces and wires. We bent the hot metal apart with our bare hands without feeling pain.

We freed ourselves and ran through a sea of fire. It was like a dream. Our bodies had no weight. They floated like stars through space.

Margaret Mather's Account

I was leaning out of an open window in the dining saloon with many others including the young aviator, who was taking photographs. He told me that he had taken eighty during the trip. When there were mysterious sounds from the engines I glanced at him for reassurance.

At that moment we heard the dull muffled sound of an explosion. I saw a look of incredulous consternation on his face. Almost instantly the ship lurched and I was hurled a distance of fifteen or twenty feet against an end wall.

I was pinned against a projecting bench by several Germans who were thrown after me. I couldn't breathe and thought I should die suffocated, but they all jumped up.

Then the flames blew in, long tongues of flame, bright red and very beautiful.

My companions were leaping up and down amid the flames. The lurching of the ship threw them repeatedly against the furniture and the railing, where they cut their hands and faces against the metal trimmings. They were streaming with blood. I saw a number of men leap from the windows, but I sat just where I had fallen, holding the lapels of my coat across my face, feeling the flames light on my back, my hat, my hair, trying to beat them out, watching the horrified faces of my companions as they leaped up and down.

Just then a man—I think the man who exclaimed "Mein Gott" as we left the earth—detached himself from the leaping forms, and threw himself against a railing (arms and legs spread wide) with a loud terrible cry of "Es ist das Ende." 6

I thought so too but I continued to protect my eyes. I was thinking that it was like a scene from a medieval picture of hell. I was waiting for the crash landing. 7

Suddenly I heard a loud cry: "Come out, lady!" I looked and we were on the ground. 8

Student A

All of a sudden there was complete silence and not a sound from the motors of the airship. Everybody in the airship "stiffened." Leonhard Adelt suddenly "heard a dull detonation from above, no louder than a beer bottle being opened." L.A. knew that the "airship was aflame." The only way to save one's life was to jump. This meant the jump was for 120 feet. All of a sudden, "the airship crashed to the ground with terrific" speed. The force was so high that Margaret Mather "was hurled a distance of fifteen to twenty feet against an end wall."

Student B

"At that moment we heard the dull and muffled sound of an explosion. Almost suddenly the ship lurched and I was hurled a distance of 15 or 20 feet against an end wall." This is the beginning described by two passengers that were on the Hindenburg of 1937. After a long voyage over the Atlantic and being so close to their destiny, this was too much of a shock for them to handle. All the passengers had to escape death. Some were fortunate, others weren't. "I was pinned against a projecting bench by several Germans who were thrown after me. I couldn't breathe, and thought I should die, suffocated, but they all jumped up." Everyone ran for their life.

Student C

Adelt: "The motors were silent"

Mather: "Dull muffled sound of an explosion"

Adelt: "I turned my gaze toward the bow and noticed a rose glow. . . ."

Mather: "The ship lurched and I was hurled a distance of fifteen or twenty feet against an end wall."

Adelt: "Its impact threw us from the window to the stair corridor."

Mather: "Then the flames blew in"

Mather: "I saw a number of men leap from the windows."

Adelt: "We leaped from the airship."

Student D

before crash:

Adelt: "The motors were silent" "I heard a light, dull detonation from above. . . ."
"I turned my gaze toward the bow and noticed a delicate rose glow"

Mather: "Mysterious sounds from the engine" . . . "dull muffled sound of an explosion" . . . "then the flames blew in, long tongues of flame, bright red
and very beautiful"

after crash:

Adelt: "'Through the window!' I shouted to my fellow passengers. . . ." ". . . how
we leaped from the airship. The distance from the ground may have
been 12 or 15 feet," . . . "impenetrable darkness of black oil clouds, shot
through with flames" . . . "a sea of fire."

Mather: ". . . where they cut their hands and faces against the metal trimmings.
They were streaming with blood."

Student E

"I turned my gaze toward the bow and noticed a delicate rose glow, as
though the sun were about to rise." The blimp catches on fire: the only means of
escape is jumping to the ground. Distance from the ground approximately 12 or
15 feet when couple jumped out of "airship." People "beat the hot metal apart
with our bare hands without feeling pain." How mind works when in life and
death situation. No pain. People had to run through fire one at a time.

Mather: "mysterious sounds from the engine." She was leaning out of
the dining saloon, heard sounds of explosion. People thrown 15 or 20 feet after
hearing explosion. Flames came into room after people thrown. "lurching of ship
threw them repeatedly across furniture and the railings."

Student F

There was an inexplicable silence followed by a "light, dull detonation
from above, no louder than the sound of a beer bottle being opened." Then it
was discovered that the airship was on fire looking like "the sun were about to
rise." There was the realization that the only chance for survival was to abandon the ship. By the time the decision to jump and the action itself was implemented, the ship had crashed (from 120 feet). Upon impact, everything in the
ship (chairs, tables, people) was tossed about. Reality became suspended "as
though fate in its cruelty was yet compassionate enough to withdraw from its
victims the consciousness of their horror."

EXERCISE 35

Reread the three articles dealing with the Cocoanut Grove Fire of 1942 at the end of Chapter 6. Head one group of cards or one sheet of paper "The Causes of the Fire," and take a set of notes on that topic. Head another group of cards or sheet of paper "The Fire's Intensity and Speed," and take a second set of notes on the second topic. Each set of notes should make use of all three sources.

EXERCISE 36

Assume that you are planning an essay about gender and advertising and that you have come across the following source in the library. After doing a preliminary evaluation of the passage, take a set of notes for an essay entitled "Marketing Products Through Sports" and another set of notes for an essay entitled "Advertising's Use of Fantasy."

Sports serves as a metaphor for the male: a special arena free of life's contradictions and contaminations, where a man can test himself and be tested. Sports terms and icons are used to sell a remarkable range of goods, from jackets to tires, from shoes to savings bonds. Once again, we find the qualities of the product transferred to the consumer. TAG-Heuer watches possess endurance and precision, qualities found among "those who thrive on pressure." Dial soap provides "extra inning relief." Sports stars, such as Orel Hershiser and Jim Palmer, transfer their magic to the product, allowing the consumer to share vicariously in their achievements. [1]

The world of sports is colorful and challenging. It is, above all, a man's world. By comparison, the real world seems dull and banal. While there is a certain amount of macho posturing in the presence of high technology, in the computer rooms and at desktop terminals, it is not the same thing as being physically tested by a physically demanding job. [2]

Not surprisingly, a number of advertisements take the consumer back to his past. For it is only there that a secure sense of manhood can be recaptured, in however mythic a form. The highly successful movie, *Field of Dreams*, resurrected long-dead baseball players, who looked like the strong, simple, mostly silent heroes of yesteryear. It is an image directly simulated in an American Express advertisement featuring Tom Seaver, clad in rolled-up white pants and a white singlet, standing as if contemplating a pitch, baseball behind his back, against the eerie light of evening. His trusty dog is at his side. [3]

There are many different boyhood dreams, not all having to do with baseball or dogs, although there are lots of dogs in advertisements directed at men: Men also dream of cars. Beautiful cars. [4]

Cars to kill for. One brand of men's clothes is advertised as being "as classic as a '55 Thunderbird," with most of the two-page spread taken up by the Thunderbird. The clothes only turn the reader on by association. Corvette relies upon its classic [5] dream-car status to condescend to criticize the "rag-tag collection of pseudo 'sports cars' that, over the years, have challenged Corvette's supremacy." Mazda evokes the streetscapes of small-town America, when the bright red convertible in the showroom was every boy's dream. "We stood in the glow of a streetlight, our faces pressed against the glass, hypnotized by visions of Route 66, road racing, and rock and roll."

Other dreams have to do with the romance of flight: The Ralph Lauren model in his sportsman's sweater stands confidently on the pontoon of his seaplane in the rugged lake country, the "bombardier watch" advertises "rugged precision for land, sea, or air." Sometimes a man has to travel far for adventure, leaving behind the girl foolish enough to prefer "rum you could see through." He prefers rum you can't see through, and other mysterious satisfactions of the tropics: "the club with no name, the curious but delicious daiquiri, and the waiter with the bamboo cane." 6

These are dreams of escape. Back home, in everyday adulthood, the man finds himself weighed down by the pressures of competition, achievement, and conformity. These pressures, ironically, are reinforced by the mass of advertising he encounters—even when he doesn't think he's paying attention to it. Is there really any way he can succeed on his own terms? 7

DIANE BARTHEL, from "When Men Put on Appearances"

EXERCISE 37

Read the following excerpt from an essay (printed in the August 3, 1975, issue of *The Observer,* a British newspaper) about the career and personality of George Washington. Then take *four separate sets of notes* from this passage, using four separate cards or sheets, as if you were preparing an essay on *each* of the following topics.

Topics

A. The personality of George Washington

B. George Washington's military strategy

C. War atrocities

D. How England lost the Revolutionary War

from WASHINGTON—THE TRUTH BEHIND THE LEGEND
Michael Davie

The verdict of military historians is that Washington was a competent but not a great general. The British were overconfident. The man in charge of the British armies in the field, as Secretary of State for the Colonies, was a Lord Germain who had been court-martialled for cowardice in 1760, found guilty, and declared "unfit to serve His Majesty in any military capacity whatever." George III interfered con- 1 stantly, and disastrously. In any case, as the great English republican Tom Paine pointed out at the time, it was always "very absurd" that an island should try to rule a continent.

Even so, the war went on for almost as long as the war in Vietnam. It was 18 June 1775 when Washington wrote from Philadelphia to his wife Martha, at home at Mount Vernon, to tell her of his unwillingness to part with her and the family, "not doubting but that I shall return safe to you in the fall." But it was 17 October 1781 before a white cloth appeared on the British ramparts at York-town to indicate that General Cornwallis was suing for terms, and an entire British army—7,421 men, with 7,000 muskets, 200 cannon, 450 horses—marched out to stack its arms while the band played "The World Turned Upside Down."

Undoubtedly, it was Washington who kept the struggle going. It was a brutal and bloody war: a civil war as well as a war of liberation. When the British were led at night by their Tory spies to a force of sleeping Americans at Paoli, in Pennsylvania, they went in with bayonets, stabbing until their muscles were tired. The British army, whether or not it was incompetent, was certainly not gentle. The 42nd High-landers, later the Black Watch, went into action not only with muskets and bayo-nets, but with enormous swords, like claymores. During battles, the Highlanders were liable to throw aside their muskets and lay about them with these monstrous broadswords. To oppose such savage apparitions, Washington was compelled to rely on farmboys, many of whom expected to return to their farms after a few months' service. The rich young Marquis de Lafayette, second-in-command of the French troops in Washington's forces (Lafayette later gave Washington the key of the Bastille that today hangs at Mount Vernon), described a section of Washing-ton's army as follows: "About eleven thousand men ill-armed, and still worse clothed, presented a strange spectacle. Their clothes were particoloured, and many of them were almost naked. The best clad wore hunting shirts, large grey linen coats."

Washington kept this rabble in being as a fighting force by no other means than his own force of character. He shared with his men the terrible winter ordeals of Valley Forge and Morristown, hanged deserters selectively, and showed an iron nerve in battle. He also stood up for his troops against the Congressmen who put their own interests before that of the cause. Washington's writing in time of peace was invariably stodgy and temperate, but some of his wartime papers are violent and impassioned. "I would to God," he wrote in 1778, "that one of the most atro-cious [speculators] of each State was hung in gibbets upon a gallows five times as high as the one prepared by Haman. No punishment in my opinion is too great for the man who can build his greatness upon his country's ruin."

This is the heart of the Washington legend—the patriot holding the cause to-gether. And the legend is true. The picture of General Washington that emerges from contemporary writings—especially in Tom Paine's descriptions of him, as a man "who never appeared to full advantage but in difficulties and action," a man with "a mind that can flourish upon care"—is sharp and unequivocal. No one can argue with it; no one has tried.

▪8▪

Presenting the Results of Your Research: Organizing and Writing the Essay

You should plan and write your research essay in exactly the same way that you would work on any other essay. Whatever the topic, you will probably start out with written notes—facts, ideas, comments, opinions—that serve as the raw materials for your synthesis. From these notes, you form a sequence of separate generalizations to be used as the focus of each of your paragraphs. These steps help you to work out the basic structure of your essay.

The difference between organizing the research essay and organizing the other essays that you have previously written comes from the unusually large quantity of *notes*. The term "notes" here refers to any of the products of your research, including your own *summaries* and *paraphrases, quotations, Xeroxed copies* of pages and articles, class *lecture notes,* and stories clipped from *newspapers,* as well as *your own ideas* about the topic.

TAKING INVENTORY AND DEVELOPING A LIST OF TOPICS

You search for ideas worth developing by reviewing all the major points that you have learned and thought about during your research. These ideas form the core of your essay.

You select the main ideas of your research by:

1. Carefully reading through all your notes;
2. Looking for and writing down any points that seem especially important to understanding and explaining your topic.

In other words, *you take a new set of notes from your old set*. In this way, you can reduce the accumulated mass of information to a more manageable size. The new list of generalizations can be rearranged, tried out in different versions, and eventually converted into an outline of topic sentences.

Organizing your essay involves:

- reading lists of notes,
- thinking about them,
- making new lists,
- deleting and adding items,
- rearranging the order.

You follow these steps until the list of topics—and the paragraphs of your essay—form a sequence that both makes sense and makes your point. This process is actually a more elaborate version of the synthesis that you practiced in Chapter 4.

Guidelines for Taking Inventory of Your Notes and Forming Your Paragraph Topics

1. *Do* write down *in any order* the important ideas that you find in your notes. At this point, the items don't have to be related to each other in sequence.

2. *Don't* try to *summarize* all your notes or even summarize each of your notes. At this point, you are working on a paragraph outline, not a summary of your research.

3. *Don't* try to *link* the ideas that you write down to specific sources. At this point, there is no special reason to place the names of the sources next to your new list of ideas; not every statement in your new list will be included in your essay. Later, you will decide which source to use in support of which topic sentence.

4. *Do think about your own reactions* to the information that you have collected. At this point, the many strands of your research begin to become the product of your own thinking. Now you are deciding what is worth writing about.

5. *Do use your own words*. At this point, even if you only jot down a phrase or a fragment, it should be *your* version of the source's idea. Even if the point has appeared in ten different articles (and has been

noted on ten different index cards), you are now, in some sense, making it your own.

6. *Do evaluate your list* of important ideas that are worth writing about. At this point, notice which ideas are in the mainstream of your research, discussed by several of your sources, and which ones appear in only one or two sources. Consider whether you have enough evidence to support these ideas or whether you should exclude them from your master outline. Think about eliminating the ones that seem minor or remote from the topic. Remember to look for and combine similar statements.

7. *Do think about the sequence of ideas* on your final list and the possible *strategies* for organizing your essay. At this point, consider how these ideas relate to the topic with which you began your research:

- How does your list of ideas help to establish a thesis?

- Are you working with a collection of reasons? consequences? problems? dangers?

- What kind of essay will you write: cause and effect? problem and solution? explanation of a procedure? evaluation of reasons for an argument?

If you are developing a historical or biographical topic:

- Did the event fall into distinct narrative stages?

- What aspects of the scene would an observer have noticed?

- Which of your subject's activities best reveals his or her personality?

8. *Do arrange your list of topics* in a sequence that has meaning for you, carries out your strategy, and develops your thesis in a clear direction.

USING THE COMPUTER TO ORGANIZE YOUR ESSAY

One advantage of taking notes on a computer is that you can move the items around experimentally as you develop a new sequence of key ideas. Even if you have only a limited knowledge of word processing, you'll soon find it easy to pull a quotation or a paragraph out of your notes and add it to your outline, or to place a concrete example next to the general idea that it illustrates. A more sophisticated knowledge of "windows" and other software allows you to shift back and forth from one file to another or see two screens simultaneously, giving you even more flexibility in trying out different organizational strategies.

As you work with your notes on the computer, remember to *make a duplicate file of your notes,* keeping one file intact as a resource should you, later on, want to abandon a half-completed outline and start over or—worst case—lose your working file completely. Above all, *save your work at regular and frequent intervals*—and back up your files on a disk—or your notes and outline may suddenly dissolve into an empty screen.

The computer can make organizing, writing, and revising a research paper very easy. You can electronically manipulate notes, sentences, and paragraphs with miraculous speed. But you should apply the same thoughtfulness and care to working out your strategies for organization on the computer as you would if you were rearranging a stack of index cards and cutting and pasting a typed draft.

CROSS-REFERENCING

When you have developed a list of major topics that will roughly correspond to the paragraphs of your essay, you are ready to link your tentative outline to your research notes. Remember to:

- Leave plenty of space between the items on your outline; and
- Assign a number or a letter to each item.

Now, once again, *slowly reread all your research notes, this time keeping your list of topics in front of you*. Every time you come across a point in your notes that might be cited in support of a topic on your outline, immediately:

1. Place the number or letter of the topic in your outline next to the reference in your notes.
2. Place the source's name (and the number of the notecard, if you have used that system, or the page number of your notes) under the item on your outline.

For the system to work, you must complete both stages: notes must be keyed to the outline, and the outline must be keyed to each item in your research notes. The notes and the outline criss-cross each other; hence the term, *cross-referencing*.

To illustrate cross-referencing, here are three paragraph topics taken from an outline for an essay on the *Chicago Fire*. The outline for the essay is divided into three main sections: the *causes* of the fire, the *panic* during the fire, and *restoring order* after the fire. The three paragraph topics come from the last section of the outline. Figure 8-1 (on p. 372) shows an excerpt from the notes for the essay. Both paragraph topics and notes have cross-references in the margins. Notice that, to avoid confusion, the paragraph topics have Roman numerals, and the notes have arabic numerals.

Paragraph Topics

IX.   Feeding the homeless   G6/G7
X.   Providing basic services   G4
XI.   Protecting life and property   G3/G8

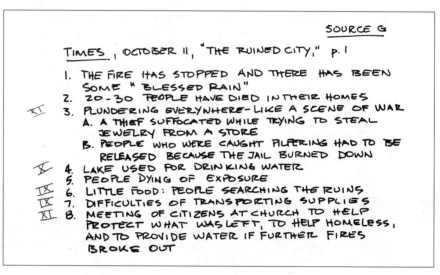

Figure 8-1. Notes: One Source per Card

Cross-referencing helps you to make full use of your notes and avoids time-consuming searches for references later on when you are writing the essay. At the end of this procedure:

- Your outline will have a list of sources to be cited for each main point, *and*
- Your research notes will have code numbers in most (but not necessarily all) of the margins.

Notice that a few items on the note card for Source G have no cross-references next to them. Some will be cross-referenced to other topics in this outline, and they have not yet been given their reference numbers. Items 2 and 5 in the notes, for example, would probably come under the heading of Casualties, in the section on panic during the fire. On the other hand, *not all the notes will necessarily be used in the essay;* some items will simply not fit into the topics chosen for the outline and will be discarded.

Figure 8-1 illustrates a method of note-taking that put all the material taken from a single source on a single card. Cross-referencing can also be used to organize *one-fact-per-card* notes, which can be sorted into piles corresponding to your topics. If you use this method, remember to put an identifying number on *each* card. In Figure 8-2, notice that:

- The code letter identifying the *source* (G) is in the upper right-hand corner.
- The code number identifying the *card* (32) is placed in the upper left-hand corner.
- The code number identifying the *outline topic* (XI) that this fact will be used to illustrate is indicated on the bottom of the card.

When you use the one-fact-per-card system, you put the relevant card number after each topic on your outline, but it is not necessary to identify the source.

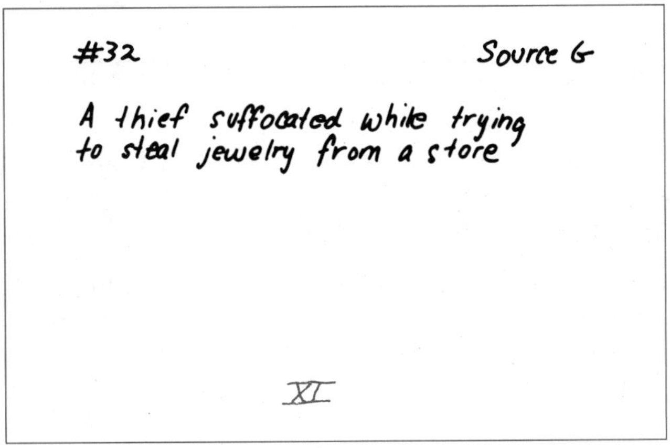

#32 Source G

A thief suffocated while trying to steal jewelry from a store

XI

Figure 8-2. Notes: One Fact per Card

Paragraph Topics

IX. Feeding the homeless
X. Providing basic services
XI. Protecting life and property

#32, #38

The third kind of notes—*one-topic-per-card/sheet*—already incorporates the cross-referencing process by planning topics at the same time that notes are taken. Since you have already grouped your materials by topic, using a special card or sheet for each topic, you need only review your notes and shift those points (usually by cutting and pasting) that have inadvertently been placed under the wrong topic. In the next stage, as you prepare to write about each topic on your outline, you will be able to refer to the exact points in your notes that you need to cite.

Of course, if you are using a computer to organize your notes, your "cutting and pasting" will be done much more quickly on the screen. But the cross-referencing process is still important. In developing a complex research topic, it is helpful to print out your outline and your notes, to identify outline topics and sections of your notes through numbers and letters, and to match up your notes with your outline by cross-referencing using numbers and letters in the margins. When you are satisfied with your organization, and the topics in your outline are fully supported by information from your notes, then you turn to the computer and "cut and paste" on the screen.

The more notes that you have collected, the more important it is to be thorough during the preliminary organization. *Don't start to write your essay, and don't even start to sort your notes or "cut and paste" your sheets, until you have completed both your basic outline and your cross-referencing.*

EXERCISE 38

Read the following set of notes, organized by source, for an essay on the Olympic Games.

1. Write an outline of topics for an essay to be called "The Commercialization of the Olympics."
2. Cross-reference the notes with your outline.

As you consider the information in these notes, remember that, if this exercise were preparation for an assigned essay, you could return to any of the sources, if you wished, and add details or examples to develop a topic that does not have enough supporting information.

Source A
Jeffery, Nicole. "Vying for the 2000 Olympics." *World Press Review* July 1993, 24–25.

1. On 23 Sept. 1993 the International Olympic Committee (IOC) meets to decide the site of the 2000 Olympic games.

2. Accusations of corruption following the choice of Atlanta to host the 1996 Summer Games have brought scrutiny to the committee's actions.

3. Investigation proves that committee members cashed in first-class plane tickets meant for travel to site locations and demanded extra tickets for friends and relatives.

4. Travel arrangements now handled by the IOC.

5. Site location choice is governed by commercial considerations: television rights and sponsors are a major factor in the selection.

6. Countries vie to host the games because of the large amount of revenue the Olympics can generate.

7. Serious bidders spend a minimum of 20 million dollars to even be considered.

8. China, a favorite for the 2000 choice, figures on spending 1.02 billion dollars if they win the right to host the Olympics: they plan on making 1.14 billion as a result of the games.

Source B
Storvik, Kjell Ove. "Gear Wars." *The Sciences* Jan./Feb. 1994, 31–34.

1. 10 Feb. 1982 Paul Enoch breaks world record in 3,000 meter speed-skating due to his novel outfit: he wore his wife's stockings; this begins a revolution in sports outfits.

2. Renovations in skating/athletic outfits by sports clothing manufacturers begin an unprecedented industry.

3. Olympic games become a trade exposition as rival designers pit their equipment against one another.

4. Even the symbolic torch has undergone redesign and the new high-tech torch will never go out in the worst snowstorms.

5. The games within the games: athletes vie for product endorsements; industries competing against other sports equipment companies.

6. Is the trade sideshow of the Olympics true to its origins as a celebration of amateur athletes?

7. Do advances in technology put athletes from poorer countries at a disadvantage?

8. Swedish skier Boklov's change in ski-jump styles led to an increase in research concerning aerodynamics for winter sports.

9. Changes in technology lead to a shattering of world records.

10. Norwegian Ski Association hires a professor of fluid dynamics to design skis for the 1994 Olympics, signaling a shift in how countries employ technology to win the games—and then sell the technology.

Source C
McCallum, Jack. "Dreamy." *Sports Illustrated* 17 Aug. 1992, 14–19.

1. Speculation as to whether or not the USA Dream Team was a one shot compilation of professionals or a shift in the make-up of Olympic athletes.

2. USA Dream Team stars Michael Jordan and Charles Barkley refuse to wear official Team USA jerseys because they are made by Reebok and both have promotional contracts with Nike.

3. All Dream Team members hide product labels on U.S. Olympic team gear during interviews for fear of endorsing rival companies: the American Olympic Committee allows them to do so.

4. The American professional basketball players defeat their opponents by an average of 43.8 points per game: displaying the enormous difference between American professionals and other amateur players.

5. NBA scouts travel to Olympics to search for talent capable of playing against the American stars and who could play either professional or college ball in the U.S.

6. Coach Chuck Daley praised for bringing together a collection of highly paid individuals and making them into a team: unlike their opponents the U.S. did not play together very long but in fact were mostly rivals.

Source D
Edwards, Phil. "A Gold for Subsidiarity: Olympic T.V." *New Statesman and Society* 7 Aug. 1992, 34.

1. The hope for the first post–cold war Olympics displaying a revitalized Europe and signaling the new European Community was muted.

2. The unified team—composed of the former Soviet Union—now comprised athletes from 12 different countries played under the Olympic flag displaying the best sense of Olympic spirit.

3. U.S. athletes criticized for their aggressive competitive spirit: lacking a sense of what the games are about.

4. T.V. coverage criticized for being biased towards Americans: presenting them as the world's favorites.

5. The television coverage fails to show lower-profile sports or inform audiences about the rules for lesser-known competitions: preferring to cover bigger-named athletes for sponsorship reasons.

6. British athletes praised for their lack of financial or pharmaceutical aid while still in possession of Olympic spirit, and their ability to win.

Source E
Benjamin, Daniel. "Pro vs. Amateur." *Time* 27 July 1992, 64–5.

1. The debate over who an Olympian can be is raised by the 1992 American basketball Dream Team—composed of professional NBA players.

2. A shift from obscure amateur athletes representing their countries to highly trained professionals representing sponsors.

3. The USA Dream Team collectively earns $33 million a year for playing the sport they will play in the Olympics.

4. Will truly amateur events—archery, Greco-Roman wrestling—become even more marginalized?

5. Is current trend so different from Greek tradition? Greek athletes were city champions and sponsored by patrons.

6. Amateurism brought to the games in 1896 believing it would result in fair play.

7. Jim Thorpe, winner of two gold medals in the decathlon, was stripped of his medals when it was discovered that he played summer league basketball in college for $25 a week in 1910: medals later restored.

8. Soviet Bloc nations had put athletes on government payrolls, granting them bogus titles and allowing them to train full time.

9. Western athletes support themselves by sportswear and other product endorsements.

10. In 1981 the word amateur stricken from IOC charter.

11. Rules of eligibility for athletes for different sports shifted from IOC to different sport federations.

Source F
"The Olympics Go Better with Coke." *The Economist* 22 Sept. 1990, 24.

1. Atlanta spends seven million dollars up front on its bid to win the right to host the 1996 Summer Games: will spend 1.16 billion over the next six years to prepare.

2. Speculation arises over possible bribery: one African delegate remarked that Delta promised free tickets to all African tourists to the Olympics if they were in Atlanta.

3. Athenians accuse IOC of "selling its soul for a buck and a proverbial case of Coca-Cola."

4. Coca-Cola USA spent at least $350,000 towards Atlanta's efforts to host the games.

5. Coca-Cola Great Britain refused to spend any money to help Manchester's bid for it would be "inappropriate" to oppose its Atlanta headquarters.

6. Television rights will secure Atlanta half of its Olympic capital with an additional $342 million coming from corporate sponsors: ticket sales are expected to cover the rest of the expenses.

Source G

Janofsky, Michael. "Olympics Are at a Point to Start Looking Ahead." *New York Times* 9 Aug. 1992, 5.

1. At end of 1992 Olympics, officials are anticipating 1996 in Atlanta. A reference to the "romance of Las Ramblas" in Barcelona being replaced by the "malls of Atlanta."

2. Juan Antonio Samaranch, president of the International Committee, expressed a concern about limiting the number of participating athletes to 10,000. (Much interest is anticipated since this is the centennial of the first modern Olympics.) Samaranch wants to avoid having nations taking advantage of free room and board for their athletes at the Olympic Village and having athletes attending to "vacation" and going to the beach rather than taking part in the competition.

3. Another member of the International Committee expressed concern about the elimination and reduction of events in so-called elite sports. As new "popular, low-cost sports" are included, such sports as yachting, equestrian, and fencing may be lost.

4. The really popular sports, like swimming and track and field, are unlikely to lose their prominence in the Olympic schedule because television audiences like to watch them.

INTEGRATING YOUR SOURCES INTO PARAGRAPHS

Writing a research essay resembles putting together a *mosaic*. Each paragraph has its basic design, determined by its topic sentence. To carry out the design, a paragraph might contain a group of reasons or examples to illustrate its main idea, *or* an extended explanation to develop that idea in greater detail, *or* a comparison between two elements introduced in the first sentence. These are the same paragraphing patterns that you use in all your writing. What makes the research essay different is the fact that the materials are assembled from many sources, *not* the way that they are organized or presented.

Imagine that the notes that you have taken from several different sources are boxes of tiles, each box containing a different color. You may find it easier to avoid mixing the colors and to work *only* with red tiles or *only* with blue, or to devote one corner of the mosaic to a red pattern and another to a blue. In the same way, you may find it both convenient and natural to work with only one source at a time and to avoid the decisions and the adjustments that must be made when you are combining different styles and ideas. But, of course, it is the design and only the design that dictates which colors should be used in creating the pattern of the mosaic, and it is the design or outline of your essay that dictates which evidence should be included in each paragraph.

When you decide to discuss a topic in a given paragraph, you must work with all the relevant information that you have gathered about that topic, whether it comes from one source or from many. Of course, you may have *too much material*; you may find it impossible to fit everything into the paragraph without overloading it with repetition. These rejected pieces may not fit into another part of the essay; instead, they will go back into their boxes as a backup or reserve fund of information.

The criteria for judging the quality of a paragraph remain the same—*clarity*, *coherence*, and *unity*.

■ Do integrate your materials so that your reader will not be distracted by the differing sources or made aware of breaks between the various points.

■ Don't integrate your materials so completely that you forget to provide appropriate acknowledgment of your sources.

As you will learn in Chapter 9, the documentation that you insert acts as a running record of your research. Observing the names and page numbers of your sources in parentheses, your reader becomes aware of the diverse origins of these smoothly integrated pieces of information.

Guidelines for Constructing Paragraphs in a Research Essay

1. *Each paragraph should possess a single main idea, usually expressed in the topic sentence.* That topic or design controls the arrangement of all the information in the paragraph. Everything that is included should develop and support that single idea, without digressions.

2. *The body of the paragraph should contain a combination of information taken from a variety of sources.* The number of different sources that you include in any one paragraph depends partly on the number of authors in your notes who have touched on its main idea and partly on the contribution each can make to the development of your topic.

3. *The topic sentence of each paragraph should support the development of your essay's thesis.*

PROVIDING A CLEAR ACCOUNT OF YOUR EVIDENCE

What do you do if you have so much information that you risk overcrowding your paragraph? You may have collected four or five examples from several different sources, all illustrating your topic sentence. Each of these examples in its original source may have filled several sentences, several paragraphs, or several pages. Interesting as they all may be, you can't give each of them the same amount of space. If you run rapidly through a long series of brief examples, your reader may not understand their significance and your reasons for including them. Instead, you select a few examples and either disregard or briefly refer to the others. Your goal is to supply just enough information about each example to make your reader appreciate its interest and its relevance to your topic.

In the following complete paragraph, there are only two examples, but each is presented as an afterthought:

> Advertising uses women amorally. This condition should be publicized, and the sooner the better for every member of the reading public. For the past half century, the giant and not-so-giant corporations have succeeded in portraying an image of women that ranges from downright stupidity (Parker Pen: "You might as well give her a gorgeous pen to keep her checkbook unbalanced with") to the object of sadistic sex (Vogue's "The Story of Ohhh . . . " which included shots of a man ramming his hand into a woman's breast). Women today are being awakened to these debasing and degrading tactics.

The parentheses in this paragraph are being used to wedge the writer's examples into an already overloaded sentence. This writer is counting on having an exceptionally patient reader, someone who will pause long enough to interpret the significance of the material in parentheses.

In contrast, the next paragraph is from an essay about the novelist F. Scott Fitzgerald, in which four different explanations of an incident are presented, each at suitable length. Formal documentation of the sources has been omitted; but, to emphasize the variety and complexity of the research, the names of the sources and the attributing verbs and phrases have been underlined. The writer is describing an affair between Fitzgerald's wife, Zelda, and Edouard Jozan, a young Frenchman.

> There is a lack of agreement about the details of the affair as well as its significance for the Fitzgeralds' marriage. According to one of Fitzgerald's biographers, Jozan and Zelda afterwards regarded it as "nothing more than a summer flirtation." But Ernest Hemingway, in his memoirs, wrote much later that Scott had told him "a truly sad story" about the affair, which he repeated many times in the course of their friendship. Gerald and Sara Murphy, who were present that summer and remembered the incident very well, told of being awakened by Scott in the middle of a September night in order to help him revive Zelda from an overdose of sleeping pills. The Murphys were sure that this incident was related to her affair with Jozan. Nancy Milford, Zelda's biographer, believes that the affair affected Zelda more than Scott, who, at that time, was very engrossed in his work. Indeed, Milford's account of the affair is the only one that suggests

that Zelda was so deeply in love with Jozan that she asked Scott for a divorce. According to an interview with Jozan, the members of this triangle never engaged in a three-way confrontation; Jozan told Milford that the Fitzgeralds were "the victims of their own unsettled and a little unhealthy imagination."

This paragraph gives a brief but adequate account of what is known about the events of that summer of 1924. The writer does not try to rush through the four accounts of the affair, nor does he reduce each one to a phrase, as if he expected the reader to have prior knowledge of these people and their activities. In the context of the whole essay, the paragraph provides enough information for the reader to judge whose interpretation of the affair is closest to the truth.

DOING JUSTICE TO YOUR SOURCES

Perhaps the greatest disservice that you can do your sources is to distort them so that your reader is left with a false impression of what they have said or written. Such distortion is most likely to happen when you are writing an argumentative essay. You may want to review the earlier section on "Logic and Argumentation," pp. 31–37.

Mistakes to Avoid When Summarizing an Argument

1. Don't be one-sided; present *both* sides of an argument.
2. Don't omit crucial parts of the source's reasoning; provide a complete account of the argument.
3. Don't quote ideas out of context: make sure that you—and your reader—understand whether the source really supports the idea that you are citing.
4. Don't twist the source's ideas to fit your own purpose; provide a fair presentation.

---

1. **Present both sides of the argument.**

One way of shading an argument to suit your own ends is to *misrepresent the strength of the opposition*. Let us assume that you are working with a number of articles, all of which are effectively presented and worth citing. Some clearly support your point of view; others are openly opposed; and a few avoid taking sides, emphasizing related but less controversial topics. If your essay cites only the favorable and neutral articles, and avoids any reference to the views of the opposition, you have presented the issue falsely. Using ostrich tactics will not convince your reader that your opinions are right; on the contrary, your unwillingness to admit the existence of opposing views suggests that your point of view has some basic flaw. Your reader may be familiar with some of the arguments on both sides and will expect you to locate and cite sources that represent both. A one-sided presentation will make you appear to be either biased or sloppy in your research. If the sources are available and if their views are pertinent, they should be represented and, if you wish, refuted in your essay.

2. **Provide a complete account of the argument.**

Sometimes, distortions occur accidentally, because you have presented only a *partial* account of a source's views. In the course of an article or a book, authors sometimes examine and then reject or accept a variety of views before making it clear which are their own conclusions. Or an author may have mixed opinions about the issue and see merit in more than one point of view. If you choose to quote or paraphrase material from only one section of such a work, then you must find a way to inform your reader that these statements are not entirely representative of the writer's overall views.

3. **Make sure that you—and your reader—understand whether the source really supports the idea that you are citing.**

Ideas can get distorted because of the researcher's misunderstanding, careless note-taking, or hasty reading. Remember to check the entire section of the article or all your notes before you attribute an opinion to your source, to make sure that you are not taking a sentence out of context or ignoring a statement in the next paragraph or on the next page that may be more typical of the writer's thinking. Writers often use an argumentative strategy that sets up a point with which they basically disagree in order to shoot it down shortly thereafter. Don't confuse a statement made for the sake of argument with a writer's real beliefs.

4. **Provide a fair presentation.**

Occasionally, you may be so eager to uphold your point of view that you will cite any bit of material that looks like supporting evidence. To do so, however, you may have to twist the words of the source to fit your ideas. This is one of the worst kinds of intellectual dishonesty—and one of the easiest for a suspicious reader to detect: one has only to look up the source. *If you cannot find sufficient arguments and if your sources' evidence does not clearly and directly support your side, then you should seriously consider switching sides or switching topics.*

Here is a fairly clear instance of such distortion. In an essay on the need for prison reform, Garry Wills is focusing on the *deficiencies of our society's penal system;* he is not directly concerned with the arguments for or against the death penalty. But the student citing Wills in a research essay is writing specifically in support of capital punishment. To make Wills's argument fit into the scheme of this essay, the student must make some suspiciously selective references. Here is a paragraph from the research essay (on the left), side by side with the source.

Although the death penalty may seem very harsh and inhuman, is this not fair and just punishment for one who was able to administer death to another human being? A murderer's victim always receives the death penalty. Therefore, the death penalty for the murderer evens the score, or, as stated in the Bible, "an eye for an eye, and a tooth for a tooth." According to Garry Wills, "take a life, lose your life." Throughout the ages, society has demanded that man be allowed to right his wrongs. Revenge is our culture's oldest way of making sure that no one "gets away with" any crime. As Wills points out, according to this line of reasoning, the taking of the murderer's life can be seen as his payment to society for his misdeed.

The oldest of our culture's views on punishment is the *lex talionis,* an eye for an eye. Take a life, lose your life. It is a very basic cry—people must "pay" for their crimes, yield exact and measured recompense. No one should "get away with" any crime, like a shoplifter taking something unpaid for. The desire to make an offender suffer equivalent pain (if not compensatory excess of pain) is very deep in human nature, and rises quickly to the surface. What is lynching but an impatience with even the slightest delay in exacting this revenge? It serves our social myth to say that this impatience, if denied immediate gratification, is replaced by something entirely different—by an impersonal dedication to justice. Only lynchers want revenge, not those who wait for a verdict. That is not very likely. Look at the disappointed outcry if the verdict does not yield even delayed satisfaction of the grudge.

In the essay, the writer is citing only *part* of Wills's argument and thus makes him appear to support capital punishment. Wills is being misrepresented because (unlike the writer) he considers it fair to examine the views of the opposing side before presenting his own arguments. The ideas that the student cites are not Wills's, but Wills's presentations of commonly accepted assumptions about punishment. It is not entirely clear whether the writer of the research essay has merely been careless, failing to read past the first few sentences, or whether the misrepresentation is intentional.

INTEGRATING YOUR SOURCES: AN EXAMPLE

To illustrate the need for careful analysis of sources before you write your paragraphs, here is a group of passages, all direct quotations, which have been gathered for a research essay on college athletics. The paragraph developed from these sources must support the writer's *thesis:*

Colleges should, in the interests of both players and academic standards, outlaw the high-pressure tactics used by coaches when they recruit high school players for college teams.

The first three statements come from college coaches describing recruiting methods that they have observed and carried out; the last four are taken from books that discuss corruption in athletics.

I think in the long run, every coach must recognize this basic principle, or face the alumni firing squad. Recruiting is the crux of building a championship football team.

STEVE SLOAN, Texas Tech

Athletics is creating a monster. Recruiting is getting to be cancerous.

DALE BROWN, Louisiana State University

You don't out-coach people, you out-recruit them.

PAUL "BEAR" BRYANT, University of Alabama

It is an athletic maxim that a man with no special coaching skills can win games if he recruits well and that a tactician without talented players is a man soon without a job.

KENNETH DENLINGER

There is recruiting in various degrees in every intercollegiate sport, from crew to girls' basketball and from the Houston golf dynasty that began in the mid-50's to Southern California importing sprinters and jumpers from Jamaica.

J. ROBERT EVANS

The fundamental causes of the defects in American college athletics are too much commercialism and a negligent attitude towards the educational opportunity for which the college exists.

CARNEGIE FOUNDATION, 1929

[Collier's magazine, in 1905, reported that] Walter Eckersall, All-American quarterback, enrolled at Chicago three credits short of the entrance requirement and his teammate, Leo Detray, entered the school before he even graduated high school. In addition the University of Minnesota paid two players outright to play in a single game (Nebraska: 1902). A quarterback and an end also from Minnesota admitted shaving points during the 1903 Beloit game.

JOSEPH DURSO

Examining the Sources

Your paragraph will focus on *recruiting high school stars,* as opposed to developing students who enter college by the ordinary admissions procedure. Which of these ideas and observations might help to develop this paragraph? In other words, which statements should be represented by *paraphrase* or perhaps by *direct quotation*?

> I think in the long run every coach must recognize this basic principle, or face the alumni firing squad. Recruiting is the crux of building a championship football team.
>
> (STEVE SLOAN)

This very broad generalization seems quotable at first, largely because it sums up the topic so well; but, in fact, because it does no more than sum up the topic, it does not advance your argument any further. Therefore, you need not include it if your topic sentence makes the same point. (In general, you should write your own topic sentences rather than letting your sources write them for you.) The phrase "alumni firing squad" might be useful to quote in a later paragraph, in a discussion of the specific influence of alumni on recruiting.

> Athletics is creating a monster. Recruiting is getting to be cancerous.
>
> (DALE BROWN)

Coach Brown's choice of images—"cancerous" and "monster"—is certainly vivid; but the sentence as a whole is no more than a *generalized opinion about recruiting,* not an explanation of why the situation is so monstrous. To be lured into quoting Brown for the sake of two words would be a mistake.

> You don't out-coach people, you out-recruit them.
>
> (PAUL "BEAR" BRYANT)

This is the first statement that has advanced a specific idea: the coach may have a *choice* between building a winning team through recruiting and building a winning team through good coaching; but recruiting, not coaching, wins games. Coach Bryant, then, is not just making a rhetorical point, as the first two coaches seem to be. His seven-word sentence is succinct, if not elaborately developed, and would make a good introduction to or summation of a point that deserves full discussion.

The remaining four statements suggest a wider range of approach and style.

> Walter Eckersall, All-American quarterback, enrolled at Chicago three credits short of the entrance requirement and his teammate, Leo Detray, entered the school before he even graduated high school. In addition, the University of Minnesota paid two players outright to play in a single game (Nebraska: 1902). A quarterback and an end also from Minnesota admitted shaving points during the 1903 Beloit game.
>
> (JOSEPH DURSO)

This passage is as much concerned with corruption as recruiting and indicates that commercialism is nothing new in college athletics. Although the information is interesting, it is presented as a list of facts, and the language is not worth quoting. You may, however, want to summarize the example in your own words.

> The fundamental causes of the defects in American college athletics are too much commercialism and a negligent attitude towards the educational opportunity for which the college exists.
>
> (CARNEGIE FOUNDATION)

This extract from the 1929 Carnegie Foundation study is phrased in *abstract* language that is characteristic of foundation reports and academic writing in general. This style can be found in most textbooks (including this one) and in many of the sources that you use in college. The foundation presents its point clearly enough and raises an important idea: an athlete recruited to win games (and earn fame and fortune) is likely to ignore the primary reason for going to college—to acquire an education. Nevertheless, there is no compelling reason to *quote* this statement. *Remember that you include quotations in your essay to enhance your presentation; the quotation marks automatically prepare the reader for special words and phrasing.* But the prose here is too colorless and abstract to give the reader anything to focus on; a paraphrase is preferable.

> There is recruiting in varying degrees in every intercollegiate sport, from crew to girls' basketball and from the Houston golf dynasty that began in the mid-50's to Southern California importing sprinters and jumpers from Jamaica.
>
> (J. ROBERT EVANS)

This statement presents a quite different, more *detailed* level of information; it lists several sports, including some not known for their cutthroat recruiting practices. But details do not necessarily deserve quotation. Will these references be at all meaningful to the reader who is not familiar with the "Houston golf dynasty" or Jamaican track stars? To know that recruitment is not limited to cash sports, such as football, is interesting, but such specifics date quickly: in a few years, they may no longer be a useful frame of reference for most readers.

> It is an athletic maxim that a man with no special coaching skills can win games if he recruits well and that a tactician without talented players is a man soon without a job.
>
> (KENNETH DENLINGER)

Largely because of parallel construction, the last comment sounds both sharp and solid. In much the same way as Coach Bryant's seven words, but at greater length, Kenneth Denlinger sums up the contrast between coaching and recruiting, and suggests which one has the edge. Because the statement gives the reader something substantial to think about and because it is well phrased, Denlinger is probably worth quoting.

Should the writer include the statements by Bryant and by Denlinger, both of which say essentially the same thing? While Bryant's firsthand comment is commendably terse and certainly authoritative, Denlinger's is more complete and self-explanatory. A solution might be to include both, at different points in the paragraph, with Bryant cited at the end to sum up the idea that has been developed. Of course, the other five sources need not be excluded from the paragraph. Rather, if you wish, all five may be referred to, by paraphrase or brief reference, with their authors' names cited.

Here is *one* way of integrating this set of statements into a paragraph. (Note that, in this version, there is no documentation: none of the sources—except those quoted—is cited.)

In college athletics, what is the best way for a school to win games? Should a strong team be gradually built up by training ordinary students from scratch, or should the process be shortened and success be assured by actively recruiting players who already know how to win? The first method may be more consistent with the traditional amateurism of college athletics, but as early as 1929, the Carnegie Foundation complained that the focus of college sports had shifted from education to the material advantages of winning. Even earlier, in 1903, there were several instances of players without academic qualifications who were "hired" to guarantee victory. And in recent years excellence of recruiting has become the most important skill for a coach to possess. Kenneth Denlinger has observed, "It is an athletic maxim that a man with no special coaching skills can win games if he recruits well and that a tactician without talented players is a man soon without a job." It follows, then, that a coach who wants to keep his job is likely to concentrate on spotting and collecting talent for his team. Coaches from LSU, Alabama, and Texas Tech all testify that good recruiting has first priority throughout college athletics. According to Bear Bryant of Alabama: "You don't out-coach people, you out-recruit them."

One problem that can arise as you are crafting your paragraph is what to do with material that casts doubt on or flatly contradicts the point you're making. (Frequently, you come across that material *after* you have worked out your thesis and structure.) Here, for example, is an excerpt from *College Sports Inc.* by Murray Sperber. How does it fit with the paragraph on recruiting to win?

Coaches who cheat do so for the same reasons that some gamblers try for an illegal advantage. They are extremely competitive, obsessed with winning, and will bend or break the rules to obtain the winning edge. They subscribe to the dictum that "winning is the only thing," that losing is not merely defeat but also a loss of self-worth. When gamblers or coaches cheat and succeed, they consider themselves "smart" and they show no remorse or inclination to stop. Only when caught do recriminations and blame—"Pressure from the school made me do it"—appear.

Richard "Digger" Phelps, head of Notre Dame's men's basketball program, has long argued that external pressure is not the main source of coaches' cheating. He says of himself and his colleagues, "You choose the job you want to take. You decide who you want to recruit—the type of person. You also decide who you want to have surround that program as far as alumni, boosters, and friends. . . ."

The coaches referred to in the earlier student paragraph about recruiting assume that winning is the point of college athletics. The author of the paragraph is focusing on the best way to win—recruiting—and the only criticism of the primacy of winning is a slight complaint by the Carnegie Foundation about the materialism of college athletics. Now, not only does Sperber denigrate the "win at all costs" philosophy, but he (and Phelps, his source) suggests that the impetus to win and cheat (and, presumably, recruit at the expense of good sportsmanship) comes from the egoism of the coaches themselves, rather than the pressure from college officials and alumni.

What do you do with this excerpt from Sperber? Should you rewrite your paragraph on recruiting to include Sperber's (and Phelps's) opinions and attempt to reconcile them with the material provided by your other sources? In this situation, do two things:

1. **Examine the new source more completely to see if the author provides a broader context for these contradictory opinions.**

   In fact, Sperber also has a good deal to say about the commercialism of college sports, pointing out that athletic departments resemble business enterprises, with program directors who are in the "entertainment business." His book indicates that the "winning is everything" philosophy derives as much from institutional (and media) expectations as from the competitive obsessions of individual coaches.

2. **If the point made by the new source is worth developing, it may be preferable to do so in a separate paragraph.**

   The "recruiting" paragraph focuses on *what* coaches do to win, not why they do it. Sperber, however, is more concerned with motivation—quite a different topic and an equally interesting one. Your essay may benefit from an exploration of this point, but to develop and support it properly, you will probably have to find more sources that deal with the pressures to compete to win. The more you read, the more new directions you are likely to find for the development of your essay.

SELECTING QUOTATIONS

Now that you are working with a great variety of sources, you may find it difficult to limit the number of quotations in your essay and to choose quotable material. If you are doubtful about when and what to quote, review the sections on quotation in Chapter 2 and Chapter 4, starting on pp. 88 and 215. As a rule, the more eminent and authoritative the source, the more reason to consider quoting it.

Guidelines for Quoting

1. *Never quote something just because it sounds impressive.* The style of the quotation—the level of difficulty, the choice of vocabulary, and the degree of abstraction—should be compatible with your own style. Don't force your reader to make a mental jump from your own characteristic voice and wording to a far more abstract, flowery, or colloquial style. Of course, the need for consistency of style does not mean that your essay should lack all variety; nor are you expected to exclude significant but difficult quotations by authors whose style is so distinctive that it cannot be paraphrased.

2. *Never quote something that you find very difficult to understand.* When the time comes to decide whether and what to quote, stop and observe your own reactions. Rapidly reread the quotation. If you find it difficult to understand on the first try, then either attempt to paraphrase the point or leave it out entirely. If you become distracted or confused, your reader will be, too. In the long run, the writers that you will want to quote will be the ones whom you understand and enjoy.

3. *Primary sources are often worth quoting—if they are clear and understandable.* When you are working on a biographical or historical research essay, you may encounter special problems in deciding whether or not to quote. Primary sources often have a special claim to be quoted. For example, you would be more likely to quote one of Hemingway's own descriptions of Paris in 1925 than a comparable sentence by one of his biographers. A person who witnessed the Chicago Fire has a better claim to have his original account presented verbatim than does a historian decades later.

4. *Use single and double quotation marks to differentiate between primary and secondary sources.* When quoting primary sources, it is essential to make the exact source of the quotation clear to your reader.

The need for these guidelines is illustrated in this excerpt from a student essay describing Charles Dickens on holiday in France in 1853:

Unclear Use of Quotation

On first beholding Boulogne, Dickens was enraptured. He immediately wrote home to a friend expressing his delight in the beauty of the French countryside and of the town. "He raved about the rustic qualities of the people. . . . " He raved about the "fresh sea air" and about the "beauty and repose of his surroundings."

The first "He raved" tells you at once that the biographer, not Dickens, is being quoted, but you cannot be sure which of the two is responsible for "fresh sea air" and "beauty and repose," since the biographer may, in fact, be quoting from Dickens's letters. Single quotation marks inside the double quotation marks might have been used to show who wrote what.

The placement of the quotation marks in the next excerpt makes it clear that the words are Dickens's own; on the other hand, they may not be worth quoting. The novelist is describing the house that he has rented, the Chateau des Moulineux:

Excessive Use of Quotation

Dickens rattled off a list of phrases in his attempt to describe this idyllic place. It was to become his "best doll's house," "our French watering place," and "this abode of bliss." More than anything else it would become a "happy, happy place."

Such a list of separately quoted phrases creates an awkward, disconnected effect, which, if used too often, will become tedious to read.

Descriptions are often more difficult to paraphrase than ideas; as a result, they tend to be presented in such a sequence of quoted phrases. If your source states that the walls of the room were painted sea-green and the furniture was made out of horsehair and covered with light-brown velvet, you may find it next to impossible to find appropriate synonyms to paraphrase these descriptive terms. "Crin de cheval" covered with fuzzy beige fabric? Mediterranean colors decorating the walls? The result is hardly worth the effort. If the man's eyes are described as dark blue, don't alter the phrase to "piercing blue" or "deep azure" or "ocean pools." If you place "dark blue" in a sentence that is otherwise your own writing, you may omit the quotation marks.

EXERCISE 39

The following unfinished student paragraphs are followed by brief excerpts from sources.

1. Decide which excerpt contains the most appropriate sentence for quotation. (It is not necessary to quote the entire excerpt.) For the purposes of this exercise, assume that all the sources are qualified authorities.

2. Paraphrase the other excerpts.

3. Complete the paragraph by using both paraphrase and quotation, citing two *or* three sources. Maintain a consistent tone and (except for the quotation) a single voice. Do not digress too far from the topic sentence.

Student Paragraph A

Violence at sporting events can be generated by both the players and the audience. Certain sports seem to legitimize an aggressive stance which communicates itself from the athletes on the field to the fans in the bleachers. . . .

Sources

Players use a complex moral logic in attempts to coordinate the goal of winning with the need to respect limits to egocentricity. Some athletes identify the rules as the final arbiter of legitimacy, but most appeal to less formal criteria. Themes such as intimidation, domination, fairness, and retribution are continuously woven into participants' fabric of thought, providing a changing picture of what constitutes legitimate action.

BRENDA JO BREDEMEIER and DAVID L. SHIELDS

The emerging view [among psychologists] is that the particularly brutal and angry aggression that is a virtually integral part of some forms of competitive athletics increases the likelihood of imitative violence among crowds dominated by young adult males. One theory holds, for example, that anonymity and excitement allow fans to put aside more readily the inhibitions that would keep them from being openly aggressive in other situations. Violence on the playing field then holds out to them an example they are more likely to follow.

DANIEL GOLEMAN

In some sports—basketball, baseball, soccer—violence is occasional (and usually illegal); in others, like hockey, it is incidental; in others still, car racing, for example, it is accidental. Definitive violence football shares alone with boxing and bullfighting, among major sports. But in bullfighting a man is pitted not against another man, but against an animal, and boxing is a competition between individuals, not teams, and that makes a difference.

GEORGE STADE

So much aggression seems to be expressed in games that to many an observer a game appears to be like a war, that outstanding example of aggressiveness. Though some sports seem to have been invented to promote physical fitness, skill and dexterity, or for the purpose of using up surplus energy enjoyably, others—archery, fencing, shooting, judo, evidently, and conceivably boxing, wrestling, dressage, running, weight lifting, and the relay—have instead a military origin or a military objective. These, and perhaps others, refine and promote activities which are parts of the art of war.

PAUL WEISS

Student Paragraph B

In recent years, Americans have invested great faith in and at the same time professed great disillusionment with what they read in the newspapers and see on the evening news. Yet the public's dissatisfaction with the content and presentation of the news cannot be entirely attributable to malicious intent—or even self-interest—on the part of journalists, newspaper proprietors, or network chiefs. . . .

Sources

The American press is malleable. It can be easily hurt and easily influenced. It really has no obligation to tell the truth about anything. None. We would *like* it to tell the truth. But there is nothing that says that it must.

FRANCES FITZGERALD

The importance of an event is immediately measured by the extent to which radio and television stations interrupt their normal schedules. Without on-site inspection or interpersonal verification, the average person is limited to the news media for authentication. During a time when cynicism is fashionable, an extraordinary amount of trust is placed in media organizations with whom the public has no immediate relationship.

GARY GUMPERT

Today's journalism is increasingly an amalgam of fact and fiction. This isn't done with evil intention, but because journalists work in the usual alloys of flawed information and unconscious bias. . . . Journalism is sculpture in the snow. To have the expectation that it's somehow cast in stone—that it will reveal the truth to us—is to load it down with a burden it can't carry.

LEWIS H. LAPHAM

People may have come to expect too much of journalism. Not of journalism at its worst; when one is confronted with lies, cruelty and tastelessness, it is hardly too much to expect better. But that is not a serious problem because lies, cruelty and tastelessness are the freaks of the trade, not the pillars. The trouble is that people have also come to expect too much of journalism at its best, because they have invested too much power in it, and in so doing have neglected or forfeited other sources of power in their lives.

ROGER ROSENBLATT

ASSIGNMENT 15

You have been assigned to write a research paper on one of the following broad topics:

    A. Changing Concepts of Masculinity

    B. Men and Women in Modern America

    C. Sports, Violence, and Masculinity

Each of the readings in Appendix E relates to one or more of these topics.

1. Read through all the passages. (In a full-scale research project, these readings would form a substantial part, but not all, of your sources. Check with your instructor about whether you may use additional sources.)

2. Write down a tentative list of main ideas, based on these sources, that should be discussed in an essay dealing with your subject. Also include your own ideas on the subject.

3. Develop an outline based on your list of ideas, and consider possible theses for the essay and the strategy that will best fit your thesis and sources.

4. After you have compiled a substantial list of topics and developed a tentative thesis, reread the passages, cross-referencing the topics on your list with the relevant paragraphs from the essays. While you do not have to use up everything in all of the readings, you should include all relevant points.

5. Develop this outline into an eight- or ten-page essay.

·9·

Presenting the Results of Your Research: Acknowledging Your Sources

When you engage in research, you continually come into contact with the ideas and the words of other writers; as a result, the opportunities to plagiarize—by accident or by intention—increase tremendously. You must therefore understand exactly what constitutes plagiarism.

Plagiarism is the unacknowledged use of another person's work, in the form of original ideas, strategies, and research, or another person's writing, in the form of sentences, phrases, and innovative terminology.

- Plagiarism is the equivalent of *theft*, but the stolen goods are intellectual rather than material.

- Like other acts of theft, plagiarism is against the law. The copyright law governing publications requires that authorship be acknowledged and (if the borrowed material is long enough) that payment be offered to the writer.

- Plagiarism violates the moral law that people should take pride in, as well as profit from, the fruits of their labor. Put yourself in the victim's place. Think about the best idea that you ever had, or the paragraph that you worked hardest on in your last paper. Now, imagine yourself finding exactly the same idea or exactly the same sentences in someone else's essay, with no mention of your name, with no quotation marks. Would you accept the theft of your property without protest?

- Plagiarists are not only robbers, but also cheats. People who bend or break the rules of authorship, who do not do their own work, will be rightly distrusted by their classmates, teachers, or future employers, who may equate a history of plagiarism with laziness, incompetence, or dishonesty. One's future rarely depends on getting a better grade on a single assignment; on the other hand, one's lifelong reputation may be damaged if one resorts to plagiarism in order to get that grade.

But plagiarism is a bad risk for a more immediate and practical reason. As you observed in Exercise 13, an experienced teacher can usually detect plagiarized work quite easily. *If you are not skilled enough to write your own essay, you are unlikely to do a good enough job of adapting someone else's work to your needs.* Plagiarism represents a confession of failure, an inability to do—even to attempt to do—the job.

Anyone can learn to write well enough to make plagiarism an unnecessary risk.

Finally, you will not receive greater glory by plagiarizing. On the contrary, most instructors believe that students who understand the ideas of their sources, apply them to the topic, and put them in their own words deserve the highest grades for their mastery of the basic skills of academic writing. There are, however, occasions when your instructor may ask you not to use secondary sources. In such cases, you would be wise to do no background reading at all, so that the temptation to borrow will not arise.

ACKNOWLEDGING YOUR SOURCES

Acknowledging your sources—or *documentation*—means telling your reader that someone other than yourself is the source of ideas and words in your essay. Acknowledgment can take the form of *quotation marks* and *citation of the author's name*—techniques that are by now familiar to you—or more elaborate ways to indicate the source, which will be explained later in this chapter. There are guidelines to help you decide what can and what cannot safely be used without acknowledgment, and these guidelines mostly favor complete documentation.

DOCUMENTING INFORMATION

By conservative standards, *you should cite a source for all facts and evidence in your essay that you did not know before you started your research.* Knowing when to acknowledge the source of your knowledge or information largely depends on common sense. For example, it is not necessary to document the fact that there are fifty states in the United States or that Shakespeare wrote *Hamlet* since these facts are common knowledge. On the other hand, you may be presenting more obscure information, like facts about electric railroads, which you have known since you were a child, but which may be unfamiliar to your readers.

Technically, you are not obliged to document that information; but your audience will trust you more and will be better informed if you do so. *In general, if the facts are not unusual, if they can be found in a number of standard sources, and if they do not vary from source to source or year to year, then they can be considered common knowledge, and the source need not be acknowledged.*

Let's assume that you are writing an essay about *Lawrence of Arabia* for a course in film studies. The basic facts about the film—the year of release, the cast, the director, the technicians, the Academy Awards won by the film—might be regarded as common knowledge and not require documentation. But the cost of the film, the amount grossed in its first year, the location of the premiere, and the circumstances of production are relatively unfamiliar facts that you would almost certainly have to look up in a reference book. An authority on film who includes such facts in a study of epic films is expected to be familiar with this information and, in most cases, would not be expected to provide documentation. But a student writing on the same subject would be well advised to do so.

Similarly, if you are writing about the 1994 World Cup and know who won a specific match because you witnessed the victory on television, then it would probably not be necessary to cite a source. (If you were writing about the 1990 World Cup, you would probably have to consult an almanac—and give it credit for the information.) Issues surrounding the 1994 World Cup—such as the use of steroids—are less clearly in the realm of common knowledge. You may remember news broadcasts about which athletes may or may not have taken steroids before a match, but the circumstances are hardly so well defined—or so memorable in their details—that you would be justified in writing about them from memory. The articles that you consult to jog your memory would have to be documented.

Documenting Ideas Found in Your Source

Your objective is both to acknowledge the source and to provide your reader with the fullest possible background. Let us assume that one of the ideas that you are writing about was firmly in your mind—the product of your own intellect—long before you started to work on your topic. Nevertheless, if you come across a version of that idea during your research, you should cite the source, *even though the idea was as much your own as the author's.* Of course, in your acknowledgment, you might state that this source is confirming *your* theories and indicate that you had thought of the point independently.

Documenting the Source of Your Own Ideas

Perhaps, while working on an essay, you develop a new idea of your own, stimulated by one of your readings. You should make a point of acknowledging the source of inspiration and, perhaps, describing how and why it affected you. (For example: "My idea for shared assignments is an extension of McKeachie's discussion of peer tutoring.") The reader should be made aware of your debt to your source as well as your independent effort.

PLAGIARISM: STEALING IDEAS

If you present another person's ideas as your own, you are plagiarizing *even if you use your own words*. To illustrate, the paragraph on the left, by Leo Gurko, is taken from a book, *Ernest Hemingway and the Pursuit of Heroism;* the paragraph on the right comes from a student essay on Hemingway. Gurko is listed in the student's bibliography and is cited as the source of several quotations elsewhere in the essay. But the student does not mention Gurko anywhere in *this* paragraph.

Source	*Student Essay*
The Hemingways put themselves on short rations, ate, drank, and entertained as little as possible, pounced eagerly on the small checks that arrived in the mail as payment for accepted stories, and were intensely conscious of being poor. The sensation was not altogether unpleasant. Their extreme youth, the excitement of living abroad, the sense of making a fresh start, even the unexpected joy of parenthood, gave their poverty a romantic flavor.	Despite all the economies that they had to make and all the pleasures that they had to do without, the Hemingways rather enjoyed the experience of being poor. They knew that this was a more romantic kind of life, unlike anything they'd known before, and the feeling that everything in Paris was fresh and new, even their new baby, made them sharply aware of the glamorous aspects of being poor.

The *language* of the student paragraph does not require quotation marks, but unless Gurko is acknowledged in a note, the student will be guilty of plagiarism. These impressions of the Hemingways, these insights into their motivation, would not have been possible without Gurko's biography—and Gurko deserves the credit for having done the research and for having formulated the interpretations. After reading extensively about Hemingway, the student may have absorbed these biographical details so thoroughly that he feels as if he had always known them. But the knowledge is still secondhand, and the source must be acknowledged.

PLAGIARISM: STEALING WORDS

When you quote a source, remember that the quoted material will require *two* kinds of documentation:

1. *The acknowledgment of the source of the information or ideas* (through a system of documentation that provides complete publication information about the source and possibly through the citation of the author's name in your sentence), and

2. *The acknowledgment of the source of the exact wording* (through quotation marks).

It is not enough to supply the author's name in parentheses (or in a footnote) and then mix up your own language and that of your sources. The author's name tells your reader nothing at all about who is responsible for the choice of words. Equally important, borrowing language carelessly, perhaps in an effort to use paraphrase, often garbles the author's meaning.

Here is an excerpt from a student essay about Henrik Ibsen, together with the relevant passage from its source:

Source

When writing [Ibsen] was sometimes under the influence of hallucinations, and was unable to distinguish between reality and the creatures of his imagination. While working on *A Doll's House* he was nervous and retiring and lived in a world alone, which gradually became peopled with his own imaginary characters. Once he suddenly remarked to his wife: "Now I have seen Nora. She came right up to me and put her hand on my shoulder." "How was she dressed?" asked his wife. "She had a simple blue cotton dress," he replied without hesitation. . . . So intimate had Ibsen become with Nora while at work on *A Doll's House* that when John Paulsen asked him why she was called Nora, Ibsen replied in a matter-of-fact tone: "She was really called Leonora, you know, but everyone called her Nora since she was the spoilt child of the family."

P. F. D. TENNANT,
Ibsen's Dramatic Technique

Student Essay

While Ibsen was still writing *A Doll's House*, his involvement with the characters led to his experiencing hallucinations that at times completely incapacitated his ability to distinguish between reality and the creations of his imagination. He was nervous, distant, and lived in a secluded world. Gradually this world became populated with his creations. One day he had the following exchange with his wife:
Ibsen: Now I have seen Nora. She came right up to me and put her hand on my shoulder.
Wife: How was she dressed?
Ibsen: (without hesitation) She had a simple blue dress.
Ibsen's involvement with his characters was so deep that when John Paulsen asked Ibsen why the heroine was named Nora, Ibsen replied in a very nonchalant tone of voice that originally she was called Leonora, but that everyone called her Nora, the way one would address the favorite child in the family (Tennant 26).

The documentation at the end of the student's passage may refer the reader to Tennant's book, but it fails to indicate the debt that the student owes to Tennant's *phrasing* and *vocabulary*. Phrases like "distinguish between reality and the creatures of his imagination" must be placed in quotation marks, and so should the exchange between Ibsen and his wife. Arranging these sentences as dialogue is not adequate acknowledgment.

In fact, the problem here is too complex to be solved by inserting a few quotation marks. The student, who probably intended a paraphrase, has substituted some of her own words for Tennant's; however, because she keeps the original sentence structure and many of the original words, she has only succeeded in obscuring some of her source's ideas.

At times, the phrasing distorts the original idea: the student's assertion that Ibsen's hallucinations "incapacitated his ability to distinguish between reality and the creations of his imagination" is very different from "[Ibsen] was sometimes under the influence of hallucinations and was unable to distinguish between reality and the creatures of his imagination." Many of the substituted words change Tennant's meaning: "distant" does not mean "retiring"; "a secluded world" is not "a world alone"; "nonchalant" is a very different quality from "matter-of-fact." Prose like this is neither quotation nor successful paraphrase; it is doubly bad, for it both *plagiarizes* the source and *misinterprets* it.

EXERCISE 40

Here are some facts about the explosion of the space shuttle *Challenger.* Consider which of these facts would require documentation in a research essay—and why.

1. On January 28, 1986, the space shuttle *Challenger* exploded shortly after takeoff from Cape Canaveral.
2. It was unusually cold in Florida on the day of the launch.
3. One of the *Challenger*'s booster rockets experienced a sudden and unforeseen drop in pressure 10 seconds before the explosion.
4. The explosion was later attributed to the failure of an O-ring seal.
5. On board the *Challenger* was a $100 million communications satellite.
6. Christa McAuliffe, a high school social studies teacher in Concord, New Hampshire, was a member of the crew.
7. McAuliffe's mission duties included conducting two classroom lessons taught from the shuttle.
8. After the explosion, classes at the high school were canceled.
9. Another crew member, Judith Resnick, had a Ph.D. in electrical engineering.
10. At the time of the explosion, President Ronald Reagan was preparing to meet with network TV news correspondents to brief them on the upcoming State of the Union address.
11. The State of the Union address was postponed for a week.

EXERCISE 41

Here are two excerpts from two books about the Industrial Revolution in England. Each excerpt is followed by a passage from a student essay that makes use of the ideas and the words of the source without any acknowledgment at all.

1. Compare the original with the plagiarized passage.
2. Insert the appropriate quotation marks.
3. Underline the paraphrases.

Source A

   Materially the new factory proletariat was likely to be somewhat better off [than domestic workers who did light manufacturing work in their own homes]. On the other hand it was unfree, under the strict control and the even stricter discipline imposed by the master or his supervisors, against whom they had virtually no legal recourse and only the very beginnings of public protection. They had to work his hours or shifts, to accept his punishments and the fines with which he imposed his rules or increased his profits. In isolated areas or industries they had to buy in his shop, as often as not receiving their wages in truck (thus allowing the unscrupulous employer to swell his profits yet further), or live in the houses the master provided. No doubt the village boy might find such a life no more dependent and less impoverished than his parents'; and in Continental industries with a strong paternalist tradition, the despotism of the master was at least partly balanced by the security, education, and welfare services which he sometimes provided. But for the free man entry into the factory as a mere "hand" was entry into something little better than slavery, and all but the most famished tended to avoid it, and even when in it to resist the draconic discipline much more persistently than the women and children, whom factory owners therefore tended to prefer.

   E. J. HOBSBAWM, *The Age of Revolution 1789–1848*

Student Essay

   The new factory proletariat was likely to be better off materially than those who did light manufacturing in their homes, but it was unfree. There was strict control and discipline imposed by the owner and his supervisors. They had no legal recourse and only the very start of public protection. The despotism of the master was at least a little bit set off by the security, education, and welfare services that he sometimes provided. But entry into the factory as a hand wasn't much better than slavery.

Source B

   Most of the work in the factories was monotonously dreary, but that was also true of much of the work done in the homes. The division of labor which caused a workman to perform over and over only one of the several processes needful for the production of any article was intensified by the mechanical inventions, but it had already gone so far in the homes that few workers experienced any longer the joy of creation. It was, indeed, more of a physical strain to tend a hand loom than a power loom. The employment of women and children in the factories finally evoked an outcry from the humanitarians, but the situation was inherited from the domestic system. In the homes, however, most of the children worked under the friendly eyes of their parents and not under the direction of an overseer. That to which the laborers themselves most objected was "the tyranny of the factory bell." For the long hours during which the power kept the machines in motion, the workers had to tend them without intermission, under the discipline established by the employer and enforced by his foreman. Many domestic laborers had to maintain equally long hours in order to earn a bare subsistence, but they were free to begin, stop and rest when they pleased. The operatives in the factories felt keenly a loss of personal independence.

W. E. LUNT, *History of England*

Student Essay

Factory work was monotonous and dreary, but that was also true of work at home. Humanitarians cried out against the employment of women and children, but that was inherited from the domestic system. What annoyed the laborers the most was the dictatorship of the factory bell. The workers had to stay at the machines without intermission, maintaining long hours to earn a bare subsistence. Those who worked in their homes were free to begin, stop, and rest whenever they felt like it. Factory workers keenly felt a loss of personal freedom.

EXERCISE 42

In 1991, the *New York Times* reported that H. Joachim Maitre, then Dean of the School of Communications at Boston University, had been accused of plagiarizing the content and language of an article written by Michael Medved, a film critic for the Public Broadcasting System, and published in the February issue of the journal *Imprimis*. The alleged plagiarism occurred in a commencement speech given in May of that year.

Here, side by side, as published in the *Times*, are parallel excerpts from Medved's article (on the left) and Maitre's speech. Examine them and determine whether, in your opinion, Maitre has plagiarized Medved's work.

Apparently some stern decree has gone out from the upper reaches of the Hollywood establishment that love between married people must never be portrayed on the screen. . . . The top grossing film of 1990 was "Ghost," one of a series of sex-after-death fantasies that the movie industry has churned out in recent years.	Apparently, some stern advice has come from the upper reaches of the Hollywood establishment that love between married people must never be portrayed on the screen. The top-grossing film of 1990 was "Ghost," one of the series of sex-after-death fantasies that the movie industry has churned out in recent years. In this

| In this crafty tear-jerker, the film makers seemed to make a point of the fact that the central couple, connected by a love so deep that it survives into the afterlife, have never taken the trouble to get married. | crafty tearjerker, the film makers seem to make a point of the fact that the central couple, connected by a love so deep that it survives into the afterlife, of never taking the trouble of getting married. |
| As part of the continuing struggle we must do more than protest the bad; we should also begin promoting the good. . . . Keep in mind that the entertainment industry is one area of endeavor in which a few gifted individuals can still make an enormous difference. The American people have shown that they are ready to respond when given the opportunity, as witness the utterly unexpected $100 million success of a wholesome, life-affirming project like "Driving Miss Daisy." | As part of the continuing struggle, we must do more than protest the bad, we must fight it actively. As we can do that. . . . Keep in mind that the entertainment industry is one industry, in one area of endeavor in which a few gifted individuals can still make an enormous difference. The American people have shown that they are ready to respond when given the opportunity, as witness the utterly successful film, bringing in $100 million recently, "Driving Miss Daisy." |

USING DOCUMENTATION

In addition to using quotation marks and citing the author's name in your text, you also need to provide your reader with more detailed information about your sources. This documentation is important for two reasons:

1. By showing where you found your information, you are providing *proof that you did your research.* Including the source's *publication history* and the *specific page* on which you found the information assures your reader that you have not made up fictitious sources and quotations. The systems of documentation that are described in this chapter and in Appendix B enable your reader to distinguish your ideas from those of your sources, to know who was responsible for what, by observing the parenthetical notes or numbered notes.

2. Documentation also enables your readers to *learn more about the subject of your essay.* Methods of documentation originally developed as a way for serious scholars to share their findings with their colleagues—while making it entirely clear who had done the original research. The reader of your research essay should be given the option of going back to the library and locating the materials that you used in writing about the topic.

Of course, the essay's *bibliography* can serve this purpose, but not even the most carefully annotated bibliography guides readers to the book and the precise page that will provide the information that they need. Documentation, then, provides a direct link between an interesting sentence in the paper and the source in the library that will satisfy your readers' interest.

Using Parenthetical Notes

The most widely accepted system of documentation is based on the insertion directly into your essay of the author's name and the page on which the information can be found, placed in parentheses. This style of documentation is called the Modern Language Association (MLA) style. It has replaced footnotes and endnotes as the most common form of documentation, and it will probably be the style you use in writing general research essays, especially those in the humanities. Documenting through parenthetical notes is much less cumbersome than preparing an additional page of endnotes or placing footnotes at the bottom of the page. MLA style also allows your reader to see the source's name while reading the essay, instead of having to turn to a separate page at the back. Readers who want to know more about a particular source than the author's name and the number of the page containing the information can turn to the "Works Cited" page, which provides all the necessary details of publication.

Another frequently used kind of parenthetical documentation is the one recommended by the American Psychological Association (APA) for research in the social and behavioral sciences. APA style is described on pp. 484–494 of Appendix B.

For those writing essays on a computer, many software packages (especially those, like Nota Bene, specializing in academic writing) provide documentation automatically, in a choice of styles—provided that basic information about each work cited has been entered into the computer.

MLA Format

Here is what an excerpt from a biographical essay about Ernest Hemingway would look like using MLA style. Notice that the parenthetical notes are meaningless unless the reader can refer to an accurate and complete bibliography placed at the end of the essay on a page titled "Works Cited."

> Hemingway's zest for life extended to women also. His wandering heart seemed only to be exceeded by an even more appreciative eye (Hemingway 102). Hadley was aware of her husband's flirtations and of his facility with women (Sokoloff 84). Yet, she had no idea that something was going on between Hemingway and Pauline Pfeiffer, a fashion editor for Vogue magazine (Baker 159).

She was also unaware that Hemingway delayed his return to Schruns from a business trip in New York, in February 1926, so that he might spend more time with this "new and strange girl" (Hemingway 210; also, Baker 165).

Works Cited

Baker, Carlos. Ernest Hemingway: A Life Story. New York: Scribner's, 1969.

Hemingway, Ernest. A Moveable Feast. New York: Scribner's, 1964.

Sokoloff, Alice Hunt. Hadley: The First Mrs. Hemingway. New York: Dodd, 1973.

Many of the basic rules for using MLA style are apparent in the previous example. Here are some points to observe.

1. **Format and Punctuation.**

   The placement of the parenthetical note within your sentence is governed by a set of very precise rules, established by conventional agreement. Like rules for quotation, these must be followed without any deviation.

   a. *The parenthetical note is intended to be a part of your sentence, which should not end until the source has been cited.* For this reason, terminal punctuation (period or question mark) should be placed *after* the parenthetical note.

   Incorrect

   Unlike most American writers of his day, Hemingway rarely came to New York; instead, he spent most of his time on his farm near Havana. (Ross 17).

   Correct

   Unlike most American writers of his day, Hemingway rarely came to New York; instead, he spent most of his time on his farm near Havana (Ross 17).

   b. *If the parenthetical note follows a quotation, the quotation should be closed before you open the parentheses.* Remember that the note is not part of the quotation and therefore has no reason to be inside the quotation.

   Incorrect

   Hemingway's farm consisted of "a domestic staff of nine, fifty-two cats, sixteen dogs, a couple of hundred pigeons, and three cows (Ross 17)."

Correct

Hemingway's farm consisted of "a domestic staff of nine, fifty-two cats, sixteen dogs, a couple of hundred pigeons, and three cows" (Ross 17).

c. *Any terminal punctuation that is part of the quotation* (like a question mark or an exclamation point) *remains inside the quotation marks.* Remember also to include a period at the end of the sentence, *after the parenthetical note.*

Incorrect

One critic reports that Hemingway said of The Old Man and the Sea, "Don't you think it is a strange damn story that it should affect all of us (me especially) the way it does" (Halliday 52)?

Correct

One critic reports that Hemingway said of The Old Man and the Sea, "Don't you think it is a strange damn story that it should affect all of us (me especially) the way it does?" (Halliday 52).

d. *When you insert the parenthetical note, leave one space before it and one space after it*—unless you are ending the sentence with terminal punctuation (period, question mark), in which case you leave no space between the closing parenthesis and the punctuation, and you leave the customary one space between the end of that sentence and the beginning of the next one.

Incorrect

Given Hemingway's intense awareness of literary tradition, style, and theory, it is strange that many critics and readers have found his work primitive(Cowley 47).

Correct

Given Hemingway's intense awareness of literary tradition, style, and theory, it is strange that many critics and readers have found his work primitive (Cowley 47).

2. **Placement.**

The parenthetical note comes at the end of the material being documented, whether that material is quoted, paraphrased, summarized, or briefly mentioned. By convention, your reader will assume that the *parenthetical note signals the end of the material from that source.* Anything that follows is either your own idea, independently developed, or taken from a new source that will be documented by the next parenthetical note later in the text.

One critic has remarked that it has been fashionable to deride Hemingway over the past few years (Cowley 50). However, though we may criticize him, as we can criticize most authors when we subject them to close scrutiny, we should never forget his brilliance in depicting characters having grace under the pressure of a sterile, valueless, painful world (Anderson 1036).

3. Frequency.

Each new point in your essay that requires documentation should have its own parenthetical note. Under no circumstances should you accumulate references to several different sources for several sentences and place them in a single note at the end of the paragraph. All the sources in the Hemingway paragraph cannot be covered by one parenthetical note at the end.

Incorrect

> The sources of Hemingway's fiction have been variously named. One critic has said he is driven by "personal demons." Another believes that he is occupied by a desire to truly portray reality, with all its ironies and symbols. Finally, still another has stated that Hemingway is interested only in presenting "fragments of truth" (Cowley 51; Halliday 71; Levin 85).

Correct

> The sources of Hemingway's fiction have been variously named. One critic has said he is driven by "personal demons" (Cowley 51). Another believes that he is occupied by a desire to truly portray reality, with all its ironies and symbols (Halliday 71). Finally, still another has stated that Hemingway is interested only in presenting "fragments of truth" (Levin 85).

4. Multiple Notes in a Single Sentence.

If you are using a large number of sources and documenting your essay very thoroughly, you may need to cite two or more sources at separate points in the same sentence.

> Even at this early stage of his career, Hemingway seemed to have developed a basic philosophy of writing. His ability to perceive situations clearly and to capture the exact essence of the subject (Lawrence 93–94; O'Faolain 113) might have stemmed from a disciplined belief that each sentence had to be "true" (Hemingway 12) and that a story had to be written "as straight as you can" (Hemingway 183).

The placement of notes tells you where the writer found which information. The reference to Lawrence and O'Faolain must be inserted in mid-sentence because they are responsible only for the information about Hemingway's capacity to focus on his subject and capture its essence; Lawrence and O'Faolain are not responsible for the quoted material at the end of the sentence. The inclusion of each of the next two parenthetical notes tells you that a reference to "true" sentences can be found on page 12 of the Hemingway book and a reference to "straight" writing can be found on page 183.

5. Multiple Sources for the Same Point.

If you have two sources to document the same point, you can demonstrate the completeness of your research by placing both in the same parenthetical note. The inclusion of Lawrence and O'Faolain in the same note—(Lawrence 93–94; O'Faolain 113)—tells you that much the same information can be found in both sources. Should you want to cite two sources but emphasize only one, you can indicate your preference by using "also."

> Hemingway's ability to perceive situations clearly and to capture the exact essence of the subject (Dos Passos 93–94; also O'Faolain 113) may be his greatest asset as a writer.

There is, of course, a limit to how many sources you can cram into a single pair of parentheses; common sense will tell you what is practical and what is distracting to the reader. Usually, one or two sources will have more complete or better documented information; those are the ones to cite. If you wish to discuss the quality of information in your various sources, then you can use an explanatory endnote to do so (see p. 415 on explanatory notes).

6. Referring to the Source in the Text.

In the previous examples, the writer of the Hemingway essay has chosen not to cite any sources in the text itself. That is why each parenthetical note contains a name as well as a page number. *If, however, you do refer to your source as part of your own presentation of the material, then there is no need to use the name twice; simply insert the page number in the parenthetical note.*

> During the time in Paris, Hemingway became friends with the poet Ezra Pound, who told Hemingway he would teach him how to write if the younger novelist would teach him to box. Noel Stock reports what Wyndham Lewis saw when he walked in on one of their boxing sessions:
>
> > A splendidly built young man [Hemingway] stript to the waist, and with a torso of dazzling white, was standing not far from me. He was tall, handsome, and serene, and was repelling with his

> boxing gloves—I thought without undue exertion—a hectic as-
> sault of Ezra's. (88)

Because Stock's name is cited in the text, it need not be placed in parentheses; the page number is enough. Stock's book would, of course, be
included in the list of "Works Cited." Also notice that the parenthetical
note works just as well at the end of a lengthy, *indented* quotation; but
that, because the quotation is indented, and there are no quotation marks
to signify its end, it terminates with a period placed *before* the parenthetical note, which follows separated by *two* spaces.

7. Including the Source's Title.

*Occasionally, your bibliography will include more than one source by the same
author or sources by different authors with the same last name. To avoid confusion and to specify your exact source, use an abbreviated title inside the parenthetical note.* Had the author of the Hemingway essay included more than
one work by Carlos Baker in the bibliography, the parenthetical note
would look like this:

> Yet, she had no idea that something was going on between Hemingway
>
> and Pauline Pfeiffer, a fashion editor for Vogue magazine (Baker, Life Story
>
> 159).

If you are working from a newspaper or periodical article that does not
cite an author, use an abbreviation of the article's title in your parathet-
ical note (unless you have referred to the title in your text, in which case
you need only include the page number in your note).

8. Referring to a Whole Work.

*Occasionally, you may refer to the overall theme of an entire work, citing the ti-
tle and the author, but no specific quotation, idea, or page. If you refer to a work
as a whole, no page numbers in parentheses are required.*

> Hemingway's The Sun Also Rises focuses on the sterility and despair per-
>
> vading modern culture.

9. Referring to a Source by More Than One Author.

*Occasionally, you will need to refer to a book that is by two, or three, or even
more authors. (If you have mentioned the authors' names in your text, just include a page reference in parentheses.) If you refer to a text by more than three
authors and you have not mentioned them in your text, it is acceptable (and saves
space) to cite the name of the first author followed by et al., unitalicized, and
then the page number, all within parentheses. Et al. is Latin for "and others."*

> *Two Authors*
>
> We may finally say of the writer Hemingway that he was able to depict the
>
> turbulent, often contradictory, emotions of modern man in a style as

starkly realistic as that of the sixteenth century painter Caravaggio, who,
art historians tell us, seems to say, "Here is actuality . . . without deception or pretence. . . . " (Janson and Cauman 221).

More than Three Authors

Hemingway did what no other writer of his time did: he captured the
plight and total disenchantment of his age in vivid intensity (Spiller et al.
1300).

10. Referring to One of Several Volumes.

You may use a single volume from a set of several volumes. If so, refer to the
specific volume by using an arabic numeral followed by a colon. In your "Works
Cited," be sure to list all the volumes. (See Appendix B for proper bibliographic entry of a set of volumes.)

Perhaps Hemingway's work can be best summed up by Frederick Coppleston's comment concerning Camus: both writers prove that human
greatness is not shown in escaping the absurdity of modern existence,
but "in living in the consciousness of the absurd and yet revolting against
it by . . . committing . . . [one]self and living in the fullest manner possible" (3:393).

11. Referring to a Work of Literature.

If you refer to specific passages from a well-known play, poem, or novel, then
you need not cite the author; the text's name is sufficient recognition. Use arabic numerals separated by periods for divisions such as act, scene, and
line in plays and for divisions like books and lines in poems. For novels,
cite the page number followed by a semicolon, "ch.," and the chapter
number.

Play

Hemingway wished to show reality as truly as he could, even if he found
man, as did King Lear, nothing but "a poor, bare, fork'd animal . . . "
(3.4.106–7).

Poem

Throughout his career as a writer, Hemingway struggled to make sense of
the human condition so powerfully and metaphorically presented in The
Waste Land: "Son of man/ . . . you know only/ A heap of broken images"
(2.21–23).

Novel

In The Sun Also Rises, toughness is an essential for living in the modern
age, but even toughness has its limits in the novel; as Jake says, "It is

awfully easy to be hard-boiled about everything in the daytime, but at
night it is another thing" (34; ch. iv).

12. **Referring to a Quotation from an Indirect Source.**

   *When you quote a writer's words that you have found in a work written by some-
   one else, you begin the citation with the abbreviation "qtd. in."* This form shows
   the reader that you are quoting from a second-hand source, not the original.

   In "Big Two-Hearted River," Hemingway metaphorically captures the
   pervasive atmosphere of his time in the tersest of descriptions: "There
   is no town, nothing . . . but the burned over country" (qtd. in Anderson
   1027).

13. **Referring to Sources That Do Not Appear in Print.**

   Sometimes you may cite information from nonprint sources such as interviews, films, or radio or television programs. If you do, be sure that
   the text mentions (for an interview) the name of the interviewer and/or
   the person being interviewed or (for a film) the name of the producer,
   director, and/or scriptwriter; these names should also appear in your
   list of "Works Cited." (For proper bibliographic form of nonprint sources,
   see Appendix B.)

   Interview

   In an unpublished interview conducted by the writer of this essay, the
   poet Phil Arnold said that a lean style like Hemingway's may be just as
   artificial as an elaborate one.

Preparing to Document Your Essay

- Whether you take notes or use photocopies of your sources, remember always to write down the information that you will need for
  your notes and bibliography.

- Look at the front of each book or periodical and jot down the publication information.

- As you work on the first draft of your essay, include the author's
  name and the relevant page number in parentheses after every reference to one of your sources, to serve as a guide when you document your essay. Even in this early version, your essay will resemble
  the finished product, with MLA documentation.

- Finally, when the essay is ready for final typing, read through it
  again, just to make sure that each reference to a source is covered
  by a parenthetical note.

MLA Style: A Sample Page

Reference to quotation, author mentioned in text	Michelle A. Cawley defines passive euthanasia as "cooperating with the patient's dying" (959). Failing to resuscitate a patient who has suffered a massive heart attack is one example of passive euthanasia. Another is deciding not to feed a terminally ill patient who is unable to feed himself. In contrast, removing the feeding tube from a patient who is being fed that way would be considered active euthanasia. Similar to passive euthanasia is "assisted suicide," in which a doctor or other person provides a terminally ill person with the means—pills, for example—and the medical knowledge necessary to commit suicide (Orentlicher 1844).
Reference to an entire work, no page reference required	Derek Humphrey's 1991 book *Final Exit*, which describes ways to painlessly commit suicide, and the organization Compassion in Dying, which helps terminally ill patients end their lives, are both recent examples of "assisted suicide" (Belkin 50; also Elliott 27).
Reference to two sources in which same information can be found, emphasis on "Belkin"	The professional people who care for the sick and dying think there is a great difference between active and passive euthanasia, or "assisted suicide." A recent panel of distinguished physicians declared themselves in favor, by a margin of 10 to 2, of doctor-assisted suicide for hopelessly
Standard reference, author mentioned in note	ill patients who request it (Orentlicher 1844). In a survey taken in 1975, 73% of the nurses questioned were in favor of withholding treatment that would prolong the lives of dying patients who don't want their lives sustained in that way—in other words, passive euthanasia. But only 17%
Reference to an article with no author listed	were in favor of using active means to end lives of dying patients who request euthanasia ("Taking Life" 40).

Constructing a "Works Cited" Page

None of the parenthetical notes explained above would make complete sense without a "Works Cited" page. The technical forms for bibliographic entries according to MLA style are described in Appendix B (pp. 476–484). Below is a sample "Works Cited" page for all of the parenthetical notes about Hemingway found earlier in this chapter.

Works Cited

Anderson, Charles W. Introduction. "Ernest Hemingway." American Literary
    Masters. Ed. Charles W. Anderson. New York: Holt, 1965. 1023–114.

Arnold, Philip. Telephone interview. 3 Nov. 1993.

Baker, Carlos. Ernest Hemingway: A Life Story. New York: Scribner's, 1969.

Coppleston, Frederick. Maine de Biran to Sartre. New York: Doubleday, 1974.
    Vol. 9 of A History of Philosophy. 9 vols. 1946–1974.

Cowley, Malcolm. "Nightmare and Ritual in Hemingway." Hemingway: Twentieth
    Century Perspectives. Ed. Robert P. Weeks. Englewood Cliffs: Prentice,
    1962. 40–51.

Halliday, E. M. "Hemingway's Ambiguity: Symbolism and Irony." Hemingway:
    Twentieth Century Perspectives. Ed. Robert P. Weeks. Englewood Cliffs:
    Prentice, 1962, 52–71.

Hemingway, Ernest. A Moveable Feast. New York: Scribner's, 1964.

------. The Sun Also Rises. New York: Scribner's, 1964.

Janson, H. W., and Samuel Cauman. A Basic History of Art. New York: Abrams,
    1971.

Lawrence, D. H. "In Our Time: A Review." Hemingway: Twentieth Century
    Perspectives. Ed. Robert P. Weeks. Englewood Cliffs: Prentice, 1962. 93–94.

Levin, Harry. "Observations on the Style of Ernest Hemingway." Hemingway:
    Twentieth Century Perspectives. Ed. Robert P. Weeks. Englewood Cliffs:
    Prentice, 1962. 72–85.

Ross, Lilian. "How Do You Like It Now, Gentlemen?" Hemingway: Twentieth Century
    Perspectives. Ed. Robert P. Weeks. Englewood Cliffs: Prentice, 1962. 17–39.

Shakespeare, William. King Lear. Ed. Frank Kermode. The Riverside Shakespeare.
    Boston: Houghton, 1974. 1249–305.

Spiller, Robert E., et al. Literary History of the United States. 3rd ed., rev.
    London: Macmillan, 1963.

Stock, Noel. The Life of Ezra Pound. New York: Pantheon, 1970.

Signaling the Transitions between Sources

The student who wrote the research essay on Ernest Hemingway chose to write about her subject by citing sources in her parenthetical notes and leaving them out of her own sentences. However, since many students go to considerable trouble to find and select the right materials to support their ideas, they tend to paraphrase and to use their sources' names as a way of keeping them before the reader's eye. Of course, the sources' names should appear only when necessary so that the reader is not distracted by their constant appearance.

In general, the citation of the author's name signals to your reader that you are starting to use **new** *source material; the parenthetical note signals the* **point of termination** *for that source.*

If the name is not cited at the beginning, readers may not be aware that a new source has been introduced until they reach the parenthetical note. Here is a brief passage from an essay that illustrates this kind of confusion:

> The year 1946 marked the beginning of the postwar era. This meant the de-mobilization of the military, creating a higher unemployment rate because of the large number of returning soldiers. This also meant a slowdown in industry, so that layoffs also added to the rising rate of unemployment. As Cabell Phillips put it: "Motivation [for the Employment Act of 1946] came naturally from the searing experience of the Great Depression, and fresh impetus was provided by the dread prospect of a massive new wave of unemployment following demobiliza-tion" (292–3).

Here, the placement of the citation—"As Cabell Phillips put it"—creates a problem. The way in which the name is introduced into the paragraph firmly suggests that Cabell Phillips is responsible for the quotation and only the quo-tation. (The fact that the quotation is nothing more than a repetition of the first three sentences, and therefore need not have been included in the essay, may also have occurred to you.) Anyone reading the essay will assume that the ref-erence to Phillips covers only the material that starts with the name and ends with the page number. The coverage is not expected to go back any farther than the beginning of the sentence. Thus, in this passage, *the first three sentences are not documented*. Although the writer probably took all the information from Phillips, his book is not being acknowledged as the source. "Probably" is not an adequate substitute for clear documentation. Phillips's name should be cited somewhere at the beginning of the paragraph (the second sentence would be a good place); alternatively, an "umbrella" note could be used (see pp. 419–420).

You may need to insert a parenthetical note in midsentence if that single sen-tence contains references to *two* different sources. For example, you might want to place a note in midsentence to indicate exactly where the source's opinion leaves off and your own begins:

> These examples of hiring athletes to play in college games, cited by Joseph Durso (6), suggest that recruiting tactics in 1903 were not as subtle as they are today.

If the page number were put at the end of the sentence, the reader would as-sume that Durso was responsible for the comparison between 1903 and the present; but he is not. Only the examples must be documented, not the con-clusion drawn from these examples. In this case, the *absence* of a parenthetical note at the end of the sentence signals to the reader that this conclusion is the writer's own.

Here is a passage in which *the techniques of documentation have been used to their fullest extent* and *the transitions between sources are clearly indicated.* This example is taken from Jessie Bernard's "The Paradox of the Happy Marriage," an examination of the woman's role in American marriage. At this point, Bernard has just established that more wives than husbands acknowledge that their marriages are unhappy:

> These findings on the wife's marriage are especially poignant because marriage in our society is more important for women's happiness than for men's. "For almost all measures, the relation between marriage, happiness and overall well-being was stronger for women than for men," one study reports (Bradburn 150). In fact, the strength of the relationship between marital and overall happiness was so strong for women that the author wondered if "most women are equating their marital happiness with their overall happiness" (Bradburn 159). Another study based on a more intensive examination of the data on marriage from the same sample notes that "on each of the marriage adjustment measures . . . the association with overall happiness is considerably stronger for women than it is for men" (Orden and Bradburn 731). Karen Renne also found the same strong relationship between feelings of general well-being and marital happiness: those who were happy tended not to report marital dissatisfaction; those who were not, did. "In all probability the respondent's view of his marriage influences his general feeling of well-being or morale" (64); this relationship was stronger among wives than among husbands (Renne 63).[2] A strong association between reports of general happiness and reports of marital happiness was also found a generation ago (Watson).
>
> [2]Among white couples, 71 percent of the wives and 52 percent of the husbands who were "not too happy" expressed marital dissatisfaction; 22 percent of the wives and 18 percent of the husbands who were "pretty happy" expressed marital dissatisfaction; and 4 percent of the wives and 2 percent of the husbands who were "very happy" expressed marital dissatisfaction.

This paragraph contains *six parenthetical notes* to document the contents of *seven sentences.* Four different works are cited, and, where the same work is cited twice consecutively (Bradburn and Renne), the reference is to a different page. The material taken from page 64 of Renne covers a sentence and a half, from the name "Karen Renne" to the parenthetical note; the remainder of the sentence comes from page 63. Finally, there is no page reference in the note citing Watson, since Bernard is referring the reader to the entire article, not a single part of it. Notice also that:

- Bernard quotes frequently, but she never places quotations from two different sources together in the same sentence.
- She is careful to use her own voice to provide continuity between the quotations.
- The reader is never in doubt as to the source of information.

Although Bernard does not always cite the name of the author, we are immediately told in each case that there is a source—"one study reports"; "the author wondered"; "another study based on a more intensive examination of the data on marriage from the same sample"; "Karen Renne also found." These phrases not only acknowledge the source but also provide vital transitions between these loosely related points.

EXERCISE 43

The following paragraph, taken from a research essay about the Industrial Revolution, is based on the source materials in Exercise 41 on p. 399. Compare the paragraph with its sources, and then decide where the parenthetical notes should be placed. Insert the notes, making sure that you distinguish the source material from the writer's own contributions to the paragraph.

The Industrial Revolution caused a major change in the working environment of most people in England. Historians have described the painful transition from working in the home and on the farm to working in the factory. E. J. Hobsbawm points out that most factory employees were at the mercy of the master and his foremen, who controlled their working hours with "draconic discipline." According to W. E. Lunt, those who previously did spinning and weaving in their homes had worked as long and as hard as the workers in the new textile factories, but they had been able to maintain more control over when and how they performed their tasks. It was the male workers who especially resented their loss of freedom and tended to be more resistant to discipline, and so manufacturers found it desirable to hire women and children, who were more passive and obedient. The long hours and bleak and unhealthy environment of the factories must have been particularly hard on the women and children who worked in them. Indeed, Lunt observes that it was their plight that "finally evoked an outcry from the humanitarians." Ultimately, then, an improvement in working conditions came about because of respect for the frailty of women and children, not because of respect for the rights of all workers.

Using Explanatory Notes

You will have noticed that, in the excerpt from Bernard on p. 414, following the second parenthetical reference to Renne, there is a number. This calls the reader's attention to a separate note appearing at the bottom of the paragraph. (In the actual essay, the note would appear either at the bottom of the page or, together with other notes, on a separate sheet at the end of the essay.) Jessie Bernard is using an *explanatory note* as a way of including information that does not quite fit into the text of her essay.

If your research has been thorough, you may find yourself with more material than you know what to do with. It can be tempting to use up every single point on your note cards and cram all the available information into your essay. But if you include too many extraneous points, your reader will find it hard to concentrate on the real topic of your paragraph. To illustrate this point, here are two paragraphs dealing with the domestic life of Charles Dickens: one is bulging; the other is streamlined. The first contains an analysis of Dickens's relationship with his sister-in-law; in the second, he decides to take a holiday in France.

Paragraph 1

Another good friend to Charles Dickens was his sister-in-law. Georgina had lived with the family ever since they had returned from an American tour in June 1842. She had grown attached to the children while the couple was away (Pope-Hennessy 179–80). She now functioned as an occasional secretary to Dickens, specifically when he was writing A Child's History of England, which Pope-Hennessy terms a "rather deplorable production." Dickens treated the history of his country in a very unorthodox manner (311). Dickens must have felt close to Georgina since he chose to dictate the History to her; with all his other work, Dickens always worked alone, writing and correcting it by himself (Butt and Tillotson 20–21). Perhaps a different woman would have questioned the relationship of her younger sister to her husband; yet Kate Dickens accepted this friendship for what it was. Pope-Hennessy describes the way in which Georgina used to take over the running of the household whenever Kate was indisposed. Kate was regularly too pregnant to go anywhere. She had ten children and four miscarriages in a period of fifteen years (391). Kate probably found another woman to be quite a help around the house. Pope-Hennessy suggests that Kate and her sister shared Charles Dickens between them (287).

Paragraph 2

In 1853, three of Dickens's closest friends had died (Forster 124),[5] and the writer himself, having become even more popular and busy since the publication of David Copperfield (Maurois 70), began to complain of "hypochondriacal whisperings" and also of "too many invitations to too many parties" (Forster 125). In May of that year, a kidney ailment that had plagued Dickens since his youth grew worse (Dickens, Letters 350), and, against the advice of his wife, he decided to take a holiday in Boulogne (Johnson 757).[6]

[5]The friends were Mr. Watson, Count d'Orsay, and Mrs. Macready.

[6]Tillotson, Dickens's doctor, who had been in Boulogne the previous October, was the one to encourage him to go there.

The first paragraph obviously contains too much information, most of which is unrelated to this topic. Pope-Hennessy's opinion of the history of England and the history of Kate's pregnancies are topics that may be worth discussing, but not in this paragraph. This extraneous material could be shifted to other paragraphs of the essay, placed in explanatory notes, or simply omitted. Its placement depends on the shape and structure of the entire essay.

The second, much shorter paragraph suggests that related but less important detail can usefully be put into explanatory notes where, if wanted, it is always available. Readers of the second paragraph are being given a choice: they can absorb the essential information from the paragraph alone, or they can examine the topic in greater depth by referring also to the explanatory notes.

Explanatory notes should be reserved for information that, in your view, is useful and to some degree relevant to the topic; if it is uninteresting and way off the point, simply omit it. If you indulge too often in explanatory notes, your notes may be longer than your essay. Also remember to find out whether including explanatory notes is acceptable to your instructor.

EXERCISE 44

Read each of the following paragraphs, paying special attention to unity and coherence. Draw a line through any material that you find entirely unrelated to the topic. Any information that seems loosely related to the paragraph's focus should be placed in explanatory notes.

Paragraph 1

Since Dickens tried to pack so much activity into each day of his holiday, one wonders when he had time for his nine children—Charles, born in 1837; Kate, 1839; Francis, 1844; Sydney, 1847; Mary, 1838; Walter, 1841; Alfred, 1845; Henry, 1849; and Edward, 1852 (Johnson Genealogical Chart 5). Since July 3, the children had been with their parents, and on that day, their father wrote to a friend in London that the children had arrived "all manner of toad-like colors" from their trip across the channel (Johnson 759). In this description and in other references to them in letters to his wife, we can see evidence of Dickens's feeling for his children: very often he refers to them as "the darlings," sends them his love (Dexter 159–60), and refers to them by nicknames that perhaps only another father might appreciate: "Keeryleemoo" (either Walter or Francis); "the jolly post boy" (Henry); "Lucifer Box" (Kate); and "Plornishghenter" (Edward) (Dexter 167; Johnson 751; Dexter 175). Many of the boys had been named for great literary men of the time, which suggests their father's hopes for their future: Edward Bulwer-Lytton, Henry Fielding, Sydney Smith, and Alfred Tennyson (Pope-Hennessy 373).

Paragraph 2

A day after the major league strike of June 1981, baseball was not as much concerned about hits and runs as about concepts that are more relevant to labor unions. According to Pete Axthelm, "deadlocked negotiations and empty ball parks and a hopelessly disputed clause in the collective bargaining agreement between players and management began to dominate headlines" (57). Axthelm paints a good picture of how baseball was before the strike. The head-to-head confrontation between Rose and Ryan is what makes baseball so special. This was the final stage of a long and controversial struggle between the owners and players that dated back to the beginning of baseball. The strike was caused by a disagreement between players and owners on how to compensate teams that lose free agents (Axthelm 57). In 1975, pitchers Dave McNally and Andy Messersmith had challenged baseball's reserve clause and declared themselves free agents. Before their action, all players were bound to the teams that they first signed with until they were either traded or retired from baseball (Phillips 55). In 1971, Curt Flood tried to do the same thing as McNally and Messersmith, but he failed to succeed. These two pitchers triumphed over a reserve clause that had stood for 92 years. The reserve clause meant that once a player completed his contract he was free to offer his services to the highest bidder. This gave the owners a chance to go out and spend their money on the best players available with hopes that they could win a World Series (Falls 17). Falls, whose articles appear in the Detroit Free Press, disapproves of buying world championships by buying players. The owners began plunking down tremendous amounts of money to secure ballplayers who had become free agents.

Avoiding Excessive Notes

Complex research was needed to gather the numerous details found in the biographical essays about Ernest Hemingway and Charles Dickens, and the writers of these essays use numerous parenthetical notes to document their sources. Here is a brief example:

Dickens's regular work habits involved writing at his desk from about nine in the morning to two in the afternoon (Butt and Tillotson 19; Pope-Hennessy 248), which left a good deal of time for other activities. Some of his leisure each day was regularly spent in letter-writing, some in walking and riding in the open air (Pope-Hennessy 305, quoting Nathaniel Sharswell). Besides this regular routine, on some days he would devote time to reading manuscripts which Wills, his sub-editor on <u>Household Words</u>, would send to him for revision and comment (Forster 65; Johnson 702).

In this passage, three parenthetical notes are needed for three sentences because a different biographer is the source for each piece of information. To combine all the sources in a single note would confuse, rather than simplify, the acknowledgments. In addition, the writer of this essay is not only making it clear where the information came from, but is also providing the reader with a *choice of references*. The writer has come across the same information in more than one biography, has indicated the duplication of material in her notes, and has decided to demonstrate the thoroughness of her research by citing more than one reference. Since the sources are given equal status in the notes (by being placed in alphabetical order and separated by a semicolon), the reader can assume that they are equally reliable. Had the writer thought that one was more thorough or more convincing than another, she would either have omitted the secondary one or indicated its status by placing it after "also" (Johnson 702; also, Forster 65).

But an abundance of parenthetical notes does not always indicate sound research. As the following example demonstrates, excessive documentation only creates clutter.

> In contrast to the Dickenses' house in London, this setting was idyllic: the house stood in the center of a large garden complete with woods, waterfall, roses (Forster 145), and "no end of flowers" (Forster 146). For a fee, the Dickenses fed on the produce of the estate and obtained their milk fresh from the landlord's cow (Forster 146). What an asset to one's peace of mind to have such a cooperative landlord as they had (Pope-Hennessy 310; Johnson 758; Forster 147) in the portly, jolly Monsieur Beaucourt (Forster 147)!

Clearly, this entire passage is taken from three pages in Forster's biography of Dickens, and a single note could document the entire paragraph. What information is contained in the sentence leading up to the triple parenthetical note that justifies citing three sources? And what does the last note document? Is it only Forster who is aware that Monsieur Beaucourt is portly and jolly? To avoid tiring and irritating his readers, the writer here would have been well advised to ignore the supporting evidence in Pope-Hennessy and Johnson, and use a single reference to Forster. The writer was undoubtedly proud of his extensive research, but he seems more eager to show off his hours in the library than to provide a readable text for his audience.

use sparingly

Using Umbrella Notes

what it is?
write out example,
use once or twice

As in the previous example, sometimes the logical sequence of your ideas or information requires you to cite the same source for several sentences or even for several paragraphs at a stretch. Instead of repeating "Forster 146" again and again, you can use a single note to cover the entire sequence. These notes are sometimes called *umbrella notes,* because they cover a sequence of sentences as an umbrella might cover more than one person. Umbrella notes are generally used in essays where the sources' names are not often cited in the text, and so the reader cannot easily figure out the coverage by assuming that the name and the parenthetical note mark the beginning and ending points. An umbrella simply means that you are leaving the reader in no doubt as to how much material the note is covering.

An umbrella note consists of an explanation of how much material is being covered by a source. Such a note is too long to be put in parentheses within the text and generally takes the form of *an explanatory note placed outside the body of your essay.* Here is an example:

> [2]The information in this and the previous paragraph dealing with Dickens's relationship with Wilkie Collins is entirely derived from Hutton, Dickens-Collins Letters 41-49.

Inside your essay, the superscript number 2 referring the reader to this note would follow right after the *last* sentence that uses material from Hutton to discuss Dickens and Wilkie Collins.

Of course, umbrella notes work only when you are using a single source for a reasonably long stretch. If you use two sources, you have to distinguish between them in parenthetical notes, and the whole point of the umbrella—to cut down on the number of notes—is lost.

Umbrella notes must also be used with caution when you are quoting. Because the umbrella provides the reference for a long stretch of material, the citation usually includes several pages; but how will the reader know on which page the quotation appears? Sometimes you can add this information to the note itself:

> [2]The information in this and the previous paragraph is entirely derived from Hutton, Dickens-Collins Letters 41-49. The two quotations from Dickens's letters are from pages 44 and 47, respectively.

However, if you use too many umbrella notes, or if you expect a single note to guide your reader through the intricacies of a long paragraph, you will have abused the device. Your essay will have turned into a series of summaries, with each group of paragraphs describing a single source. That is not what a research essay is supposed to be.

EXERCISE 45

Improve the documentation of the following paragraphs by eliminating unnecessary notes, placing the remaining notes in the proper places, and introducing umbrella notes if they seem appropriate. If necessary, eliminate repetition and rearrange the sequence of information in the text.

Paragraph 1

Many students are highly uncertain about their future careers. Sometimes, they change their career goals many times while they are undergraduates. Some who enter college with a career already chosen later discover that they are really interested in new and different professions (Van Doren 119). Even students who have graduated from college or graduate school and have entered their chosen profession may find themselves doing completely different work 25 years later (Van Doren 119). Mark Van Doren observes that "most undergraduate students cannot predict . . . what careers they will follow, what turns those careers will take, or what specialized preparation they will need for their later opportunities" (Van Doren 121). For this reason, the best security for the future lies in a broad liberal arts education, which is the best way for young students to prepare for the professions that await them (Van Doren 119–121).

Paragraph 2

Japanese students receive a very thorough education because they are so well disciplined. For one thing, students in Japan spend more time in school than Americans do. "Japanese adolescents are in school sixty days more each year than are their American counterparts" (Rohlen 274). Even their weekends are cut short because they have to go to school on Friday nights (Rohlen 274). Students in the United States are usually partying on a Friday night, and the thought of going to school instead would seem hilarious to them. The sixty days spent in school by Japanese students are used as holidays and vacations by American students. What is so amazing about the students in Japan is that, although they spend a tremendous amount of time in school throughout the year, they have an average attendance rate of no less than 99 percent in the elementary and lower secondary schools (Cogan 464). They also spend a great deal of time studying, an average of two hours a night and three hours on Sunday, in contrast to the American average of less than one hour a night (Rohlen 276). Even the top five percent of our students do less homework than the average Japanese (Rohlen 277)! Clearly, in Japan, studying and going to school become "the unequivocal central pivot of a student's existence" (Rohlen 161).

THE FINAL BIBLIOGRAPHY

While the bibliography is always an essential part of the research essay, it becomes especially important when you use MLA documentation, since *it is the only place where your reader can find publication information about your sources.*

Which works you include in your final bibliography may depend on the wording and intention of your assignment. There is an important difference between a list of works that you have *consulted* or *examined* and a list of works that you have *cited* or actually *used in writing your essay*. Many instructors restrict the bibliography to "Works Cited," but you may be asked to submit a list of "Works Consulted." Remember that one purpose of a "Works Consulted" bibliography is to help your readers to find appropriate background information, not to overwhelm them with the magnitude of your efforts. Don't present a collection of thirty-five titles if you actually cite only five sources in your essay.

> *An appropriate final bibliography of "Works Consulted" for an undergraduate essay consists of all the sources that you examined (in other words, actually held in your hand and looked at) that proved to have a clear bearing on your topic, whether or not you actually used them in your essay.*

If you consulted a book in the hope that it contained some relevant information, and if it provided nothing useful, should you include it in your final bibliography? You might do so to prevent your readers from repeating your unnecessary research and attempting to consult works with misleading titles in the belief that they might be useful, but only if your bibliography is *annotated* and the book's lack of usefulness can be pointed out. Finally, if you have been unable to locate a source and have thus never examined it yourself, you may not ordinarily include it in your final bibliography, however tempting the title may be.

THE ANNOTATED BIBLIOGRAPHY

Annotating your bibliography (which was described in Chapter 5, pp. 302–304) is an excellent way to demonstrate the quality of your research. But, to be of use, your brief annotations must be informative. The following phrases do not tell the reader very much: "an interesting piece"; "a good article"; "well-done";

Guidelines for Bibliographical Entries

(Additional models can be found in Appendix B, p. 476)

1. The bibliography is always listed on a *separate sheet* at the *end* of your research essay. The title should be centered, one-half inch from the top of the page.

2. Each entry is *double-spaced*, with double spacing between entries.

3. Each bibliographical entry starts with *the author's last name at the margin;* the second line of the entry (if there is one) is indented *five spaces*. This format enables the reader's eye to move quickly down the list of names at the left-hand margin.

4. The bibliography is in *alphabetical order,* according to the last name of the author.

   ▪ If there are two authors, only the first has the last name placed first: "Woodward, Robert, and Carl Bernstein."

   ▪ If an author has more than one work included on your list, do not repeat the name each time: alphabetize or arrange chronologically by publication date the works by that author; place the name at the margin preceding the first work; for the remaining titles, replace the name with three hyphens, followed by a period and one space.

   Freud, Sigmund. Civilization and Its Discontents. London: Hogarth, 1930.

   ---. Moses and Monotheism. New York: Knopf, 1939.

   ▪ A work that has no author should be alphabetized within the bibliography according to the first letter of the title (excluding "The"); the title is placed at the margin as the author's name would be.

5. A bibliographical entry for a book is read as a list of three items—author, title (underlined), and publication information—with *periods between each piece of information.* Each period is followed by *one* space. All the information should always be presented in exactly the same order that you see in the model bibliography on p. 424. Place of publication comes first; a colon separates place and name of publisher; a comma separates publisher and date.

6. A bibliographical entry for a *periodical* starts with the author's name and the article title (in quotation marks), each followed by a period and one space. Then comes the name of the periodical, followed by one space (and no punctuation at all). What comes next depends on the kind of periodical you are citing.

   ▪ For *quarterly and monthly journals,* include the volume number, followed by a space, and then the year in parentheses, followed by a colon.

   ▪ For *weekly or biweekly journals,* include only the full date—day, month, and year—followed by a colon.

   All periodical entries end with the inclusive pages of the article, first page to last, followed by a period.

   Tobias, Sheila, and Carol Weissbrod. "Anxiety and Mathematics: An Update." Harvard Educational Review 50 (1980): 61-67.

   Winkler, Karen J. "Issues of Justice and Individual's Rights Spur Revolution in Political Philosophy." Chronicle of Higher Education 16 April 1986: 6-8.

7. Each entry of the bibliography ends with a period.

another source of well-documented information." What is well done? Why it interesting? What is good about it? How much and what kind of informa-..on does it contain? A good annotated bibliography will answer some of these questions.

Examine the following bibliography carefully, noting the way it presents the basic facts about the author, title, and publication, as well as some *evaluative information*. If the annotations were omitted, these entries would still be perfectly correct, for they conform to the standard rules for bibliographical format. Without the annotation, one would simply have to change the heading to "Works Consulted" or "Works Cited."

HEMINGWAY: AN ANNOTATED BIBLIOGRAPHY

Baker, Carlos. Hemingway: A Life Story. New York: Scribner's, 1969. 563 pages of biography, with 100 pages of footnotes. Everything seems to be here, presented in great detail.

Donaldson, Scott. Hemingway: By Force of Will. New York: Viking, 1977. The material isn't organized chronologically; instead, the chapters are thematic, with titles like "Money," "Sex," and "War." Episodes from Hemingway's life are presented within each chapter. The introduction calls this "a mosaic of [Hemingway's] mind and personality."

Griffin, Peter. Less Than a Treason: Hemingway in Paris. New York: Oxford UP, 1990. Part of a multivolume biography. Covers Hemingway's life from 1921–1927, exclusively. Griffin says in the preface that his goal is not to "analyze this well examined life" but "to recreate it." Not surprisingly, it reads like a novel, with an omniscient narrator with access to Hemingway's emotions.

Gurko, Leo. Ernest Hemingway and the Pursuit of Heroism. New York: Crowell, 1968. This book is part of a series called "Twentieth-Century American Writers": a brief introduction to the man and his work. After fifty pages of straight biography, Gurko discusses Hemingway's writing, novel by novel. There's an index and a short bibliography, but no notes. The biographical part is clear and easy to read, but it sounds too much like summary.

Hemingway, Ernest. A Moveable Feast. New York: Scribner's, 1964. This is Hemingway's own version of his life in Paris. It sounds authentic, but there's also a very strongly nostalgic tone, so it may not be trustworthy.

Hemingway, Leicester. My Brother, Ernest Hemingway. Cleveland: World, 1962. For 1924–1925, L.H. uses information from Ernest's letters (as well as commonly known facts). The book reads like a third-hand report, very remote; but L.H. sounds honest, not as if he were making up things that he doesn't know about.

Hotchner, A. E. Papa Hemingway. New York: Random, 1955. This book is called a "personal memoir." Hotchner met Hemingway in 1948, evidently hero-worshiped him, and tape-recorded his reminiscences. The book is their dialogue (mostly Hemingway's monologue). No index or bibliography. Hotchner's adoring tone is annoying, and the material resembles that of A Moveable Feast, which is better written.

Meyers, Jeffrey. Hemingway: A Biography. New York: Harper, 1985. Includes several maps, and two chronologies: illnesses and accidents, and travel. Book organized chronologically, with every year accounted for, according to table of contents. Well documented critical biography, with personal anecdotes taking a back seat to literary. Less gossipy, more circumspect in claims than Griffin.

Reynolds, Michael. Hemingway: The Paris Years. Cambridge, Mass.: Blackwell, 1989. Second of three-volume biography. Includes a chronology covering December 1921–February 1926 and five maps ("Hemingway's Europe 1922–26," "France," "Switzerland," "Italy," and "Key points for Hemingway's several trips through France and Spain").

Sokoloff, Alice Hunt. Hadley, the First Mrs. Hemingway. New York: Dodd, 1973. This is the Paris experience from Hadley's point of view, most of it taken from her recollections and from the standard biographies. (Baker is acknowledged.) It's a very slight book—102 pages—but there's an index and footnotes, citing letters and interviews that some of the other biographers might not have been able to use.

Weeks, Robert P., ed. Hemingway: Twentieth Century Perspectives. Englewood Cliffs: Prentice, 1965. Contains many important essays on Hemingway's life and art. Offers a selected annotated bibliography.

Young, Philip. Ernest Hemingway. Minneapolis: U of Minnesota P, 1959. A short psychobiography of Hemingway's life. Offers stimulating insights, but suffers from the limitations of psychoanalysis.

EXERCISE 46

Correct the errors of form in the following bibliography:

Becker, Howard S, Geer, Blanche, and Everett C. Hughes. Making the Grade: New York (1968) Wiley.

Dressel, Paul L.. College and University Curriculum, Berkeley (California): McCutcheon, 1971

(same)----Handbook of Academic Evaluation. San Francisco (California): Jossey-Bass: 1976.

J. F. Davidson, "Academic Interest Rates and Grade Inflation," Educational Record.   56, 1975, pp. 122–5

(no author). "College Grades: A Rationale and Mild Defense." AAUP Bulletin, October 1976, 320–1.

New York Times. "Job Plight of Young Blacks Tied to Despair, Skills Lack," April 19, 1983: Section A page 14.

Milton Ohmer, Howard R. Pollio and James A. Eison. GPA Tyranny, Education Digest 54   (Dec 1988): 11–14.

Leo, John. "A for Effort". Or for Showing Up. U.S. News & World Report, 18 Oct, 1993: 22.

Kennedy, Donald. What Grade Inflation? The New York Times June 13, 1994: All.

Bretz, Jr., Robert D. "College Grade Point Average as a Predictor of Adult Success: a Meta-analytical Review and Some Additional Evidence" Public Personnel Management 18   (Spring 1989): 11–22.

·10·

Read by Wednesday

The Research Essay

An effective research essay will integrate all the skills that have been explored throughout this book as overlapping stages in the writing process. However, a research essay must also conform to a few basic mechanical rules:

1. Type your essay on a typewriter or a word processor. If you use a typewriter, make sure that your ribbon is dark. If you use a word processor, make sure that you use a letter-quality printer.

2. Double-space throughout the essay.

3. Use 8½-by-11-inch paper; leave 1½-inch margins.

4. If you type, use only one side of the page.

5. Number each page.

6. Proofread your essay and insert minor corrections neatly, in ink.

7. Do not include graphics or illustrations unless your instructor requests them.

8. Include your name, the name of the course, the date, and the title of the essay, either on a separate title page, or on the first page of the essay.

Check with your instructor for any other special rules that may apply to the assignment.

THREE SAMPLE RESEARCH ESSAYS

The following three student research papers, on three very different sub-jects, use three different kinds of documentation.

The first writer is analyzing an issue. In presenting some of the reasons why some people advocate and others condemn the practice of euthanasia, the writer is also constructing an *argument:* his essay is intended to persuade his readers that terminally ill people should have the right to choose the time of their deaths. The writer documents his sources with MLA documentation. He sum-marizes, paraphrases, or quotes one source at a time, which makes it practical to use brief and unobtrusive parenthetical notes at the ends of the sentences. Almost everything that the writer wants to say is said within the body of the essay, so there are only a few endnotes.

The second writer uses a *narrative* structure, with a great deal of precise de-tail, to describe a real event—the aftermath of a plane crash in the Andes Mountains in 1972. This essay will help you to understand why many history instructors—and also instructors in some other humanities disciplines—still prefer the traditional footnote or endnote and bibliography form of documen-tation. The writer frequently refers to a group of sources to support specific points; she also presents a great deal of background information that cannot be included in the body of her paper. The separate endnotes provide enough room to cite all the sources and explain some of the points that they are making.

The third writer combines *narrative and analysis* by describing the after-math of the strange event that happened in 1908 at Lake Tunguska, Siberia, and then analyzing some of the many theories that have been used to explain that event over the last seventy years. The bibliography for this essay contains relatively few sources, which are cited less frequently than the sources are in the first two essays. The writer's purpose is to help his readers understand what might have happened at Lake Tunguska and to clarify the scientific ex-planations. He is not using numerous sources to reconstruct the event in com-plete detail, or trying to convince his readers, by citing authorities, that his conclusions are the right ones. Like many essays in the behavioral sciences, this paper uses the author-year variation of parenthetical note documentation. (This method, often called APA after the American Psychological Association, is described in Appendix B, on pp. 486–494.) Having the date, as well as the author, included within the body of the essay is especially useful when you are reading about scientific theories developed over a span of eighty years.

A Research Essay Checklist

As you read these essays, keep the following questions in mind. Then, when you have completed the next-to-the-last draft of your own research paper, check the list again to see if you can answer yes to most of these questions.

1. Does the essay have a single focus that is clearly established and main-tained throughout?

2. Does the writer have a thesis or a consistent point of view about the events or issues being described?

3. If it is a narrative essay, does the narration have a beginning, middle, and end?

4. Does the essay begin with an informative introduction?

5. Does the essay end on a conclusive note?

6. Does each paragraph have a clear topic sentence?

7. Does each paragraph contain one and only one topic?

8. Are the paragraphs long enough to be convincing? Is each point supported by facts and information?

9. Does the development of the essay depend entirely on a dry listing of facts and events, or does the writer offer explanations and relevant commentary?

10. Does the writer use transitions to signal the relationship between separate points?

11. Does the reader get a sense of the relative importance of the sources being used?

12. Does the writer use one source for very long stretches at a time?

13. Is there an appropriate number of notes rather than too many or too few?

14. Is it clear how much material is covered by each note?

15. In essays containing endnotes, do notes provide important explanatory information?

16. Are the quotations well chosen?

17. Is paraphrase properly used? Is the style of the paraphrase consistent with the style of the writer of the essay?

18. Does the writer use enough citations? Does the text of the essay make it clear when the writer is using a specific source, and who that person is?

19. Is the essay convincing? Did you believe what you read?

Jorge Catto

English 102

Spring, 1990

What your paper should look like

Euthanasia: The Right to Die

Someone you love is suffering from terminal cancer. He asks you to inject a lethal drug into him so that he can die without prolonged agony. Would you do it? Should you? Incidents such as this one, in which one person asks another for help to die, are called euthanasia. At the center of this problem is the right of a person to die with the least suffering and the most dignity and comfort. In this essay, I will consider some of the reasons why euthanasia is so vigorously opposed, and why, in spite of that opposition, we must insist on our right to decide for ourselves when to end our own lives.

Euthanasia is usually divided into two kinds: active and passive. According to Michelle Anne Cawley's definition in The American Journal of Nursing, active euthanasia involves directly causing the death of another person through an intended action (859). Administering a fatal drug to a dying person, injecting an air bubble into the bloodstream, or giving him some other means to shorten his life constitute active euthanasia. The most famous recent example of active euthanasia is Dr. Jack Kevorkian, the doctor from Michigan who helps patients to die with the help of his "suicide machine," a tank of carbon monoxide and a mask (Belkin 50; Elliott 27).

Passive euthanasia can be described as helping someone to die by doing nothing. It is also called, Cawley writes, "cooperating with the patient's dying" (959). Failing to resuscitate a patient who has suffered a massive heart attack is one example of passive euthanasia. Another is deciding not to feed terminally ill patients who are unable to feed themselves. In contrast, removing the feeding tube from a patient who is being fed that way would be considered active euthanasia. Dr. David Orentlicher, in the Journal of the American Medical Association, categorizes "assisted suicide" as a form of passive euthanasia. In assisted suicide, a doctor or other person provides a terminally ill person with the means--pills, for example--and the medical knowledge necessary to commit suicide (1844). Derek Humphrey's 1991

Catto 2

book Final Exit, which describes ways to commit suicide painlessly, and the
organization Compassion in Dying, which helps terminally ill patients to end
their lives, are both recent examples of instruction in "assisted suicide"
(Belkin 50; also Elliott 27).

The professional people who care for the sick and dying think that
there is a great difference between active euthanasia and passive euthanasia
or "assisted suicide." A recent panel of distinguished physicians declared
themselves in favor, by a margin of 10 to 2, of doctor-assisted suicide for
hopelessly ill patients who request it (Orentlicher 1844). In a 1975 survey,
73% of the nurses questioned were in favor of withholding treatment that
would prolong the lives of dying patients who don't want their lives sustained in that way--in other words, passive euthanasia. But only 17% were
in favor of using active means to end the lives of dying patients who request
euthanasia ("Taking Life" 40). ← *article without author*

In the past, euthanasia was not such a topic for public speculation
and censure. In part, this was because death did not usually take place in
a public place, and therefore no one except family members or a doctor
was likely to know whether the patient was or wasn't helped to die. Also,
doctors lacked the knowledge and the means to try to prolong a dying person's life. But, as Sonia Rudikoff points out in Commentary, this acceptance that death was inevitable and not to be avoided may also have been
related to the idea that death was a significant and sacred event and even
a welcome one, because it was the prelude to a better existence in the
afterlife (62).

Today, as a result of advances in medical science, it has become
both possible and, many say, desirable to try to prolong a dying person's
life. Indeed, it is considered criminal not to try to do so. Fifteen years ago,
Peter Hammerli, a doctor in Switzerland, was arrested for "murdering" his
patients. He was accused of not taking steps to prolong the lives of the terminally ill people that he was treating.[1] Thus, most controversies over euthanasia center around the issue of who, if anyone, has the right to end a
sick person's life. Those concerned in this issue include the patient, the patient's family, and the doctor and nursing staff, all of whom may be affected
by their differing conceptions of God or divinity or fate.

Endnotes are used for info. that does not go into the flow of the paper.

In a Gallup poll in 1975, slightly over 50% of Americans said that they do not believe that an individual has the right to end his or her own life ("Taking Life" 40). Most of these people probably share the belief that life is a gift from God and that our bodies and lives are not our private possessions, but are held in trust (Cawley 869). As Rudikoff puts it, they believe that "the breath of life in each of us is a part of a spirit or life, or a community of spirit over which we do not exert ultimate control" (63). To these people, only God has enough knowledge and power to have the right to take away life. They associate euthanasia with murder, and quote Biblical phrases such as "Thou shalt not kill" and "The Lord giveth and the Lord taketh away" as the basis for their belief (Rudikoff 66). They argue that no human being--not even the dying person--can ever be certain when death is about to happen or whether euthanasia is really necessary. So, they want to turn the matter over to God, to whom they attribute perfect objectivity and omniscience.

Advocates of euthanasia think that this argument is a way of avoiding human responsibility. The ideals of our society include the belief that we are all individuals capable of self-determination. A Catholic theologian has observed that, in this respect, man is different from the rest of living creation, because he is "the only animal who knows he is going to die and who also knows he can bring about his own death" (Maguire 57). Before becoming ill, most patients were free to choose their style of life, to decide when to eat, when to sleep, and how to take care of themselves. Why, then, should they not have the right to choose whether to live or to die? (Rudikoff 63). Writing in the New York Times about a decision he once made to end his life if his illness grew more serious, Edward M. Brecher makes the point that it is perfectly acceptable for veterinarians to put extremely sick animals out of their misery, but the same privilege is not usually extended to human beings (72). It is as if one's ability to reason and make moral choices no longer matters when someone is dying.

This issue is made even more painful by the fact that, very often, the dying person is experiencing great suffering. Peter Hammerli became a practitioner of euthanasia because he could not bear to prolong the misery of the patients whom he saw suffering ("Hammerli Affair" 1273). Similarly, a

licensed practical nurse reported that she had "seen an elderly terminal patient bite through his I.V. tubing to prevent prolonging of the inevitable. I
think it was horrible that we drove that man to such extremes" ("Taking Life"
40). On the other hand, such incidents may be the exceptions, and these reactions may, to some extent, be extreme and unnecessary. According to a
report made by the British Medical Association, most people, no matter how
serious their illnesses are, do not die in agony, but rather peacefully and
with dignity ("Against Euthanasia" 220).

    The right to die with dignity is regarded as almost as important as
the right to die without suffering excessive pain. In earlier times, people of
all ages died at home, in a natural and familiar setting, with their loved ones
about them. According to a survey in Time, as recently as 45 years ago,
more than half the deaths that took place in the United States occurred at
home (Tifft 68). Today, however, four out of five Americans die in institutions
("Right to Choose" 22). Kathy Fackelmann points out in Science News that
patients and their families are especially frightened by "the frantic commotion and turmoil that surround a dying patient." Those who aren't used to
the new equipment and the hospital procedures intended to prolong lives
think that what goes on is a form of torture inflicted on helpless victims (232).

    The person making unpleasant decisions about euthanasia is often
not the patient nor one of the patient's relatives, but rather the patient's
doctor. The majority of doctors are strongly opposed to both passive and active euthanasia, arguing that the Hippocratic Oath, which they must swear
when they receive their medical degrees, pledges them to save lives, not to
end them. Few would approve of Dr. Walter W. Sackett, a general practitioner in Miami, who has publicly stated that he has prescribed euthanasia
for hundreds of his patients during thirty years of medical practice (Maguire
64).[2] Most doctors tend to share the attitude of the British Medical Association: "No doctor or nurse should be asked to hold responsibility for deciding
when euthanasia may properly be administered, or for administering it"
("Against Euthanasia" 220).

    One reason that doctors frequently cite for their refusal to accept any
form of euthanasia is that an error may have been made, that the case may
not be hopeless, and that, as the British Medical Association puts it, "errors

Catto 5

of judgment in euthanasia cases would be irreversible" ("Against Euthanasia" 220). Some patients with symptoms that suggest a terminal illness have been known to survive for months or years. If euthanasia were an accepted practice, how could such patients be protected from a possible premature death? By prolonging life and postponing death, doctors are also buying time in the hope that a cure might soon be found for a disease that appears to be hopeless (St. John-Stevas 422; Fackelmann 233). To some extent, this concern over possible errors and possible cures may be connected to a fear of being sued. Each year more and more lawsuits are being brought against doctors who have supposedly failed to use every possible means to ensure that the dying live as long as possible ("Right to Choose" 23). As Richard Lamm notes in his New Republic article, if it can be proven that a doctor has failed to do everything possible to prolong life, then she may be faced with a malpractice suit, and the resulting bad publicity could seriously affect her future career (21).[3]

Another strong professional objection to euthanasia is based on the special relationship that is supposed to exist between doctor and patient. Doctors have traditionally promoted and preserved human life; euthanasia may change the doctor's role, some fear, to that of a hired hand who simply caters to the whims of one person's individual idea of the good life (Callahan, "Euthanasia Debate" 15). More important, people trust doctors because they assume that a doctor's sole object is to save lives. Daniel C. Maguire makes the point that doctors are not supposed to differentiate between good death and bad death: "As medicine has developed, it is geared to promoting life under all circumstances. Death is the natural enemy of the healing science" (59). According to the British writer Norman St. John-Stevas, it is vital that patients continue to regard doctors as a force for life, not as a potential giver of death (422). The British Medical Association confirms that "to be a trusted physician is one thing; to appear as a potential executioner is quite another" ("Against Euthanasia" 220). But there are those who criticize this attitude, suggesting that doctors get considerable personal satisfaction from their almost godlike ability to keep people from dying.[4] Some nurses have criticized the almost proprietary attitude of doctors and other health-care professionals toward their patients:

Catto 6

[handwritten annotation: Indented 10 spaces, double space, no quotation marks.]

In a sense aren't we playing God? If God has called a patient *[handwritten annotation: parenthetical citation goes outside period]* to meet his Maker, what right does a nurse or doctor have to prolong his suffering if there is no hope?

A patient does not belong to the nurses or to the physician.

We saved him, if you can call it that. What it amounts to is an ego trip for us. ("Taking Life" 41)

[handwritten annotation: Umbrella note goes in the 1st sent. of a para.]

These statements suggest that doctors and nurses may be reluctant to practice or even permit any form of euthanasia because of their own fear of failing to carry out their mission (Fackelmann 232). Conversely, conscientious physicians may find the ethical ramifications of euthanasia too disturbing to accept, for, as Leon Kass of the University of Chicago asks, "How easily will they be able to care wholeheartedly for patients when it is always possible to think of killing them as a 'therapeutic option'?" (35).

Cases of comatose or irreversibly vegetative patients, or of infants born with terminal diseases or generally fatal malformations, present additional ethical problems. In theory, these patients have little to live for, yet they are, of course, unable to request euthanasia for themselves. Who will determine whether euthanasia is appropriate in such instances? Opponents of euthanasia argue that it is impossible for anyone to determine what any individual's "likely quality of life" will be regardless of that individual's present condition (Koop 3), and that "it will be difficult--if not impossible--to develop the requisite calculus of degradation or to define the threshold necessary for ending life" (Kass 33).

One important point is that the mission of the medical profession may have changed as a result of new advances in medical science and technology. The Hippocratic Oath was relatively simple to maintain centuries, even decades ago, before drugs, equipment, and techniques were invented that could prolong the natural course of a patient's life. An article in Science News describes "the high-tech atmosphere" existing in most hospitals today, especially in intensive care units, that supports the idea that science is stronger than death, and that encourages doctors to think of death as "an unacceptable outcome of medical therapy" (Fackelmann 232). Some hospital teams seem to regard patients as the objects of scientific experiment: Lamm cites the case of a dying woman who was resuscitated 70 times in one 24-hour period (22). Professor George J. Annas of the Boston University School of Medicine considers whether patients have the right to refuse to have their lives prolonged and concludes that "the proper role of medical technology" is at the center of the debate over euthanasia: "Is technology going to be our master or our servant? Is technology going to take on a life of its own such that we give it rights of its own? Or are we going to reassert our dominant role in controlling technology and using it for human ends?" ("Symposium").[5]

An important factor here is the high cost of these technological miracles. Maintaining a comatose patient can cost hundreds of thousands of dollars. Even if much of the financial burden is placed on health insurance agencies or the government, the gain may not be worth the cost. Noting that, in 1983, the national bill for health care was $355 billion, Lamm observes that "the time is not far off when there will be a direct conflicts [sic] between the health of the individual and the health of the society" (21). Given the limited amount of money available to pay for chronic and terminal illnesses, it may be necessary to make some unpleasant choices. Providing the latest medical equipment for one patient may drain resources that might be used to pay for more nursing personnel and a more pleasant environment for other patients. There are also those who believe that available resources should be spent on preventive medicine: according to one doctor writing in The New England Journal of Medicine, "the costs of trying to preserve the life of one cirrhotic patient with bleeding esophageal varices might be used to treat and prevent alcoholism in many persons" (Lamm 21).

The final argument against euthanasia that must be given serious consideration is that it is dangerous for any society to legalize the killing of a certain class of its citizens. Daniel Callahan of the Hastings Center argues that a society that condones euthanasia condones a fundamental moral wrong, namely to give one individual

> ultimate power over another. It is to create the wrong kind of relationship between people, a community that sanctions private killings amongst its members in pursuit of their individual goals. (5)

In the Hastings Report Special Supplement, Richard Fenigsen further cau-
tions that the line between voluntary and involuntary euthanasia--between
euthanasia and "crypthanasia"--is inherently impossible to distinguish and
that members of some societal groups, the elderly for instance, may submit
to euthanasia against their will if they feel pressured to do so by relatives,
doctors, or society at large (25). Furthermore, according to those who reject
euthanasia, it is too easy to enlarge the category of people marked for euthanasia to include the handicapped, the mentally ill and retarded, those
convicted of serious crimes, and other groups rejected by society. Eventually, once the barriers begin to break down, the whole attitude of a society
toward its members may undergo an "ominous shift":

> Instead of the message a humane society sends to its mem-
> bers--"Everybody has the right to be around, we want to keep
> you with us, every one of you"--the society that embraces
> euthanasia, even the "mildest" and most "voluntary" forms
> of it, tells people: "We wouldn't mind getting rid of you."
> (Fenigsen 26)

In light of Washington State's 1991 Initiative 119, a narrowly defeated refer-
endum that would have made it legal for doctors in Washington to help terminally ill patients commit suicide (Belkin 51), opponents of euthanasia
believe they have even more reason to fear the "slippery slope" syndrome:
once a society makes it legal to kill one patient, then what's to stop it from
unfairly killing many (Elliott 26)?

Some critics of euthanasia express concern about its implications as
a social policy. St. John-Stevas points to the terrible precedent of Nazi Germany and the eugenics movement, which attempted to eliminate everyone
who did not meet a certain standard of social excellence and desirability
(421). Rudikoff fears that we will create "euthanasia mills," which would
make the termination of life a routine matter (66). It is true that, as one
psychiatrist put it, euthanasia can never be "a logical decision. It is not
one that you can make by a computer model" (Fackelmann 233). It is important to have some degree of personal involvement in each decision, to
consider each case individually, and to assert, as Dr. Peter Hammerli did,
that "I have never done anything to my patients that I would not do for my

own mother and father . . . if they were in such a position" ("Hammerli Affair" 1272).

If euthanasia is going to become acceptable social policy, it is important to have some guidelines so that hospitals and nursing homes will understand when and by whom each decision will be made. Otherwise, John Ladd observes in Ethics, euthanasia will eventually take place at random: "Sometimes someone, no one knows who it is, will turn off the ventilator or will turn it on again after it has been turned off, because he thinks that one ought to let the patient die or ought not to let him die." These communication breakdowns can happen easily enough when everyone thinks it is his or her particular duty to intervene--or to stop someone else from intervening. Eventually, Ladd continues, "the patient becomes a football tossed around among those with different and competing interests and ideologies" (138).

One solution to this problem is, whenever possible, to allow individuals to assume the responsibility for deciding when they are ready to die (Modell 908). The report of the Presidential Commission in 1983 determined that a dying patient, if competent to make a decision, should be informed of all the available options and that "those who decline life-prolonging therapy should not be denied other forms of care needed to relieve pain and to maintain dignity" ("Right to Choose" 23). But doctors may not always be sure when patients are competent to make a responsible decision or whether they may have been coerced by family members for whom a lingering illness may be a continued burden (Rudikoff 66–67). For this reason, supporters of the right to euthanasia frequently recommend that each individual write a "living will" relatively early in life while still healthy and undeniably competent to make decisions (Rudikoff 64; "Hammerli Affair" 1272). Such a legal document would state that, should the person be incapable of making such a decision, he or she is establishing certain preferences among the options that might be available for his or her care. Typically, such wills, which have been authorized by numerous states, instruct doctors not to start or to stop any procedures intended to sustain life if the condition is terminal (Modell 908).

Of course, a living will is no assurance that the patient would still choose euthanasia. What if the patient has changed his mind since he wrote the living will? (Fackelmann 233; Rudikoff 66). A nurse who frequently cares for the dying notes that many patients do change their minds--sometimes more than once--as death approaches: "Since the patient may be unresponsive by this time, and since hearing is the last thing to go, I have wondered if it wouldn't be a terrible thing to be laying [sic] there and each time someone came in, wondering if they were coming to kill you" ("Taking Life" 42). That is, of course, a horrifying picture. But so, too, is the picture of a patient lying there longing for death and unable to convince anyone to carry out that wish.

Today, for most of us, the dread of death is so great that we go to any lengths to avoid it for those we love, as well as for ourselves. However, death in the right circumstances is everyone's right. It may be that the right to choose euthanasia would never have become a vital issue if death were a more integral part of our lives and if the circumstances in which death took place were easier to bear. St. John-Stevas argues against euthanasia by asserting that "dying can be a vital period in a person's life, reconciling him to life and death and giving an interior peace" (422). But this kind of ideal acceptance of death is possible only if there is a lot of care and love provided by all those in charge of the patient. At present, we seem to be more concerned with keeping people alive than with the quality of the lives that are being prolonged. Until we can have some assurance of a compassionate death--without unbearable cost to others and to society--we should not be intimidated by the church, the law, or the medical profession. Just as we choose the way we live, so should we be able to choose the way we die.

We have to use end notes.

Notes

[1]When there seemed to be no hope at all of a return to consciousness for those elderly people who were being kept alive by artificial feeding, Hammerli and his staff decided against continued treatment. Defending his actions, Hammerli insisted that he did not "believe in giving extensive treatment to a patient who is hopelessly ill: sometimes it is better to allow a person to die in peace" (26).

[2]Sackett suggests that, whether they admit it or not, 75% of all doctors have acted similarly at some point in their careers.

[3]The president of a Presidential Commission on the question of euthanasia is concerned that this fear of legal action may affect doctors' medical judgment. He imagines "a future horror scene in which a dying patient looks up from his deathbed to see the doctor flipping through a thick docket of legal cases" (Fackelmann 233).

[4]Of those few (17%) nurses who favored active euthanasia, only half would allow patients themselves the means to end their own lives; the other half believe that only professionals should be allowed to make and carry out that decision ("Taking Life" 40).

[5]The case of Elizabeth Bouvia is a good illustration. A quadriplegic who is regarded as mentally competent, Bouvia has been prevented from carrying out her expressed wish to end her own life by hospital staff, who insist on force-feeding her. Ernest van den Haag compares this with force-feeding convicts who go on hunger strikes, and argues that it is acceptable to force food on convicts since they are not entitled to the same liberties that free people are. "A hospital . . . may be liable for failing to artificially feed patients who cannot eat by normal means, or are incompetent. But not a patient who will not eat. He has a perfect right to decline food, or medicine, or an operation, if he so wishes and is competent to understand the consequences" (45–46).

Works Cited

"Against Euthanasia." The Lancet 30 Jan. 1971: 220.

Belkin, Lisa. "There's No Simple Suicide." New York Times Magazine 14 Nov. 1993: 48–55+.

Brecher, Edwin. "Opting for Suicide." New York Times Magazine 18 Mar. 1979: 72–80.

Callahan, Daniel. "Can We Return Disease to Death?" Hastings Center Report Special Supplement Feb. 1989: 4–6.

------. "The Euthanasia Debate: A Problem with Self-Determination." Current Oct. 1992: 15–19.

Cawley, Michelle Anne. "Euthanasia: Should It Be a Choice?" American Journal of Nursing May 1977: 859–61.

Elliott, Carl. "Dying Rites: The Ethics of Euthanasia." New Scientist 20 June 1992: 25–27.

Fackelmann, Kathy. "A Question of Life or Death." Science News 9 Oct. 1982: 232–33.

Fenigsen, Richard. "Euthanasia: How It Works: The Dutch Experience." Hastings Center Report Special Supplement Feb. 1989: 22–30.

"The Hammerli Affair: Is Passive Euthanasia Murder?" Science 26 Dec. 1975: 1271–74.

Humphrey, Derek. Final Exit: The Practicalities of Self-Deliverance and Assisted Suicide for the Dying. Eugene: Hemlock Society, 1991.

Kass, Leon R. "Neither for Love or for Money: Why Doctors Must Not Kill." Public Interest Winter 1989: 25–26.

Koop, C. Everett. "The Challenge of Definition." Hastings Center Report Special Supplement Feb. 1989: 2–15.

Ladd, John. "Euthanasia, Liberty, and Religion." Ethics Oct. 1982: 129–38.

Lamm, Richard D. "Long Time Dying." New Republic 27 Aug. 1984: 20–23.

Macguire, Daniel C. "Death By Chance, Death By Choice." Good Housekeeping Jan. 1975: 57–65.

Modell, Walter. "A 'Will' to Live." New England Journal of Medicine 18 Apr. 1971: 907–08.

Orentlicher, David. "Physician Participation in Assisted Suicide." Journal of the American Medical Association 262 6 Oct. 1989: 1844–45.

"The Right to Choose." Economist 26 March 1983: 22–23.

Rudikoff, Sonia. "The Problem of Euthanasia." Commentary Feb. 1974: 62–68.

St. John-Stevas, Norman. "Euthanasia: A 'Pleasant Sounding Word.'" America 31 May 1975: 421–22.

"Symposium: When Sophisticated Medicine Does More Harm Than Good." New York Times 30 Mar. 1986: E6.

"Taking Life Away." Nursing 75 Oct. 1975: 4050.

Tifft, Susan. "Debate on the Boundary of Life." Time 11 Apr. 1983: 68–70.

van den Haag, Ernest. "A Right to Die?" National Review 4 May 1984: 45–46.

Joan Smith

History 101

December 10, 1993

The Quest for Survival in the Andes Mountains

What was meant to be a pleasure trip for forty-five people flying from Montevideo, Uruguay, to Santiago, Chile, on October 13, 1972, turned into the horror of instant death for some and of slow starvation in the freezing Andes temperatures for others. The Old Christian Rugby Team and families and friends of the team--forty-five in all--flew out of Montevideo with nothing more on their minds than a rugby match with a Chilean team and a few days of skiing. But a terrifying plane crash in the rugged peaks of the Andes changed everything. What ensued for those who survived first the crash of their plane and then a crushing avalanche a short time later was a long ordeal of hunger and cold. The events that took place during these seventy-two days high in the icy Andes remain a fascinating story of the tenacity of the human will to survive at almost any cost, even the cost of eating human flesh.

According to a comprehensive newspaper account, the rugby team departed from Montevideo on October 12, 1972, in a propeller-driven Fairchild F-227, a Uruguayan Air Force plane, and after a night in Mendoza because of bad weather, they resumed their flight on Monday, October 13, at midday. The plane would cross an Andes mountain range that had peaks up to 21,000 feet in a blizzard.[1] As Piers Paul Read describes it, though the weather was inclement, everyone was assured that the flight was perfectly safe because the plane would be able to stay above the clouds. As the plane approached Santiago, the co-pilot Lagurara radioed Air Traffic Control at 3:35 to announce the plane's location and altitude. The controllers authorized him to lower the plane to 10,000 feet as he neared the airport of Pudaheul. However, when he brought the plane down 3,000 feet, it began to shake as it entered the clouds. The plane continued to jump and shake more vigorously as it entered other cloudbanks; the passengers began to panic and pray.[2]

Apparently, as the plane continued through clouds, it got caught in an air pocket, sank quickly in seconds, and broke apart against the side of an 11,500-foot mountain.[3] According to Benales' account, the tail section somersaulted down a mountain slope, killing those in the back of the plane immediately, while some still in their seats were swept out of the front of the plane because of the force of the air. The front section of the aircraft, or fuselage, slammed onto an area between peaks in the Hilario range of the Andes. Jose Luis Inciarte, one of the survivors interviewed by Benales, later described the scene as the fuselage slid over the snow: "Blood spurted all over me, people were screaming and I could smell fuel and cold air rushing in from outside, when suddenly with one big bump we came to rest."[4] Twelve of the forty-five people on board were killed in the crash.[5]

The first twenty-four hours were the worst for the survivors of the crash. Many were seriously or fatally injured, almost all were in a state of shock, and all of them froze in subfreezing temperatures of an Andes blizzard. Gustavo Zerbino, another survivor, remembers the first night as a nightmarish series of the "injured screaming, crying, dying. . . ."[6] Those who survived the first night did so by wrapping up in the ski clothes they had brought for their holiday[7] and by covering up in the seat covers they ripped from the seats of the plane. The group was almost totally exposed to the cold air, with only a makeshift barrier of seats and luggage protecting them. Worse than the cold was the hysteria.[8] It is miraculous that any survived that first night; the day after the crash, Chilean authorities said the chance for survival was "virtually nil" because those who hadn't died in the crash would die in the freezing blizzard.[9]

Suffering through the first night was the first of many trials for the sixteen who would live to tell the story. All of those who survived the crash had sustained some type of injury. In fact, three more people died during that first night. The wounded had to be attended to; fortunately, the survivors had among them an innovative medical student named Robert Canessa. Under Canessa's supervision, the survivors fought to keep their wounded alive. With the few makeshift medical tools they had, they tried several surgical operations. Cologne was the only disinfectant they had, and the harsh environment simply would not let the wounded heal properly.[10] Some would suffer from gangrene.[11] The fuselage also had to be made livable. The men of the rugby team worked tenaciously to pack the open back of the plane with whatever they could find to block the wind; they continued to rip the covers off the seats for more blankets; they made hammocks for the wounded out of cable and cord and metal plates ripped from the side of the plane.[12]

And they worried about how to get food and water. For ten days after the crash, the survivors lived off the meager rations that were found on the wrecked plane. During that period, each of the twenty-seven who survived the initial ordeal lived on a daily ration of one square of chocolate, one teaspoon of jam, a bit of toothpaste, and a small mouthful of wine in a deodorant cap.[13] Thirst was a big concern. In temperatures often descending to 25°C below zero, melting snow for water was a problem. Eating snow was no substitute for drinking water, as it burned the survivors' chapped lips and gave them stomach cramps.[14] They used the metal sheets from the wreck to rig up reflectors that tediously melted the snow into bottles. This process was slow, however, and the survivors were forced to carefully ration water.[15]

Meanwhile, the survivors had hope of rescue. A transistor radio was found in the wreckage, and Carlos Rosque, the plane's mechanic and only surviving crew member, said that batteries for it could be found in the other half of the plane. Three of the strongest survivors, including Canessa and Fernando Parrado, the two who would eventually succeed in hiking out of the mountains, went in search of the lost tail. After a strenuous hike, they located it, but the batteries were too heavy to carry back to the wreck. The three returned and the next day found it easier to carry the relatively light radio back to the tail. Roy Haley, who was knowledgeable about radios, went with them, and eventually figured out a way for them to listen to Radio Spectator in Montevideo. Listening to the radio, however, may have turned out to be more tragic than hopeful. On October 21, eight days after the crash, Haley heard that the rescue mission had been called off because there was little reason to believe anyone could survive the crash and the cold.[16]

After hearing that the search had been called off, the survivors knew that they would have to discover another source of food if they were going to live. Their meager rations were quickly running out, and the men were beginning to feel the effects of starvation.[17] They considered all possible options for sustenance. No plant life that might provide food survived in the harsh weather of the Andes; they found only lichen on the exposed rocks, which was worthless as sustenance.[18] For several days, many of the men had been silently concluding that the only way they would survive was to eat the bodies of those who had died. Canessa, the medical student, finally had the courage to openly suggest the possibility of consuming human flesh. He urged that, since the rescue had been called off, the only way the group would live was by rescuing themselves, and they could only do this if they had food. Further, he admonished that they had the moral duty to stay alive, that they had been given the gift of life and were responsible for sustaining it. Though many had serious reservations about eating the flesh of their families and friends, they felt the force of Canessa's arguments.[19] Several others supported Canessa, clothing their arguments more and more in religious language. God wanted them to live, they argued; He had spared them from the crash and had given them the bodies to eat. It would be wrong to reject this gift on the grounds of squeamishness.[20]

On the tenth day after the crash and the second day after the crushing news about the cancellation of rescue efforts, after much heated discussion, Canessa, with the support of most of the twenty-six other survivors, cut into a corpse with a shard of glass and ate the flesh.[21] The group calculated that each corpse would last five days if they carefully rationed their intake.[22] Two metaphors helped them to justify their actions. The group compared their consumption of flesh to a heart transplant; just as a heart is taken from one person at death to keep another alive, so the dead bodies sustained the breath of the living. But the most powerful metaphor for the survivors, most of whom were Catholic, was the sacrament of the Holy Communion.[23] Survivor Eduardo Deigrado later said, concerning their decision, "We thought of Jesus and how in the Last Supper He had divided his body and blood to all the apostles. We understood that we had to do the same, to take His body and blood which had been reincarnated and that was an intimate communion among us. It was what helped us to subsist."[24] Catholic priests would later support the survivors' decision. Two priests said that the men had "acted justifiably" and within the bounds of religious morality; a person is permitted to eat human flesh, they said, if there is no other means for survival. They called the Communion metaphor "not unreasonable."[25]

In fact, the group's shared religious beliefs helped them through the many life-threatening difficulties they faced. As Jose Luis Inciarte said later, "When we got really low in spirits, we said our rosary together and we were overcome with such strong faith that it bubbled up inside of us."[26] Carlos Paez led the men in a nightly rosary throughout the ordeal.[27] But it was not only religion that kept them alive; their youthful good health, as well as the teamwork and discipline developed on the rugby field, also worked to sustain them.[28] As Claudia Dowling describes it, the survivors, all aged from nineteen to twenty-six, worked together unselfishly, making rules and organizing chores. Adolfo Staunch, Eduardo Staunch, and Daniel Fernandez, all cousins, initially took charge of apportioning labor and of the unpleasant task of flaying the bodies. Others, like Canessa and Parrado, also emerged as leaders. The men knew that to survive they must construct and follow communal rules. Their discipline and teamwork kept them from consuming too much food too quickly and encouraged them to look after each other's needs. They knew that any selfish behavior might lead to death. The fact that the men were friends from the same town definitely made their community more harmonious than it might have been in other circumstances. Inciarte remembers that when he was down to half of his body weight and barely able to move, Adolfo Staunch gave him an entire bottle of his precious water. Such unselfish behavior, generated by both religious belief and friendship, kept the men alive.[29] Dowling points out that the survivors "never degenerated into Lord of the Flies primitivism, never turned on one another. They worked together as a tribe so all might survive."[30]

Not all groups have behaved so harmoniously under the duress of cold and starvation. The comparable incident of the Donner Party, trapped in the Sierra Nevada mountains of California in the winter of 1846–47, provides a gruesome foil to the ordeal of the Uruguayan rugby team. The party, comprised of ten unrelated families and sixteen other individuals and headed by the Illinois farmer George Donner, was snowbound in the Sierra Nevadas as they were making their way west. What ensued during that winter shares with the Andes incident the same tenacious struggle to survive under similar conditions, but greed, selfishness, and possibly murder taint the story.[31] As hunger overtook the party, families with food often refused to help those with less, or charged them exorbitant prices for meager portions[32] and then seized their goods when they could not pay.[33] After the food ran out, the party agreed that cannibalism was the only means of survival. They waited impatiently for someone to die. When a bachelor in the group accidentally caught his hand on fire, they refused to save him; he died and they ate him.[34] As one member of the party wrote in his journal, certain people then began to talk freely about shooting and eating those who were probably going to die anyway.[35] Later, a woman, after eating a corpse, shot, killed, and ate the two Native Americans in the party. Finally, after some of the party had finally hiked out of the mountains and returned to rescue the others, a man named Keseberg was found alone, surrounded by several mutilated corpses and incredible filth. Though he said they had died naturally, he was frank about eating their flesh and enjoying it, and valuables of the dead were found on his person.[36]

Though physically taxed to the same limit as the Donner Party was, the Andes survivors maintained a sense of charity and morality. It is testimony to the group's fortitude that they held together in relative harmony and survived. As the days passed, their ordeal only became more dire. One week after eating their first flesh, they were struck by another tragedy. The group of twenty-seven was reduced to nineteen after an avalanche crashed into the fuselage in the middle of the night, and killed eight while wrecking the carefully arranged barrier against the cold.[37] The avalanche struck suddenly; the men all felt a push on the plane, and then all were buried, giving themselves up to die. Again, only the strength of those lucky enough not to be fully buried prevented the number of deaths from increasing. They worked vigorously to pull others from the snow and revive them with mouth-to-mouth resuscitation.[38] Those who did survive did so miraculously. Inciarte recalls his good fortune: "It [the avalanche] got me with my hand in front of my face, so I managed to make a little cavity and breathe a bit. I heard screaming. . . . I moved my hand about a bit but couldn't get out. I think it was the worst moment of all because I really gave myself up for lost."[39] But he was finally pulled out.

Though the group had found a way to sustain themselves and made rules for running an efficient community, the days after the avalanche threatened their morale. Not only did the men grieve over the deaths of their friends, but they also had to witness the slow deaths of three others due to starvation or injuries suffered in the crash or the avalanche. Among these was Numa Turcatti, one of the strongest and most fit of the group. During the days after the avalanche, he had suddenly lost the will to live; he refused food to the point that he essentially let himself die in early December.[40] Others seemed to follow Turcatti's lead, as despair set in for the group. Strife over cigarette rations was a constant irritation; discord started to threaten the group's harmony.[41]

A numbing boredom made matters worse. The men were well aware that they were miles from civilization, and that almost impassable mountains separated them from the nearest village.[42] In the face of such slim odds for survival, the group often had bouts with apathy. Through the long cold days and nights of November, they underwent long periods of silence.[43] They tried various ways to invigorate their spirits. Aside from the daily routine of melting snow for water and eating their sparse meals, they engaged in group discussions on pre-arranged topics,[44] planned what they would do when they returned to Montevideo, listed the best restaurants in their town, and held small birthday celebrations with red wine for the three men whose birthdays came during their ordeal.[45]

The survivors also continued to consider how they might rescue themselves. After several failed attempts to use the radio to call for help, they decided that the only chance for survival lay in hiking out of the mountains.[46] Throughout their stay in the mountains, the group had been sending out small scouting parties on trial expeditions. These short excursions allowed them to determine who the strongest of the group were and what clothing and methods for carrying food were the most effective.[47] As December approached, the weather began to warm as spring approached in the seasonal cycle of the Southern Hemisphere. Canessa, Parrado, and Antonio Vizintin were selected to make the trek out of the mountains.[48] The group began gathering food and the best clothing for the expeditioners, and tore felt covers from the heating tubes in the aircraft to make sleeping bags for them.[49] But the scouting trips did not provide much information on the group's exact location. They knew Chile was to the west, and had the aircraft compass to point them in that direction. Otherwise, the three knew they would be wandering blindly through the rugged, freezing peaks of the Andes.[50]

At the end of the first week of December, after the group had been trapped on the mountain for fifty-six days, two condors appeared and circled the sky. These were the first of several signs of spring. The weather warmed; the group heard from the radio that the search had resumed. They had planned for Canessa, Parrado, and Vizintin to leave as soon as the weather improved; the preparations for the journey were almost finished. However, the normally strong-willed Canessa began to procrastinate. As Read's account and the film based on it illustrate, strife broke out between Canessa and the others when he began finding excuses for not going on the journey. The others knew the effort would fail without him and felt that he was letting them down for the first time. Just before their greatest attempt to overcome their plight, the group seemed to be falling apart.[51]

It took another death to persuade Canessa that he must go. Turcatti finally breathed his last on December 10, reducing the number of survivors to sixteen. Canessa realized that he could wait no longer; the group's morale could stand little more. Others were on the verge of death as well.[52] Many had dropped in weight from two hundred to one hundred pounds.[53]

On December 11, the three set out, loaded with as many clothes and as much food as they could carry. On the third day of strenuous travel, during which the hunger-weakened travellers averaged only four miles a day,[54] they reached the top of a high mountain; there they saw a distant valley between the only two mountains that weren't snow-covered. They realized then that there was not enough food for the three of them to reach the valley. They decided that Vizintin must return to the plane so that Canessa and Parrado would have enough food to complete the journey.[55]

The two resumed a journey that would end seven days later. Of the many hard-fought victories over death during the ordeal, this ten-day trek was the most triumphant and the most difficult. Canessa recalls those "unending days of travel--intense cold at night, intolerable heat at midday. We rationed the water and the food and said, 'if we don't walk so far, then no food for us.'"[56] The two were near death from exhaustion and hunger when they saw a rancher's hut in Chile on December 20. The hut belonged to Sergio Catalan Martinez, a forty-four-year-old cattle hand, living in San Fernando, who at 9 p.m. heard the faint shouts of the men across the roaring Tinguiririca River. He saw what seemed to be two tramps shouting at him on the other side of the water. When he still couldn't hear them, he threw over a stone with a paper and pen attached. Parrado quickly wrote,

> I come from the plane that crashed in the mountains.
> I am Uruguayan. We have been walking like this for
> 10 days. My friend is injured [from the hike]. There are
> still 14 injured people in the plane. We have to get out
> of here quickly because we have nothing to eat. We can
> walk no more.[57]

He threw the rock back to Sergio, who immediately went for help; patrols reached them by 12 p.m.

Canessa and Parrado made it out just in time. By the time the men back at the plane heard the message on the radio that they would be rescued, they had almost given up hope. Each day brought the prospect of death by starvation. Christmas was approaching, and their pessimism grew each day that they heard no news of Canessa and Parrado. Only the remnants of their incredible will to stay alive kept them from sinking totally into despair like Turcatti.[58] But everything changed on the morning of December 20. As the men heard the news, euphoria spread through their camp. They abandoned their daily tasks; they made their remaining cigarettes into Havana-style cigars. Two days later, on the afternoon of December 22, most of the men were taken out by helicopter; the rest were removed the following day.[59] The seventy-two-day ordeal was over. They had survived.

The aftermath of the ordeal caused a major stir in Uruguay. As the survivors revealed their story and their methods of survival, the reaction from the media was one of admiration and sympathy. Experts were amazed that the men could walk and remain mentally lucid after such starvation.[60] People were moved by the religious metaphors the men used to describe their consumption of flesh. But the dead were not forgotten. The twenty-nine victims were given a Christian burial in a common grave near the snow-covered wreckage.[61]

The survivors' celebrity status has not waned in their home country, and now it is international in the wake of the recent film Alive. Dowling suggests that, while the survivors cannot forget their great victory for the force of life, they also won't forget the sacrifice and the pain. They were made soberer and wiser from the ordeal, with striking insights into what a human is capable of. Many survivors felt a religious depth on the mountain they have never again experienced.[62] As Canessa said in a recent interview about his reaction to the film Alive, "I think it's a family film because it values religion and friendship, if in a touching and different way."[63] This remark perhaps best sums up what the victory of the survivors can mean for us; life and friendship are precious and powerful gifts, and not to be taken lightly.

Notes

[1]Carlos Benales, "70 Days Battling Starvation and Freezing in the Andes: A Chronicle of Man's Unwillingness to Die," New York Times, 1 Jan. 1973: A3. This article was the first comprehensive one on the Andes story. It was issued from the South American news agency LATIN.

[2]Piers Paul Read, Alive (New York and Philadelphia: Lippincott, 1974), 36–37. Of the many books written about this Andes mountain incident, Read's is considered the most authoritative, so I have chosen to use it to elucidate certain points of the story. The survivors of the group authorized this book so that the truth could be known about the many rumors surrounding their story. The other books on the subject did not receive authorization and Frank Marshall chose Alive as the most accurate basis for his 1993 film portraying the story. The book is written in the form of a novel; it is based on actual events that Read has brought to life in more detail. Read's book contains all information that appears in this essay; I have specifically drawn on it to elucidate certain scenes that the periodical articles either did not cover or dealt with only briefly. Other unauthorized, novelistic accounts of the story may be found in Enrique Hank Lopez's The Highest Hell (New York: Pocket Books, 1973), Clay Blair Jr.'s Survive! (Berkeley: Berkeley Books, 1973), and Richard Cunningham's The Place Where the World Ends (New York: Sheed and Ward, 1973).

[3]Claudia Glenn Dowling, "Still Alive," Life, 16 Jan. 1993: 50.

[4]Benales.

[5]Several of the survivors later blamed the crash on a pilot's error. Terry Clifford, "Staying Alive," Chicago Tribune, 15 Jan. 1993: 5:3.

[6]Don Podesta, "Echoes of a Crash Unheard of: The Tales of 16 Uruguayans Are Still as Chilling as Their Survival 20 Years Ago," Washington Post, 21 Dec. 1992: C1. Benales reported that the co-pilot spent the entire night groaning for water and for his revolver.

[7]Benales.

[8]Read, 47.

[9]"Uruguayan Plane with 45 Is Missing on Andes Flight," New York Times, 14 Oct. 1972: A9.

[10]The information in this paragraph up to this point comes from "Cannibalism After Air Crash Reported," New York Times, 27 Dec. 1972: D2. Canessa extracted a steel bar, for example, from the intestines of a wounded person, who nevertheless died, as did two others who died over the next few days.

[11]Rick Miller, "A Nightmare Revisited: 20 Years Later, with the Film's Release, Andes Survivors Recall Ordeal," Boston Globe, 21 Jan. 1993: 1:2.

[12]Benales.

[13]Dowling, 50. Also, "8 Survivors of Crash Picked Up in Andes," New York Times, 24 Dec. 1972: A9.

[14]Benales.

[15]Benales; Podesta.

[16]This account of finding the batteries and listening to the radio is taken from Benales. Though official searches were called off, the parents of those on the plane continued to search throughout the ordeal. Most notably, Carlos Paez Vilaro, the father of Carlitos Paez, searched diligently for his son, plotting clairvoyants' visions of maps, hounding the authorities, and searching by means of airplanes, on a mule, and on foot. Dowling, 58.

[17]Read, 81. Read describes their hunger: "Starvation was taking its effect. They were becoming weaker and more listless. When they stood up they felt faint and found it difficult to keep their balance. They felt cold, even when the sun rose to warm them, and their skin started to grow wrinkled like that of old men."

[18]Read, 82. Benales reports that the group also tried to make a soup out of the lichens and water.

[19]Miller.

[20]Read, 84–85.

[21]Dowling, 51.

[22]Benales.

[23]"Cannibalism." Both metaphors are described in this article.

[24]"Survivors of Andes Air Crash Admit Dead Saved Their Lives," New York Times, 29 Dec. 1972: A9. Canessa also justified their actions later when he said, "I've . . . thought that if I were dying, I would be proud that a friend could use my body." Clifford, 5:3.

[25]"Two Catholic Aides Defend Cannibalism in Chilean Air Crash," New York Times, 28 Dec. 1972: A8.

[26]Benales.

[27]Podesta.

[28]Benales.

[29]Dowling, 50, 55.

[30]Dowling, 50. Dowling goes on to aptly link the men's friendship, religion, and consumption of flesh:

> At the most basic level, friendship is founded on the sharing of food; the word companion comes from the Latin "he with whom one shares bread." Sharing flesh has even more resonance. In primitive agricultural societies, the sacrifice of animals was often a sacred celebration of tribes. Jewish Passover and Christian Communion are based on such traditions.

[31]Eric Linklater, Preface, Ordeal By Hunger, by George R. Stewart (London: Jonathan Cape, 1936), p. 9. Stewart's book offers a thorough and riveting account of the Donner Pass incident.

[32]Jared Diamond, "Reliving the Donner Party," Discover 13 March 1992: 103.

[33]Patrick Breen, The Diary of Patrick Breen, One of the Donner Party, ed. Frederick J. Terrgart, Academy of Pacific Coast History Publications, Vol. 1 (Berkeley: University of California Press, 1910), p. 280. Breen's diary provides a terse day-by-day account of the ordeal; he briefly alludes to the dissension and the cannibalism.

[34]Diamond, 103.

[35]Breen, 284.

[36]Diamond, 105.

[37]Dowling, 50; Benales.

[38]"Cannibalism."

[39]Benales.

[40]Benales. Another of the group, Bobby Francois, was also reluctant to preserve himself. He refused to do his chores, and often just sat around smoking. The others told him if he didn't work, he couldn't eat. He said that sounded fair. The survivors fed him anyway, and kept him alive. Dowling 57.

[41]Read, 204–205.

[42]Podesta. The group learned how isolated they were when some men on early scouting excursion ascended a 14,000-foot slope and saw only 100 miles of snow-covered mountains in every direction.

[43]Benales.

[44]"Cannibalism."

[45]Benales.

[46]Read, 204–208.

[47]Benales.

[48]Dowling, 51.

[49]Read, 213.

[50]Benales.

[51]All information in this paragraph comes from Read, 213–215, and the film Alive, directed by Frank Marshall (Touchstone and Paramount, 1993), which was adapted by Patrick Stanley from Read's novel. The box office success of the film proves the story's lasting interest.

[52]Read, 218.

[53]Benales.

[54]Dowling, 51.

[55]Read, 227–228.

[56]Benales.

[57]Benales. Read, 271, reports an expanded version of the encounter with Martinez and the note.

[58]Read, 244.

[59]All information after note 58 to this point comes from Benales.

[60]Benales. Weathered mountaineers especially were amazed at the survivors' relative good health after such wear and tear on their minds and bodies.

[61]"29 Victims in Andes Crash to Receive Common Burial," New York Times 26 Dec. 1972: E12.

[62]Dowling, 58.

[63]Clifford, 5:3.

Bibliography

Benales, Carlos. "70 Days Battling Starvation and Freezing in the Andes: A Chronicle of Man's Unwillingness to Die." New York Times 1 Jan. 1973: A3.

Breen, Patrick. Diary of Patrick Breen, One of the Donner Party. Academy of Pacific Coast History Publications, Vol. 1. Ed. Frederick J. Terrgart. Berkeley: U of California P, 1910. 269–84.

"Cannibalism After Air Crash Reported." New York Times 27 Dec. 1972: D2.

Clifford, Terry. "Staying Alive." Chicago Tribune 15 Jan. 1993: 5:3.

Diamond, Jared. "Reliving the Donner Party." Discover 13 Mar. 1992: 100–105.

Dowling, Claudia Glenn. "Still Alive." Life Feb. 1993: 48–59.

"8 Survivors of Crash Picked Up in Andes." New York Times 24 Dec. 1972: A9.

Linklater, Eric. Preface. Ordeal By Hunger. By George R. Stewart. London: Cape, 1936.

Marshall, Frank, dir. Alive. Touchstone and Paramount, 1993.

Miller, Rick. "A Nightmare Revisited: 20 Years Later, with the Film's Release, Andes Survivors Recall Ordeal." Boston Globe 21 Jan. 1993: A2.

Podesta, Dan. "Echoes of a Crash Unheard of: The Tales of 16 Uruguayans Are Still as Chilling as Their Survival 20 Years Ago." Washington Post 21 Dec. 1992: C1.

Read, Piers Paul. Alive: The Story of the Andes Survivors. Philadelphia and New York: Lippincott, 1974.

"Survivors of Andes Air Crash Admit Dead Saved Their Lives." New York Times 29 Dec. 1972: A9.

"29 Victims in Andes Crash to Receive Common Burial." New York Times 26 Dec. 1972: E12.

"Two Catholic Aides Defend Cannibalism in Chilean Air Crash." New York Times 28 Dec. 1972: A8.

David Morgan

Natural Science I

December 15, 1991

Explaining the Tunguskan Phenomenon

The Tunguska River Valley in Siberia has always been an area of swamps and bogs, forests and frozen tundra, sparsely populated, and remote and inaccessible to most travelers. It was at dawn on June 30, 1908, that witnesses in the Tungus observed a light glaring more brightly than anything they had ever seen. This cosmic phenomenon, they said, was bluish-white in color and gradually became cigarlike in shape. Just as terrifying to the few people inhabiting that part of Siberia was the tremendous noise that accompanied the light, a noise that was reported to have been heard 1,000 kilometers from the site (Parry, 1961). Some who were in the vicinity were deafened, while others farther away apparently became speechless and displayed other symptoms of severe trauma. The Tungus community refused to go near the site or speak of the occurrence, and some even denied that it had ever happened (Crowther, 1931). The event was so frightening to these simple peasants that many believed it had been an act of divine retribution, a punishment by a god demanding vengeance (Baxter & Atkins, 1976).

Since 1921, when the first perilous expedition to the Tungus region confirmed that a remarkable event had indeed taken place, scientists have attempted to explain what it was and why it happened. Almost 80 years later, the various theories developed to explain the explosion in the Tunguska Valley have become almost as interesting a phenomenon as the original occurrence. Like doctors trying to diagnose a disease by examining the symptoms, scientists have analyzed the fragmentary evidence and published theories that supposedly account for it. However, no theory has been entirely convincing. The purpose of this essay is to provide a brief description of some of the major interpretations of the Tunguska occurrence and to suggest that, in their efforts to substantiate their theories, scientists can be fallible.

At dawn on that day in June 1908, a huge object evidently came from space into the earth's atmosphere, breaking the sound barrier, and, at

7:17 a.m., slammed into the ground in the central Siberian plateau. Moments before the collision, a thrust of energy caused people and animals to be strewn about, structures destroyed, and trees toppled. Immediately afterward, a pillar or "tongue" of fire could be seen in the sky several hundred miles away; others called it a cylindrical pipe. A thermal air current of extremely high temperature caused forest fires to ignite and spread across forty miles, melting metal objects scattered throughout the area. Several shock waves were felt for hundreds of miles around, breaking windows and tossing people, animals, and objects in the air. Finally, black rain fell from a menacing-looking cloud over a radius of 100 square miles. It is no wonder that the peasants of the Tunguska River Valley thought that this was the end of the world (Krinov, 1966; Baxter & Atkins, 1976).

For a variety of reasons, this devastating occurrence remained almost unknown outside Russia--and even outside central Siberia--for many years. The Tungus was extremely remote, even for Russia, which is such a vast country that transportation and communication between places can be slow and difficult. The few people living in the area who actually witnessed what happened were mostly peasants and nomadic tribesmen, and did not have much opportunity or inclination to talk about what they had seen. There was little publicity, and what there was was limited to local Siberian newspapers (Krinov, 1966). During that summer, there was a lot of discussion in the newspapers of the European capitals about peculiar lights and colors seen in the northern skies, unusually radiant sunsets, some magnetic disturbances, and strange dust clouds (Cowan, Atluri, & Libby, 1965). But, since news of the events at the Tungus River had hardly yet been heard even in Moscow, there was no way for scientists in other countries to see a connection between these happenings.

It was only in 1921, when Russia was relatively stable after years of war, revolution, and economic problems, that the first expedition to investigate the event at Tunguska actually took place (Crowther, 1931). That it occurred then at all was largely because an energetic Russian scientist, Leonid Kulik, had become fascinated by meteorites. He read in an old Siberian newspaper that, in 1908, a railway train had been forced to stop because a meteorite fell in its path--a story that was quite untrue. Kulik thought that he might become the discoverer of the greatest meteorite ever found on earth and determined to search for evidence that such a meteorite existed. Authorized by the Soviet Academy, Kulik led a series of expeditions to the Tungus River. In 1921, he did not even reach the site, for the route was almost impassable. In 1927, and annually for the next few years, Kulik did, indeed, explore the devastated area and was able to study the evidence of what had happened and listen to the oral accounts of the event provided by those inhabitants who were still alive and who were willing to talk to him. Finally, in 1938–39, Kulik traveled to the Tungus for the last time, for the purpose of taking serial photographs that might confirm his meteorite theory (Baxter & Atkins, 1976).

Kulik and his fellow investigators believed that whatever had happened at the Tungus River had been caused by a meteorite. So, what they expected to find was a single, vast crater to mark the place where the meteorite had landed. Such a crater, however, was simply not there (Cowan, Atluri, & Libby, 1965). Instead, he found a vast devastated and burned area, a forest of giant trees with their tops cut off and scattered around (Crowther, 1931). In 1928, without the benefit of an aerial view of the region, Kulik concluded from his various vantage points on the ground that, around the circumference of the area where the meteorite had landed, there was a belt of upright dead trees, which he named the "telegraph pole forest." Scattered around the perimeter of the frozen swamp, which he called the "cauldron," were groups of fallen trees, with their tops all pointing away from the direction of where the blast had occurred (Cowan, Atluri, & Libby, 1965). None of this was consistent with Kulik's meteorite theory, and he could only attribute the odd pattern of upright and fallen trees to a shock wave or "hot compressed-air pockets," which had missed some trees and affected others (Baxter & Atkins, 1976). The account of his discovery in the Literary Digest of 1929 states that "each of the falling meteoric fragments must have worked, the Russian scientists imagine, like a gigantic piston," with compressed air knocking trees down like toothpicks (What a meteor, 1929, p. 34). Kulik continued to insist that the fire and the resultant effect on the trees was the result of a meteorite explosion. But the Russian scientist V. G. Fesenkov estimated that such destruction could only have been caused by an object of at least several hundred meters, and that, if anything of this size or force had hit the ground, it would have left a crater (Baxter & Atkins, 1976).

Kulik found other evidence that could not easily be explained by the meteorite theory. Although there was no trace of a single large crater (Cowan, Atluri, & Libby, 1965), there were numerous shallow cavities scattered around the frozen bog (Olivier, 1928). For several years, Kulik attempted to bore into the ground, seeking evidence that these pits and ridges were formed by lateral pressure caused by gases exploding from the meteorite's impact. Kulik described the scene as "not unlike a giant duplicate of what happens when a brick from a tall chimney-top falls into a puddle of mud. Solid ground actually must have splashed outward in every direction." In this account, the supposed meteorite became "the great swarm of meteors" that "must have traversed" the atmosphere for several hundred miles, pushing ahead of it a "giant bubble of superheated atmosphere" that was "probably responsible" for the burned countryside (What a meteor, 1929, p. 33). All the "must have's" and "probably's" make a good narrative, but are not scientifically convincing.

Similarly, Kulik endeavored to explain eyewitness accounts of the huge fireball in the sky that burned one observer's shirt off his back and threw him off his porch (Cowan, Atluri, & Libby, 1965). Such extreme heat waves had never before been known to have accompanied the fall of a meteorite, but Kulik decided that this meteorite was much larger than those previously recorded and that therefore it would have released much more energy upon impact and that would account for such radiant heat (Baxter & Atkins, 1976). So obsessed was Kulik with the idea that somewhere buried in the Tungus swamp was a phenomenal meteorite that he focused the efforts of all the expeditions to the area during his lifetime on digging beneath the frozen tundra and to some extent neglected the examination of other evidence that might have further threatened the theory that he was determined to prove (Parry, 1961). Initially, he was successful in convincing the scientific community that his theory was correct. It is most interesting to read excerpts from The American Weekly of 1929 flatly asserting that a meteorite had fallen in Siberia and that Professor Kulik had brought back photographs of the giant crater that he found, as well as small samples of meteoric materials. The article is accompanied by a photograph of Professor Kulik measuring "the main crater, where the largest mass of this celestial visitor buried itself in the earth" (Quoted in What a meteor, p. 34).

While Kulik's expeditions were still searching for evidence of a meteorite, other scientists were hypothesizing that the Tunguska explosion might have been caused by a small comet, which would account for the absence of a crater. Comets are composed of ice, frozen gases, and dust, and as they travel around the sun, they develop a long tail. Upon impact, a comet might give off a trail of gases and dust which would create a bright and colorful night sky similar to that observed after the explosion. This would not be true of a meteorite, which has no gaseous trail and thus leaves no trace in the atmosphere. It has also been suggested that the observed direction of the object's travel was more typical of a comet than a meteorite (Florensky, 1963). If the comet had blown up approximately two miles above the site, that would explain why some trees survived while others did not (Parry, 1961). On the other hand, there is no evidence that a comet had ever crashed on earth before, or caused a comparable change in magnetic and atmospheric phenomena, or even come so close without being sighted (Baxter & Atkins, 1976). Those scientists supporting the comet theory have suggested that, although it is unusual for any comet to come that close to earth without anyone sighting it, the one landing at Tunguska might have been small enough to go by unnoticed. But that idea is contradicted by Fesenkov's estimate that, to cause such destruction, the nucleus of the Tunguskan comet--if there was one--would have been only slightly smaller than those of well-documented comets that were visible at great distances (Cowan, Atluri, & Libby, 1965).

The next major explanation for the cosmic phenomenon at Tunguska could only have been formulated after World War II, when the scientific community had learned how to make atomic explosions and had become familiar with their aftermath. Aleksander Kazantsev, a Russian scientist and (equally important) science-fiction writer, had visited Hiroshima after the atom bomb explosion and had studied the data describing its impact and aftermath. Because of certain similarities in the blast effects--the burnt yet upright trees, the mushroom cloud, the black rain--Kazantsev and other

scientists concluded that the blast of 1908 was an atomic explosion estimated at a minimum of ten times the strength of the one at Hiroshima
(Parry, 1961). Witnesses had described the blinding flash and withering heat
at Hiroshima in much the same way that the Siberian peasants described
the frightening blast at Tunguska. The melting heat that Kulik found so inconsistent with his meteorite theory was more consistent with an atomic explosion (Baxter & Atkins, 1976). It is worth pointing out that scientists went
on to develop the hypothesis that a nuclear explosion had occurred at
Tunguska even though their theorizing was largely based on stories told by
ignorant peasants, believers in devils and wrathful gods, who could quite
easily have exaggerated what had actually happened to improve their stories.
Even though these eyewitness accounts were gathered twenty or more years
after the actual event, and had quite possibly entered the folklore of the
countryside (Krinov, 1966), they were still regarded as the purest evidence.

To test whether a nuclear explosion might have occurred, scientists
examined the trees for radioactivity and for any unusual increase in normal
growth patterns, shown by greater spacing between the age lines, that might
have been the result of radioactivity. What they found was that some trees at
the site grew to be four times greater than what would normally have been
expected. Similarly, scabs that appeared on the hides of local reindeer were
explained as being the result of radioactive contamination (Baxter & Atkins,
1976). This evidence, by no means conclusive (Florensky, 1963), was cited
as proof that such an atomic explosion had taken place, just as Kulik had
cited the existence of shallow pits in the terrain as proof that a meteorite
had exploded.

Assuming that what happened at Tunguska was the result of an
atomic blast, and faced with the fact that nuclear fission was not within
man's grasp before the 1940s, Kazantsev and his colleagues concluded that
the phenomenon must have involved extraterrestrial beings and that the
explosion was caused by a UFO, propelled by atomic energy, that crashed
(Parry, 1961). The pattern of devastation on the ground, as seen from the
air, suggested that the object took a zigzag path, changing its direction as it
came closer and closer to earth. Advocates of the UFO theory argue such a
change in direction would not have been possible with a natural object like a

meteorite or comet, and that the object--a spacecraft--was driven by intelligent beings who were trying to land without hitting a more densely populated area. They hypothesize that the craft had some mechanical problem that made it necessary to land but that the initial angle of its trajectory was too shallow for landing and would only have bounced the craft back into space. So the navigators tried to maneuver and correct the angle, but swerved, came down too sharply, and exploded (Baxter & Atkins, 1976). On the other hand, it seems just as possible that a natural object swerved or that debris from a nonatomic explosion was thrown in zigzag directions than that navigators from outer space ran into mechanical troubles and crash-landed. If probability is going to be disregarded in order to support one theory, then the same suspension of the natural order of things can be used to confirm an equally unlikely theory.

In the late 1950s, an exploratory team examined the Tunguska site with an advanced magnetic detector and, in 1962, scientists magnified the soil and found an array of tiny, colored, magnetic, ball-shaped particles, made of cobalt, nickel, copper, and germanium (Baxter & Atkins, 1976). According to extraterrestrial-intelligence specialists, these could have been the elements used for electrical and technical instruments, with the copper used for communication services and the germanium used in semiconductors (Parry, 1961). However, controlled experiments would be necessary to make this atomic-extraterrestrial argument convincing.

Scientists who find the UFO and extraterrestrial explanations less than credible have turned to the most recent theories of physics and astronomy to explain what might have happened in the Tungus. Some (including Kazantsev) argue that such an explosion might have been caused by debris from space colliding with the earth (Morrison & Chapman, 1990), or by anti-matter, which exploded as it came in contact with the atmosphere (Parry, 1961). Alternatively, the explosion might have been caused by a "black hole" hitting the earth in Siberia and passing through to emerge on the other side. Those opposing these theories point, again, to the absence of a crater and to the numerous eyewitness accounts that describe the shape of the object and the sound of the blast, all of which would be inconsistent with antimatter or black-hole theories (Baxter & Atkins, 1976). However, a 1973 article in

Nature asserts that a black hole would not, in fact, leave a crater, but would simply enter the earth at a great velocity and that a shock wave and blast might possibly accompany its entrance (Jackson & Ryan).

What is most fascinating about the Tunguska Valley phenomenon is that, despite all the advances in science over the past 80 years, investigators cannot now be any more certain of the cause of the blast than they were in 1921, when Kulik first came near the site. None of the theories presented is wholly convincing, for all of them rely to some extent on human observers, whose accounts of events are notoriously unreliable, or hypotheses based on ambiguous evidence, without the support of controlled tests and experiments. The formulation of a radically new body of scientific knowledge might provide a new theoretical context for examining the evidence and establishing a more convincing explanation. But, as it is, with the trail getting colder, finding a solution to this mystery seems to become more and more unlikely.

Examining these explanations about what did or did not land and explode in Siberia does teach us that scientific theories are sometimes based on the selective interpretation of evidence and that scientists, like everyone else, tend to believe their own theories and find the evidence that they want to find. Although the language that they use is very different, the accounts of what happened at Tunguska according to Kulik, Kazantsev, and their other scientific colleagues are not so very different from what the local peasants say that they saw. Both have a closer resemblance to science fiction than science fact.

References

Baxter, J., & Atkins, T. (1976). The fire came by: The riddle of the great Siberian explosion. Garden City, NY: Doubleday.

Cowan, C., Atluri, C. R., & Libby, W. F. (1965, May 29). Possible antimatter content of the Tunguska meteor of 1908. Nature (London), 861–865.

Crowther, J. G. (1931). More about the great Siberian meteorite. Scientific American, 144(5), 314–317.

Florensky, K. P. (1963, November). Did a comet collide with the earth in 1908? Sky and Telescope, 268–269.

Jackson, A. A., & Ryan, M. P. (1973, September 14). Was the Tungus event due to a black hole? Nature (London), 88–89.

Krinov, E. L. (1966). Giant meteorites. London: Pergamon.

Morrison, D., & Chapman, C. R. (1990). Target earth: It will happen. Sky and Telescope, 261–265.

Olivier, C. P. (1928). The great Siberian meteorite. Scientific American, 139(1), 42–44.

Parry, A. (1961). The Tungus mystery: Was it a spaceship? In Russia's Rockets and Missiles (pp. 248–267). London: Macmillan.

What a meteor did to Siberia. (1929, March 16). Literary Digest, 33–34.

Appendix A

Some Useful Reference Sources

GUIDELINES FOR USING REFERENCE WORKS

1. You can find sources for your essays by looking
   - in the library's *on-line database of books* or *card catalog;*
   - in the *bibliographies of standard works* on your subject;
   - in the brief bibliographies at the end of *encyclopedia articles;*
   - under the broad subject headings in *general-interest bibliographies* and *periodical indexes;* and
   - in the *indexes and abstract collections* that deal with the specific subject of your research.

2. Some reference sources are entirely bibliography: they consist of long lists of articles and (sometimes) books, each followed by the essential publication information. These indexes are usually arranged by topic. You may have to check several broad headings before you find the articles that you need. If, for example, you are doing research on educational television, you would look up "education," "television," and the names of some of the programs that you intend to write about. Most indexes are cross-referenced.

3. Some reference sources are called "abstracts" because they contain abstracts or paragraph summaries of many (but not all) of the articles published each year in that discipline. Abstracts often have two sections: the first contains a series of summaries of articles, chosen for their special in-

terest or excellence and arranged by subject; the second contains a list of all the articles published in that field in that year. (Occasionally, you will find a modified form of abstract, in which several articles are each given a one-sentence summary.) First you look up the specific subject that you are interested in and glance at the summaries. Then you get the publication information about the articles relevant to your research by looking up their *authors* in the second section of the reference work. Although abstracts give you a convenient preview, you will find that many of the articles are highly technical and may therefore be difficult to read and write about.

4. Some of the periodical articles that you want to consult may be available only on microfiche or microcards. Ask the reference librarian to help you to use the system and its apparatus. With the proper explanations, even the most unmechanical people can become adept at using these tools of the modern library.

5. Many bibliographies and indexes are available on-line. Ask the reference librarian to show you the commands that you need to use at the computer monitor. *Those reference sources that are available on-line and/or on CD-ROM as of this date are asterisked.*

6. If you can't find a specific reference work or if you are not sure which one to use, check with a librarian. As long as you can tell librarians the broad or (preferably) the narrow subject of your research, they will be willing and able to help you.

GENERAL ENCYCLOPEDIAS

Collier's Encyclopedia. 24 vols. with annual supplements and revisions. 1995. Easier to read and understand than the old *Britannica* or *Americana.*

Encyclopaedia Britannica. 14th ed. 24 vols. with annual supplements and periodic revisions (through 1973). 1929. Dated and more sophisticated than the 15th edition, but retained by many libraries for the excellence of its articles.

Encyclopedia Americana. 30 vols. with annual supplements and revisions. 1995. Use the index volume to locate your subject within the longer encyclopedia.

New Columbia Encyclopedia. 5th ed. 1993. A single-volume encyclopedia, especially good as a starting point.

New Encyclopaedia Britannica. 15th ed. 32 vols. with annual supplements and periodic revisions. 1995. Divided into a "Micropaedia" of brief articles, a "Macropaedia" of longer articles, and a "Propaedia" that serves as a guide to the "Micropaedia" and "Macropaedia." The three-division arrangement can be inconvenient to use.

SPECIALIZED ENCYCLOPEDIAS

Encyclopedia of American Art. New York: Dutton, 1981.

Encyclopedia of Biological Sciences. Ed. Peter Gray. 2nd ed. New York: Van Nostrand, 1970.

Encyclopedia of Computer Science and Technology. 14 vols. New York: Dekker, 1980.

The Encyclopedia of Education. Ed. Lee C. Deighton. 10 vols. New York: Macmillan, 1971.

The Encyclopedia of Human Behavior: Psychology, Psychiatry, and Mental Health. Ed. Robert M. Goldenson. 2 vols. New York: Doubleday, 1974.

Encyclopedia of Psychology. Ed. Raymond J. Corsini. 2nd ed. 4 vols. New York: Wiley, 1994.

Encyclopedia of Sociology. Ed. Edgar F. Borgatta and Marie L. Borgatta. 4 vols. New York: Macmillan, 1992.

Encyclopedia of World Art. 17 vols. New York: McGraw, 1959–87.

An Encyclopedia of World History: Ancient, Medieval, and Modern Chronologically Arranged. Ed. William L. Langer. 5th ed. Boston: Houghton, 1972.

International Encyclopedia of the Social Sciences. Ed. D. L. Sills. 17 vols. New York: Macmillan, 1972.

McGraw-Hill Encyclopedia of Physics. Ed. Sybil Parker. 2nd ed. New York: McGraw, 1993.

McGraw-Hill Encyclopedia of Science and Technology. 7th ed. 20 vols. New York: McGraw, 1992.

McGraw-Hill Encyclopedia of World Drama. 2nd ed. 5 vols. New York: McGraw, 1984.

The New Grove Dictionary of Music and Musicians. Ed. Stanley Sadie. 20 vols. New York: Macmillan, 1980.

VNR Concise Encyclopedia of Mathematics. Ed. S. Gottwald et al. 2nd ed. New York: Van Nostrand, 1989.

GENERAL INDEXES

*Book Review Digest. New York: Wilson, 1905–present. Includes excerpts from reviews as well as lists of references.

*Book Review Index. Detroit: Gale Research Co., 1965–present. Lists reviews of books on literature, art, business, economics, religion, and current affairs.

*Books in Print Plus. Lists books currently in print in the United States, with prices. Full text of book reviews is available for some titles.

*British Newspaper Index. 1990–present. Indexes major British newspapers.

*Editorials on File. New York: Facts on File, 1970–present. Selected editorials on subjects of contemporary interest, with each editorial preceded by a summary of the issue being discussed.

*Facts on File. New York: Facts on File, 1941–present. Summaries of issues and events, with selected bibliographies.

Milner, Anita Check. *Newspaper Indexes: A Location and Subject Guide for Researchers,* Metuchen, N.J., and London: Scarecrow, 1982.

*National Newspaper Index. 1990–present. Combined indexing of five major newspapers: *The New York Times, The Wall Street Journal, Christian Science Monitor, Washington Post,* and *The Los Angeles Times.*

*New York Times Full-text. Indexes the most recent years of *The New York Times,* as well as providing the text of the articles.

New York Times Index. New York: New York Times, 1851–present.

Periodical Abstracts Ondisc. 1986–present. Indexes and abstracts over 950 general-interest periodicals from the United States, Canada, and the United Kingdom.

Popular Periodical Index. Camden, N.J.: Popular Periodical Index, 1971–present. Includes magazines such as *New York, Playboy, Rolling Stone,* and *TV Guide.*

Proquest Image. Indexes and abstracts articles from hundreds of news and general-interest magazines and some scholarly journals; provides the full text for many articles.

Readers' Guide to Periodical Literature. New York: Wilson, 1905–present. Includes listings of articles in many general-interest magazines, especially news magazines and women's magazines.

Vertical File Index. New York: Wilson, 1932/1935–present. Lists pamphlets on all subjects.

BIOGRAPHICAL SOURCES

Annual Obituary. New York: St. Martin's, 1980–present. Annual collection of profiles of prominent individuals who died during the year, arranged by month of death date.

Biography Index. New York: Wilson, 1947–present. Organized like the *Readers' Guide,* listing articles about contemporary celebrities.

Current Biography. New York: Wilson, 1940–present. Consists of full-scale articles (like encyclopedia entries) about prominent people. Use the index to find the right year for the person that you are researching.

Dictionary of American Biography. 10 vols. New York: Scribner's, 1980. Articles contain basic information about notable figures in American history. (Do not use this source for contemporary figures.)

New York Times Obituary Index 1858–1990. New York: New York Times.

SEMISPECIALIZED INDEXES AND ABSTRACTS
Humanities

Art Index. New York: Wilson, 1929–present. Covers the literature of art and art history in periodicals, yearbooks, and museum bulletins. Subjects include architecture; archaeology; art history; fine arts; crafts and folk art; film and photography; graphic arts; industrial design.

Humanities Index. New York: Wilson, 1974–present. Annual volumes include reviews of books and performances as well as a listing of articles on issues and new developments in all the humanities.

MLA International Bibliography of Books and Articles in the Modern Languages and Literature. New York: MLA, 1921–present. Indexes critical documents on literature, language, linguistics, and folklore. Articles from more than 3,000 journals, serials published worldwide, conference papers and proceedings, handbooks, dictionaries, and bibliographies are indexed. Includes works on literature transmitted orally, in print, or in audiovisual media.

The Music Index. Detroit: Information Coordinators, 1949–present. Includes reviews listed under composer and title.

The Philosopher's Index. Bowling Green, Ohio: Bowling Green State U, 1967–present. Articles on philosophy and its relation to art, religion, the humanities in general, and history.

Physical and Biological Sciences

Applied Science and Technology Index. New York: Wilson, 1958–present. Includes references to a large number of scientific and technological periodicals.

Biological and Agricultural Index. New York: Wilson, 1964–present.

Chemical Abstracts. Washington: Amer. Chemical Soc., 1907–present. The on-line and CD-ROM databases are called *CA Search*.

Engineering Index. New York: Engineering Information, 1906–present. The on-line and CD-ROM databases are part of *Compendex*.

General Science Index. New York: Wilson, 1978–present. Includes articles in 109 English-language science periodicals of general interest.

Science Abstracts. London, Eng.: Inst. of Electrical Engineers, 1898–present. Summaries of articles about physics.

Science Citation Index. Philadelphia: Inst. for Scientific Information, 1945–present. Includes citations to the literature of science, technology, medicine, and related disciplines from 3,300 science journals worldwide. The on-line and CD-ROM databases are part of *SciSearch*.

Social Sciences

Almanac of American Politics. Ed. Michael Barone. Boston: Gambit, 1972–present. Lists sources for information about local and national public affairs.

America: History and Life. Santa Barbara, Calif.: ABC-Clio, 1964–present. Includes references to 2,000 publications dealing with past, recent, and present history. Part A consists of abstracts; Part B consists of one-sentence summaries of articles, grouped under topic headings.

Ethnic Newswatch. Stamford, CT: Sofline Info. Indexes and provides full text of articles from ethnic and minority newspapers and magazines across the U.S. Subjects include current events covered with a specific ethnic focus and topics related to specific ethnic groups.

Guide to U.S. Government Serials and Periodicals. McLean, Va.: Documents Index, 1964–present. A cumulative index directs the user to the correct volume.

Historical Abstracts. Santa Barbara, Calif.: ABC-Clio, 1955–present. Part A deals with modern history from 1450 to 1940; Part B deals with mid-twentieth-century history. The index is in the Winter issue.

International Bibliography of Economics. Paris: UNESCO, 1952–present.

International Political Science Abstracts. Paris: International Pol. Sci. Assn., 1951–present. Summaries of articles on political science and international relations.

Psychological Abstracts. Washington: American Psychological Assn., 1927–present. Use the three-year cumulative subject and author indexes; for example, the years 1978–1980 are indexed together. The on-line database is called *PsycInfo,* and the CD-ROM database is called *PsycLit.*

Public Affairs Information Service Bulletin. New York: PAIS, 1915–present. Includes pamphlets and government documents and reports as well as periodical articles. Covers an unusually large number of periodicals. Emphasizes factual and statistical information.

Sage Public Administration Abstracts. Beverly Hills, Calif.: Sage, 1979–present. Summaries of books, articles, government publications, speeches, and research studies.

Social Sciences Index. New York: Wilson, 1974–present.

Sociofile. A cumulation of *Sociological Abstracts* and *Social Planning, Policy and Development Abstracts.* Indexes over 1,500 serials published worldwide in sociology and its related disciplines.

INDEXES AND ABSTRACTS FOR PROFESSIONAL STUDIES

Business

ABI/INFORM. Ann Arbor: UMI, 1971–present. Provides abstracts from more than 800 business and trade journals for the last five years. Subjects include accounting and auditing, banking, data processing and information management, economics, finance, health care, human resources, labor relations, public administration, and telecommunications.

Accountants' Index. New York: Amer. Inst. of CPAs, 1944–present. Lists articles about accounting, data processing, financial management, and taxation.

Business Periodicals Index. New York: Wilson, 1958–present. Lists articles from more than 100 periodicals dealing with new developments and methods in business management.

Corporate Text. Current. Copies of annual reports for companies traded on the New York Stock Exchange, American Stock Exchange, and NASDAQ exchange and over the counter.

Personnel Literature. Washington: U.S. Civil Service Commission, 1969–present. Lists articles about administration, supervision, management relations, and productivity.

Education

CIJE: Current Index to Journals in Education. Phoenix: Oryx, 1969–present. The on-line and CD-ROM databases are part of *ERIC.*

Education Index. New York: Wilson, 1929–present.

ERIC. Indexes and abstracts journal and technical literature in education and related fields, including psychology and sociology. Information is compiled from *Resources in Education* (RIE) and *Current Index to Journals in Education* (CIJE).

Law

Index to Legal Periodicals. New York: Wilson, 1908–present. In addition to listing articles by subject and author, there is a table of cases and a group of book reviews.

Library Science

Library and Information Science Abstracts. London: The Library Assn., 1970–present. Materials about information dissemination and retrieval, as well as library services.

Nursing and Health

Aidsline. Provides detailed coverage of all aspects of the AIDS crisis, focusing on clinical aspects but including health planning implications and cancer research from more than 3,000 journals. Information is derived from the U.S. National Library of Medicine's *Medline, Health Planning and Administration,* and *CancerLIT* databases.

Chem-Bank. Indexes descriptions of and toxicity information on thousands of chemical substances in the form of lists prepared by four government agencies: RTECS (Registry of Toxic Effects of Chemical Substances), from the Department of Health and Human Services; OHMTADS (Oil and Hazardous Materials Technical Assistance Data System), developed by the Environmental Protection Agency; CHRIS (Chemical Hazard Response Information System), produced by the Coast Guard; and HSDB (Hazardous Substance Databank), from the National Library of Medicine.

Cumulative Index to Nursing and Allied Health Literature. Glendale: CINAHL Information Services, 1977–present. Articles listed include health education and social services as they relate to health care. The on-line and CD-ROM databases are called *Nursing and Allied Health Database.*

Index Medicus. Bethesda: National Lib. of Medicine, 1960–present. Lists articles of medical interest and includes a bibliography of medical book reviews. The on-line and CD-ROM databases are part of *Medline.*

International Nursing Index. New York: Amer. Journal of Nursing, 1966–present.

Medline. Database of the U.S. National Library of Medicine; contains bibliographic citations and abstracts of biomedical literature, and full indexing, with MeSH thesaurus terms. Indexes articles from approximately 3,400 journals published in more than 70 countries.

OSH-ROM. Produced by National Institute for Occupational Safety and Health; provides citations and abstracts from journals, books, and technical reports dealing with occupational health and safety. Subjects include environmental health, toxicology, safety engineering, and industrial pollution.

Social Work

Human Resources Abstracts. Beverly Hills, Calif.: Sage, 1965–present. Covers developments in areas such as poverty, employment, and distribution of human resources.

Journal of Human Services Abstracts. Rockville, Md.: Project Share, 1976–present. Summarizes articles concerning the provision of public services as they relate to public administration, education, psychology, environmental studies, family studies, nutrition, and health services.

Sage Family Studies Abstracts. Beverly Hills, Calif.: Sage, 1979–present.

*Social Work Research and Abstracts. Albany, N.Y.: National Assn. of Social Workers, 1965–present. Selected research articles as well as abstracts of other articles in the field of social welfare. Computer database is called *Swab Plus.*

INDEXES TO STATISTICAL COMPILATIONS

American Statistics Index: A Comprehensive Guide and Index to the Statistical Publications of the U.S. Government. Washington: Congressional Information Service, 1973–present.

*County and City Plus. Indexes statistical information for counties, cities, and other designated places. Subjects include population, age, race, income, labor force and unemployment, local government education expenditure, hospitals, crime, climate, and more.

Statistical Yearbook. New York: UN Dept. of Economic and Social Affairs, 1949–present. International statistics.

*STATMASTER. Indexes statistical publications issued by the U.S. government, U.S. state governments, international governmental organizations, professional and trade associations, business organizations, commercial publishers, and university and independent research organizations.

Appendix B

Some Basic Forms for Documentation

MODELS OF MLA BIBLIOGRAPHICAL ENTRIES AND PARENTHETICAL DOCUMENTATION

The following is a list of model bibliographic and parenthetical entries for MLA style. The proper bibliographic form that will appear in alphabetical order on your "Works Cited" page is followed by a sample parenthetical documentation that might appear in the text. The sample documentation in this list will always contain the author's name; but remember that in your essay you will often mention the author's name in your text, thus making necessary only the parenthetical documentation of the page(s) of your source. You can find guidelines for preparing MLA documentation in Chapter 9, on pp. 403–412. See also the list of "Works Cited" in the student essay "Euthanasia: The Right to Die" in Chapter 10.

1st question   put in correct form

Book by a Single Author

Veysey, Laurence R. The Emergence of the American University. Chicago: U of
5 spaces Chicago P, 1965.   *Double space*

(Veysey 23)

476

Book by Two Authors

Postman, Neil, and Charles Weingartner. Teaching as a Subversive Activity. New
York: Dell, 1969.

(Postman and Weingartner 34–36)

Book by More Than Three Authors

Spiller, Robert E., et al. Literary History of the United States. London:
Macmillan, 1946.

(Spiller et al. 67)

Edited Collection Written by Different Authors

Wheelwright, Philip, ed. The Presocratics. New York: Odyssey, 1966.

(Wheelwright 89)

Essay from a Collection Written by Different Authors

Webb, R. K. "The Victorian Reading Public." From Dickens to Hardy. Ed. Boris
Ford. Baltimore: Penguin, 1958. 205–26.

(Webb 209)

Book Published in a Reprinted Edition

Orwell, George. Animal Farm. 1946. New York: Signet, 1959.

(Orwell 100)

Book Published in a New Edition

Baugh, Albert C. A History of the English Language. 2nd ed. New York:
Appleton, 1957.

(Baugh 21)

Work in Translation

Lorenz, Konrad. On Aggression. Trans. Marjorie Kerr Wilson. 1966. New York:
Bantam, 1969.

(Lorenz 45)

Book Published in Several Volumes

> Tocqueville, Alexis de. Democracy in America. Ed. Phillips Bradley. 2 vols. New
>   York: Knopf, 1945.
>
> (Tocqueville 2: 78)

One Volume in a Set or Series

> Granville-Barker, Harley. Prefaces to Shakespeare. Vol. 2. London: Batsford,
>   1963.
>
> Gaff, Jerry G. Institutional Renewal through the Improvement of Teaching. New
>   Directions for Higher Ed. 24. San Francisco: Jossey-Bass, 1978.
>
> (Granville-Barker 193)
>
> (Gaff 45)

Book in an Edited Edition

> Kirstein, Lincoln. By With To & From. Ed. Nicholas Jenkins. New York: Farrar,
>   1991.
>
> Jenkins, Nicholas, ed. By With To & From. By Lincoln Kirstein. New York:
>   Farrar, 1991.
>
> (Kirstein 190)
>
> (Jenkins xiii)

The second entry indicates that you are citing the work of the editor (not the author); therefore, you place the editor's name first.

Introduction, Preface, Foreword, or Afterword

> Spacks, Patricia Meyer. Afterword. Sense and Sensibility. By Jane Austen. New
>   York: Bantam, 1983. 332–43.
>
> (Spacks 338)

Article in an Encyclopedia

> "American Architecture." Columbia Encyclopedia. 3rd ed. 1963.
>
> ("American Architecture")

Notice that no page numbers are needed for either the bibliographical entry or the parenthetical reference when the source is an encyclopedia. If the article is signed by an author, list the author's name at the beginning of the bibliographic entry and identify the source in your parenthetical documentation by using the author's name. If you are citing a little-known or specialized encyclopedia, provide full publication information.

Publication of a Corporation, Foundation, or Government Agency

Carnegie Council on Policy Studies in Higher Education. Three Thousand Futures: The Next Twenty Years for Higher Education. San Francisco: Jossey-Bass, 1980.

United States. Bureau of the Census. Abstract of the Census of Manufactures. Washington: GPO, 1919.

Coleman, James S., et al. Equality of Educational Opportunity. U.S. Dept. of Health, Education, and Welfare. Washington: GPO, 1966.

(Carnegie Council 34)

(Bureau of the Census 56)

(Coleman et al. 88)

Pamphlet or Brochure

The entry should resemble the entry for a book. If the author's name is missing, begin the entry with the title; if the date is missing, use the abbreviation *n.d.*

More, Howard V. Costa de la Luz. Turespana: Secretaria General de Turismo, n.d.

(More 6)

Classic Work

Job. The Jerusalem Bible. Reader's Edition. Ed. Alexander Jones. Garden City: Doubleday, 1968.

Homer. The Odyssey. Trans. Robert Fitzgerald. Garden City: Doubleday, 1963.

(Job 3:7)

(Odyssey 7.1–16)

2nd question

Article in a Scholarly Journal with Continuous Pagination

Title of article   *Title of Journal*

Shepard, David. "Authenticating Films." The Quarterly Journal of the Library of Congress 37 (1980): 342–54.

(Shepard 350) *Volume #*

The four journals comprising Volume 37 are treated as a single continuous work for purposes of pagination. The first journal in Volume 38 will start again with page 1.

Article in a Scholarly Journal without Continuous Pagination

Burnham, Christopher C. "Expressive Writing: A Heretic's Confession." Focuses 2.1 (1989): 5–18.

(Burnham 7–8)

Article in a Monthly Periodical

Loye, David. "TV's Impact on Adults." Psychology Today Apr. 1978: 87+.

(Loye 87)

The plus sign after the page number indicates that the article is not printed on consecutive pages, but skips to later pages.

Article in a Weekly Periodical

Meyer, Karl E. "Television's Trying Times." Saturday Review 16 Sept. 1978: 19–23.

(Meyer 21)

Article in a Newspaper

Goldin, Davidson. "In a Change of Policy, and Heart, Colleges Join Fight Against Inflated Grades." New York Times 4 July 1995, late ed.: 8.

(Goldin)

No page number is required in a parenthetical citation of a one-page article. If the issue of the *Times* or another newspaper is divided into separate sections, the page number in both the bibliographical entry and the citation should be preceded by the section, e.g., *B6*.

Article without an Author

"How to Get Quality Back into the Schools." US News & World Report 12 Sept. 1977: 31–34.

("How to Get Quality" 33)

Letter to the Editor

Kropp, Arthur J. Letter. Village Voice 12 Oct. 1993: 5.

(Kropp)

Editorial

"Justice Berger's Contradictions." Editorial. New York Times 27 June 1995, late
ed.: A16.

("Justice Berger's Contradictions")

Review

Appiah, K. Anthony. "Giving Up the Perfect Diamond." Rev. of The Holder of
the World, by Bharati Mukherjee. New York Times Book Review 10 Oct.
1993: 7.

(Appiah)

Personal, Published, or E-Mail Letter

Hans, James S. Letter to the author. 18 Aug. 1991.

Keats, John. "To Benjamin Bailey." 22 Nov. 1817. John Keats: Selected Poetry
and Letters. Ed. Richard Harter Fogle. New York: Rinehart, 1952. 300–303.

Wittreich, Joseph. E-mail to the author. 12 Dec. 1994.

(Hans)

(Keats 302)

(Wittreich)

Unpublished Dissertation

Eastman, Elizabeth. "'Lectures on Jurisprudence': A Key to Understanding
Adam Smith's Thought." Diss. Claremont Grad. School, 1993.

(Eastman 34)

Previously Printed Source Accessed from CD-ROM

Burke, Marc. "Homosexuality as Deviance: The Case of the Gay Police Officer."
British Journal of Criminology 34.2 (1994): 192–203. PsycLit. CD-ROM.
SilverPlatter. Nov. 1994.

(Burke 291)

Previously Printed Source Accessed from an On-line Computer Service

> Riesman, David, and Judith McLaughlin. "A Primer on the Use of Consultants in Presidential Recruitment." Change 16.6 (1984): 12–23. ERIC. On-line. Pipeline. 5 July 1995.
>
> (Riesman and McLaughlin 18)

Source Not Previously Printed Accessed from an On-line Computer Service

> "The $100 Million Club." 20 May 1995. Hollyweb. On-line. Pipeline. 6 July 1995.
>
> ("$100 Million")

Source from an Electronic Journal or Conference Accessed through a Computer Network

> Thomas, Gail. "Geomancy: A New Form for the Making of Cities." Gnosis 33 (1994): 2 pp. On-line. Internet. 7 July 1995. Available gopher.well.sf.ca.us
>
> (Thomas)

Personal Interview (Conducted by the Researcher)

> Nussbaumer, Doris D. Personal interview. 30 July 1988.
>
> Albert, John J. Telephone interview. 22 Dec. 1989.
>
> (Nussbaumer)
>
> (Albert)

Broadcast or Published Interview

> Kennedy, Joseph. Interview with Harry Smith. This Morning. CBS. WCBS, New York. 14 Oct. 1993.
>
> Berger, John. Interview with Nikos Papastergiadis. American Poetry Review. July–Aug. 1993: 9–12.
>
> (Kennedy)
>
> (Berger 10)

Lecture

Auchincloss, Louis, Erica Jong, and Gloria Steinem. "The 18th Century Woman."
Symposium at the Metropolitan Museum of Art, New York. 29 Apr. 1982.

(Auchincloss, Jong, and Steinem)

Live Performance

Tommy. By Pete Townshend. Dir. Des McAnuff. St. James Theater, New York. 3
May 1993.

(Tommy)

Film

Dr. Strangelove. Dir. Stanley Kubrick. Columbia Pictures, 1963.

Kubrick, Stanley, dir. Dr. Strangelove. Columbia Pictures, 1963.

Put the film first if you wish to emphasize material from the film; however, if
you are emphasizing the work of the director, list that name first.

(Dr. Strangelove)

(Kubrick)

Television or Radio Program

Serge Pavlovitch Diaghilev 1872–1929: A Portrait. Prod. Peter Adam. BBC.
WNET, New York. 12 July 1982.

(Diaghilev)

A radio program is entered the same way, with a listing of the program, the director or producer, the producing network, the local station and city, and the
date. In citing television or radio programs, if you wish to emphasize the work
of the producer or director, enter that name first.

Audio Recording

Tchaikovsky, Piotr. The Tchaikovsky Collection. Audiocassette. CBS Special
Products, 1989.

(Tchaikovsky)

Videocassette

> *Wuthering Heights*. Dir. William Wyler. 1939. Videocassette. Embassy, 1987.
>
> (Wuthering)

Work of Art

> Brueghel, Pieter. *The Beggars*. Louvre, Paris.
>
> (Brueghel)

Map or Chart

> *Spain, Portugal, and North Africa*. Map. American Automobile Association,
>
> 1993–4.
>
> (Spain)

Cartoon

> Trudeau, Garry. "Doonesbury." Cartoon. *Charlotte Observer* 23 Dec. 1988: B12.
>
> (Trudeau)

AMERICAN PSYCHOLOGICAL ASSOCIATION (APA) PARENTHETICAL AUTHOR-YEAR DOCUMENTATION

The format for documentation recommended by the American Psychological Association is used primarily in the social and behavioral sciences, especially sociology and psychology. It is also often employed in subjects like anthropology, astronomy, business, education, linguistics, and political science.

Like MLA style, APA documentation is based on parenthetical references to author and page. The chief difference is that, in the APA system, you include the work's *date of publication* after the author's name, both within parentheses.

MLA

Primitive religious rituals may have been a means for deterring collective violence (Girard 1).

Brain Theory suggests two extremes of writing style, the appositional and the propositional (Winterowd and Williams 4).

APA

Primitive religious rituals may have been a means for deterring collective violence (Girard, 1972, p. 1).

Brain Theory suggests two extremes of writing style, the appositional and the propositional (Winterowd & Williams, 1990, p. 4).

As with MLA style, if you cite the author's name and/or the date of publication in your sentence, it is not necessary to repeat them in the parentheses.

In 1972, Girard suggested that primitive religious rituals may have been a means for deterring collective violence (p. 1).

According to Winterowd and Williams (1990), Brain Theory suggests two extremes of writing style, the appositional and the propositional (p. 4).

Here is what the bibliography for these two entries would look like in MLA style and in the style recommended by APA for student papers.

MLA

WORKS CITED

Girard, René. Violence and the Sacred. Baltimore: Johns Hopkins UP, 1972.
Winterowd, W. Ross, and James D. Williams. "Cognitive Style and Written Discourse." Focuses 3 (1990): 3–23.

APA

REFERENCES

Girard, R. (1972). Violence and the sacred. Baltimore: Johns Hopkins University Press.
Winterowd, W. R., & Williams, J. D. (1990). Cognitive style and written discourse. Focuses, 3, 3–23.

These are some of the ways that APA bibliographical style for student papers differs from MLA style:

- Authors' first and middle names are designated by initials. When there are multiple authors, all are listed last name first, and an ampersand (&) is used instead of *and*.

- Two or more works by the same author are listed chronologically. Instead of using a dash for repeated names (as in MLA style), you start each entry with the author's full name.
- The date of publication (in parentheses) is placed immediately after the author's name.
- In the title of a book or article, only the first word and the first word of the subtitle are capitalized.
- The title of a section of a volume (e.g., an article in a periodical or a chapter of a book) is neither underlined nor surrounded by quotation marks.
- The volume number of a journal is underlined.

Since the identification of sources greatly depends on the dates that you cite, you must be careful to clarify the dating, especially when a single author has published two or more works in the same year. Here, for example, is an excerpt from a bibliography that distinguishes among three sources published in 1972:

> Carnegie Commission on Higher Education. (1972a). The campus and the city: Maximizing assets and reducing liabilities. New York: McGraw-Hill.
>
> Carnegie Commission on Higher Education. (1972b). The fourth revolution: Instructional technology in higher education. New York: McGraw-Hill.
>
> Carnegie Commission on Higher Education. (1972c). The more effective use of resources: An imperative for higher education. New York: McGraw-Hill.

And here is how one of these sources would be documented in the essay:

> In its report The More Effective Use of Resources, the Carnegie Commission on Higher Education recommended that "colleges and universities develop a 'self-renewal' fund of 1 to 3 percent each year taken from existing allocations" (1972c, p. 105).

For an example of the use of APA author-year documentation, look at "Explaining the Tunguskan Phenomenon," the third research essay in Chapter 10.

MODELS OF APA BIBLIOGRAPHICAL ENTRIES AND PARENTHETICAL DOCUMENTATION

The following is a brief list of model entries for APA style. Each bibliographic form that will appear in alphabetical order on the "Works Cited" page is followed by a sample parenthetical reference as it might appear in your text. Whenever there is an author, the sample parenthetical references in this list will contain the author's name; remember that, in your essay, you will often mention the author's name (and the date) in your text, with only the page of the source needed in the parenthetical reference.

Book by a Single Author

Veysey, L. R. (1965). The emergence of the American university. Chicago:
> University of Chicago Press.

(Veysey, 1965, p. 45)

Book by More Than One Author

Postman, N., & Weingartner, C. (1969). Teaching as a subversive activity. New
> York: Dell.

(Postman & Weingartner, 1969, p. 143)

When a source has three to five authors, name them all in the first text reference or parenthetical note; then, in all subsequent references or notes, list only the first author's name followed by "et al." For sources with six or more authors, use "et al." in the first reference or note as well. Always list all authors in bibliographical entries.

Edited Collection Written by Different Authors

Wheelwright, P. (Ed.). (1966). The presocratics. New York: Odyssey.

(Wheelwright, 1966, pp. 2–3)

Essay from a Collection Written by Different Authors

Webb, R. K. (1958). The Victorian reading public. In B. Ford (Ed.), From Dickens
> to Hardy (pp. 205–226). Baltimore: Penguin.

(Webb, 1958, pp. 210–212)

Work in Translation/Work Published in a Reprinted Edition

Lorenz, K. (1969). On aggression. (M. K. Wilson, Trans.). New York: Bantam.
> (Original work published 1966.)

(Lorenz, 1966/1969, p. 75)

Work Published in a New Edition

Baugh, A. C. (1957). A history of the English language. (2nd ed.). New York:

Appleton-Century-Crofts.

(Baugh, 1957, p. 288)

Book with No Author

World atlas. (1984). New York: Simon and Schuster.

(World atlas, 1984)

Article in an Encyclopedia

American architecture. (1963). Columbia encyclopedia. (3rd ed.). New York:

Columbia University Press.

(American architecture, 1963)

Publication of a Corporation, Foundation, or Government Agency

Carnegie Council on Policy Studies in Higher Education. (1980). Three thousand

futures: The next twenty years for higher education. San Francisco:

Jossey-Bass.

(Carnegie Council, 1980, p. 110)

Article in a Periodical Numbered by Volume

Plumb, J. H. (1976). Commercialization of childhood. Horizon, 18, 16–29.

(Plumb, 1976, p. 20)

Article in a Monthly Periodical

Loye, D. (1978, April). TV's impact on adults. Psychology Today, 87+.

(Loye, 1978, p. 87)

Article in a Weekly Periodical

Meyer, K. E. (1978, September 16). Television's trying times. Saturday Review,

19–23.

(Meyer, 1978, pp. 19–20)

Article in a Newspaper

Goldin, D. (1995, July 4). In a change of policy, and heart, colleges join fight against inflated grades. The New York Times, late ed., p. 8.

(Goldin, 1995)

Article without an Author

How to get quality back into the schools. (1977, September 12). US News & World Report, 31–34.

(How to get, 1977, p. 32)

Unpublished Dissertation

Eastman, E. (1993). "Lectures on jurisprudence": A key to understanding Adam Smith's thought. Unpublished doctoral dissertation, Claremont Graduate School.

(Eastman, 1993)

Film

Kubrick, S. (Director). (1963). Dr. Strangelove. [Film]. Columbia Pictures.

(Kubrick, 1963)

On-line Journal Article

Weintraub, I. (1994). Fighting environmental racism: A selected annotated bibliography [14 p.]. Electronic Green Journal [On-line serial], 1(1). Available: Telnet: gopher.uidaho.edu Directory: University of Idaho Electronic Publications File: egjol.txt

(Weintraub, 1994)

Material from an Electronic Information Service or Database

Belenky, M. F. (1984). The role of deafness in the moral development of hearing impaired children. In A. Areson & J. De Caro (Eds.), Teaching, learning and development. Rochester, NY: National Institute for the Deaf. (ERIC Document Reproduction Service No. ED 248 646)

(Belenky, 1984)

NUMBERED BIBLIOGRAPHY

In this method, used primarily in the abstract and engineering sciences, you number each entry in your bibliography. Then, each citation in your essay consists of only the number of the work that you are referring to, placed in parentheses. Remember to include the page number if you quote from your source.

> Theorem 2 of Joel, Shier, and Stein (2) is strengthened in the following theorem:

> The following would be a consequence of the conjecture of McMullen and Shepher (3, p. 133):

Depending on your subject, you arrange your bibliography in alphabetical order (biology or mathematics) or in the order in which you cite the sources in your essay (chemistry, engineering, or physics). Consult your instructor or a style sheet that contains the specific rules for your discipline.

ENDNOTE/FOOTNOTE DOCUMENTATION

Until about ten years ago, documentation for most research essays was provided by *footnotes* or *endnotes*. In this system, a sequence of numbers in your essay is keyed to a series of separate notes containing publication information, which appear either at the bottom of the page (footnotes) or on a separate page at the end of the essay (endnotes). It also includes a standard bibliography as part of the essay. Many authors still use footnotes or endnotes, and some of your instructors may ask you to use this system of documentation.

This brief excerpt from a biographical essay about Ernest Hemingway shows you what the endnote/footnote system looks like.

> Hemingway's zest for life extended to women also. His wandering heart seemed only to be exceeded by an even more appreciative eye.[6] Hadley was aware of her husband's flirtations and of his facility with women.[7] Yet, she had no idea that something was going on between Hemingway and Pauline Pfeiffer, a fashion editor for Vogue magazine.[8] She was also unaware that Hemingway delayed his return to Schruns from a business trip to New York, in February 1926, so that he might spend some more time with this "new and strange girl."[9]

> [6]Ernest Hemingway, A Moveable Feast (New York: Scribner's, 1964) 102.

> [7]Alice Hunt Sokoloff, Hadley: The First Mrs. Hemingway (New York: Dodd, Mead, 1973) 84.

⁸Carlos Baker, Ernest Hemingway: A Life Story (New York: Scribner's, 1969) 159.

⁹Hemingway 210. Also Baker 165.

If your instructor asks you to use endnotes or footnotes, do not put parenthetical source references, as in MLA or APA style, anywhere within the text of the essay. Instead, at each place where you would insert a parenthetical reference, put a number to indicate to your reader that there is a corresponding footnote or endnote.

When *inserting the numbers,* follow these rules:

- The note number is raised slightly above the line of your essay. To do this with a typewriter, move the roller up one half-turn. Many word processing programs have provision for various styles of documentation, including inserting footnotes/endnotes. If yours does not, leave two spaces in the line and insert the number neatly by hand in the first space, slightly above the line, once the essay is finished.

- The notes are numbered consecutively: if you have twenty-six notes in your essay, the number of the last one should be 26. There is no such thing as "12a." If "12a" appears at the last moment, then it becomes "13," and the remainder of the notes should be renumbered.

- Every note should contain at least one separate piece of information. Never write a note that states only, "See footnote 3." The reader should be told enough to make it unnecessary to consult footnote 3.

- While a note may contain more than one piece of information (for example, the source reference as well as some additional explanation of the point that is being documented), the note should have only one number. Under no circumstances should two note numbers be placed together, like this: ⁶,⁷.

When you prepare the documentation for your essay, you will have two lists to make: the list of works cited, and the list of notes.

The *format of the bibliography* closely resembles the "Works Cited" format for parenthetical documentation that was described in Chapter 5 and Chapter 9: the sources are alphabetized by last name, with the second and subsequent lines of each entry indented. The entries themselves closely resemble the forms for MLA bibliographical entries listed at the beginning of this appendix.

The *format of the list of notes* resembles the bibliography in reverse: the first line of the note is indented five spaces, with the second and subsequent lines at the margin; the note begins with a raised number, corresponding to the number in the text of the essay; the author's name is in first name/last name order; author and title are separated by commas, not periods; publication information is placed in parentheses; and the note ends with the page reference and a period. Notes should be double-spaced throughout.

Here is a list of five notes, illustrating the most common forms, followed by a bibliography consisting of the same five sources:

NOTES

¹Helen Block Lewis, Psychic War in Men and Women (New York: New York UP, 1976) 43.

²Gertrude Himmelfarb, "Observations on Humanism and History," in The Philosophy of the Curriculum, ed. Sidney Hook (Buffalo: Prometheus, 1975) 85.

³Harvey G. Cox, "Moral Reasoning and the Humanities," Liberal Education 71.3 (1985): 196.

⁴Lauro Martines, "Mastering the Matriarch," Times Literary Supplement 1 February 1985: 113.

⁵Carolyn See, "Collaboration with a Daughter: The Rewards and Cost," New York Times 19 June 1986, late ed.: C2.

WORKS CITED

Cox, Harvey G. "Moral Reasoning and the Humanities." Liberal Education 71.3 (1985): 195–204.

Himmelfarb, Gertrude. "Observations on Humanism and History." In The Philosophy of the Curriculum. Ed. Sidney Hook. Buffalo: Prometheus, 1975. 81–88.

Lewis, Helen Block. Psychic War in Men and Women. New York: New York UP, 1976.

Martines, Lauro. "Mastering the Matriarch." Times Literary Supplement 1 February 1985: 113.

See, Carolyn. "Collaboration with a Daughter: The Rewards and Cost." New York Times 19 June 1986, late ed.: C2.

Another kind of endnote or footnote, known as the *short form*, should be used when you are citing the same source more than once in your essay. The first time you cite a new source, you use the long form, as illustrated above, which contains detailed information about publication history. The second time you cite the same source, and all subsequent times, you write a separate note, with a new number, but now you use a shorter form, consisting of the author's name and a page number:

⁶Lewis 74.

The short form can be used here because there is already a long-form entry for Lewis on record in a previous note. If your bibliography contained two works by Lewis, then you would have to include an abbreviated title in the short form of the note:

> [6]Lewis, Psychic War 74.

The short form makes it unnecessary to use any Latin abbreviations, like *ibid.* or *op. cit.,* in your notes.

For an example of the use of endnote documentation in a full-length essay, see "The Quest for Survival in the Andes Mountains," in Chapter 10.

NOTES PLUS PAGE NUMBERS IN THE TEXT

If you are using only one or two sources in your essay, it is a good idea to include one footnote at the first reference and, thereafter, cite the page number of the source in the text of your essay.

For example, if your essay is exclusively about Sigmund Freud's *Civilization and Its Discontents,* document your first reference to the work with a complete note, citing the edition that you are using:

> *Sigmund Freud, Civilization and Its Discontents (Garden City:
>
> Doubleday, 1958) 72. All further citations refer to this edition.

This single note explains to your reader that you are intending to use the same edition whenever you cite this source. All subsequent references to this book will be followed by the page reference, in parentheses, usually at the end of your sentence.

> Freud has asserted that "the greatest obstacle to civilization [is] the
>
> constitutional tendency in men to aggression against one another . . . " (101).

This method is most useful in essays on literary topics when you are focusing on a single author, without citing secondary sources.

Remember: The choice of documentation for your essay is not really yours. Ask your instructor which method is appropriate for your course and your paper topic.

Interviewing and Field Research

As well as the books, articles, films, videos, and other research materials available at your library, personal interviews and field research can provide worthwhile information for your research essay. A well-conducted interview with an expert in the field, if it is carefully focused on your topic, can give you information unavailable from any other source. A personal interview can also enrich your essay with details, based on actual experience, that will capture and hold your audience's interest. Similarly, your own observation of an event or environment can be a source of valuable information. Through close observation of the river flowing past a sewage treatment plant or of the behavior of people during a political demonstration, you can collect data to support your thesis, to supplement the texts you have read, and to suggest alternative interpretations of the issues and ideas developed in your essay.

As you progress through your college's general education curriculum, you will probably find that some professional fields and academic disciplines, such as literature or history, depend most on library research, while others, such as sociology or science, often call for direct observation and interviewing by the researcher. For many of the topics that you explore across the curriculum, your essays will benefit from a combination of both library and personal investigation.

INTERVIEWING

Sources for Interviews

You will want to interview experts or authorities who are both knowledgeable and appropriate sources of information about your specific topic. First, consider the faculty on your campus, not only as direct sources of information but as sources of referrals to other experts in the field at nearby colleges and universities. If your general topic is the Holocaust, for example, you may want to interview a faculty member with that specialization in your college's history, sociology, or Judaic studies department. You may, in fact, come across the names of appropriate faculty at your college in the course of your library research.

An entirely different source of direct information is a person who has had personal experience with some aspect of your essay topic. As you talk about your research on the Holocaust, one of your friends might tell you about an aunt living nearby, someone who, for example, survived the concentration camps at Auschwitz. That woman's recollections can be just as appropriate and important an addition to your essay as a professor's more theoretical comments, lending it human drama or highlighting a particular issue that interests you.

Some essays can be enhanced by interviewing several sources. For example, if you were preparing a report on an environmental issue in your town—let's say the purity of its water supply—you would want to learn about the impact of the new sewage treatment plant on the local environment. Of course, you would want to talk to the plant's manager; but you might also consult the managers of local businesses to determine some of the economic implications, and to some public health officials to learn about the kinds of health hazards the plant is intended to avoid. In this case, a single source would not cover the possible spectrum of responses.

Interviews can be time-consuming, and direct information derived from interviews will probably have to be combined with notes taken from your reading. You need to know in advance what kinds of interview will be most useful and appropriate—if any—and, thus, not waste your time and that of your source.

Planning an Interview

Whether in person or on the telephone, interviews require careful planning and preparation. First, you have to establish a courteous and professional relationship with your subject (that is what the person you are interviewing is generally called). Most potential interview subjects will be pleased to participate in your research. Your interest enhances the value of their knowledge and experience, and they are likely to enjoy being cited as authorities and having their ideas quoted and read.

You are more likely to get someone to consent to an interview if you write or phone first to make an appointment. Arrange your appointments as soon as possible once you have focused your topic and identified candidates for interviews. Since your potential subjects are likely to have busy schedules, allow enough time to make initial contact and then to wait a week or two, if necessary, until the person has enough time to speak with you at length. This way you can avoid having your initial conversation turn into an interview before you are quite prepared for it—which can be awkward if you don't have your questions ready.

When you call or write to those whom you hope to interview, politely identify yourself; then briefly describe your topic and the special focus of your essay. Ask for an interview of 20 to 30 minutes at a later time convenient for the subject. If appropriate, mention the name of the person who suggested this source, or refer to the publication in which you saw the subject's name. Your objective is to convey your own serious interest in the topic and in your subject's knowledge of the topic. Be friendly, but professional. If someone is reluctant to be interviewed, you should retreat gracefully. At the same time, don't hesitate to ask for a referral to someone else who might be in a better position to provide helpful information.

Preparing for an Interview

Because your interview, whether in person or on the phone, will probably be brief, you need to plan in advance what you intend to say and ask so that you can use the time effectively. Careful preparation is also a compliment to your interview subjects and shows respect for their expertise.

Reviewing your research notes, make a focused list of questions in writing beforehand, tailoring them to your specific paper topic and to your source's area of knowledge. If, for example, you are going to interview the manager of a sewage treatment plant on the Hudson River about the effective removal of PCB's from the water, you don't want to use up ten minutes asking about plant management. It can be helpful to prepare a questionnaire, leaving space between the questions for you to take notes. You can use the same questionnaire, with variations, for a whole series of personal interviews.

Recording Information during an Interview

During the actual interview, you will be listening intently to your subject's responses and thinking about your next question. But as a researcher, you have another challenge. You need to take away with you a comprehensive record of the interview so that you can quote your expert accurately and cite information authoritatively. Most successful interviewers use one of two techniques to record the interview, or a combination of both: tape-recording and note-taking.

Tape-recording

If you plan to use a tape-recorder, make sure you ask your subject's permission in advance; test the equipment beforehand (especially if it's borrowed for the occasion); and know how to operate it smoothly. Bring it to the interview with the tape already loaded in the machine, and be sure the batteries are fresh. (Bring along a second tape in case the first one jams or breaks, and carry extra batteries. When the interview is about to begin, check again to see if your subject has any objection to your recording the conversation. Then, to avoid making your subject self-conscious, put the tape recorder in an unobtrusive place. After that, don't create a distraction by fiddling with the machine.

Note-taking

Even if you plan to tape-record the interview, come prepared to take careful notes; bring notebook and pens, as well as your list of questions or questionnaire. One way of preparing for detailed note-taking—the kind that will provide you with accurate direct quotations to use in your essay—is to rehearse. Pair off with a classmate who is also preparing for an interview, and practice interviewing and note-taking (including handling the tape-recorder). Also review the instructions for Assignment 8 and Assignment 9 in Chapter 4 (pp. 256–259). If your subject presents a point so well that you know you'll want to quote it, write it down rapidly but carefully, and—then and there—read it back to make sure that you have transcribed the statement correctly.

Conducting the Interview

Arrive on time (not late and not early)! Once you've been invited to sit down and your equipment is set up, *briefly* remind your subject of the essay topic and your reason for requesting the interview. Then get right down to your "script": ask each question clearly, without hurrying; be alert to recognize when the question has been fully answered (there is usually a pause); and move briskly on to the next question. Otherwise, let your subject talk freely, with minimum interruption. Remember that you are the receiver, not the provider, of information, and let your subject do almost all the talking.

Sometimes, a particular question will capture your subject's interest, and you will get a more detailed answer than you expected. Be aware of the time limit for the interview; but if you see a promising line of questioning that you didn't anticipate, and your subject seems relaxed and willing to prolong the conversation, take advantage of the opportunity and ask follow-up questions. What if your subject digresses far away from the topic of your essay? At the first opportunity, ask whether there is a time constraint. If there is, politely indicate that you have three or four more questions to ask and you hope that there will be enough time to include them.

No matter how careful your preparations, a good interview won't go exactly as you planned. You should aim to participate in a conversation, not direct an interrogation. At the end, your subject should feel that the time has passed too quickly and, ideally, offer to speak with you again, if necessary, to fill up any gaps. To maintain that good impression, be sure to send a brief note of thanks to your subject no longer than a day or two after the interview. Later on, you may want to send a copy of the completed essay.

Using Interview Sources in Your Essay

Since the purpose of the interview is to gather information (and to provide yourself with a few apt quotations), you need to have clear notes to work from as you organize your essay. If you used a tape-recorder, you should transcribe the interview as soon as you can; if you took notes, you should go over them carefully, clarify confusing words, and then type a definitive version. Otherwise, you may find yourself deciphering your almost-illegible notes at a later time or searching through the entire tape to find a specific sentence that you want to quote. Transcribe the interview accurately, without embroidering or revising what your subject actually said. Keep the original notes and tapes; your instructor may want to review them along with your essay.

Working with notes from an interview is almost exactly the same as working with notes from library research. As you organize your essay (following the process described in Chapter 8), you cross-reference your notes with a list of the topics for your essay, choosing information from the interview that might be cited to support the major points in your outline. When you begin to choose quotations, you may want to review the section on "Selecting Quotations," pp. 388–392. Remember that it is the well-chosen and carefully placed source that carries authority, not the number of words quoted. Finally, document each use of material taken from your interview, whether it is ideas or words, with a parenthetical reference. (See Appendix B for the appropriate bibliographical entry.)

FIELD RESEARCH

Like interviewing, field research is a way of supplementing the material you take from texts and triggering new ideas about your topic. When you engage in field research, you are gathering information directly, acting as an observer, investigator, and evaluator within the context of an academic or professional discipline. If you are asked by your anthropology instructor to describe and analyze a family celebration as an ethnographer would, your observations of Thanksgiving dinner at home would be regarded as field research.

In many of your college courses, you will be expected to engage in field research. When, for example, the nursing program sends students to a nearby hospital for their clinical practice and asks for a weekly report on their work with patients, these students are doing field research. Other students may participate in a cooperative education program involving professional internships in preparation for potential careers; the reports these interns prepare on their work experiences are based on field research. Whatever the course, your instructor will show you how to connect your field research activities to the theories, procedures, and format characteristic of that discipline. Still, there are certain practices common to most kinds of field research that you need to know from the beginning. Let's follow that process from assignment to essay as you develop a simple topic based on field research.

Your sociology professor has suggested that, although college students like to think of themselves as unique individuals, certain patterns clearly underlie their characteristic behavior. As an example, he asserts that both male and female students prefer to work and relax with members of the opposite sex. He is asking each of you to test this hypothesis by choosing a place on campus to observe students as they go about their daily routine, keeping in mind two questions: are there patterns one can observe in these students' behavior? what might be the significance of these patterns? If you were assigned this project, your work would fall into three stages: gathering the information, analyzing that information, and writing the essay.

Gathering Information

According to your instructor's guidelines for this essay based on field research, you will need to perform at least six separate observations for 20 to 30 minutes each at a site of your choice and, later, be prepared to hand in copies of your accumulated observation notes along with your essay. So your first important decision concerns the location for gathering information about students' behavior: the cafeteria? the library? a particular class? the student union? the college bookstore? a classroom or another place on campus where students congregate? You decide to observe students gathered at the row of benches outside Johnson Hall, the busiest classroom building, extending from the bookstore on the right to the student union building on the left; these benches also face a field where gym classes meet and the baseball team practices. Since this area is an important junction on the campus, you can assume that enough students will appear to provide basic information for your field research.

Planning the Observations

To conform to your instructor's requirements and obtain all the information you need for your essay, you should prepare for your observation sessions quickly and carefully. First, establish a schedule that will fulfill the guidelines for the assignment. Since your first class in Johnson Hall is at 11 AM, and you are free before that, you decide to schedule your observations for the half hour before class, that is, from 10:30 to 11:00 AM on Monday, Wednesday, and Friday, for the next two weeks.

You will need to set aside a separate notebook for recording your observations. For each session, start a fresh page, and indicate the date and the times when you begin and end your sessions. Such specific information is what establishes your authority as a field researcher. Before your first session, consider making a diagram of the site, roughly sketching in the location of the buildings, placing the seven benches correctly, and assigning each a number.

As with interviewing, a list of prepared questions will help you to spend your time profitably. This time, however, your object is not to ask for information, but to set up a framework for your observations and, possibly, a potential structure for your essay. For this assignment, you are basically trying to find out:

- How many students are spending time at this site?
- Where are they and what are they doing?
- Do they stay for the whole observation period, or do they come and go?

Engaging in Observation

Your work consists of careful observing and precise note-taking. You are not trying to write a narrative or, at this point, understand the significance of what you are seeing; you are only trying to record your subjects' activities accurately to provide notes for future reflection.

Some people may feel self-conscious to have an observer watching them closely and writing down everything they do. To avoid potential questions or confrontations, try to do your observing and note-taking unobtrusively, without staring too hard at any one person. If someone asks what you are doing, be prepared to say that you are working on an assignment for a college class, that you aren't going to identify anyone by name, and that you would be grateful for the person's cooperation. As with interview subjects, you will find that most subjects of field research are sympathetic and helpful. If someone speaks to you, take advantage of the opportunity to combine observations with a little formal interviewing, and possibly gain a useful quotation for your essay. If someone objects to being included in your study, however, you should immediately turn your attention elsewhere, or move on and try again at another time.

A portion of your notes for one session might look like that shown in Figure C-1.

After a couple of sessions, you may feel that you have a general idea of the range of students' behavior at the site, so you can begin to look specifically for repeated instances of certain activities: studying together or individually, eating, relaxing. But you will need to keep an open mind and eye about what you might observe. Again as with interviewing, your subjects' behavior may not absolutely conform to your planned questions, so you may need to add new questions as the sessions progress. For example, you may not have realized until your third session that students sitting on the benches closest to the playing field are focusing on the sports activities there; from then on, you will be looking for that behavior.

For this assignment, you would continue observing until you complete the number of observations specified; but for your own field research in a project for a course in your major field, you might conduct observations for most of a semester. As a professional researcher (like Margaret Mead when she was observing Pacific Island adolescents for her classic book *Coming of*

Monday, April 3; 10:30 am.

3 students at bench 3 -- 1 male & 2 females.
Females sitting on bench. Male, between
them, standing with 1 foot up on bench,
smoking. They're talking quietly. About
5 minutes later, another male arrives on
bike & stands, straddling bike, in front
of the bench. Conversation continues, now
with 4 participants. At 10:50, females
get up & walk into Johnson, along with
1st male. 2nd male rides off toward
library.

At benches 4 & 5, 2 people at each. At 4,
1 male reads book, stopping now and
then to use a highlighter. 1 female has
bunch of 3x5 cards, & she looks at
each one for a second, then flips it,
then goes to next one. At 10:35, another
male comes over to her, she gets up,
& they both go to bench 6, where no
one is sitting. There she continues
going through her cards, but now
she seems to read something from
each card, as male responds with
a word or 2. They continue to do this
for another 10 minutes.

Figure C-1

Age in Samoa), you might even live with a tribe, studying their culture for a
year or more.

Analyzing Your Information

When you have all your observations recorded, you are ready to move on to
the next stage: reviewing your notes to understand what you have seen, and
analyzing what you have learned. You have probably noticed that this over-
laps with the previous observation stage; as you watched students in front of
Johnson Hall, you were already beginning to group their activities into several
categories: studying, casual conversations, watching sports, eating, sleeping.

Once you establish these categories, you pull out of your notes the specific
references that match the category, noting the date and time of each instance.
So now you have several new pages that look like those shown in Figure C-2.

Studying

girl and guy with flash cards 4/6 10:35
group of 5 with science notes 4/8 10:30 – 10:58
   (they told me about their 11 am quiz —
   all in same class)
guy with book and highlighter 4/6
   10:30 – 10:45

Sports watching

observations 2, 4, 5, 6: groups of 2 – 5 guys at
   benches 1, 2, 3 (facing sports field).
   Groups generally talked, pointed,
   laughed, while gym classes did
   aerobics.

observations 4, 5: during baseball team
   practice, guys in small groups
   cheered, pointed; several stood up
   and walked over to edge of path
   that overlooks field.

female pairs watching sports
   during 4, 5, but no groups.

observations 1, 2: no sports scheduled
   then; few people on benches 1, 2,
   and 3.

Figure C-2

You may want to chart your observations to represent at a glance such variables as these: how many students studied, or watched sports, or socialized? Which activities were associated with males or with females? If your sessions took place during different times of the day, the hour would be another variable to record on your chart.

As you identify categories, you need to ask yourself some questions to help you characterize each one and define the differences among some of your subjects' behaviors. For example: are these differences determined by gender, as with the sports watchers, or by preferred methods of learning, like solitary or group study? As you think through the possible conclusions to be drawn from your observations, record them in your notebook, for these preliminary analyses will later become part of your essay.

Writing the Essay

An essay based on field research generally follows a format appropriate to the particular discipline. Your instructor will provide detailed guidelines and, perhaps, refer you to an article in a professional journal to use as a model. For the essay analyzing student behavior, you might present your findings according to the following outline:

Purpose: In the first section, you state the problem—the purpose of your field research—clearly indicating the question(s) you set out to investigate.

Method: Here, you explain your choice of site, the times and number of your observation sessions, and the general procedure for observation that you followed, including any exceptions to or deviations from your plan.

Observations: Next, you record the information you gathered from your observations, not as a list of random facts, but as categories or groupings that make the facts coherent to the reader. In many disciplines, this kind of information can be presented through charts, graphs, or tables.

Analysis: The heart of your essay, here is where you explain to your readers the significance of your observations. If, for example, you decided that certain activities were gender-related, you would describe the basis for that distinction. Or you could discuss your conclusion that students use the benches primarily as a meeting place to socialize. Or you might make the connection between studying as the most prevalent student activity outside Johnson Hall and the scheduling of midterms during the time of your observations.

Conclusions: At the end of your essay, you remind your readers—and the instructor who is evaluating your work—that your purpose throughout has been to answer the questions and clarify the problems posed in the first paragraph. What did you discover that can illuminate your response to your professor's assertions about students' behavior?

Using Field Research

There are several important points to remember about using field research:

1. In actual practice across the curriculum, field research is usually combined with library research. As part of your investigation, you will often be asked to include in an early section of your essay a "literature search," that is, a summary of some key articles on your topic. This summary shows that you are familiar with an appropriate range of information and, especially, the major work in the field.

2. Whether you emphasize library or field research depends on the purpose and nature of your essay. If field research is integral to your topic, you will be acting as the principal investigator and interpreter

of new data, and the library research will serve only as a supplement to your field research. Otherwise, you should integrate your field research into your essay as you would any other source of information.

3. For field research, careful documentation is especially important since you are asking your reader to trust the data that you yourself have gathered and upon which your speculations and conclusions are based. You can create this trust by making careful and repeated observations, recording them in detail and accurately, and presenting them in a clear and logical manner.

4. The methods of analyzing data obtained through field research are, in most cases, specific to particular disciplines. So you should indicate to your readers, by reference to authorities or models, that you are observing the conventions of the field you are working in. It is especially important that, after consultation with your instructor, you use the appropriate method of documenting both your field research and your library research, so that a reader can clearly distinguish the work of the previous investigators who are your secondary sources from your own primary contributions.

Appendix D
Writing Essay Examinations

Instructors give essay examinations for three reasons:

- To make sure that you have read and understood the assigned reading;
- To test your analytical skills;
- To find out if you can integrate what you have read with the ideas and information that you have learned in lectures and class discussion.

Since your instructor is usually not trying to test your memory, essay examinations are often open-book, allowing you to refer freely to the source. But in any exam, even a take-home assignment, there is likely to be some time pressure. To prepare, you should have read all the material carefully in advance and outlined, underlined, or annotated the text.

READING THE QUESTION

You determine your strategy by carefully examining the wording of the question before you begin to plan and write your essay. First, you must accept that someone else is providing the topic for your essay. The person who wrote the question wants to pinpoint a single area to be explored, and so you may have very little scope. However restrictive it may seem, you must stay within the boundaries of the question. If you are instructed to focus on only a small section of the text, summarizing the entire work from beginning to end is inappropriate. If you are asked to discuss an issue that is raised frequently throughout the work, paraphrasing a single paragraph or page is pointless. Do not include extraneous information just to demonstrate how much you know. Most teachers are more impressed with aptness and conciseness than with length.

The controlling verb of the question will usually provide you with a key. Different verbs will require different approaches. You are already familiar with the most common terms:

summarize; state; list; outline; condense; cite reasons

What is sometimes forgotten under pressure is that you are expected to carry out the instructions literally. *Summarize* means condense: the reader expects a short but complete account of the specified subject. On the other hand, *list* should result in a sequence of short entries, somewhat disconnected, but not a fully developed series of paragraphs.

Other directions may be far broader:

describe; discuss; review; explain; show; explore; determine

Verbs like these give you a wide scope. Since they do not demand a specific strategy, be careful to stay within the set topic, so that you do not explain or review more than the readers want to know about.

Still other verbs indicate a more exact method of development, perhaps one of the strategies that you have already worked with in Assignment 3 in Chapter 3:

compare and contrast; illustrate; define; show the reasons; trace the causes; trace the effects; suggest solutions; analyze

Notice that none of the verbs so far has provided an opportunity for personal comment. You have been asked to examine the text, to demonstrate your understanding of its meaning and its implications, but you have not been asked for your opinion. However, several verbs do request commentary:

evaluate; interpret; criticize; justify; prove; disagree

Although these verbs invite a personal response, they do not give you freedom to write about whatever you choose. You are still confined to the boundaries of the set subject, and you should devote as much of your essay as possible to demonstrating your understanding of what you have read. *A brilliant essay that ignores the topic rarely earns the highest grade.* If you have worked hard to prepare for the essay, you would be foolish to ignore the question. Don't reinterpret the directions in order to write about what is easiest or what would display your abilities to best advantage or what you figured out earlier would be asked. Just answer the question.

PLANNING AND DEVELOPING THE ESSAY

Even when you have worked out what you are expected to write about, you are still not ready to start writing. Your reader will also judge the way in which your essay is constructed, so organize your thoughts before you begin to write. No elaborate outline is necessary.

Guidelines for Planning and Developing Your Essay

1. *List some of the main points that come into your head, reduce the list to a manageable number, and renumber the sequence.* This process does not take very long and it can prevent unnecessary repetition, unintentional omissions, mixed-up sequences, and overemphasis.

2. *Develop each point separately.* Don't try to say everything at the same time. Consult your list, say what is necessary about each item, and then move on to the next.

3. *Develop each point adequately.* Each reason or cause or criticism deserves convincing presentation. Unless you are asked for a list, don't just write down one sentence and rush away to the next item. You will write a more effective essay by including some support for each of your points. Do not make brief, incomplete references to ideas because you assume that the reader will know all about them. It is your responsibility to explain each one so that it makes sense by itself.

4. *Refer back to the text.* Whenever possible, demonstrate that you can cite evidence or information from the assigned reading. If you think of two possible examples or facts, one from the source and one from your own experience or knowledge, and if you haven't enough time to include both, the safe choice will come from the source. However, you must always mark the transition between your own presentation of ideas and your reference to the source by citing its title, or the name of its author, or both.

ANALYZING AN ESSAY
AND AN ESSAY QUESTION

Carefully read through George Stade's "Football—The Game of Aggression." Assume that you have previously read this essay and that you have between forty-five minutes and an hour to answer the following question:

Although he acknowledges that it can be violent, George Stade suggests that football may serve a constructive social function. Considering some of his descriptive comments about the sport, explain why football may not be as healthy for society as Stade implies.

FOOTBALL—THE GAME OF AGGRESSION
George Stade

There are many ways in which professional football is unique among sports, and as many others in which it is the fullest expression of what is at the heart of all sports. There is no other major sport so dependent upon raw force, nor any so dependent on a complex and delicate strategy; none so wide in the range of specialized functions demanded from its players; none so dependent upon the undifferentiated athletic *sine qua non,* a quickwitted body; none so primitive; none so futuristic; none so American.

Football is first of all a form of play, something one engages in instinctively and only for the sake of performing the activity in question. Among forms of play, football is a game, which means that it is built on communal needs, rather than on private evasions, like mountain climbing. Among games it is a sport; it requires athletic ability, unlike croquet. And among sports, it is one whose mode is violence and whose violence is its special glory.

In some sports—basketball, baseball, soccer—violence is occasional (and usually illegal); in others, like hockey, it is incidental; in others still, car racing, for example, it is accidental. Definitive violence football shares alone with boxing and bullfighting, among major sports. But in bullfighting a man is pitted not against another man, but against an animal, and boxing is a competition between individuals, not teams, and that makes a great difference. If shame is the proper and usual penalty for failures in sporting competitions between individuals, guilt is the consequence of failing not only oneself and one's fans, but also one's teammates. Failure in football, moreover, seems more related to a failure of courage, seems more unmanning than in any other sport outside of bullfighting. In other sports one loses a knack, is outsmarted, or is merely inferior in ability, but in football, on top of these, a player fails because he "lacks desire," or "can't take it anymore," or "hears footsteps," as his teammates will put it.

Many sports, especially those in which there is a goal to be defended, seem enactments of the games animals play under the stimulus of what ethologists, students of animal behavior, call *territory*—"the drive to gain, maintain, and defend the exclusive right to a piece of property," as Robert Ardrey puts it. The most striking symptom of this drive is aggressiveness, but among social animals, such as primates, it leads to "amity for the social partner, hostility for the territorial neighbor." The territorial instinct is closely related to whatever makes animals establish pecking orders; the tangible sign of one's status within the orders is the size and value of the territory one is able to command. Individuals fight over status, groups over *lebensraum*[1] and a bit more. These instincts, some ethologists have claimed, are behind patriotism and private property, and also, I would add, codes of honor, as among

[1] Literally, living space. The word is often most associated with the territory thought by the Nazis to be essential to Germany's political and economic security.

ancient Greeks, modern Sicilians, primitive hunters, teen-age gangs, soldiers, aristocrats, and athletes, especially football players.

The territorial basis of certain kinds of sports is closest to the surface in football, whose plays are all attempts to gain and defend property through aggression. Does this not make football *par excellence* the game of instinctual satisfactions, especially among Americans, who are notorious as violent patriots and instinctive defenders of private property? . . . Even the unusual amity, if that is the word, that exists among football players has been remarked upon. . . . And what is it that corresponds in football to the various feathers, furs, fins, gorgeous colors by means of which animals puff themselves into exaggerated gestures of masculine potency? The football player's equipment, of course. His cleats raise him an inch off the ground. Knee and thigh pads thrust the force lines of his legs forward. His pants are tight against his rump and the back of his thighs, portions of the body which the requirements of the game stuff with muscle. . . . Even the tubby guard looks slim by comparison with his shoulders, extended half a foot on each side by padding. Finally, the helmet, which from the esthetic point of view most clearly expresses the genius of the sport. Not only does the helmet make the player inches taller and give his head a size proportionate to the rest of him; it makes him anonymous, inscrutable, more serviceable as a symbol. The football player in uniform strikes the eye in a succession of gestalt[2] shifts; first a hooded phantom out of the paleolithic past of the species; then a premonition of a future of spacemen.

In sum, and I am most serious about this, football players are to America what tragic actors were to ancient Athens and gladiators to Rome: models of perennially heroic, aggressive, violent humanity, but adapted to the social realities of the times and places that formed them.

[2]I.e., perceptual.

ANSWERING THE QUESTION

At first, you may have some difficulty determining the focus of your essay since the question includes more than one key word to help you work out your strategy. The main verb in this question is *explain*. You are being asked to account for something, to help your reader understand what may not be entirely clear. *Explain* also implies persuasion: your reader must be convinced that your explanation is valid.

- If the question asked you to explain *something that is confusing* in Stade's essay, your task would be to provide an interpretive summary of some part of the text. For example, you might have been asked to explain the differences, with illustrations, between violence that is occasional, incidental, and accidental, discussing the implications of these distinctions for sports in general.

- If the question asked you to explain *some related point that Stade omits* from his discussion, your task would be to extend his reasoning, perhaps to discuss causes or effects, or to contrast and compare. For example, you might have to explain why football lends itself to a greater degree of violence than other sports, or explain the parallel between the way football players and animals defend their territory.

- If the question asked you—as it does—to *evaluate the author's reasoning* in forming his conclusions, you would then examine Stade's "almost serious" conclusions and demonstrate—explain—the limitations of his arguments and examples.

The essay question raises the point that Stade may have underestimated the harmful effects of football, a sport so violent that it could undermine the social benefits that it otherwise provides. To answer the question, then, you must accept the assumption that Stade may be overenthusiastic about football, *whether or not you agree,* and proceed to point out the implications and the shortcomings of his analysis. In a sense, writing a good essay depends on your willingness to allow your views to be shaped by the examiner's, at least for the duration of the exam.

The question defines the *limits* as well as the strategy of your essay. It does not permit you to dispute Stade on grounds that are entirely of your choosing. You are firmly instructed to focus your attention on the conflict between violence and social benefit. It would be foolish to ignore these instructions and write only about the glories of football or to condemn the sport for reasons unrelated to the violence of its play.

What should you be evaluating in your essay, and how many comments are "some"? Stade makes the following points in support of his view that football can be a useful social ritual:

- It fosters individual strength and determination.

- It develops cooperation and teamwork.

- It teaches players how to acquire and defend territory and thus encourages nationalism and the patriotic defense of one's country.

- It provides players and spectators with the opportunity to act out their aggressions in a controlled and relatively harmless way.

These points should certainly be on the list of paragraph topics that you jot down as you plan your essay. Since these ideas are embedded within the paragraphs of Stade's essay, you should use your own ordering principle—least violent to most (potentially) violent might be a good choice. Each of your paragraphs should begin with a description of one characteristic of the sport as Stade presents it, followed by your own explanation of the social disadvantages or benefits that might result.

Resist the temptation to devote too much space to a single aspect of the sport. For example, if you spend too much time discussing Stade's comments about uniforms and the extent to which the football player is magnified and dehumanized by his padding and his helmet, you may not be able to develop your discussion of whether football encourages patriotism or a more divisive and dangerous nationalism. Stade's essay is based on his belief that people participate in sports as a way of expressing passions and impulses that have no place in our normal daily occupations. He implies that, if this outlet is eliminated, our instincts for violence may spill over into activities where they would be far more dangerous. This argument has often been used to justify violence as depicted on television and in the movies. While you are not expected to analyze the issue with the expertise of a trained psychologist or sociologist, your essay should reflect your awareness of and your views on Stade's conception of football as a way of controlling our aggressive instincts.

INTRODUCING YOUR TOPIC

Examination essays, like all essays, require an introduction. Before beginning to explore some of the issues inherent in George Stade's analysis, you should provide a short introduction that defines the author's topic and your own. Your later references to his ideas will need a well-established context; therefore, try to define Stade's conception of football (which might differ from someone else's) right at the outset of your essay. Although the introduction need not be longer than two or three sentences, *cite your source*—the name of the author and the name of the essay, both properly spelled—and state exactly what it is that you and your author are concerned about. To demonstrate the frustration of reading an introduction that is shrouded in mystery, look at the first paragraph from a student essay answering the question that has just been analyzed:

> The attitude of the author of this essay is highly supportive of a sport that may
> be the most violent in the world. It is true that players acquire a lot of skills and
> learn about teamwork, as well as receiving huge sums of money and becoming
> public idols. However, there are also risks and dangers that result, for specta-
> tors and those watching on television, as well as for those on the field wearing
> team uniforms, which he fails to point out in this brief essay.

"He," of course, is George Stade, and the sport under discussion is football. The student had read and understood the source essay, but is so eager to begin commenting on Stade's ideas that she fails to establish a context for her arguments. Here is a more informative introduction:

> In "Football--The Game of Aggression," George Stade presents the game of foot-
> ball as a necessary evil and a useful social ritual. He does not deny that the
> game, more than most sports, is based on a potentially lethal kind of aggression.
> But, contrasting football with other sports, he finds that it also encourages a
> sense of teamwork and an instinct for patriotism, which can be valuable both to
> the individual and to society. Left unclear is whether ritualizing violence through

sports does, in fact, result in a less violent society, or whether watching football players maul each other in weekly combat only encourages spectators to imitate their heroes.

PRESENTING YOUR ESSAY TO THE READER

Students often choose to divide their time into three parts. For example, if you have forty minutes during which to write an essay, try the following timetable:

- ten minutes to analyze the question and plan a strategy
- twenty minutes to write the essay
- ten minutes to proofread and correct it

During in-class examinations, students often waste vital minutes by painstakingly transcribing a new copy from their rough drafts. While *your handwriting must be legible,* it is not necessary to hand in a clean copy. Teachers expect an exam essay to have sentences crossed out and words inserted. They are used to seeing arrows used to reverse sentences and numbers used to change the sequence of paragraphs. It makes no sense to write the last word of your first draft and then, without checking what you have written, immediately take a clean sheet of paper and start transcribing a copy to hand in. Because transcription is such a mechanical task, the mind tends to wander and the pen makes errors that were not in the original draft. Take time to proofread your essay, to locate grammatical errors, and to fill in gaps in continuity. As long as your corrections and changes are fairly neat and clear, your instructor will not mind reading the first draft and will probably be pleased by your efforts to improve your writing.

Appendix E

Readings for a Research Essay

The essays in this appendix are sources for you to work with if your instructor asks you to write a research essay based on Assignment 15 (p. 393). That assignment asks you to choose one of the following topics:

A. Changing Concepts of Masculinity
B. Men and Women in Modern America
C. Sports, Violence, and Masculinity

The following list includes readings that you can find in other parts of this book (indicated by asterisks), as well as the essays contained in this appendix. Taken together, these sources could form the entire bibliography for your research essay. Or you may wish to supplement these essays with additional sources from the library.

Readings for Assignment 15

*Diane Barthel, from "When Men Put on Appearances: Advertising and the Social Construction of Masculinity," in *Men, Masculinity, and the Media.* Ed. Steve Craig. Newbury Park, California: Sage, 1992 (pp. 365–366).

*Bill Buford, "The Hate Behind the Game," *New York Times*, June 16, 1994 (pp. 24–26).

Helen Fisher, from *Anatomy of Love: The Mysteries of Mating, Marriage, and Why We Stray.* New York: Fawcett Columbine, 1992.

Kathleen Gerson, from *No Man's Land: Men's Changing Commitments to Family and Work.* New York: Basic Books, 1993.

David Gilmore, from *Manhood in the Making: Cultural Concepts of Masculinity*. New Haven: Yale University Press, 1990.

*Christopher Lasch, from "The Corruption of Sports," *New York Review of Books*, April 28, 1977 (pp. 166–70).

Michael Messner, from *Power at Play: Sports and the Problem of Masculinity*. Boston: Beacon Press, 1992.

Norma Pecora, from "Superman/Superboys/Supermen," in *Men, Masculinity and the Media*. Ed. Steve Craig. Newbury Park, California: Sage, 1992.

Ray Raphael, from *The Men from the Boys: Rites of Passage in Male America*. Lincoln: University of Nebraska Press, 1988.

*William Rhoden, "In 'Minor' College Sports, Big Pressure," *New York Times*, January 7, 1990, p. 1 (pp. 68–73).

E. Anthony Rotundo, from *American Manhood*. New York: Basic Books, 1993.

Richard Slotkin, from *Gunfighter Nation: The Myth of the Frontier in Twentieth-Century America*. New York: Atheneum, 1992.

*George Stade, from "Game Theory," *Columbia Forum*, 1966 (p. 508).

*Lance Strate, from "Beer Commercials: A Manual on Masculinity," in *Men, Masculinity, and the Media*. Ed. Steve Craig. Newbury Park, California: Sage, 1992 (pp. 197–207).

from ANATOMY OF LOVE:
The Mysteries of Mating, Marriage, and Why We Stray
Helen Fisher

Body Talk

In the 1960s Irenaus Eibl-Eibesfeldt, a German ethologist, noticed a curious pattern to women's flirting behavior. Eibl-Eibesfeldt had used a camera with a secret lens so that when he directed the camera straight ahead, he was actually taking pictures to the side. This way he could focus on local sights and catch on film the unstaged facial expressions of people near him. In his travels to Samoa, Papua, France, Japan, Africa, and Amazonia, he recorded numerous flirting sequences. Then, back in his laboratory at the Max Planck Institute for Behavioral Physiology, near Munich, Germany, he carefully examined each courting episode, frame by frame.

A universal pattern of female flirting emerged. Women from places as different as the jungles of Amazonia, the salons of Paris, and the highlands of New Guinea apparently flirt with the same sequence of expressions.

First, the woman smiles at her admirer and lifts her eyebrows in a swift, jerky motion as she opens her eyes wide to gaze at him. Then she drops her eyelids, tilts her head down and to the side, and looks away. Frequently she also covers her face with her hands, giggling nervously as she retreats behind her palms. This sequential flirting gesture is so distinctive that Eibl-Eibesfeldt is convinced it is innate, a human female courtship ploy that evolved eons ago to signal sexual interest.

Other gambits people use may also come from our primeval past. The coy look   4
is a gesture in which a woman cocks her head and looks up shyly at her suitor. A
female possum does this too, turning toward her suitor, cocking her snouty jaw,
and looking straight into his eyes. Animals frequently toss their heads in order to
solicit attention. Courting women do it regularly; they raise their shoulders, arch
their backs, and toss their locks in a single sweeping motion. Albatross toss their
heads and snap their bills between bouts of nodding, bowing, and rubbing bills together. Mud turtles extend and retract their heads, almost touching noses. Women
are not the only creatures who use their heads to flirt.

Men also employ courting tactics similar to those seen in other species. Have   5
you ever walked into the boss's office and seen him leaning back in his chair, hands
clasped behind his head, elbows high, and chest thrust out? Perhaps he has come
from behind his desk, walked up to you, smiled, arched his back, and thrust his upper body in your direction? If so, watch out. He may be subconsciously announcing
his dominance over you. If you are a woman, he may be courting you instead.

The "chest thrust" is part of a basic postural message used across the animal   6
kingdom—"standing tall." Dominant creatures puff up. Codfish bulge their heads
and thrust out their pelvic fins. Snakes, frogs, and toads inflate their bodies. Ante-
lope and chameleons turn broadside to emphasize their bulk. Mule deer look askance
to show their antlers. Cats bristle. Pigeons swell. Lobsters raise themselves onto
the tips of their walking legs and extend their open claws. Gorillas pound their
chests. Men just thrust out their chests.

When confronted by a more dominant animal, many creatures shrink. People   7
turn in their toes, curl their shoulders, and hang their heads. Wolves tuck their
tails between their legs and slink. Subordinate lobsters crouch. And many species
bow. A bullied codfish curls its body downward. Lizards move their whole bodies
up and down. Deferential chimpanzees nod their heads so rapidly and repeatedly
that primatologists call it bobbing.

These "crouch" and "loom" positions seen in a host of creatures are often man-   8
ifest in courtship too. I recall a cartoon in a European magazine. In the first box a
man in swimming trunks stands alone on an empty beach—his head sags, his stomach protrudes, his chest is concave. In the next box, an attractive woman is shown
walking along the beach past the man; now his head is erect, his stomach sucked in,
his chest inflated. In the last box, the woman is gone and he has resumed his normal, sad-sack pose. It is not uncommon to see men and women swell and shrink in
order to signal importance, defenselessness, and approachability.

from NO MAN'S LAND:
Men's Changing Commitments to Family and Work
Kathleen Gerson

Before the rise of industrial capitalism, economic survival required that all able-   1
bodied family members contribute to the common family enterprise of economic

survival. Even youngsters were not treated as children—that is, economic dependents—for very long. In all but the most affluent households, all family members
contributed what they could, as soon as they could, to secure the family's survival
amid the natural and social uncertainties of rural, farm, and small-town life.

Although husbands and wives shared the economic burdens and domestic hard-
ships of preindustrial life, their relationships faced a shaky future. High rates of premature death and desertion made unpredictable and untimely marital breakup
common. Life expectancies for both sexes were shorter than they are today. Deaths
among mothers with young children, often from complications with pregnancy and
childbirth, left many men to rear their offspring alone or to find surrogate parents
to look after their children. Male death and desertion left widows and abandoned
wives in a similar plight. Despite the low incidence of legal divorce, short life spans
meant that young married couples could not safely assume that they would share a
long life together. As many analysts have pointed out, divorce has merely replaced
death as a modern form of marital disruption.

Contemporary American men have inherited an ambiguous legacy. The "lone
man against the world" image extolled in popular myth has its roots in the early
period of preindustrial expansion, when men could, and often did, leave home and
family to seek their fortunes alone. Yet the preindustrial period also offers a vision
of men and women jointly shouldering the risks and responsibilities of work and
family. Both visions have persisted in American mythology, but each lost a large
share of real-life adherents as industrial capitalism developed throughout the nineteenth and twentieth centuries. The rise of the wage-earning worker produced a
new definition of manhood and, indeed, a new kind of man.

The birth of the industrial system did not immediately produce the primary
breadwinning model that today is mislabeled "traditional." Women were heavily
represented among early industrial workers—for example, in the emerging textile
industries. As the traditional weavers of cloth in the home before the advent of
factories, many women initially followed the shift from production in the home to
production in a communal workplace. As the economic organization of production
shifted from personal use and barter exchange to earning a wage, it was not preor-
dained that men would become the primary earners while women became economically dependent on men. Rather, the breadwinning male—as a pattern of
behavior and as an ideal—was constructed through protracted conflict. The sequence and causes of this transformation remain a matter of debate, but the process of change was clearly marked by political struggle.

As the physical and economic separation of home and work grew, wage workers
began to organize in an effort to gain some control over the terms and conditions
of their work. According to the economist Heidi Hartmann, male workers struck a
fateful bargain with owners and employers, who agreed to exclude women and
children from important sectors of the emerging occupational structure in order to
improve male workers' bargaining power with employers as well as their leverage
over women. Of course, women also faced convincing reasons to pursue domes-

ticity instead of wage work, since working conditions were generally poor and it was not easy to meet the needs of children while in the public workplace. Whatever the causes, protective labor legislation and other policies of occupational sex segregation eventually took hold. The belief eventually emerged that a "family wage" or "living wage" should pay men enough to support their wives and children.

None of these developments encompassed all families, of course. Real wages often fell short of the family-wage standard. And women have always worked: working-class, minority, and poor women have usually had no choice but to find low-wage work in the least desirable sectors of the economy. Single women, whether never married, divorced, or widowed, have always had to support themselves and their children. It follows that even when breadwinning became the predominant form, it was never as widespread as commonly assumed—especially outside the white middle class. Nevertheless, as the nineteenth century drew to a close, most men and women occupied separate economic, social, and spatial spheres.

The rise of the primary-breadwinning husband, based on the ideal of a family wage and the "protection" of women and children, provided some obvious benefits. It afforded middle-class women and children relief from the sometimes dangerous and often squalid conditions of early industrial workplaces. It freed children from the burdens of wage earning, allowing them an extended childhood devoted to learning and play under the watchful eyes of mothers, teachers, and other female caretakers. As the sociologist Viviana Zelizer points out, children became economically "useless," but socially "priceless."

Despite these real benefits, the barring of women from highly paid, secure jobs reinforced and exaggerated inequality between men and women and between adults and children. The "modern family" became synonymous with a sharp differentiation between the sexes, a glorification of the mother-child bond, and an expectation that men should provide economically for their wives and children.

The consolidation of the modern family, with its reliance on a male family wage, transformed the justification for male control over women and children. Patriarchal dominance could no longer be easily asserted as a male birthright; men now had to earn it through economic success in the marketplace. Male power and privilege became tied to good jobs that paid enough to support the family in a certain degree of comfort. In exchange for assuming economic responsibilities, men "earned" the right—and gained the economic power—to head the household and to control the family purse strings.

Many men, of course, were never able or willing to conform to these new standards of manhood. Working-class jobs often paid too little, and poor men were hard-pressed to find any work at all. Periodic recessions and depressions swelled the ranks of the unemployed, but even during good economic times many men fell short of these new definitions of success. A significant proportion of working-class women, and even children, have always supplemented their husbands' limited incomes or lived without the help of any male support. Similarly, men, especially those with poor labor market prospects, have always been able to use desertion or

6

7

8

9

10

divorce to escape the economic burdens of breadwinning. These alternatives did not disappear, but they became harder to choose and defend as the breadwinner-homemaker model became the dominant cultural ideal, if not the only behavior in reality.

A range of ideas emerged to justify and reinforce male breadwinning and female homemaking. A "cult of domesticity" arose in the mid-nineteenth century, which held that a woman's proper place is in the home, providing for her family's emotional needs and moral education. The advent of psychoanalysis at the end of that century transformed the case for male breadwinning and female domesticity into scientific language, suggesting that these arrangements were not just morally superior but biologically necessary. These ideas were first and most enthusiastically accepted among the middle class, where more families could afford to heed their prescriptions, but they eventually spread throughout the common culture. An ideology of manhood as "good providing" could not force men to conform, but it did judge those who would not or could not to be inadequate husbands, failed fathers, and immature adults.

Yet even as male primary breadwinning came to predominate, the social foundations that made it possible showed signs of eroding. By the turn of the century, white-collar and service jobs were expanding and women were beginning to fill them. Although their numbers were small at first, the growth of white-collar and service jobs in the early twentieth century foreshadowed the postindustrial revolution that was to take place after World War II. Men were among the first clerical workers, but a ready supply of educated women began to replace them (at lower wages) in the early decades of the twentieth century.

In this early period, the growth of the female labor force did not appear to threaten the preeminence of the male breadwinner. After all, the vast majority of women workers were young, single, childless, and only temporarily employed. Marriage and pregnancy sent most employed women home to care for newly acquired husbands and children. The economic prosperity that followed the Great Depression and World War II, coupled with veterans' benefits and preferential treatment for male workers, gave male breadwinning a new boost and temporarily suppressed the long-term erosion of the good-provider pattern. However insignificant the emergence of large numbers of employed women may have appeared at the outset, it was a portent of more widespread changes to come.

When changes did become apparent, they made a revolutionary transformation in women's lives. Streaming into the labor force in ever-increasing numbers, women have developed a commitment to the workplace that has come to resemble the career pattern once reserved for men. A burgeoning proportion has also postponed or rejected marriage, reduced their reproductive rates to an unprecedented low, and fashioned a variety of alternatives to full-time mothering. By the mid-1970s, over half of all American women of working age were in the labor force, and the birthrate had dropped below the replacement rate of 2.2 children per woman for the first time in American history.

Since then, women's movement into the work force has continued unabated, 15
topping 58 percent for all working-age women in 1990 and accounting for two out
of every three mothers with preschool children. Since the precipitous rise in women's
employment rate is fueled by the entry of younger rather than older cohorts of
women, the percentage of mothers with young children who are employed has
risen faster than the percentage of all women who are employed. Most employed
women have entered female-dominated occupations, but a notable proportion has
broken the barriers to entry into male-dominated fields such as law (up from
4 percent in 1972 to 21 percent in 1990), medicine (up from 10 percent to 19 percent), computer programming (up from 20 percent to 36 percent), and even bus
driving (up from 34 percent to almost 52 percent). Other women have not been so
fortunate, however, as rising marital instability and the decline of male support have
left them economically vulnerable in an economy that continues to allot most of
the best-rewarded jobs to men.

Men have also undergone a revolution in family and work commitments, albeit a 16
quieter one. Since 1970, men's earnings have stagnated, eroding their ability to earn
a "family wage." From 1979 to 1988, the median hourly wage for men fell 5 percent,
and the bottom 75 percent of the male work force experienced wage reductions.
For white men serving as a family's only breadwinner, median inflation-adjusted income fell 22 percent between 1976 and 1984. Families have been able to maintain a
comparable standard of living only because women have joined the work force and
experienced slightly rising wages. Men's relative economic contributions to family
survival have thus declined over the last several decades, while pressure for them
to share in the work of the home has mounted.

Although the economic prospects of most men have contracted, their options 17
about whether to share their earnings with women and children have expanded.
The rise in divorce, nonmarital sexual partnerships, and out-of-wedlock childbear-
ing has given men an escape hatch from the demands of primary breadwinning. Many
men may now find it difficult to support a family alone, but they have a choice about
what to do instead: they can rely on an employed partner to share the pressures of
economic survival, or they can simply remain single and thereby keep their earnings to themselves.

Few Americans now live on farms or in small towns, where preindustrial men, 18
women, and children joined in a common physical and economic struggle to survive. Men no longer depart the household to seek their fortune on an expanding
frontier. Outside the inner city, premature and unexpected death is less likely to
take young men from wives, lovers, and dependent children. Social conditions have
changed irrevocably, but the historical ambiguity and diversity of male commitments have reemerged in a new form.

Now, as in an earlier era, "good providers" vie with "autonomous men" and "in- 19
volved husbands and fathers" for ideological and social support. But no clear suc-
cessor has taken the place of the once-ascendant but now embattled ethos of male
breadwinning. Contemporary men—whether primary breadwinners, husbands and

fathers in dual-earner marriages, or confirmed bachelors—face new choices and circumstances. Models from the past, however unambiguous or attractive, provide little help in navigating these uncertain waters.

from MANHOOD IN THE MAKING:
Cultural Concepts of Masculinity
David D. Gilmore

Aside from potency, men must seek to provision dependents by contributing mightily to the family patrimony. This, too, is measured by the efficiency quotient, by results (Davis 1977:77). What counts, again, is performance in the work role, measured in sacrifice or service to family needs. What has to be emphasized here is the sense of social sacrifice that this masculine work-duty entails. The worker in the fields often despises manual labor of any sort, because it rarely benefits him personally. For example, the rural Andalusians say that work is a "curse" (D. Gilmore 1980:55), because it can never make a man rich. For the poor man, working means contracting under humiliating conditions for a day-wage, battling with his fellows for fleeting opportunities in the work place, and laboring in the fields picking cotton and weeding sunflowers from dawn to dusk. Synonymous with suffering, work is something that most men will freely admit they hate and would avoid if they could.

Yet for the worker, the peasant, or any man who must earn his bread, work is also a responsibility—never questioned—of feeding dependents. And here, as in matters of sex and fatherly duty, the worker's reputation as a citizen and a man is closely bound up with clearly defined service to family. A man who shirks these obligations renounces his claim to both respectability and manhood; he becomes a despised less-than-man, a wastrel, a *gamberro*. The latter term means an irresponsible reprobate who acts like a carefree child or who lives parasitically off women. Although it is true that women in Andalusia are often wage-earners too, the husband, to be a real man, must contribute the lion's share of income to support wife and family like a pillar and to keep the feminine machine of domestic production running smoothly. A man works hard, sometimes desperately, because, as they say, *se obliga,* you are bound to your family, not because you like it. In this sense, Spanish men are, as Brandes notes (1980:210), like men everywhere, actively pursuing the breadwinning role as a measure of their manhood. The only difference is that they rarely get pleasure or personal satisfaction from the miserable work available to them.

In southern Italy, much the same attitude is found. John Davis (1973:94–95) writes of the town of Pisticci: "Work is also justified in terms of the family of the man who works: 'If it were not for my family, I'd not be wearing myself out' (*non mi sacrifico*). The ability of a husband to support his wife and children is as important a component of his honour as his control of his wife's sexuality. Independence of others, in this context, thus implies both his economic and sexual honour. . . .

Work, then, is not regarded as having any intrinsic rewards. Men work to produce food and some cash for their families."

This sacrifice in the service of family, this contribution to household and kin, is, in fact, what Mediterranean notions of honor are all about. Honor is about being good *at being a man,* which means building up and buttressing the family or kindred—the basic building blocks of society—no matter what the personal cost: "[Mediterranean] honor as ideology helps shore up the identity of a group (a family or a lineage) and commit to it the loyalties of otherwise doubtful members. Honor defines the group's social boundaries, contributing to its defense against the claims of equivalent competing groups" (Schneider 1971:17).

The emphasis on male honor as a domestic duty is widespread in the Mediterranean. In his seminal survey of the literature, John Davis, like Jane Schneider in the quote above, finds confirmation for his view of masculine honor as deriving from work and economic industry as much as from sexual success: "It should be said at the outset that honour is not primarily to do with sexual intercourse . . . but with performance of roles and is related to economic resources because feeding a family, looking after women, maintaining a following, can be done more easily when the family is not poor" (1977:77).

Sometimes this kind of economic service can be quantified in terms of money or other objects of value, or it can be expressed in material accumulations that are passed on to women and children, such as dowries. For example, Ernestine Friedl (1962), writing about a Greek peasant village in contemporary Boeotia, describes the honor of fathers as grounded in their ability to provide large dowries in cash and valuables to their daughters. This success assures them of the best in-laws, contributes to family prestige, and consequently enhances their image as provider. Manhood is measured at least partly in money, a man's only direct way of nourishing children. Manhood, then, as call to action, can be interpreted as a kind of moral compunction to provision kith and kin.

Man-the-Protector

After impregnating and provisioning comes bravery. Being a man in Andalusia, for example, is also based on what the people call *hombría.* Technically this simply means manliness, but it differs from the expressly virile or economic performances described above. Rather, hombría is physical and moral courage. Having no specific behavioral correlatives, it forms an intransitive component: it means standing up for yourself as an independent and proud actor, holding your own when challenged. Spaniards also call this *dignidad* (dignity). It is not based on threatening people or on violence, for Andalusians despise bullies and deplore physical roughness, which to them is mere buffoonery. Generalized as to context, hombría means a courageous and stoic demeanor in the face of any threat; most important, it means defending one's honor and that of one's family. It shows not aggressiveness in a physical sense but an unshakable loyalty to social group that signals the ultimate deterrent to challenge. The restraint on violence is always based on the capacity for violence, so that reputation is vital here.

As a form of masculine self-control and courage, hombría is shown multitudinously. For example, in Fuenmayor, a group of young men may wander down to the municipal cemetery late at night after a few drinks to display their disdain for ghosts. They take with them a hammer and a nail or spike. Posturing drunkenly together, they pound the nail into the cemetery's stucco wall. Challenging all manner of goblins and ghouls, they recite in unison the following formula to the rhythm of the hammer blows:

Aquí hinco clavo	I here drive a spike
del tio monero	before goblin or sprite
venga quién venga,	and whatever appear,
aquí lo espero!	I remain without fear!

The last man to run away wins the laurels as the bravest, the most manly. Sometimes adolescents will challenge each other to spend a night in the cemetery in a manner of competitive testing, but otherwise hombría is nonconfrontational, as the defiance is displaced onto a supernatural (nonsocial) adversary. Nevertheless, as the above example shows, it is competitive and, like virility and economic performance, needs proof in visible symbols and accomplishments. Hombría judges a man's fitness to defend his family. Pitt-Rivers (1961:89) has depicted it best: "The quintessence of manliness is fearlessness, readiness to defend one's own pride and that of one's family." Beyond this, "*un vero uomo*" (a real man) is defined by "strength, power, and cunning necessary to protect his women" (Giovannini 1987:68). At the same time, of course, the successfully protective man in Sicily or Andalusia garners praise through courageous feats and gains renown for himself as an individual. This inseparable functional linkage of personal and group benefit is one of the most ancient moral notions found in the Mediterranean civilizations. One finds it already in ancient seafaring Greece in the voyager Odysseus. His very name, from *odyne* (the ability to cause pain and the readiness to do so), implies a willingness to expose oneself to conflict, risk, and trouble and to strive against overwhelming odds in order to achieve great exploits. "To be Odysseus, then, is to adopt the attitude of the hunter of dangerous game: to deliberately expose one's self, but thereafter to take every advantage that the exposed position admits; the immediate purpose is injury, but the ultimate purpose is recognition and the sense of a great exploit" (Dimrock 1967:57).

But Odysseus's ultimate goal is not simply one vainglorious exploit after another. All his wayfaring heroism is directed at a higher purpose: to rescue wife and child and to disperse the sinister suitors who threaten them both. The real man gains renown by standing between his family and destruction, absorbing the blows of fate with equanimity. Mediterranean manhood is the reward given to the man who is an

8

9

efficient protector of the web of primordial ties, the guardian of his society's moral and material integuments.

Autonomous Wayfarers

The ideals of manliness found in these places in the Mediterranean seem to have three moral imperatives: first, impregnating one's wife; second, provisioning dependents; third, protecting the family. These criteria demand assertiveness and resolve. All must be performed relentlessly in the loyal service of the "collective identities" of the self.

10

One other element needs mention. The above depend upon something deeper: a mobility of action, a personal autonomy. A man can do nothing if his hands are tied. If he is going to hunt dangerous game and, like Odysseus, save his family, he needs absolute freedom of movement. Equally important as sex and economic resourcefulness is the underlying appeal to independent action as the starting point of manly self-identity. To enter upon the road to manhood, a man must travel light and be free to improvise and to respond, unencumbered, to challenge. He must have a moral captaincy. In southern Spain, as reported by Brandes (1980:210), dependency for an Andalusian peasant is not just shameful; it is also a negation of his manly image. Personal autonomy is the goal for each and every man; without it, his defensive posture collapses. His strategic mobility is lost, exposing his family to ruin. This theme, too, has political implications in Spain.

11

An example comes from George Collier's account of the Spanish Civil War in an Andalusian village. Collier (1987: 90) points out the role played by masculine pride in the labor movements of workers and peasants in western Andalusia. He describes the critical political connotations of what he calls the "cultural terms in which Andalusians relate autonomy to masculine honor" and the virtues attached to asserting this masculinity (ibid.:96). Collier's discussion of the violent conflicts between landowners and laborers during the Second Republic (1931–36) in the pueblo of Los Olivos (Huelva Province) shows that a driving force behind their confrontations was this issue of personal autonomy. The peasants and workers were defending not only their political rights but also their self-image as men from the domineering tactics of the rich and powerful. Autonomy permitted them to defend their family's honor. Encumbered or dependent, they could not perform their manly heroics. Their revolutionism, as Collier brilliantly shows, was as much a product of a manhood image as their political and economic demands. This was particularly true of southern Spain, but Collier sees this mixture of political ideology and masculine self-image as something more widely Mediterranean:

12

> Villagers in Los Olivos held to the ideal of masculine autonomy characteristic of property relations and the system of honor in the agrarian societies of the Mediterranean. . . . The prepotent male discouraged challenges by continually reasserting this masculinity and potential for physical aggression while he guarded against assaults on the virtue of his women and stood up to others to protect

his family's honor. . . . The ideal of masculine autonomy thus charged employer-employee relations with special tension. In having to accept someone else's orders, the employee implicitly acknowledged his lack of full autonomy and his vulnerability to potential dishonor. (Ibid.:96–97)

To be dependent upon another man is bad enough, but to acknowledge dependence upon a woman is worse. The reason, of course, is that this inverts the normal order of family ties, which in turn destroys the formal basis for manhood. For instance, in Morocco, as reported by Hildred Geertz (1979:369), the major values of *rajula,* or manly pride, are "personal autonomy and force," which imply dominating and provisioning rather than being dominated and provisioned by women. There is indeed no greater fear among men than the loss of this personal autonomy to a dominant woman.   13

In Morocco there is in fact a recurrent anxiety that a man will fall under the magical spell of a powerful woman, a demonic seductress who will entrap him forever, as Venus entrapped Tannhaüser, or as Circe attempted to enslave Odysseus, causing him to forget his masculine role (Dwyer 1978). The psychological anthropologist Vincent Crapanzano has written an entire book about a Moroccan man who lived in terror of such a demonic female *jinn.* He tells us that this anxiety is widespread: "This theme of enslavement by a woman—the inverse of the articulated standards of male-female relations, of sex and marriage—pervades Moroccan folklore" (1980:102). There, as in Spain, a man must gain full and total independence from women as a necessary criterion of manhood. How can he provide for dependents and protect them when he himself is dependent like a child? This inversion of sex roles, because it turns wife into mother, subverts both the man and the family unit, sending both down to corruption and defeat.   14

from POWER AT PLAY: Sports and the Problem of Masculinity
Michael A. Messner

The institution of sport is extremely hierarchical, with the highest value placed on winning, on being "number one." A few years ago, I observed a boys' basketball camp organized by a professional basketball coach and his staff. The youngest boys, about eight years old (who could barely reach the basket with their shots) played a brief scrimmage. Afterward, the coaches lined them up in a row in front of the older boys who were sitting in the grandstands. One by one, the coach would stand behind each boy, put his hand on the boy's head (much in the manner of a priestly benediction), and the older boys in the stands would applaud and cheer, louder or softer, depending on how well or poorly the young player was judged to have performed. The two or three boys who were clearly the exceptional players looked confident that they would receive the praise they were due. Most the boys, though, wore expressions ranging from puzzlement to thinly disguised terror as they awaited the judgments of the older boys.   1

This kind of experience teaches boys that it is not "just being out there with the guys—being friends," that ensures the kind of attention and connection they crave; it is being better than the other guys—beating them—that is the key to acceptance. Most of the men in this study did have some early successes in sport, and thus their ambivalent need for connection with others was met, at least for a time. But the institution of sport tends to encourage the development of what sociologist Walter Schafer calls "conditional self-worth" in boys. As boys become aware that acceptance by others—fathers, coaches, peers—is contingent upon being a "winner," narrow definitions of success, based upon performance and winning become increasingly important to them. As Willy S. said, by the time he was in his early teens, "It was *expected* of me to do well in all my contests—I mean by my coaches, my peers, and my family. So I in turn expected to do well, and if I didn't do well, then I'd be very disappointed." This conscious striving for athletic success eventually became the primary means through which many of these young males defined themselves, as well as their relationships with others. Given the fact that one's own "success" is the flip-side of another's "failure," organized sport encourages boys to view other boys not as intimates, but as rivals. Within this competitive world, the chief question a boy may ask himself when confronted with another boy is, "Can I take him?"

from SUPERMAN/SUPERBOYS/SUPERMEN
Norma Pecora

In the 1930s Superman was introduced as a champion of the "oppressed":

> Unlike his predecessors [in science fiction], Superman not only chooses a place for himself in society, he also identifies with and aids his fellows and in turn is accepted, even glorified, by them. He is the embodiment of society's noblest ideals, a "man of tomorrow" who foreshadows mankind's highest potentialities and profoundest aspirations but whose tremendous power, remarkably pose no danger to its freedom and safety. (Andrea, 1987, p. 125)

Superman of the 1930s was at base "human," incorporating the characteristics of kindness and caring. In the early episodes he:

> [S]aves an innocent woman from being electrocuted, stops a wife-beating, halts corrupt politicians . . . deals with the [issues] of the rights of accused persons to fair and impartial justice . . . crooked unions and corrupt municipal officials, and with prison brutality, slum conditions, and other pressing social issues. (Andrea, 1987, p. 130)

He brought, as Kimmel suggested, compassion and ambition together.

During World War II and the 1940s, Superman presented an ideal for the young men going off to war ("Superman Slipped," 1987). Although he was classified as 4F during the war, he maintained his representation of goodness (see Uslan, 1979, pp. 43–58). He became the embodiment of patriotism and, by extension, a true American hero. However, no longer was his fight against social injustice, his struggle turned to a defense of private property (Andrea 1987, p. 131). Although he was still the personification of good versus evil, the definition of evil shifted. Later we were told by the 1953 television adaptation that Superman fought for "truth, justice, and the American way." However, racism and sexism were accepted as the norm; in the comics, as in real life, simplistic solutions were offered for cultural conditions (Skidmore & Skidmore, 1983).

With the 1960s came enlightenment to both society and the *Superman* comics. Issues became more topical and comic book characters more relevant. Lois Lane became a "marginal" feminist, protesting denial of a dangerous assignment with: "That's not fair, Perry. You're discriminating against me because I'm a woman! I protest" (VanGelder & VanGelder, 1970, p. 39). And, acting out another vignette from real life, the *Daily Planet* was taken over by a multinational conglomerate with broadcasting interests, and Clark Kent moved to television (VanGelder & VanGelder, 1970, p. 39). 3

By the 1980s many of the growing number of superhero characters became "real." Although the characters, and particularly Superman, maintained the machismo qualities of power, control, goodness, and competence, reality was beginning to be a part of the superheroes' life. For example: 4

> Richard and Susan Richards of the *Fantastic Four,* often had to find a sitter for their son before venturing out to save the Universe. (*Fantastic Four,* 1983, 1985)

> Sam Guthrie, the Cannonball, was forced to contend with school dress codes and failing grades. (*New Mutants,* 1985)

> Matt Murdock, the Daredevil—the man without fear, is blind.

> Box, a member of the Canadian team Alpha Flight, is a double-amputee.

> And Charles Xavier, mentor of the X-Men, leads his group from a wheelchair.

Contemporary comic-book heroes now confronted such concerns as the threat of nuclear war, institutionalized racism, organized crime, corrupt government, inept judicial systems, environmental protection, and teenage prostitution. 5

During each decade, *Superman* comic books appeared to reflect the time: 1940s–1950s, isolationism and a quiet conservatism; 1960s, liberalization and radicalization; 1970s, humanization; 1980s, political and social conservatism of the Reagan era (Pecora & Gateward, 1989). 6

Most of us are familiar with the story of Superman and his journey to Earth, his susceptibility to kryptonite, and his alter ego, Clark Kent. We grew up with Superman's friends, Jimmy Olsen and Lois Lane, and his archenemy, Lex Luthor (who, until recently killed, had become an evil corporate executive). Our memories are of battles of good versus evil, of kindness and chivalry. He was described, in a story 7 line that included several heads of state, by a representation of Ronald Reagan as follows:

President of the United States: Superman hasn't let [down] the good people of the United States *or the world yet* . . . and by golly he's not about to yet.

Leader of "Russian-like" country: He is going to . . . to . . .

President of the United States: . . . to show you what a true American hero can *do,* Mr. Premier. (*Superman #387,* 1983)

A careful reading of the comics demonstrates a less-than-benign text, revealing a world where violence is used to solve problems; women, if present, are victims and nuisances; and racism reinforces a world of second-class citizenry. Such a reading supports the argument by Kaufman, presented earlier, that racism and sexism are forms of institutionalized violence. The Superman of the eighties supported a fantasy world with Superman acting as a vigilante, solving problems with violence, while maintaining the status quo. A reading of the character of Superman reveals not the simple battles of good versus evil, but rather a vigilante operating without legitimate authority. Answerable to nothing except his own code of ethics, Superman utilizes violence and physical strength as his primary method of operation.

His lack of respect for civil liberties became so intense during the 1980s that in one story line, he functioned as judge, jury, and executioner: roles he previously left to the legal system. In a story titled "The Price," Superman denied three Kryptonian villains a trial. Seeing himself "forced to stop the three of them for once and for all," Superman exposed them to deadly kryptonite. Though they begged for mercy, Superman resisted their pleas and reduced them to piles of dust (*Superman #22,* 1987).

Popular culture has been described as important because it is:

[A] realm within which racial ideologies have been created, produced, and sustained . . . not that of misportrayal, but of invisibility. (Omi, 1988, pp. 114, 121)

And certainly the *Superman* comics have contributed to such ideologies. In an analysis of 8 years of *Superman* comic books (1980–1988) examined, it was found that the world of Superman excluded people of color, class, and gender (see Pecora & Gatewood, 1989). The reader was presented with a white world, where problems were solved with violence, and women were victims. In the few stories that included people of color, the representations remain negative stereotypes. If, indeed, the media present us with social rules and courtesies, the comic books offer the young reader a world where violence and exclusion are acceptable.

Virtually every issue of the *Superman* comics offers themes of violence. Terrorists bomb embassies (*Superman #399,* 1984) and national monuments like Mt. Rushmore (*Superman #396,* 1983). The earth is conquered by Vikings (*Superman #394,* 1984) and aliens too numerous to count. In a particularly violent story line, Bloodsport, a psychotic draft-dodger, is used as a lure by Lex Luthor. Bloodsport becomes a sniper, believing he is in the jungles of Vietnam and shooting at anyone he sees in the streets.

Bloodsport is one of the many black Americans portrayed as victims in the *Superman* comics. In several story lines, black women and children live in a ghetto tenement and are burned out of their homes. Unable to do anything but cower in fear, they are, of course, rescued by Superman (*Superman #352,* 1980; see also *Superman #394,* 1984). The most dominant trend in these comics was the depiction of blacks as unskilled labor. Because the characters had virtually no "speaking parts," they served no purpose other than to "color" the background. The jobs at which they were employed included security guards, cab drivers, and truck drivers. The only recurring black character was Frank, the doorman of the high-rise building in which Clark Kent/Superman lives. The only professional presented was a corporate lawyer, referred to as a "shyster" by the chief of police, who appeared only in the last few frames of one comic (*Superman #10,* 1987).

One of a few black characters representing the criminal element was a young man who served as a lackey. In a group of five, this character, in terms of spatial representation, was consistently drawn behind the other criminals and was the only member without a weapon—denying him equality even as a criminal (*Superman #346,* 1980). Baron Sunday was the major black opponent to Superman but, unlike other *Superman* villains, he did not utilize science and technology to achieve his goals, rather his sole source of power was voodoo magic (*Superman #26,* 1988).

Another group featured in the stories was Native Americans and they, too, were subject to treatment similar to that of the black characters. In one issue, as an attack was made on Superman, he exclaimed: "Now I know what Custer felt like at Little Big Horn" (*Superman #377,* 1982). Of all the issues examined, Native Americans played a prominent role in one, a story titled "The Master of Wind and Storm" (*Superman #348,* 1980). It concerned an elderly Native American who perceived of himself as a powerful individual. He was mistaken, however, because he was actually being tricked and used by an alien. Superman saved the community from a disaster caused by the old man and closed the issue with the comment: "He's just a harmless old man with dreams." Thus the writers and artists managed to simultaneously insult both the elderly and the Native Americans.

Other groups were also represented as ethnic or racial stereotypes. The Italian was in organized crime (*Superman #385,* 1983); the Hispanic was a priest (*Superman #352,* 1980); Mrs. Goldstein talked of "bubelah" (*Superman #393,* 1984), and the lesbian was an unfit mother (*Superman #15,* 1988).

Though the women of the *Superman* comics are more visible than other groups, they are no less victims. They are old ladies with cats (*Superman #390,* 1983) or silly girls (*Superman #358, #362,* 1981). And though Lois Lane and Lana Lang, the two female protagonists, are both professional journalists, their main function has been to depict the "damsel in distress syndrome," continually in need of rescue by Superman (For example: *Superman #346, #348, #350,* 1980; *#370,* 1982; *#392,* 1984; *#1,* 1987; *#21,* 1988). Lois has long pined for Superman to no avail. More often than

ways thought that was kind of a chicken way out. Then when I tried to get aggressive I started forcing my shots. If I missed a few shots and lost my sense of confidence, I'd get more conservative and more nervous than ever. I'd worry about whether I'd double-fault, and then of course I'd double-fault. I wouldn't open up and take advantage of opportunities.

I don't know what it's like for other guys, for guys who are real successful in tennis. Maybe when they come down to an important point or an important match they take on a more arrogant stance. I don't know what their internal experience is, whether they have the kind of self-anguish that I always had at those moments—"Oh, God, can I do it?"—or whether they think, "I'm just great. Of course I can do it." I never really had that kind of blind self-confidence. I always had the sense that my outward success was precarious and that I might just blow it at any moment.

When I first got to college I went right up to the coach and started playing a lot of tennis. He ranked me third on the freshman tennis ladder, but it was just informal at that point because the season didn't start until spring. I played a lot of squash that winter to keep in shape, but when spring finally came I couldn't seem to make the adjustment back to tennis. I lost a couple of challenge matches on the tennis ladder and then I got into this losing frame of mind. I lost ten challenge matches in a row, dropping down the ladder from three to thirteen. It kept getting worse and worse. Every time I'd walk out onto the court I'd have this weird trip in the pit of my stomach and I wouldn't really see that good and I'd be sweating before the thing would even start. I was too tensed up: my neck was tight, my muscles were tight, and I would say to myself, "Oh no, here we go again!"

In between challenge matches, when it didn't count, I could still play well. I could beat a lot of those same guys in practice games. I could serve well, I could hit well, I could just beat 'em. But something was happening when it counted that was awful. I couldn't pull myself out of it. My ego investment was too extreme. It was very difficult for me to separate having a bad day on the tennis court and being a bad person. My sense of being personally okay was seriously threatened. It got worse and worse till finally I just quit playing competitive tennis for the next ten years.

So what good has come out of Ken B.'s spotty career in interscholastic sports? Athletic competition, which is supposed to help a young man establish his strength and self-assurance, seems to have had the opposite effect. Although Ken has in fact excelled in fields extraneous to sports . . . his athletic activities have apparently had little to do with the development of manly ideals such as confidence, courage, or self-reliance. Even now, years later, Ken is still burdened with insecurities which seem exaggerated, not relieved, by his participation in sports:

Just last year a fellow came into town, Jack, who's a real serious player. It's a *big* part of his life. He makes his living at it, he's a professional. He heard I could play and he kept seeking me out as someone who could help him break a sweat.

I was real flattered, so I got serious about tennis again and we started playing together. He's younger and stronger and a more experienced player, so he always won. I don't think I've ever beat him. There were a couple of times when he got a little bit down and I got on a roll and we got to where a couple of points would become crucial. Then he'd always come on a little harder and I'd always not quite pull it off.

About a month ago we got out on the court and I started thinking: "All right, he's beat me every time for the last twenty times. Now *this* time I'm going to really have at it." I got myself worked up to a frenzy. At one point I got really mad at him because he seemed to be questioning one of my calls. That's very emotional for me—I hate the thought that somebody thinks I might be cheating. So I got in a stew. Then later in the set when it was still close—the games were tied—I put away an overhead and got ahead forty-fifteen. I went to serve and he stopped me from serving. He dried off his hand on his towel. I went to serve again and he stopped me again and said he had to change his sweatband. He walked clear across the court, and meanwhile I was there in this stew. I got so mad at him that I could hardly see the ball anymore. I said to him something like, "I don't need to learn any more about hitting tennis balls to beat you; what I have to learn is how to compete psychologically with this stuff." I can't remember my exact words, but it was some stinging phrase that I was sure would make him crumble. Of course he just thought I was acting weird and went on to trounce me.

I'm a fairly easy-tempered person, but this time I was in a stew all day. I was really wrought up, and I kept talking to people about it. I thought, "This is a little extreme here. Why am I so wired up? What's got ahold of me?"

Failure in war is tragic; in sports it's almost comic. The developmental quest for manhood becomes transformed into an absurd Sisyphusian task: we are forever trying to climb a ladder that has no inherent meaning. Why do we strive so hard to achieve such apparently pointless goals? What's in it for us, anyway? Or, more specifically: What *has* got ahold of Ken B.? Why has this personable, sane, and otherwise rational young man allowed himself to take his games so seriously—even though he obviously knows better?

The actual games that Ken plays are fine; even the aggression is fine, the satisfaction of a primordial urge. The only problem lies in the interpretation of the results. The metaphor has become too real. Through sports, Ken hopes to determine his place on the pecking order: whom can he beat? Is he on the top or the bottom of the ladder? Or (as is much more likely) is he somewhere in between?

The promise of a competitive sport, for all aspiring athletes, is to provide a linear ordering of reality; we either win or lose, and that clearly defines us as better or worse than the others. We reduce the complex world of everyday affairs to a finite field with a well-defined set of rules, and on that field we try to pinpoint exactly where we stand with respect to all our rivals. The multi-dimensional tasks of life get reduced to the one-dimensional task of beating our opponent. By diverting complex questions of right and wrong into more comprehensible questions of winning and losing, sports can even supply us with a simplified sense of moral purpose. This simplification offers an antidote to some of the ambiguities of our pluralistic culture, where questions of meaning are hard to answer and a precise definition of rank is often difficult to achieve. Is a baker higher or lower than a butcher? Is he better or worse? Is he more or less of a man? It's hard to say—but when they face off head-to-head out there on the ball field or the tennis court, one will win and the other will lose and they will both know where they stand.

But even this simplified paradigm, in the end, often defies our quest for linearity—and that tends to cause us great concern. Like Ken B., we might win one day and lose the next, possibly to the very same opponent. Except for a rare handful of unbeatable champions, our place in the pecking order is forever in question. We climb a few rungs up the ladder, but we are always in danger of falling back down. Even Jack, the seasoned professional, must struggle to beat out his nervous rival. Success, once attained, must still be defended, so all that remains constant is the anxiety caused by uncertainty. 8

from AMERICAN MANHOOD: Transformations in Masculinity from the Revolution to the Modern Era
E. Anthony Rotundo

Northern men had engaged in physical games and contests almost from the time that British settlers came to New England. Wrestling matches and informal team games were played on special occasions under the loosest of rules. Boys did not wait for special occasions; from the colonial era to the nineteenth century, they enjoyed physical contests and indulged in them as often as they could. The Puritans and their Yankee descendants approved of such games, which they considered wholesome exercise, as long as they were not played on the Sabbath or at times that interfered with work. In the middle of the nineteenth century, however, these games took on new meaning and heightened importance for Northern men. 1

By the 1840s a new game called "baseball" was spreading rapidly. With roots in several ball games that were common in the Northeast, baseball became a vehicle for expressing rivalry between towns, neighborhoods, and businesses. These rival groups organized their best players into teams that championed local honor in hotly contested "match games." In the large cities of the 1840s and 1850s, baseball rivalries focused especially on work-based groups. The teams, at first a middle-class phenomenon, spread later to working-class men as well, but the spectators for the games continued for many years to be middle class. Meanwhile other sports were finding favor. During the 1840s and 1850s, rowing enjoyed a great vogue, with clubs springing up in business and professional circles. The first great intercollegiate contests were the rowing regattas of the late 1850s. During the antebellum years, fencing and boxing lessons even became acceptable for aspiring clerks and well-bred students. 2

The significance of sport went beyond its growing popularity as a pastime; it was also important as a cultural phenomenon. This dimension was what gave athletics 3 its special significance for the redefinition of manhood at the turn of the century. Before the Civil War, athletics was seen as a form of physical culture that strengthened the body, refreshed the soul, and increased a man's resistance to luxury and vice. In the postbellum period, on the other hand, athletics came to mean competition and not mere exercise. At Phillips Exeter Academy, for instance, late-century students demanded more of the school than simple physical training. Student sentiment urged "the boy to drop his chest weights, and don boxing gloves; to stop jogging on the track, and race; to quit signal practice and scrimmage. There is a difference between physical culture and athletics, and that is it."

The same rage for competitive sports was emerging at Exeter's rival academy. In   4
the 1890s, the letters written by Andover students showed an "exultation in the fanfare surrounding each contest with Exeter." Andover boys at the time often dressed for the Sunday chapel service in their athletic uniforms. By the close of the 1800s, team sports had taken on a moral and social significance that far outstripped their old relationship to physical culture.

Between 1860 and 1890, baseball moved beyond local rivalries to become the   5
national pastime. At the same time, collegiate rivalries spread from crew races to football games, baseball matches, and track meets. Golf became a popular pastime for businessmen at the end of the 1800s, and tennis emerged in the 1870s as a new passion for male youth. The traditions of one affluent family claim that when a daughter in the house wanted to meet young men, she had a tennis court built in the backyard. The story may be apocryphal but the basic point remains: young men were preoccupied with sports, often to the exclusion of romance.

What was the meaning of competitive athletics to those who advocated them?   6
Men seeking a peacetime equivalent to war often turned to team sports with hope. Francis A. Walker believed that the manly traits inspired by Civil War experience were best taught in peacetime by "the competitive contests of our colleges." Cultural confusion between military combat and athletic combat was widespread, especially in the last two decades of the century when the Civil War experience was valorized. Walter Camp, the father of modern football, wrote at the turn of the century that there was a "remarkable and interesting likeness between the theories which underlie great battles and the miniature contests of the gridiron." Camp's contemporaries referred to quarterbacks as "field generals," and called linemen "soldiers" (after World War I, linemen would be said to "battle in the trenches"). Perhaps the most dramatic instance of this confusion between team sports and war came from a conversation that poet Hamlin Garland had with novelist Stephen Crane. The author of *The Red Badge of Courage* had never gone to war, so Garland asked him how he knew about it. Crane responded that he had played football and that its strategy and emotion were like a war, with the other team serving as the enemy.

In a cultural setting where war and athletics were equated and war was thought   7
to breed a new, forceful manhood, people readily came to the position that athletics, too, fostered the new form of manhood. At the start of the new century, the president of Princeton praised competitive sports as tests of manliness, "gentle-

manly contests for supremacy." And, in 1901, an education writer insisted that "manly social games, like football, basket-ball, baseball, are our best resources in developing . . . almost every characteristic of virility."

The claims for athletics as a source of manhood were so vast and varied that they can best be understood in several categories. First of all, athletic contests were praised as breeding grounds for the fighting virtues. These included determination, "coolness, steadiness of nerve, quickness of apprehension," "endurance against hunger, fatigue, and physical distress," and—above all—courage.

Through the experience of team play, athletics were also credited with the development of social, cooperative, and even submissive virtues. In 1905, Cunningham LaPlace wrote in a magazine called *The Outlook* that team contests taught a youth "the subordination of the unit to the total, the habit of working with his fellows, of touching elbows." Luther Gulick, a noted leader in work with boys, made the point most emphatically in 1899: team sports bred "heroic subordination of self to the group." To most middle-class men in the nineteenth century, the phrase, "heroic subordination," would have been a contradiction in terms. To men like Gulick at the turn of the twentieth century, the phrase made fine and noble sense. Courage, strength, and endurance meant more to them than independence, especially if a man subordinated himself to the right cause.

If the traits encouraged by team sports contradicted some of the republican values that infused nineteenth-century manhood, they did support some others. Competitive athletics, according to their advocates, counteracted one of the greatest sources of worry for republicans: those "dangerous tendencies in modern life" that often "produce neurotic and luxury-loving individuals." Team contests demanded a strength, vigor, and physical assertiveness that undermined the ease and debility of modern affluence. Other proponents of sports, concerned with the greed of Gilded Age tycoons and politicians, claimed that the experience of team contests restrained "the selfish, individualistic tendencies of the age."

According to popular belief, athletics also served as a moral force by thwarting those habits that the nineteenth century labeled collectively as "vice." As one historian has argued, athletic training required precisely the sort of ascetic self-denial that might stop a youth from masturbating. Organized sports seemed to check other forms of vice as well. Henry Dwight Sedgwick recalled a group of schoolmates who swore, gambled, lied, and did very little work. He observed that none of the four played football, and speculated that the game would have had an "educational effect" on their moral tone.

When supporters insisted that competitive athletics built character, then, they were claiming more than just the development of martial virtues; they were arguing that organized sports taught self-control, which would enable a boy to govern selfishness or sensual impulses. This line of thinking had an undertone of gender politics; luxury and self-indulgence—"effeminacy"—were considered quintessential female flaws which athletics could counteract. More than that, advocates of sport were claiming new cultural and social ground away from women. For a century, moral instruction had been regarded as a woman's task, but now men asserted that all-male competition could do the job. Beneath this assertion lay an implied complaint that young males were reaching their teens and twenties without the moral training that they should have received from their mothers.

Even as the advocates of athletics were making dramatic new claims about sports   13 and morality, they pointed to academic benefits as well. Many agreed with Theodore Roosevelt that "those boys who take part in rough, hard play outside of school will not find any need for horse-play." While sports siphoned off "animal spirits" so that boys could concentrate in the classroom, they could also teach a new respect for intelligence and cultivated skill. Ellery Clark, a former Harvard track star, testified that "a great light . . . burst upon [his] mind" when he realized that, in athletics, "skill was greater than strength, brain than muscle; and that the man who once thoroughly mastered the method of performing an event could thereafter hold his own with those infinitely his superiors in strength and size."

By the start of the twentieth century, then, the claims on behalf of the athletic   14 experience were broad. Team sports seemed to offer benefits in every aspect of life. In fact, the men of the time treated athletics as a metaphor for life, or as a mirror that reflected the situations of life with a peculiar clarity. Here we find the historical roots of a cultural habit that, at the end of the twentieth century, seems timeless. For example, financier Charles Flint, recalling his years as a hunter, "observed an indifference to sports on the part of men of leisure as compared with the intense delight of those who are transformed from business hustlers into hustlers after game." This facile equation of business with sport, so familiar in later years, was a product of the turn-of-the-century era. It was an equation commonly made. Essayist Rafford Pyke used common athletic imagery to make a different sort of point about manly honesty: "Fair play and the rigor of the game is a masculine ideal; men will trust and like and honor those who live up to its strict requirements." The most famous comparison of life to athletics in this era came from that master of aphorisms, Theodore Roosevelt, when he said: "In life, as in a foot-ball game, the principle to follow is: Hit the line hard; don't foul and don't shirk but hit the line hard." Sport, in sum, both reflected and illuminated men's lives. It also served as "a means of preparation for the responsibilities of life" because it taught "qualities useful in any profession."

Most of all, athletics seemed to teach the qualities men needed in life because it   15 was a competitive endeavor. Cunningham LaPlace, reflecting in 1905 on his son's college experience, turned a favorable eye on intramural sports. LaPlace wrote that student fun "should take the form of a contest, since life is so constituted that this is its law. Every man who obtains a position of responsibility and of corresponding remuneration does so because some man or group selects him from a field as the one who is considered to be best qualified." "A young man," wrote LaPlace, "can best learn" this phase of life from competitive games. Henry Sheldon, a scholar of student customs, shared LaPlace's view of life as inherently competitive. Commenting on college sports, he wrote:

Athletics have flourished in proportion as the competitive feature has been emphasized. In many colleges the chief motive power is not an interest in physical training, but a craving for distinction, an ambition to beat some one. Among nations of Anglo-Saxon descent the desire for exercise is chiefly the result, not the cause, of competitive contests.

Whatever the source of this "ambition to beat some one," everyone seemed to agree that athletics took their value and their appeal from their reflection of life's "inherently" competitive nature.

Increasingly, the appeal of the athletic contest exerted its sway over spectators   16
as well as youthful participants. In the last quarter of the nineteenth century, middle-class males provided a mass following for professional baseball and college football. The popularity of these spectator sports was intimately related to the fact that they were competitions. Historian Leonard Ellis has analyzed their deep structure in a way that links their appeal persuasively to their rivalrous nature. Football pitted one team against the other in the conquest and defense of territory. It emphasized teamwork, an elaborate division of labor, a hierarchy of roles, and intricate strategies in the service of team competition, thus rendering the experience of bureaucratic work—which was just emerging at the end of the century—in dramatic physical form.

As Ellis analyzes it, baseball had a very different sort of structure. The two teams   17
did not engage in direct combat, but rather took turns in an exercise at home-leaving and successful return. From the safety of "home," one individual after another attempted to enter a hostile territory and negotiate a safe arrival back at home. The constant repetition of home-leaving and return mirrored the daily journeys of men into the world and back again. Baseball embodied not just the competition of nineteenth-century manhood but also the organization of male life into zones of striving and safety. Sports seemed to mirror men's lives, and that was the greatest source of athletics' appeal as public drama, as a teaching device, and as a means for building manly character.

from GUNFIGHTER NATION:
The Myth of the Frontier in Twentieth-Century America
Richard Slotkin

High Noon (1952): *The Hero in Spite of Democracy*

The ideological implications of this approach to the Western were developed   1
with striking clarity in Stanley Kramer's production of *High Noon,* directed by Fred Zinneman and written by the blacklisted screenwriter Carl Foreman. The film was both a critical and a commercial success. Academy Award nominations went to the film (as Best Picture) and to both Zinneman and Foreman; Gary Cooper won an Oscar as Best Actor. The film editors and Dmitri Tiomkin's score received Oscars

as well. It was also an extremely influential film, spawning many imitations (including the TV series *Gunsmoke*) and one major "rebuttal": Howard Hawks' *Rio Bravo* (1959). Although nominally a "town-tamer" Western, its hero is envisioned in ways that link him to King's Jimmy Ringo, and the formal structure of the film mirrors and exaggerates *The Gunfighter*'s clock-driven narrative.

The hero of *High Noon* is Will Kane (Cooper), who is about to marry and then   2
retire as Marshal of Hadleyville. Kane is a lean, dour, iron-gray man who wears the lawman's costume of white shirt and gray vest like a set of vestments. His wife (Grace Kelly) is a good deal younger and is a Quaker; it is because of her religion that he is giving up his gun and his badge. As the two are about to leave, they learn that Frank Miller is out of prison and will return on the noon train. Miller had ruled Hadleyville from his saloon and had terrorized the town with his penchant for insane cruelty until Kane decided to put on the badge and clean up. Now Miller is returning to kill Kane and the others who had a hand in his overthrow. The townspeople insist that Kane not change his plans, assuring him that they can take care of themselves and that Kane's callow deputy Harvey (Lloyd Bridges) can protect them till the new marshal arrives. But after starting off on his journey, Kane turns back, despite his wife's passionate objections and her insistence that she will leave him if he decides to fight.

From this moment the film begins a dramatic countdown in pace with the real   3
passage of time—one minute on screen equals one minute closer to "high noon." As Kane tries to rally his old deputies to oppose Miller's return and to talk his wife out of leaving on the train that will bring Miller back, the camera continually refers us to the clock, to the narrowing time/space within which Kane's heroism (like Ringo's fame) has entrapped him.

Like Ringo, Kane is isolated from society by the very qualities that have given him   4
honor. The difference is that Ringo is alone from the moment we meet him; Kane does not discover his alienation until, through the action of the narrative, he tries to engage his community's sense of solidarity and decency in defeating Miller. One by one, everyone he approaches refuses to take up arms against Miller's return. (The series of encounters parallels the narrative plan of *Gunfighter* and even engages the hero with some of the same conventional types.) Kane's mentor and predecessor is too old and arthritic; most people (like the judge who sentenced Miller) are simply too frightened. Some cover their fear by professing to believe that Miller may have grown soft in prison. The young deputy is jealous of Kane. The minister is in a snit because Kane was not married in his church.

The crisis arrives when Kane addresses the townspeople in the church and re-   5
minds them of what life was like under Miller's rule—asking, in effect, if they have learned the lesson of their history. What follows is a parody of democracy. At first the townspeople are all for helping Kane; then "cooler heads" prevail, particularly the mayor (Thomas Mitchell). The defeat of Miller (he says) meant progress for the town, and that progress is about to culminate in a wave of new investment—important people in the state capital have heard about Hadleyville! But if a gun-

fight takes place in the streets, Hadleyville will seem like "just another wide open town." Thus the traditional sanctions of "progress" become motives for cowardice rather than incitements to heroism. The community, in a virtual town meeting, declares that it does not want Will Kane to fight its battles a second time.

But just as he rejects the moral authority of his wife's religion, Kane rejects the "will of the people" and prepares to face Miller and his henchmen alone. At this moment, he has been deprived of the classic sanctions that authorized the town-tamer's use of violence. He has no official entitlement to the badge he has re-assumed after retiring that morning; the Mayor has defined his action as anti-progressive; and the town meeting has made it clear that it no longer wants him to act as its agent. He is, in effect, a vigilante: a private man assuming the power of the law without submitting himself to the democratic process. In these circumstances, what principles can justify his decision to face Miller? 6

There is a personal element in his decision, which at first predominates. Kane knows that Miller will pursue him wherever he goes and prefers to face him now rather than spend a lifetime looking over his shoulder. But other feelings and ideas move him as well. He is a professional: his badge was his calling, the expression of his pride and honor, and Miller's expulsion was his most meaningful victory. He can't leave the job unfinished, and Miller's return will undo the work of his life. There is also a social component among Kane's motives. His work was meaningful because it transformed Hadleyville into a "progressive" little town where it is safe for women and children to walk the streets. He cannot permit society to revert to the savage regime of Miller, even if the people who constitute that society are willing to permit it. In effect, the principle on which he acts is the same as that to which Wister's and Dixon's vigilante heroes and Ford's cavalrymen appealed: that the defense of "civilization" is more important than the procedures of "democracy." 7

But Kane's ultimate appeal is to the authority of his "character" and his "manhood"—the same "red-blooded" principles to which Judge Henry and the Virginian appealed in justifying the lynching of rustlers. Kane is the only man with knowledge, skill, and power enough to defeat Miller; and his conscience, like that of Sheridan and Yorke, holds that (in cases like this) possession of the power to act entails an absolute responsibility to act, whether or not the action is legal or acceptable to the public. But Foreman and Zinneman do not provide an excuse like the capture of the children to cover his action. Kane forthrightly asserts the need for preemptive violence to prevent atrocities which he (apparently alone) believes are certain to follow Miller's return. 8

Kane understands Miller's savage character, because, like "the man who knows Indians," there is a side of Kane's nature that is akin to Miller's. The hint is there in the name "Will Kane," which combines the suggestion of "will" as the drive to power with a homonym of the Bible's first murderer. When Kane talks to the old marshal who first persuaded him to put on the badge, their conversation confirms that Kane might have gone "bad" if the marshal hadn't turned him around. But the dark potential in Kane is most vividly defined by Helen Ramirez (Katy Jurado), who 9 owns the town's saloon (and presumably its attendant gambling and prostitution). Helen was originally Frank Miller's moll and is presently the mistress of Kane's deputy Harvey. But she was once the lover of Will Kane, who freed her from Miller's sadistic control and may have enabled her to replace Miller as owner of the saloon, become a wealthy woman, and repay the town's scorn of her for being a "Mexican woman." Helen is therefore to be believed when she tells Harvey that the difference between him and Kane is that Kane "is a *man*." The emphasis and context of the remark identify Kane's manliness as a lover with his power to confront and overcome Miller.

There are precedents in earlier Westerns for the sharing of a woman between hero and villain, and if we are aware of these (as an audience) Helen's suggestions will carry a bit more resonance. A similar quartet of figures—gunfighter, gambler, Mexican woman, Christian woman from the East—set the terms of the moral drama in Hart's *Hell's Hinges* (1915); but Hart's turn-of-the-century morality insists on the (racial) purity of Blaze Tracey's sexual inclinations. The foursome of marshal, gambler, Mexican woman, and virginal Anglo maiden also forms the central group of the Wyatt Earp/O.K. Corral story, most recently remade by John Ford in *My Darling Clementine* (1946). In that film Wyatt (Henry Fonda) becomes marshal of Tombstone in order to avenge the killing of his brother and the rustling of his cattle. Far from "cleaning up" Tombstone, Wyatt forms a close friendship with the murderous gambler Doc Holliday (Victor Mature), who owns a saloon and keeps as mistress the Mexican singer Chihuahua. Although Ford's movie ultimately reaffirms an essentially "progressive" view of the town-tamer, the Earp/Holliday relationship suggests an element of darkness and violence in Earp that belongs to an earlier stage of civilization. Earp, however, is moving toward a more civilized way of life, a direction indicated by his falling in love with Clementine, an aristocratic easterner who is virtually the reincarnation of the Virginian's Molly Stark. But Clementine was once Doc Holliday's fiancée, and his abandonment of her indicates that his path will be the reverse of Wyatt's, toward atavism and death.

Foreman and Zinneman use the same group of characters but alters their relationships to emphasize the "dark" and "Miller-like" aspects of Kane's past. The sympathetic Holliday becomes the vicious Miller (whose name is the same as that of the villain in *Hell's Hinges*), and the woman they share is not the pure Anglo maiden but the "dark" Mexican woman. The capacity for "dark" sex and "dark" violence is the key to Kane's power, the definition of the virility Helen praises. Kane can defeat Miller because he could have been Miller. He too is willing to impose his will on the citizens. The difference between them is Kane's latent instinct for goodness, which shows in his jilting of Helen and his love for a Quaker woman. Like the Virginian, the "essential" goodness and manliness of his character provide the only "authority" to which he can appeal in justification of his actions. And the movie says it is enough.

The gunfight is the center of the film's formal structure, the iconic moment toward which the clock-driven narrative inexorably drives and its moral resolution as well. Only the gunfight can prove that Kane really does "know Indians" and is there-

10

11

12

fore morally entitled to set his will against that of the townspeople. The gunfight it-self has a ritual quality. Kane's preparations and his solitary walk up the empty street tell us not only that he *must* fight Miller but that he has to do it in a certain way, playing by certain rules. Even Miller and his henchmen move in formal order and make symbolic gestures, the most significant of which is a gunman's shattering a shop window to steal a woman's bonnet—an act that validates Kane's prediction that if Miller wins neither women nor property will be safe, and that coincidentally warns Kane of the gang's presence. The ritual proceeds through passages of quick-draw confrontation, chases, and ambushes (which visually echo similar passages in earlier Westerns). At the end, Kane's moral vindication is perfected, first by the "conversion" of his Quaker wife—who grabs a gun and shoots one of Miller's men in the back—then by a "captivity/rescue" in which Kane kills Miller while Miller is holding Mrs. Kane as a shield.

In the classic town-tamer Western, Kane's personal redemption would have been mirrored in the triumph of the community. But the social implications of Kane's vic-tory are anti-canonical. Instead of vindicating Kane discredits the community, which proves itself unworthy of the sacrifices he has made for it. At the end, Kane con-temptuously drops his badge in the dust at the mayor's feet and rides out of town. The people have been saved, but they have less value than the man who saved them.

13

Sipher, Roger, "So That Nobody Has to Go to School If They Don't Want To." *The New York Times*, December 19, 1977. Copyright © 1977 by The New York Times Company. Reprinted by permission.

Singleton, Carl, "What Our Education System Needs Is More F's." *The Chronicle of Higher Education, 1984*. Reprinted by permission of the author.

Ventura, Michael, "Someone Is Stealing Your Life." *Utne Reader,* July/August 1991, pp. 78–80. Excerpted with permission from *Letters at 3 am—Reports on Endarkenment* (Spring Press) by Michael Ventura.

Mathabane, Mark, "Appearances Are Destructive." *The New York Times,* August 26, 1993, p. A21. Copyright © 1993 by The New York Times Company. Reprinted by permission.

Maslin, Janet, "Old Miser Bringing Up the Cute Girl Is (a) Marner (b) Martin?" *The New York Times Film Review,* September 2, 1994, p. C31. Copyright © 1994 by The New York Times Company. Reprinted by permission.

Lasch, Christopher, "The Corruption of Sports." *The New York Review of Books,* April 28, 1977. Reprinted by permission of The New York Review of Books and Nell Lasch.

Steele, Shelby, "The New Sovereignty." *Harper's* magazine, July 1992, pp. 47–54. Reprinted by permission of the author.

Strate, Lance, "Beer Commercials: A Manual on Masculinity." *Men, Masculinity, and the Media,* Steve Craig, ed., pp. 79–92. Copyright © 1992 by Sage Publications, Inc. Reprinted by permission of Sage Publications, Inc.

Sapolsky, Robert M., "On Human Nature." This article is reprinted by permission of *The Science* and is from the March/April 1994 issue. Individual subscriptions are $18.00 per year. Write to The Sciences, 2 East 63rd Street, New York, NY 10021 or call 1-800-THE-NYAS.

Essay reprinted from *The New York Times,* September 21, 1967. Copyright © 1967 by The New York Times Company. Reprinted by permission.

Clines, Francis X. "City Layoffs Hurt Minorities Most." *The New York Times,* February 20, 1990. Copyright © 1990 by The New York Times Company. Reprinted by permission.

Dubler, Nancy Neveloff and Nimmons, David, specified excerpt from pages 130–132 of *Ethics on Call* by Nancy Neveloff Dubler and David Nimmons. Copyright © 1992 by Nancy Neveloff Dubler and David Nimmons. Reprinted by permission of Harmony Books, a division of Crown Publishers, Inc.

Extracts from *Readers' Guide to Periodical Literature 1992–1993.* Copyright © 1993 by the H.W. Wilson Company. Material reprinted by permission of the publisher.

Encyclopedia Americana, entry on "anorexia nervosa." Encyclopedia Americana 1994. Grolier, Inc. Danbury, CT. Reprinted by permission of the publisher.

Van Thorre, Mary Deanna and Vogel, Frances X., "The Presence of Bulimia in High School Females." *Adolescence,* volume XX, Spring 1985, pp. 45–51. Reprinted by permission of Libra Publishers.

Gordon, Richard A., from *Anorexia and Bulimia* (1990). Reprinted by permission of Blackwell Publishers.

Wolf, Naomi, excerpt, pp. 205–208, from *The Beauty Myth: How Images of Beauty Are Used Against Women* by Naomi Wolf. Reprinted by permission of William Morrow & Company, Inc. and Random House of Canada Ltd.

Bers, Susan A. and Quinlan, Donald M., "Perceived-Competence Deficit in Anorexia Nervosa." *Journal of Abnormal Psychology,* August 1992. Reprinted by permission of the American Psychological Association.

Anderson, Judith, "Battling Bulimia: My War Story." Copyright © 1993 by Judith Anderson. Reprinted by permission. The article from which this passage is excerpted was originally published in *Glamour.*

Baker, Carlos, excerpt from *Ernest Hemingway: A Life Story,* 1969. Copyright © 1969 by Carlos Baker and Mary Hemingway. Reprinted with permission of Charles Scribner's Sons, an imprint of Macmillan Publishing Company.

"300 Killed by Fire, Smoke and Panic in Boston Resort," *The New York Times,* November 30, 1942. Copyright © 1942 by The New York Times Company. Reprinted by permission.

"Boston's Worst," *Time,* December 7, 1942. Copyright 1942 Time Inc. All rights reserved. Reprinted by permission from TIME.

DeVoto, Bernard, "The Easy Chair," *Harper's,* February 1943. Copyright © 1943 by Harper's magazine. All rights reserved. Reprinted from the February issue by special permission.

Barthel, Diane, "Masculine Nostalgia." *Men, Masculinity, and the Media.* Copyright © 1992 by Sage Publications, Inc. Steve Craig, ed., pp. 150–151. Reprinted by permission of Sage Publications, Inc.

Davie, Michael, "Washington—The Truth behind the Legend." *The Observer.* Copyright © The Observer. Reprinted with permission.

Stade, George, "Football—The Game of Aggression." Excerpt from "Game Theory." Reprinted by permission from *The Columbia Forum.* Copyright © 1966 by The Trustees of Columbia University in the City of New York. All rights reserved.

Fisher, Helen E., Ph.D. "Body Talk." *Anatomy of Love: The Natural History of Monogamy, Adultery, and Divorce* by Helen E. Fisher, Ph.D. Reprinted by permission of W.W. Norton & Company, Inc. Copyright © 1992 by Helen E. Fisher.

Gerson, Kathleen, specified excerpt from pages 17–22 of *No Man's Land* by Kathleen Gerson. Copyright © 1993 by BasicBooks, A Division of HarperCollins Publishers, Inc. Reprinted by permission of BasicBooks, A Division of HarperCollins Publishers, Inc.

Gilmore, David D., "Beyond Sex," "Man-the-Protector," "Autonomous Wayfarers." *Manhood in the Making: Cultural Concepts of Masculinity* by David D. Gilmore, 1990, pp. 42–51. Copyright © 1990 by Yale University Press. All rights reserved.

Messner, Michael A., selected excerpts from pages 33–34 of *Power at Play* by Michael A. Messner. Copyright © 1992 by Michael A. Messner. Reprinted by permission of Beacon Press.

Pecora, Norma, "Superman/Superboy/Supermen: The Comic Book Hero as Socializing Agent." *Men, Masculinity, and the Media,* Steve Craig, ed., pp. 66–71. Copyright © 1992 by Sage Publications, Inc. Reprinted by permission of Sage Publications, Inc.

Rotondo, Anthony, specified excerpt from pages 239–244 of *American Manhood* by Anthony Rotondo. Copyright © 1983 by BasicBooks, A Division of HarperCollins Publishers, Inc. Reprinted by permission of BasicBooks, A Division of HarperCollins Publishers, Inc.

Slotkin, Richard, specified excerpt from pages 391–395 of *Gunfighter Nation: The Myth of the Frontier in Twentieth-Century America.* Copyright © 1992 by Richard Slotkin. Reprinted with the permission of Scribner, an imprint of Simon & Schuster.

Index